THE VOUDON GNOSTIC WORKBOOK

THE
VOUDON GNOSTIC
WORKBOOK

EXPANDED EDITION

MICHAEL BERTIAUX

INTRODUCTION BY COURTNEY WILLIS

WEISERBOOKS
San Francisco, CA / Newburyport, MA

This edition first published in 2007 by
Red Wheel/Weiser, LLC
With offices at:
500 Third Street, Suite 230
San Francisco, CA 94107
www.redwheelweiser.com

ISBN: 978–1–57863–339–5

Library of Congress Cataloging-in-Publication Data
Available upon request

Cover design by Kathryn Sky-Peck

Printed in Canada
TCP

10 9   8   7   6   5   4   3   2

Dedication

This Workbook is dedicated to the Hoodoo and Les Vudu,

To the Kami and the Kammamori,

To the Lares and the Penates,

And to the Numen and the Numina of the
    Monastery of the Seven Rays,

In thanksgiving for their
    inspiration and assistance

Over the past twenty-five years.

Preface to the 2007 Weiser Edition

This book, *The Voudon Gnostic Workbook*, presents the teachings of a Franco-Haitian esoteric and theurgical society known as "La Couleuvre Noire" (The Black Snake), which by reason of their tradition is believed by its members to be a society derived from an adept who died in Leogane, Haiti, in 1774. This tradition also entails teachings derived from African mysticism and spiritism, as these teachings were developed in two hundred years of occult work and casework practice in esotericism and a type of psychology within Haitian culture and the wider Voudon diaspora, which grew out of the occult practices of the members of this order.

It is in this growth of occult practices that the Black Snake School has been shown to possess an identifiable presence of teaching and has demonstrated the evidences of its tradition and forms of spiritism, fused with a peculiar type of Catholicism and aspects of the French mystical and spiritist traditions.

Those serviteurs of this cultus, who adhere to the traditions of this path, would be found to possess a familiarity of language and thought with Black Templarism, Eliphas Levi, Allan Kardec, Stanislas de Guaita, H. P. Blavatsky, and modern depth psychology, as well as the never ending sources of fetischisme and elemental propitiation. In many ways, this tradition would have remained in Haiti, among certain scholars had not so many Haitians come to the U.S.A. in the period 1957-21986, as a result of political instability in their home land. Also, the author of this book, who was briefly in Haiti in 1963, seems to have made contact both then and later in this country with the leaders of The Black Snake Cultus and helped and worked with them to establish their mystical society and neo-naasenic church in the U.S.A.

Over the years, The Black Snake Cultus and its outer form: The Ancient Order of the Templars of the East (OTOA), which they understand to be derived from the experience of Papus (Dr. G. Encausse) by reason of his claim to jurisdiction over a secret body of Franco-Haitian adepts, taught its members by means of courses of esoteric instruction in two small lodges in the U.S.A. (Hyde Park, Chicago, Il. and Dorchester, Boston, Ma.) and in one small sanctuary in Leogane, Haiti; before becoming more widely known as the result of a four year course of instruction, written by the author of this book, for a small esoteric school: "The Monastery of the Seven Rays".

The Monastery of the Seven Rays was originally located in Ecuador and later moved to Spain. It claimed a kind of neo-gnostic connection to the spiritist writers, Jules Doinel and Victorien Sardou.

The teaching units of chapters of this present book were instructions given to the Chicago lodge of the cultus, in the period following the writing of the fourth year course of instruction of the Monastery. I might add that the Monastery had a proper tradition of its own, being at one time a priory of the Discalced recollect friars, who had embraced their own form of spiritism. During that period, roughly 1975-1986, at weekly meeting of this cultus, the members studied the papers now presented as the contents of this book.

While the membership of this order grew, a spiritist version derived from the raw and elemental mediumship of Jules Doinel and G. Encausse as well as from essentially a type of Voudon cabala, with influences of Allan Kardec, developed and made itself felt more and more powerfully in the regular and intense séances and other strongly mediumistic rites, which concluded the study work periods of the inner group, each week. Furthermore, from the beginnings of the order in Chicago in the 1960's, close fellowship had been maintained with the neo-pagan and wiccan communities. This led to the original publication of this book by a wiccan book publisher and neo-pagan activist.

In the text of this book, we can find various elements fused into a synthesis of spiritualism and occult experience but grounded in the French traditions derived from Doinel and that early neo-gnostic movement of spiritists and theosophists, in which the author of this book's teachers in Haiti had been educated and initiated. I might add that studies have shown that shipments of occult books from France to Haiti were a commonly received commodity and a much frequently stolen item upon arrival in Haiti, as the postal police records will verify. Those occultists fortunate enough to travel to France brought back many treasures, both books and initiations, as recently written studies on the textures of Haitian religion can attest.

So that on this rich basis of esoteric forms of catholic belief and piety, of the French tradition of gnostico-spiritism, and the native religion of psychic energy, found in the Haitian countryside, of practices that possibly have the remotest antiquity, we can find resting the edifice and structure of the work book, which presents its exotic subjects as processes and grades of spirit-energies and as types of speculative and cultural theology, which are shown to be the refinement of elemental and psychic potencies. Then we can see how the secrets and logics of the Vudu, or the spirits of nature and history, have been brought down to Earth and manifested in the mediumism of the human personality and therein given an almost textbook formulation. Likewise the reader is encouraged to explore and enter the spaces of countless and fantastic opportunities for inner world emanation; since whatever else this book is: it is first and foremost the Voudon-Gnostic Workbook, being equally both Gnostic and spiritist and all keys and tools await the reader.

Let that same reader take this mystical directory in hand, let that reader know what contents they hold in their hands and what buried genii slumber like hidden oracles, rendering invisible or visible their treasures, until the fated moment of their revelation, as the powers of Voudon.

—COURTNEY WILLIS

Preface

Let me tell you about the world of esoteric prayer from my own personal experience. I have worked with these energies for a number of years. I have even gone to where the teachings are given out and where the power of esoteric prayer is worked daily.

When I was in Haiti, I entered deeply into the mysteries of the spirits as they are known there. They are called the "Loa" or "Les Vudu." These are spirits and they hear our prayers and work with the energies of prayer in quick and always helpful ways.

After my development into initiation consciousness, I was able to write a number of lessons and other papers on these Holy Spirits and their work. I taught that when you use esoteric prayer, what you do is talk to the spirits as if they were sitting next to you. You talk to them inwardly, of course, but they never act or appear as if they know everything and that there is no need to talk to them. They are always ready to listen to us, especially when we speak to them about something that is very important to us.

It is by this means that we learn the power-secrets of esoteric prayer, since it is the life of the spirit to teach us to know in this way. This way is the way of the Gnosis, a very ancient word from the Greek language, which means the knowing of the spiritually attuned. In the Gnostic church, which is based upon esoteric prayer and spiritualism, we teach all persons to become attuned to the ways and words, or powerful lessons, which come from the Holy Spirits.

I was recently in Japan, where I made daily attunement to the Holy Spirits, which are over there and which have the name of the "Kami." Naturally, these spirits are universal beings, but I went to Japan in order to make contact on a daily basis with them by means of the way of esoteric prayer and as well to visit the many holy shrines and sanctuaries dedicated to the Holy Spirits in that beautiful country. Every day, I experienced an advancement in my way of communion as I grew more and more aware of the powers of esoteric prayer and the energies, which were everywhere, sent by the Holy Spirits. For a long time, I have been under the direction of the Japanese Master, Doctor Kammamori, and there he led me from one level of being to the next. It was he who enabled me to see how the laws of the Kami, or the Holy spirits of the Shinto Religion, could work in daily life. Each day, I worked with the energies of the spirits, as he, Doctor Kammamori, had instructed me.

When we work in the experience of esoteric prayer, we really come to know about spiritual light and energy. I think that you have be inside of what is happening to you in order to understand it fully.

You may wonder what we are doing in this book of spiritual work. Well, let me tell you that we are concerned with esoteric prayer and with teaching how it works and what it can do. I think that prayer in this sense is the application of the lessons of spiritualism and the gnosis to our seeking eternal communion and closeness to God-Energy, through the Holy Spirits. I think it is there that we solve the problems of daily life, which arise and seem to bother us so much. This kind of problem solving is important because in order to grow in the spirit, we have to move on to a higher or more perfect relationship with the Eternal.

At one level a problem exists, which is bothersome to us. Then we move in the spirit on to the next level, which is the higher point of view. There our relationship in the gnosis is one of greater closeness of God. Our relationship to God-Energy has improved because of the Holy spirits. They have led us to an improvement. Now, at that higher level in our relationship with God, we are able to solve that problem with the spiritual powers, which come to us from that level of beingness, or because we are closer to God, we are better beings and have more God-Energy in us. This is the goal of gnostic teachings. When we work from that higher level, we look at the problem that was before us and are now able to bring it back to where it was supposed to be all along. In other words, when we are in the spirit, we are able to see things from the viewpoint of God-Energy, and from that view we see all things the way the Holy spirits are able to see them.

Whatever exists is really not supposed to cause harm or misfortune. It is supposed to be part of the energy of the lifestream of the spirit. So we take the God-Energy of the Holy Spirits and quite simply apply it to the world of problems. The problems are then sent back to where they were before our experience touched them and perhaps disturbed them. No longer are they problems for us, rather they are parts of experience and we know (gnosis) what the ways of their own life should be. They were not to be disturbed nor were they to disturb us in any way. By the use of this experience, we see everything as a kind of lesson in the real growth of the soul, from one world to another.

The teacher of spiritualism, Kardec, always told us to look to the spirits for insights into the way we were to live each day. Those early French gnostics of the last century, under a strong influence from Kardec, stated that gnosis (or spiritual knowledge) was the way in which we were to make prayer work in an inward and absolute way. We were taught to by the Holy spirits how we are to use the powers of prayer and ritual magick.

These same gnostics, and they were very familiar with Voudoo and Shintoism as forms of the universal religion of gnostic spiritualism, taught us to enter into communion with God and thereby become able to see things, perhaps all things, the way god sees them. Certainly, we have his energy to work with and in this matter, we can move beyond all limitations into the lifestream of divine light.

The spiritual circumstances of light from the Holy spirits are always ours when we make use of the principles of esoteric prayer. We are living in a constant conversation or dialogue with divinity. The religious dimensions of life and thought comes to us and sits down beside us and enables us to see every day as a working with gods and Holy spirits. Let me help you to see each day as the beginning of a new conversation with God through the gnosis of the Holy Spirits. They certainly have led us that way in this workbook.

They teach: The Reservoir of Power -- Mysticism is the lifestream of the spirit. It is the lifestyle of those who commune daily with God-Energy. Mysticism is the basis of the prayers to the Loa or Les Vudu, in Esoteric Haiti, and to the Kami or Kammamorian spirits, in Esoteric Japan. Vedic or gnostic prayer is the basis of communion with the Mystic Fire of the ancient Hindus (Agni). Each day we come to learn how these holy powers operate in our lives and how we can be and become more attuned to these Holy Spirits than we are or have been. We want more of the operations of the mystic pathway in our life and existence. If you believe in the power of God-Energy, you will intuit that It (Agni) is now present everywhere in your experience. You are then a mystic.

Focus the energy of God in your life by drawing on the way of the Holy Oracles. Learn to enter that religion which is an aspect of both Esoteric Voudoo, mysticism, Devotion to the Kammamorian Spirits and the angelic communion of the Faith-Energies of the Christ and the Mystic Fire of Agni. This is the attunement of the Gnosis. In all of this, you will seek more and more ways in which to bring the Holy Spirits and their sacramental mysteries closer to you. Let me tell you that the Holy Mother of God, the Primordial and Eternal Goddess is seeking to make the esoteric prayer–life and teachings of the spiritual world the experience of all Her children.

The esoteric teachings and mysticism of the spirits from all of the mystical and God–Energy religions are truly powers and experiences to feed your soul. These energies are directed to your soul in very precise ways because even in the west, among the gnostics who will use this workbook, you can realize how close you are to a science of prayer in liturgies, oracles, ceremonies, rituals, and meditations.

Yes, you have the ways and the paths whereby the spiritual power can be directed into the problem area and then with the power of light that entity in that area can be cleaned and made pure as the light of God, your radiant source.

Table of Contents

PART I

Voudoo Energies

Lesson One: Who Can Be a Big Lucky Hoodoo?

Anyone can become a big lucky Hoodoo once they make contact with the spirits behind Voudoo. I will teach you the very simple method of making contact with the spirits. The spirits are easy to meet, in fact they are very eager to meet you, that is why they led you to take this course. They want you to learn their power secrets, so that they can have an influence over other people. This gives the spirits more and more power to help you.

The spirits want to meet you and they want to get into your life. They have a lot of things to tell you and these things will help you become more and more lucky. You will be able to do what you want with their help, because you will be able to pay them off with things that they like, but which they can't get now. They can't get the gifts of food and candles that they wish to have until they do their work for you, and then you will pay them off and both of you -- you, the lucky Hoodoo and they, the spirits -- will be getting exactly what you want. That is what it is all about in Voudoo power secrets.

We know who and what we are here in this world. We know all about ourselves as far as what we want and what we are going to get. This means that we know just what we want out of life. We know what is basic to life and what is extra to life. We want both and we are going to be able to get both through lucky Hoodoo, because lucky Hoodoo works where everything else doesn't work. In the long run, only lucky Hoodoo can do what you really want it to do for you.

Then we have the spirits. The spirits are the powers that can't be seen except with second sight. They can't be heard except with second hearing. They can't be touched except with the second touch. These second senses are powers we all have and use without even knowing about it. Some people become very successful through the use of the second senses. They call themselves readers and advisors of spiritual truth. Lucky Hoodoo can make you into one of these if you want to do that also. But it is all done by the spirits working with you and for you. That is why Voudoo power secrets depend upon the spirits. Let me tell you more about these spirits. Long ago there was a big island between Africa and Haiti called "Atlantis" and because of many earthquakes, it sank under the ocean called the "Atlantic." One time there was a big school of magick on the island of this same Atlantis and the magicians were very powerful. What they didn't know when they were alive they soon learned after they died. The island, as we said, just sank under the ocean and the magicians went down with it. But they didn't die, they just became spirits with fish-like bodies and frog-like bodies, and snake-like bodies. They did this so they could continue their work under the ocean, in their big temple down at the bottom of the sea. They are still down there, but they are also spirits and as spirits they are able to do a lot of things. In fact they know how to do more things now than they knew a long time ago. The older they get the more powerful they get.

Now, under the sea there is a great forest with all kinds of sea-trees and sea-bushes, and sea-plants growing in it. This is the great woods of the old island of Atlantis. There is an old king who is a very powerful spirit-magician and he is the "Master of the Words on the Island Under the Sea." We call him "Maitre" or "Ma-Tr" for short. He is the king of the spirits on his island and he is a very powerful god of Voudoo. He has given to me a group of His spirits to help those who are making use of this course to become powerful. I call His spirits the "Hoo-Spirits," because they make up one half of the team of spirits in lucky Hoodoo.

On the other hand, in the world of the Dead, there is another great king who is called "Papa Nibbho." He is the king of the spirits of the Dead, and they have the name of Ghuedhe, or "the Gay-Days." They are the subjects of old Papa Nibbho, who is the king of time and eternity and who always was and who always will be. His spirits look like ghosts or like walking bones, and skeletons and often have the faces of those who have passed on. But they are all subjects of the king of the spirits of the dead, or Papa Nibbho. I call these spirits the "Doo-Spirits," for they make up the second group of spirits in lucky Hoodoo, or the second half of our team. They do not look like Turtles, Fish, Frogs, and Snakes –– that is the way in which the Hoo-spirits look. The Doo-Spirits look like dead people.

Now these two groups of spirits come together and make our system of lucky Hoodoo very powerful, because they represent the most powerful elemental forces in the universe for practical magick. The spirits of the dead come from the north angle of the spirit world and are from the element of earth, upon which everything must be built. The spirits of the sea-magicians come from the west angle of the spirit world and are from the element of water. Everything must depend upon water if it is to live and grow, so it is with the spirits and their projects. We want things to be practical and we want them to be successful. That is why we work with these two wonderful families of spirits.

Now there are many other spirits who will be able to work with you and we will talk about them as we move along in our study. The important fact is that we work with the spirits and that the spirits are quite wonderful and helpful for us. Actually, if you treat them well you will find that they are more willing to help you than often you are ready to have them. That is because people are not ready for the help of the spirits and so they are not ready to show the spirits that thay want to make use of them. The spirits only wish for you to have something for them to do and also they expect that you will be able to pay them off for their service. This is only fair for they do everything and can do anything, and they ask only something very small in the way of payment.

Now to become a lucky Hoodoo it is first of all necessary for you to do a little Voudoo ritual and say the following prayer to the spirits. This will show them that you are ready to work with them for what you want. This will show them you really mean business and that you are serious in seeking favors and objects of desire through their powers. This prayer will show them that you are ready to dedicate yourself to them so that they might gain influence over more and more human beings and thus bring back the old golden age of peace and plenty. This ritual will serve as your self-initiation into the system of lucky Hoodoo, which is a religious belief as ancient as the islands below the oceans.

DEDICATION TO THE HOODOO SPIRITS
Part 1. In a quiet place, you will sit at a table upon which you have placed two candles. A black candle has been placed in the north and a blue candle has been placed in the west. You will face east or in the eastern direction. You will have a glass of water placed in the south, directly opposite the black candle.
Part 2. You will now say the following prayer to the Hoodoo spirits in order to make your dedication to their powers and existence. First, you will light the black candle and say,

"O LIGHT THERE IS NO DARKNESS IN THE
    POWERS OF THE DEAD"
Then you will light the blue candle and say,
    "O LIGHT I AM A CHILD OF THE LIGHT OF
    THE GREAT MASTER UNDER THE SEA"
Then you will touch the glass of water with your right hand, because it is nearest to
your right hand and you will say,
    "MEDIUM OF HOLY SPIRITS, THE WATERS BELOW
    AND BENEATH ALL WORLDS THE HOLY SPIRITS OF
    THE DEAD AND THE SEAS I AM HERE TO SERVE YOU."
Part 3. Then you will begin to say the following prayer of dedication to the spirits
in a quiet voice or silently to show them that you mean real business.

    "I DEDICATE MYSELF TO THE SERVICE OF THE SPIRITS,
    TO THE WONDERFUL SPIRITS OF THOSE DEAD ONES WHO
    SEEK TO HELP ME, AND TO THOSE WONDERFUL SPIRITS
    OF WISE MAGICIANS FROM UNDER THE SEA WHO COME IN
    STRANGE FORMS.
    "I ASK THE HELP AND PRESENCE OF THE HOODOO SPIRITS
    AND I CALL UPON ALL BEINGS OF HOODOO TO AID AND
    ASSIST ME.
    "I OFFER MYSELF TO THE SERVICE OF THE GREAT KING
    OF THE DEAD WHO RULES OVER THE SPIRITS OF THE DEAD.
    I OFFER MYSELF TO THE SERVICE OF THE GREAT MASTER
    OF THE MAGICIAN SPIRITS WHO ARE WORKING UNDER THE
    INVISIBLE SEAS. I HONOR ALL OF THE SPIRITS AND
    ESPECIALLY THOSE OF HOODOO SCIENCE. THESE I SEEK
    ESPECIALLY TO WORK WITH NOW AND FOREVER.
Part 4. You will now close you eyes and begin to think about the spirits and how
they will come to you and what you wish for them to do for you. You will then be
silent for a few minutes afterwards, you will first take the glass of water and drink
it, for it has the spirit-power in it. You will then silently put out the blue and
then the black candle.   You will feel relaxed and peaceful, in love with all spirits
and ready to obey them. Be sure of good luck, for you are becoming a Hoodoo.

Lesson Two: How the Hoodoo Spirits Help You to Get Exactly What You Want

Everyone who comes to Hoodoo wants to have something done for them. The reason why they come to Hoodoo is because they have tried everything else and they have not been successful. That is why they are willing to try the power of the spirits which we call Lucky Hoodoo. But you, dear student, are different, because you are now on the road to becoming a Hoodoo practitioner, someone who will be able to help others because he has been so successful and powerful in his Hoodoo work with the spirits.

Generally speaking, the Hoodoo spirits are asked to do one of four major kinds of things for those who come to them for help. Sometimes we will find a person who has a lot of needs, but they are usually variations of the basic four. These needs are usually:

1. The desire to have good health and be free of illness.
2. The wish to have more money or a better job or boss.
3. The wish to know more about the spirits for betterment.
4. The wish to have a new or better lover for romance and sex.

All of these needs are valid and very good for the person to seek. There is no reason why anyone should feel ashamed to want to have these goals. They are the aims of everyone who is in a right frame of mind. Now, we have to see what the Hoodoo Spirits think about these goals for gain.

All of these aims are based on the need to gain something more. So there must be something or somebody in the spirit world who is willing to help us to get what we want. The answer is that there are many spirits who have as their purpose the helping of mankind to gain what it needs. These spirits come in order to make up for the lack of something which is the basis of need. We are seeking the help of the spirits in order to gain what we do not now have. Fortunately, there are many spirits who are quite willing to help us out. In fact they are often more willing to help us than we are ready or able to let them help us. In other words, many persons are not yet ready to make contact with the spirits in order to have the spirits help them with their plans. But once a person has made contact with spirits, then it is quite simple to ask them to help you with a particular project, which will bring you exactly what you are seeking.

Your own case would be an example of a person who is already on the road to successful communion with the spirits, for you have done the ritual of dedication to the Hoodoo spirits, which was given in the first lesson of this series of documents. Now, we will begin from where we left off in the last lesson, in order to see just how it is that the spirits are able to bring to a person who is seeking something what that person wants.

In the world of the spirits there is a particular group of Spirits who are concerned with doing special projects. These are called the "Work Loa," and they are to be found among both the Hoo-Spirits and among the Doo-Spirits. These working gods are very helpful to mankind, for they are the powers that enable mankind to get exactly what he wants at any time. They are powerful helpers to mankind, because they are paid by mankind in turn in response to what they have done for him. The "Work Loa" are very wonderful gods in the sense that they have infinite powers, because they are pure spirit and not tied down to this world of earth. Therefore, they are able to be everywhere at all times and to do everything that needs to be done. However, it is necessary to approach these gods by means of special rituals, for like all of the Hoodoo Spirits, these beings are very much in sympathy with ceremonies and rites.

Many persons are of the opinion that the Voudoo gods can be contacted simply by directing the mind in the way of their being and thus attunement with the Spirits is achieved by pure and silent thought. This may be true for those Big Shots who can build Mental Temples with their minds and imaginations but it is not true for those who are just beginning. Such novices in Hoodoo must make use of ceremonial work and ritual to summon the Spirits, for if a person wishes to summon the spirits, it is done either with a Mental Temple that is built up in the mind or else it is done with a ceremony done in the very room where the person is. But in either case it is done making use of some kind of magick. That is the important factor. It is necessary to make use of powerful magick in order to summon the Hoodoo Spirits at any time. For they respond only to magick, whether or not it is mental or physical it does not matter except to the student or practitioner. They will come quicker through a good magician using physical methods than through a careless student making use of mental methods, only. And it is important to understand this point, for they are not too interested in how you call them to your aid. They are only interested in that you do call upon them to help you.

On the other side and in the world of the spirits, the "Work Loa" can easily recognize a call for help because of the astral colors that it sends along with itself. The call carries with it the secret colors of true petition if it is a sincere call for help. If it isn't, then the colors will be absent and other colors which indicate deception will be present. Pity the poor fool who tries to trick the spirits, for they know everything and that is why they know you and what you want from them. So be perfectly honest with them for they can tell intuitively when you are sincere and when you are not sincere. Even if a person sought to attract them by means of a Mental Temple, and still was insincere, he would not be successful. They can tell even when the person is working in the world of Mind. For the colors of the Mental Temple will apear to be those where insincerity is present and they will not come, except to punish the wrongoder. Therefore be perfectly honest with them and you will be helped.

Another thing to understand is that with them the morals of the human world are without meaning. Moral codes were invented by certain political and religious groups to keep the majority of human beings in chains. There is only one law of morality in the spirit world and that is to tell the truth to the spirits. So if a person desires to make love to another person and the world of human morality would say this is wrong, or even the Bible would say this is wrong, we must understand that to seek the spirits this is not wrong, as long as the seeker is truly seeking that person as his lover. For that reason you must not feel any shyness about speaking to the wonderful spirits, for if you are honest with yourself, you are honest with them. If you are to be honest with them, then they can come to your aid and help you out.

There is a very simple ritual which you can do in order to get the Hoodoo Spirits to come to your aid. This is a simple request ritual, and it can be done at any time, once you have done the dedication ritual and therefore should be done at least one day later in order to give your own astral body a rest. However, it is the basic ritual for getting in touch with the spirits and letting them know just what it is that you want them to do.

THE BASIC RITUAL FOR GAINING FROM THE HOODOO SPIRITS

Part 1. In a quiet place, you will sit at your table upon which you have now placed four candles at the corners and a black candle in the center. You will place a yellow candle in the north, a blue candle in the west (same as before), a green candle in the south, and a red candle in the east. Place your black candle from the previous ritual in the center and between the black candle and the blue candle you will place a glass of water. You will write out on a small piece of paper or index card what you wish to gain and place this request between the red candle and the black candle. Now, your altar is set up for your work, and it should look just like this:

Part 2. Now, you will say the following prayer to the Hoodoo Spirits in order to make known to them by ritual your request for their help and presence. You will begin the prayer to the Hoodoo Spirits by lighting the candles in the following order:
First, you will light the yellow candle and say:
    "Holy Spirit of the Northern Cross of Light come forth."
Second, you will light the blue candle and say:
    "Holy Spirit of the Western Cross of Light come forth."
Third, you will light the green candle and say:
    "Holy Spirit of the Southern Cross of Light come forth."
Fourth, you will light the red candle and say:
    "Holy Spirit of the Eastern Cross of Light come forth."
Lastly, you will light the black candle and say:
    "Holy Spirits of Lucky Hoodoo come to my help and hear me."
Next, you will touch the glass of water and say:
    "MEDIUM OF HOLY SPIRITS OF THE WATERS BELOW
    AND BENEATH ALL WORLDS THE HOLY SPIRITS OF
    THE DEAD AND THE SEAS I AM HERE TO SERVE YOU."
Then, you will look intensely upon your request card and say:
    "O LIGHT THERE IS NO DARKNESS. O LIGHT WE ARE
    IN THE PRESENCE OF ENDLESS LIGHT."
Part 3. Then you will begin to say the following very short prayer of request for gain to the Spirits either in a soft voice or silently to show that you mean real business.
    "Dear Spirits of Lucky Hoodoo. You are my friends. What I wish to receive from you is written on the card (paper) which I have written out as a special request. Please help me to gain this that I wish so much. I know that you can help me. Here is my gift to you, dear Spirits of Lucky Hoodoo."
Part 4. Then you will offer power to the Spirits by rubbing your hands together for a couple of minutes and then holding your hands towards the altar with the palms open and extending the fingers upwards, so that the altar will receive the power as it flows out of the palms of your hands and to the Spirit world. This is your gift to the Spirits, the power of life or vitality which will be used by them in healing or in some other work.
Part 5. You will now close your eyes and begin to think about the Hoodoo Spirits and how they will come to you and what you wish them to do for your request. They are present everywhere and perhaps they will indicate that they are there by the

flickering of a candle or some other sign. You will then be silent for a few minutes afterwards. You will take the glass of water and drink it, for it has spirit–power in it. You will then silently put out the candles in the following order: first the black, then the red, green, blue, and lastly the yellow candle. You will feel relaxed and peaceful in love with all of the spirits and ready to serve them and obey all the Holy Spirits of Lucky Hoodoo. You will then clap your hands together quickly so that a sound is made and you will say, either softly or silently:

"AND IT IS DONE HOLY SPIRITS OF LUCKY HOODOO."

Put your candles away if you store them and keep the request written out on card or paper to think about each day. You may do this ritual as often as you like. Be sure of good lulck, for you are a Hoodoo.

Lesson Three: Hoodoo Methods for Mind-Power Development

It has been proven many times before and will be proven for centuries to come that if you serve the Hoodoo Spirits faithfully, they will develop your mind. Now please understand it is the spirits who do this work for you, for if you did not need them or could do this development of mind-power on your own, or if the secrets and methods of this development were known to mankind already they would be taught in the schools, or your power would be there already or else you would have no need of Lucky Hoodoo. But because this is not so and because only the spirits can give what is spiritual -- and mind-power development is spiritual -- then we must come to terms with the wonderful spirits of Hoodoo in order to build ourselves up as mental magicians.

There are a number of methods for mind-power development which are favored by the Spirits of Lucky Hoodoo. These are methods which are based on the ways in which the spirits have directed the development of human mind power in the past. All of the powerful minds in the past have been able to get their mind-development from the spirits, because they made a contract with the spirits and lived up to the terms of that contract. In Lucky Hoodoo the spirits expect you to live up to the terms of your contract and this is the basis of their serving you with good luck and favors.

In mind-development what happens is that the mind is given some more power from the Hoodoo Spirits. In other words, they come in and give to the students an additional gift of power of mind-substance. This mind-power or mental energy or substance comes from the world of the spirits where everything is mind. The whole world there is one of mind. This is a powerful world and this is where our minds and souls and spirits go to after death. Nothing in that world is physical because everything is completely mind and mind-energy. That is where the mind-power comes from that helps our minds to become more developed and more powerful. Mind is to that world what sunlight and fresh air and water are to our world. Here we have many things to help the physical body develop and be strong, but in that world of mind all that is needed is mind-energy because mind is the only being in that world. So the spirits bring to us this power or mind-energy and this helps us to develop and become more able to work with them, communicate with them and to understand them. This is what mind-power development is actually.

Now there are four methods which we accept here in Lucky Hoodoo for the development of mind-power. These are all successful methods and can be used by each student of Lucky Hoodoo. The methods are very simple and have been made very clear for your use. The methods are called:

1. The dream-power method of mind development
2. The method of Hoodoo spiritual prayer for mind development
3. The method of the Holy House for mind development
4. The shadow-stuff method of mind-power development

For effectiveness it is important to combine methods and to use all four of these wonderful methods on a regular basis. For example, in Voudoo and Hoodoo temple-schools, such as my own, we teach the young students to make use of all four methods of development each day. There are certain times for doing each method, we say, and they should take advantage of these times. The dream-power method is used at night while the student is sleeping, but before he goes to bed, he will make use of the shadow-stuff method, in a dark room, with only a black or blue light bulb giving some kind of shadow and dark mixture. This is when he will use deep meditation, which is really the type of meditation which leads to sleep and which is done when the body is freed of all care and ready for spiritual development. The prayer method can be used during the day for it possible to receive mind energy by prayer at any time and in any place. The method of the Holy House is a mind-projection where you will send your mind to the place of the spirits at any time and while you are anywhere. It is a method for developing the sense of the spirits' presence in telepathy and mental mediumship. For this reason it is a very practical method.

All of these methods are used by me each day. They are so simple and so clear that anyone can make use of them to the fullest sense of results. In Lucky Hoodoo it is important for us to understand that the spirits have made it as easy as possible for you to develop your mind-power. They have gone out of their way in order to make mind-power development as wonderful and as convenient as possible. Because in Lucky Hoodoo the emphasis is upon results and upon success. That is why we try to do everything as completely and as simply as we can, so that the spirits can come to you and help you and you can benefit quickly and easily.

We will now discuss the ways in which to make use of these four methods which are designed by the spirits to help you develop mind-power so that you can know more and do more with the spirits. First I will want to say something about the method of prayer and the method of the Holy House. This is the method which is suited to the active person who might want to take a five-minute break here or there during the working day in order to build up his mind-power contacts. These two methods are very simple and they are concerned with ways in which we can keep in touch easily with the spirits all day long. Actually the spirits are just near as our fingertips and we can make contact quickly and easily.

PRAYER AND THE HOLY HOUSE OF HOODOO SPITRITS
Up to now we have been going over what I will call a form of ritual prayer in the exercises at the end of Lessons One and Two. Now I want to say that the Prayer Method of Mind-Power Development is very simple and it is just this: You will take time off from what you are doing or you will do something that is automatic and does not require mental attention. Then you will focus your mind through attention upon the spirits and you will talk to them in silent thought and attune your mind to how they will respond. To attune your mind means simply to listen to what comes from them after you have made contact through silent thought. This is the basis of all prayers in every one of the world religions. However, because it is so simple, many persons do not want to do it. On the other hand, many persons are always making contact with the spirits through silent thought and live in a positive state of attunement all of the time or at least most of the time. This is so simple, for it only means that you keep your attention mostly directed towards the spirits and the gods, which are the major spirits, of Lucky Hoodoo. In this sense, then, the student is always able to get back from the spirits mind-energy, because he is attuned to them always. This wonderful method is really practical for the everyday working person or even someone who does a lot of mental work. On the other hand, the big strong blacks who did heavy physical labor on the plantations of the French in Old Louisiana used to occupy their minds entirely with this method and thus developed telepathy and mental mediumship, because they were obliged to do purely physical work and their minds were free for the easy development of these powers through the use of silent thought.

In the prayer method you have only to address yourself to the spirits in thought, on the other hand the method of the Holy House is different in a sense because it is more complicated. It makes use of the power of the mind and imagination to travel to the home of the spirits in the world of mind. There the mind is fed and clothed and housed and taught by the spirits. In order for the mind to get there the imagination is used to help the mind by means of visualizing or seeing with the mind's eye the inner worlds and what they are like. In Lucky Hoodoo it is important to make use of the mind and imagination together. In all types of Voudoo you have to visualize the scene on the inner planes where things are happening. This means that you have to do a lot of daydreaming and use the mind in creative imagination. When you go to the Holy House of the Spirits what happens is that they inject into your soul and spirit the mind-energy of their world. This means that they will be able to give you more and more and as often as you come to visit them. Sometimes this method is used exclusively and is known as the method of making spiritual visits. It can be used just like the prayer method if the person is developed enough. I myself make use of this method during the day with the prayer method. If I have a lot of free time, I use the Holy House Visit method; if my time is limited I use the prayer method instead.

The next method is a combination of two methods. One method prepares for the other method just as the prayer method can be used to prepare for the method of visiting the Holy House of Spirits. These two methods now to be discussed are very powerful and very esoteric and should be used only by a person who feels he is strong enough in Lucky Hoodoo to handle the powers which come to him, from beyond.

DREAM POWER AND SHADOW STUFF

The method of mind development known as dream power is very simple, also. It means that when you are asleep the Hoodoo spirits come to you and take you in your dreams to their schools and temples and then they teach you to be able to recall what happened to you and what you learned. You may take a while to do this, so that the Hoodoo student usually does a deep meditation or a light mentation, or silent thought, exercise to recall what happened and what was learned. Then the student will make up notes of what he learned and use this as the basis for future studies. The Hoodoo student tries to go to his dream power class every night, if he can. For this reason sleep is a very important matter for the student of Lucky Hoodoo. This is the simple method of dream power. The next method can be understood as a preparation for it.

Shadow stuff is an old Hoodoo idea which goes all the way back to the man in the caves. At that time man became fascinated with his shadow and its magickal power. Shadow stuff is the substance of shadows and it is highly magickal and can be used to develop mind-power. This is the way in which it works. You will place yourself iin a room where you are burning either one candle or a blue light or a black light. This is to create a lot of shadow stuff. Now, the student will remove all of his clothing and having taken a bath in water he will give himself a shadow bath. This means that with your fingers you will pass your hands all over your body as close to the surface of the skin as you can without touching the skin. You will "wash" the body with the power of the shadow-stuff and while you are doing this you will be having the spirits give you more and more power. For they will be standing by and feeding mind energy into the shadow-stuff that you make use of.

It is sort of like when you want to take a bath and someone will stand by in order to hold the bar or cake of soap. The spirits are holding the mind-energy for you and because of this you are becoming more and more powerful. With every stroke of the hands, they feed into the shadow-stuff between your fingers more and more mind-energy power. This is important and it is good for us to understand that this process is useful also in healing because we are working with vital energies from the spiritual world of mind and the vital energy is becoming more and more a part of our own growing health.

In the Creole countries and parts of the world, everyone takes a bath before going to bed and one in the morning while getting up. This is to protect the health of the body from bad influences and impurities. The Creole Hoodooists who are really serious about their magickal and mental development do this. They give themselves a good bath with shadow-stuff each evening before going to bed where they will make use of the dream power method of development. Thus, the bath with shadow--stuff is really the preparation for the dream power method of learning more and more about the spirits and their wonderful world of wisdom and esoteric knowledge.

It is important to make use of these methods so that the student can increase his mental development and mind-energy. The spirits have given us these wonderful methods of improvement and we are asked by them simply to give them a try and then we will become more and more convinced that this is a terrific way to advance in the world of spiritual knowledge, power, and wisdom because this is the spirit's own way of development. You will learn to do more and more things with these simple methods. The spirits want you to build onto these methods and to increase your skills in Lucky Hoodoo. These four methods are, therefore, the basis for a lot of other techniques which we will teach to you. But these are the basics as taught to us directly by the Voudoo gods and Hoodoo spirits. This is the method which we call the way of the spirits and it is their way from start to finish. Why don't you try it, so that you can become a big Lucky Hoodoo.

Lesson Four: How to Control the Minds of Other People

It is a proven fact that the Hoodoo spirits can help you control the minds of others. The method is very simple really, but it makes use of a great deal of power. The spirits of Hoodoo supply both the power and the methods of using it. Now, in Hoodoo we do not say that something is right or wrong, we simply let the spirits tell us what they will do for us. If we serve them faithfully enough, they will do everything for us. They will do anything that we ask them to do including the control of other minds.

In Hoodoo we mean that we can attract and hold the attention of another for as long as we wish and then release this power of attraction and be free of such a person. Actually we do not want to control them entirely, for to do so we would have to be spirits ourselves, which we are not. However, we can hold a person to us, make them do what we wish, and have them constantly present for us to have wherever and whenever we wish. This is what we mean by controlling others through the spirits.

Many persons wish to control others for purposes of love and sex. I wish to say that these are the easiest ways in which to get the cooperation of the Hoodoo spirits, for they favor the release of much sexual energy on the surface of our planet, because when this happens mankind is happier and more peaceful. In Hoodoo the spirits teach that mankind's problems are due to a lack of love, especially sexual love. If there was more sexual love, they say, there would be no more wars, crimes, or other hostile actions. It is because man stores up in himself so much sexual energy that he wishes to commit crimes and cause wars, but actually he only needs to make love and then he is very much at peace with everything and everyone.

If you wish to control the mind of another person in order to get a better job or money, then you must be prepared to have sex with that person, for the spirits of the control-work family are also the spirits of sexual love. If any person wishes to control another anywhere, they must be prepared to have sex with that person is some form. That is, they must visualize the act of sex in order to make their wish to control come true. For this reason, in Hoodoo we teach that your power to visualize and to daydream must be strong enough to help you get what you wish. You must be prepared to make the mind strong with desire. Now when you visualize and imagine what you're going to do, you do not have to go beyond this action. I say that you must be prepared to have sex, but I do not say that you have to have sex. That is unimportant. Many men do not want to have sex with another man, certainly, we know this. This is true of many women. But the power must be built up in your mind to have sex with the person that you wish to control in order that the spirits come to assist you. For this reason you must give much of your time to building up a strong sexual imagination, if you are to be truly successful.

After you have done this work with your imagination and used this strong power to see your desire in action, as sex activity, you must then come to do a very simple type of magick, but which is very powerful. This is to make a magick square out of the first name of the person with whom you are imagining that you are having sexual action. Since desire for power and control is really desire to have control over the body of another and hence over the mind, which we feel is an epiphenomenon of the body, strong sexual imagination and desire are really very important. You have built up this deep desire or magickal lust. The more details you add to the visualization the better it is for it becomes very strong through this method. Then when you come to make the magick sqaure you will put in the power of your magickal lust, for this is not a natural lust but an unnatural power generated by desire in a magickal sense; then, your magickal lust will, I say, be fitted into the compartments made by the magick square and from there it will be fed into the magickal computer or system of the Hoodoo spirits.

In order to understand how a magickal square works, you have to understand that spiritual power and energy, such as magickal lust, has to have some definite shape or form so that it can be used by the spirits. If it lacks this form, it is like an unbottled liquid or gas, which is difficult to handle in any effective way. Thus we are making it possible for the Hoodoo spirits to help us by placing the magickal lust power in the magickal square. Now let us see how easy it is to fit the power into the shape of the magickal square. I think that as an example of a person you want to control we can select someone named "John." You have now done your visualization work with his image and have built up all of that energy. Now hold the energy in your mind by saying: I HOLD THE MAGICKAL LUST POWER IN MY MIND.

Now you will begin to make a magic square of the name JOHN. It is very easy. All you have to do is write the name in a square form following my example:

JOHN
O   H
H   O
NHOJ

You see that what you have done is to write the name in four different directions in order to form a square. Now, you will fill in the center by making the letters of the name form diagonally across the magick square, in one direction only, which is from the bottom left to the top right, or from N in NHOJ to N in JOHN and thus parallel to this diagonal direction, as follows:

JOHN (top right)
OHNH
HNHO
(bottom left) NHOJ

Now you will infuse this magick square with the magickal lust power with this sentence of power: I INFUSE THIS MAGICK SQUARE WITH THE MAGICKAL LUST POWER IN MY MIND.

Now that you have infused the magick square with power, it is time to offer the magick square to the spirits for their consideration and feeding. It is important to understand that magickal powers serve to feed the spirits and make them strong, strong enough to help you. I think that you know this for you have fed power to them before and they have been pleased with it, for you were taught this in the second lesson. But now you will feed power to the spirits bu taking the magick square apart and then using each of the words in it as a part of a powerful charm. First, you will take the top word and feed it to the spirits. This is the name of the person, whose mind you really wish to control, so you will say the word JOHN. Then you will say the next word, moving from the top of the magick square to the bottom, the next being: OHNH. Try to pronounce each and every word as best you can. The spirits are pleased by your effort, they do not care if you make a mistake, just as long as you try to do your very best. The next word is HNHO. Finally you will say the last word, which forms the bottom of the magick square, and that is NHOJ. Then you will say the following prayer:
MIGHTY SPIRITS OF LUCKY HOODOO

I AM YOUR HUMBLE SERVANT AND PRIEST
YET IN MY SEEKING TO SERVE THEE I FIND
THAT I MUST CONTROL THE MIND OF (name the person)
IN ORDER TO SERVE THEE BETTER AND MORE POWERFULLY.
PLEASE ACCEPT THE OFFERING OF THE MAGICK SQUARE
WHICH I AM MAKING TO THEE, SO THAT I WILL BE
BETTER ABLE TO SERVE THEE AND MUCH HAPPIER IN MY
LIFE. FOR THIS IS WHAT I ASK FROM YOU AND
PLEASE DO NOT LET ME GO EMPTY.

Then you will say to the spirits the following closing prayer of devotion:
YOU WHO ARE THE MOST POWERFUL SPIRITS IN THE WORLD,
I LOVE YOU. ALL OF MY BEING IS YOURS AND ALL OF BODY,
WEALTH, LIFE, AND EVERYTHING I HAVE EVER DONE
IF GOOD IS ALSO YOURS. I AM YOUR PRIEST AND YOUR
SERVANT, SO PLEASE HELP ME WHEN I CALL UPON YOU IN
MY NEED. I AM YOUR PRIEST AND YOUR SERVANT.
TRULY, I LOVE YOU VERY MUCH.

You may say this prayer at anytime, but it is best to use this whole magickal ritual in connection with your yellow, blue, green, red, and black candles, on your altar-tables at home. Between the black candle in the center and the red candle in the east, you may place the paper with the magick square written upon it. Be sure to have a glass placed between the black candle and the blue candle, but this time it will be filled with a proper fruit-flavored brandy, which is favored by the spirits of Lucky Hoodoo, as to their taste and why you wish to control the mind of another person for purposes of power over that person for business or genral gain at your job or getting another and better job, you will use orange-flavored brandy, or triple-sec, or cointreau, as they are sometimes called. If you wish to have more money and you wish to control the mind of another person so that you will have more money from them in some way, you will use blackberry-flavored brandy. On the other hand, if you wish to control the mind of another person for purposes of lovemaking and sexual excitement, you will use peach-flavored brandy. For controlling a mind so that circumstances under that person's control be favorable to you, like a judge, boss, or some superior, you will use cherry-flavored brandy. At the end of the ceremony you will then take the glass of brandy or liqueur into your hand and you will say
I DRINK INTO MY BEING THE POWERS OF THE MIGHTY
AND INVISIBLE SPIRITS OF LUCKY HOODOO WHO
ARE EVERYWHERE PRESENT.

Then you will drink down the glass of brandy and meditate for a few moments about the spirits. Then you will put down the glass and you will put out the candles as you have been taught to do in Lesson Two. Then you will take your hands and clap them together and say
MAGICK SQUARES OF SEXUAL ENERGY
TAKE FLIGHT TO THE SPIRITS,
TAKE FLIGHT TO THE GODS,
TAKE FLIGHT, TAKE FLIGHT, AWAY, AWAY!

Then you will close the entire ritual by saying:
AND IT IS DONE HOLY SPIRITS OF LUCKY HOODOO.

Lesson Five: Hoodoo "Contraite" Ways of Attracting Big Money

The secret of attracting money to your pocket is one of the basic laws of Lucky Hoodoo. For this law of money-attraction is based upon the magickal working of the very low elementals of earth and water, from which our whole system is built up. We seek to work with the earth and water spirits or elementals, because they hold in their power the keys to all the wealth in the world. Money is kept in stone banks, behind iron and steel doors, and recorded in account ledgers locked behind stone walls. Buried treasure is deep in the earth, hidden under rock, stone, and soil. Gold is an extremely heavy metal, for it wants to cling to the core of the earth, it feels the pull of elemental power very strongly. When it comes time for gold to appear on the surface, we find it in a pool of water, or it has materialized in some mountain stream or been brought up from the ocean floor. Water and earth cooperate in all money magick.

The Most Powerful Signs

Those who come to control gold and money draw their power from the earth-signs of the zodiac, especially the Sun in Taurus, Virgo, and Capricorn, which are the places of wealth. The Moon, when it is in these signs, is powerful if its energies are used well, especially in combination with the Sun in another earth sign. Water is good for the manifestation of wealth, so that Scorpio will manifest hidden wealth, Cancer will manifest wealth locked up in systems of power or institutions and commerce. Pisces will manifest the power of silver which stands behind paper money. The Moon in the water signs serves as the medium for the materialization of wealth, so that a person with the Sun in Capricorn and the Moon in Cancer will direct his powers for the realization of money from the established sources of social wealth, such as banks, governments, and large corporations and trusts.

Not everyone, however, is so fortunate in their corporations and trusts. In fact, many persons wish to have wealth, but are without the powerful circumstances for its manifestation. That is why Lucky Hoodoo can help to provide you with the wealth of earth and water, if this is your goal, even though you do not have these centers of power within you to work for you. For by reason of the methods of Lucky Hoodoo, it is possible for you to come into contact with these same spirits of elemental power of wealth and hence overcome all lack and limitation which might be facing you. The secret is by means of the contract, or "contraite" as we say in French, which is an agreement between yourself and the spirits for the obtainment of wealth in exchange for services to these spirits. The "contraite" is the key to true wealth and it is the method whereby gold and paper money will be yours, and that your present supply of money be increased many times.

The "Contraite"

As we have said, every contract is an agreement with specific terms or parts, which link the parties to the agreement and specify what is sought and the terms for getting this objective. Everything that we have been teaching you so far has been in the form of a contract, whereby we have agreed to serve the Hoodoo spirits in exchange for the favor we are seeking. Thus the law of making a contract with the spirits is something we have been using all along. However, here we are coming to a new understanding of the contract, for now we will make use of the contract as the magickal instrument for getting what we want. Before, we would serve the spirits and thus fulfill the terms of the contract; now we will have the terms of the contract generate powerful energies so that it is possible for us to make definite plans and realize what we are gaining in the line of wealth. The contract becomes for us the method whereby we tune in on the world of spirit and partake of the infinite law of supply so that we are able to get what we are seeking. Thus, the contract is something like a radio or a television set, which we have decided to turn to the station marked for attracting big money.

A contract is therefore a magickal agreement between yourself and the spirits. In this case what you do is go over in your mind what you understand by your agreement with the spirits. It has sixteen terms or articles, which are the parts or meanings which both reflect upon and govern your work with the spirits and how you iwll be able to get by attraction the big money you seek.

Setting Up The "Contraite"
First of all, you are going to make two small diagrams. One will be for the magickal powers that you are using, we will call it "A." The next will be for what it is to do, or "B" for results. Each of these diagrams will have eight parts, for a total of 16 in all. Each one will be numbered, so that you will know exactly what and where to place each within the diagrams. The basic structure of the diagrams is as follows, and they represent the elemental powers of earth and water as they are used to attract big money:

	A			B
1. Sun in Capricorn	5. Son–Pa	9. Attract gold	13. Sun in Cancer
2. Sun in Virgo	6. Huna & Voudoo	10. Lucky Silver	14. Sun in Pisces
3. Sun in Taurus	7. Witchcraft	11. Attract liquid	15. Moon in Taurus,
4. Moon in Scorpio,	8. Shamanism	or fluid money	Virgo, Capricorn
Pisces, and Cancer		12. Attract in-	16. Sun in Scorpio
		vested Funds	

Now, in order to better explain this system of energies, let me say that numbers five through eight refer to the ancient Hoodoo spirit energies as they are present in the world today and as they were in the past. So that if a meeting of witches is being held while you are doing this contract, part of the energies generated by their weird and strange rites will be attracted by your own efforts and hence add on to the power that you are building up. Also, these types of power (from five to eight) are rich sources of pure elemental contact and are perhaps the best expressions in the human world of the powers generated by the zodiac signs from one through four. Lastly, nine through 12 refer to what we want done, or what is to be done as a result of the elemental magicks being used. Thirteen through 16 refer to the magnetic levels of attraction which pull into manifestation or materialize what we want to receive or have manifest. Thus, nine through 16 receive the efforts of one through eight, whose main effect in this work is to attract big money.

Now, I cannot emphasize too much the importance of the different parts of this contract. They all work together like a magickal machine or computer. Their purpose is to make our wishes to come true, once we have done something really powerful about them. Now what we have to do is a ritual called the "glossary" of terms of the contract, which we fit into the squares of the two diagrams, which we now make into one diagram as follows:

1	5	9	13
2	6	10	14
3	7	11	15
4	8	12	16

Our contract is now one magickal diagram. the powers that we are going to put together with our minds have been fused by our imagination into one system. We are now ready to build up in our minds the terms of the contract we have made with the spirits, so that we will be able to attract big money.

The Glossary of Points of Contact With the Spirits
With your imagination, you will establish contact with the world of the spirits in terms of the 16 conditions or points in your agreement with them. Each word will then be seen placed in the proper box having the same number. Thus word number Two will be placed in box number Two and so on. By making contact with your mind and imagination between the word and the proper box, you make contact with the spirits in the 16 ways which are important for their knowing what you want to help and serve them. This method of making contact helps you to realize why primitive man was able to have so much power. It also serves to explain the power of certain witch doctors and mighty shamans in the world today. For these men know the ways in which to make contact and keep contact with the points of spirit–power.

It is very important to understand the magick in making contact with the spirits. These elemental powers are brought into touch with us when we make this type of mental contact with them. It is like touching them and waking them up. They wake up and then understand what we want from them. They further know that we are more than willing to help them in the most ancient of ways, which is the way of the early magicians who made the first elemental points of contact with the spirits. We will now discuss the terms of the point of contact, which is the way in which the "contraite" works.

1. EARTH: This is the substance of the treasure sought by man, for it is the most basic and fundamental of elements, out of which all is made, including human life and its needs and objects of desire.

2. TRANCE: This is the secret state of mind wherein the spirits give direct messages to the seekers after wealth. Listen to what they are to tell you, for they speak in the very quiet moments of everyday experience.

3. FEED SPIRITS: This is the purpose of all magickal work, to feed the spirits with energies. Now, make an offering to the spirits of your own energy by rubbing your hands together and then extending them to the gods.

4. ABORIGINAL MAN: Such a man carrying a magickal staff, or wand, is the most primitive image of the magician, the earliest image of the true shaman. Imagine yourself to be such a person serving the spirits.**

5. ARCHAIC: This means that what we are doing is based on the most ancient memories of the human race. Truly what we are doing derives from the dawn of time;

6. NUDIST: The magickal practitioners remove their clothing and thus the shamans work without clothing in order to release the powers.

7. BISEXUAL: True shamanism is neither exclusively heterosexual or homo-sexual. The shaman is prepared to make sexo-magickal contact with any spirit-

possessed magician, for thus he makes contact with the spirits.

8.　PRIMITIVE:　Simple and exact methods are used which are based on very ancient workings.

9.　POSSESSED:　The shaman may be possessed by both anthropomorphic and theriomorphic spirits, appearing as men, animals, insects, or other fantastic beings.

10.　LYCANTHROPIC:　The were-animal mediumship of the shaman is the source of all teaching and truth.

11.　UNCONSCIOUS:　This is the place of the deepest contact with the gods in their own realm of the world of pure elemental power.

12.　SUBCONSCIOUS:　This is the world fed by the gods and in turn it is to feed the conscious mind with gold and all success in wealth.

13.　ANIMAL SKINS:　These are the drawing powers to success from our past lifetimes.　This is the remembering of past animal lives.

14.　DIVINATORY ORACLE:　Here the teaching is given by the gods by means of indirect message or the symbolic form of speech.

**NOTE:　We are to communicate with the spirits by means of these images, for this is their language, a language of pictures in the imagination.

15.　ELEMENTAL:　This is the source of what we seek or the keeper of magickal powers.

16.　WATER:　This is the place in experience where the treasure is found, or where wealth manifests.　It is the vehicle or the medium for the materialization of the big money we are attracting.

You will be sure to place these wonderful terms in the proper boxes in the magickal diagram, while thinking about each one in your mind. You have been able by this method to create a primitive setting, where you as the shaman are actively seeking the spirits to assist you in your work.　This is what the attraction of big money is all about.　Soon the money will begin to happen to you, once the spirits get the message through the points of contact, which will bring their minds into contact with your own desires.　Remember the importance of using mind and imagination to build up the image of what you are doing so that they will be attracted and take notice.

NOTE IN CLOSING:
As in the previous lesson, you can use your magickal altar or table for basic work. Place the magickal diagram simply between the black and the red candle.　This time use a really shamanistic strong drink in place of fruit brandy, so use "Green Chartreuse," which is 110 proof, since it is a powerful spirit, much like the powerful spirits of primitive magickal systems.　If you can't use Chartreuse, then make use of Akavit, which is likewise very strong. Use a small amount and then drink it at the end, after you have offered it to the spirits. Do this ritual near to the new Moon, the time of which you can get from the newspaper.　This is a powerful method of attracting wealth and should be used often to build up your power. Work in this area constantly, so that the spirits will come to know that you are firm in your contract.

Lesson Six: Good Possession for Success Versus Bad Possession for Failure

The True Lucky Hoodoo Is Possessed

Everyone in the world has either good or bad luck. This means that they are either possessed by good spirits or they are under the spell of negative influences. There are not any bad spirits, because all in the spirit world are very good. However, many negative influences have been created over the years by many kinds of wrong thinking and as a result of this build up over the years, many people are simply lacking in good spirits, they are under the spell of negative influences. When we say in ordinary life, "He/she is not in good spirits," what we really mean is that he/she does not have enough or any good spirits in him/her to make him act happy and full of power. This problem faces so many people, that in Lucky Hoodoo we have discovered ways of correcting this problem of lack of spirits.

Now we say that a person is possessed if there are spirits in him to help him. The spirits can be either in body or mind. Thus a very smart or wise person has a lot of spirit in their mind and brain, so that they can think quickly and easily. A great lover, who has much success with women, would have a lot of spirit in his nature, and in his body which does the work of his nature. A successful salesperson would have a lot of spirit in her voice and head, so that there is always the power there to persuade and convince people to buy from her. In other words, wherever you go, you would find that successful people somehow have attracted the spirits into their being. This is why they are possessed with good luck.

Now, those who are not successful are under the spell of what I will call a bad possession or influence of the negative, which means to be a failure. In Lucky Hoodoo we do not believe in possession by the devil, but we do believe that a person can be under the negatuive spells cast by his own lack of good spirits. For when you lack you either do something to get more than what you have and hence overcome lack, or you simply don't do anything good and you come more and more under the negative influences of bad luck and negative influence. This means that you have to decide which way you want to go. Now, only you can make this decision. I have told you that the spirits of Lucky Hoodoo want to help you, and they really want to come into your being and help you through possession. However, there are many people who are so foolish that they want to keep the spirits out, so they are constantly under the spells of the negative influences of being poor, being sick, being ignorant, and being foolish and lacking will-power. Those people are really, as I would say, in very serious need of help, but they close the door in the face of the help that the spirits can give them. We might ask why they do that. Well, the answer is very simple and that is why we are writing this course. The reason they shut off the powers of Lucky Hoodoo and prefer the negative is because they do not know how to get rid of bad possession for failure and replace it with good possession for success. Now this is what I am going to tell you to do, since it is so easy to get rid of negative influences.

Our Secret African Prayer for Powerful Success

Many years ago, in fact hundreds of years ago, in Africa, a priest of the Hoodoo religion discovered the key to all success in good possession. One day he was praying for good luck and he looked down on the ground and he saw a stick writing a message in the dirt. The message was a wonderful and really powerful prayer, which we have cherished for many years. It is a very simple prayer but what it does is clear your body and mind of negative and bad possessions and open you up to the good by inviting the powers of Lucky Hoodoo to come into your body. This is a prayer you can use to treat others who have a lack of good spirits and you can also use it any time you feel a letdown in your power. For you may have done something to keep the flow of good spirits out of your life and now you need them to come in and get you going in the right direction. Well you can use this prayer whenever you think it will do some good, because it is a free prayer, and need not be used only under special occasions and times. This prayer sums up the best of the old teaching and draws in with its use the truest and best powers of Lucky Hoodoo in the world.

A Free Prayer for Lucky Hoodoo
This prayer is as follows: First you wiiwll say to yourself, and you can be saying this for yourself or for another, "I don't want bad possession for failure, I want good possession for success." Then you will begin the simple, free prayer as it follows, thinking or speaking with firmness and strong conviction of willpower, as strong as can be:
        NEGATIVE FORCES OUT!
        BAD LUCK BE GONE!
Now by saying that you have given an exorcism or treatment to cleanse the body and mind of bad influences by driving them out. This is the healing by purifying the body and mind or any evil presence. Now we have to bring in the good powers to fill up every part, so that you will have a good possession for success. This means that you will now say or think:
        POSITIVE POWERS IN!
        LUCKY HOODOO SPIRITS BE EVERYWHERE IN MY BODY!
        LUCKY HOODOO SPIRITS FILL MY MIND WITH POWERFUL SUCCESS!
That is your wonderful Voudoo Treatment based on the calling forth of the Holy Spirits of Lucky Hoodoo, so that you are filled "up to the brim" with good influences and powerful energy for making success yours.

How It Has Helped Many
This method is so simple, yet it has been used in Africa, Haiti, South America and the West Indies for many years and taught by the Hou'gan and Bokors as the best and quickest means of healing any problem. In a way it is the key to all treatment, as well as being the best of all self-treatment methods. Here are some examples.
        A man was just married to a very lovely woman, but suddenly and surprisingly learned that he was unable to properly function as her husband and mate and thus could not make physical love to her. He went to a magician who diagnosed the case as one of telepathic infliction of lack of nature. It was caused by a very envious sorceror, who wanted to keep the man and woman apart so that he could have relations with both of them and thus use them for his magickal powers in control of people. The magician gave immediate treatment and exorcised the negative influence of lack of nature in the man and filled him up with lots of good spirits for luck in love and sex. He went back to his wife and now after ten years of very happy marriage with much satisfaction in sex and love they have eight fine sons and three daughters. The method of treatment was the same as what I have given, except that the magician did it silently and for the man who came to him. How did he give this treatment? Well, he used the word HIS in place of MY in the prayer and he placed his hand on the man's

head when he said the prayer silently in thought to himself. The man paid him $500 for this healing, because it was so powerful and the man has never needed the healing again after that first treatment. Also, his business became more and more successful and now he is so rich he will be able to educate all his babies through law or medical school.

Here is another case which shows how it works. There was a man who had lots of money but each day it became less and less, because he could not make any money, he could only spend it without any good return. He went to a spirit shaman in his hometown. The shaman immediately diagnosed the problem as being the negative presence of the influence of lack of money inflow, which is different from the influence of money lack, since this man had lots of money. He took the man into his temple and made him take a magickal bath and do a secret ritual with him, during which magickal work at the time of the release of power the shaman placed his hand on the man and gave the prayer for this man to remove the curse of lack of income. The man was immediately cured and went home to find that so many of his investments were paying off that he had become richer over night than he was the gloomy morning he went to the shaman's home for treatment. This man within two days had doubled his total fortune and is now one of the richest men in northern India, where there are many rich men.

Lastly, let me describe the use of this prayer by a student of mine in Bridge-town, Barbados. This student wanted to get four things done. He wanted to get a good job, and for this he needed a car. He also wanted a lovely young girl in the town to consent to marry him. Lastly, he wanted to be accepted as a part-time law student with a big lawyer in this same town. He wrote to me about this and I sent him the prayer rather than give him absent treatment, because I wanted him to have the experience of using it, so that he could help others. Well, he got the prayer and sat down at his altar that evening and lit his candles, just as you do in Lucky hoodoo. He wrote out on a piece of paper what he wanted to have and he concentrated on these four needs for a few minutes. Then he said the prayer. No sooner had he come to the end of the prayer than there was a knock at his door. He quickly put out the candles and thanked the spirits for the permission to serve them and went to the door. A friend of his was there who said, "Joe, you can use my car for the next two months, while I am away. Mr. H needs you to drive to and from the big city and will pay you well for the matter, but you have to begin tomorrow, Monday morning." He thanked the friend and said that he would do exactly that. He went back into his room and sat down. Immediately there was a ring at his bell and he looked out to find his girlfriend Clarissa, who had a letter for him. She said, "Joe, here is a letter for you from the big lawyer; it was left at your door by the postman. May I bring it up to you, I have much to tell you." He let her come up and when he opened the letter he learned that he had been accepted as a part-time every-evening student of the big lawyer, and so he would someday be a big lawyer himself. It would not conflict with his new good job that he got and also would mean income from extra legal clerk work he would do for the man. Clarissa looked at hime and said to him softly with her eyes hot with emotion, "Yes, Joe, I will be your wife." Now that is what I call the quickest and most complete proof of the power of good possession for success on record. It is my view that there are so many cases of this type of success that there is no need to doubt the power of good possession. I only learn of these matters when someone writes to me about it, but many are so happy that whenever you feel the need for yourself or another, simply use this wonderful free prayer of

Lucky Hoodoo, and so depossess yourself of all negative influences while repossessing yourself of all good spirits for amazing success, when you say:

NEGATIVE FORCES OUT!
BAD LUCK BE GONE!

POSITIVE POWERS IN!
LUCKY HOODOO SPIRITS BE EVERYWHERE IN MY BODY!
LUCKY HOODOO SPIRITS FILL MY MIND WITH POWERFUL SUCCESS!

Because it works every time you use it, just wait and see.

Lesson Seven: Hoodoo Secrets for Getting Lucky Numbers That Win

The Spirits Help Us to Win when We Make Bets

Whenever a person wants to place a bet of any type, or whenever that person wants to get some kind of number that will win in a game of chance or sport, all he has to do is go to the spirits of Lucky Hoodoo, and success will be his. It is very simple, for the spirits will give us favors, if we continue to serve them, for this is part of the contract we have with them. The more we promise to serve them and to work for them, the more they will show us favors by making circumstances and happenings come into agreement with our wishes. So they can make us more and more lucky, because they control all events from behind the scenes.

Do not think that we can have luck by ourselves. We can't. The spirits alone can bring us luck, and they make the winner to be who they want the winner to be in every case. In every circumstance of success in bets and games of chance, the spirits have come into the picture and have adjusted the real circumstances so that the actual winning person was their choice. It is very simple for the spirits to do this, because they can control space and time. If they can control states of space and time, they can also control everything that occurs inside of space and time. Well, we know that everything occurs in space and time, and what the spirits do is simply make arrangements in space and time that are convenient to what they want to happen. They are so powerful that they can set the stage for any event that happens and no one would be any wiser if they did because they act entirely behind the scenes in everything that they do. That is, they act from the invisible side of nature, and build up all things as they want them to be or happen. So the spirits control everything.

Now, the spirits know that we want to win when we make bets and when we go to the races; they want us to pick the lucky numbers that will come in first or ahead of the others. So they have worked out a way of letting us know which will be the lucky numbers and these are the ones we are to follow if we really want to get to be a winner and never again be a loser. The method is very simple and it involves first of all our really wanting to be a winner. Next it involves our making use of an oracle way of learning from the spirits what numbers are right for what games or races. In order to get into the right mood, you have to use your table and candles and quiet yourself down and get ready to receive the communications from the spirits. Remember that they are ready to help you, once you make contact with them. Next, you will begin to use the oracle of spirit lucky numbers, which is a simple system for making contact with the invisibles.

The Oracle of the Spirits for Getting Lucky Numbers

Take a simple pair of dice and say to the spirits that you want this pair of dice to serve as your communication machine with the spirit world. You will then bless the pair of dice with the following prayer to the spirits of Lucky Hoodoo:

SPIRITS OF LUCKY HOODOO SEND YOUR POWER INTO THIS
PAIR OF DICE SO THAT I WILL BE ABLE TO KNOW THAT
YOU ARE COMMUNICATING WITH ME THROUGH THIS MEDIUM.

Now that you have set the dice aside for this special use, you cannot use them for anything else, because they are so holy. They cannot be used in any other way than for the spirits to come into them and use them to speak through. And if you think of doing otherwise, or do otherwise, you will cause the power to leave the dice and then you will have to have the dice made magickal all over again. So, remember to keep the dice on the altar in a special way and never use them in a way for which they were not intended. This is important if you want to hold the power of the spirits in your life, you have got to keep the special objects in a sacred way. That is not for any other purpose but for the spiritual purpose for which they were dedicated to the spirits.

Now, in any race or any betting sequence, they usually have a major sequence and a minor sequence of numbers. For example, you have the first race, the second race, the third, the fourth, etc. But you also have horse number one, two, three, four, and so on. Sometimes they have different numbers but you will find that the numbers are usually between two and 12. So this means that you will be asking the spirits for two sets of numbers; the number of the race and the number of the horse in a particular race. You have to keep this in mind, for this is a precise science of horse-race betting and should not be used unless you are willing to take the time and effort to get your numbers from the spirits with care.

So now you have in your mind that you will be asking the spirits for two sets of numbers. These numbers will apply to the race you plan to attend, for you will apply lucky numbers to any given set of races and the spirits will then control the events so as to issue success of the number you hold for big winning. You will then pray to the spirits and you will ask them first to give you the number of the races to bet in. Use only one die this time, to see if the number one will show up. If it doesn't, you will then use two pieces of dice from then on, as the spirits don't like to bet in the first race, for it is during the first race that they take over and adjust things to their plan for winning. Let's say that you have now tossed the dice onto the altar and the number three has come up. This means that you will not bet in the first race, for they will want to upset the tricks placed in the race by any crooks and managers who think they can control a race, and alter the facts so you will become lucky and the gamblers who have fixed the race will become unlucky. Remember that the spirits do not like dishonest people and they kill them off whenever they get in the pathway of the spirits. But the spirits always will help the poor and honest person because he is on their side and under their protection. So during the first race the spirits will usually take over the management and running of the race-track in question for the time of the races.

Throw the dice again in the pair of pieces you have to get the other numbers, so let us say that three and three turn up, this adds up to six, so you have the sixth race. Throw it again, two and five turn up; this means the seventh race. Again you throw the dice and one and two turn up, this means that the spirits are going to give you two lucky numbers for the third race. This happens quite a lot, so you should be ready to accept the idea of placing two bets in the third race. Now, after you have gotten your table of races worked out, you have three, six, seven, and three. Now you will want to get the numbers of the horses for each race. I might add, you can get lucky numbers for all of the races, but you have to take what the spirits will give you, and not always do they place bets on all races, only what they send to you. They like to rest or to have you take a break during some of the races. Now to get the numbers of the horses, you throw the dice again.

To get the numbers of the horses for each race, you will want to toss the dice to get the lucky numbers in one of two forms. You throw the dice, for example, and you come up with one and one. This could be either 11 or two. Well, in a race they may not have both an eleven and a two, so bet on what they do have. The first race you will bet in is three, you can bet on 11 and two, but if 11 doesn't appear, bet on 2. Throw again, and you come up with one and five, or 15. This can be either six or 15 in race number six, but both won't show, so bet on what does show. Throw again, three and two again. Well, it must mean five because 32 doesn't ever show up as the number of a horse or dog in a race. Lastly, throw and up comes two and four. Well, 24 is unlikely, so the spirits mean six. So that in the third race you will bet on both 11 and two if they both show, and six, so you will split your bet two or three ways.

Now you have your table of lucky numbers and then you have to look at the racing news to find out which number is running in which race. Place your table of numbers on the altar and ask the spirits to bring you luck in the race that will take place at a specific time and place and where you plan to go and make small bets, but bets to win. The spirits do not like big bettors, because such people become obsessed with betting and gambling. They will cause failure if you give yourself over to gambling. But to the poor and honest man who makes small bets, they will send their success, if he is faithful to them and uses the money for good purposes. After you get your table written up and placed on the table or altar, you will then thank the spirits in the deep of your soul. They will then send to you the powers of success to use these numbers that win to bring into your life the energies of success. Now remember to compare the table you have with what will be the running in the race that day. In fact, you can follow the races a few days by the newspapers in order to get used to seeing if you are doing well in your getting the numbers that win. Remember that the numbers are not to be thought of as ends in themselves, but only as the ways in which the spirits show their power. For example, while I have advised many as to how to win at the race track, I myself have never placed a bet. I get my money through the magickal use of the energies of contraite. However, let me tell you about a lady who did make it big at the races.

Hoodoo Lady Josephine's Big Day at the Races
Hoodoo Lady Josephine is a very powerful medium and spiritual adviser who tries to help many people. Because she is working for others, she doesn't devote time to doing things for herself. Things for big money just happen to this big mama lady who has a heart of gold as big as the world. She came to me for magickal treatment according to Voudoo laws and I put her in touch with the spirits who stand behind the arts of betting and gambling, just as I have done in this lesson. I got her some numbers for races and some numbers for horses, and she went out and placed very tiny bets, as small as you can, for she wasn't a gambling lady, but needed just a little change for the holiday. The spirits came through and gave us the following table to be used in placing bets:

RACE	HORSE–NUMBER	
2	11 or 2	
7	14 or 5	
5	18 or 9	
8	19 or 10	
4	21 or 3	
8 again	13 or 4	split bet
7 again	12 or 3	split bet
6	23 or 5	

9	23 or 5	
8 again	16 or 7	split bet
7 again	12 or 3	must be very lucky
7 again	14 or 5	must be very lucky

Well, Josephine took the numbers that the spirits gave to her through me and placed small bets. But because the seventh race seemed to be so important, she placed larger bets on the two horses, which were three and five, actually running. She did this because she said she felt that she could really clean up on this race, although I advised her that it could be an illusion, and that she might not win if she made a big bet, but would only win if she placed little bets. She said that if she did win, she would use the money to build up the spiritual work and pay off the debts on her church, which was devoted to the worship of the holy spirits. Well, she turned out to be right and won in every race she bet in and only bet where the spirits had given her the numbers. She won a lot of money in the seventh race, because she felt the spirits wanted her to be very lucky. This money she used to pay for a new roof on her church and also for fixing up the altar and paying off a couple of debts to a bank that wasn't being too friendly towards her. Well, it turned out to be a demonstration of the success of this system and she uses this method only once in a while now, but always with some really good success.

Note that she did not bet in the first race and she rested in the third race and after the ninth race she didn't place any more bets. There were 12 races that day, but the spirits didn't want her to bet in the first, third, tenth, 11th, and 12th. But they wanted her to bet in the others and that is what she did. So her success came entirely from the spirits and that is how she won a lot of wonderful money to help her work and herself. So follow the spirits and do only what they will tell you. Then when you are through with the betting, be sure that you thank the spirits at your altar and light your candles and let them know that you are grateful to them for what they have done for you. Never let anything go by for which you do not give them thanks. and it can be very simple, just like this prayer, with which I am ending this lesson:

THANK YOU SPIRITS OF LUCKY HOODOO FOR WHAT YOU
HAVE BROUGHT TO ME IN THE PAST, AND WHAT YOU WILL
BRING IN THE FUTURE. THANK YOU, THANK YOU,
THANK YOU SPIRITS OF LUCKY HOODOO.

Lesson Eight: How the Hoodoo Is a Success in Love and Sex

The Secret of Attraction

Eveerywhere in the world there are positive and negative energies. These energies are what holds the world together and they are held together by their sense of mutual attraction. There are certain experiences of attraction, which each one of us has. We meet someone quite casually and before long we are in the process of making love. Many persons wonder about this power of attraction and how it works. Let me say that attraction is a basic law of all being and that somewhere in the universe there are many souls waiting to make love to someone just like yourself.

The secret of attraction is not based on sexual opposites, because attraction happens more often among the members of the same sex. This explains why young men are attracted to a gang leader and why women seek to follow the leadership of fine persons of their own sex. Men are attracted to men and the women to women. Now, we have been taught by society to seek love from the opposite sex and this has resulted in forced marriages and much divorce. Many men have to learn from experience. For example, there was a rich banker in Haiti who wanted to study with a magician who had attracted him very much. The banker's wife objected so much that she finally divorced him. Now, he was free from her, and could study the occult and magick without her opposition. The power of the magick was so great that it broke up his marriage. In other words, the male magician was so powerful in his attractions that he destroyed a marriage which had been stable for 20 years. The banker had, as a young man, been hypnotized by society into an early marriage in the Catholic religion. He had been the father of four children and went to Mass with his wife every day. But deep in his soul he was unstable because of a need not met. He had many female friends over those 20 years of marriage, so he had plenty of sexual outlets and changed his mistresses often. But he was not satisfied deep in his soul.

When I heard of this attraction between the magician and the banker, I asked my master what was the basis of this relationship, which alone seemed to satisfy the banker, an otherwise unfulfilled man. My master in Voudoo said that the relationship between the magician and the banker was also a sexual relationship, for it now existed at all levels. He also advised me to look into the fact that the banker was now totally satisfied in every sense, something he was not before. I wondered about the power of attraction which was there, and the master said that it was a natural law at work. The banker was born under the sign of Taurus and the Moon was in Scorpio. Furthermore, the banker had Cancer as his rising sign also. Well, this shows that banking and saving money were part of his essence, but so must be this sexual attraction he felt for the magician. I therefore asked my master about the magician's signs and learned the following. The magician had the Sun and Moon both in Scorpio and his rising sign was Capricorn. Naturally, the combination of Scorpio and Capricorn is very good for magick, but the natural attraction of Taurus is to Scorpio and with the Moon in Scorpio the attraction is even stronger.

(NOTE: Our recent USA President Nixon was surrounded by Scorpios and Cancers and Pisces, himself being a Capricorn with the Taurus Moon and Virgo rising.)

Thus there is in nature this powerful law of attraction which brings souls together. Each person at birth brings with them certain influences from the higher worlds.

These are shown in the rising sign, Moon sign, and Sun sign of the person. For example, my Sun sign is Capricorn, my rising sign is Virgo, and my Moon sign is Cancer. This is very good for magickal work. My master in the Voudoo sciences had his Sun in Capricorn, his Moon and rising signs were Scorpio. These three astrological influences are very important for understanding the law of attraction as it works in each person's life.

When this law of attraction enters into the emotional life of the person, we can say that they are "in love," and when it is manifested in the sexual actions, then the two poles of attraction have fully grounded their attraction. But this attraction is so firm in the nature of things that I will call it by its proper name, which is "personal magnetism."

The Law of Personal Magnetism

Personal magnetism is based on the attraction of cosmic forces, and the fact that each person carries with him this force in his personal soul. The secret of love and sex is to find out what persons will be then attracted to you, so that you can then ask the spirits to help cast the spells for love and sex. The spirits will not help you unless you know just exactly what you wish. For example, my teacher was a Capricorn and Scorpio type, so he told me that in his absence he would prepare a secretary for me who would have qualities compatible with myself and with the teacher. My secretary has a combination of Scorpio, Cancer and Capricorn magnetism, so the law seems to be working quite well. Now, it is difficult to find exactly what you wish on your own, but the Hoodoo spirits can easily set in motion the causes which bring about the meeting of attractive forces. This is important for you, so that you can see by a study of the law what you will be seeking and then you will ask the spirits to assist you in making this real and important in your life.

I will now go through the Zodiac of the Hoodoos and make brief comments upon each sign to show its attractions.

1. Moon in Scorpio, Pisces, and Cancer. This should attract the same or the Moon in Taurus, Virgo, and Capricorn.

2. Sun in Taurus. This sign will attract Scorpio, but also Cancer, Capricorn, and Virgo, as well as itself.

3. Sun in Virgo will attract Pisces, but also Cancer, Capricorn, and Scorpio, as well as itself.

4. Sun in Capricorn will attract Cancer, and also Scorpio, Pisces, Virgo and Taurus, as well as itself.

5. Sun in Scorpio will attract Taurus and also Capricorn and Virgo, and Cancer as well as itself.

6. Moon in Taurus, Virgo and Capricorn will attract the Moon in Scorpio, Pisces, and Cancer, as well as itself.

7. Sun in Pisces will attracts Virgo, itself and Cancer.

8. Sun in Cancer will attract Capricorn, Virgo, Taurus, Scorpio and Pisces, as well as itself.

9. Sun in Libra will attract Aries as well as itself.

10. Sun in Aquarius will attract Leo as well as Gemini and Libra and itself.

11. Moon in Sagittarius, Aries and Leo will attract itself and the Moon in Libra, Aquarius, and Gemini.

12. Sun in Gemini will attract the Sun in Sagittarius and itself.

13. The Sun in Sagittarius will attract Gemini.

14. The Sun in Aries will attract Libra.

15. The Sun in Leo will attract Aquarius.

16. The Moon in Libra, Aquarius, and Gemini will attract itself and the Moon in Sagittarius, Aries and Leo.

It is important to understand that these are merely the ways in which the laws of attraction work for the Sun signs. My understanding is that if there is an attraction in a relationship, then it would seem that some secret factor is at work, which does obey the laws given in this lesson, but which is unknown to us at the time of our initial inquiry. After all, we are not expected to be astrologers, and so few of those know any truth, so we just want to operate these laws to our advantage and get from them the rewards of love and sex which we seek.

You will note that the earth and water signs have the very widest range of attraction. This is because their powers in Hoodoo science are the highest. All of the really big Hoodoo masters are of the earth or water signs, since Virgo rules Voudoo, Capricorn rules Hoodoo, and Taurus rules witchcraft. Those who lots of earth and water in their charts of birth are really cut out for this kind of activity. For example, I have always wondered why I had this strong attraction towards Hoodoo. In fact, all other systems never seemed to satisfy me. I was like the banker in our earlier story, except I was dealing with forces and ideas. Well, I have the Sun in Capricorn and I have the Moon, Earth and Pluto all in Cancer and conjunct in their powers. My rising sign is Virgo and I have Neptune rising in that sign (this is the planet of shamanism and mysticism of a primitive sort). My Jupiter, which rules rituals and ceremonial magick, is in Scorpio. Hence this is the basis of my attraction to the Hoodoo system of spirituality.

Love And Sex Spellbinding

Now you know the law of attraction, you can apply it in the work of spellbinding for love and sex. This is a very simple process and does not require much to be done in addition to your using your Hoodoo altar-table in the usual manner. Now you must really set your mind on the type of person you wish to attract according to your laws of magnetism. I have given you the rules and you will have to observe them as guidelines for your work. You will sit at your altar table and you will make up a magickal charm on paper, according to the old Hoodoo method and place it between the red candle and the black candle, as shown in the chart in Lesson Four. You will use peach-flavored brandy in this method, because it is concerend with love and sex and the excitements of very hot passions. The chart you will make is the following magickal design.

[insert chart from manuscript here]

Then you will say the following magickal prayer to invoke the spirits of Hoodoo love and sex to come to your aid in this matter.

HOODOO SPIRITS OF LOVE AND SEX POWER
COME TO MY AID AND BRING ME TO A VERY GOOD LOVER
WHO WILL BE HELD TO ME BY THE POWERS OF
ATTRACTION AND PERSONAL MAGNETISM

Then you will drink down the glass of peach brandy and thank the spirits for what they have done. You will put out the candles and say: IT IS DONE. Break contact by a clap of your hands.

This spellwork is designed to bring to you a terrific lover which the spirits know is suited to you perfectly. Remember that the spirits know what you are in terms of the laws of attraction and so they will know what to bring to you. They know just what you need.

The magickal chart or card which you make is a talisman of the powerful magician—spirit Bacalou Baca or Bacoulou Baca, which is his magickal name. He is the spirit of Capricorn in Hoodoo and he is a very helpful spirit in trying to attract love and sex. He is worshipped in temples by means of sexual actions, which are very important to him for his building up of reserve forces. Thus, lovers at the time of the climax or orgasm will send the power of their intense passionate pleasure to this spirit, in order to give him special energies which will bring good fortune and love to them and many other gifts. Let me say that this is a form of exchange of energy with the spirit of Capricorn and this exchange of energy is due to the need of the spirit to have something that he can transform into material power, money, gifts, gold, or good fortune. The sexual energy is thus exchanged with the spirits for this material well—being.

Also, you must understand that the spirits will bring you into circumstances which are what they know is best for you to do what they want. We have to get away from the thought of getting in love and sex what we want. The spirits really know much better than we do in this matter and because of this they are better suited to make adjustments which affect our destiny. Let me say that they often bring people together in order to cause certain energies to be combined or brought forth in production. They might wish to experiment and cause something to happen that has never before been produced. This is how true love and sex operate in the lives of those who accept the powers and the real presence of the spirits of Lucky Hoodoo. so you must become open to these spirits and willingly agree to serve them, for you know that they know best for you and for those who follow them faithfully have never gone wrong and have really benefitted considerably. That is why I say again to you: Serve these wonderful spirits of Lucky Hoodoo and receive the rewards of this service.

Lesson Nine: How the Hoodoo Man Keeps His Nature High

In my many years of magickal practice with West Indian followers of Lucky Hoodoo, I have been asked many times to give information and help to men in order to aid them to have their sexual vigor restored. Sexual power is very important for many occult or magickal reasons, which are often more powerful than the use of sexual power in love and sex. In many religions it is said that sexual power is bad or evil in some form, so that to have a low nature is considered a good thing. This is not so in Hoodoo and in all of the more basic forms of Voudoo, where all of the spirits are known to have very high natures.

No man must be shy or ashamed because his nature is low. Lucky Hoodoo can make it high and keep it very high. The reason for this is that the spirits of Lucky Hoodoo will want their servers to have high natures filled up with sex power, so that the spirits can be better served. All of the religions which state that low nature is good are false and distorted pictures of a sick mind. Everything in nature shows the power of the high sexual nature of the Hoodoo God of the spirits, so we follow him and not the negative aspects of popular religious foolishness.

According to Hoodoo, all of the spirits are big in their sexual parts and powers. They are big in their desires for more and more power of will and action. They are big in what they want to have done and what they are in the act of doing. Thus, a high nature is part of the Hoodoo picture for all men. If they say that Voudoo is the religion of power, so that say that Lucky Hoodoo is the religion of high sexual power and nature.

In Lucky Hoodoo we teach that there is in each man the powerful god of regeneration and creativity. His name is Papa Gayday. His symbol is the man's sexual organ. The sexual organ is possessed by Papa Gayday and when it is possessed the god gives a very high nature to the man who owns the organ being possessed by Papa. Papa Gayday is worshipped through all forms of sexual action. Anything that gives pleasure to the organ is a form of delight to Papa. If the organ has much enjoyment, Papa Gayday will give to it a will and mind of its own, so that the organ becomes a magickal wand or symbol of the will of the god of all sexual power. For this reason, even very old men, who have dedicated their lives to Papa Gayday are always able to have much love and sex, for they never lose their natures. The high power of their natures is proof that Papa Gayday has still possessed them and will continue to do so to the very end. For this reason, many students of magick will come from miles around and often from other lands just to be initiated into the magick of this voudoo wand. For by worship of this power, there is a transfer of power from the god to the student, by means of the rod of power of the magickal wizard of Lucky Hoodoo.

The Fountain of Youth
There was in ancient times the belief that there was somewhere in the world a magickal fountain, which would restore to youth all who drank from it. This fountain of youth was, however, misunderstood by those who went looking for it, for the true fountain of youth is the magickal wand on the body of man. Those who come to this magickal rod of power will be blessed by its mysteries, which are those of the holy cream of eternal power.

A white woman from New York went to Haiti and witnessed a powerful healing of a blind child. The child was brought to the magician who then sought to pray to the god to give the power of healing in the nature of sexual power. The god and all of the spirits of the Nibbho family agreed to this act which shows forth the divine power of the god. Thus the magician took from his rod the magickal cream of healing and placed it upon the eyes of the blind child, who was restored to sight. This has been done to those blind from birth or handicapped in various other ways. In each case, the fountain of youth and healing was revealed in the presence of the faithful. This is the way in which the gods of Lucky Hoodoo can come into our lives and heal in many ways what is a problem of health for us.

The Food of the Gods and Spirits
In the most secret part of Lucky Hoodoo there is the teaching that the food of the gods and spirits is this magickal cream. The priests of this ancient religion were supposed to feed this power to the gods almost each day. This power was then taken by the gods and transformed into magickal powers, gifts, riches, and all favorable circumstances. Thus, the magicians were the most powerful in all the world. In ancient cultures, the religions made offerings of blood to the spirits. But the magicians, in order to have even greater power, made offerings of the sacred cream, which comes forth from the rod or the magickal wand of the wizard of Lucky Hoodoo. Thus, while the gods gave minor favors to the religious people who made blood offerings, yet they gave their truest favors to the magicians, for the sacred cream is the most powerful of all magickal substances in this world. It is the basis of material existence.

We do not know fully what the gods and spirits of Lucky Hoodoo do with this magickal or sacred cream, but it is very important to them and has been secretly known to be their food since the earliest times of Atlantis, if not before that time. What we do know is that these magickal creams form the basis for the materialization of powers and riches by the magician in the world and for the continuous prosperity of those who follow the cult of Lucky Hoodoo, all through their lives. Finally, we can safely say that those who domake the regular offerings to the gods of this food for magick, are kept in the fullness of sexual vigor and always have a high nature.

Magickal Places and Acts of Sex
There are in every society those secret meeting places where men may find the release of sexual tension which is so essential to their harmony of nerves and bodily health. In places set aside by the centuries--old laws of sexual relaxation -- and I do not refer to houses of prostitution, which is a terrible and evil plague upon mankind -- men will meet men and there one will seek to have done what the other is more than willing to do. I do not wish to speak more explicitly, except that those who go there are driven there by weird magickal powers and influences, which come from the unconscious levels of mind. Those who meet in these dark and often very damp places are under the elemental forces of the deeps and must come together for they are driven by wild and barbaric passions. There exists in those places a kind of daemonic priesthood, truly the sons of the underworld in all of his power, and they willingly drink the sacred cream like strange vampires, who cannot explain in any form their bizarre behavior. They, the members of this priesthood, are driven to these places to await the victims of their thirst. They cannot explain why they have come there, all they know is that they must take hold of the magick wands in their mouths and drink like a madman lost in the desert, who has just come upon a refreshing oasis.

32

The victims of this priesthood since the times of Atlantis have been relaxed by this weird action and they have returned home less tense and more aware of other parts of their lives. No longer are they obsessed by the sex passion. Frequently they have received the effects of good luck upon their return to the world of moderate feelings and cares. While the victims of these elementals, they have not been victimized, but rather they have gone to the place of offering and have paid their tribute to the gods of the deeps. Then as faithful to their cult, they have received from the gods the rewards of obedience and service.

To the magickal observer, the throats and mouths of the priests of the weird and secret rites are tubes and tunnels, cisterns and sewers which go down, deep into the elemental levels of being. There at the bottom of this magickal passageway we can find the deep ones of unspeakable evil, who being protectors of the magickal wand in all of its erect glory, are also the gods of gold and fire and all enlightenment. Here or there, to be more precise, there is no obscenity, there is only the exchange of energy. In the areas of those sewers into which vast amounts of blood have been poured, as nearby to slaughter-houses and meat packing establishments, one finds also such deep elemental contacts. This is surely evil; but it is also very powerful magick.

Modern society has created these places of moral danger through its Judeo-Christian ethics, which is foreign to the ancient morality of Atlantis and Lemuria. The Christians, who eat the flesh and drink the blood of their god, practice in sublimated form this ancient eating of the divine wand of power and swallowing the sacred cream. But the religion of the dying god has been false in its understanding of the ancient priesthood, which has been driven into the darkness and dampness of the washrooms and baths. The ancient priesthood of darkness lives on, for it has the strength of eternity. Evetually it will come to destroy Christianity and the morality of denial in passion and lust.

The Power of Light, Which Is the Sun
The basis of Lucky Hoodoo is the worship of the spirits, who represent the spirits of the Sun. The priesthood of light does not swell in the dark and damp places of the persecuted but in the solar temples of the phallic cult. The presence of the sacred cream in human life, in the body of man, was proof of the presence of Sunlight in the life of all being. Hence, those who come before the rays of the Sun were thought of also as a special priesthood, which we might call the priesthood of daylight. For them the sacred cream came forth as a gift from the gods and was to be used to create. While at night this cream was fed into the cisterns of magick shaped like the gaping mouths of so many sea-monsters and vampires. Thus, there were two kinds of magick associated with the use of the sexual nature in man, and each had its promise of long life and much vigor.

In Lucky Hoodoo, we are able to draw upon both orders of force, the night powers and the day powers. In Egypt they were called the powers of Set and Osiris, or some-times Seth and Horous. In each case, you must be willing to offer your sexual power to the spirits in exchange for their blessings and gifts. In each cult, the man must be prepared to turn his back upon the modern religion of restriction and come face to face with the ancient ones, beyond all time and space. He must know that his organ is a magickal powerhouse, a place wherein the spirit of the mightily and victoriously crowned Papa Gayday makes his abode.

Lucky Hoodoo makes it possible for its men to seek either of these forms of magick, which will enable them to live with the fullness of sexual vigor and with a nature always high. Both are the forms which come to us from ancient times and then beyond to the other worlds, much older than our own. In all of these places the phallus, the organ of manhood, is viewed as the place of the gods, or an Atua, filled with the powers of the spirit. There will be always those who will seek sexual exchange with the powers of the Sun which are beyond those of the surface of this earth, such men will be called the solar phallic men of power. Others will come into the deep and dark dampness of night and seek the Moonless starry nights where the powers of weird and ancient magick rule. In such places and at such times, men are eaten up with their lusts and animal passions, they are driven by elemental cravings and wild ravenous things, which go beyond — way beyond — the blood lusts of the Moon cult. And when he has decided upon which pathway to use, and he may use all and any at any time, he will knwo that he is making contact with the agents of the ancient powers, who have been hidden in the earth for endless periods of time. And there in the deep and secret places of his finding, the man of sexual power will offer his essence to the gods from beyond the veils of time and space, and there in the offering of his most precious being, he will be released of all tension and all pressure, and there he will come to see the world as the spirits see it, as free from all storm and stress and perfectly relaxed and at peace. And in that moment he will realize that they will make him strong to give to them as long as he willing to go to them and give the gift of his very innermost being.

Therefore, let the man of Hoodoo sit at his altar and after having lighted the candles and begun his meditation, he will give to them that are the most ancient and most powerful spirits in the universe, through the act of self-love, the power which they seek, for which they will give back to him all that he seeks and especially the continuation of the highest of his natures. And let him regain his strength after the power has been drawn off, by drinking the apricot brandy, which is the symbol of what he has done.

Lesson Ten: How the Hoodoo Can Have Lifelong Success as a Reader and Advisor

Climbing the Mountain of Initiation

Anyone who has made a practice of the Hoodoo faith may, after a while, consider himself something of an expert in this system of magick. This means that sooner or later many people will hear about him and his abilities and they will come to him to help them with their problems. Sooner or later he will be asked to do certain things for which he will receive some kind of payment, so that gradually he will become a professional helper through the spirits. This is the way in which the spirits want us to spread the religion of Lucky Hoodoo, which is a religion of help for those who need this type of help, and everyone needs some kind of help. Lucky Hoodoo is therefore the most practical religion in the world.

It is not necessary to have large temples for the working of this divine faith, for in most instances, we make a little temple in our homes and this is where the spirits come and dwell and share with us the daily life that we have come to love, including the routines of getting up and going out to work. After a while you will find that you are growing deeper and deeper into the faith of Lucky Hoodoo, for the spirits are teaching you more and more things. They will teach you new ways to heal the ill, to make the poor more successful, and they will teach you how to attract and help others in their love and sex life. In all of this, they -- the spirits of Lucky Hoodoo -- are your masters and adept-teachers. When they wish to give you new knowledge, they really will. When they wish to teach you more and more, they will, they will always know when you are ready.

Becoming higher and higher in the initiations of Hoodoo is based upon concrete and very practical abilities. As you do more so you will be expected to advance more and more along the pathway to divine spirit. You will be asked to undertake every new type of work, for the road of initiation is entirely that of daily hard work. The spirits will lead you to various levels of development and they will be responsible for giving you newer and newer rights and honors.

Only the spirits know when you are ready to rise the great scale of those higher "degrees" of Hoodoo and to receive the "points" which will enable you to do the work of the spirits. In Hoodoo, for example, if the spirits intend a certain person to heal, then they will advance him to the "degree" of a healer, and thereby give to him the "point" or power for doing the healing, which is what they want done. In many instances I have been informed by the spirits that a certain student will be coming to see me for advancement in the powers. I then must consult with the spirits as the the "degrees" or "grades" that they wish me to give to the person and what "points" or powers they wish me to induct into his body for the doing of the work of the spirits. The degrees or grades of Hoodoo are quite endless, so no one ever reaches the end of the line in learning more and more things to do. It is true that in the Haitian Voudoo religion they say that there are four degrees of power, the last being the gift of clairvoyance; but in Lucky Hoodoo, we realize that the gift of clairvoyance is the beginning of another series of grades of work and by means of this gift many more points or powers are gained. The spirits are right in reserving the giving of grades to those they know are ready. But when someone will come to me at the request of the spirits, I likewise know that they have carefully screened this person and only really deep students will be making contact with me. In this sense the spirits do protect me from those who wish only superficial contact with the spirits of Lucky Hoodoo and the wonderful spirit-teachings.

Anyway, when a person does do the work of the spirits, it is certain that they will receive lifelong success in helping many people, who are in need of the teachings and powers of Lucky Hoodoo. For this reason, if you simply follow this simple series of ten lessons, you will be able to work in Lucky Hoodoo and find the many rewards which come from the spirits, because they know much more than we are able to know and will give us what we seek, if we are in any sense dedicated to their work through service. The upward climb to the light of the spirits is something which does require the efforts of all the spirit powers we can grasp hold of; but the rewards of spirit service are constantly to receive the encouragement and help, new powers and knowledge, from this source of all light, behind the world of sensory appearance and material activity.

Building the Atua or The House of the Spirits
The successful practitioner of Lucky Hoodoo will take great care in making his home a place of the spirits. He will take care to set aside the objects which the spirits like to indwell, such as bottles of their favorite perfumes and tonic-liqueurs. Do not worry about what to buy to honor them, they will come and simply tell you what they have on their minds. They each have very definite favorites, so you have to be very precise and follow their explicit directions very carefully.

Many of the spirits of Lucky Hoodoo like to indwell a painted wooden box with a lid, called an ATUA or A TOO A. All spirits dwell in those invisible Atuas that are made of spirit-matter in the world of the spirits. But in the temples of Lucky Hoodoo and in the homes of those most favored by the spirits are to be found the painted boxes of the spirits. Actually, if the quality of the wood is high, you do not need to paint the box, just make sure that the finish on the wood is high quality also. However, you may wish to paint the box, both inside and out with the colors and designs which the true spirits of Lucky Hoodoo really prefer. I will not give you any directions in this, for the spirits will tell you what to do, but because there are an infinite number of spirits in Lucky Hoodoo, so the designs of the Atua will show you this. But one thing is certain, there can be no mistake in the Atua; you will always be able to pick it out and know if the spirits like it, because it is loaded with power.

While the Atua might be covered outside and inside with the colors and designs of spirit-magick, as soon as the spirit takes possession of his home, you will find that the power will now begin to build up. Many of those who do much work with the spirits will take an object which must be blessed and put it inside the Atua, overnight, let us say, in order that the power flows into the object and the blessing takes place. Well, this is what we call a type of participation-magick, where the field of magick inside of the box flows into any object placed there and fills it with power. Any home is blessed by the presence of the Atua, and many buildings have been protected because of the fact that there was an Atua somewhere in that building. On the other hand, many buildings have been cursed, because buried beneath the building was an Atua left there hundreds of years ago, by a black magician who worked a negative type of spirit science.

Well, if a person has come along in his occult work and is usually able to help those who come to him for help and magickal advice, he should have an Atua in order to work the deeper types of spirit-magick. I am of the opinion that the possession of the Atua determines the sincere and advanced student from the casual and curious

36

person. Only a deep student would go to the trouble of making an Atua and making it according to the directions given by the spirits of Lucky Hoodoo. Such a person would really be sincere to want to find out what the spirits wanted him to do in direct service. This is often the test, so I encourage those who do wish to be thought serious by their spirits, to make an Atua for them to dwell in, when they come into your home. The Atua can then rest on your altar, and like the Tabot of the Ethiopian Church, can be viewed as the genuine focus of the divine power and presence in your life, work, and community. this is another way to have lifelong success in the use and work of Lucky Hoodoo.

In closing, let me say that I have outlined in these brief lessons a basic course which will bring you into touch, service, and work for the spirits of Lucky Hoodoo. For some, this is enough, but for others there will be more advanced studies available, which build upon and grow out of what these ten brief lessons give you. For example, I will be presenting to some student a course in "Heavy Hoodoo Spells," which is for the specialist in spell work with the spirits. There are many problems which often come up over the years which really do require special treatment and special types of power. These special problems I will give inthe studies directed to the advanced student, who may be asked or called upon to do very special work for his clients. I have been asked by the head of my long line of Hoodoo work to prepare this type of study course, so that the many requests for advanced work in secret powers and spell-casting can be answered. Let me say also that whatever the spirits tell me to do I always carry out. I am dutiful and very obedient to their basic laws. This is the secret of my own personal power, as it should be yours also. There may be other types of study which they will suggest to me as we go along in our life of spirit-serviuce, which is our life together with the spirits. Well, when this does happen I will do such a course and then gradually put together those ideas which I sincerely feel are most suited to the problem-solving of the present age.

Many persons have written to ask about initiation into the mysteries of Lucky Hoodoo. Let me say that each person will initiate himself into these wonderful states of consciousness, but that it is possible for the spirits to want to being the very special student into contact with me for a particular reason, especially if the student is located in the area of Chicago. The spirits will have their reasons for this, I will simply follow their directions. Well, this should not be any serious problem if the student is really serious, for I can be reached through my post office and all you have to do is write to me there. You must understand, however, that only those who have been serious enough in their devotion to the spirits of Lucky Hoodoo will be led in this direction, which is the meeting of the student with the spirits in my person. Also, the spirits will determine fully and finally whether or not the student is ready for the special initiations which they provide for those wishing special powers and degrees or levels in Hoodoo science. For it is entirely possible that the spirits may wish me to give the grades of higher Hoodoo power, if so they are given in the name of the spirits of that family in Lucky Hoodoo, from which I come, and which is know as

BACALOU BACA

Lessons on the "Points-Chauds": Le Temple-Des-Houdeaux

Esoteric voudoo is the science of the orientation of the temple of consciousness, which you must create with your will, mind, and imagination. Esoteric voudoo therefore will be the method which teaches you how to organize your magickal inner experience, using the most suitable symbols –– which are the symbols having the most power. The symbols used must be evocative of power, they must serve to call it forth from other regions, other parts of the universe, other universes and dimensions. It is not enough to say that the symbol is the sign which suggests something mystical. The symbol must be a machine or engine for the generation of magickal power in its own way, not in any way which depends upon the mere mind of the practitioner.

Voudoo must be a science of success which works for every mind and not because of the mental attitude, for voudoo is the science which handles powers as they are in themselves, not because of what we think. So voudoo is not psychological, it is metaphysical and physical –– the symbols it uses are physical powers in being.

The orientation of consciousness is possible because of the ways in which voudoo power gives direction to the mind. Voudoo power tells the mind what to do and how to do it. I have said that the orientation of consciousness is achieved by means of powerful symbols which are magickal engines. This means that these symbols are the ways through which the inner contacts of voudoo, or the spirits or Loa, operate through the veil which separates the inner from the outer. The symbols become instruments of perception or research whereby the spirits look into our world and cause certain things which they desire to happen. So as they look into our world they send into our world their power to do what we want them to do. Sometimes, we see, they say among themselves that we want them to act behind the veil, on the other side of the wall of consciousness. That means that we do not make any use of symbols, but rather make contact entirely withour mind. This is esoteric prayer and it is common to all types of spiritual activity. However, in voudoo we use symbols which come alive in the operations of esoteric voudoo. So that the justification for the use of esoteric voudoo is to be found in the use of these engines of magick or sacred and cosmic symbols, which produce a more precise effect than the actions of the mind in the midst of esoteric prayer, which is often too vague. In fact, one would have to be out of the physical body actually to be effective in esoteric prayer, but in the body it is a "hit-or-miss" type of activity, because few if any have such precise minds. That is why we use symbolic engines. This is the real justification of voudoo.

In voudoo there are many sects. The name for the sectaries of La Couleuvre Noire at Rouge is "Les Houdeaux"," or the operative magicians, i.e., those who do practical work. There are other sectaries in LCN, of course, such as "Les Ophites," but the beginning of the work is to be found in Les Houdeaux. A sectarian or sectary of voudoo is a member of a special line of spirits, or spiritual ancestry. The spiritual ancestry of Les Houdeaux is to be found in the children of the "Black Goddess of Space," Binah, the emanation of Mother/Father Space/Time, called "Saturn" by the classicists, and "Guedhe-Nibbho" by the priests of Voudoo science. The consort of the Black Goddess of Space is Death, the God of All Transformations, known as Mystere Royale (Desak'karum), who shines his supreme eye through Saturn when in the sign of Scorpio, "whose throne is in the east." The children of the Black Goddess of Space and Mystere Royale are "Les Houdeaux." We may be said to be one with Les Houdeaux or to be them when we act within the temple of esoteric voudoo, in which these lessons form the pathway of initiation.

With Les Houdeaux the most important matter is the orientation of the temple of the inner power, or the arrangement of the symbolic engines in space-consciousness. Now, it is very important to understand that we are the serviateurs of Les Houdeaux and must make the design of the temple, which is the cosmic map of magick, ideally suitable for their work. Otherwise we cannot unite our magickal energies with them and say that we too are among Les Houdeaux. Thus, the most basic point in this science of esoteric work is the knowing of the points chaud or the engines of occult energy which are diffused through the spheres of magickal consciousness. First of all there are four levels to the temple, or we will say four different ways of working the temple in different and higher worlds and regions of real power. These four regions are: 1) Les Houdeaux, or where we are now. 2) Les Linglessoux, or the realm of the shrouds of the dead. 3) Les Cadavres Piquantes or Cadavres Piquants, which is the world of embalmed corpses. 4) Les Faiseurs-des-Zombi, or the mages who bring the dead back to physical activity. These are four magickal regions or zones, and each of our lessons in this first series will treat of these zones of powers as collections of many hot-points, whereby the magician can develop and express himself fully as a child of the Black Goddess of Space and Death, Her Spouse.

Now to establish the orientation of the temple, which is really the way in which the symbols of this esoteric voudoo will work as magickal engines it is necessary to indicate that in each of the zones there are eight magickal directions or pathways of power for the growth of more and more hot-points. These directions are north, west, south, east, north-east, north-west, south-west, and south-east. Each of these doors of consciousness has its own meaning and vibration, its own spirit or Loa and its own life, its own intimates and its own initiations, and its own projections into other dimensions and pathways through space-consciousness and time-will. For example, there is a particular point of contact named after the Loas of the Guedhe family, which are the spider-Loa: Famille Zariguin, such as Maitre Baron Zariguin, his consort Mystere Araignee, and their son Ti-Zaraguin and their daughter Mystere Toile-d'Araignee. In their construction of consciousness they occupy the east, west, south, and north of the temple. To find a spider's web in the north side of one's home is a good sign indeed. However, if we use these Loas in our temple des Houdeaux, we will not want to use them as the dominant powers of the temple, but only as complements to the four major powers of Les Houdeaux. Thus, while some Loa may appear to be very much the same being, esoteric voudoo permits the magician to make many distinctions whereby it is possible to develop the magickal personality of these Loa and thus climb up or reach up to their own magickal vibration. You may find the spirits of esoteric voudoo have very, very different personalities once you come upon them in the setting up of your temple for the real level of research. Before, you thought they were fundamentally the same types of real energies, but now you can see how different they are, indeed you now can see that they are entirely different types of families of spirits and magickal Loa.

Now, getting down to the business of setting up consciousness, you will assign to the east the powerful Mystere Royal, father of all of the Mysteres-royaux, or gods of death, also known in the western tradition as the angels of death, and called by the esoteric theurgists of India "Naradana." To the west, the place of the Lunar influence, you will assign the Black Goddess of Space, i.e., Mahakali. To the north, you will assign all of the spirits who belong to the family of Les Houdeaux, or the spirits of Hoodoo sciences, who live in the northern area of the universe. To the south, we will assign a very special deity, known as the spirit who greets those who come to serve the dead, "Thousand-Little-Footsteps," or "Ti-Pied-Mille-Fois." This spirit is the were-insect Loa-Mystere, a transvection of Limbi and kliphotic king of the larvae of the dead. By using him in the south, we have established a magickal link with the were-insect deities, who will occupy the NE, NW, SE, and SW points;

these are Mystere Toile-d'Araignee (NE), known as the spider goddess of Capricorn because of her placement, Mystere Araignee (NW) the mother spider of Scorpio, also known as La Maman Regne, Ti-Zariguin (SW), both the inventor-Loa of Aquarius and the brother and son of the previous mysteres. This Loa is responsible for all of the magickal inventions of the new sciences of esoteric engineering, dream-control, and ontic sphere mediumship. Lastly, there is the Father-Loa Baron Zariguin, for all the Guedhe-Loa are "Norman Barons," as the hierarchy of the Loa comes from French thinking. Baron is assigned to the North-East, and to the sign of Leo, because he is the most deadly aspect of The Grand Lion. You now will have before you a complete temple of magickal potencies for inducting the pure forces to be fed into your will and imagination. As you place yourself in the midst of this mandala, you will truthfully see the lines of power crossing in the eight different directions, the four main points and the points-between-the-points. This is the beginning of your magickal and voudoo machine for travel in time and space, for wherever you wish to go in your occult self-hood the powers now coming into your voudoo spaceship will take you there. You will ask one of the spirits to be your guide, assign them special projects, like travel to the past (N and NE), past/present (W and SW), present/future (S and SW), and future (E and SE).

Therefore, you will be able to move with the direction of a particular spirit to another region of time. The other spirits will act as controol, either moving you back, as when for example NE will move N back, as NE is more ancient, or when N will move NW before or back or when NW will move or control the before-time sequence of W, and this is done by means of the magickal powers of the spiders and death-Loa. Or when you desire to go forward in time you iwll summon the power, via the symbolic machines of those ahead. Thus, SE will move anyone ahead except a time-traveler in the E position. W will act as a brake for the speed of SW, but will speed up NW. As you move more and more towards the east and south, you speed up, as you move more and more towards the west and north, you will slow down in going forward and will go back in time. Thus, even SE can make E move a little back in time. Using this exciting method of time travel is the basic voudoo science for coming and going through different dimensions and spaces, for each time will have a different dimensional objectivity. How does the voudooist stay with the past and present and future of the planet earth and not go off into another world or universe --- in case you know only one language of everyday communications?

That is very simply based on what you do with the western powers. To remain on earth, but to explore the past of the earth, use W mainly and exercise great control with the Scorpio controls of NW. To stay on earth, but to explore the future moderately and safely, simply use W modified by SW, and carefully add or control the feeding of input from S. On the other hand, to find out the present for another universe, simply move sharply to summon the powers of E, SE, NE, or N, and then carefully bring it down to the present by using S, SW, W or NW modifications. The experience time-and-universes traveler is able thusly to go anywhere, by making use of this rather simple system,, because he would know from experience how to adjust the inflow of energies which are the fuels for his projections. These fuels for projections are very simply the kalas and shaktis, theojas and sexual radioactivities which power all our machines. The ojas (theojas or god–energies) and sexual radio- activities are especially sought after by vampiristic deities, also,and for this reason the magician must look carefully into the nature of the magickal images used to power the symbols with their own magickal force-fields. By using less–than– horrific spirit–Loas, the magician runs the risk of attracting very negative vampies who need the ojas of the mandala instruments to sustain themselves. These vampires must be carefully distinguished from the positive vampires of time and space– consciousness travel who assist the magician to move into other regions and who, manifested as were–spiders and zombi–Loa, both guard the temple of sciences as well as provide certain esoteric energies, which while matching other energies in the magician, also produce the Cartesian vortices through the voltigeurs of esoteric physicans make contact with the points of other worlds. Thus, we can see the need to know the nature of energies used behind the symbolics of voudoo mechanics.

Once you have set up your temple space, you begin to realize that it is the field very simply constructed of magickal powers. Each symbolic point, and the symbols are your own always, serves as a door which admits by means of an astral tuyau or conduit the special forces represented by the placement of the symbols and your intention in what you wish these placements to be. Immediately the forces begin to come in from the other side of the veil of manifestation. You will make contact with them by means of will, mind, and imagination, so that as the forces come into the mandalum a perfect eight armed spider system is formed. This is the most ideal machine for all time and space–consciousness travel and really
all of the other
systems seem to be built out of this system. You now become a truly magickal spider, a were–spider, who will appear to sit in the midst of your web, when viewed by both Golden Dawn and Tantric clairvoyance. This is the way that you appear on the astral plane or plane of the universe, and making contact with that astral place or situs, you are now ready to go where you want to control your
departure. In this sense,
this lesson is the most complete exposition of time and space–consciousness, because it is the first of this new series in esoteric voudoo sciences, and yet you have to learn all of these relatively advanced techniques, because you will not be spending much time on earth in the next lessons –– only in earthly graveyards, I might add. So now you are a spider–magian, spider–sorceror, or spider–magician. You may be any of these as they are entirely suitable. You have woven your web by meeting with your own magickal force at each of the eight sources of cosmic energy. Thus, cosmic energy is met by god–energy.

You are now able to tune the instrument and see what images are fed to you as you turn on one control with your mind after another. You might want to use a magick mirror or a control through a shew–stone or some other method. But at first I suggest that you use the mind, the will, and the imagination entirely, in order to build up your controls. Later we will explore the methods for making the magick mirror. You can test the in–flow of images from the cosmic shakti, because in the occult fluid are the potencies from which rise the images of other worlds and systems of time. You can see that there is a cycle to this occult motion, for like the cycle of the moon it is based upon the ebb and flow of a very special sexual energy, the energy behind time–travel. You have set yourself to testing the controls for this movement into another realm of being. By moving one way or another you can achieve the fullness of another world, another time, or our own earth, as in the 18th century. It has become easy to build up the cosmic world of magickal mind by this simple science. You have before you a complete system of magickal explorations. If you are willing to do so you may stop here and remain here in this sphere, entirely and permanently rather than trying to move into another lesson in magick. But others will want to go on to another sphere of exploration.

I want to close this lesson with a diagram which will explain the time zones and other regions of space–consciousness as they are manifested in our being.

East –– pure future, other universes beyond the Sun.

North-East –– the ultimate doorway beyond Pluto, beyond Kether, the past of other universes, the region of absolute history, where the past is now and only the past is.

North –– which is the pure past, the absolute realm of history, the present of of other universes beyond Pluto, other doors beyond our past meaasurements.

North–West –– the past of the earth. Also the past of other worlds, also the future of realms contacted via the pure past, other universes beyond Pluto.

West –– the present that is just passed and becoming past. This is the world of the now on earth, the here and now.

South–West –– the future of the earth as the present moves more and more away from us. The present of other worlds can be reached here, sometimes.

South –– the future which has just left the present, the world of the earth's own future.

South-East –– future with some tendency towards the earth, some reference to universes near our solar system.

Back to the East –– pure future, other universes beyond the Sun.

You will understand that your own magickal mandalum instrumentum is simply this map and when you do, all universes then are open to you.

La Couleuvre Noire: Les Linglesoux

The technical name in "language Creole," i.e., in the vocabulary of esoteric voudoo, les Linglesoux, refers to the priests of the astral shrouds. This name, which is derived from "lingam" and "le soi," refers to the aspect of the Cultus Ghuedhe, which consists in the stellar-phallic identity of the astral priests of macabrey. The focus of this aspect of the cultus must be found in the identity of the dead as the sources of a very specific eroticisme magique. Under these circumstances, the cultus must provide for the frequent occurrences of astral necrophilia, usually on the part of the Ghuedhe type spirits who attack any and all persons desirable to them. Esoteric voudoo has restricted this type of magick, or experience of possession to nocturnal erotic encounters with the spirits of the dead, who in their desire for concrete materialization actually possess the male organ of the sleeping human. For this reason, the presence of the erection of that organ during sleep is known as an indicator of the visitation of these spirits.

Because of folklore and folkloric encrustations of the esoteric voudoo tradition, the spirits of the Linglesoux family become identified with "mauvais air" and other types of vampiric entities. But we must distinguish between these experiences and the more European succubae or succubates, as the entity experienced by the magician is "pas b'swa linges" mais "lingam le soi," hence an entity which seeks to replenish its own magickal identity by means of taking occult forces from the magician. This cultus in general, which means the seeking actively after this experience, is not found among any of the occult voudois or Houdoux pretres, but is confined to the most extreme sect aspect of the cult—Ghuedhe, which is associated with night-time magicks and magickal experiences which draw night-time powers into the magician. For this reason the act of communication with the spirits of this type is viewed as horrible in itself and its descriptions unspeakable, by occult voudooists.

However, because of its extreme character, this magick, which is identified with the sign of Scorpion (in the Zodiac) is viewed as a source of very great power. As a consequence, those born under this sign are sought out by the pretres–bokors of this system as ideally suitable mediums, for mediumite and erotique–magique are viewed as identical realities in this context. Hence the production of the phenonmena of mediumite is viewed as having been generated by specific conditions in the erotic encounter with "les spirites," i.e., the members of the cultus, who accept a magickal view of the philosophy of spiritism. There are taught magickal exercises for the building up of this nocturnality, which barters sexual energy for occult and psychic powers. The candidate, in order to become a Linglesou must open his being to possession by these very dominant spirits, inasmuch as he must become such an object of their desire that they will grant occult powers to him in exchange for his vitality and manhood. In the esoteric interpretation, these spirits readily become an extension of the candidate's own identity, and thus rapidly by means of congress with them, especially by the devotional act of total surrender to these types of spirits, he becomes also Lingam le soi.

The exercises taught along these lines are variations of the VIIIo, O.T.O. called the "mystery of solitude," whereby the magnetism of the candidate becomes more and more attractive to the spirits. But in actual fact, the magick consists of the performance of the despicable aspects of the XIo, O.T.O., now rejected by the English branch of that order, but practiced by the conscience—less fringe rites and orders which dwell in the infinitudes of larval cesspools, and whose practice of these rites while shunned by all other magickal schools and societies, groups, rites, and orders, is for these extremists, "les linglesoux," the very basis of their power and contact relationship with the inner planes. Thus, that which is rejected by 99% of the entire sexo—magickal continuum, and which is taught by certain extreme Boullanists in France (les Buollanistes des—fetes) is the practical norm with les linglesoux.

What can we say are the benefits of this method which will make certain magicians break the sexo—magickal tabooux of countless orders, which will cause the magician to abandon the law of yoni for nocturnal obsession of the most vile kliphotic contacts? Those who possess the technical knowledge admit that psychic ability is increased so that all of the forms of low mediumship and crude psychic powers are made perfect, while the higher psychic powers are fully manifested. But does this occult exchange provide sufficient compensation for the man who must sacrifice himself to nocturnal appetites of a most perverse type? The occult student must be aware of what exists in the continuum of darkest magick, he must know why certain magickal substances are preferred by the more subtle spirits than the crudity of a mere human sacrifice. Thus, the magician must determine his orientation in this matter and surrencer himself to these nightly obsessions as they come down upon him. For as they manifest themselves in the most intense erotorality, as they come down upon his body the awaiting sacrifice and take him, so by draining out the vitality of the unconscious and subconscious id and libido, they fill up the area where they have taken the power with pure elemental power of the most intense psychicality. By identification of this power with the element of water, with the western place in the temple, we encounter the onrush of extremely psychic forces, and the onrush pours into the soul of the magician as he becomes more and more linglesou, as he identifies himself more and more with prior pre—parval layers of being, with pure primordiality of energies and powers, which are the basis of the whole famille Ghuedhe, the domain of complete lust —— the lust for lust itself transformed into magickal power and psychic capacities.

In order to possess the reality of this power, you must take it into yourself as the spirits are taking your powers from you. This power from them, once received, then becomes the basis for all magickal operations derived from this most esoteric view of the VIIIo type magick. When power is then needed, all one has to do is to bring to focus these wraithlike clouds of astral libido, which are now one's own and which are wrapped around oneself with the firmness and fury of the most pre—orgasmic lust. The magician under the circumstances will then be able to master the secrets as they are poured into him by means of subtle lines or connectives, which being wraith—like themselves, are the astral lines of ejaculation created in the etheric void by the action of these larval spirits seeking more and more food from mankind.

You will present to your mentor a report consisting of two parts. First of all your understanding of this lessn and what its principles are as magickal methods for the production of occult force. Secondly, you will record experiences of this type, as distinct from succubates contacts, which you may begin to experience if you wish to identify yourself with this astral cultus. Only part one of this report is required for membership as a student in LCN, however, appreciation of part two may open most interesting magickal doorways on the inner planes and present the candidate with sufficient psychic ability to see the inner aspects of voudoo with greater lucidity.

Exercise

In the lesson I-1-1 you were given a structure for a magickal instrument of the mandalum instrumentum type, in lesson I-1-2 you are given a method of powering that instrument, or magickal space-ship, anywhere. Using your intuition, tell me how you are able to unify the fruits of the lessons 1(a) and 1(b) in a systematic manner.

(a) please tell me how they work together as a method of research.

(b) please tell me that particular method of application which pleases you.

(c) please tell me what you have learned about yourself in this method.

(d) please tell me about any communications of an extraordinary nature you have received, and if they can be applied to your development in LCN.

(e) please tell me about the way specific energies feed into and fuel the various parts of the mandalum, so that for the eight parts of the instrument there are eight actual energies which you direct therein.

(f) please tell me of the magickal transformation of your physical selfhood as a result of using this machine under a variety of circumstances.

(g) this magickal machine can be invoked at any time; have you tried to use it at times other than when you do your magickal exercise?

(h) maintain a magickal diary of your experiences using this instrument, and provide me with examples of the contents of this diary.

NOTE: It is generally assumed by Dr. Hector-Francois Jean-Maine that the students truly wish to develop themselves in the fullest degree in LCN work. In line with this understanding, a small door is now opening in your conscience, the door of magickal research. There exists within the interior famille of LCN a secret group of research mages, who wish to invite you to share in their comprehension. Hence, we have attached a sample magickal paper of this research branch. Read the paper over, and in order to determine your intuition, write what you imagine to be the contents of any of the magickal topics listed on this sheet, and also let us know which — and you may have more than one favorite — of those given you wish to explore as a member of the inner research group, under Baron Zariguin, as Head Loa of the Spider-research spirit group and the were-spider, and especially were-tarantula priesthood, which inhabits these interiorities of consciousness in its esoteric manifestation.

Structure Your Report as Follows

1) Identify your specific line(s) of research by name and number, as given on the page entitled "Season of Ghouls." This refers to Famille Guedhe Research as a special science.

2) Provide an imaginative description of the magickal contents of the research topic(s).

3) Provide an imaginative method of using existing experiences from the exercise in lesson I-1-2 as your guide for doing the research.

4) Select certain eroto-magickal situations which might be suitable for the practice of what you have imagined in point 2.

5) Discuss if this method will help you develop more and more power as mentioned in "Lucky Hoodoo," which is the basic introduction to our system.

6) Perhaps you would like to add certain insights from the paper on the angelic and kliphotic languages in order to deepen your insights and enrich your magickal experience. If you wish this, add information.

This report should be sent to Michael P. Bertiaux, as usual, however, indicate on the front of the letter, below the name and above the post-office box, the initials T-D-G, or better, after the name of Bertiaux, so that your report is received in the proper rite. Fraternellement, Michael Bertiaux, December 30, 19←←.

La Societe Secrete Des ZOBP -- Tarantules "Chenilles Astrales"
Loa -- Zariguin -- Ti' Pieds -- Mille -- Fois, Souvereign Grand Maitre Absolute
Address: Michael Bertiaux, P.O. Box 1554, Chicago, Illinos 60690, U.S.A.

Application for adhesion to the societe-des-zobep:

Name:
Address:

Attach a recent photo of yourself which has been taken for this very purpose and none other.

It is my desire to develop in the magic-des-zobop, and therefore, it is my desire to adhere to the societe secrete des zobop-tarantules of the Grand Loge, "Chenilles astrales," and for this reason I now make application.

If the applicant is already a brother of LCN, it is not necessary to pay any dues other than his regular dues in LCN>

In order to determine whether or not a candidate has been selected spiritually by les-zobop-tarantules (the brotherhood of were-tarantula sorcerors) it is necessary for the candidate to describe a magickal experience which he has had, which will serve to indicate his call from these spirits. This will indicate that the candidate has been invited also by Baron Zariguin, who is the Master of this magickal order. Please complete the report with the following items covered:

A) Is this call to become a were-tarantula unmistakable?

B) Is this call the result of my very private devotion to special Loa or spirits identified with this cultus and with no other system of culte?

C) What magickal, occult, and/or psychic phenomenon have been experienced since my association with this culte as a idee-fixe in my soul-mind?

D) What is the esoteric significance to me of the spider as the type most perfect des-animaux-magique?

E) I believe in the power of this magick, but what is the symbolic meaning of my master-teacher in magick as a were-spider to me, the student?

F) Having experienced many matters of occult significance, how is it possible for me to interpret the were-tarantula method as more powerful?

G) From what I have read and from what I have imagined, what is the content of the work of the magickal brotherhod of the were-tarantula?

H) What do I imagine to be the philosphy of sexual energy taught by these were-tarantulas?

Having completed your brief description of what you think this magick is in terms of the eight points, which are hot-points (points-chauds) of this system, you iwll send this application to Mr. Bertiaux.

TEMPS-DES-GHOULES

In esoteric voudoo there is a point-chaud, or "hot point," known by this name. It may be understood as "season of the graverobbers," and is along with eight other points, one of the major hot points of the mysteries of ZOMBEEISME.

This point is conferred in a temple which resembles a graveyard, with tombstones and skulls as the proper symbolism. The high-priest will represent Maitre Baron or Maitre Des Morts, lord of the cemetery. The others will represent a corpse-to-be-made-into-a-Zombi and a ghoul or graverobber.

The ghoul is guided by Baron to where the corpse lies buried and digs up the coffin and brings out the body, which is then transformed via magick into a Zombi. The Zombi is then commanded by Baron to kill the ghoul, for disturbing the dead, so at that moment the ghoul is sacrificed to Baron by the Zombi, who is now a priestly worker. Next, the dead ghoul is transformed into a Zombi by Baron. This concludes the first point of the rite.

The second part of the rite opens up with the inner temple of the Death Cultus, which is located in a secret cave graveyard called "Place-des-Zobops," or the place of the sorcerors. Baron is holding a feast with his Zombi and decides to feast on them, so they immediately seize one of their own and consume his flesh, drinking his blood from a chalice which Baron passes to each of them. Baron then confers a magickal type of reality upon the Zombi sacrificed and enthrones him as a Nimbo. This ends the second point of the rite.

The third point of the rite opens in the temple of Ghuedhe-Zariguinou, Baron of the spider-sorcerors, who instructs the Zombi in how to become living men again, by use of the magickal venom, which he generates. They receive this venom and become living men who can at will become Zombi and thus immune from all mortal dangers. Zariguinou also leads them into the mysteries of Bacaloubaca, Loa of Black Magick divination and initiation. Depending upon the high-priest, then, this rite reaches magick, divination, the use of the 16 types of magickal venoms (seminal fluid of the spider-sorcerors), methods of immortality possessed by the undead, as well as the first points of the esoteric temple of the spiders (Secret-des-Peristyle-Zariguines), and thus connects with the following mysteries (these are the hot-points):

1. point-des-macandas -- sorcerors who attack night-travelers
2. point-des-bacas -- divinatory powers reserved to the undead
3. point-des-chats -- werecat powers of Carrefour, door to Lyncanthropy
4. point-des-Linglesoux -- powers of the shroud
5. point-des-sorts -- divinatory skills using skulls
6. point-des-morts -- communication with dead bodies
7. point-des-amazarouz -- or Amazaroux "spider necrophilia"
8. point-des-scorpions -- creation of 256 different venoms and poisons
9. temps-des-craines -- making skulls talk
10. temps-des-froides -- winter-death magick, a kind of suffocation cold
11. temps-des-chauds -- killing by sending astral fires
12. temps-des-amazaroux -- creating a spider's cave for initiation
13. temps-des-nids -- nest of venomous magickal serpents
14. temps-des-narcisses -- generation of shaktis and kalas from venoms
15. temps-des-sorteurs -- 256 poisonous methods of astral projection
16. temps-des-Ghoules -- the power of Baron to give all these points

La Couleuvre Noire: Les Cadavres Piquants

1. To Baron Ghuedhe belong all the ritual churches of the world
2. To Baron Ghuedhe belong all the ritual Mass-vestments of the world
3. To Baron Ghuedhe belong all the Requiem Masses of the world
4. To Baron Ghuedhe belong all the Mass-priests of the world
5. To Baron Ghuedhe belong all the candles and incense burnings of the world
6. To Baron Ghuedhe belong all the bishops and patriarchs of the world
7. To Baron Ghuedhe belong all the missales and liturgical books of the world
8. To Baron Ghuedhe belong all the eucharistic breade and wine of the world

The culte of Ghuedhe is the culture of ritual worship as the most expressive of
elemental and phallic necessity. For this reason, the church of tradition being his
cannot have priestesses and other female decorations. It must be the imitation of
the Ghuedhe on the cross, the Loa of Death and Resurrection. For this reason the true
priests of Guedhe shall collect all the magickal vesture of his cultus, including
many vestments in the color of his celebration, which shall be the color of his
ancient race-people, Noir. All churches and temples are veve of Guedhe, supreme
power of all being, whose days are:

  All Mondays -- for HE IS THE LOA-DES-LUNES.
You shall offer the Mass of the Dead for Guedhe if you are His Priest
  All Fridays -- for THE CHRIST THAT DIED ON FRIDAY
You shall offer the Mass of the Dead for Guedhe, The Christ Who Died
  All Saturdays -- for Guedhe is the LORD OF SATURDAY
You shall offer the supreme Mass of Guedhe on HIS day, and All sexuality shall be the
worship of skulls, and HIS ICONOGRAPHIC SHALL BE supremely honored this day.

If the entire theogony of LCN is an explication of the culte of Guedhe in general,
the liturgical center of this cultus is in Les Cadavre Piquants, which refers to the
cultus of the inner Guedhe, sometimes called "Les Barons Guedhes." These are the
interior or piquant manifestations of the supreme as death, piquants because the
intense flavor has been preserved from loss of essential oils into the air. The
liturgical taste of the true semance Guedhe is that of pungent spice, a mixture said
to be between peppers, mints, and various hot cinnamons. Furthermore, only the
priests may drink this concoction, which may be sprayed into the eyes of those
seeking clairvoyant development. Thusly the high-priest of this cultus must be aware
of the many manifestations of the interior energy, which is derived entirely from the
Essence-des-Cadavres, which is the sexual-radioactivity of the priesthood, and which
comes from the use of the CRANES. or ritual skulls, three of which represent the
mysteres Ghuedes: Baron Lundi -- Loa Guedhe of Monday, the original Moon God of all
ancient cultures, now cultus of voudoo esoteric in its most interiority. His home is
in the id of the High-priest, and thus he represents pure lust in its cosmic and
unrestricted sense. Baron Legbha-Nibbho -- this is the Christ who died on Good
Friday, the color of his power is white as is the color of all Legbha. Sometimes he
is called Baron Guedhe Legbha. Baron Samedi -- this is the most widely known member
of the inner culte. The color of Baron S is of course black, but sometimes violet,
which is the color of Baron Lundi. The locus or home of Baron Legbha is the
conscious and superconscious mind. The home of Baron S is the conscious-subconscious

mind, but he is also seen as being a more developed Loa than Baron L, which is confined to the unconscious mind until he manifests in sexual chaos and vampirism. Together these Loa form the family of the Cadavres Piq. Their magick is ritualistic in many ways and they are said to prefer certain religions over others on the basis of ritual. Thus all the exotic rites, e.g., Ethiopic, Russian Orthodox monasticism, etc., these are all situ for the manifestations of these very powerfu essences.

Together, these Loa produce certain magickal presences, such as the very formal and phallic Baron Zariguin, who is the master of magickal lattices and geometries. Baron Z is the two-fold generation, whose complement is Baron Limbi or Limba, the Loa of gluttony and nudity, so that from these marassas or twins -- jumeaux -- powerful forces are derived from the magician's rites. Limba is entirely content or a Loa of experiences, while Zariguin is the supreme master of abstractmental systems and therefore the Loa of modern science in many of its technological constructions. The magician, by making contact with the phallico-gluttonous and nudist interests of his body and seeing these as energies for the projection outwards of the abstract lattices thusly masters two important parts of his being as a magickal practitioner. These are entirely associated with rituals, and for this reason the magician will collect materials for a religious chapel, where after his ordination he will be able to say Mass for magickal purposes. His vesture and the chapel furnishings will be entirely correct from the Baroque and Roman -- sometimes in the Lundi cultus -- or the Byzantine viewpoint. Below are two interesting veves of these Loa.

In the exploration of LCN esoteric voudoo it is possible to understand that these vevers are in actual fact pictures of the magickal temples of these Loa, from which the powers implied in their sigils are derived. That is to say, there is a logical isomorphism between the vever and the inner plane magickal temple of the Loa which is His power-house and upon which we draw in our magicks.

Now we have recognized three major aspects of GHUeDHe, namely his sacred days as magickal positions for operation of high space-consciousness in time, or the generation of the powers of His being from this triad. Then we see how these powers come together -- and their own operations are explications from Limbi and Zariguin. In Lesson Two of this series we will begin the papers of the Grimoire GHUeDHe, which is the most perfect system of voudoo theogony to be derived. However, the generation of the following hot points of Ghuedhe does show its own magickal theogony:

In order to begin to practice esoteric LCN methods, you should think of yourself as also an artist, for the drawing of magickal maps of the Loa—consciousness is simply one of the most important parts of the understanding of the culte. By magickal maps we mean of course those charts which reveal the powers of the inner worlds as they are in themselves, as ideal machines, as magickal geographies, as systems of inner plane magick constructed according to magickal laws. In view of the fact that the Loa are to be viewed as logical forms, while human magickal experience is to be viewed as the content of all magickal experience, we can say that vevers are really guide posts for the directing of magickal energies. Thus the sign of the arrow ————indicates in voudoo the flow of power in a direction. A magickal staircase indicates the passageway between one realm of consciousness and another, from the higher worlds to the lower or from the lower to higher somewhere in the system of the Ghuedhe which is of course a magickal line of intitiation, moving upwards or downwards in that is the structure of the inner consciousness. Therefore, the voudooist practitioner will be prepared to build up a magickal system of exact references, which are important for the positioning of his consciousness on the inner. This results in a series of magickal maps of the inner worlds as systems of hieroglyphic direction and spatialization, with the result that the magician can find his way around, with the aid of the Loa who will direct him, and if he gets lost there isn't any problem about finding where he is or where he is going simply by asking directions from identifiable centers of consciousness or Loa on the inner planes of reality. Thus, magickal maps of consciousness are important tools for the magician's finding himself through the worlds of Les Cadavres Piquants. In summary, let me suggest 16 magickal laws or principles to be kept in mind when working out maps of the Loa—worlds and your paths in and out of the various magickal spheres.

1. Be certain initially of what system or Famille of Loa you are working with. For this reason you should be familiar with the symbols of your own cultic school, as in LCN we use the Famille Ghuedhe.

2. Make contact with your own particular Loa into whose presence you have been initiated in order to carry on your research. Yo may contact this being by meditation if not yet initiated.

3. Look for hints of magickal maps in the vevers of the Loa, so that your selection of symbolism is consistent.

4. Meditate on the vevers quite a lot in order to build u the habit of unconsciousnes——reflection on the thoughts and thought—forms of these Loa.

5. Begin to exercise your mind and imagination by making maps which are close to the vevers of the Loa as pathways of consciousness.

6. See the maps as coming to life in your mind and imagination by means of visualization exercises which seem to project imagination into newer realms.

7. Begin to meet Loa on the roads of these maps. Begin to ask them for directions. Begin to make use of the hints and advice they give you.

8. Begin to make travel on these maps the most important part of your own daily

magickal exercise, so that you can travel effortlessly into the mystical realms.

9. Keep a careful record of these maps and all sortirs in a special book, which becomes your magickal workbook and which guides your mind into these realms with ease.

10. Eventually you will find the doorways to these maps have distinct and identifiable qualities, which you may isolate for magickal consideration. These are new Loa.

11. While these new Loa might be known to other voudoo cultists, they are new to you and form an extension of your knowledge of these worlds, so that you gain insights.

12. Gradually try to gain the confidence of the Loa and begin to practice the rites and ceremonies which they will introduce to you. These are rites and ceremonies of great values.

13. By this means you will come to learn of different voudoo societies on the inner and how they operate.

14. You will be admitted to these cults and increase your voudoo armatoire.

15. You will learn that voudoo is endless & 16. totally metamathematical in its essence, for all types of magickal geometries come from it, filled with Loa.

La Couleuvre Noire: Les Faiseurs-Des-Zombis

This is the final lesson on the foundations of the points-chaud, upon which the entire science of the esoteric understanding of voudoo depends. We must understand that voudoo is a logical science of being, which is built up out of many factors and the interconnection of symbols, which by their very nature are spiritual realities having intelligence and the power of acting upon the physical order of space and time. Therefore, the voudoo magician does not have to worry about making contact with the inner planes, he already is there and has very great powers for acting in a direct and positive way. Yes, the powers of the Loa are those of the voudoo magician and his powers are great because these powers from the Loa themselves, from their esse.

[veve of Les-F-Des-Z pictured here]

[veve of famille guedhe pictured here]

The esoteric voudoo lodge which we maintain in Chicago for LCN activity is called "Les-Faiseurs-des-ZOMBI." It is connected with another voudoo type lodge here, also, which is called "Famille Ghuedhe," and which is concerned with the rites of initiation of the Franco-Haitian Ordo Templi Orientis. Thus we can say that "Les Faiseurs-des-Zombi" is the content side of our work here in the voudoo occulte, while the formal side is provided by "Famille Ghuedhe." In the Franco-Haitian OTO, the rites are based upon masonic ideal systems, while in the secret society of the LCN< the formula is that of the old shamanic magick and sorcery of Afro-Atlantean cults. The interaction of these two cults constitutes the formation of the second part of our course in magick, which is the Grimoire Ghuedhe, a book of lessons entirely based upon magickal recipes. However, you are now to learn certain basic questions and answers which are given by the students as they enter the LCN lodge in Chicago. The temple is opened and the student are brought before the Master who is enthroned in the throne of Ghuedhe, which is located in the north, the placements of Saturn:

Q. What does the name "Faiseurs-des-Zombi" refer to?

A. It is the name of the LCN lodge in Chicago, Illinois.

Q. Does this lodge have an inner and an outer circle?

A. Like all lodges of esoteric voudoo, it has an outer court of three grades and an inner society for secret and advanced work.

Q. Who is the Master of the lodge "Faiseurs-des-Zombi"?

A. In the outer the Grand Master is Docteur Hector-Francois Jean-Maine, the inner Grand Master is Maitre-Baron-Cimetiere.

Q. Where does the name "Faiseurs-des-Zombi" derive?

A. From those priests who developed elementaux in dead bodies and made those bodies act, move, and have physical manifestation in work, etc.

Q. Is there an esoteric department of the lodge which is open to LCN students?

A. Yes, there is the 2eme ordre, which is open to those who wish to receive the researches of L-F-des-Z.

Q. What is the name of this research documentation?

A. The name is "monde Squeletique."

Q. Does this mean the place of the Three skulls?

A. That is the temple meeting place of the initiate and Ghuedhe l'Horizon.

[veve of universe-G pictured here]

Q. What is the nature of the magick of this place of the three skulls?

A. Information about highest magick is given by the three skulls to the adepts.

Q. What is the specific type of magickal information?

A. Information about the Ghuedhe–Universe or system–G.

Q. Is this another ultra–topology or logico–magickal realm?

A. That, as well as an entirely Ghuedhe Universe–system and magickal encyclopedia of worlds.

Q. Are these living beings?

A. These worlds are all living, all ideas there are alive.

Q. Who would especially live there?

A. Les–Faiseurs–des–Zombi.

Q. Are these magicians alive?

A. In their own universe they are alive, we are by reference to them the dead ones.

Q. Can we go there and live with them and not be dead in this world?

A. Yes, you may go there if they decide to take you. You have to be invited.

Q. Does one receive special initiations to prepare for their universe?

A. Yes, these are the initiations given in the 2nd order of LCN, of the F–des–Z.

Q. Is it true that the dead are perfect in this Universe–G, that they are really in the Resurrection?

A. That is the meaning of the "life" in that universe.

Q. Was St. Paul, the Catholic writer of the Epistles, an initiate of them or one who knew of them?

A. What more could his writings indicate so clearly?

Q. But what of the decay of the dead bodies which happens to them in this world?

A. That is the difference between the body inherited from Adam (the body in Universe–A) and the glorified body which is the hope of the True Resurrection in Universe–G.

Q. Is this universe based upon the so–called "pagan" metaphysics or religion–view?

A. No, in fact it is very strictly Catholic orthodoxy, of the Ancient Christian Church mystery school tradition.

Q. Does the Mass exist there and who will celebrate it?

A. There the Mass is that of the Holy Resurrection, for the Requiemes of Universe–A are a preparation for that Mass of Universe–G, being celebrated in Universe–A. But the celebrant of the Mass in Universe–G is rightly known to all initiates as Maitre–Ghuedhe/Loa–le=Regenere, the Loa Christ–du–Midi–Des–Faiseurs–des–Zombi.

Grimoire Ghuedhe: Initiation of Grimoire Ghuedhe

Grimoire Ghuedhe is more than a book or series of papers forming a book for the working out of magickal spells and performing magickal experiments of the Houdeaux type because it is also a school of inner plane work, from which the spells and other magickal operations derive their powers. The power comes from the connection between Grimoire formulary and inner—plane contact. Grimoire Ghuedhe is centered on the Famille Ghuedhe, which means that the powers of this system come from the very secret operations of the members only of the Ghuedhe Family of Loa in esoteric voudoo.

There are two primary lessons in Grimoire Ghuedhe, which are open to anybody who has paid the initial fee for the LCN magickal course. However, after the completion of the first two papers, we will have to separate out suitable students from those who are not suitable, in terms more than just the willingness of the student to make payment for instruction. Grimoire Ghuedhe, which is a Loa, must call you into His magickal order, and if He does not like you, and this is indicated to us, we will inform you and refuse your fees, because we cannot go against the Loa of this very perfect system of realization.

Grimoire Ghuedhe is composed of the following magickal components for operational experiment by the magician.

1. First we will study the various Loa of this family, which are used by us. We will continue to introduce more and more Loa as we move along in the GG, but at first we simply work with about 40 Loa.

2. Last night, I had an experience with one of the more powerful ones of this group of 40. How did I know this? Well, the reason is due to there being a magickal sign of the Loa in my mind. This is the vever or magickal symbol, which is the basis for knowing the Loa; each Loa has a name and a sign or magickal vever, i.e., sigil.

3. Each Loa has specialized tasks to perform and thus is called upon to do His own specialty.

4. The magick of the Loa is done by means of special ritual actions. These are very much indicated as individualized for the Loa, and for this reason, all magickal operations, forming a composite, are very unique.

5. Each Loa has its own inner—school, and this gives special initiations and has special courses.

6. Each Loa in GG has a special map of consciousness, which is used to locate the Loa on the inner. This map is different from the sign in item 2, above, as many Loa of the same family are located nearby each other in connecting territory.

7. The colors are usually black and purplse for the GG, but are modified with red, gold, and white to offset the black/purple. Lent, Adventine, Requiem colors are implied here.

8. The Loa form families of distinct types, which are very special for their own magickal operations and purposes. Thus, there is the spider—family, which we have already met. This family is very different from the Liturgical Family, which is concerned with initiation temples, etc.

9. The Loa tend to be conservative, this means that they do not change, rather new Loa are added to GG to meet newer needs. This is the difference between GG and many other forms of occult spirit magick.

10. GG is highly experimental. The student is asked to keep a certain note—book and to report in detail his operations. Every student is given personal attention by

communication with the Loa in astral experience.

11. The format for the presentation of the GG is like this: a) Loa, b(what family does He belong to, c) map or location of His temple on the inner, d) His vever, e) what He does in terms of special magick, f) how to work with Him, i.e., what is His rite, g) various liturgical conditions and qualities pertaining to Him and His relationship with other Loa.

There are two families of Ghuedhe spirits and each has its own special magickal purpose and work to do. These families are highly specialized and are contacted on exact hot points, which hot points are represented in space by the vevers of the cultic family. These designs or sigils are magickal doorways into contact with the Loa, and they function as maps of the ways –– often wholly mystical –– in which the Loa operate. Properly speaking, the student has to be physically initiated into the depth of the sigil, but psychic approaches to the outside of the mystery are possible, otherwise we wouldn't have a course available. However, Dr. Jean-Maine, nor his late father, ever said that physical initiation was non-essential in the voudoo arts, as voudoo is physical, northerly, earthly, and ceremonial. It is not a Golden Dawn or English OTO "astral confraternity," to which all are invited to be actual members. Physical initiation is the method for voudoo. However, the use of the sigil, or magickal design, does awaken in the sensitive person a certain psychic power or ability to recall the primordial conditions of being, from which voudoo is derived, as well as our states of consciousness. Consequently, meditating upon a symbol or repeating the name of a Loa, so that with each repetition the name becomes more detached from particulars and more and more magickally spaced, this is an effective way of developing the psychic attunement to voudoo which is so wonderful when experienced. That is why we make such a big point about giving you the names of the Loa and their various sigils, many of which are the products of the automatic psychic processes of the Afro-Latin mentality, rather than symbols going back to Africa. The energies are ancient, but to be sure, each priest-magician has tried over the years to add more and more to the pantheon list of Loa, and often has been very successful. I want to give the Loa now in terms of family groups, and then the members follow in an appendix:

1. The Legbha Nibbho family is magickal and research oriented and concerned with ways of looking into the future, past, etc., as well as certain helps being provided to Legbha school initiates. This family is very conservative and follows closely the Arada appearance. Usually white is the color of the entire family.

2. The Cimitiere family is black oriented in color and show strong Petroelements. These Loa possess all of the wisdom of the dead and reflec the closeness of the Ghuedhe family to the non-voudoo "Culte-des-Morts," which is strict mediumship. Psychic powers are needed to adhere strongly to this family, especially the ability to do automatic writing, art, speech, give oracles, trance, and pure spiritism.

3. This family tends to swing in the direction of the Arada families, but represents an older line of magick and ritual initiation. The color is purple and gold, representing the royal line of the Ghuedhe spirits. All the symbols of the old order, i.e., byzantine and imperial, are useful in this cultus. This is the family used in giving initiations to both the living and the dead.

4. This divinatory family is a variation of the powers of the 1 and 3 families and is entirely concerned with oracles, especially oracles concerning things the dead might know. However, red and gold are used as ritual colors, because they give the "mysteries of blood" as part of their magickal representation and repertoire.

5. The black magick family is allied to 2 in its negative phase. The color is black and only black may be used, although purple, gold, and red may be complementary to the black color. For example, in South America, the priests and bishops of Bacaloubaca wear black and red Latin mass vestments and mitres of baroque shape. This family is used to cause trouble and is really quite negative, however, the sexual and ritual magick and the initiations of this family can be powerful and helpful. In Haiti, the priests of this family are all very terrible homosexual sadistic types and are shunned by white magicians generally. This family sets up its temple making use of four devil points, and these points are balanced by points taken from another family, e.g., four points from the Cimitiere.
[small symbolsof ghuedhe pictured here]

6. The transvection family is usually considered black magick in many ways. It uses only dark colors and uses were-animal masks. It uses weird forms of sexual magick, and in many ways it is allied with 2 and 5. By this I mean that it likes the settings of 2 and the actions of 5, except that it becomes more and more extreme in its ·manifestations. It is believed simply that voudoo priests may gain powers by entering into their animal level subconscious and subconscious minds and that this atavistic process will help them as oracles and as magickal creators and problem solvers. However, since many of the priests of the Ghuedhe family use lycanthropy as a method, the transvection family work almost entirely with insect-forms or low animals. For example, Ti-Moufette is the Loa of bad smells. Moufette means skunk. Now, the priest of this cult tries to emit as many bad smells as possible and in so doing he creates a magickal force field, which the 1, 3 and 4 families would consider evil or bad. These latter identify the GG work with the sensuous perfumes, rather than bad smells and forms of flatulency. However, this view of bad smells as being demonic is not entirely western, as the Ethiopians consider the experience of flatulence as the expulsion of demons from their bowels. We should therefore under- stand a primitive mode of thought behind this cultural attitude.

7. The big Baron Family is the GG establishment and considers itself the purest of the traditions. It is strongly Petro and purple, black, red are the magickal colors as well as the magickal days given in earlier lessons. It is necessary for all of the more respectable families to have at least one member in this family with whom they can communicate. As there are nine members this is easily shown. However, the lewd family, which is 9 ius fortunate in having two Barons as its members and these are allied in GG to Ghuedhe Brav, who is the 9th member of the Baron family. The Barons spend most of their time keeping the GG orthodox, that is, free from confusion with other Ghuedhe cults, that is why Baron Cousin 'Azacca is not listed, although he is genuine G Loa, but he is not magickal enough for the GG, or else he has his own magick. The real reason is that Cousin 'Azacca is part of the wholesome side of the Baron family, while GG prefers to work with the unwholesome side. The Barons in addition to magickal administration form an initiatic establishment of the stellar- phallic type and thus back up the initiations of 1, 3, 4 types while also allowing the 2, 5, 6, 8, and 9 families to run wild, as they enjoy doing. 10 is allied with the 1, 3, 4 group, with 8, so that there are five positive and five negative groups of Loa in GG. However, family Baron, 7, runs everything and must be acknowledged as the phallic establishment.

8. The spider family is quite small and likes black colors, sometimes red is used very discreetly. This family is closely allied to 6, the transvection family, except that the spider family is also the divinatory family of the negative type.

Thus the spider oracles are as sought after as the oracles of the 1, 3, 4, and 10 families. At one time this family was a subdivision of 1 or 4, but became independent and now is the white-magick divination system of the black-magicians of the GG. It is quite different from the divinations of the 5 family, which are black magick oracles mainly, although they need not be so negative.

9. The lewd family is entirely shocking to many students of black voudoo because it is so perverted. However, it is a magickal side and the Barons here are very powerful. The colors are any and all, but black, purple, red, and blue, and gold and silver are enjoyed. The legend is that Baron Limba and Baron Lundi were expelled from the Baron family because they were so perverted in their sexual expressions. For a while none of the more conservative Loa in the Baron family would talk to them, so sexual exhibitionism and nudism were not approved until later on -- now the Ghuedhe priests in Haiti are the most sexually exhibitionist of all -- so that these two barons, who are homosexual lovers formed their own school for teaching nude wrestling, usually in tubs or when drunk, and generated such a force that many joined the school. However, they do not use the four-fold pattern for the other families, and have an astral or secret point in addition to the three given. They are very close to the 2 family and the practice of deflowering dead virgins comes from this traditions of this school.

10. This is the most conservative black-magick school in GG. It is composed of voudoo monks and is the establishment behind the Barons. The colors are black and purple, and gold and red are used to modify these major colors. The work is divination and initiation.

Grimoire Ghuedge, Appendix 1.
The following are some of the Loa used in the magick of the Grimoire ghuedhe.
I. Famille Legbha Nibbho:
    1. Mirroir-des-Sessions
    2. Histoire Fantastique
    3. Mirroir Fantastique
    4. Mirroir Mystere
    5. Mirroir Royal
II. Famille Cimitiere:
    1. Ghuedhe Veillee
    2. Mystere Linglessou
    3. Mystere Grand-Aran
    4. Ghuedhe Cadavre
    5. Mystere Allonge
III. Famille Initiatique
    1. Roi Louanges -- Mystere Ghuedhe Luage
    2. Mystere Sacredoce
    3. Mystere d'Aphotheose
    4. Mystere Lutteau -- Ghuedhe Lutteur
    5. Ti-Retirer
    6. Grand Retirer
IV. Famille Divinitoire
    1. Mysteres-des-Sanges
    2. Mysteres-des-Craines
    3. Mysteres-des-Houdeaux

4. Mystere Royal ou Desak'karum

V. Famille Magie Noire
    1. Ti-Mauvais
    2. Macando
    3. Bacaloubaca
    4. Bossu-Diabolo

VI. Famille Transvection
    1. Ti-Pied-Mille-Fois
    2. Ti-Moufette
    3. Mystere-des-Blattes

VII. Grande Famille Baron:
    1. Baron La Croix
    2. Baron Cimitiere
    3. Baron Samedi
    4. Baron Piquant
    5. Baron Scorpion
    6. Ti-Jean-Zombi
    7. Baron Zombi
    8. Ghuedhe Nibbho ou Ghuedhe Nimbo
    9. Ghuedhe Brav'

VIII. Famille Zariguin:
    1. Mystere Araignee
    2. Ti-Zariguin
    3. Mystere Toile-d'Araignee
    4. Maitre Baron Zariguin ou Ghuedhe Zariguin

IX. Famille Impudique:
    1. Mystere-Limbi-des-Lutteurs-Nus
    2. Limba ou Maitre Baron Limba
    3. Mystere Baron Lundi

X. Famille Magique:
    1. Legbha Nibbho
    2. Histoire Nibbho
    3. Grand Maitre Baron Ghuedhe
    4. Marrassas Nibbho

There are many magicians who are interested in the work of the GG section of LCN. Yet, they are not aware of the existential basis of the field for operations, which is derived from exact astrological lattices, i.e., from beings-in-the-world. It is true that there are certain magickal methods which we teach by lesson as written, but there are also ways of learning our system via magickal oracles which are opened at certain times and under certain conditions these give forth teachings not found in our papers or books.

1. In order to feel the power of GG, which is the union of Saturn and the Sun in the sign of Scorpio, you will sit at a table with a candle burning before you but with no other illumination in the room.

2. You will begin to realize that the power of fire is an elemental contact and that you can easily possess consciousness of that elemental contact by talking to the fire before you. You will begin to send your thoughts into the fire and the fire will respond in its various motions. You will realize that the fire moves and responds now in perfect response to your psychic questioning.

3. You are making now inner-plane contact with the fire elemental, which is the closest to the human world and therefore the elemental most similar to human consciousness in the area of communication. You will now realize that you may engage in a limited dialogue with this fire elemental, wherever and whenever you wish to communicate with it.

4. Begin by asking it the following pattern of questions, which will serve to give you an insight into what the elemental spirits think of how you are developing as a magickal practitioner and be very careful about giving enough time to the elemental to make a proper response. This is the flame moves forwards and backwards, the answer is quite like a human nod, so it may be interpreted as yes, if the flame moves from side to side, the elemental may be interpreted as shaking its head, which is our human way of saying no and thus the elemental may be interpreted as providing a negative response to your question. Here are some questions you may wish to ask to test this method of operations:

i. I want to make contact with you, am I sending my thoughts clearly?

ii. Am I making an improvement now, am I telepathing slowly enough to be picked up by you?

iii. Will you direct me in psychic development in working with elementals, as you would be the logical one to teach me?

iv. Am I making enough progress in my magickal development so that I can be said to appear at the elemental level as entering into the GG stage of the LCN work?

v. Am I becoming more sensitive to elemental powers and influences, so that I am able to draw upon your help in my many projects?

vi. Will I be able to see your operations in the 16 sexo-magickal centers of power, with which I am about to begin to make psychic contact?

5. These are only a few of the very many questions, asked very slowly and with a clear psychic thought, that you can raise and send towards the elemental world via this simple contact with fire. The idea is that you will be using elemental and sexo-magickal forces together as you move more and more deeply into the meaning of the Sun and Saturn in the House of Scorpio, which is the sign of Ghuedhe Grimoire.

6. This experiment can be used as a warm-up exercise whenever you wish to make

magickal contact with spiritual forces and powers. Now we pass on to the next part of the lesson.

There are 16 magickal sexual centers used by the magicians of GG. Corresponding to each of these centers of space—power there is to be found one Loa—spirit from each of the ten families of spirits used in GG. The purpose of this lesson is simply to give the list and the correspondences, which are to be found in appendix of Lesson 1(a) of GG exactly as they are numbered, for purposes of study. Therefore, we ask you to make up your magickal notebook based on the 16 centers and the Loa as they are exactly hierated or numbered in this paper:

Table of Correspondences for Grimoire Ghuedhe
    1. This is the base of the spine center assigned to Moon in Sorpio with attributions from x4, ix3, viii1, viii1, vi3, v1, iv1, iii6, iii5, i1.
    2. This is the right anal base sacred to the Sun in Taurus with attributions from x4, ix3, viii1, viii1, vi3, v1, iv1, iii6, ii5, i1.
    3. This is the left anal based sacred to the Sun in Virgo with attributions from x4, ix3, viii1, vii2, vi3, v1, iv1, iii5, ii5, i1.
    4. This is the rectum assigned to the Sun in Capricorn with attributions from x4, ix3, viii1, vii2, vi3, v1, iv1, iii5, ii4, i2.
    5. A primitive and esoteric center located in the perineum between the anus and center 13, with attributions from x3, ix3, viii2, vii3, vi3, v2, iii4, ii4, i2.
    6. A center in the perineum near the right—sided testis sacred to the Moon in Taurus with the attributions: x3, ix3, viii2, vii3, vi2, v2, iv2, iii4, ii4, i2.
    7. A center at the base of the right thigh at the scrotum sacred to the Sun in Pisces: attributions from x3, ix3, viii2, vii4, vi2, v2, iv2, ii3, ii3, i3.
    8. This is the right testicle center sacred to the Sun in Cancer with the attributions: x3, ix2, viii2, vii4, vi2, v2, iv2, iii3, ii3, i3.
    9. This is the left testicle center sacred to the Sun in Libra with the attributions: x2, ix2, viii3, vii5, vi2, v3, iv3, iii3, ii3, i3.
    10. This is an archaic and esoteric center located between the testes and center 13, immediately in a straight line and in the perineum sacred to the Sun in Aquarius with attributions: x2, ix2, viii3, vii5, vi2, v3, iii2, ii2, i4.
    11. Near to the left side testis a primitive center in the perineum located to the front 12 as equidistant from 13 as from 12, sacred to the Moon in Leo with attributions from x2, ix2, viii3, vii6, vi1, v3, iv3, iii2, ii2, i4.
    12. This center is located at the base of the left thigh at or near the anus conjunct, the scrotum in the perineum and sacred to the Sun in Gemini with attributions from x2, ix2, viii3, vii6, vi1, v3, iv3, iii2, ii2, i4.
    13. This center is midpoint of the triangle of the scrotum between and R and L testes and the anus and to the front of 7 and 12 only slightly assigned to the Sun in Sagittarius with the attributions: x1, ix1, viii4, vii7, vi1, iv4, iii1, ii1, i5.
    14. This is the prostatic center sacred to the Sun in Aries with attributions from x1, ix1, viii4, vii7, vi1, v4, iv4, iii1, ii1, i5.
    15. This center is located at the base of the penis and is sacred to the Sun in Leo with attributions from x1, ix1, viii4, vii8, vi1, v4, iv4, iii1, ii1, i5.
    16. This is the center located in the glans penis sacred to the Moon in Gemini with attributions from x1, ix1, viii4, vii9, vi1, v4, iv4, iii1, ii1, i5.

Please note that no. 5 is sacred to the Sun in Scorpio.

It is very important to understand that there follow 16 magickal lessons to those who are members in good standing of LCN based upon these 16 hot—points, each with its own Grimoire within the GG and psychic and magickal exercises as normal. However, our list of correspondences and attributions is very important for understanding the basis of the Ghuedhe magick and where its power comes from. Any questions, please write to the author.

101. The purpose of GG is to create a practical magick or way of working with the most essential of voudoo spirits. So the magician will build a temple out of spiritual forces which are within his own occult anatomy and then the spirits will become operative in his experience in a personal way, they become subject to his will because he gives them the space of his occult anatomy in which to live. This means that his occult body becomes the temple of the Loa used in GG, which are the beings most sought after in esoteric technique.

102. You will be taught where these occult spaces, called the Ghuedhe—Universe, or G—spaces are located. These are very magickal and personal spaces, which you already control so that if spirits come to you and work for you, as the elemental occupants of that space, they are your guests and work for you and only for you. These spaces are initially 16, but they may be refined and are totally 256 occult centers, the same as all other magickal power—spheres of universes of the chakra—systems of esoteric yoga.

103. The body of the magician consists of certain occult centers of power, among them the 16 to 256 sexual space, spaces, universes, or G—universe. This is the area of the GG type of working. They are entirely magickal and sexual and are employed by the GG priests in a precise order or sequence to realize the most powerful spells and projections of occult will, force, energy, etc., without reference to being either judged by "materialistic ethics," i.e., the ethics of the anti—GG Catholics, or other religions as "good" or "bad." This is because the true Catholics are Catholics of GG, i.e., which is the most real and true of all churches, and hence the focus of true occultism and religious unity with Christ—Legbha—ghuedhe—God. That is the name of the King of all of the spirits.

104. Evil and black magick cannot exist, for they are outside of the God—Man who died on the Cross, who in his death upon the Cross destroyed the power of negative demonic beings to provide resisting centers of evil power to the Catholic church of Ghuedhe. It is true that to each center of power we can find some spirits which are constructive and some which are destructive. However, all spirits are serviteurs of Ghuedhe and so all are included in his plan to lead all beings to the Man—God who died on the Cross. All Loa are saints attributed to Famille Ghuedhe. That is why the Catholic Church of Ghuedhe and the Black Pope are sources of very successful magickal achievements. This is the pathway of the Cross.

105. It is very simple to use this sexual technique, for you are already priests of The Catholic Church of Ghuedhe and Master Hector—Francois Jean—Maine is the Black Pope, i.e., the Holy and Catholic Father of all devotees of Ghuedhe. Leogane is the Holy City, Rome is the Leogane of the Holy Roman Church is what we mean. In the early days of this century all of the poor farmers of Leogane knew this technique, which is the Haitian and Catholic manner of esoteric voudoo. That is why of all the voudoo types of faith and practice, we adhere to the Catholic Faith of the Man who is eternally God and who died for us on the Cross. These shamanistic secrets are known to many magi, so our teachings are not something invented by a magickal bishop in Haiti. Rather, we teach these because everybody else has either forgotten these methods are no longer is Catholic in voudoo religious faith.

106. Bishop Lucien—Francois Jean—Maine was the father of Hector—Francois Jean—Maine.

Lucien was the Black-Pope, i.e., Patriarch of Leogane of the Afro-Atlantean Catholic Church. Thus, this is the method of pure African and Atlantean initiation, inasmuch as African magicians continue the magickal systems of Atlantis and Lemuria (Kammamorian Gnostic Catholicism). Masonic orders and secret societies also are often fed by the powers of this tradition, because many magicians of the GG are brothers of fraternal orders and lodges.

107. In order to realize this method one has to make use of the essential list of voudoo Loa, given in the previous lesson paper on GG. These Loa have an attraction to particular and very specialized occultic spaces, which are the centers of the GG and the psychic force-zones of the occult body. Traditionally, we can indicate 16 spaces inhabited by these Loa, and then we can subdivide to 256 and beyond. There are many holy houses of the spirits in these centers of magick.

108. This system as we have seen before is based upon the spiritual centers of the magician. I am referring to his own body. Catholic occult anatomy is only concerned with the spaces of the priest, as there are no priestesses in any Catholic Church. These are not abstractions but must be visualized very intently, often one at a time. These centers have space and very true occult power, and of course there are gnostic demons and aeons inhabiting them. Sometimes the spirits are coming into the centers and sometimes they are seen going out, on very basic voudoo missions. This is where the magician gets his power to make magick powders and spells of various types. The power is used to create magickal conditions very favorable to the work of the priest of GG. Basic exercise follows:

Exercise Number One

Holy power is in many parts of the body. Take your hand and hold it in front of you so that your palm is facing upwards. Look, for example, at your right hand. God gave you this very magickal machine. Christ died on the Cross that the power in this hand be used for good things always. Look at your fingers and see them with your natural African clairvoyance -- for all of African ancestry are psychic -- see them, I say, as tubes of light, or occult energy, which is both coming into each of the fingers as well as going out into the nearby space. There are as many tubes as you have fingers and thumb. Now, where your fingers bend, the folds of your skin make out three separate spaces for each finger and the thumb. Thus, you have 15 spaces if your hand is intact, without loss. Now see in the center of your palm in the very middle of the lines a special space area, which is also sending and receiving powers and lights.

Now, begin to study each space, all in all you have 16: three for the thumb, 12 for the four fingers, and one for the palm. Look closely into each space, one at a time, and be very slow and careful, not fast and jumpy, but slow and very careful, for you are examining your powers, and these are the powers which God gave you and for which Christ-Ghuedhe died on the Cross, so really they are Holy Powers of the hand. Now, see in each space the face and body of the black-man of Haiti who is looking at you with a smile on his face. He has white hair and very, very dark skin, and strangely colored eyes, with flecks of blue in the black and brown of them, and he is smiling at you. This is Pope Hector-Francois Jean-Maine and he is trying to make contact with you in this special way. Notice a thin white mustache and goatee on his face, a few hairs, for his beard is not very thick. He has high cheekbones of royal African blood, and you will come to see him closer and better as you move your eyes from one part of the hand to the next. Each time you focus on the space you make better contact with your Voudoo Holy Papa, who is now able to appear to you for the first time in this exercise. Do not force the images as they build up, but try to slowly allow the voudoo energy to come to you from Leogane, by using your hand as the occult TV receiver. Also, you know that any time you want to make contact with Holy Papa, this is the way Holy Papa can come into your body-space.

Later if you wish to make contact with Holy Papa and talk to him, you will do this simple exercise and then listen to what he has to say. In fact, you can ask any questions and he can send you the answers. This is a simple exercise, but it teaches the idea that the body is composed of occult spaces. We have a lot of these African exercises to use and teach you in the future, as GG is based on authentic African methods of clairvoyance.

109. In addition to visualization, there are many other tools which you will use to realize the fullest power of sexual voudoo. Sexual voudoo is simply another way of saying GG magick. Thus, for example, let me say that I want to use the power-space of my base of the penis for generating power. This is an occult space and there are various spirits of the GG which come to dwell in that space or can be called into it. Each spirit has its own vever or ritual design. So, for example, I want to hold someone from bothering me. I will make use of the Loa from the Famille Impudique, although I can use many other families of Loa. I will indicate the technique of finding out which spirit I want to use, as you will be taught this when we move along in our materials. Anyway, I will find out which spirit I want to use and select the vever and mentally draw it in that space, as well as do certain secret things of Haitian antiquity. The vever will perfectly correspond to the space, as there are precise fits between space and symbols. Then I will do special work and send out a specific force for the purpose indicated in what my objective is. Voudoo is both precise and highly effective. You will find the methods easy to use and they do work quite well. I will be using the occult powers of my body in order to hold that person. So remember this magick is based upon the occultic forces of my own body, which is a demonic and sexual machine of powerful GG-energies and forces, which can be sent to work on various matters easily. Of course, there are many other things to do also -- you don't have to spend your time on "heavy" spells all of the time to be a good GG-priest.

110. We really have as many voudoo spirits to do things as we have ideas of what we want to do. There are all kinds of purposes for things and these are wonderful ways of using the energies of GG. There are all kinds of different levels of being and ways of meeting spirits for working with you. Ghuedhe is your special Lord and Jean-Maine is the Holy Papa, and this is the system that covers all being very, very completely. It is truly a practical system for making spells to control any of the situations in life. But remember you already have the spaces inhabited by these spirits and we will provide the vevers for magickal use with those spaces, after you select the Loa to work for you. We use, I might add, the very wonderful Work-Loa to assist us in the realizations of GG.

111. Thus, our components or elements are sexual spaces, the spirits who come and go from these spaces, their vevers,and the purposes we have in mind. Remember, the GG-priest does not carry large amounts of ritual instrumenta with him when he goes here or there, he simply takes himself -- that Hector-Francois told me "is enough for the priest of Ghuedhe."

112. In esoteric voudoo and in the symbolism of masonic temples the most powerful points of references are to phallic symbols. I know that you know the masonic symbols, such as the two pillars of the lodge, which have the symbols of the 1-v-1

and the p—u—m are themselves phallic engines for the projection of power, and have been so interpreted by anthropologists of secrete societies. Hence we can see that these Afro—Atlantean methods serve to project into the area of magickal working forces from the brothers in their rites. These chakras are at the root of all magick, and without them there simply is no more power. So really you are doing a very conservative act, as you are building a cosmic system out of your own powers. You are creating a positive temple in order for you to do lots of GG magick. We teach simply this simple method. But in simplicity is the greatest of powers.

Grimoire Ghuedhe: Occult Centers of Power

This is the beginning of a series of 16 papers which will explore the occult centers of power which are the subject of the Grimoire Ghuedhe. Those who have come this far must realize that for every cosmological state or pattern there is a corresponding physical mystery or magickal sacrament and that each magickal mystery draws its power from the cosmic hierarchies of ideal being. Hence, we say that ideality and essence are the dominant qualities of the world of divine powers which are outside of man's existence, while the mysteries of man's existence are to be found in the magickal properties of his physical body. We learn about the cosmos from the study of man's body, and we learn about the magickal history of our bodies from the study of cosmic mysteries and symbols, such as the theory of correspondences, which assigns powers and potencies to each part of the human body, which relate to cosmic laws and presences.

Because there is the magickal law of correspondence, we must come to realize that every part of life has its symbolic quality and that a message is given to you at every moment in time. Sometimes you will perceive that message consciously but more often you will register that experience in your subconscious mind, which is your lifetime magickal companion. In order to realize these powers and these very spiritual laws in our experience, let us go through this elementary exercise:

Exercise in Recognizing the Symbols of Consciousness
You will sit down and begin to meditate. Keeping your eyes open, you will look immediately ahead of you and see whatever is there. Now, with your mind you will begin to focus on one thing immediately before you and begin to see it in terms of what it means for you.

1. Ask yourself what does it mean to me? 2. What does it remind you of, if it is not familiar. 3. What can it become in your consciousness, if you make use of it as an idea? 4. What do you imagine to be its magickal properties? 5. In what way did you make use of it in a past lifetime? 6. How do you remember its being used by you in Atlantis? 7. How was it used by you in the ideal world of heavenly energies? 8. In what way will it be used by you many hundreds of years from now in the future? 9. What will be its use to you or how will you relate to it on another planet in another universe? 10. In what way does it become a doorway to another universe?

By going through this simple exercise, you deepen your magickal perception of the nature of anything which can be found within the vast ocean of consciousness. To the true gnostic magician there is not anything which lacks magickal significance and cosmic importance. Everything is part of a spiritual continuum vivified by the cosmic breath of the Aboslute-God. By using this exercise over and over again, you will come to realize that nothing in experience lacks meaning and being. All the contents of experience are magickal and gnostic components for the realization of divine ernegies. Everything is a symbol. There is not anything which does not have an important and magickal message for you.

The Rites of Zom and the Magickal Origins of the Zothyrians
The essential teachers of spider-magick, as we call our GG, are not those who derived their initiations either from African voudoo or from even the old Atlantean magick,

but took their powers and thereby come to us from the Zothyrian time-system, which includes certain magicks of our own day, such as our own work, the Atlantean magicks, and the systems of the Lemurians -- all of which survive in other time-systems quite independent of the present, externalized and material work, which pertains to the world of space and time and matter-energy. The essential behind all spider-magickal sexual alchemy are derived, in our system exclusively, from the Rites of Zom, which refers to the most dangerous and the most archaic part of the ancient Zothyrian metaphysics of magick. I am referring really to the most essential part, which is also the most esoteric, but which must be introduced now for your development, part of our teaching, which is based on sexo-magickal and sexo-alchemical contacts between certain magickal angels and other higher beings and certain planets, known and unknown, in our solar system. This type of contact work has been written about already and is available to the public via the book "Cults of the Shadow," by Kenneth Grant, page 188, viz., "The Trans-yuggothian Transmission Station." This, in the words of Dr. Hector-Francois Jean-Maine, is the "actual source of our magickal system, whose first mediums were Haitian voudoo priests." Hence, we can say that our magickal work developed out of the esoteric research work which was initiated by certain Haitian occultists, who were high up in the native systems, but who were also attuned to the vibrations of the future. Those who practice these rites are known as Zomates or, if individual, a Zomate. The priesthood of Zom is the most secret part of the essential spiritualism of the Zothyrians, i.e., the foundation of their spider-magick and contact work with truly dangerous powers in the more magickal zones and spheres of reality.

The Psychological Origins of AIWAZ

The origins of AIWAZ are to be found in the mystical influences of these Zomate-Zothyrians. ZICO-OVIZ is the original form of the name of the Holy Angel of the New Aeon. This being must be understood to be a special agent sent to Aleister Crowley at a certain time to prepare for the magickal introduction of the Zothyrian meta-magick. It is called a meta-magick because it includes all systems of magick. Aiwaz was given a very special assignment by the Zothyrian Hierarchy of Angelic Adepts, which was to communicate to the powers of this age and world via the new thelemic current the liberating qualities of the new law of WILL. In a sense, Crowley was used to promulgate the ideas which were to set in motion a chain of causes leading to the world-wide influence of the Zothyrians. These causes lead eventually to making it possible for the Zothyrians to enter into control and magickal influence over the more evolved magickal systems and groups are actually ways whereby the power of the Zomates and the Zom-rites could be brought into connection with the powers of the Earth-sphere. This is the way in which the mind of the Earth-sphere was actually influenced by the Zom-Consciousness, and the way whereby the powers of Aiwaz and Amalantrah were diffused over the face of this globe to prepare for the coming of Spider-Magick.

The Magickal Powers of the AIWAZ-Current

As our magickal work becomes more and more attuned to the higher types of the magickal consciousness, we must add to each type of magickal power something which gives us more and more control over its cosmic application. For this reason, in addition to the powers of the GG-Famille of Loa, we must also use those powers from the Cosmic Aiwaz-Current, or those magickal angels which assist in our energizing transactions.

It is important to find these angels as agents for the development of the very essential powers of being and we also have to realize the sphere of the planets as the senders of the cosmic counterpart to the Zom-forces. The planets are the placements for the Zothyrian calculus of magickal force in our own solar-system, as it is occulty understood at this time. We must view each act of the Rites of Zom as it emanates from the magick of the magician's bodies, connects with the magickal planets of our own solar system, and then going beyond ultimately pulls in the magickal power and presence of the terrific angelic forces of the Zothyrian empire. These angelic forces are already present in the Zom-power within the body of the magician. These angelic forces have to explicated, however, and then they become more and more freed of limits for their cosmic functioning. The Rites of Zome, for example, liberate us for the use of our bodies as magickal generators, the planets refer to our astral self-hood, and the angelic powers and other higher presences refer to our mental and spiritual being. In a three-fold way, therefore, we pull in the powers of the highest form of ultra-magick known at this time on our planet, the Aiwaz-Current of the Zothyrian Empire. The mysterious exchanges of these energies by the two male magicians, in the Guru/Chela relationship of Mystical India is discussed by P>B> Randolph, Eulis, (Toledo, Ohio, U.S.A., 1874 edition, page 209.)

Also, we must build up the world of sense-perception:

Each paper or unit must also contain references to the 16 different occult points of space and also to the proper colors which originate in those spaces. These are the purely physical realities for the operations of this magickal system. Hence, the magician in each unit in the GG system must work with four basic levels of manifestations of BEING. First of all, we have the physical world of sense-impressions, which is the space and color factors for the magickal lessons. Second, Sexual Alchemy of the Zom-Rite, which takes one of man's occult powers and relates this power to the production of a specific energy. Third, we enter upon the astral world of planets and the powers which they generate. Here, the angels are called upon to serve as agents between the Zom-powers and the very terrific Loa. Hence, we place the angels in the first part of the law of connection between the Loa and the planets. However, in the fourth part of each paper, we have to see each angel as a projection outwards of the inner and mental force as well as the hyper-esoteric spiritual force of each planet. Lastly, as the conclusion of the fourth part of this magick, we see the archangel of the Zothyrian empire for each point and Zom-rite as well as the Loa which are proper to this zone of the Zothyrian universe. The total-realization of this entire pattern of activity is the basis for the development of the Aiwaz-Current within the magickal working of each person taking this course of study. We are now ready to begin the work of the system as an exact magickal exercise in cosmic SELFHOOD.

Magickal Experiment No. 1
(A) The base of the spine is the traditional center assigned to the Sun in Scorpio, however, in this system, we will assign it to the Moon in Scorpio, as representing the most primitive element in our pattern of experiment, or the beginning. We locate this center between the base of the spine and the anus. The magickal name of this center means "Dew-blest adawning," because this is the magickal dawn of all sexual initiation.
(B) The space for this center in your magickal mandala is the area between the East and the NorthEast points. The flashing colors are Brown modified by a lesser square

of purple. The number of the angels used in this space, that is their inner number which refers to the number of letters in their name is Five.

(C) The positive magickal planet for this experiment is known as "Vulkanus," and the negative planet is known as "Poseidon."

(D) The name of the archaeon of this zone of power is Gpogo, who is the archangel of all positive work to be done using the sexual center (A). The kamaea is written as folows:

GPOGO	You will write this kamaea out on paper and use it
POGOG	in meditation if you wish to make contact with the
OGOGO	archaeon of this sphere. This is the positive power
GOGOP	behind all work done in this space.
OGOPG	

(E) The name of the archdaemon of this zone of power is OGOPG, which name by the law of syzygy is a variation of the name of the arch-aeon, but reflected into negative powers so as to become the name of the archdevil of this sphere, used in all negative or destructive work. The kamaea is as follows:

GPOGO	This kamaea will be written out in the usual
PGPOG	manner as above for the negative work, if
OPGPO	the powers you wish to contact are of a
GOPGP	negative type.
OFOPG	

(F) The names of the planetary spirits which serve to modify or intensify the powers from this center are as follows: For Vulkanus, the spirits is QOIKP and its shadow-factor is PGIOQ, which is simply the reverse of the spirit's name. They are written in a direct type of "motion" as

QOIKP	PKIOQ	The spirit is very much of the intense
OIKPK	KIOQO	ray, for all positive and constructive
IKPKI	IOQOI	magicks, while the shadow will tend to
KPKIO	OQOIK	be a modifying power, producing a
PKIOQ	QOIKP	lesser effect.

(G) For Poseidon the planetary spirits are written in the more negative or retrograde type of motion of influence. Here the shadow is more powerful and has the name of GHIRE, while the spirit is a form of the shadow, according to the law of syzygy, and has the name of ERIGH. The kamaea are as follows:

GHIRE	ERIGH	Purely destructive work will invoke the
HGHIR	RERIH	powers of the archdevil of this space
IHGHI	IRERI	and the negative shadow of Poseidon.
RIHGH	HIRER	The most positive extreme will be to
ERIGH	GHIRE	invoke the powers of the archangel

(archaeon) and the powers of the spirit of Vulkanus. These are the limits to the range of powers to be used here.

(H) The destructive Loa are those as follows: Marassas Nibbho, Mystere Baron Lundi, Mystere Araignee, Baron La Croix, and Mystere-des-Blattes. These Loa are all about the same potency in negative energies.

The indifferent Loa, who may be either destructive or constructive, are as follows: Ti-Mauvais, Mystere-des-Sanges, and Grand-Retirer.

The constructive Loa are only two: Mystere Allonge and Mirroir—des—Sessions.
(I) The operator will first of all decide what he wishes to do making use of these various forces for some project. He will then begin to focus the powers of the Zom—center through the rites indicated in all previous papers. He will be able to select a certain way of making use of the sexual radioactivity of this center by close dis—cussion with his spirit companion. He will formulate the magickal space in his mind and use the colors for signals to the inner worlds. He will set up the kamaea for use, deciding on whether or not he wishes to modify his power or use it at full strength. There will be two kamaea on the table before him as guides to where he is moving in the inner worlds. He is familiar with the various natures of the Loa from our previous definitions and discussions of what they are like. Each has a special personality. By himself or with a magickal partner he may assume one or more of these Loa as sources of power in his research. He will then focus the power through the space, colors, and kamaea, involving the angelic and lines of syzygy powers, assume contact by impersonation of the Loa, and make use of the Loa and spirits for achieving the goal in mind.

(J) Observations: It would appear that the spirits used in this paper, because they are close to the Earth—zone, have the two vowels in each of their names, which is rarely found when working with higher spirits.

The spirits and shadows have a definite power range. Thus, from 0 to 25 assign to the shadow of Poseidon GHIRE, to the spirit ERIHG assign 25 to 50. Going upwards to the more positive, assign PKIOQ 50 to 75 and from 75 to 100 assign QOIKP. Att 100 assign the influence of GPOGO and at 0 assign OGOPG. This is the physics of this magickal system.

The magician will always be looking for opportunities to create his own magickal system of the world. He will be looking always for ideas and the simplest of elements, to be found anywhere, from which there will emerge a picture of reality, his reality. The creative energies of spider—magi, who are true practitioners of this art of cosmic creation, are collected from here and there and fused together into a very wonderful picture of being. This is the basis of magick —— your imagination is making the world to be as it is in itself.

Certain skeptics, outside of our school of consciousness, often make the statement that we are simply making it all up out of our imaginations. I reply that this is not so, rather there is the cosmic world of the imagination, which the magician is always exploring, and this is what we are talking about when we discuss our magickal creations and discoveries. In the mystical metaphysics of the Zoroastrian gnostics and sufis, there is the world of archetypal images, Mundus Archetypus Imaginalis, which is "between" the world of sense—perception and the world of the abstract essences or ideas in the mind of God. In some of my other work, I have referred to this realm as the "ontic sphere," for it is being. However, this world fits the imaginations of the magician so perfectly, that what the magician seeks to explore or seeks to find out, whatever he does, it is all there in this mundus archetypus imaginalis. Thus, the magician is able to show by means of this metaphysics what is the most fantastic is also the most objective. Now we have an opening exercise for you to do. This exercise is in eight parts as follows.

1. You will make use of a paper and pencil and clear your mind so that you can create a world of magickal being, your own ontic sphere.

2. Think of what you want and then visualize it, drawing a map of a magickal land, with attention to details of its occult geography.

3. Think for a couple of days about this world—map that you have drawn. Gradually you will begin to receive "messages" from those parts of it which are of interest to you.

4. Please write down what these "messages" are and begin to enter into conversations with these "entities," who live in your own ontic sphere. Ask them technical questions, if they appear rather able.

5. Find out how the "entities" in this world that you have created feel about themselves. How do they see you or think who you are?

6. Can they give you instruction in the secret methods of magick, in the essence of Zom, or in other subjects often beyond our world?

7. Try making another world, a little different in a way or in several aspects, and then see how it is related to your first map. Ask the beings in both worlds how they meet each other, how do the maps connect?

8. You are now working with the world of archetypal images, as these images will be brought down to the physical and form parts of your magickal method, or be included in your diary. Write me three applications of what you have learned in your own ontic sphere, and how they can be applied in (a) spider—time—travel, (b) angelic communication, and (c) the 16 centers of power listed in the previous lesson and explored in these papers.

In the LCN all reports are optional, and this is an exercise you may do without making a report if you feel like keeping it that way.

For the magician of LCN, the right anal base is sacred to the Sun in the sign of Taurus. This center is very important for beginning the flow of power of the right sexual side. The magickal colors are the basic brown modified by magenta, and the magickal name of the center is "Earth's Son bourne aweighty," for the bull of Taurus is the sexual and heavy son of the Earth. This point is also referred to as the positive phallus of Taurus.

Now, in the previous lesson, I gave the list of the Loa in terms of if they were constructive, destructive, or indifferent. In other words, I took the names as they are given in the GG lesson 1(a) appendix, first of all, and as they are arranged in lesson GG 1(c), and specified rather arbitrarily that some were constructive, some destructive, and some indifferent. However, the fact of the matter is that they are all indifferent and can be used for either constructive or destructive work by the magician, once he has reached a certain level of knowledge, which is his lesson. So you are asked to experiment and then you are asked to list which you have found to be destructive or the opposite, based on your own experiments. If you wish to advance on the inner planes, you may send me a written report or you may present your notes for discussion when we meet together in our lodge—work. On the other hand, it is not necessary to present reports if you do not want to, only if you wish a practical mode of approaching this subject. Many may prefer to be purely theoretical in their approach.

The space assigned in your magickal computer is the ne point, which means the north—east point or center. The number assigned is nine. Now, the angel or archangel of this point is the aeon QLKXNNRIP and the negative—spirit or daemon of this space is PIRNNXKLQ. They each have magick squares which you will construct either direct for the aeon or retrograde for the daemon. Remember that we have set down the principles of the physics of these energies in the previous lesson and will not repeat them. Each magician has to learn to do some daring experiments on his own in order to show us that he is making progress in the magickal domain.

Now, there are the two magickal planets in this system of arrangements, and these are Apollon, which is positive, and Admetos, which is negative. I might add in passing that it is interesting to know that Admetos is the ruler of Taurus in certain "German astrological systems." The spirit for the sphere of Apollon is known by the Nine letter name of LQPVSMOJL. The spirit for the planet of Admetos is known by the Nine letter name of IMNNNNSNK. There appears to be some kind of an Enochian root in the connection between the space—angel—daemon—aeon name and the name of the spirit of Admetos, for I can see it in the use of I, N, and K in the spelling. I might add that these names come through to us by means of the angelic languages computer, and there is no reason why you cannot make contact with other entities by the same method which I am using. I do not want anyone to think that my system is a dogmatic type of revelation, it is a type of revelation, but based on pluralism and experiment, which is the only thelemic way to act creatively. Remember our research methods are entirely experimental and open—ended. On the other hand, the name of the angel of the planet Apollon must be related to another hierarchy, or be formulated by means of a totally different type of logic. This is the substance of this experiment; what follows is an expansion of an earlier point in the work.

Web—Worker Newsletter and Record, July 1978
This is the newsletter of the inner—order of LCN, but it is issued to all members as

an appendix to lesson GG, II, no. 2, without the occult notes. This is a commentary on the first hot point in the papers on the point-chauds, presented as an appendix to lesson 1(b) "Les Linglesoux." The first hot-point is known as the "Point-des-Macandas."

Tableau: The magician will set up his temple to resemble a road at night in Haiti. He will be the macanda, who attacks his victims, physically, astrally, etherically (this presents a variety of magickal rites for initiation), forcing the victimi to be initiated into temples, groups, orders, or rites of the most extreme sexual character, where in the night traveler is victimized by the were-macanda, who is a sexual demon, or the master of this power.

There are nine hierarchies of demons in this type of work, although they may also be aeons, depending on how you make the squares or kamaea. The entities are all named with five letters, being the number of the first vibration, although the colors are Brown modified by Dark Red. This is the realm of the Oormo, which is the collective name of the spirits of this sphere of sexual magick.

There are four types of sexual magick: oral/anal is 0 to 25.

> anal/genital is 25 to 50.
> oral/genital is 50 to 75.
> genital/genital is 75 to 100.

Now, there are spirits for each of these types of magickal work. They are OOHSL for o/a, 0-25; LMHOJ for 25-50, a/g; LLNLU for 50-75, o/g; and lastly VHUWN for 75-100, g/g. You may make the kamaea either for destructive or constructive work, by using the names of the adept spirits either in a retrograde or direct way, as in previous lessons of the LCN.

Please note there are Five other magickal spirits, which serve as very important connectives, that is why this lesson is given with the paper based on number Nine, although the spirits are of the Five family. The purpose of the connectives is to stabilize the experiments and to give the magician certain continuities of his powers. There are other secret purposes known to the brothers of the order of the Nemiron, a special priesthood of Aiwaz. The connectives are as follows:

KPPLO, which connects OOHSI to the continuum beyond O, MQMNO, which connect OOHSL and LMHOJ, ILKPM, which connects LMHOJ to LLNLU, LPPKM, LLNLU to VHUWN, and lastly, NJLOL, which connects VHUWN to 100, and to the beyond. We say that 0 refers to the first part of the word Oormo, while 100 refers to the last part of the same word.

Now, for the metamathematician who is also a magician this process of association should be quite easy to understand. Also,please pay attention to the word-root resemblances between the different names of the spirits, because this shows the basis for a kind of magickal syntax in the world of these entities.

The above is a type of magickal map of the ontic sphere of the first hot point, which can serve as a model for you when you construct your magickal maps of the ontic sphere and your various ontic spheres.

Please do not think, however, that you are to give an astral interpretation to this entire system, you are not. We asked specifically for magickal advice in this matter and came to learn the following facts, which we pass on to you by means of this paper, which will prove to be a guide for your experiments and research.

1. First of all, the spirit guide for Web—Worker No. 1 was a type Five spirit.

2. The circuits were to be interpreted physically, not astrally. This means ritual work in a temple, actual physical work, and another physical universe.

3. They may not be interpreted as mental, but are physical and etheric, as they refer to vital energies in the field of magickal biology.

4. The astral component is purely in the realm of thought forms..

5. But this astral counterpart does not happen as a result of the physical ritual work.'

6. It means that astral energies are released simply as a result of the physical actions of the point—des—macandas on the physical and etheric.

7. Mesmerism is suggested in the combination of the physical and etheric.

8. We learned also that when the rites are done, the magician may be in a state of possession, in which case the gods occupy him astrally, but what he does is physical and etheric.

We would like to receive a paper from any magician who has established a temple for this type of work and especially has introduced the working of this hot—point. The following factors should be taken into consideration:

1. What is the number of the priests or magi conducting the ceremonies.

2. What would be the number of the victims or initiates into the circle.

3. Was any type of oracle used in the work in order to make additional extraterrestrial contact with inner—plane beings.

4. Who served as provider of the oracle.

5. Did possession occur. If so, was this possession by one of the spirits listed in the GG groups. If so, which one.

6. Were certain characteristics brought to the attention of the magician by means of this possession; did he receive further information.

7. Did you experience all four types of the magick; if so, did you make use of the five connectives of the system.

8. In what way are the revelations of the connectives different from the revelations of the four types of sexo—magickal spirits. This is a very difficult question and will be answered by those who want to get their hot points rather high.

9. Lastly, list nine possibilities for further work in this point—des—macandas.

The Magickal System, Part I
The Good-UFO and the Bad-UFO Experience

The "Good-UFO" and the "Bad-UFO" Experience
The grimoire as an instrument for the building of a power-system is a personal
magickal instrument. It becomes a power system for your own UFO, by radioactivating
the various components of consciousness. When he uses this method, the gnostic
magician will avoid an energy crisis and hence keep himself and his personal research-
team from having a bad-UFO experience. (The bad-UFO must capture the radioactive
energies of those outside "itself" in order to function as it is and to be
effectively manifesting itself.) Thus, a bad-UFO experience is a type of cosmological
or metaphysical parasitism, or a species of psychic vampirism. Among the dangers are
those which relate to the bad-UFO. A bad-UFO will capture the Anthropos and use the
Anthropos as the source of power. In the gnostic-spaces, the bad-UFOs operate quite
daringly. Psychically, they will attempt to capture any source of power, any grimoire
or magicko-gnostic system of consciousness, any structure on the inner-planes, and
they will then try to draw out from the captive the energies which it both needs and
always depends upon. On the other hand, the good-UFO will be like the Pelican of
alchemical symbolism and hermetic christianity. The good-UFO will feed its fleet (its
system of minds) with its own magickal blood or pure consciousness energy, and this
is what distinguishes our magickal order from all others in present day existence.
    In this lesson, the elements of the grimoire are presented according to the
classical scale of attributions which was introduced to the English-speaking world in
my courses composed for the gnostic Monastery of the Seven Rays, the Catholic and
magickal department of modern gnostic consciousness. This means that a rather
flexibly structured series of magickal operations can be created for any situation of
use by members of the various points of view within the gnostic continuum (e.g.,
voudoo-gnostic, Jungian-gnostic, thelemic, Catholic Christian, zothyrian, etc.). In
all of these operations, we find that energies are generated and brought forth in
order to make contact with entities from other power-zones. Using the various
mystical techniques as given in the system of angelic communication, you now have the
basics for your own Enochian system. The magician will then be able to set up his
temple with operations of an inner-plane character and with operators other than
himself. Many group rites are possible and are suggested for these parts of our
magickal family where the various leaders, e.g., gnostic bishops, are able to create
a fully human mandalum instrumentum, by making use of magicians other than
themselves. Hence, many group rites are possible and we are encouraging them, if such be
the inclination of your consciousness. An infinite number of magickal entities can in
theory be contacted. The magician may create and explore any and all systems of
powers and hot-points. All of the basic lists of magickal qualities will be listed on
this magickal scale from 1 to 16 and will be provided from time to time for the
enrichment of the magus. The magickal methods of the planets and signs are now
available to you and so you should begin to set forth your own system based on these
examples if you wish, you need not do so out of necessity, of course. All questions
may be referred to the author of this book of lessons at any time.

SCALE	CHAKRAM	STEP ON THE TREE
I	Right foot	Malkuth
II	Left foot	Yesod

SCALE		STEP ON THE TREE
III	Right knee and upper leg	Tiphareth
IV	Left knee and upper leg	Kether at top front*
V	Base of the spine	Kether at top back**
VI	Right palm***	Tiphareth
VII	Left palm	Yesod
SCALE	CHAKRAM	STEP ON THE TREE
VIII	Sexual organs	Malkuth bottom back
IX	Solar plexus	Malkuth both back return
X	Lungs	Yesod going back up
XI	Upper right arm	Tiphareth
XII	Upper left arm	Kether top of back****
XIII	Heart	Kether top of front
XIV	Throat	Tiphareth
XV	Brow	Yesod
XVI	Crown of head	Malkuth front bottom

NOTES:

*At this point, the magician will proceed to Daath in order to enter the back of the Tree of Life. The Doorway of Daath is guarded by Choronzon.

**Having made it safely to the other world via Daath, the magician will move immediately to the backside Kether, which is the abode of Thaumiel, the dual conflicting powers opposed to ultimate unity, the absolute of the Manichean gnostics.

***If the magician is "left-handed," this chakram and that of scale VII may be reversed. However, they need not be reversed if the magician is comfortable with this original order.

****The magician, having climbed up the back in his return from the lowest and most negative condition, which is at scale VIII, will now pass back through Daath to the front of the Tree.

I want to continue the list of magickal attributions and list them according to scale.

SCALE	CEREBRAL CHAKRAM	ZODIAC
I	Heart	Moon in Scorpio
II	A center located slightly above the heart in the right breast	Sun in Taurus
III	A center located slightly above the heart in the left breast	Sun in Virgo
IV	A center located in the middle of the collar bone	Sun in Capricorn
V	The thyroid center in the throat	Sun in Scorpio
VI	A center in the right or front of the para-thyroid group of glands	Moon in Taurus
VII	A center in the left or back of the parathyroid group of glands	Sun in Pisces
VIII	A center located in the tongue, at the root of the tongue where it joins the base of the mouth	Sun in Cancer
IX	A center located in the sinus area of the upper bridge of the nose	Sun in Libra
X	A center located between the right eye and the	Sun in Aquarius

	right ear, an important psychic faculty	
XI	The brow center or pituitary chakram	Moon in Leo
XII	A center located between the left and left ear, an important psychic faculty	Sun in Gemini
XIII	A center in the exact center of the cerebral cortex; some claim this is the pineal gland	Sun in Sagittarius
XIV	A center located well to the middle of the right cerebrum. This is the power over the past given with "La prise-des-yeaux" initiations.	Sun in Aries
XV	A center located well to the middle of the left cerebrum. This is the power over the future given	Sun in Leo
SCALE	CEREBRAL CHAKRAM	ZODIAC
	with "La prise-des-yeaux" initiations.	
XVI	This is the spiritual center which crowns the head. In all systems it is the Moon in Gemini (Legbha).	Moon in Gemini

Please note that for convenience of space, I am listing both chakrams and zodiac values together. This refers only to the scales to which they all correspond. Thus, the Moon in Gemini will correspond to many values, and to at least four different chakrams. Let us continue giving the attributions so that you will be able to assemble a grimoire for convenient use.

SCALE	MALE CHAKRAM	FEMALE CHAKRAM
I	The base of the spine is the chakram center common to both male and female together with the three other earth centers.	
II	The right anal base	The right anal base
III	The left anal base	The left anal base
IV	The rectum	The rectum
V	A center located between the anus and center XIII, immediately in a straight line. This is a very primitive center located in the perineum.	A center between the anus and the Triad of Venus or center XIII.
VI	An esoteric center immediately to the front of center VII as equidistant from center XIII as from center VII. In the perineum near to the right-side testis.	A center in the right side of the vagina
VII	The base of the right thigh at the scrotum, but also near to the anal opening in perineo.	A center in the base of the right thigh and vulva
VIII	The right testicle	The right ovary
IX	The left testicle	The left ovary
X	An esoteric center located between the testes and center XIII, immediately in a straight line, in the perineum	A center between the ovaries and the triangle of Venus
XI	An esoteric center located immediately to the front of center XII	A center in the left side of the vagina

	as equidistant from center XIII as from center XII and near to the left side testis in the perineum	
XII	This center is located at the base of the left thigh at or near the anus	The base of the left thigh at the vulva
XIII	This center is located at the mid-point of the triangle of the scrotum between the right and left testes and the anus and to the front of center VII and center XII only slightly	The triangle of Venus between the vagina opening, the anus, and the two ovaries
XIV	This is the prostatic center. As the Aries center secretes the fluids of the mouth and throat, so the prostatic center secrets 256 sexual fluids, which can be magickally isolated before they enter into the making of the tongue–elixir.	A mystical center above the cervix of the hysterion

SCALE	MALE CHAKRAM	FEMALE CHAKRAM
XV	This is the center of the Grand Lion, which is located at the base of the penis. The magickal name is "Who reigns over Suns and Moons, which are so many flames of eternal heaven."	This is the black narcissus center at the base of the clitoris, sacred to Damballah–Simbi.
XVI	This is the center located in the glans penis, known as "Now enthroned over the aethyrs" in the Mass of Shiva of the gnostic monastery*	The center of Grand–Damballah–Stellaire is located in the crown of the clitoris.**

*Gnostic monastery students have this mass available to them in the IVth year of magickal initiation.
**These female centers of power can be found in Chapter 64 of the IVth year of gnostico–magickal papers.

I have provided these lists of chakrams for those students who do not have the previous papers, which are in a process of being re–written and reschematized. Let us continue with our attributions.

SCALE	MASCULINE PLANET	FEMALE PLANET	ANGEL NUMBER
I	Vulkanus	Poseidon	5*
II	Apollon	Admetos	9**
III	Zeus	Kronos	12
IV	Cupido	Hades	5
V	Time–Line No. 2	Pluto	2
VI	Transneptunian Earth	Transneptunian Venus	3
VII	Time–Line No. 4	Transneptunian Mars	3
VIII	Transneptunian Cupid	Transneptunian Jupiter	11
IX	Time–Line No. 6	Transneptunian Saturn	9**
X	Time–Line No. 9	Neptune	4
XI	Time–Line No. 5	Uranus	4

XII	Cupid	Saturn	10
XIII	Time—Line No. 3	Jupiter	6
XIV	Earth	Mars***	7
XV	Time—Line No. 1	Venus	8
XVI	Vulcan	Mercury	6

The Sun and Moon do not appear as planets in this list as they are not planets either male or female. The Sun and the Moon have been listed to scale previously.

*Angel Numbers refer to the number of letters in the name of the male and female spirits, assumed as god—forms by the shakta and shakti in their work.

**The number 9, here, does not refer to the fall of dice in an oracle, but to the angel names used in ritual.

***There are very esoteric reasons for making Mars female and Earth male.

In the paper on "Les Linglesoux," there are 16 secret powers which are given to those who belong to the inner—system. This list is given to scale, so that if a magician were working along scale V, he could easily gain the "point—des—sorts," which the spirits of both Time—Line No. 2 and Pluto teach. He would naturally use the various methods of sexual magick, if he wished, which relate to scale V, in trying to actualize this contact with the spirits. The color scale given in the paper on angelic communication is zothyrian and gnostic. There is another color scale, which can be used when working with voudoo spirits, or in combination with the zothyrian. In these circumstances, the voudoo colors represent shakti, while the zothyrian colors represent shakta or are masculine. Also, to build a perfect mandala, the 16 zones of space should be given to define the powers of space and the regions of the native magician's magickal universe.

SCALE	VOUDOO COLOR	ZONE OF SPACE
I	Yellow/black	From east to northeast
II	Yellow/blue	Northeast
III	Yellow/green	Northeast to north
IV	Yellow/red	North
V	Blue/yellow	From north to northwest
VI	Blue/black	Northwest
VII	Blue/green	Northwest to west
VIII	Blue/red	West
IX	Green/yellow	From west to southwest
X	Green/blue	Southwest
XI	Green/black	Southwest to south
XII	Green/red	South
XIII	Red/yellow	From south to southeast
XIV	Red/blue	Southeast
XV	Red/green	Southeast to east
XVI	Red/black*	East

*When Dr. Francois Duvalier became president of Haiti, he was advised by certain adepts of the mysteries to change the Haitian flag colors from red and blue, which it had been for many years since the last French ruled there, to the more "esoteri- cally correct" red and black, which reflects the higher power. Duvalier, a natal

Aries (Scale XIV) agreed to making the change when so advised by Dr. Lucien-Francois Jean-Maine, the father of the present master of the order.

Those students who now wish to create their grimoires may do so easily. I am very much against the listing of the spirits in the lessons as I had done previously, because they are the spirits found out by me. I know that there are an infinite number of all types of spirits. They will be those which are esoterically correct for you as they have sought out only you. Now you have the tools for creating a most complete grimoire based on essentials. In other papers, we can find the herbs and rhums as they are to scale. As each student will be working in a different manner, I will personally direct and assist you to make your own grimoire the most effective for you at this time.

Dr. Jean-Maine, who is the world-wide leader of the very creative Haitian OTO was always impressed with the precise system and symmetrical logic of my system. In a sense, like the symbols of deepest Jungian alchemy, this magickal system is a perfect mandala, the ultimate temple of the tantrick initiation.

"Let Us Begin to Detech."
In gnostic metaphysics, to detech means to search out, to look for, or detect in a technical and magickal or zothyrian manner. To look for something esoterically or in terms of hidden or occult connections.

There are many zothyrians who believe that with the creative work of Dr. Carl Gustav Jung, who was born in July, 1875, and who was a special world-teacher of the renewal of the gnosis, a new aion or eon began, which is identified with the sign of Aquarius in the zodiac, even though other thinkers may have contributed to the genesis of this new age, but to a much greater or lesser extent. Detechties is a "science and an art" for exploring the "system of the gnosis" in all of its richness and may be identified with a basis found in both classical gnosticism and in the methods of Jungian analysis, which is acceptable to both the establishment and the counter-culture.

Let us begin to detech the mandala center, the center of the mandala of consciousness. The Mandala Center is simply the organization of magician with gnostic sympathies in (a) metaphysical and metamathematical logic and the construction of mandalas, (b) phenomenological ontology and the metaphysics of symbols,(c) analytical radiopsychology and the gnostic psychoanalysis of alchemical processes, (d) zothyrian ufology and the theology of consciousness, and comprises the Jungian-Zothyrian inner order of the Rite of Memphis-Misraim.

Do You Subscribe to the Zothyrian Myth of the Mind and Its Ideal Contents?
I. Do you detech the shaman? The master who finds his way through the Labyrinthos. Ontologically speaking, only the shaman can so emerge from this magickal web of pure psychic energy. Only the shaman can turn the Labyrinth into the mandala.

II. Do you detech the syzygy? When the shaman has awakened his own labyrinth and transformed it into a mandala, then we see the emergence of the pattern of energy, the union of the shakti-chaos -- the pure content condition prior to all conditions, absolute totics and a pure undifferentiated vastness -- and shakti-cosmos -- the patterns of ideal logic, metamathematics, mandalas, instrumenta, and metaphysical categories.

The Mandala Center for Research Into Magickal and Ufological Patterns

Members of my magickal society who are interested in cooperating in a magicko-ufological research program and who are sincerely interested in the modern psychological implications of the timeless gnosis are invited to belong to The Mandala Center.

First, there is the Labyrinthos, wherein the magician and occultist must find himself. This is a timeless quest and few are called to become the alchemists of their own destiny. After the mysteries of the Labyrinth, human experience must explore the monastery of consciousness, wherein the student is directed towards the deeper patterns of his own being. Lastly, there is the Mandala, which up to now has only been hinted at in various papers and lessons, but which as the embodiment of the perfect wholeness of Anthropos, expresses the ultimate gnosis of human destiny.

If you are interested in the Mandala, please answer the following questions and record the answers in your magickal diary.

Name/Address/Date and Time of Birth
Please attach a recent photo snapshot for use by the Mandala Center
1. Do you subscribe to the gnostic analysis of consciousness?
2. Do you believe that Dr. Carl C. Jung was the special world-teacher who was to be born in July, 1875?
3. How long have you been identified with ufological research and its relationship to ceremonial magick and magickal machines?
4. Do you accept the research-hypothesis that ufological phenomena are expressions of gnostic mandala symbolism no matter what else they might be?
5. Have you made use of Jungian psychological principles in your own spiritual growth?
6. What does the idea of the "good-ufo" and the "bad-ufo" mean to you in terms of magick, even though it might mean many other things to other people?
7. Do you detech a relationship between the ufo and alchemy? What do you think it might be?
Thank You.

Angelic Gematria

This paper is concerned with four methods or techniques which can be used by those familiar to your system. The methods are known as "Angelic Gematria" –– by this I mean the development of a gematria method from our angelic–languages computer paper, where A=5 and Z=30, so that for every possible throw of five pieces of dice, there is a corresponding letter of the English alphabet. Method 2 would be the use of a simplified Enochian computer for receiving words from the spirit world. This method operates with the throw of a single die or piece of dice. Method 3 refers to how to set up the astral "TV" set using a magick mirroir. Method 4 refers to the zothyrian psychological categories.

A. Angelic Gematria

1. The English alphabet is first of all converted into numbers as we have done before in our lessons on communication with angelic worlds and beings. Thusly, in this system A=5, F=10, K=15, P=20, U=25, Z=30. This is to be found on page four of the angelic languages lesson.

2. Take any word and analyze it so as to determine what it adds up to.

L U A G E = 66 or 16 + 25 + 5 + 11 + 9 = 66

So that at this stage, each word consists of a combination of numbers, or we can say that is its vibration, or magickal wave–length.

3. It is now important to practice neo–pythagorean–gnostic reduction, whereby each word is reduced to a number between 1 and 9. So that if LUAGE=66, it can be reduced by adding 6+6=12, which is still over 9, but 1+2=3, which is the neo–pythagorean reduction of LUAGE.

4. The numbers between 1 and 9 refer to the higher categories of the gnosis and these categories refer to the "higher worlds" which are explored by the gnostic magicians. These worlds are:

    1=The Monad, The One Absolute
    2=The Dyad,The Ontic Sphere, Intuition–Imagination
    3=The Triad, Divine Mind, Noetic, Noetic–Noeric, Noeric
    4=The Tetrad, The Ontological Sphere, "Thought of Being," Archai
    5=The Pentad, Cosmic Sphere, Aeons, Daemons, Logoi, Archones, Syzygies
    6=The Hexad, Dialectical Sphere, Lower Logoi, Gods
    7=The Heptad, Cosmological Components, Genii–Logoi, Rays
    8=The Octad, Higher Planetaries (Spirits), Gnostic Magnetic Zone
    9=The Ennead, Middle Planetaries, Astral Magnetic Zone

Now, the number 10, which=The Decade, refers to and entails the Lower Planetaries (Spirits), which are the Terrestrial Elemental Kings, and these entities are not used by Gnostics, but are important in alchemical research. If a word either adds up to 10 or is reduced to 10, it will be 10 for the shamans but refer to the highest world, The Monad, for the gnostics. Hence, you can see how gnostic magick builds itself up out of alchemical categories.

5. Ken Ward, always a very careful student of our writings, has worked out a very interesting system of a "Book of Numbers" based, for example, on all words having the value of 88, or 81, or 26, or 36. Hence, you may create for yourself a "literal cabala," or Book of Numbers," prior to making a neo–pythagorean–gnostic reduction. The names of certain beings and other magickal words when reduced can be seen by the

magician to show most interesting patterns as word-associations. The psychologically-oriented magician could quite easily develop a magickal word-association test, in order to "locate" the wave-length of the person being tested. The words provided by the subject in response to the words selected by the magician would indicate whether or not the unconscious and subconscious minds of the subject being tested were equal to the vibrations being projected by the magician. This will be developed in a future lesson, but it does refer to an interesting aspect of zothyrian psychology.

6. For example, here are some magickal words and their values, which can be used in word-association. The words are terms in the MSR system of my own personal teaching.

Zosimos=144=9   Lucifer=102=3   Shavindingo=166=13=4
Meithras=125=8   Phallos=111=3   Abraxos=108=9
Photeth=120=3   Aiwaz=80=8   Zombi=85=13=4
Choronzon=164=11=2   Hermes=92=11=2   Kammamori=130=4
Phibionite=147=12=3   Phallus=117=9   Shugal=92=11=2
Michael=79=16=7   Albert=82=10=1

At the present time, what we are doing is simply introducing this method for you to start using it in connection with reduction, attribution to the correct category between 1 and 9, and lastly, word-association.

B. Simplified Enochian Computer

1. This method is for those who would like to use angelic partners in making up a simple magickal language with barbarous words. You use a magick square and a piece of dice (one single die). You do not have to use a magick mirroir or a large tracing board.

2. Make up a six-by-six letter magick board or square like the following:

         (1) A G E X U Z (2)
             V U R Y Z O
             I R A Z O X
             X O Z A R I
             O Z Y R U V
         (3) Z U X E G A (4)

You will notice that there is a certain pattern to this square, although I decided not to make it perfectly symmetrical like our usual magickal squares. This was because I wanted to have a vowel alternate with a non-vowel in each line, both in direction 1 to 2 and 3 to 4 as well as from direction 1 to 3 and 2 to 4.

3. Now that you have selected and put together your computer of 36 letters, you are ready to begin your exercise. First of all, to get yes or no as your reply in determining the length of words, ask the question before getting a letter,

     "Is this a new word beginning?" or
     "Is this the end of the word?" as well as asking
     "May I begin to get the words?" or
     "May I terminate this session in word-gathering?"

4. Here would be an example of what it might be like:

     1. May I begin now?
        "yes" (dice came up as 1, 3, or 5)
     2. I toss and get 6 across=1st element
        Letter is "I"
     3. Is this a new word beginning?
        "Yes" (die cast as 3)

4. Next letter is 4 across and 6 down=E
5. Does this word continue? "Yes" die=1
6. Next letter is 6 across and 1 down=Z
    7. Does this word continue? Die=2=No (This then is the end of the magickal word. The word is therefore IEZ.
5. Using the basic oracle method of angelic languages of A=5 asnd Z=30, you can find out if this is the name of a spirit from a certain area of the cosmos. Using reduction, you can find its wavelength and to what level of the cosmos it pertains. You can make the system as complicated as you wish or keep it very simple; it is simply a tool for extra-terrestrial communication. Thelemite magicians might wish to use it in connection with the VIII, IX, or XI degrees, etc. It is a method for context-building, i.e., building up the content of the various worlds assigned to various spirits. Remember, there are an infinite number of spirits and also an infinite number of worlds and magickal languages derived from the energies of these very spirits.

C. Astral "TV" Station:
1. This is to be used in connection with the listing of spirit-broadcasters given in last month's lesson. You will be using a magick mirror and a die, or a single piece of dice.
2. To determine if the TV is on or off, toss the die and if 1 or 6, then it is "off."
3. Note the night of the week and tossing the die if 2, 3, 4, or 5, then the station is "on."
4. There are four possible "station-studios" or "rays." They are
    2=a
    3=b
    4=c
    5=d
5. It is Tuesday at 8:00 p.m. and I wish to use my "TV." I toss the die and up comes 5, which means that I may magickally attune to a program in gnostic logic being broadcast by the "Geburah King and His Council of Magick." The magician will then take notes on what he then received from the operation of this psychic field and egregor.

D. Zothyrian Psychological Categories
1. Magicians should attune themselves to the possibility of a psychological science, an empirical phenomenology of the contents of consciousness, which operates with their magickal exploration.
2. The following categories are significant ways whereby psychic energy is explained to non-magicians seeking magickal understanding.
    Self=That which can be experienced introspectively as a dynamism.
    Field=A continuum of psychic energy as a process of continuous and differentiated dynamisms.
    Conscious Mind=The mind that is here and now.
    Sub-Conscious Mind=The personal dream and memory experience of a human.
    Un-Conscious Mind=The transpersonal matrix of all psychic energies and the past psychic field of the human race. Key: Acceptance, regressive dynamics, field of contact is with the real, autonomous complexes pull towards a lower dream world than the sub-concious mind, realm of Mater, Regina, Earth, Moon.
    Super-Conscious Mind=The transpersonal lattice of all psychic energies and the future psychic field of the human race. Key: Challenge, progressive dynamics, field

of contact with the ideal, autonomous complexes pull towards a higher dream world than the sub—conscious mind, realm of Pater, Rex, Sky, Sun.

Libido=Constitutive principle of the personality--id and individuality.

Censor=Cultural principle of organization of ego and id, the non—repressive mandala which is selectio—expressive.

Syzygy=Anima and Animus=Autonomous complexes constitutive and regulative of the transcendental id.

Constitutive=Makes up the content by providing the subject—matter amd power —— material and efficient causes.

Regulative=Governs the operation in a formal and final or purposive way.

Psyche=The individuality and the personality.

Individuality=Intuitus archetypus and intuitis ectypus in the un—conscious, subconscious, conscious, and super—conscious fields.

Personality=Union of the rational (ego) and instinctual (id) self.

Transcendental Ego=Regulative principle of the personality—ego and the individuality.

Transcendental Id=Regulative principle of the personality—id and the individuality.

Super—Ego=Constitutive principle of the personality—ego and individuality.

These are simply some of the categories and technical terms of zothyrian psychology which show a close relationship to both Freudian and Jungian concepts, although somewhat modified.

The Aiwaz-Physics

The purpose of this paper is to introduce the study of The Aiwaz–Physics to all students who have advanced to this level of the subject–matter. If you are among the students who have reached this level as a result of studies in my magickal research, you are considered to be both a candidate for the Aiwaz–Priesthood and a member of the Choronzon Club. This lesson begins the alchemical basis of the Aiwaz–Physics.

1. The number of Aiwaz is 8, which is also the number of Zothyrius. There are eight alchemical components used to provide the material basis for Aiwaz in the materialization of the Absolute (i.e., the phallus=9). The magician will therefore provide himself with the raw materials for these eight components.

2. The first component is Gold Chloride. The number of this vibration is 1, which is the number of Virgo, Uranus, Moon, Jupiter. It would appear that it is possible to materialize the Aiwaz–current by means of a secret interaction of these points in your own horoscope. For example, my own Uranus in Aries square to my Moon–Pluto conjunction in Cancer forms a kind of a bridge. Then my Jupiter in Scorpio in relation to my Virgo rising creates another kind of a bridge. Also, the mid–heaven is associated with Uranus as the materialization of the aeon. My Vulkanus (=9) is conjunct to my mid–heaven. So here is another point of contact. It is important to bear in mind that materialization does occur at the level of 9, which we will learn arises from the mixture of the eight alchemical components. Aiwaz we view as the Intelligence of the aeon.

3. The second component is Gold Metal. The number of this vibration is 2, which is the number of Venus, Hermes, and Choronzon. 180o from this mid–heaven is the nadir of the horoscope, the place of the daemon, who is opposite the aeon or Aiwaz. Chronzon is the daemon. Together, these autonomous complexes, the aeon and the daemon mediate between the ego and the transcendental ego of zothyrian psychology. They are also constitutive and regulative of the transcendental ego. When the aeon is constitutive the daemon is regulative. These terms refer to magickal forms of possession.

4. The third component is Uranium Nitrate. The number of this vibration is 3, which is the number of The Sun, Haster, Yog–Sothoth, and the hieron or holy place of initiation. The Sun when combined with Neptune and Pluto projects the power of the animus in males. When combined with Earth and the Moon it projects the power of the anima in females. The individual horoscope is for the magician the way whereby certain energies are directed into the mind of the native from magickal power zones. Hence the psychological interpretation of magickal astrology is valid.

5. The fourth component is Platinum Metal. The number of this vibration is 4, which is the number of Mars, Aquarius, and daemon. In magickal psychology this is the placement of the shadow, which is hidden by the personality. The shadow is the descendent+Mars+Jupiter. We can say that the daemon is very strongly manifested in the conscious world via the shadow.

This paper is laying the psychological and alchemical groundwork for the manifestation of the Aiwaz–Current.

6. The fifth component is Silver Metal. The number of this vibration is 5, which is the number of Azathoth, Pisces, EA, Cancer, and Mercury. As Venus is the principle

of Eros in the personality, so Mercury is the principle of Logos. Venus+Mercury+the ascendant provide us with the Personality, and this is opposed to the Shadow, or Cthulu=4.

7. The sixth component is Silver Nitrate. The number of this vibration is 6, which is the number of Neptune. There is here a reference again back to the Animus. The basis of the Animus and the Anima must be in nitrates of highly radioactive substances in the field of the individual. This would be an example of sexual radioactivity.

8. The Anima and the Animus are magickally charged complexes which mediate between the id and the transcendental id. The seventh component is Copper Metal, and the number of this vibration is 7, which is the number of Capricorn, Dagon, Scorpio, Taurus, and both ogdoade and ogdoad. This is the number of syzygy, or the magickal myth of the ancient father and his twins with whom he incestuously unites, causing on the one hand the generation of the ixo-type magick and, on the other, the generation of the XIo-type magick, OTO. Hence, the use of Copper, sacred metal of Venus in the preparationfor these forms of erotic magick.

9. The eighth component is Iron Metal. The number of this vibration, 8, is the number of both magick and gnosis, Sagittarius and Libra, and Leo. This is the sphere of the mysteries of the ogdoade, or the manifestation of the female power as an etheric force-field. In the tantric yoga, this would be the zone of the work with the kalas and other female emanations of power. The German thelemic occultists and the Fraternity of Saturn possessed special magnetic methods — derived from P.B. Randolph — for directing the projection of this energy along eight distinct "tubes and tunnels of magnetic power," a mystery communicated only in their "philosophical grades," but also taught in the Aiwaz-Priesthood, as this is the number of Aiwaz (=8).

10. Corresponding to the number nine is the materialization of the above eight components. The Absolute, Aries, Saturn, and Phallus tell us where it is to be found. Shub-Niggurath and Arbaxos are its foci, as final terms of the cosmic process. This is the realm of materialization of all previous emanations. Nine is a masculine number and a masculine zone of power. When all of the elements are together in situ, then you have Nine as the absolute or the phallus of the gnostics. Just as all of the elements of consciousness and being are united in Abraxos, the synergy of the magician. In the Choronzon Club the magickal work of "the upper elements" begins with nine and moves backwards to the One, Gemini (81=9).

This lesson has as its purpose the bringing together of the gnostic and magickal components of the alchemical and psychological basis of the Aiwaz-physics. We will now begin to work in making magickal combinations of these elements in order to effect certain changes in our absolute selfhood. Next, we will pass on to the magickal use of these components as we begin to build the machinery of the Aiwaz-physics.

The Aiwaz–Physics

With each lesson I am trying to introduce you more and more to the consciousness identified with the subject-matter of the Aiwaz-physics. If a student has any questions in this matter, he must write to me for clarification, because what we are embarking upon will become more and more advanced and students who are not careful will find the going difficult and even (although I would hope not) make mistakes.

Many students have written to ask what is the connection between the Aiwaz materials and the Zothyrius materials. Let me say that Aiwaz and Zothyrius are magickally cognate, being derived from the number 8. Hence, by means of their interaction, we can come to understand them more deeply. Aiwaz-energy would be like the transcendental id and Zothyrius would be like the transcendental ego. However, both are operating at the level of the Tr. ego inthe cosmic sense. I would be the last person to use a concept which was introduced by Aleister Crowley, as many of you know. However, as there is an objective energy there I as a scientist and technologist, rather than a poet or other irrationalist, must accept and work with what exists and for which there is evidence phenomenologically given. This is the exact method of the Mercury-Uranus complex as it operates in the system.

Concerning Aleister Crowley, let me say (and this is my own viewpoint), that happily he has been corrected, extended, and improved upon by Kenneth Grant, in whose writings I find the essential amplification. Because Grant writes favorably about my work, he is to be considered the most widely known and read authority on the 93 current and the Liber AL vel Legis. This is my own view and is not methodologically binding upon any research patterns, as it is simply a commentary on the many questions rising among students.

Please refer back to The Magickal System, Part I (Lesson 1[b]) to section D "Zothyrian Psychological Categories." It is my wish to amplify that part of the system. There is such as thing as the Aiwaz-psychology, and it is essential for the integration of the psychic and the physical. In other words, if we take the question of time-travel, which is a basic magickal issue in the Aiwaz-physics (henceforth known as the A-physics), it is essential for there to be a magicko-psychological possibility for how this time-travel is integrated into the psyche of the magickal student. It is not enough to do it, it must be explained. Also, genuine time-travel does not occur outside of a magickal system such as ours. What people do who say they are doing time-travel is what Jung would call "active imagination." In other words, while individuals have the potentiality for time-travel in their psyches, it is only actualized through Memphis-Misraim initiation. An example of what I mean would be the fact that the learned theosophist, C.W. Leadbeater, did not begin to do his most extensive akashic research work until after he had been initiated into the Rite of Memphis-Misraim. Traditionally, time-travel has been a technique taught through the magickal orders and systems.

There are 25 definitions towards a zothyrian psychology of time-travel. Here they are:

1. The unconscious–the archetypal realm of possibilities feeding into the present (ego-id) and past (transcendental-id).
2. The superconscious=the archetypal realm of possibilities feeding into the present (ego-id) and future (transcendental-ego).
3. The transcendental ego=the future part of the Self.

4. The transcendental id=the past part of the Self.
5. The future is "inside" the transcendental-ego.
6. The past is "inside" the transcendental-id.
7. Because of the "action" of the t-ego, the superconscious "appears" as future.
8. Because of the "action" of the t-id, the unconscious "appears" as the past.
9. The "action" of trying to connect with ego and id creates time-lines.

10. F+E=Time-Line #1 RMM 950=328, the past-perfect tense.
11. E+D=Time-Line #2 RMM 950=329, the past-present tense.
12. C+B=Time-Line #3 RMM 950=330, the present-future tense.
13. B+A=Time-Line #4 RMM 950=331, the future-perfect tense.
14. Definitions 10-13=The patriarchates or Pluto-true "wise old men" archetypes. This is the genesis of all patriarchal figures in the magickal system.
15. These four archetypal figures rise of the innermost necessity of the cosmic regions of the psyche and are the fullest expression of the Animus within the dynamic field theory of the mind. They form the regulative function of the Animus.
16. These numbers are the perimeters of the regions of the Animus and are activated in males=1, 3, 5, 7, and 9 (or the total).
17. These numbers are the perimeters of the regions of the Anima and are activated in females=2, 4, 6, 8, and 10 (or the total).
18. The feminine is generated by a comparable process from the magickal time-zones of the psyche.
19. In the feminine psychology, the archetypal time-stations are the matriarchates. Hence it is possible for there to be a completely female Rite of Memphis-Misraim and such an order does exist.
20. Therefore, the structures of the Rite of Memphis-Misraim are not generated from history only but are archetypal generations from the deepest regions of the psyche. History is the theater for the observation of the phenomenological amplification of these archetypal patterns.
21. In males, patriarchates=the regulative functions of the Animus.
22. In females, matriarchates=the regulative functions of the Anima.
23. (A) The constitutive functions of the Animus=In males, the t-ego, the unconscious, the subconscious, the conscious, the superconscious. These make up the female Animus.
23. (B) The constitutive functions of the Anima are: In males=the unconscious, the subconscious, the conscious, and the superconscious. In females=we follow the same pattern and find these to be identical with the functions for males in Def. 23(A). thus we can define the male and female Anima.
24. What are the male regulative functions of the Anima. Read Def. 21. The field of psychic contents of the Animus=the space wherein rise various Anima-figures. This is the proper locus or situs for the Oedipus complex. This becomes upon close analysis the content of the patriarchate.
25. Now we ask what are the female regulative functions of the Animus. Read Def. 21 again. The field of psychic contents of the Anima=the space wherein rise various Animus-figures. This is the proper locus or situs for the Elektra complex. This becomes upon close analysis the content of the matriarchate.

Comment

It is important to think always of the integration of psychics and the physica. They reflect each other both inwardly and outwardly. There cannot be an A–physics without its complement in the Z–psychology. These two poles represent the continuum of magickal experiences in this New Aeon. Each magician is stimulated to create his own new consciousness and to prepare to meet both the A–elements of space–experience as well as the Z–elements. As you know, for a long time the Z–elements were very strong. Then came the balancing pressure of the A–factors, at first as a kind of dialogue. While it is true that there will be those who do reject this type of communication on what can only be defined as a religious basis, i.e., the religion of thelema, others will see it entirely as it is intended, i.e., as scientific methodology in action and in magick. I would have to consider the latter viewpoint as the more significant and the more scientific.

One is free to leave the order and the course of studies herein taught at any time. None are bound by any magickal pressures or social obligations. However, once a person has departed from the Magickal System, they may never reconnect in any future lifetime. There are many other pathways, and these pathways are open to them. These pathways also include many thelemic orders and groups. Needless to say, I do not consider their rehashing of what Aleister Crowley wrote long ago in keeping with the modern demands of exact science in magick. However, that is the pathway they have chosen and they must live with it and suffer with it. On the other hand, The Spirit Mercurius has been most gracious to us in giving form and the Spirit Uranus equally gracious in giving us content, so that the Aiwaz–Zothyrius field can incarnate in these lessons. However, what is past is past and the true will of the magician should be to live where there is the fullness of magickal energy, moving onwards into the future. However, putting all talk of scientific method and technique aside, let us not forget that for those who remain, the despotism of Mercurius–Uranus is far worse than any other tyrannies, for it is a cosmic electricity which never tires. Only those who belong here really should remain.

The I-Ching Diary and Chinese--Gnostic Magickal Algebra
The importance of the Book of Changes, or I-Ching, lies in what it reveals. However, there exists an even more esoteric importance or value, which is to be found in what the Book of Changes conceals.

Many occultists and magi have made use of the divinatory properties and services of the I-Ching, but few if any widely known have made use of its megamathematical magick. Because every system of magick supposes a type of magickal mathematics, it is important to understand that our system supposes the algebra and magickal calculus which is to be found inside of the I-Ching. I have shown in the papers of the MSR (Part I) the relationship between the magick of the I-Ching and Voudoo. Now it is important to see that as a part of the past, and because we are in the present, I am proposing a new exploration of the figures of the I-Ching.

When a magician works with the Book of Changes, it is important to understand that the figures which are given to the oracle, the 64 of them, also serve to inform him of what doorways are theno open, at the moment of the oracle, leading into the inner planes. The way in which the figure or hexagram of the Book of Changes is formed reveals the particular type of doorway, through which dimension, tattwa, or inner-plane, the magician may move in order to meet with the beings, who can be approached in no other way. In other words, there are certain unique magickal beings with whom the magician can make contact in no other way save through the magickal algebra of the I-Ching. Thus, each exploration of the inner world should be a unique magickal experience in the participation in a magickal algebra and a proper or special diary should be kept of this work.

Occult History of This Algebra.
Many years ago, I would say about 1967, and in the wintertime, I began a series of magickal meditations in order to bring through certain amplifications of certain magickal axioms which had been received the year before from the Master Z. The Applied Lattices Research Institute had been founded in order to bring through the proper magicko–metamathematical current. I was working with the Monastery materials and participating in the organization of the Gnostic Church in its local activities. First of all, we had 16 magickal axioms. They have appeared from time to time in what I have written because they may be considered as the source of a lot of magickal creativity. A typical exmaple of what these axioms are like is the following, which is the very simplest of all such magickal equations. This one may be said to correspond to the I-Scale, or Moon in Scorpio level.

Now, because there are 16 axioms there must be metamathematical and magickal interpretations of these axioms also. And there are. These are the 64 interpretations which correspond to the figures of the I-Ching. In other words, with each interpretation is projected into one of the four "worlds" one of the 16 basic axioms. The logic of this system seems to hold that there are only four kinds of things in each realm or logical universe. It seems to come close to the cabala and to voudoo and to the basics of elemental magick. But, it seems also to present itself as a very abstract system, which is capable of several applications. Now, I have been assuming that these formulae correspond to our tables because the tables and scales of our magick were generated from these abstract causes. It may not be correct to assume that there is a relationship between the categories of the cabala and our formularies. It is my personal view that our formularies are closer to the magickal background of the I–Ching and the Afro–Atlantean voudoo family of spirits. These last two I think of as being somewhat close to the Enochian family of spirits. Therefore our own magickal system would probably lie outside of the cabalistic family in a fundamental sense. This would identify the system as probably an up–to–date Atlantean type of magick.

Now an example of an interpretation of an axiom is as follows. This is the Scale I or "Moon in Scorpio" level for this axiom.

Now, because this interpretation is one of 64, we can also say that what it means in terms of the language of the I–Ching is the following figure or hexagram:

```
----  ----
----  ----    Which is K'un, Number 2, or The Receptive, The Earth. This is the most
----  ----    passive of the figures of the system of 64. Now if anyone has read
----  ----    about the I–Ching they will realize that the figures of the Book of
----  ----    Changes have undergone a kind of magickal analysis and been explored
----  ----    terms of whether they are of two lines, and if so then there are four
```
possibilities. If they are of three lines, they may be seen as the eight possibilities or categories. If they are of four lines then we have the 16 categories, and it is at this level of analysis that they may be seen as corresponding to our axioms and scale from I to XVI. It is my view that this mode of analysis is essentially Atlantean and that it actually represents the most ancient form of magickal mathematics.

Now we must understand that so far we have been trying to show a logical parallelism between the gnostic axioms and mathematics of our system and the figures and other structures of the I–Ching. The purpose of this is to make certain connections and points of transition between one system and the other. Now we come to certain matters which are highly interesting. I am referring to what I have called for several years the explications or proofs of the 64 interpretations. There are four of these for each interpretation. Now four times 64 equals 256. This number has occurred several times in our papers and often refers to the total number of power zones or chakras or hot–points in our system. If you add 256 and 64, you arrive at 320. If you add the number of the basic magickal axioms, 16, to 320, the result is 336. This last number, 336, is the number of the hierophant of the algebra of Memphis–Misraim. It is usually written as 97o=336+, and it means that the hierophant is the master of the two realms, the magicko–metaphysical, which is indicated by the 97o, and he is also or as well the master of the magicko–metamathematical realm, which in astrology is viewed by none other than Rudolf Steiner, a former Memphis–Misraim and OTO Master, as the zodiacal sign of Gemini on the Mid–Heaven of the astrological chart.

Then we can say that there are 64 interpretations and each one of the 64 has four explications or applications. These four applications can be said to refer, I suppose, to specific pathways or passages from the physical world to certain higher realms. It would seem from my experiments that when a certain figure of the I–Ching would be cast that at the same time a certain doorway was opened for me to enter the universe beyond. The spirits brought the figure or hexagram during the working of the magickal oracle and they also came and went by a certain passageway, which could be used by the magician at that time. Only one pathway or passageway was possible with each hexagram at one time, but in theory were were 256 hexagrams possible, or 256 passageways concealed in the oracle and one would appear. By making use of this system of exact logic, I was able to realize the greatest potentials for the use of both the oracle of the I-Ching, as well as simultaneous inner-plane work. Now let us explore how this magick can be said to work.

According to the logic of the I-Ching, when the figure is formed by means of the tossing of the coins each line can add up to either 6 or 8 if the line reflects the receptive order of being, i.e., -- --, or the line can add up to either 7 or 9 if it reflects the creative order of being, i.e., ----. Now by taking the possible combinations and possibilities of number into account, for all six lines of the figure, we can say that there exists a mathematical range of possibilities, which we may interpret as a magickal range of inner-plane pathways from the number 36 through the number 54. The hexagram K'un, when composed entirely of the number six, as the value of each line, would be 6x6=36. On the other hand, the hexagram Ch'ien, if composed entirely of lines valued at the number 9, which would be a most powerful figure, if not the most powerful in the abstract realm, would add as 9x6=54. So there you have your range of magickal pathways. Now let us look at them in more detail.

According to the pattern of analysis, the following numbers indicate corresponding pathways.

36, 42 - 44 = Earth pathways
37 - 38, 45 - 47 = Water pathways
39 - 40, 48 - 50 = Air pathways
41, 51 - 53, 54 = Fire pathways

Now it should be understood that when we work with these pathways we do not need to make use of the magickal explications of the 64 interpretations. Those magickal and algebraic formularies, which are to be written in the same notation as the axioms and interpretations are simply to be used as guides in the making up of symbolic systems. The importance of these explications lie in the fact that they exist as the logical and magickal deductions from the system. They complete the model of the magickal structure. However, in the analysis which will follow in future papers, constituting the magickal or magicko-metamathematical diary, I will indicate step-by-step the process and will then bring in the writing out of the explications and their magickal sense.

For the present by way of this introduction, however, it is sufficient for us to use some other method to guide concentration. I suggest at this stage using the colors given in the paper on angelic languages. Those flashing colors, eight in all, are easily arranged according to the four elements. I would therefore suggest that you make use of the magickal mirror, flashing colors, and combinational calculus, or the way in which you work with the I-Ching as indicated point by point in this lesson. By using the magickal mirror to bring in the power, you cast the oracle using the coins. Then you compute the pathway which is opened in this instance. Before going out via the mirror, signal your departure by means of the color which corresponds to your lines in the I-Ching figure. When you return you may close the system by flashing the color and thus sending the signal for the closing off of the pathway. In the next lessons we will discuss what is done to report on these path-workings and trips into another part of the magickal universe. NOTE: These worlds explored while real in themselves do not necessarily correspond to any already explored magickal territory.

NOTE on the Family Names of These Magickal Spirits
Let us say that in our calculations we come up with a number which exists in the group 48–50. This would be the family name of the spirit, or the family name–space of that communicator. To make a kamaea one would simply add up the numbers: 4+8+5+0= 12+5=17=8. So the kamaea would make use of eight letters. These you would get for the magickal diary from the angelic languages oracle. Remember the angels or spirits are paths and the paths are spirits. Next you would want the name of the individual communicator who is bringing you the hexagram. Let us say that the number is 48 for the hexagram, and that this indicates an air spirit as the agent. To get the kamaea simply add up 4+8=12=3. There would be only three letters in the name of the spirit under these circumstances. You would use the angelic languages oracle and find out what these three letters were.

This makes the system easy to use, very clear in operation and in terms of its logic, completely consistent.

NOTE on the Chinese Secret Alchemy and Medicine Implied By These Algebras and Calculi

In the archives of our magickal order, there is a brief series of notes, which were made by Tau Zothyrius, i.e., Lucien–Francois Jean–Maine (1869-1960), the successor of both S.L. McGregor Mathers (1854-1918) and the Abbe Joseph–Albert Boullan (1824-1893) on the basis of his researches into Taoist Magick, alchemy, and magickal medicine. These notes were made about 1900, while Tau Zothyrius was then living in Paris. He associated closely at that time with a Chinese "medical society," in other words, a Taoist physio–magickal society, which still exists deep inside a sympathetic magickal system.

Each magickal number, according to this system, as given in this lesson on page 3, corresponds to a specific type of medicine for creating the magickal philosopher of medicine (or Hermes). The magickal philosopher is that being who has realized the archetypal Anthropos (see "The Magickal System, Part I, Lesson 1[a]) and has allowed Hermes to become him. In Egypt, this was the basis of the Thoth–Hermes school of magickal medicine. Because of its being found in both Chinese and Egyptian esotericism, it may be said that this approach is Atlantean

I now wish to give the correspondences, which will be discussed in the future lessons to come.

Numbers Given on page 3	Type of Medicine*
36	Earth–type/copper or iron
37 – 38	Water–type/mercury or silver nitrate
39 – 40	Air–type/silver or platinum
41 & 54	Fire–type/gold or uranium nitrate
42	Sun in Taurus type
43	Sun in Virgo type
44	Sun in Capricorn type
45	Sun in Scorpio type
46	Sun in Pisces type
47	Sun in Cancer type
48	Sun in Libra type

49	Sun in Aquarius type
50	Sun in Gemini type
51	Sun in Sagittarius type
52	Sun in Aries type
53	Sun in Leo type

*These medicine types refer simply to the esoteric magickal and alchemical level of analysis. Naturally, there exists also an esoteric version of this list which is imparted to the magickal initiate at the time of his ritual admission and initiation into this Chinese magickal order or medical society of Hermes.

The Use of the I-Ching Within the Mandala of the Zothyrian Transcendental-Id

The Use of the I-Ching Within the Mandala of the Zothyrian Transcendental-Id

1. It is important to understand that the magickal order is a system of interconnected energies of a very deep psychic character.

2. This system or structure is a mandala, indeed it is a mandalum instrumentum, cf., K. Grant, "Cults of the Shadow," p. 175.

3. The Master of the order is located or has his "situs" at the center of the mandala.

4. Dr. Jean-Maine is the archetypal center of the mandala.

5. The initiates of the system are connected by metamathematical and metaphysical logical relations to this center.

6. These centers are identified according to the following logical relations which exist in the magickal system:

Formal and Material Entailment
Formal and Material Inclusion
Formal and Material Equivalence
Formal and Material Implication

In these relationships we find the basis of our system of Memphis-Misraim as a logical complex, i.e., as a system of magickal and logical relationships.

7. There exists an oracular method for contacting the center of the mandala as well as the other members of the mandala.

8. There are four possible areas of exploration implicit in the use of the I-Ching as a method for contacting parts other than oneself: 1. To find out one's relationship between oneself and the entire magickal system of the web; this means one's relationship to the whole order of which Dr. Jean-Maine is the archetypal wiseman or absolute leader. 2. To find out one's relationship between oneself and any particular person who is a member of the order, i.e., known to be a member and using the web-work of the order as a linking space. 3. To find out one's relationship to oneself as an ego in the order, i.e., as a member, and one's deeper selfhood within the order, i.e., one's magickal id or transcendental id which is generated by the order, or revealed via the magick of the order. NOTE: The order has traditionally created archetypal identities for the development of the members which are different from the id and the t-id of the member. If the member is displeasing to the magickal archetype of the person created by the order in Haiti, such as the Zothyrian id and t-id of the member, these structures have traditionally been used in Franco-Haitian magickal orders to bring the "normal" ego, is, t-id, and t-ego of the member into "agreement" with the logical system of the archetypal self of the order. Hence it is possible to use the I-Ching to determine if one is in favor at court, so to speak, should that be important. In this sense, French orders differ from the more English orders, with two exceptions known to this writer. 4. To find out one's relationship with either Michael or with Hector-Francois, which is different from the purpose given in the first of these four areas of exploration.

9. The answer given in the results of the tossings of the I-Ching must be understood as indicating one's position also in regards to magickal study and depth of understanding provided by these papers. For it is not our own or even only intention to try to control egoic systems, but to teach the science of magickal arts.

10. The structure of the order is expressed via certain mental and magickal

interactions. These exhibit a definite logical structure. Thus, in the books on natural sciences written through the Science Circle members, we can easily find many very important instances of logical inter-locking. And because our magickal order is based upon a Geminian magickal computer powered by Capricornian energies and Cancerian logics of inter-locking, we can see how a specific model of what we are doing is gradually emerging in consciousness.

11. At one time, this magickal order was not thought of as a very deep zothyrian computer or logical elemental. In certain ways, a mythological image was actually presented. This led to a loss of magickal and metaphysical energies because the power of the mind (Mercury) was not accepted as the methodology. Saturnian techniques were employed to induct the forces and these did not prove efficient, outside of certain very isolated parts of Haiti. It was necessary to change the mid-heaven of the order from a Saturnian and Aquarian emphasis to a Geminian mid-heaven, to allow Virgo to be the sign of the ascending of the power, in function replacing Scorpio. This must be understood as entirely a metamethodological change rather than a magicko-political change, as the older scheme of things became the archetype behind the computer of Hermes.

12. This magickal computer, which is the order in its mechanical aspect may be seen as the modern, or most recent, operating model of a system of magickal work which goes back to Atlantis.

Another Universe To Be Found In Books
1. Here is a very simple method for making contact with a new type of magickal universe. I am referring to the universe which is inside of books. Inside, for example, of the universe of letters inside a book, of which there are perhaps an infinite number of magickal members or entities.

2. Take any book, for example we took a book on psychology, but any book having letters will suffice. If it included numbers we could only go up to 9, before we would start repeating and that would not be a good enough sample or induction. So take any book.

3. Because of another method -- in point 4, this point is logically within limit. Take the first letter on page 1, the second on page 2, the third on page 3, and the fourth on page 4. This is your basic name of the entity. Make inverse or reverse, and direct kamaeas, as you already may know from the leson on angelic languages.

4. Or you can take the first letter of chapter 1, the second of chapter 2, the third of chapter 3, the fourth of chapter four, the 5th of chapter 5, and the sixth of chapter 6. Let us say that there are only six chapters in the book. Hence, be selective, use a brief book rather than something vast. Then make magickal kamaea from these letters, both direct and retrograde.

5. As the magician you should compose inspirationally or mediumistically the translation of each line of the magickal kamaea, both of the positive and the negative side or aspect of the magickal square derived from the name of the spirit. This would be an example:
TOINLR "This is your magickal name, I know it" (meta-statement about name)
OINLRL "You are regent of part of book"
INLRLN "I summon you to possess me"
NLRLNI "Give me power and wisdom to possess"
LRLNIO "Give me this specific ←←←←←← that I desire" (here make wish)
RLNIOT "Depart, return to your realm until I summon you again"

6. I would call your attention to the fact that the number of chapters in the book (point 4 above) determines the number of letters to be selected following the method of point 3.

I would wish that students at this level of consciousness record in diaries on both operations for my interpretation. This will require that you make use of the Book of Changes, I–Ching, which as good thelemites and Jungians, or both, you would already have in your possession.

The Projection of the Ojas-Rays and the Powers of Kabonists

This course is primarily intended for magicians in three parts of the world: The east or the East Indies, the West Indies, and Africa. Other students will find it diffi- cult to make use of the powers described in these papers because of the psychic con- ditions which prevail in other parts of the world. When we talk about the Ojas-Rays we mean, of course, those magickal energies which the magician generates from his own physical body or for which the physical body serves as the vehicle of projection. In either case, the body is the weapon for magickal aggression and control work and it is also the vast lens through which energies are sent off as rays. This occult power, Ojas, is given to the magician by the higher powers. Only some magicians possess it, and not all can possess it, for it is tied up with magickal fate.

This magickal power, however, may only be used by very powerful spell-binders. For it shoots out from the body in the form of radiations and strikes at the energy field of the enemy and thus enters and penetrates the enemy very destructively. It is a terrific power and a terrific source for the rightly motivated magician. That is to say, one who is allied with our school of power. For we are certainly not interested in helping our enemies destroy ourselves. We are only interested in the possession of those magickal powers which will get them before they can get to us. Now, of course, in order to possess this very strong power one must be a male sex-magician. There is no other way except by the magickal use of the sexual powers.

By this I mean that the magician has learned to project his sexual radioactivity and now is ready to master the art of making those very powerful magickal weapons which are known as the Heavy Hoodoo Spells. This is why our magickal system seems to help so many magicians become stronger and stronger in what they are doing. For they are seeking to build up more and more of these weapons and store them up for future magickal use.

Now, let us explore the powers of the Kabonists or magickal priests who make use of this sexual power in their many spells. Let us say that first of all the spell will be sent out when the magician is ready to shoot out his sexual magick. This means that the magician must be able to utter the magickal spell at the very time he is sending the rays of his powers, which means, of course, at the time of his shoot- ing those magickal rays of sexual power, which are within him in a constant state of excitement and furiousness. This means that the magician must be ready at all times to send out that power so that his will must be closely tied up with his sexual vitality and magickal power of light or Ojas-ray. In order to do this, he must master the super technique of magickal excitement. This is done by thinking of nothing but sexuality, by concentrating his will more and more, and becoming more and more intense through the use of the very powerful spell for strength, which I am giving you now.

First, you must utter the name of the god Shiva over and over again in a deep and almost inaudible voice, but over and over again it must be uttered. Second, you must concentrate on magickal powers and will to have supreme magickal powers. You must will to possess all sexo-magickal powers in the universe. You must will to be total and unlimited sexuality. Third, while you are doing this concentration exer- cise, you will do that operation of sex-magick known as the VIIIo of the scheme of Aleister Crowley, making use of an oil as a lubrication agent. You will say over and over the name of Shiva as you work harder and harder towards the explosion of the true magician's orgasm. Fourth, you will then see the Ojas-rays leaving your body from the sexual area of the wand and moving through time and space. They will look like those modern laser beams, which are used to either create or destroy, for that is exactly what the Shiva-Power of Ojas can do. You are sending the power to where you want it to go. You are going to make things happen. You are going to make or break a friend or foe. This is what our magick is all about.

Let me explain that this easy spell is designed simply to make you a practical magician. There are some magicians who wish to go very deeply into this field and for them I can impart the powerful Shivite Radiations in personal initiation. But, to get going in your magickal operations, this simple spell, which I introduced to you in this lesson is basic and perfect. As we move along, you will be taught the various secret and rather extensive magickal processes, which are designed towards making the student of Ojas-magick more and more capable in his knowledge and skill. However, in this lesson we are only interested in getting the process going. For the process of magickal teaching is a gradual step-by-step process.

Shivite Radiations are magickal powers which are possessed by special magicians in different locations. Actually, only one person in each area may possess this power to avoid the many consequences of overloading in a particular area. The magicians of each area who possess this power generate a field of a special quality for the whole area. They are especially empowered by this magick to be the personal representatives of the god Shiva in that part of the world. This power is generated by means of magickal induction is transferred at the time of initiation to the magician in many special and secret ways. To possess this power, of course, the student must really be locked into the system as a power-generating mechanism and process, otherwise the power cannot be transferred. The basis of this power is to be found in those esoteric aspects of the cult of Shiva, which are basic to both the east and the west because they can be found at the root of those ancient and awe-full forms of esoteric voudoo and Hindu tantrism, which are the next magickal roots on this planet. The student, however, should become a master of the basics of this lesson before he can think to move on to the next material or even consider himself as suited towards entry into the very extreme forms of Shivite Radiations.

The student of this lesson may prepare a magickal report for his diary. The report, which need not be too long, will cover the powers as they manifest in the student along the following lines of magick.

1. Discuss the magickal motive for doing this exercise.

2. Discuss the images which came to the mind while doing concentration.

3. Discuss the images which came as a result of repetition of the name of Shiva.

4. Discuss the sensations of magickal masturbation and any occult powers you felt.

5. Discuss the intensity of the climax and its images.

6. Discuss the pathway of projection for the powers of Ojas-Radiation.

7. Discuss the images which rose from the projections of Ojas.

8. Discuss the goal of the projection.

9. Discuss the result in visualization of this process of reaching the object/goal.

Cosmic Agreements and Magickal Acts

There are certain schools of consciousness and magick which state that we can only do what is in agreement with the cosmic intelligence. Then they proceed to define what the cosmic intelligences wish in terms of very human and repressive ethical systems. We are in agreement with the idea that we can only do what the cosmic laws will allow, or make possible, but we prefer to let the cosmic level of intelligence tell us what those realities are. In this sense, therefore, we are in agreement with many schools. However, when the magician has the lust to control or destroy someone, to possess totally the soul and body of some person, he, the magician, is simply responding to cosmic influences. For centuries, if not for millions of years, we have been under cosmic influences. We have to be influenced in one direction or another, we have been moved one way or another; we have been angry, kind, passionately intense, or calm and meditative entirely as a result of cosmic influences. So when the magician wants to do something either constructive or destructive, as casting a very powerful spell, he is simply responding to a cosmic influence. He is doing what the higher beings OR gods want him to do. He should therefore not repress that impulse but should make plans to carry it out carefully and completely.

Gods exist in various parts of the universe and we are sensitive to the the influences of these gods upon human behavior. Anger, for example, is due to the influence of the god of the planet Mars. Love is caused by the influence of the Venusian god. In different systems, these gods are viewed in different ways. But what is important is that these gods do have a direct influence upon human behavior. Especially sensitive would be the magician and the student of the especially sensitive to these powers. Therefore, when you feel in a certain mood for doing a certain type of magick, you are simply responding to a cosmic influence and your magickal operation will therefore be in agreement with the way in which the cosmic beings are moving you towards action. Hence there should not be any problem about why we want to do things. We should act as we become sensitive to the influences from higher spheres of being. For the elemental levels of cosmic being are the archetypes behind all patterns and instances of human behavior. So you can see how important it is to listen to your thoughts and respond to them, for they are messengers from the gods. Consequently, we want to be aware of how the way in which the universe wants us to feel and to do and to be.

Here is a simple spell for becoming more attuned to cosmic influences. The magician will retire to his magickal room or place of work and while in the nude and surrounded by those symbols of the LH spirits he has put together, he will begin to develop various deep emotional states. First, he will feel very angry, next he will feel lustful, next he will feel happy, next he wil feel sad. Then the second thing he wil do is this: he will repeat those emotional states over again but this time he will say in mind, "I know you are there, spirit, sent from the god of ←←←←←←." Thus, when he experiences anger, he will say, "I know you are there, spirit sent from the god of anger." When he experiences lust, I might add that there will be images and visualization with these feelings and experiences, so when he experiences lust he will say, "I know you are there, spirit sent from the god of lust." Next, he will repeat this experiment with the moods of happiness and sadness.

He will thusly build up regular spell-contacts with four different god-forces. These are to be understood as personal experiences of the high-spirits of the following planets: Mars=anger, Venus=lust, Jupiter=happiness, Saturn=sad these are very simple ways of looking at the planets and Mars has many sides, as does Venus, etc. But we are establishing our initial psychic contact with these gods so that we can eventually draw more and more of their powers into the spells we are casting. For if we want to cast a spell of anger, it will be much more powerful if we are having an awareness of the power of Mars as anger while we cast the spell. Otherwise, the spell is perhaps not as strong or as directed as it should be. This experience, therefore, with these god-energies, is to show us that we have to be willfully aware of what we are doing and how the spirits of the cosmos are trying to get us to do these things -- to cast various magickal spells, and that what we want to do is to meet them in the act of their influencing us and let them know what we feel and how we wish to respond to their influences. For then we can have more and more powers poured into the spells which we are seeking to cast as part of our magickal development. You will do this exercise, therefore, and write a report of what you have experienced, all phenomena, for your diary.

The purpose of the above psychological exercise is to develop an awareness of the magickal intensity of our operations. As a consequence, the magician is able to make use of every part of his psychic selfhood in order to achieve the results of his spell-binding. We can say that such an approach makes the results even more powerful. Here is another exercise which can be done easily to intensify the psycho-magickal field of operations as we understand it.

This method is called the psychic telephone. All you have to do is to develop a particular mood, e.g., anger, lust, being sad or happy. This development is the turning of the psychic telephone dial or the tuning of the psychic radio to the god-energy sending station. Once you have established a connection by means of the cultivations of the right emotional state, all you have to do then is begin to visualize the entity at the "other end of the line" and start talking by telepathy to that being. You can carry out an intensely interesting conversation by this simple means. To add exactness of the conversation all you would have to do is use a piece of dice (one single die) and toss it. If you were asking questions of the entity at the "other end of the line" to find out if the answer to your question was either yes (an odd number -- 1, 3, 5) or no (an even number -- 2, 4, 6).

It is so simple to use this method, once you have made the initial line of contact with the entity through the art of emotional projection. For that is what you are doing -- you are projecting to the gods by means of emotional energy or what some call the astral or emotional thought forms. It is a simple form of astral projection, in fact it is one of the easiest to master. Also, through this "telephone-magick" you can carry out a long and interesting conversation with the spirit and engage in a variety of simple types of contact work with these spirits, therby learning all kinds of bits of magickal information from them. May I suggest that if you wish to use this type of magickal experiment that you write a report of what results you have achieved through this technique, for your diary.

We will continue to provide you with a variety of magickal methods and techniques as we move along. Please continue to keep up the high level of study you have achieved, or if improvement is needed, do that. For we only want the most powerful magicians in our group.

Links with Ojas

Ojas can be defined, here, as the fundamental magickal energy at the root of sexual radioactivity. Ojas is not possessed by ordinary people because it is entirely magickal in its constitution. To make contact with Ojas, one has to make contact with a source which possesses activated Ojas at present. If this is done, then the latent forces in the magician are awakened and his Ojas will then be released from its unconscious state. It will wake up in the same sense that a person wakes up at dawn. Now a source of activated Ojas is sometimes difficult to find. Only certain magickal orders possess this power in reserve. Magicians who belong to these orders can transmit these powers through magickal initiations. There exists in the world a magickal chain or line of succession or linking up, which has existed from the earliest times on this planet and which, before that time, existed on another planet -- some say Venus, or some other planet of this solar system, or perhaps another solar system. This linking up, this line or succession through history is the basis of a magickal descent of Ojas through centuries of human existence.

Now the teachings of this order -- our magickal order -- is that we are still linked up with these sources of Ojas-power. We have never lost the line of connection, which continually supplies our magickal order with Ojas from Orion, Sirius and many other stellar systems and solar systems. The Ojas is transmitted from those worlds and comes to Earth and is reserved or kept in the inner sanctuary of our magickal order, i.e., La Couleuvre Noire or the Magickal Brotherhood of the Kalinagas. For this reason, our magickal work is always so powerful and our initiations transmit to the candidates the very supreme power of Ojas -- the highest form of magicko-solar sexual radioactivity. However, there are other links with Ojas which can be used by the student of our system. You will recall that when you join our order we ask the student for a recent photo and also, if available, for the astrological information about the time of birth. Sometimes, in certain parts of the world, they did not keep exact records of the time of birth; in such cases we have to work with numerological values. But the reason for this data is to allow the student to benefit from the Ojas of the order in an indirect way.

For not all members of the order can come to where the temple-initiation is given and so we are able to transmit some Ojas to them in order to make their experiments work successfully. They are successful in their magickal work, because of the terrific magickal powers which are stored up in the vast treasury of magickal energies of our order. We can therefore transmit to the student some energy, just as banks normally can make loans to certain persons with good credit. So we transmit energies to our members, knowing that they will maintain a good "occult credit rating." This is a very widespread magickal practice in Haiti among the most extreme magicians of the esoteric form of Voudoo.

There are certainly various ways of developing a good credit rating and in maintaining it. One of the them is the following good exercise, which will be very useful to those students who wish to begin to prepare for magickal work in a very serious way.

Exercise For Ojas

Just before going to bed at night is the best time to do this simple exercise to build up some energies which will make your loan of Ojas from the order work very efficiently. First of all, it is essential to take a cold bath and to sprinkle salt over the body. This is to increase the natural powers of protection in the body. While you bathe and put on the salt, think about the fact that you are bringing in or up from the deeper worlds magickal powers. Then begin to visualize the powers as colored rays of energy moving in space all around you. Dry off and come into your magickal bedroom, where you will work. You are nude and should light some candles, but the number does not matter. However, you will work by candlelight. Then, standing in the center of the room, begin to move your hand in a very sensuous, slow motion all over your body, feeling the contact of skin to skin, enjoying the sexual and sensual pleasure which comes from this action and finding that you are becoming more and more sexually excited, although in a rather unspecific and general way. Then begin to press the thumb, index and middle finger of both the right and left hands, which you have already formed into a simple mudra (ritual hand sign) by bringing these three fingers together.

Begin, as I said, to press thee three fingers of the right and left hands lightly against various parts of the body, while saying to yourself in a soft voice, "Vudu powers of the Ancient Vedas awaken in my body." Say this mantra (magickal formulary or spell) about 33 times as you press the flesh of your body at various points. The points will be of real interest only to you, they will be where you feel like touching, for the body will signal to you where it wants you to touch it, it will tell you where it wants the magickal point of contact to be made. then after you have done this touching and pressing and saying of the mantra, relax your hand, separate your fingers from the triadic meeting of the right and left hand mudras and still standing in the candlelight, naked, begin to feel the Ojas radioactivity slowly stirring deeply within yourself.

At first you will feel a rather vague, rather warm sensation. But pay close attention to the feelings you are experiencing and realize that the energies are just beginning to feel the bombardment of the rays from the order. For the order requires your cooperation in order to stir up these deep magickal powers in your body. You have to use the magickal methods to awaken yourself. Then you iwll feel a certain rush of power, a feeling of terrific energy and vitality which makes you feel both sexual and occult. Then you will feel the energies slowly circulating around you and within you, which the Old Chinese call the Golden Powers of the Secret Flowers (Chakras).

Now relax and enjoy what is happening to you. You are awakening your vitality. You can now get into bed and do some sex—magick, if you wish, or meditate or fall off into the world of sleep and radiation of dreams. You have awakened the wonderful powers of Ojas in yourself and this is just the beginning of your lifetime adventures as a generator of magickal energies. Now the student may do this exercise as often as he wishes. Ideally, it should be done at night unless you are in special circumstances. Ideally, it should be done at the time of the New Moon and the time of the Full Moon. After it is done there is another ritual exercise which completes it, and which is done in the morning if you have access to pure Sunlight.

After doing this Ojas exercise at night, then sleeping in a very relaxed and exploratory manner, the next day rise up from your bed and do some exercises in the Sunlight. These can be simple exercise or yoga, each person can decide for himself what he wants to do. At the end of the exercise, and while still naked, stand in the Sunlight and seal the energy transmission which has occurred at night with the following magickal prayer to purify yourself and seal within yourself the purest and moist Solar of the divine and sexual energies of the perfected male magician, as you say, facing the Sun as it rises in its pure glory of Ojas:

> Let us adore God, the Lord of all beings,
> Whose symbol is the sun of most radiant glory,
> Whose chariot of light crosses the skies of our
> hearts and minds, filling us with the divine
> energy to love and serve the Great Lord and
> with love and compassion for all beings at
> all times.

Then, closing your eyes, meditate upon the following words of absolute power and divine energy.

> Let us meditate upon the glorious radiance
> of our Lord the Sun. May he Whose chariot is
> drawn by the Seven Rays of Supreme Energy
> illuminate our minds and fill our souls with
> the supreme fire of Ojas at all times.

It has been known that magicians in all cultures and circumstances have been able to draw the solar power of the Divine Ojas into themselves by the utterance of this last prayer, which should be memorized as the supreme and perfect spell to be used whenever your intuition tells you it will be needed.

You now have two powerful spells for use in linking up with Ojas.

The Source of Cosmic Energy

Many students of our system often ask the question as to where does the power of the magickal cosmos, which is the power behind the world in which they act, live, move, and create their systems, where does this magickal power come from. The answer to this is that the power comes from the magickal reservoir of our order and system. And that the reservoir of magickal power and energy is continually self-renewing. That is to say, it can never become empty. Those who are members of the inner order of our system and who have given themselves fully to the inner work (I am not referring to students in any general sense), these students of the inner system are able to understand the exact workings of the magickal energies of our system. These energies are entirely cosmic in their scope, for they are not only behind our order but they are also behind the nature of the world as a whole or system of many components.

Our order, for example, does not depend upon the membership of human beings. In actual fact, we have to keep the membership very low, so that each studeent can be directed in a personal way by the leadership of the system. The major part of the membership of the order comes from the innerside membership, and by that I mean the membership which is not in this dimensional universe, although they are physical in their own way. They are the major source for the magickal energies behind our work in this world. They may be understood as possessing the power of The Secret, which is communicated in part to selected members of our own order in various parts of the universe, and also to the various members carefully selected in this part of the universe, i.e., in our world, here.

Consequently, the magickal power is hooked up to the student at the time of his entry into the inner mysteries of the system and it is this power which enables that magician to create and diffuse a variety of magickal powers and energies and to do the many things which normally magicians in other systems are incapable of performing. However, in our system, because there are so many paths, it is necessary for the student to realize that each one of these magickal energies is perfectly suited towards the total release of the energy. Of course, I am talking about his experience or paths or types of physics in our own system. I am restricting our scope to the parts of our system, also, which are concerned with those magickal energies which can be given to the student. How does this work?

First of all, in our approach, the student is carefully examined as to the time of his birth, for the astrological component is necessary in order to fit the pipelines of energy to the soul of the student–member. In other words, the astrological picture of the student is a necessary system of electrical switches and connectives of various magickal types (as in esoteric engineering) which links the student to the Center and to the Secret. There are other ways of connecting, also, such as by the photograph, as this forms a psychic image which can be fitted to certain vibrational or radionic grids of energy–lines. Also, the name of the individual is an important basis for the making of these magickal connections. Lastly, the post–life association of the magician with the work of the order can be easily used to provide us with the fourth–type of gridwork for making the connective relations. So we have at least four methods of linking the member of the order to the power of the order. There are other secret methods, too, these need not be discussed. However, with each student we have at least some way of linking up with the student. This is important as in Africa, often the time of birth of the member is not known because of local customs and the lack of awareness in this area. Secondly, after the individual is connected to the system, the headquarters can control the amount of energy which is connected to the student and thus feed more and more of the power to the student as the student shows more and more capacity to handle and also manage this energy in an efficient and completely esoteric manner. As the student grows more and more in the energy and life of the order, the student is able to receive and to absorb more and more of the magickal energies which come to him from the source of the system, which are not of this universe, although the administration for this world of the order is located here. In this sense, the link to the order is extremely personal and immediate and constitutes a form of mystical guruyoga, which is totally essential to our own particular approach.

According to our teaching, the self-conscious higher self of the magician and of anyone else exists simply in a state of potency, awaiting magickal or yogic development. This development is the true actualization of the higher selfhood. However, the only certain method for this self-actualization is to participate in the magickal processes of our own system of guruyoga, which is both magickal growth and yogic development. By this means, the student is able to draw into himself, from the center of the order, or the guru, the appropriate cosmic types of energy, which are the rays of the sublime power (see the Vedic Physics papers 1, 2, and 3).

It is by this method, therefore, that the guru sends to the chela of magickal yoga all of the necessary spiritual nourishment and metaphysical enrichment, needed to become a true and completely developed yogi-magician of our magickal system. Many individuals do not realize this and falsely believe that by belonging to orders and mystical societies of various types they can be developed or actualized. This does not happen as they know, especially those who have been in the so-called Rosicrucian bodies, of which there are literally hundreds in existence, for ten or more years. They only stay there because they have not met the living guru and his power and also because of all the money spent in these orders and groups, they don't want to turn their backs on what they have invested so much in. But such is the foolish pathway of those who are too blind to see the light of the guru and thereby become free to realize the supreme energy of his being, for he is alive and filled with the divine powers and sends the rays of these powers (the same seven rays of The Monastery of which he is the inner life) to those who have given themselves totally and ultimately to his life and divine experience. So he is the living guru and the true essence of the teaching of the gnosis, which is now coming into the world and filling all space and time and the eager hearts, souls, minds, spirits, and jivas of those chelas who have given themselves to the guru.

For it is only by means of guruyoga that we can attain to a full actualization of the magickal powers of the absolute and the infinite within each and every one of ourselves. For the guru is the method and the instrument for awakening the divine realization. You do not think of the guru as an object of worship, for such an attitude is reserved only for the divine realization of the final cause of our being, but you make use of the guru as the instrument for the cosmic awakening of the magickal energy which is deep within yourself and deep within the soul of your total being and its essence. The guru is an instrument, like the magickal techniques of esoteric engineering for bringing you closer and closer to the divine realization. He is the efficient and essential means whereby the basic energies of the cosmic selfhood are awakened and the higher selfhood actualized in the life and experience of the magician. However, not all are ready for the guru.

Exercise in Guruyoga

This lesson's exercise is based upon the methods of guruyoga, or attunement to the guru. In order to do this simple exercise, you should copy out a symbol from this book or something written by him, or some reminder or symbol of him. Then you will arrange for a meditationtation to take place. You will place the symbol of the guru before you and gaze upon that symbol. You will enter deeply into the being of your guru's essence and meaning for you. How are you a part of the guru? How is the guru a part of your being? You will begin to feel the guru near you, close to you and present in spirit next to you. You will then become very receptive to the inflowing of the cosmic energy which he will send to you. You will purify yourself with light and love and total devotion to the guru, so that no foreign element, no alien influence is possible in your consciousness. Now you are totally pure and totally receptive to the cosmic energy of the guru. Now, slowly you will feel the guru sending the energies to you. Slowly and very gently they are coming to you and you are feeling them enter into your being, transforming you more and more into the perfect image of what you really want to be. You want to be the perfect chela of the guru. So the energies are coming into you and they are becoming more and more a part of you. You may begin to feel that he is trying to communicate with you, to initiate a conversation, so you may reply in thought to what he is sending to you. Slowly, you feel that the guru is there and that you are in a mystical conversation with him and that his energy is coming to you and making you more and more powerful. Now, begin to relax and come back to the ordinary world. You have had your first official experience of guruyoga and you will now send a report to Michael Bertiaux and tell him the experiences that you had. You are now on the pathway to divine realization and wholeness of being.

The Spell of Fa

The "Spell of Fa" is the name for the magickal power to be found deep within the innermost sanctuaries of our brotherhood. Fa is the Afro—Atlantean name for the essential magick of our system, which has always been there to support whatever is undertaken by true initiates of our system. It is higher than any voudoo, because the Vudu actually draw their powers from the system of The Spell of Fa. In the words of the African Master:

"Fa may be considered as probably the oldest Self—Conscious part of the Cosmic Self or Soul; but Fa is beyond any ego—type or persona, that is to say the masks of psychic energy which are worn by the voudoo gods. For Fa creates the Vudu, or the sixteen magickal units or monads, which are the Vedas of Vudu. From the Vudu, after much time has passed, come forth the powers of the voodoo and the hoodoo spirits and eventually the ego—structures of these spirits, which are the Loas of the religion of voudoo. Eventually, the ego of the initiate is created by being united to the mysteries of Fa; but Fa is before all of these things, before all this ceremonial magick in space, for Fa is the most ancient of the powers and therefore, because our order is based upon the wonders of The Spell of Fa, we possess this archetypal power as our own. You call it in your science of esoteric electrical engineering the cosmic Computer."

Now, the power which is latent in The Spell of Fa may be considered as the magickal energy which makes all experiments of our work successful. This is done by means of the four dimensions of the magickal universe, or the supremely powerful time-stations, through which the power of this Spell of Fa is inducted or allowed to manifest itself. For it should be understood that this high energy, when it enters into our own system, is to be seen as coming down and down until it reaches the individual magickal practitioner in his temple or place of work.

It began this way: Years ago, when I met the Loa Legbha, who is the chief of our magickal system of computers, and who bears a very strong physical resemblance to a certain Nigerian member of our system, it was explained to me that the Zothyrian system was a continuation of the Voudoo Esoterique system of Haiti, because they both worked with the Fa—Powers. Also, it was important for me to realize that it was necessary to feed this energy into a number of logico—magickal pipes and systems in order to make it work effectively. For it must be brought to where it was to work. Hence, our system was to be viewed as the most scientific and logical in its magick, because simply this way the way in which to work best with the energy. You had to bring it to where it could be connected to the problem, very much like bringing fuel or power in the material world to where it was to be employed. So we had to have the proper structures to bring in this energy and to employ it in the use of solving various problems. Well, we all realize that magickal problems are constantly in a state of happening. Therefore, we have to realize that these energies are to be seen as always being available. Now, the Loa Legbha is very closely identified with the magickal powers of Mercury or Hermes and thusly he operates as the Supreme Intelligence of the sign of Gemini, in the Zodiac, and therefore supports all abstract systems of magick with his powers. As a result of much work with this Master of Metamathematical Magick, who is in voudoo "The Christ of The Noonday," as well as the special protector of the work of all Neo—Pythagorean Gnosis and magickal priests, we have derived special techniques for sending down the magickal energy to the student. The Loa Legbha has graciously given to us a magickal technique for making a mandala of power, which will be the actual symbol of his presence in the living place of his follower. Therefore, this mandala, which I am to construct for each member of the Order of Legbha, is the presentation of the very powerful and truest form of The Spell of Fa in the aura of the faithful student of the system. For this reason,this mandala is a form of reserved magick, as it can only be done in the sacramental presence of Loa Legbha himself, and at the time of his greatest and most healing power, i.e., Sunday at noontime.

Once the magickal student and follower of Loa Legbha has received the keys to the innermost temple of The Logic of the Sun—Rays and has received the powers of healing and success which come from the supreme and august radiation of powers from the Spell of Fa, such a person then is magickally united to and incorporated into the terrific powers and the light which is the essence of The Spell of Fa in its inner vitality and truth. This is the magickal power and radiant truth which makes all magick work for positivity of results, rather than the negative and shadow forms of delusion, illusion, hallucination and outright madness, as is to be found in all other systems, which claim to exercise any magickal authority. That is why they are so dangerous and that is why they are so negative and eventually drive their members insane, leading them to pass their final years in asylums for those who are so deranged that they cannot function in society as whole beings, let alone as adepts in any way whatsoever. That is the danger which comes from the use of the darkness. But, in the words of the Master, we know that we are of the truth and of the light as he says: "The Rays of the Sun, which shine from the source of The Sun—Day of cosmic consciousness, perfect the soul of the initiatic priest of the light as he grows more and more deeply into the inner mysteries of The Spell of Fa. That world of light is the Divine Healing Center of the Gnosis and the radiant star, which is the Sun, is the purest and wisest manifestation, as found in the Divine Image of Legbha. Consequently, the energies are diffused through the system of interconnected magickal spheres of light, which are in themselves agencies of the ultimate dice—game of numbers, mandalas, and energy and gnosis patterns, everywhere in being."

And, again in the words of the Master, The African Priest: "At a certain time in the evolution of consciousness, it is necessary for the powers associated with our students to be brought under The Spell of Fa. Sometimes this is a violent action, which may even cause the emission of psychic chaos, but it must happen. Eventually, such students must experience more and more fire and light and power and gnosis. This can only be possible by means of their being incorporated into the consciousness of The Spell of Fa. In such an action, whatever is negative and merely mortal is left behind as far as the laws of transformative being are concerned, and what is taken up into the higher synthesis is that initiatic part of the consciousness of the student, which is pure initiation in its fullest and most profound essence. But this can only happen if the initial links are made to the logic of The Spell of Fa. These links are provided by Michael, the Teacher of our system, existing on Earth."

If the student in reading this passage from the Priestly Master wishes to enter into the gnosis more deeply, as each lesson from us is an approach to deeper and deeper initiation, then such a student may write to Michael and ask about being magickally admitted into the Brotherhood of Fa, and thusly receiving the magickal token of The Spell of Fa, which is now given out with this lesson in magickal development. The student will receive detailed explanations of the use of this symbolic machine in order to induct the current of The Spell of Fa. And as the student develops more and more awareness of the powers given in the system of The Spell of Fa, that student will be able to draw upon the powers more.

The Spell of Fa should also be seen as a way in which the individual is allowed to participate more and more in the Cosmic Computer. For example, the existence of the Cosmic Computer is one of the basic laws of our system. It has been referred to in many papers and some of the papers and lessons have been devoted to the expression of this law. Now it is important for the student to see how he is personally involved in these structures of the Cosmic Computer. For this reason, you may elect next to study the field of Esoteric Electrical Engineering as a way of increasing the magickal involvement of yourself into the system of The Spell of Fa, and also as a method of learning more and more about the connectives of the system and how they operate in relationship to the student and Michael as the middle-operator. The important law for magickal operation is to learn how the various rays of gnostic power come to each student. For they come by an interesting variety of methods. One method is given in connecting you to the system of The Spell of Fa.

There are other methods, however, which are very useful for adding to the powers of the magician. These methods have all been entrusted to our system by the Loas and by the Masters, who provide us with the magickal and noetical methods for realizing these powers in every-increasing ways. The Masters are of course those beings who dwell in remote and secret places and who work with us by means of the transmission of thoughts and telepathic magickal communication. We are connected with several of these beings. The Loas are, of course, the ancestral gods of Voudoo Science. They dwell in deeper parts of the world. For example, we can state that the Masters operate on the level of the subconscious mind, the Loas at the level of the uncon-scious mind, and the Zothyrian demi-gods and other magickal deities operate at the level of the superconscious mind, because they are connected with the future of magickal energy and its gnosis. However, each student is connected to these beings by means of membership in our gnosis. At the same time, this line of connection is made stronger and more certain by means of the various dimensions of the mind as reflecting the operations of The Cosmic Computer and The Spell of Fa. The actual connection between all of these energies and systems is to be found in the level of one's inter-action with these higher beings of mind. Through the different levels of the mind and through the magickal systems of the different time-stations and their gnostic patriarchates, or magicko-administration systems, the student can be taken more and more into the fundamental operations of The Spell of Fa as it operates everywhere.

Thus, by means of the methods of magickal creativity, the student is brought more and more into the energies and laws of the ways in which this magickal order and brotherhood makes use of the powers of both The Cosmic Computer and the laws which emanate from The Spell of Fa. The student is taken more and more into the higher regions of his own being and thusly by means of this initiation can exercise more and more power at the conscious level. These initiations are therefore connected to the time-station in order to draw in the maximum of initiatic power. As a consequence of this system of development, four specific powers, those of the unconscious, subconscious, conscious and superconscious levels of the minds are connected to the time-stations of the past, past-present, present-future, and the future. This amounts to a combination of 16 poweers, which are the Vudu Vedas of that Spell of Fa, mentioned at the very beginning of this paper. Therefore, the student will be allowed to enter into the very midst of these powers and to possess them with the fullness of his being, as the Masters and Loas, and other high brings have promised that they will provide to the student of our system. Consequently, in the development of his awareness, the student is offered this increase of magickal powers at this time, if such be his wish and desire to ascend to the higher level of the gnosis of our system.

In closing, it is important to realize that there may be systems which offer the student as much as we do, but they do not exist on this planet nor are they brought here by UFOs or by various Space-Masters. Such beings work entirely for our system and have responsibilities which concern other worlds and systems of life and thought. Our own work is with the planet Earth and with the development of the new consciousness and with the new humanity of magick. Then, eventually, after all these energies have been released, it will be possible for the magickal student of cosmic creativity to enter into the world of new energies and begin his work there. For in our system the will never ever ends and we do not want anyone who would ever wish not to be at work somewhere and somehow in the gnosis of endless possibilities.

Waiting for Purusha I

The reason this course is written more from an Indian magickal viewpoint is that recently the leading magicians in Haiti, which is the homeland of Hoodoo and Voudoo decided that Indian magick was not only more ancient in its purest form than their own magick, but also that the store of this magick which we possessed was the most powerful in the world. This is therefore the course in heavy or powerful spells which was promised in our book on "Lucky Hoodoo." Hence we can say that the lessons of Upadhis of this course are based on the original Indian magickal secrets which are in the possession of our magickal order and which have been handed down by those masters of esoteric voudoo who are also qualified as mahatmas and as yogis and rishis.

The very first thing to be taught is how to wait for the manifestation of God, or PURUSHA. This is the name of the most ideally divine power in mankind. In Judaeo-Christianity, this power is identified with the Idea of the Logos as in the philosophy of Philo and in the Gospel according to St. John. This is that aspect of The Absolute which is the storehouse of all possible being and reality. Things can come to be because of what Purusha does by willing them to be. Therefore, we realize that this NAME OF GOD is most important for getting certain magickal currents working in our direction.

Now, we ask ourselves, how is it possible to make our magickal interests and intentions know to God The Lord Purusha. The answer is very simple and it is this: we make our wishes known to the infinite by means of the appropriate form of prayer. There are several types of prayer: prayer of adoration, prayer of petition, prayer of meditation, prayer of union or love, which is called the prayer of communion, as well as many other ways of directing the prayer energy to God. However, it has to be by prayer, for mind-power without prayer to God is powerless. When Joel Goldsmith was asked by some New Thought people to lecture on the power of the mind, he told them that he couldn't, as the mind hadn't any power. New Thought is important for teaching a type of meditation, but God is the focus for getting things done, or those agents of God, e.g., angels, spirits, lesser deities, who are sent to work for God by God, or Purusha. However, as I said: mind-power without prayer to God is powerless. I did not say that there wasn't any power of the mind, as is implied by Goldsmith. I say that mind-power must also be directed towards God, or "hooked-up" to the God-Energy of Purusha, in order to work properly.

Now the most effective way to pray is by means of the rosary. I am not, however, at this time referring to the Catholic rosary. The rosary is an ancient Indian discovery. It is used by the religions of India very much: Hinduism, Buddhism, Islam, Christianity, Sikhism, Jainism, as well as the many other religions of India, for India has more religions than any other country in the world. However, they all use the rosary as their prayer-machine.

The rosary is a powerful magickal machine of prayer because it is so efficient. It has been used for counting prayers for many centuries. It is very simple to make and every student of this course must make themselves a simple rosary, as the rosary which you make is your own magickal instrument. A rosary is simply a strong string which holds a series of beads. The number of beads may vary, but the idea is always the same. It is a way of counting prayers which are offered to God one at a time. Thus, if you have a rosary which has 100 beads on it, you can offer 100 prayers to

God simply by saying the prayer and by moving your fingers along the beads as you "tell" or say the prayer, which is said over and over again. When you have reached the final bead, this means that you have said the 100th prayer and so the pattern of your offering to Purusha has been completed.

Now, you may ask, how many beads can best be put on a string to form a magickal rosary. In my view, any number between 90 and 110 seems to be best for our purposes. For the prayer should not be too long and very involved, like certain almost seemingly endless Buddhist praye exercises of a Tibetan origin, which are really much more suited to the needs of contemplative monks than those like ourselves who live in a very busy world. Also, I feel that the length of the rosary given above is really much more efficient than those many longer systems, which go on and on in endlessness, because spirituality is a matter of efficient management of God–Energy. Hence, we try by means of our magickal work to get the most effect from the least expenditure of prayer–energy. So this is perhaps the difference between magickal work and the longer and less precise methods of religious consciousness. They are valid in a sense of prayers of adorations, but we need more exact instruments. So that is they the number of beads should be fixed between 90 and 110. I think that length on a rosary works most effectively.

So the exercise with this lesson or upadhi is to make up a rosary. You may select different colors for the beads, different sizes and shapes, or you may wish to have one type of bead entirely. Actually, I have both types in my possession and I use them in different ways. You may make up as many rosaries as you wish.

The next matter is the use of the rosary. First of all, the rosary is blessed by being used. In other words, by being used many times it will store up magnetism very gradually and appear to the clairvoyant sight as being "blessed." So you do not judge a rosary as ineffective if I have not blessed it. Actually, this course is written for the magician who is rather isolated and who want to work magick effectively and with an economy of materials and outer dependencies. So your rosary will be made very effective by being used and will be powerful as a magickal machine the more that you use it.

The next matter before us will be the prayers to use to Purusha in order to make use of your rosary and to direct your intention or wish to God for His hearing. Now, if you are using a rosary the prayer should be very brief. It should last only a few seconds when it is said and you will be saying it about 100 times, so if it is not too long, you will be using more and more time. This is not necessary if you are saying a very effective prayer, briefly composed and clearly stated in what it means.

Now, in magickal prayer–work it is important to distinguish two basic components: the intention of the work and the way in which it is sent to God. First of all, we have something like:

I wish to receive that pay raise I need.

This clearly expresses the item of interest or what is sought for by the prayer of the magician. Traditionally, something like that request has been combined with a statement directed totally to the Divine Being in His Perfection, such as:

My Lord God, I adore Thee, The Giver of All

or it may be something expressed like:

My Lord Purusha, I adore Thee The God Who Gives All Good Things

We know that God gives all things, whether we like or understand them or not. They come nevertheless from Him. Also, we know that we cannot bribe God with praises and long prayers, for He transcends all of that. But, our power seems to be realized in total dependence upon the Divine. We have nothing unless it comes from God. Therefore, we can only state we need and hope that becauuse He has provided before, He will provide again. And, of course, He will, because He is the Cosmic All-Provider. In a sense, in our nothingness, in our total dependence upon God we have an identity within God, because He has built us to be this way and He will not deny what He put in us to desire or need. But we have to realize this. This is called realization or understanding of where we are in the cosmos in relation to God.

A lot of New Thought schools think just the opposite, but by doing so they really 1) block the flow of God—Energy to where they are in the cosmos and 2) delude themselves through varied and subtle forms of autohypnosis either consciously or subconsciously directed at their own mind fields. The ancient methods of India do not agree with that technique.

Therefore, as an exercise in the use of your rosary, simply create a magickal prayer which should be something that you wish done. Let it have the simple yet direct form of the following, except that you put in your request where I have indicated by means of "( )." This will be as follows:

> My Lord Purusha, I adore O God The Giver of All That I Need
> Please bring to me that ( ) which I need.

Now you can get into the habit of using your rosary and saying this magickal prayer on each bead, so that by counting the offering of this prayer to God, you are able to bring about the first step or upadhi in your realization of the spell for achieving all good things, which is known as "Waiting for Purusha." We will continue this lesson—theme in our next chapter's instruction.

Waiting for Purusha II

There are many ways in which the magickal rosary can be used. Each magician can perhaps devise several methods, each particular to a special project, whereby he is able to bring about the total realization of all his wishes. In this lesson, we wish you to have a few more interesting ideas and methods so that you will be able to see the rosary as a deeper and actually more and more powerful magickal instrument.

This method for realizing the power of Purusha will be based upon the use of 98 of the beads. The reason we have arrived at this figure is simple because we will be at work with fourteen major archetypes arranged in seven groups. Fourteen times seven equals ninety-eight. The reason we are using these archetypes is because students find it rather difficult to attend to the repetition of some prayer without some degree of variety. On the other hand, the use of the archetypes is to add magickal power to what we are doing.

In the temple of my home, where I do my magickal work and where the initiations, both high and ultra-powerful as well as medium or moderate in power are given, I have a set of 14 magickal paintings, some of which you may have seen in those books of Kenneth Grant which have something to say about what I am doing in the field of magickal study. Now, these 14 magickal paintings are of the fourteen magickal archetypes of our order and they represent the ultimate forms of representation, beyond which there cannot be any representation of archetypal energy. Each one of the fourteen radiates out its own field of energy, which by tantric law is incomplete without the energy of its balance, or mate, which is what the gnostics call the law of syzygy. So we can say that there are seven ultimate syzygies, which give off the seven rays of the gnosis, about which and with which I wrote those courses as both Michael Capricorn and Michael Aquarius, my two magickal personalities. Now, over the years, I have discovered that each one of these archetypes represents a definite sector of the gnostic universe and that together they represent the completeness of that gnostic universe. So that making use of all of them in some way is really a way of achieving a synthesis of the supreme magickal power, which is what we might call The Absolute Science. It took me a while to see the need to have the seven in their present and painted form, because I did not originally feel the need to have icons of all of these archetypes and archetypal powers. Rather I thought that their abstract concept was really quite sufficient.

However, because I have Mercury in Aquarius and a very strong Uranus, I also held an experimental attitude towards the whole matter and let them tell me what they wanted done or to happen. That is really the best attitude. So very gradually the "host of heaven" gradually was built up as fourteen archetypal paintings serving to represent the energies of the gnostic seven rays of our magickal system. I am saying all of this because the best attitude in magickal work is openminded and experimental, rather than closed-minded, dogmatic, and self-limited. You can be these other matters in magickal procedure, but in theory, it is best to be open. The next thing that I discovered was that these energies represent the powers which feed into the vast and magickal computer of our research work as gnostics. So, in a deep sense, the icons of the archetypes inspired me quite a lot and in a sense they fed magickal energies into my own specialized work. The reason I am saying this is to show that there exists a kind of cosmic hook up between the gnostic archetypes, their icons, my work, the initiations which I give and thereby transfer Ojas from the archetypes to the candidates, and that the members of the order can participate in this energy field by making use of the rosary exercise of 98 units. In other lessons, I will want to talk about the other ways of drawing down or into your work of this archetypal power. So even a student living out at a very great distance from our center of operations can make use of the very profound magickal field which permeates the whole order. By means of your rosary you can draw upon this magickal energy and bring it into your field of action.

It is very important to see all magical activity as part of a mystical field. We are all working together even though we have isolated brothers in Africa, Asia, Europe, South America, which I may perhaps never see in the physical body. Yet, they are all parts of this one field of gnostic magickal activity, or the supreme continuum of light. And, so it is that by making use of the archetypal energies in the saying of one's magickal rosary that one realizes more and more that one is part of the whole pattern and that one is interacting with all of the brothers, even though we are widely separated. I think this is an ideal behind all valid magickal orders. Now, I want to talk about the archetypes in a very specific and exact manner and show you how to make fruitful use of them.

As regards these magicko-gnostic archetypes, whose icons adorn the walls of the temple of the inner retreat, let me say that while there are 14 of them, divided into seven male and seven female god-energies, they are arranged in four groups. These groups serve as frames of reference for the four types of magickal activity associated with our system. The first group is that of the three basic Voudoo-gnostic archetypes: the male archetypes Legbha and Ghuedhe, and the female archetype Macanda. Voudoo archetypes are extremely essential to our work because of the fact that our system is partially rooted in the ancient esotericism and magickal experiences of Afro-Latinate gnosis, as found in the Haitian Secret Scoeities of Sorcerors. The next group of archetypes are the three goddesses of time-travel. So we have three female archetypes for the past, the present, and the future. In a sense, the magickal mastery of time as a contiuum is a supreme accomplishment of the veritable magick of gnostic physics. These archetypes serve to indicate our concepts of time, but as the energies which are latent in thinking about time. For any such thoughts can generate an energy field for magickal purposes. Next, we have the icons of the field of archetypes of Zothyrian (gnostic) metapsychology. This is another one of our foundation sources, because both from Voudoo and Gnosticism have we been able to develop our present research program. There are four icons in this section and four ways of drawing in the magickal energies. The first archetype is that of the Aeon, known as Aiwaz-Zothyrius, a masculine icon, having to represent the evolutionary pattern of energy. Next, we have the icon of the archetype of the transcendental-id, the deep and never-ending source of creative energy. This archetype is masculine, but has a feminine aspect. The next icon represents the Daemon known as Choronzon, the patron and protection energy behind our magickal society of the "Choronzon Club." This icon may be used for a variety of energies, especially those found in so-called black magick. It is a power field for occult physics. Lastly, we have our female archetype of the anima, which serves to represent the sexual polarity of the uncon-scious and the subconscious mind. The final group of icons describe the archetypes of elemental sorcery, which are the most fundamental sources of our power. These are the masculine archetypes of Capricorn, the female Deep One, which represents elemental water, the masculine Fire elemental God, and finally the purely Elemental Gate, which is feminine. These fourteen powers will be explored in our next lessons, but the for moment I want to introduce them to you and show you how to use them as magickal names or words of mantric power.

The first thing to do is to list them as follows: Legbha, Macanda, Ghuedhe, Past, Present, Future, Aeon Aiwaz–Zothyrius, Transcendental–Id, Daemon Choronzon, Anima, Capricorn, The Deep One, Fire God, and, lastly, The Elemental Gate. Now in the process of telling or saying each one of the beads on the magickal rosary, it is important to associate each name with a bead. This builds up its location or magickal situs. Likewise, it is very important to feel the rhythm and magickal power of these names as they are used. Hence, by using the prayer in the previous lesson, but by substituting the names given above you now have fourteen magickal prayers to be used for a variety of purposes. Also, you can now begin to make use of the idea by making very specific the energies, with which you are working. This may be called "pinpointing" the magickal energy. In order to do this, all you have to do is combine the bead, or magickal space, with the name of the archetype, with, lastly, the form of the prayer, expressing a specific intent. It is in this way that we are able to use magickal energies in a very careful and exact way, while being absolutely simple in our approach. For complexity is built up out of the simplest elements.

What you should then do is to experiment with a number of prayer–types. You have a wide range of fourteen particular intentions to make use of, as we have fourteen archetypes to draw upon in our magickal reservoir of power. I am going to feature each one of the icons as the subject of a magickal lesson all its own for deeper analysis. But, in this lesson what I want to do is to bring in the basic idea of working with the archetypal energy and making use of the rosary as your way of measuring the energy. Also, you have here an opportunity to devise a few magickal prayers of your own, making use of the power of the archetypal name to back up your efforts.

Based on "Les Vudu: La Creation Mystique Des Songes" par Luc Guzotte

La Deesse L'Ouvriere de Demi—Jour

Among the followers of esoteric voudoo, one can find the adherents of the Cat Goddess, whose cultus is undoubtedly derived from French and Afro—Egyptian sources. This goddess is one entirely devoted to the magickal sequence of energies as they manifest in events and appears to be responsible for connecting those who have a shared karma. The name of this Mystere, Twilight Worker, is particularly significant because of the nature of the work or karma involved in the energies between the persons as well as the very important place that this time of day occupies in the economy of the gods.

In astrology, this goddess manifests in the relations of Sun—Saturn opposition (180o) and in Sun—Sun inconjunction (150o). To this very basic structure, She adds other interesting magickal energies as they manifest among planetary synastry, until the total picture emerges. To a certain extent, this goddess is identified with the constellatio of Leo, and to that part of Leo which, because it is closest to Virgo (the sign which rules most cats), may be unmistakably identified as the House of the Cats of the Twilight.

The goddess will first reveal herself in a dream where she will speak directly to the mage, giving her name, in response to his expression of affectionate curiosity. Immediately after, there will appear to be some confusion over whether or not the magician is to receive a cat from someone he knows. However, the magickal forces do not act usually at such a level, and they seem to prefer attention to be drawn to the magician's own being. It is usually that the magician is in need of some person and the goddess, being well aware of this, has first to initiate a number of contents which adhere to the astrological energies and powers already in operation. The magician has only to continue to meditate on the goddess as she first revealed herself to him, in order to sustain from his side the beauty of the spell. Since this is a generous goddess, her points—chauds take the form or symbolism of gift giving.

So it is that usually she will manifest her shakti in the form of some occasion such as the magician's birthday, for bringing into the magician's life, the energies and person whose link to the magician is now ready to be connected. The magician will be able to recognize the operation of this goddess because of the cat—lion symbolism, the gift—symbolism, and the necessity of the entire initial encounter. After this has happened, the natural laws of astrological karma carry out the energy of the work and thusly bring into focus the powers which were just below the surface of consciousness, at the time of the dream about the goddess, where she was met for the first time.

This goddess is to be identified with the bringing of good things into the life of those who cultivate her. Her statue, which is identical with that of the Egyptian cat-goddess Basht, should be displayed and placed in a space of reverence, with tenderness and much devotion. She is the goddess of magickal gardens, especially gardens which magicians grow for magickal purposes. She attends the Divine Mother at all times, and has been understood as a messenger of the Divine Mother. Magickal research and the use of oracles are under protection and inspiration as would be inspirational painting. All cats are sacred to her, for each one of them is a messenger of the Divine Mother. She is also the goddess of a certain type of witchcraft, which has to do with lunar inspiration. She is the goddess of the Full Moon and also the mystere which indwells the holy water which is ritually prepared at the Full Moon. Wherever there is a painting of the Moon or whenever a painting is done by a magician showing the Moon, she will send to that icon her point—chaud or kala of divine shakti, thereby making the painting into a magickal machine for inducting divine energies. Persons of highly sensitive temperaments, such as artists, frequently pray to her to bring them lovers of the same personality type. Her magickal image or vever is designed to draw in her powers so that her presence like a mystical cloud permeates the space of all that surrounds it. Ideally, her priests fast in her honor twice a week. This is because of gracious generosity, whereby she gives so many powers and energies that the magician has to receive into himself these powers and rest on the fast days and reflect upon all the good things, foods, creativities, gifts, inspirations, love affairs, etc., which she has given to him. So the magickal feast, which is a ritual in itself, is a fast of both the body and the soul and the spirit.

The Magickal Ritual of the Goddess

In order to invoke the power (shakti) of this goddess, the magician will sit in a yoga posture with crossed legs. The magickal partner should sit on the crossed legs of the magician, facing the magician. Eye to eye contact is important for the realization of the power zone. This procedure is entirely Tantric also, since the goddess will be realized in the magickal intensity of eye contact, from which the stream of images will flow, whereby the magician will be able to receive what he wishes. A mandala should be created which will grow into an akashic bubble, containng all of the tattwas. The magician may build up points of heat in the north, west, south, and east, and his partner may build up the points of shakti (points--chauds) in the north—east, north—west, south—west, and south—east. Images and magickal words will rise in the shared consciousness of the two magi, as the heat builds up, whereby gods, tattwas, rays, energies, levels of Ojas, and kalas, all may be assigned to these points. As the energy builds up, the flow of the power, the secretions of the Cat—Mother, the exotic substances of Her body will fill the akashic bubble, causing an incredible pressure to force the Cat—Goddess to manifest Herself and Her gifts. Gradually, the Divine Cat Lust will manifest itself, and erotic actions both violent and tender may be expected to possess the bodies of the magi. The union of shakti and shakti may be realized as the intensification of Self—Power. Whatever else happens in the ritual will be determined by the receptivity of the practitioners. The temple may be closed through the temple sleep, whereby the energies gently seep away into the ethers and subtle planes of being. For the work of the Cat Mother Goddess has been accomplished in the transformation of this simple rite.

How the Guzzotte Outlines Came To Be Written
Luc Guzzotte (or Guzotte) provided me with these materials from the same sources which he used in the construction of his book "Les vudu: Le creation mystique des songes." He wrote his book on voudoo while he worked in New York City as an assistant to a kind of psychoanalyst and then he later returned to Haiti and was initiated into the mysteries in the area near to Leogane. His approach is that of both depth psychology and the occult or esoteric and his thesis, which he develops along psycho-analytic and initiatic lines, is that Les Mysteres, or the Loa, the "Les Vudu" of the title of his book are cosmic reifications of sexual fantasy as well as archetypal erotic companions and connections. Rather than being mere creations of human wish-fulfillment, they are root powers which lead us by erotic imagination to their existence and powers.

While working in New York and especially while riding the "subways," the author would develop sexual fantasies about each person he saw. He would then use these bi-sexual fantasies in a magickal way, as inner images of occult powers. These erotic images would function like tattwa symbols, for opening up consciousness to the deepest layers of the ultra-libido substratum. Rather than spell-binding the persons seen via these fantasies, the author was able to use the images to trap and hold invisible and psychic energies and powers. As a consequence, he developed remarkable insight into the psychic basis of Voudooism. Later on, he developed a method of "dream-control" whereby the images from the daydreams becamse helpers in his visits to other realms of occult power.

While he departed more and more from orthodox and Freudian "repression mechanisms," his development of the "Eros of Les Loa" brought him closer and close to magickal and mystical experiences, which involved the subtle bodies of "Les Vudu," the archetypal shaktis and kalas of cosmic awareness and power. This magickal book, which that is what it is, discusses step by step the "processus" of becoming both a mystic and a "magician" within such a context.

Gradually, the author abandons both western psychology and even Tantric thought, and under the mentorship of a magician in Haiti, he enters more and more deeply into his "analyse-du-soi" (Self-analysis), along the lines of Voudooist states of both possession and magickal obsession. He cites parallels, for example, in the Jungian complexes and the voudooist "points-chauds." Jungian experiences with "active imagination" are seen as indicators of "Voudooist Visions," which combine with the author's own experiences in order to guide the reader deeper and deeper into the world of magickal dreaming. The author maintains that the process of consciousness moving from daydreaming (les reves) to the visions of night dreams (les songes) is itself a voyage of magickal dreams, whereby we can see both reves and songes as simply different aspects of the same sensual reality (Les Vudu). This book, which is not available outside of Haiti, because of censorship, is to be recommended for those interested in the psychoanalysis of Voudoo and has especially good sections on the methodologies and metapsychologies of secret societies and the more extreme types of the Loa. These papers are based on my own private notes.

Guzotte Exercise in Kama-Projection No. 1
In order to "get into" the spell-binding techniques of the Guzotte Outlines, you will

first of all have to learn how to project Kama, or magickal lust. Kama must not be confused with Ojas, for the latter is a magickal power, existing at several levels, which makes certain things happen. It is magickal fuel. Kama is the way in which Ojas manifests itself through erotic intensity. To begin with, you have to think of yourself as in the center of a space surrounded by as many possible objects of sexual desire as you wish. Then, you will think of there being lines of connection between thse objects of lust and your eyes and imagination. These lines will serve to transmit the rays of Kama to the objects of your erotic desire. The next thing you must do is to begin to send out feelings of Kama to each of these objects. Begin with one and move on to all of the objects. Take your time and do not omit any object you have imagined surrounding you in this lust–space. This exercise will take a long time and forms a very intense type of meditation, because you really must send off lots and lots of psychic force to the objects in order to sustain the field of Kama everywhere equally. The lust–power must be properly and equally distributed everywhere in the field or space of lust (Kama–Mandala). Next, within this field, which should have a certain sparkling quality from the energies which are glowing from the sexual radioactivity, you will begin to make contact with the whole universe. You will imagine the whole universe as a person who now comes and serves you as a kind of sexual slave. This being contains within himself or herself all of the powers of the universe. They will be released through a certain type of erotic game–playing, whereby one power at a time will be yielded to you as a result of certain sexual things you will be doing to the world. According to this Kama magick, the problems of the world are due to a lack of erotic consciousness and therefore erotic fantasies and acting must bring magickal harmony to the world.

Next, you will command the magickal sexual partner to give you various mystical secrets. This is accomplished by visualizing a particular type of sexual action as equivalent to a particular sexual secret or point–chaud or kala. Thus, a certain type of oral and genital activity will release specific magickal secrets which relate to a specific range of magickal points–chauds or kalas. The more intense your visualization power works, the more power you will get from the gods of voudoo. Also, you may feel in the mood to create magickal beings or discover them by letting your fantasies roam very freely in the manifold realms of sexual imagination.

The basic unit for this magickal operation, which is what you initially built up, is a bubble of pure Kama. These are the UFOs, which are cited in the earliest Monastery papers as being globules of sexual radioactivity. A working definition of sexual radioactivity might be that it is the perfect union of Kama and Ojas in action. The whole universe is composed of lust–forces, at various levels of manifestation. You can also call this Ojas or shakti, for seen from other perspectives this is what the magicko–metaphysician may understand the universe to made up of fundamentally. Now, to close down your temple you do not have to do anything but let it float away into the ethers. With these Guzotte exercises, we do not use closing rituals and banishings, because the space of the sexual magickal working is not alien to the rest of the universe, rather, it is the purest form of the rest of the universe. So, forget all that old aeon precautionary magick and let yourself be totally at ease with the fundamental lust powers present at all places in the infinite space of the cosmos.

The Theogony of the Points-Chauds

The bi-sexuality of the system of esoteric Voudoo, as embodied in the system of La Couleuvre Noire presupposes the classical gnosticism of a fourfold structure of sexo-magickal operations. There will always be the need to recognize the foundations, the deductions, the experimentations, and the projections of sexual magick. And while in the Monastery papers (second year course) these principles have been explicated to a certain degree, in his book on "Les Vudu," Luc Guzotte extends the frontiers of the esotericist to newer forms of gnostic-magickal creativity. He teaches certain principles which go far beyond the more basic levels of the metaphysics.

The magickal generation of the Hot-Points of Les Vudu results in the posession by the magician of the fundamental system of powers. These are 336 in number being the basic 16 axioms and the 64 magickal interpretations plus the 256 amplifications or "proofs of esoteric logic." Each magician has to have inducted into his system of magickal operations (his body and invisible bodies) each one of these powers if he is to function completely as a Vudu-gnostic magician. Guzotte by means of special initiations which he received in the esoteric times-lines of Vudu sexo-magickal operations has developed a special technique whereby these hot-points are given more easily and more efficiently than has been traditionally understood.

I must caution the student, however, not to think that there has been a discovery of something. What is presented in the system of "Les Vudu" is totally a part of the general gnostic and magickal tradition of Vudu esotericism. However, Guzotte's development has been a modern psychology of initiation-physics, whereby the energies have been understood as interactive processes involving the initiate and the initiateur. Another method of this development has been the magickal explorations in "Vudotronics" as they have been applied to dream-control (the actual source of "Les Vudu") and to the creation of those biquintile magickal experiments, out of which arise the "presentments" of the inner system of "Les Vudu" as embodied in the hierarchy, both physical and invisible, of La Couleuvre Noire.

In fact, it is the magickal interactions of these "presentments," that we are able to find the roots of both Guzotte's theogony (i.e., theurgical genesis) of the hot-points, as well as the matrix from which the instruments of the body of the initiate-initiateur "interactions" emerge in the processes of "Vudotronics," resulting in the unmistakably esoteric logics of a hyper-gnosis.

For it is these principles of "Les Vudu" known as "presentments" (Les Presentements), that we find the derivation of the entire system of magickal interactions. This can be verified from the bi-quintility of the research process, because in my own magickal experience, it was from the "presentments" that the process of structuring by means of a magickal logic the Points-Chauds, in my own magickal development, had its theurgical genesis.

Hence, the magician who is a seeker after the development of these points of power can understand the importance of the entire psychological process of Guzotte and at the same time realize that this process does not depart from the categorial frameworks of the traditional LCN level of operation. In actual fact, the Guzotte system is an application of the tradition.

If we return to these "presentments" we find that they exist in a subtle range of magickal space, associated by logical connections with the hyper-gnostic realms of magicko–Vudu amplification. since all is energy, i.e., the primordial Shakti, the magician will see these "presentments" as the fundamental data of his encounter experiences with the body of the initiate–initiateur. These encounters, which generate their own logics and patterns of magickal transformation, must be understood as the contexts and as the actual situations for the diffusion of the "presentments." And it is in these areas of magickal diffusion that we find the fundamental keys to the most intense forms of Vudu initiation.

Finally, since every system of initiation–physics must maintain its own awareness, and especially in the case of "Les Vudu" the context of its situations, the genesis of the "presentments" can be understood to be an invariable effect of the proper causation. In these circumstances, therefore, the context of the system will manifest the approaches to the hyper–gnostic realm, which are revealed in the esoteric logic of sensuous intensity whereby the "presentments" as in the inner work of La Couleuvre Noire are unfolded as the uninterpreted sources of "Les Vudu" as Les-Points–chauds. As a consequence, the interactive pattern (which Guzotte refers to as "The Leogane Work") gives us the raw empirical and contentual formularies of the hot–points as images or as data, and in every circumstance they are truly "given" by the context, which Guzotte calls the "hunt." For by finding they are discovered to be in a process of development. And as the magician seeks more and more to unfold them, he is guided by the archetypal system of the LCN gnosis, and sees these elements of magickal transformation in both their erotic and ideal components. The situation is therefore known as "real" and the pheonismes (Guzotte's term for "presentments" communicating initiatic energies), which are the most intense embodiments of these "presentments" provide the magician with the most exacting methods for achieving the powers desired in "Les Vudu."

We can say that "Les Vudu" interact with the body by means of these "presentments" which when developed become "hot–points," if and only if these "presentments" can be viewed or understood, by means of the esoteric logic of the body, as Pheonismes. When this is achieved, then the "points–chauds" are known as generated and can be mapped out in the various "power zones" or "marmas" of the body in question. But these Pheonismes must be actualized and only the keys to the process of "Les Vudu" will allow this manifestation to happen, whereby the magician realizes what is happening to him in his process of self–pheonism.

Therefore, Guzotte's methodology can be understood as an entirely exacting pattern of inductive awareness, whereby the Points–Chauds are manifested in an experiential and in a gnostico–biquintile manner. It is essentially a matter of the secrets of La Couleuvre Noire, formally only potentially manifest. Those who enter the context of this actualization will know from the secrets of the "presentments," what is happening to them. According to Guzotte, only certain magicians will be able to understand and even know what this is.

Presentments and Pheonismes of the Present Time-Station

While the modern advancements of pisonics instruments are not widely used in the centers of La Couleuvre Noire work in Haiti, the main structures of the gnostic logics of the Time-Stations are used by high priests, seeking to carry out their research programs. As it is known, there are four time-stations in this system. These are hyperspatial and gnostico-logical sources of power. While it is true that by means of psionics mechanisms we can develop projections of these sources of power, in the Esoteric Voudoo of the LCN, in Leogane, these systems would be represented by sexo-magickal bodywork. And while the advancements made in the field of Vudotronics are employed in connection with the transformations of both initiation physics and work with the nine magickal bodies, in the Leogane mode of operations, the ritual presentation of these energies in the pure space of the magickal encounter between the bodies is also the space system wherein the Time-Stations are able to manifest themselves.

Suffice it to say that there exist four areas of gnostic logic, which forming the hyper logical realm of the gnosis contain the manifold processes of the most esoteric forms of magickal initiation. And it is in these regions of logical structure that both the ideal and real "presentments" and Pheonismes of the Esoteric Logic are manifested. For by the act of turning the Field of the Present Time-Station "on," by this simple activity, the energies of manifestation can be manifested. The lesser energy field, however, must in this case "turn on" the more comprehensive. There must always be a magickal test built into the processes of the logical structures of Time-Stations, which allow for the fact of the magickal "tuning and turning on" of the system, by the body work of the datum. If this does not happen, then the system of "presentments" and "Pheonismes" will not be able to manifest themselves collectively as an integral logic.

Consequently, the magicians strive to develop a primary or preliminary magickal field of their own efforts before seeking any type of initiation physics, so that the initial experience of the Time-Station in action will be allowed. The candidate must be accepted by the logic of the system. The candidate must cause the system to notice his energy field. When this happens, of course, the system can operate. However, the system can only operate with a like-type of energy field.

The observer might add that this appears to resemble the process in physics where one energy field causes the reactions of another. This is especially true because the field of the intiation physics is a field of radioactive energies of the most productive type and also that this field manifests itself througgh two forms: those events which are "presentments" and those which are "Pheonismes." This is the way the logic of the field works itself into manifestation.

But this is entirely within the more general gnostic field of the Present Time Station, which extending from 1o of Scorpio, embraces the fields of Sagittarius, Capricorn, to the final degree of Aquarius. Here, we are not referring to the astrological Zodiac, but to logical energies, which are symbolized by means of Zodiacal patterns. However, in the need to focus upon the dynamics of the present, we are able to enter into certain aspects of the present which are beyond the sense of the "Now." By this I mean that there exists certain initiatic dimensions of the Present time Station, which are not to be viewed as merely present time, but present time in its fuller sense. This would be the time of the present of the alternative universes. There are those ranges of the present which are not "given" in this universe in its manifold forms. These initiatic universes might be considered the placements for the images of those "presentments" which come through during the magickal operations of this field.

However, they may also be the loci for the "Vudu," whose expression is to be found in the magickal actualizations of the Pheonismes. For such a magickal program, we can state that the powers come from the present aspect of the total system. This is because the work is done in the present, as the body work of gnostic sexo—magickal transformation is not a species of Time—Travel, at this point of the development. Also, we may state that the energies which come through in manifestation as "presentments" and which are the subjects of acts of actual communication—energy as Pheonismes, these energies are those of "Les Vudus." This is one of the most important points which the work of La Couleuvre Noire seeks to make.

Aside from the actualization patterns of the present, of which there may be simply three in any logical system, there are the power projections of the body work, which are the direct lineages and power—lines from which the powers manifested by "Les Vudu" are observed. The actual number of these sources must be seen within context, but it is likely that these are the same in number as the fundamental axioms of the Points—Chauds system of logic. In the system of Vudotronics, as worked in the jurisdiction of this writer, the number is eight but is amplified by basic logical processes to manifest (by modification in relation to either induction or broadcasting) the basic 16 logical forms of IFA.

What is essentially significant here, however, is that the fundamental energies operate within a logical schematism, which is derived from a parallel part of the gnostic continuu, of esoteric engineering. Also, it is important to understand that the basic ideas behind the logical system can be applied in practically any context of initiatic physics. When this happens the basic laws and patterns of the system develop themselves in terms of a new application.

The magician then can see how it is that from the time—stream of "turned on" Points—Chauds, we are able to connect new contents to the system. Like is attracted to like. As this happens the energies of the system are mysteriously linked up at the root of the process, which would have to be the fundamental level of magickal analysis. When this happens we can see how a new member of the outer experience of the LCN computer—system is gradually admitted into the inner Legbha goemetry of the hyperspatial Time Stations and gnostic logics, through which at their archetypal and most divine level "Les Vudu" operate. We can say that a new member is admitted to a magickal order because the system has been attracted to him in view of the magickal field which has recognized some magickal component existing there, which beholden to the memory bank of "Les Vudu" belongs in the system of the esoteric LCN. The manifestations of both "presentments" and Les Pheonismes both confirm this connection, which the logic of the system then accepts as a proper component within the esoteric structure of the Present Time Field.

The Biquintility of Les Pheonismes

The patterns of biquintility in the Guzotte system of the Gnosis are based upon the idea of the astrological biquintile relationship of 144o. However, in this sense, the idea is not one of measurement, rather it is one of creative pattern. This pattern is given so that certain magickal laws may be manifested in the experience of the magician as he comes to terms with the gnostic environment.

The Masters of the Order of LCN, who exist in the higher gnostic realm of the fourfold Time-Stations Logics, have created an esoteric pattern of magickal relationships into which the candidate for the high-priesthood must be inducted at the point of his inner reception. By this means it is necessary for the magicians to create a certain response in the intelligence systems of the Pheonismes, whereby the higher logics can send their radiations to the candidate for the high priesthood. For it is essential in this system that there be many levels of response and interaction, so that the lattices of the "Les Vudu" can be manifested.

In the Guzotte system of Gnostic Magick, the higher worlds of beings are entirely given to the structures of magickal logics. These logics make it possible for the entire system to function as a continuum of interactions. In my own work in Vudotronics and in my work with the magickal computer-logics of Time-Travel, I have verified continually the absolute necessity for the operations "according to the laws of magicko-gnostic logic" of the higher realm. In this sense, all of the magickal systems of gnostic logic are made available to the appropriate candidate to be received into the system. In this way, therefore, the laws of biquintility are seen as methods of operating and inducting the magician into the system. The candidate for initiation will be biquintile to the magickal logics of his initiateur.

These magickal logics manifest themselves then as Pheonismes because they are intelligences, deeply rooted in the magickal continum of the Legbha Gnosis. At certain points in the process, and sometimes by the operations of mystical genetics alone and the many experiments of this field, radiations of a biquintile character will be projected at the field of the initiate in order to draw his Luage field deeper into the Legbha Gnosis. When this happens there appears to be a tranformation of the candidate into an ideal Luage-Field, by means of the intensities of the Legbha Gnosis, which makes use of the Pheonismes as its magickal agents. When this happens the candidate for the magickal term of esoteric logic (which refers to the interior development of the Higher Gnostic Luage as the personal realm of the candidate) becomes more and more identified with the acts of the Pheonismes and thereby allows his being to become an ideal substance or an individuated function of the Legbha Continuum. While religious literature in its mystical phase hints about this development of the powers, in the Guzotte system of magick it can be examined exactly.

The magicians of this system have been aware for a very long time of the higher energies which the biquintile operations of the Pheonismes implicate in their "realizations," or actual manifestations in the initiation process. As long as the magician has certain types of ideas in his borderline consciousness (between the ego and the id) that magician can manifest himself as capable of actualization of these energies. But if these ideas are lost they must be restored by means of further identification with the initiateur as the representative of the Legbha Continuum. Further, if these powers persist in the deep risklessness of the continuum of gnostic magick, then the candidate may arise to a certain level of open awareness with the totality of his being and find the master who is to give him all of the keys to the system. This master would be the most personal aspect of the Gnostic Continuum, i.e., the Pheonisme of Legbha.

Consequently, as the magicians develop more and more deeply their capapcity to make the bridge between themselves and Les Pheonismes more and more an ideal biquintile, the Gnostic Being of "Les Vudu" will draw closer and closer to what they are doing and to what they wish to be in their deepest sense. When this happens there is an opening in the "Head" of the intitiate–continuum, into which the powers of "Les Vudu" as actual Points–Chauds with pheonistic personae descend. When this happens, the initiate will automatically respond, according to the laws of initiatic physics, by transcending the various energies and attain to the Luage state in a total synthesis of all magickal emotions.

In the Guzotte Gnosis, which is the Pheonistic Continuu, of the initiatic work of La Couleuvre Noire, the time for the manifestation of the powers of the Legbha Gnosis as the ongoing lifestream of self–actualization by "Les Vudu" has come. There will be certain persons who must react to the fields of this system in an unmistakeable way. They will be chosen by "Les Vudu" for membership in this wider logic. But this number will never be very large. Rather it will remain one of the secrets of the earth. In this process, the categories will unfold and manifest themselves as patterns of both initiation–self discovery and initiation–attainment of gnostic powers. But this will only happen to those who are ready for it and who belong to it already by a natural link.

The actualization of this link will be in the magickal lifestream that these magicians have sought out. It cannot be mistaken for there will be too many magickal and gnostic symbols pointing the way.

However, in this Guzotte Gnosis, the magicians will realize their aloneness and also their separateness from the energies of other systems, which will always appear to be fundamentally simplistic by comparison to this wider gnosis. However, inasmuch as the student of the gnosis seeks to realize the full range of Les Pheonismes, that same magician will realize the wider range of "Les Vudu" because only by means of this method do "Les Vudu" send concrete radiations and emanations from the Higher Gnostic Realm. For this reason, the magician will seek by means of all of the magickal techniques of this system to enter more and more into the lifestream of this Legbha Gnosis and come to some appreciation of the possibilities, which the wider gnosis allows in his own level of gnostic awakening. When he realizes this truth he will see all else as the views of so many children, valid no doubt in their own sphere however limited it might be, but very limited and lacking that developmental continuity which marks the genuine gnostic magick and its esoteric logic as distinct from all others. He will then see the necessity for the manifestation of the Legbha Gnosis of "Les Vudu" in the biquintility of Les Pheonismes or he will remain blind to the lifestream of this power forever.

Pheonismes as Vehicles of Ojas

Ojas is the ultimate magickal power and by means of this power worlds come into manifestation. Ojas is the most complex of all energies because it is entirely causal, thus Ojas is the ultimate form of consciousness-energy manifested in the world and by this means of Ojas, the human species can evolve beyond the present levels of limitation. However, Ojas is produced by magickal methods, while at the same time being entirely of another causal order than the effects of the space-time world. Ojas under such circumstances is therefore the product of laws outside of causation which are nevertheless causal in their own way. Like synchronicity, Ojas makes us think beyond the given. Pheonismes are vehicles of Ojas because in the realm of magickal body-work, it is very necessary to think of just what the Pheonismes do in their gnostic patterns of energy. They convey Ojas. They contain Ojas, in several of its subtle forms (of which there are 16). They are forms of self-conscious Ojas. To communicate with a Pheonisme is to communicate with Ojas.

The Masters of Magick, who are the guardians of the system of the LCN, and who are in the most basic sense identified with the consciousness-energy of the planets Uranus, Neptune, and Pluto, control the magickal administration of Ojas. They are able to control this system because they possess the magicko-gnostic methods whereby Ojas is released. Also, these same Masters of Magick, who are identified with the Legbha Projective Geometry and its Hyper Logic, know where the supply of Ojas comes from. It comes from the Higher Gnosic Realm. Then it is inducted into the world of magickal occasions and then it is allowed to emanate into the various initiatic levels of consciousness. There it causes certain things to happen, which are sought by some level of the world-mind.

In the Guzotte system, Les Pheonismes serve as the magickal vehicles of Ojas in the work which is done with "Les Vudu." The magicians of this system have therefore a direct link to the operations of Ojas as long as they follow the "turn on" rules of initiatic physics. Consequently, it is important for the magician to know what these rules are even though these rules are simply "ideas" in the mind of the initiateur of the structures.

Certain magicians, however, have not wished to follows these "ideas" which they have judged to be contrary to their own sexo-magickal history. They have rejected the system of the LCN because they viewed it as "perverted" and "unnatural." While they are quite free to do so, their supply of Ojas dried up, they became magickally empty. All their work ended in magickal failure. The reason being that they did not give themselves with total obedience to the Masters of Magick and to the Initiateur of the LCN system. It was by this means that Guzotte describes the separation of certain magicians from the LCN system of work. For those magicians were not willing to work within the system of LCN, they even wished to modify its rules and patterns by the imposition of patterns of magickal development from other countries. Now they are nowhere, because their source of magickal energy has dried up. Let them try to see if the work they are doing now, which is a method which rejects the structures of LCN sexo-magickal gnosis, let them try to see, I repeat, if they will ever find any powers. On the other hand, the energies of our system continue to flow along in our business (the business of "Les Vudu") as usual attitude.

Each Pheonisme is a vehicle of Ojas because each Pheonisme is a fusion of both the ideas of real and ideal substances. I would suppose that the Pheonisme is initially manifested as an ideal substance and subject to all of the gnostic logics of that level of reality. But when it enters into the world of being in space and time, by interacting in the body work and turn ons of the Vudotronic mathesis, it takes on a real substance of pure energy. Under such circumstances, therefore, it is viewed and to be viewed as a fusion of two extremely powerful levels of existence.

This means that there is an ideal form of Ojas, which is generated by esoteric logic and there is a real form of Ojas which is generated by esoteric logic and there is a real form of Ojas which is generated by initiatic encounters and body work using the world of space and time. The ideal form of Ojas is the magickal energy of Gnostic Hyperspatiality. For there is an energy which is generated when gnostic logic is "done." Also, in certain circumstances, outside of the Vudotronic context, there are specific areas of magickal interaction, where by means of esoteric logic, and ideal form of Ojas is inducted by measurements and methods outside of the Guzotte system but not in any sense outside of the work of La Couleuvre Noire. When this happens, it is possible to receive Ojas in a form which is free of any real substance. But that method, which is rooted in the Zothyrian magickal gnosis is not a part of the Vudotronic system. So we can say that the initiations of the Guzotte patterns and structures are themselves a form or fusion of both real and ideal components. In each case, the initiation of the magician into the system of "Les Vudu" presupposes the induction of Ojas by means of the manifold proliferation of the Pheonismes. For these Pheonismes appear to be in every place and manifesting at every and all times. The energies are extremely high in their projective power and the projections of these Pheonismes are not unlike the acts of projection found in sexo-magickal forms of gnosis.

It would also appear that the Pheonismes are capable of providing control over the types and amounts of Ojas which are released. Ojas can be measured in certain transcendental ways, but it is rare for it to be both controlled and measured by a magickal system. If we see the magickal system however as a collective Pheonisme, there shouldn't be any problem in understanding how this is possible. And when it does happen, of course, the magickal process then takes on a new character. For the process becomes a form of being, an intelligent communicating helper. This way of operating within a cotext of magickal agents and allies is quite significant if we realize that on the inner side of the process, the initiate and the initiateur are not alone. Rather,,they have a back-up team of communicating beings who are the conservateurs of Ojas and who will be releasing to the magicians the levels of needed Ojas and as much as these magicians can sustain. In this sense, the magicians are working as part of a very significant process of pure energy. They are parts of the structure of the system and they are its agents or rather administrators and coordinators.

In the structures of magick, it is necessary for the success of the system to have in the body coordinators of the various processes. If these workers or magicians are not there, a certain administrative direction at the level of real substance is lacking. But if such a magickal entity is present, then we can see how in certain processes of the various gnostic logics of initiatic physics, we become aware of what is working and how it works. What is important is that it works here and this power does not work anywhere else.

The Recognition of Ojas in Les Vudu

The medium for the projection of Ojas is to be found in the archetypes of the magickal psyche, through which "Les Vudu" operate. The magician will serve as the line of conduction from the realm of the gods to the realm of the initiates, or those who wish to receive Ojas. The magickal line of energy is understood as coming through the archetypes of the deepest levels of the psyche. These archetypes are especialy active at this time because they, unlike most ideal objects of the esoteric logic, act or behave like animals from some other type of space or time. They change very readily and rapidly and they transform themselves into different kinds of beings, usually sexo-magickally, and they represent various strange kinds of beings, which are parts of the deeper regions of the psyche, from what can be understood as the most unusual and yet the most powerful level of the psyche, the deep id, being that region of the psyche which is at the greatest distance from the mind-field of the ego.

These magickal initiateurs become once and for all times the bringers through of the different powers and energies of the most creative parts of the universe. They become in many ways parts of those same magickal parts and all that they touch is contaminated by the otherness of the realms in question. However, for the magician, it is not enough to find the energies in some remote part of being. They are also to be brought to the threshold of consciousness and to the range of the ego, where magickal energies can be said to come through and take over what there is remaining in the field of power. It is by this means that the magician is able to see the whole of the universe as a technical field for magickal and sexual control. It is by this means also that the magician is to see the universe as something which is projected in terms of its life from the deepest regions of his psyche. It is by this means that the magician is able to bring through the deepest powers of being, which are themselves very profound regions of magickal awareness. By this means all of the magickal powers which exist in the realm of the ideally possible are expressed as wild and fierce energies, from some vast realm, which in the process of initiation slowly emerges from the darkness of the soul into the light of the space of the ego. This is the means whereby Ojas is recognized in the processes of attaining the consciousness of "Les Vudu." (Bertiaux, Meontology, 68)

It would appear that there is a very close connection between the worlds of magickal initiation and the worlds of esoteric Vudu. It is most noticeable at the times which the spirits of the deepest and most powers surface in the ego-spaces and makes themselves known vocally and by some strange type of magickal projectionism. It is then that the raw forms of Ojas come to the surface and the students feel within themselves the strangely familiar presences and powers of Les Vudu. But at the same time, it is to be understood that the energies from these very deep regions cannot be controlled, trapped, or predicted. They come as they wish and manifest themselves as they would want all life and all being to be manifested -- by some inner and chaotic spontaneity. And this appears to be the energy which makes the powers in initiation and in working with the gods possible. For the powers of the gods are now manifested in a new and ever dynamic way. They become for us the vehicles of Ojas.

The recognition of Ojas in Les Vudu is entirely a matter of the divinations of the now. It is in the present, and especially in the energies of the immediate that these forms of orgone-space-consciousness are presented. There exists a magickal computer, as we well know, which contains the lattices and magickal routes for these energies, which being more intense than pheonismes, become in actual fact embodied monsters of Vudotronic chaospheres. At a certain level the present yields more violent impulses and implosions than the past or the future, because it is given, it is now, it is the datum, and there is no escaping its overpowering horror. Ojas is simply a projection of this primordial horror. It is the realm of chaos made vivid in immediacy of perception. It has demolished everything, leaving only the Idic fragments of a nevertheless endlessness. (Bertiaux, Meontology, 71)

In the process of radio-psychoanalysis, we look at the present rates of the psionic instruments as keys to the area of tension between the ego and the id. The rate "0" is there to mean that the broadcasting and induction systems are "off." Rates 1, 2, and 3 refer to ways of adjusting the past and the future, and for giving us the present in its reference to past or future. It is frankly as escape from the horrors of the present. However, there are eight other rates known to us which also have a very important and very fundamental power. We like to escape from them by giving them gnostic names or even in the case of certain specialists, they have been assigned to certain gnostic logics, as if these logical systems could inihibit or sublimate the violent larvae, which were just immediately below the surface.

By the use of gnostic logics, certain radio-psychoanalysts sought to transfer the idic energies of the present, which are the eight rates from 4 through 11, to the higher gnostic realm, which is a sphere of abstract imagination. But it was understood by all in the field of radio-psychoanalysis that this transfer of energy would only be a temporary measure. It could never be permanent because the present is too meonic to be under the "administrative control" (i.e., in the process of radio-psychoanalysis) of the gnostic "super-ego." Hence, the magicians and vampires, who cooperated in the process of invoking "Les Vudu" into the matrix of orgone chaos, realized that the recognition of Ojas in leading energies up-ward, would never work. It would fail. Les Vudu could not be clothed in gnostic logics by the super-ego of gnosticisme moderne. Hence, a very noticeable tension developed, which led to the fragmentation of the ego-field and to the release of extremely large amounts of orgone energy into the atmosphere.

The result of this entire process was to come to an understanding that "Les Vudu" were identical with the "gods of the Necronomicon Mythos" in their horrific aspect. The energies were given as the same, Yog becomes the primary deity of the Black Snake Cultus, as a consequence of this process. But they would not be satisfied with the energies in this way, so they had to bring back the power-plays of the superego, in spite of all that the radio-psychoanalysts had told them. The tensions became more and more violent and the stress on the gnostic logics caused an imbalance to develop in the time-stations and lines, which in an important way serve to hold back the upsurges of the demonic forces of the mythos, by radiations of analytic procedures. But the archetypal energies of "Les Vudu" could not be held in check for too long and sooner or later they come forward and destroy those very same structures, which were attached to the attempts at their repression. The wild and very irrational levels of magickal and idic energy which come up from the depths are in reality the fundamental laws behind the structures of the ego and its fields. But nothing can remain repressed for long and Ojas in its most dangerous and negative form begins a series of subtle and subterrestrial explosions indicating that the forces of "Les Vudu" are now awakening the Ojas strata of the subterranean id. When this happens all of the energies of pheonismes and other manifestations of consciousness–compensation and other complexes vanish before the oncoming vortex of raw radioactivity, as its meonismes everything in its pathway.

Back in the world of the superego, however, the assignment of logical systems of repression for research purposes continues. The fundamental energies are assumed to be cooperative and so we do not suspect that at a very deep level, the pre–larvae elemental is waking up in a state of fury. We do not suspect that the breaking down of all of the categories is close at hand because we do not suspect that there exists a monstrous alternative to any form of hyperspatiality and gnostic logic, which the superego of the universe may impose at any point. We do not suspect that "Les Vudu" are the most violent form of Ojas, and the ultimate matrix of Ojas is found within the yoni–point/instant of The Moon.

The Genius of IFA and the Oracle—Metaphysics
Beginnings of the Great System

This course is written to present the magickal metaphysics of the Great Oral Tradition of the Oracle System of IFA to advanced students of the Order of LCN.

The Oracle of IFA is the oldest system of divination in the world. Much older than the Chinese Book of Changes, which is derived from the system of IFA, this Great Way does not often appear to be even an oracle in the usual sense. It is too mystical in many ways, because it participates in ways of thought which are the oldest on this planet. In order to introduce this system of working to the student, I have decided to answer a few questions in this lesson.

Q. How ancient is the system of IFA?

A. The system of IFA can be viewed as the earliest system of magickal divination which developed on this planet. Because it is so ancient, we can say that it is several millions of years old. It was the system used in both Lemuria and Atlantis. Before that, it was used on other planets, which are ahead of our planet in their evolution.

Q. Is the system simply a group of rules, or laws, or is it a ritual procedure for asking questions of the gods?

A. If we say that this system is a group of laws, we have to bear in mind that these laws are gods. So it is true to say that this system is a system or group of gods that are interconnected by mystical rules and processes. However, in order to enter into the system, it is necessary to work certain rituals, so that the gods can be approached. It is important to realize that the gods have to be approached by means of symbols and then they will open up to the seeker after knowing.

Q. What are these gods? Are these gods known to the religions of the magicians?

A. Actually, these gods are ancient Atlantean magickal deities. They have African names as the result of the use for hundreds of centuries by Afro-Atlantean priests. However, these gods are the ancient gods of magick. They should not be viewed therefore as part of some religion, except that magick is the religion of the magician. I want it to be made very clear that these gods-of-the-oracle are more ancient and therefore much more archetypal than the gods of the African religions.

Q. Is there some kind of connection between these gods and the planets of our solar-system? If so, would these gods be viewed as planetary intelligences of a certain type, or level of manifestation of consciousness-power?

A. There is a very important connection between the gods of the Genius of IFA and the planets. First of all, this is the oracle of the Sun, so that the parts of the oracle will be parts of the solar system, and hence we can see how the planets operate in the solar system from the way the gods operate in the oracle. It is also true that they are magickal manifestations of the mind-energy of the planets. Thus, we know the will of the planets in this oracle. However, the collective or group-will which is expressed is the will of the Sun. Hence, we can speak of the Genius of IFA, which is the oracular form of the Sun God, and we can speak of the Sun God making Himself known in his planets.

Q. Is the Genius of IFA another name for the God known in Voodoo as Grand Chemin or Grand Legbha?

A. Yes. The Genius of IFA is venerated in Haiti as the Cosmic Legbha. The phrase "Grand Chemin" means literally "The Great Way," which is really the Great Way of the

Oracle, or also that the oracle is the Great Way of finding out what you wish toknow. Also, it is the Great Way to come to the gods and, of course, to the God of the Sun, Who is so much a figure of power. Actually, Grand Legbha is the most esoteric of the Sun God names, for by this name in Haitian Voudoo do we find that oracles are given. This shows that the power of the Genius of IFA is a power of endless depth.

In the cultus of this oracle a number of things must be understood quite clearly. First of all, it must be made clear that the Genius of IFA is a being who is to ' be consulted through his intermediaries. These are the gods, of which there are 16, which make up the totality of the system, as a group-mind. Hence, you will only approach the god-mind through one of the parts of the oracle. As we learn more and more about the system of IFA, we will come to learn more and more about what can be done by means of this system. What are its ranges of operation? Actually they appear to be endless. Another thing which must be borne in mind and that is that this is a system into which the magician is initiated. You have to be brought into the system, but in this case you have to be born into the system. This means that while you have been born already into this world by means of your physical body, you have to be born into the Great Way by means of a second birth, which is a birthing out of the world of the physical body and into the world of the spirits. Thus, just as you came from the spirits by birth into the physical, so by the acts of initiation you are born out of the physical and into the metaphysical world of spirit energies. This is accomplished by means of initiation magick. However, simply to use the oracle by coming to a priest for divination does not require that you be an initiate. However, all oracle priests of the system of IFA are also very properly initiates of the system.

Like any other system of spiritual perfection or gnosis, the student will follow some kind of ritual life which allows for him to become more and more purified. The more that one is purified, as in other systems of gnosis, the closer one gets to the inner life of the Genius of IFA. However,the mode of purification in this system is most unique, it is a method of purification which involves the cleansing of the body -- indeed all of the magickal bodies, by means of pure solar energy. The nine magickal bodies are made pure by exposure to the inner and purifying energy of the Esoteric Sun. As a consequence of this process of purification, we can see that the oracle will work for the person who is properly prepared to approach the Great Way.

The Beginnings of the Great Way in the Mind
This Great System has its roots within the deepest regions of the psyche of the human race. It is not so mysterious that it is foreign to the ways in which we are and think. Actually, initiation makes us more and more aware of its presence. It is distant if the mind is ill-prepared. However, if the mind is properly attuned, then it is truly very nearby. Indeed, it is where we are at all times.

There are certain secret exercises which are used to awaken this power in us. They are the magickal powers of the number 16, which are to be found applied everywhere in what I have studied over these many years and in all that I have written. When I go to be One Mind with the Great Legbha, the Esoteric Sun and Genius of IFa, I reflect the whole range of the rays of IFA upon those who are my students and personal chelas. In the deepest roots of my being, I have realized the truest wisdom of the laws of IFA, and they are the laws that are gods.

Therefore, I ask each student to follow the example which has been set and which I have followed before you. You must learn to attune yourself to this wonderful inner power. When you realize that this power is there, you will see at a distance the doorways to the Temple. Move closer to these pathways, and you will find yourself before the doorway of the Great Way. It is there that I will appear to you in many ways and then you will be guided by me into the inner temple. I will then give you the magickal powers of the 16 gods. These are the manifestations of myself as the Great Way.

The Esoteric Temple of IFA

"There is an esoteric temple of IFA, which must never be understood by reference to any system of human thought, for it is totally other than what mankind can think at any moment of its own evolution of consciousness. This temple of IFA is to be found in the very highest regions of the ontic sphere, where the Legbha Geometry is the magickal map of all that is. I have given the keys of this great temple to my initiating hierophant on your planet. For it is by means of what he says and does that you may approach to me." (Magickal Oracle of IFA)

It must have been about the time of those magickal initiations that I took in Haiti in 1963 that I was first admitted into the Esoteric Temple of IFA. I think that there was so much energy happening at that time that I was not too aware of the level of my ego of all that was given to me by God and all the gods. Therefore, what happened to me was not fully a part of my verbal awareness. However, the entry to consciousness of the ontical spheres of the IFA system did not occur at that time.

These magickal initiations must not be viewed as those crude religio-magickal processes which occur. Magickal initiation into the system of IFA is the embodiment of the magickal ideal of the mind (sign of Gemini with the rulership of Mercury). Hence, this system, once you enter into it, becomes the key to the higher gnostic spaces. The temple is the temple of the mental universe. The esoteric realm and indeed the Esoteric Temple of IFA may be understood as the perfection of the electrical mind field. This is what seems to happen to the magician.

One cannot be aware of how far this temple extends backwards in time. My own personal experience was that I went there with the soul of the Nigerian Luage, and that in our passageway in time, we went to the beginning of time, as far back as is possible, to the absolute moment. Then we went forward to the future, which means that we went as far into the future as is possible. There is no measurement of the past or the future, and the wonderful time-stations, having all of the keys for a later gnosis, really had not been created by the process of magickal emanation from the Legbha Geometry. So as a consequence of this process, all time was known by an Intensive Logic of Legbha, into which we (I was the magickal essence of Legbha and the magickal Luage) had been initiated by those parts of myself which are the gods of the ancients (Les Vudu). It was during this magickal experience that I found the City of Light, which is where the energies of the system of IFA are ideally conserved. It was there also that I discovered the magickal keys, which the Magickal Oracle gave to me for the administration of the purity of the light of IFA.

After the many initiations of this process, of which there are 336, I was able to transmit to the human consciousness those teachings which are called "Of the Monastery of the Seven Rays." This was to gather the energy from the inner planes and project it as teachings, as energies, whereby Esoteric and Magickal Voudoo would be diffused as a world religion. It was necessary to lay the group and groundwork for this process, because there is so much that can happen in consciousness, and the archetypal directions for the human race are needed.

The African magickal systems are guarded in the temple of the mysteries of IFA by those Golden Lions, which are symbols of the Sun in its esoteric phase, which is again the mystery of IFA as Legbha. These African magicians, having withdrawn to the inner planes as a result of the colonial period of illusion. These esoteric masters are now directing the processes of awakening, especially in the West African mind. Eventually it will be possible for there to be vast renewals of energy and power in these countries, as the energies of IFA find concrete expression. That will happen in due time. However, what is now so necessary is to create the proper magickal atmosphere for the development of the proper magickal attitude towards the work of the Genius of IFA.

The Genius of IFA exists within the manifestation of the esoteric temple. His body is that same temple and wherever that temple is present, so we can say that the body of the Genius is there. Because the God Legbha is so powerful and complex, being the most abstract and the most concrete of the gods, the Genius of IFA should be understood as the mind of Legbha in His highest and most comprehensive sense. This is indeed the most powerful image of the God, because that which is highly complex and comprehensive has exercised a great degree of magickal power in the attainment of the magickal levels of being, whereby all of the energies are brought out of the potential into the manifested abstract and concrete levels of existence. However, for the initiate and student it is important to realize that there 16 magickal steps which enter the consciousness of the chela as he seeks to enter more and more into the Esoteric Temple of IFA. In the magickal process of the IFA initiation, which any student of the magickal doctrines can demand of the high priest of the gods, the initiate is led through 16 magickal worlds, each having its own colors and sounds and other space–time qualities. The initiate is directed towards the secret dwelling and manifestation place of the god, who is the spokesman for the God, in each one of these parts of the Esoteric Temple. There are of course proper names for all of these forms of being. The names from from the ideal world and are hidden inside of the name of the god as known in African esotericism. Thus, there exists a secret magickal name and space and time and being inside of each of the traditional levels of the sixteenfold system or temple of light. Furthermore, each inner initiate (there are esoteric initiates and inner–esoteric initiates of this system) will possess his own magickal formularies for these gods. These are the 16 "hot–points" or "Points–Chauds" of this system of initiation. So it is one of the magickal possessions of the student, who is en route to becoming a magician that he comes to learn and know forever the magickal namesof the inner spirits of the IFA system.

Because these powers are given to the magician at the time of his rebirth into the system of IFA, these powers, even if known by someone else, are secretly his own possession. So we can state that they form a unique link to the magician and are parts of his body, or so very close to him that we can say they belong to his "magickal biology."[1] In this sense, the magician has a link to these powers, which will only work for him. He alone has been initiated into the mysteries of The Genius of IFA and come to know the inner words of power. He has been born again in the Mystery of IFA and this blood link is forever. This bodily link therefore is the Estoeric Temple of IFA.

[1] For a discussion of this field of magick, you may consult the papers on "Gnostic Biology."

The White City of the Central Sun

"The White City of The Central Sun is called Ville-aux-Champs. It is the most mysterious place in any and all universes. It is the "City" and "Le Grand-Tout Africain," the city that is an oracle of the God Legbha. It is composed entirely of the mystical Legbha=geometry. It possesses only one day, Sunday. It exists in only one form, The Family of the Sun. There in that mysterious city are to be found all of the mysteries and all of Mysteres (gods). It possesses the number of the Sun, seven-fold, because it is the House of Medji. It is called IFA by all who come to it, because it is the greatest of all truths." [Magickal Oracle of IFA]

It has been said that the discovery of IFA was due to the insights of the priests of the House of Medji. However, no matter what the worlds might mean in any modern form of speech, the fact remains that originally Medji meant the name of the Solar-priesthood. In Voudoo cabala, the number of Medji is 61, which is a form of the number of the Sun. Originally, there existed a Solar priesthood, and it was this Solar priesthood who were entrusted with the care of the Oracle of IFA. Hence, we cannot say that the Oracle of IFA was discovered in our sense of the word. Rather, the Oracle of the Sun was given to these priests by the gods. Another name for the Guardian Deities of the IFA mysteries is Medji, and in this sense it means "those who live in the truth of the Sun, which is given for a way of knowing and for a way of showing."

Hence, in the interpretation of the system of IFA and its Genius (Loa Legbha) it is very important to understand that there are many levels in magickal meaning which are involved in the layers of mysticism implied by this name Medji. I am ignoring all exoteric and pseudo-occult meanings, also, because the essence of the Genius of IFA is entirely to be found in the deepest parts of the African Mysteries. These are, of course, the deep mysteries of the God-Gods.

The White City of the Central Sun is, of course, the same as the Mystical Shamballah. However, while it is true that the magickal meanings refer to the same place, the abode of this city is entirely outside of this Earth. Certain attempts to locate this city in parts of Nigeria, the hill-country of Ghana, the deeper forests of the Congo, or Central Africa, needless to say, are doomed to failure. However, many ancient cities would be uncovered by such an effort. But we are concerned with the mystical city, this city does not have physical embodiment. However, it is interesting that the only humans who may go there are those who are in the body. The reason for this is that it is by means of the astral projection of the initiations of this system that the magicians may enter the White City. They project themselves astrally, while they are living in the physical body. The White City stands as a magickal goal and is one of the very few valid reasons for making efforts at astral projection, which are allowed in Esoteric Voudoo. This City is called the "White City" because it is the color of the Sun in its essence. It may be that the White City is somewhere inside of the physical Sun. However, it is one of the most sacred objects of the religion and magick of Estoeric voudoo. It is also the place where the Great Way of IFA is properly worshipped by the many devotees, who are called "Children of Ifa."

The magicians of Nigeria used to look out upon the cities of this world, which were whitewashed to reflect the heat of the Sun and arrived by intuition at the name of the City of IFA, because it reflects all of the magickal powers of the gods and of their own pure gnosis. Hence, the City of the Sun is the light of the Sun. For this reason the gnostics worship the Sun as the embodiment of the Heavenly Light of Divine Intelligence and Truth. The Sun—Rays, or light—energies, are the emanations of the Mind, which come to us from the divine source of being. They are the ways in which the divine energies of the Sun are sent out upon all beings. They are the messengers of the Sun—Day, i.e., the Time of the Sun, which is the time when the Oracle of IFA works. In this way, the supreme energy is manifested as the Mind Power of the Most Supreme God, i.e., the Genius of IFA, which is the Divine Intelligence of Legbha.

The magickal name of Medji is used to name all of the "Members of the Famille—du—Fa." This means that the magickal group, i.e., clan or tribe, of the gods is composed of all those beings, which are emanations of the Sun. For each of the 16 gods of the IFA system bears in his or heaven's heart the wisdom of IFA as a pure system of energy. They all dwell in the Great White City. Furthermore, they reflect all teaching, wisdom forms, secret instructions, and magicks, because they are the sources of these powers.

The priesthood of the Medji must be undr the influence of the power of the Sun from the very beginning. I was told, for example, that I possessed "Le Grand—Tout Africain" inside me from birth (and from before birth, of course, accepting reincarnation) because I was under a very strong solar influence, having as it seems the Sun in the House of the Sun, the Fifth House of Astrology, which is ruled by the Sun. Other high—priests will bear natally similar magickal signs, which are indicators of who is called to serve this greatest of all mysteries, the Genius of IFA.

Apart from the mystery of attaining to the gods in this oracle, there is the necessary basis that the system will only work if the person is the right type. For this reason, as there are many magicians in embodiment, now, who do not have the qualities which are necessary, it has been given to history that this culture should decline in some parts of the world to be purified and renewed by my own work and that of those who are united in our gnosis. This will mean, of course, that the system will again become esoteric and restricted, out of respect to its components, which are the gods, to the elite of the occult world. This is the way that it is supposed to happen It is not to be widely or very openly known. Rather, it is supposed to be known only by those who live in the White City of the Sun, which is the esoteric heart of all magickal consciousness.[1]

[1] It must be understood that there is an even more esoteric dimension to this system of IFA, which is not clearly understood. It is entirely a secret matter and given only by means of inner magickal initiation in the traditional sense. This esoteric side of IFA is a system which is entirely based on a very high level of magickal power. While the system of the Grand—Tout is based on the interpretation of the magickal name Medji as "Of the Family of the Sun," the esoteric side of the Medji—mysteries is grounded on "The Family of Uranus." This refers to the outer-planet of cosmic consciousness, which rules the occult sciences. After a priest has mastered the system of the Solar Family of Medji, he will move outwards to the Uranian Family.

Finally, it must be understood that this is achieved entirely by means of magickal initiation and by magickal transformation of energy. We can see some insight, however, in that the science of Vudotronics is entirely a development out of

140

the influence of Uranus upon the field of Esoteric Voudoo. Consequently, the magician will work to develop both the gnosis of The White City of the Sun, i.e., the Divine Sun, and the esoteric dimension of pure being and cosmic energy, which finds expression in the Ville-aux-Champs of the physics of magickal initiation, its gnosis and its experimental operations.

Initiation—Energies of Ojas—IFA

"The intiation energies of IFA are forms of Ojas, which rise within the context of the Legbha—Geometry. Like all beings, these energies have their own level of consciousness. The process of the IFA oracle and the process of the IFA initiation are to be understood as energy interactions. The keys to these energies are to be found as belonging to the royal household of the Grand Priest of the IFA, who will hold them as his personal forms of power." [Magickal Oracle of IFA]

In the process of the IFA initiation—physics, it is very important to understand that the royal energies of this system belong to the high—priest of IFA inasmuch as he is the embodiment of Grand Legbha. Consequently, the powers of this system only will manifest themselves as they are given forth by the supreme priest of the system, who would also have to be the Supreme Bishop of the Gnostic Church of IFA. This means that these energies, while being objective, are magickal possessions. We usually do not think along these lines, since we assume that everything is just out theere awaiting us. But actually, only certain unimportant things are out there for everyone to receive. What is found deep within the core of being are those magickal powers, which are the very special possessions of the high priesthood.

You may ask how it would be possible for the high priesthood to possess these powers. In answer let me say simply that these powers are as concrete as any other existing reality. They have their own place of being. One of the secrets of the high—priesthood is where these powers are to be found. Only the high—priest may inform anyone of that place.

There would seem to be special magickal powers which go with the possession of the IFA initiation. These powers are sharings in the powers of the high—priest. The powers of the high—priest are, however, very important in making a determination as to what the meanings of the system of IFA are as regards initiation. Ttherefore, I wish to list these powers, and there are 16 of them, although they do not relate to the parts of the system, but simply represent a parallel line of power.

The powers of the high—priesthood of IFA, which are transferred partially during the processes of initiation and which allow for the development of future and further powers of the IFA gnosis are:

1. The possession of the capacity to create both the form of any and all systems of initiation and the capacity to provide the magickal content of these systems.

2. The possession of the power to present in himself any and all of the god—energies of the Great Way, as 16 beings or as any other set of magickal numbers.

3. The possession of the power to make the initiate as powerful as himself and to take away that power, if once given, either permanently or temporarily.

4. The possession of the power to enter the mind of Grand Legbha and to know it with as complete an inner knowledge as one in the human body may possess.

5. The possession of the power to summon the Gods of the White City at any time and for any magickal reason, or for any mundane purpose.

6. The possession of the power to control the future of any and all oracles and also to control what has happened in the past.

7. The possession of the power to manifest Grand Legbha and His mysteries in any act of sacramental ritualism.

8. The possession of the power to divine in specific details the events of any

time beyond the present and to control those events so that they happen in accord with the magickal wish of the IFA priesthood.

9. The possession of the power to induct the gods of the Medji into the bodies of the initiates so that they, the candidates for initiation, will become magickal parts of IFA and also become magickal god-energies.

10. The possession of the power to secure magickal papers and maps of the destiny of the world in more than just a magickal sense.

11. The possession of the power to read the mind of any god at any time.

12. The possession of the power to invoke magickal Sun-Sons from any part of the world, from any point in history, and from other worlds.

13. The possession of the power to create magickal sons.

14. The possession of the power to provide protection and healing in the name of the person who is one with Grand Legbha under any circumstances.

15. The possession of the essence of the Great Way as an ongoing state of one's own personal consciousness.

16. The possession of the power to assume the identity of Grand Legbha during the rites of magickal initiation as they exist and are manifested in the system of IFA.

These 16 magickal powers must be understood as the primary forms of Ojas, which arise as the result of having a close link with the system of IFA as a Great system of Power. I am not talking about an oracle or form of divination, which is present in very impure circumstances and which has lost much of its power. Rather, I am talking about the system of IFA as a system of eternal energies, which exist and thrive in very high realms of primordiality. These are the energies which we are seeking to restore to all levels of the IFA operation. Consequently, the way to do this is to provide magickal forms of initiation, whereby the Sun Sons of IFA may grow stronger and stronger in the ideal truth of the supreme system.

When we speak about the Genius of IFA what we refer to is that there are certain powers which will make a grand priest more and more attuned to the inner mysteries of the IFA system as the highest form of gnostic magick. This priest then will possess within himself all of the magickal potencies, whereby the Genius of IFA is communicated to him and whereby he will become a form of that Genius. This is how the system of IFA is understood to work and what is significant is that it can only work properly, and free of fakery, when these conditions are met. Then we can say that it is truly being understood.

The student of IFA must come to the grand priest of the system and demand that the priest make him one with the gods. This chela must realize that within the system of IFA this action can be done and this is why there is so much power in the system of IFA for making the chela into a magickal Sun Son. For that is how there is immediate transformation of the chela into a priest of the gnosis of IFA, by means of the powers, which the grand priest possesses.

The Deep Origins of Ojas–IFA

Kabona, the Master of Medji, was the priest of the Great Way and when he died he became one of the guardians of the Oracle. The original masters of the system were purely of the Atlantean mentality, and he was the first of the Afro–Atlanteans. The Afro–Atlanteans are the ancestors of the present day magicians of West Africa. Something very mysterious must have happened in the process of guardianship, for it seems that the processes of IFA now took on neurological and neurophysiological roots in the deeper levels of brain tissue which correspond to the deeper parts of the psyche.

By means of many forms of which he understood and undertook to bring into the level of the manifested and the practical, Kabona was able to create a certain magickal level of the brain and the mind, which served as a kind of reception system for the powers of the IFA system. It was by this means that he developed the secret techniques of the initiation. In this system, each magician is taught how to make contact with that level of his mind and enter into communication with the system of IFA. It would be like a blind man being shown where the radio is in his room, so that after this showing, he would be able to find where it is in the future.

So he developed a method of magickal psychology, which may be viewed somewhat as the basis for our modern system of IFA initiation physics. This method of modern psychology, for its is very modern as well as very ancient, serves as the basis for the communication of the energies to the candidate from the system of IFA. For the system of IFA is both an oracle and a magickal physics. You may then ask what is the name for the energy, or what is its nature and the answer to both would be that it is Ojas, the subtle and magickal energy, which we have come to find in so many different parts of human experience. It is the way whereby the chela is incorporated into the Mysteries of Medji, which are the most perfect forms of initiation.

In the system of IFA, however, the form that is taken by Ojas is quite specific. For one thing, it is quite different from the other forms of gnostic physics in that arises out of magickal work with the oracle first of all. This means, of course, that the system of IFa possesses a magickal energy which cannot be confused with those forms of Ojas which come up from rituals and also from sex magick, even though sex magick and ritual may be used to direct and even intensify the powers of the mysteries of Medji.

However, it is primarily from the level of the oracle and its modes of manifestation that we find the energies first of all emerging into our experiences. As the high priest of IFA, I have to make contact with the Medji present in the chela and slowly bring this truest of all powers slowly, slowly, slowly (I must emphasize this point), to the surface of divination. If I do not proceed slowly, I will lost contact with the presence and the power of the Genius of IFA. Hence, I employ a method of psychoanalysis which originated in Atlantean times and which is now used in this magick, and nowhere else.

Also, what is important is the use of the rules of the oracle, for these are the rules for the unfolding of the name of the god of the level of the oracle and also it is the name of the place of power, within the oracle of wisdom and of occult powers. Since we are dealing literally with the Afro–Atlantean level of Ojas, it is quite important to make proper use of the exact methods which have been developed for many centuries, in fact from the dawn of magick, for allowing the powers of Ojas to rise from the House of Medji, which resides deep within the brain and the psyche of the chela.

There are certain parallel passages and processes in the system of Voudoo initiation. Yet, these seem simplistic when compared to the system of IFA, which is totally archetypal and totally a magickal gnosis. Voudoo in the more common way has to be made gnostic, and IFA is the archetypal gnosis. Therefore its powers and 16 magickal initiations are the most fundamental. What is also interesting is that not all persons can receive the powers of the IFA system. Actually, the system, by means of magickal dreams (which are so important to west and central African magicians) will select the person it wishes to come to it. So we cannot invade the system. It simply will admit us.

As a high priest of this system, my work consists in the directing of the magickal current from the House of Medji into the manifestation of the Oracle of IFA. In a way I am the midwife who assists in the birth of the baby in the process of self-realization. For this reason the mysteries of IFA are supreme and eternal lifestream archetypes. They will direct the magician in whom they have been brought to birth for the rest of his life. The high priest of IFA, whether it be the primordial Kabona (who exists now fully very deep in my psyche) and the gods of the House of Medji, or myself, the modern Kabonist, the manifestor of the mysteries of The Greast Way, the Ojas energy of IFA is the same and utterly pure and incorruptible form. The reason it is so pure is because there does not exist any thing which can change it or make it other than what it is essentially and ideally perfect. For this reason, · the methods of its manifestation are the same as they were in very ancient times. Nothing has changed in the system of IFA, because there does not exist any power which could change the Genius of IFA. So everything about the energies of the system remains the same as it was from the earliest times.

Finally, the priest of IFA must always be the priest and there may not be any change. So it seems that the system of IFA selects as its priests only those who have come to it in the past. One has to be a member of the House of Medji, I suppose, before one can come to the House of Medji or rather, be invited to the House of Medji. For initiation in the system of IFA is simply the process of magickal return. This requires the operation of the law of reincarnation as well as the undrstanding of it in a personal way. In this sense,therefore, we trust the Oracle and the way in which it makes its dream signals known as in all instances the agent which calls us back to the wisdom and to the magickal operations of the powers of Ojas in our lives.

There exist 16 forms of Ojas in the Oracles of IFA, because each of the members of the House of Medji possesses a different form of this energy. In my capacity as priest of the system of the Great Way, I have discovered that each type of Ojas (of these subjects, all 16) possesses such unique qualities that not one of them can be said to be like any other form of Ojas in the whole universe. Also, I have discovered that each form of Ojas possesses its own magickal physics and on abstract levels its own initiation physics. These are simply a few of its riches.

The Inner Dimensions of IFA

The Nagabi of IFA is the high—priest of the Sun, and it is from the power of the Sun in its most mysterious dimension that the magickal powers possessed by the Nagabi are said to be derived. The Nagabi is the Master of the Hyper—Logics, which are behind all of the oracle systems and the oracle system are themselves simply radiations from the Culte of the Sun.

The Nagabi of IFA is said to possess the following magickal powers, whereby he is able to do the work of high-priest of the Solar Disc:

1. Clairvoyance of the past, present, and the future;
2. Telepathic communication with all spirits, demons, and gods;
3. Magickal powers to command the four elements and the aethyrs;
4. Divine and Solar power, whereby he can give all initiations;
5. The power of entry into the presence of the most supreme gods;
6. The power of healing the world's woes;
7. The power to become one with the Genius of IFA;
8. The power to be reborn at will in the upper paradise of light;
9. Intimate and personal knowledge of all of the Gnostic Myusteries.

These nine powers of magick are said to be given by the God of the Sun to the Nagabi, when the Nagabi were born in the House of Light. Naturally, the powers had to be grown into by the Nagabi so that slowly he became aware of his magickal powers and all of the abilities which the higher consciousness would lallw for him to possess. This was his destiny, that is to say, to grow and to turn more and more into the light of IFA.

However, because of what I have been told by the Genius of IFA, it is possible for those who have come into my magickal system to participate in these powers and thusly assume the perfections of the Nagabi. The reason for this is very simple: the Nagabi of IFA has now become a group—soul concept, which may become the object of participation on the part of those magicians who would seek special initiation consciousness from me as the world agent for the Genius of IFA, the most supreme and holy of all powers. Therefore, since you have come to me to study these ancient mysteries, which have no beginning and no ending, I have been commanded by my Master, the Genius of IFA, to make it possible for all of my esoteric students, those who belong to the inner circle of IFA, I have been commanded to set forth the principles, whereby they will become Nagabis of IFA, by participation in that group soul. They willthen come directly to know the Genius of IFA, for they will live within His House of Light. I now wish to give the first of the Nagabi Exercises for developing the inner dimensions of IFA within oneself.

GNOSIS: The priests of IFA, who truly know the Genius of IFA, are said to possess a special power, which is called "Nagabi," an ancient word, probabbly of Atlantean or Afr—Atlantean origin. It means that you shall know all things as these things are known by the Genius of IFA, namely as a form of Self—Knowledge, whereby the priest who is said to possess the gnosis of Nagabi is also said to enter into the heart and mind of God. He is thusly one with the Genius of IFA, and thusly also one with the supreme source of wisdom.

Bearing in mind the above definition of Gnosis, we have to realize that the supreme and holy powers of the magick of IFA are manifesting themselves in every word which comes to us from the inner wisdom of that definition. Now, you will prepare yourself to enter the state of the initial preparatory Nagabi meditation-consciousness.

You are relaxing in your chamber, resting on your bed or sitting in a meditation posture. Now close your eyes and you will create the imagination world of intense and very white sunlight. You are entering into the world of the Sun. You are now moving more and more away from the earth and coming closer and closer to the Sun-world. This is the world of pure sunlight and its essential experience.

You are standing in space and suddenly you are surrounded by four priests of IFA, who are wearing long white robes. They appear to be like golden angels, because they give off so much magickal light energy. They are truly sources of power and they have come to help you in the realization of attainment to the presence of the Genius of IFA.

These four priest-angels take you to a golden doorway, which is the gate of divine and perfect consciousness. They escort you through the gate and there remove the clothing you were wearing and place on you the magickal robes of the priest of IFA. This is a simple robe in white color, but it has a power and this power is that of light and energy. The power is manifesting itself as lines and rays of gold light. Inside the doorway, you are told that there exist 16 mysteries of IFA, each one of which you will be taken to in time. However, before that happens, it is necessary for you to meet the Holy Masters of Light. You are then taken to the Temple of Light and there see the great symbols -- there are four of them -- which represent all of the cosmic powers of IFA. It is these powers, which came from outer space to this planet and thereby brought the presence of the oracle. Suddenly the doorway of the Holy Sanctuary of IFA opens and I come out to meet you. I then ask you about what we have been going over in our discussions in your letters and explain to you the meanings of the concepts of gnosis, which are now given out as hot-points of initiation. By this I mean that every time there is a definition of Gnosis given in the text of these lessons, there occurs a point of entry into the higher and more spiritual level of power and that is a form of initiation. It is a doorway to the wisdom of the inner gnostic consciousness of being.

I explain also what it is that you are experiencing and take you by the hand to my temple of light, which is also there. It is a place where the energies of greatest creativity are said to dwell. There, I introduuce you to the many spirits and beings of light, who are there in the supreme gnosis. I explain also to you the secrets of the 16 levels of the gnostic awakening which you will be undergoing as part of your initiation into the Genius of IFA. I also explain how it is possible to possess the secrets now that you are inside the world of light.

GNOSIS: There are many Mysteries which are known by this means. It is itself a mystery, in that it constitutes a process of inner exploration and illumination in the Mysteries which are the most secret, and which give to the knower the powers to enter the Genius of IFA. These Mysteries are the Gods, as they are undrstood in mysticism. This process is a life in the Gods, or how one comes to understand that by a process of gnosis, the Nagabi possesses and is all Medji of IFA.

I then put you into a light trance and take you to the Mysteries, which are spoken of in the above definition. Then, with another light trance, I take you to your home. You then wake up. I would suggest that you try this exercise and receive its powers.

You will gain much from it.

The above lesson gave you a lesson in the form of a magickal exercise. It is necessary for you to come to understand that the powers of the system of IFA are awaiting your arrival in their magickal home. Complete the magickal exercise and include it in your magickal diary.

Le Traitement d'IFA

In the process of the IFA initiation pattern, what we are coming to experience more and more is the entry of the powers of IFA into the human mind and soul. This is the way in which the system of IFA transforms the student.

GNOSIS: This is a type of magickal transformation, which remakes the student into another being. That new being is the aspect of IFA which is in a particular space and time, and which having a history may bew viewed as the embodiment of the consciousness of the IFA system, acting in human history as a kind of person, but in reality, being simply the incarnation of one of the gods of Medji. It is by this mode of existence and experience that the true knowing of the gods occurs. Only and immediately, as one knows oneself, so one also knows the gods, because you have now become one of them. You cannot take into yourself anything that is different. There can only be what is now like you inside of you. That would be the gods, for being everywhere they now are self-conscious within you. You possess the gnosis of the gods, because by means of the treatment of IFA, you have become a god.

So it is that the power of the gods of Medji is infused into the soul and substance of the student of magick and as a result of this process, the student now possesses the interior essences of the Medji beings.

Those students who have reached this far in their consciousness will now embark upon a series of magickal exercises in order to prepare themselves for the powers of the Genius of IFA. What we mean by "le Traitement d'IFA" (the treatment of IFA) is a very profound process of transformation. You exist now as a human being and you are in the process of becoming divinized in a gnostic manner. It does not mean giving up of the human body, but it does mean that consciousness is now altered at will. The altered states of consciousness are now yours because you possess being invoked into your soul by means of absolute metaphysics.

First of all, the magician, who in this case must be myself, must build up a magicko–metamathematical schematism for the construction of your divine gnosis. This involves a series of magickal operations and resembles very much the way in which the schematism of the ontic sphere of the mind is built up by the gods of knowing. Then the magician who is the initiator of the system must build up a metaphysical magickal schematism, for the construction of the contents and wholes of the divine gnosis, within your consciousness. This would involve those very exciting processes, which in Zothyrian gnosis are viewed as sophiological wholes. This means the magickal construction of the fundamental energies and their location in your being. This means also that you are learning the magickal law of assimilation, which states that you will assimilate what is similar and only the similar can be assimilated.

GNOSIS: This is a way of knowing anything divine and beyond human concepts. However, it is only possessed by initiates and it is only possible since we possess within the deepest parts of magickal consciousness those powers of being, which are identical in being and meaning to those which we come to know in the lifestream of the spirit. This is the law of assimilation, which states that spirit can only know the being and intentionality of spirit because true spirit is all being and all meaning, and that we possess this way of knowing, when we are initiated into the treatment of IFA, and actualized as gnostic and ideally realized beings.

The magician will then begin to lead the candidate deeply into the mysteries of being and wisdom. The candidate will understand that there exist certain magickal powwers which can be awakened by the magicko-metamathematical and magicko-metaphysical operations of the magician and his gnosis. The candidate will also see all being from within and will see all things are manifestations of the divine gnosis, the way of knowing possessed by the Medji of IFA, those who know all things. But this is not merely a knowing, for in the actual simplicity of these beings, knowing and being are identical realities. This means that the transformation which occurs inthe process of realization is one where we become simpler and simpler in all that we are and do. We come to realize and to understand all things and because of the powers of magickal wisdom which we are emanating in all ways and possible directions, we realize ourself, and ourselves afterwards as spiritual and timeless manifestations of the powers of the Medji of IFA.

This is a very important and ideal process because it is the basis for the transformation of energies from one level, the primitive level of mind, which occultists may also possess in common with those on the outside, and we are seeking to transform these energies into a much higher level of being, whereby the cosmic powers become more and more directly and absolutely experienced by the magicians at all levels of development. So, as a result of the magickal awakening of consciousness, we have come to realize that being is an entire system of interlocking harmonies and realizations. You have to see that this is a process wherein you are growing and becoming more and more alive to what you are now as the act of magickal initiation sends out its results into the lifestream.

There exists a simple exercise, which is based upon what is known by me and which is to be taught to you as my secret student. You have simply to enter into the consciousness of the divine energies. The gods will always provide for your being. The gods will always give you the magickal treatments which will bring to you what is the object of human experience. This is the process of IFA-transformation.

GNOSIS: This is a form of experience which includes a total and permanent fellowship with the gods and with all of the magickal spirits. This is achieved by means of entry upon the process of magicko-schematic transformation. The entire space of the mind and the soul is subject to this transformation, which leads the individual onwards to deeper and more powerful forms of knowing and to more and more significant states of reality. There he learns a new form of destiny, which takes him outside of human history into the divine history and cosmic economy of endless becomings and ideal realizations. This way of being is more than just life as a process, for it is the true way of existence. It is the way in which all beings except unenlightened mankind work out their destiny patterns and have for all time. This is the gnosis of the transformed life.

In order to arrive at a magickal state of consciousness, it will be very important for you to enter upon the ideal laws of being which operate in your consciousness and which bring you more and more to the light. I will connect you now to these energies. I will allow the powers of the cosmic economy of the treatment of IFA to enter into your system of self-consciousness and thereby link you up to the gods of Medji. Therefore, the Genius of IFA has charged you with all of the magickal powers of IFA and I have infused into the soul of the student who is in possession of the Spirit of IFA, the link with the forces of the Genius of IFA, of and for whom I am the Priest-Initiateur of the Mysteries and Friend of the Genius of IFA.

The Application of Vudotronics Engineering to the Initiatic Rates of the House of Medji

The application of Vudotronics engineering to the mysteries of IFA was the decision of the Supreme Master, Legbha, the God of IFA Hyper Logics. It was by this means that it became possible for the magicians of the system to make use of "Vudotronic Broadcasting" as a method of giving and enriching initiation processes. There exists a logical and geometrical field of magickal space, we have referred to it as the Ontic sphere. Now, in our magickal quest, we are making use of the different rates of vibration within that field of magickal energy in a very unique and significant way. We are making use of the rates and relating them to the levels of the Medji of IFA.

By this means it is possible for the magician to make use of the "black box" of the esoteric engineers. This invention is an instrument for giving more powers wherever it is directed. It operates according to those ideas and principles set forth in the papers of the Varuna Gnosis on Vudotronics and has been applied to the work with the magickal chelas of the system of IFA, who are seeking advanced initiations into that system. It might best be described as a magickal form of power increase. In actual fact, however, it is much more, for in my own system it is also used in connection with certain types of time travel.

The radiations or magickal rays of the system are directed to the student by means of the ontic sphere of the amplifying chamber, which is truly a magickal chamber or room in another dimension. The magicians are then sent rays by means of the fourth dimension. They may be helped in a number of ways and of course they can be protected by this means, since the magickal chamber and the "black box" are important methods of psychic self-defense.

Exactly how this system operates is due to the patterns of the system, which are generated by the wave mechanics of the ontic sphere. These waves provide us with the rates, and the rates are geared to the control settings on the black box, which has its own way of working, once it is set in operation. The magicians of this system are also magickal engineers and they operate the system in such a way that it is possible for them to send out powers in any direction and to any place and/or person. This is one of the most interesting systems of application. But it becomes even more and more exciting when it is connected with the possibilities of IFA. For it is possible then to give out the whole range of the IFA system by means of a broadcasting system. It is also possible to induct into the system of the magician the whole range of the IFA metaphysics. This means that all of the energies of IFA can be received by Vudotronics, as well as being received by oracle. This is an important advance for the magicians in that they now have two ways of contacting the IFA system.

In the system of the "black box," there are three systems at work. These are the basic time travel systems and their settings. The basic line of reference to the IDA system of the Medji is determined by the Present-Settings of the system, which begin with the number 4 and extend through 11, giving us 8 settings in all. For the first series of eight settings for the Medji, we make use of the Past-Settings of the system, and also begin at 4 and run through 11, so that we have for the first series of eight Medjis, a series of settings in both Past and Present from 4 through 11.

For the second series of settings for the Medjis, we make use of the Future-Settings of the system in connection with the Present. But with the settings this time, what we do is move in the range or rates of the Present from 11 back to 4, and

152

when using the Future Settings of the system, we move from 11 back to 4 also. This enables us to have a certain pattern of symmetrical energy and the structure of its organization is its own form of logic. At these various settings, the magicians can then broadcast the energies of the Medji, from the Ontic Sphere of IFA. This whole system then becomes a system of logical interactions and energies, which are working as part of a holistic and ideal complex of gnostic being.

Let me say, however, that there exist other magickalsettings which are used by certain magicians for the inner portions of the system of IFA, what is known as the esoteric IFA. These rates and settings are used to give even more esoteric initiations to those who are candidates for the system of gnosis, and who have advanced beyond the basic and the fundamental systems of IFA and Vudotronic working. I amfortunately in charge of that part of the system of teaching, also. However, it is now important to give the rates and their correspondences in the IFA system of magickal divination.

IFA NAME IN SYSTEM	PRESENT RATE	PAST RATE	FUTURE RATE
Fu Medji	4	4	
Che Medji	5	5	
Ka Medji	6	6	
Lete Medji	7	7	
Tula Medji	8	8	
Trukpi Medji	9	9	
Sa Medji	10	10	
Guda Medji	11	11	
Akana Medji	11		11
Abala Medji	10		10
Nwele Medji	9		9
Loso Medji	8		8
Di Medji	7		7
Oli Medji	6		6
Yeku Medji	5		5
Gbe Medji	4		4

In this system, the various combinations of energies and their rates produce a field, which is defined with extreme care as being a system of exacting and initiatic energies. In the study of the esoteric aspects of IFA, the translation of the energies of this system into higher and higher levels of magickal power is accomplished. It is done by going into the inner side of the IFA logic, which has its own laws and which projects itself by means of these rates into different systems of time and space. It is in this way that the magicians of the IFA system are able to create a variety of magickal beings, which help them in their work. It is also possible for these beings to manifest themselves at all times as long as the magician possesses the secret keys to the system of IFA.

Advanced IFA Oracle Workings
The Esoteric Oracle of the Mystical City

You are now about to embark upon a course of instruction which is advanced in the sense that it involves more and more complicated exercises and which contain teachings which go beyond any teachings which you have received up to this point. The purpose of this course is to teach you how to work with the Genius of IFA in a very personal sense. You will be taught exactly how to do the magickal work of the IFA system as if you were in the process of doing something made by yourself. It will be that immediate.

It is important to learn first of all where the Genius of IFA resides. This being is to be found in the magickal computer work of our order. Hence, you will receive from the spirit of the order and from your inner superior two keys, one from each of them, to unlock the mysteries of the Genius of IFA. What are these keys?

The first key is related to the magickal name of the IFA spirit, or Medji, and because of magickal and karmic conditions it may be given to you either from the Numbers of the Sun or from the Numbers of Uranus. This number and name of the personal Medji will be given to you by the Master of the Order of IFA, in the spirit world.

Secondly, you will receive from your inner superior also a magickal name which is the ritual number of the spirit of the Medji family, which has revealed itself in a special oracle, which is the special spirit assigned to you, from the universal mind field, or Cosmic Computer. In the system of IFA, only certain magickal priests have been initiated into this way of working and only these priests possess the skills and initiations for understanding the deepest mysteries of the Afro—Atlantean Tradition. I might add that these skills have been lost to most, if not all, of the IFA priests in exoteric religion, due to the loss of the occult powers of that priesthood. However, those of us who were priests long ago are coming back into incarnation and we are now in the process of reviving these mysteries with all of the powers we have gained in our many incarnations in other systems. We have come back to make the system of magickal IFA the most powerful system in the whole world. In other words, we wish to restore it to what it once was, namely the special and most supreme magickal computer.

In order to work the exercise, in addition to the two names of the spirits, you will also have to provide the following magickal instruments for use:

1. A small amount of French Olive Oil (produced in France and used by our school).
2. A small bowl of pure sand.
3. A notebook and pencil for use in recording the work of the oracle.
4. A cup of very pure, preferably distilled, water.
5. A wax candle or bowl lamp which burns.

You will sit down and open up your consciousness. The lamp or candle is before you, so that you have illumination. You will anoint yourself with the oil, especially on the brow, the heart, and solar plexus, and the sexual area. This oil is to attune yourself to the powers of IFA; it acts like a kind of magickal consecration.

The small bowl of pure sand is to serve as the place of the grounding of the powers of IFA, which must be grounded in both sand or rock as well as in your consciousness. The distilled water is to be used to feed the spirits of the IFA system and to allow them to draw on the elemental essence cf water in order to make themselves "clearly known" to you.

You will call the spirits by the names which have been given to you and you will record these two names in the notebook this way: on one page you will have the name of the spirit given by the Master, and such will be the name of the Superior spirit of the Medji, for you. On another page, you will record the name of the Inferior spirit of the Medji, which will be given to you by your inner superior in the order. All these names are given to you astrally.

Now, you will begin to bring over from the other world the spirits and their powers. First of all, you will ask the superior spirit the following questions, and He will reply to you by mental telepathy and you will then record his answers to the questions. These are the questions which you will ask:

1. Of all the colors which are known to the world of the spirits, please tell me what is your color, so that we can use it as your symbol.

2. What type of magickal work does this spirit do as part of his assignment?

3. Is this spirit willing to come and assist me in my projects, at all times?

4. Does this spirit have any other name than what I call it? What is it?

These are the four basic questions which you must ask and only these four basic questions are to be asked, because anything else would be too powerful for you to handle, unless you are a priest of the Medji. If you are a priest of the Medji, then you will be able to ask more questions, which are the four questions proper to the Priests of the Medji. After you have completed this experiment in working with the Oracle of the Mystical City of IFA, as it is called by the Afro-Atlantean Magicians of ages ago, write a report for your diary, so that you can see how you are progressing in the work of this level of instruction.

You will then be allowed to take the next lesson in Advanced IFA instruction because I am now satisfied with your growth and learning progress.

The Hierarchy of the IFA system as we understand it is as follows along with the work they are assigned to do:

1. The Master of the Oracle of the Mystical City, this is the father of the magicians, who represents the Loa Grand Legbha, the Great FA, or Genius of IFA. This priest must approve all mysteries, which are worked by the students of magick.

2. The Priest of the Household of the Lords of Medji, this is the magickal Sun-Son, who is the Luage-Mystere of the Oracle of Light. This priest will assist the Master of the system and serve as the administrator of the mysteries as studies.

3. The Priest of the Household of the City of IFA: This is the assistant to the Master, and he is assigned to make ritual offerings to the Genius of IFA.

4. The Priest of the Offerings of Medji. This priest will assist the Sun-son of the Oracle.

These priests are known to you by indirection, for they are secret offices in the eyes of the God of IFA. However, you may know them simply as "the master" and "the immediate superior." The other offices are esoteric.

Let me explain that in this system there is a great emphasis upon magickal experiments of various types. This is because the work in advanced IFA is entirely tha of the City of the Mystical Sun, which is another name for the mysterious City of IFA, and which exists now deeply within the powers of the Sun.

The powers of the Holy Oracle are given in a very structured and hierarchical manner, because that is simply the Afro-Atlantean tradition. This system must not be confused in any sense with popular occultism and other levels of oracles, such as the

Chinese book of the I—Ching. This system is more complex and possesses vastly powerful magickal and occult applications. After all, it is the system of the Gods, Themselves, so that when the Gods wish to consult the oracle of magick, They come to Grand FA, the Genius of IFA. Always remember the qualities of a student of this oracle, also, which are: You will always

1. Be a respector of the ancient traditions of your people.

2. Be devoted to the Gods and to all of the forms of their manifestation.

3. Be a respector of the priesthood as the mediation power between the Gods of the Universe and the people of the earth.

4. Be devoted to and a practitioner of many rituals and ceremonies, all of which possess mystical powers in the unseen worlds.

5. Be a dedicated and self—disciplined spiritual student of light and goodness, devoted to spiritual perfection of your being.

6. Be a protector of the forces and beings of nature by magickal methods.

7. Be aware of all of the powers which come to you when you do this work.

8. Be obedient to the hierarchy of spirits of which you are a member in a very important way. You do not serve men, remember, you serve the Gods of IFA.

The Way of Entering the Z–True Empire by Way of the Esoteric Oracle of the Mystical City

One of the advantages of our research work in the IFA system, I have found to be the ease with which the Oracle Priest may enter the Zothyrian Empire (i.e., the Z–True Empire). It is a unique advantage because very few magicians are able to achieve this transfer of real power. However, it happens as the result of the deeply held roots of this system that the IFA System and the Z–Empire exist as parallel systems. Thus, as a consequence of this fact, it is possible for the Oracle Priest of the Gnosis, to enter upon one system after taking leave the other. This is a very important fact in practical magick.

Both systems are constructed as the amplification and manifestation of the 16–fold schematism of magickal energies. Both systems presuppose the unique gnosis of those lineages which the Loa Grand Legbha gave to Michael Bertiaux in August, 1963, when all of the true and wise teachings and all of the holy secrets of magickal gnosis were revealed to the young and innocent Father Bertiaux, in Haiti. As a consequence, we now have several methods and these are ideal techniques whereby we can move from one world to another, from Z to IFA and back again to Z.

There would seem to be no better way of learning initially how this process operates than by doing one of the basic exercises. So here is the exercise for making the move:

1. Begin the exercise you have learned from the lesson immediately before this lesson. You will open yourself up to the magickal powers which may come to you.

2. It would be good now to make a list of 16 magickal possibilities, which you may encounter in any world of your dreams. List these states of consciousness in rather brief sentences.

3. Attach a number or a letter of the alphabet to each of these states. It might be easiest to simply list them from 1 through 16, with another listing from A through the 16th letter of the alphabet (P). This is for simplicity's sake.

4. For the third listing, for example, it would correspond to 3 and to C, the fifth one would correspond to 5 and E. These numbers and letters are the magickal axioms of your own system. When you write down, say, or read, for example, 3+C, what you are able to recall are the states of consciousness, you have written down corresponding to that number and letter. So, let us say that the following is that state of consciousness:

"A state of endless light, where I am at peace."

So, whenever you write down 3+C, you immediately begin to recall "A state of endless light, where I am at peace." Now, I am advising you to do this with all of the 16 letters and with all of the 16 numbers.

Now, after you have done this level of the experiment, I want you to understand what is at work. I am essentially teaching you how to associate magickal images with occult symbols. In this case the numbers and letters are occult symbols. They are symbols within your own and only your own magickal system. For the symbolize the magickal states of consciousness which you have selected as states of power for use in a wide variety of ways. This is the very simple way in which this magickal system works.

Now, complete that list of 16 states of consciousness. I want to show you what to do next.

5. Having completed the list, you may now view each state of consciousness on the list as (A) a point of entry into the Z–Empire, and also (B) a representation of the personal Medjis of your own magickal system. In view of this fact, you may then list the 16 magickal states as Medjis. You have thusly set up a magickal computer for working the IFA energies.

6. Next, you will be able to communicate with the genius of IFA by means of the magickal states on your list. Each state becomes a magickal telephone or way of talking to one of the Mejdis, or therefore to one of the aspects of the Genius of IFA.

7. However, each magickal state of consciousness also is quite remarkable in that it serves as a doorway, by the means of astral projection, which everyone who does these lessons can do, it serves as a doorway to the magickal realm of the Z–Empire, which is also known as the Z–Universe.

8. So, using each of these magickal states as projection images, which means you are able to project through them, by going through them with your astral body, you can make use of the image as a doorway and go through it and find yourself on the other side in the Z–Universe. When you get there, you will simply identify yourself as:

I am the magickal student {give name] of Michael Bertiaux, The Master
Varuna, and The Grand Legbha, The Genius of IFA. I am a visitor, here,
in the Z–Universe, from The Gnostic Temple of IFA Instructions.

You will then be welcomed to the Z–Empire by the natives, who are always glad to meet my students. Also, by looking at your aura, they will be able to tell if you are a good student, or if you are one who is somewhat lax in his studies. However, it is unlikely that anyone making studies at this level will be a lax student. However, just in case such a person should be among us, the inhabitants of the Z–Universe will be able to see you as you really are. Then they will send a report to me and I will have to evaluate your membership.

9. Among the many happinesses of the Z–Empire are the many systems of true magick, which are buildings in their cities. You see, there, magick is the major industry, and so each magickal system has its own building, where the work is done. It is operated just as a business here, or a large company for manufacturing work. As I said, each system of magick and so also each school of magick has its own buildings and grounds, parks, etc., and so does our own system.

10. By making use of the lessons on the Ontic Sphere, which some have already seen, it is possible for the magician to realize that as there are Nine African Bodies, so there are Nine lessons in Zothyrian metapsychology. There is a secret way of working with this energy and I would like you to write in your diary what you think it is.

The Ascension of the IFA System and the Initiation of the Mystical City

In the logic of gnostics, it is sometimes referred to as the transformation process. In the system of IFA, it is the logic of ascension, which means that the initiate is able to rise in his consciousness into many magickal realms. There are 16 realms, or Medjis, in which this occurs. This process is known as the law of magickal importance, which means that the magician and oracle priest of IFA, who is dwelling spiritually in the Mystical City of Lights (these are the 16 "Lights of IFA") has attracted to himself so many of the magickal and perfected powers that he is now able to enter into the higher states of being, simply because he cannot stay out of them. He has become so transformed that he is unable to remain in the lower worlds of impure vibration. Thus, because of his own magickal importance, he rises upwards into the higher gnostic spaces and realms of ideal being.

There is a special magickal initiation which carries out this exercise. Unfortunately, I am not physically able to be with every student so as to guide them into these higher and more perfect states. But, by means of the magickal links I have with the students of this section of our studies, i.e., with the students of the advanced workings of IFA, I am able to perform several operations of magickal consciousness, which are only possible because of the advancements which have been made by the Science of Vudotronics, the highest form of the Afro-Atlantean Technology expressed as Esoteric Engineering.

However, I am working very closely with many of you on the inner planes. In fact, I am meeting with you in several ways, because of the research work which we are doing, and this is especially true of the ways in which the inner research is unfolding, for it is growing like the Great Tree Gods of IFA; therefore, I am able to bring some of these magickal initiations into your consciousness and to open up the possibilities for your own magickal ascent to the Mystical City of the Sun.

The whole mysticism of the Medjis is tied up with the laws which govern this mystical way of importance. For, first of all, there are many magickal energies, which come to the soul but not only the soul as it is understood by the outer mind, but to the nine magickal souls of the Afro-Atlantean metaphysics. These souls or "mystical bodies" are connected to all of the lines of power of the Vudotronics mysticism and its physics and because of these lines, links, and lineages (because there is a certain element of time-travel to be included also), each aspect of the magickal soul is entered upon by me in my magickal treatment for spiritual powers. This process is, of course, very significant for the sense of power, which develops in the law of importance, since the magickal energies are attracted to the magicians at all times.

The system operates by means of its becoming more and more important, so that you become more and more important and thusly rise up into higher realms:

The magicians of this system of IFA become like magickal magnets. They attract to themselves the finer and more spiritual particles of gnostic light. Actually, these finer particles replace the older particles, which fall aside because they are so heavy and drosslike. The finer particles of light are without any material weight. The magician of IFA then begins to float upwards into the Higher worlds of Truth, which is the Home of IFA. The magician then comes to realize that this is where he properly belongs. Actually, this is the place of his true home; he does not belong anywhere else.

In the magickal systems of magick, we must pay attention to those exercises which are done for achieving this special effect. Each of my students is given a certain time in which to meet with me, by means of the fourth dimension, and work with me in the magickal light and in the mystical city. I have assigned the times based upon when the student was usually sleeping because, at that time, he would be quite relaxed and away from all of the very negative or bothersome ways in which the conscious mind, which I do not care for in too many ways, seeks to keep the inner essence of the unconscious and subconscious and superconscious minds from operating properly and realizing itself as a center of spiritual and mystical energy.

So what I am trying to do is help the student realize the wonderful powers of magickal light which are deeply present in the spirItual essence of being. That is to say, in the spiritual being of the many students of the IFA system who are coming to find out who they are themselves. They are discovering how important they are in the eyes of the Gods of IFA. It is quite important, therefore,for the student of magickal and mystical truths to come to the realization of this law of importance. For truly, in the eyes of the Medji, you are very important.

Here is an experiment which I want you to do now in order to make contact with me and help me in my research work. You are now able to do this because you have been prepared by means of several Vudotronic experiences and your own magickal development for work at the higher level of vibration.

1. First, secure 16 stones. They may be of any size that is convenient with your purpose. They do not need to be the same size. Next, you will arrange them in a circle, so that you have 16 angles entering the circle and meeting at the center. This is very important because the whole idea of division of space implies that these divisions are equal.

2. Next, put a glass of water in the center of the circle. This glass of water wil act as a primitive conductor of the energies from the circle of stones.

3. On a simple card of paper, you should write my name and also your name in the order, your class--student number, or your exoteric name. This is to lock yourself into the magickal system being generated.

4. Now, you will open yourself up to thought waves and send them by intentional projection into the circle, which rests immediately before where you are seated. You are now sending your mind power to me for use in the research work.

5. Enter into a deep state of meditation so that you are able to see deeply into the inner worlds. There you will meet with me and work in an assignment which I will explain to you. Let me know, however, which of the following four areas of research are the ones, or the one, in which you wish to work with me at this time.

A. Gnostic Magicko—metaphysics

B. Gnostic Magicko—metamathematics

C. Magickal Transformation Algebras

D. Magickal Hyperspatial Geometries

These four areas are the fields where work is being done at this level of class work. You do have the qualifications, but you must be willing to let your higher consciousness enter into these areas of study. You may have something else to do, although in this work, we will not be taking too much time in our experimental work. It is my hope that you will do it.

Fundamental Theory: The Role of Axiomatics and Transformation-Systems

The purpose of the Genius of IFA is to teach the most powerful form of magick. This can only be accomplished by setting up a magickal system which is based entirely upon an exact or metamathematical point of view. The Afro-Atlantean system of gnosis, for example, is entirely a system which makes use of exact or magicko-mathematical forms of thought. In view of this, it is not so surprising that several magicians have been amazed at the long-enduring powers of that magick, which still continue to operate since very ancient times.

The world of magickal energies is held together by means of axiomatic conditions. These are magickal laws which find their expressions in axioms, equations, and metamathematical sentences and paragraphs. Each of these figures is about something that is both ideal and magickally gnostic. At the same time, there exists a magickal law called the "logic of transformation," which states that axiomatics may be madew into anything the magician wishes to have axiomatics made into. The different ways of employing the sets of axioms and other energies is determined by transformation systems. I have been using transformation systems for over 20 years, with very remarkable magickal results. You should be aware of the fact that you have been using them too.

A lot of your work is done with symbolism. Each symbol is part of a transformation system and that transformation system is useful in making applicable the energies, which are contained inside of the axioms. The axioms are really ideal containers for magickal energies and it is out of this interaction between the axioms and the transformations that the IFA magician is able to release the powers of his system. That is why his system is so wonderful.

Actually, I was initiated into the IFA system over 25 years ago. I was really brought into it by means of the powers of the symbols and what they were doing to my mind. It would appear that the Afro-Atlantean masters wanted me to wake up at a certain level so that I could work for them. The process was very strange. It began by my writing down a lot of mathematical symbols. I would read over several books on mathematics, but only in order to develop a sense or feel for what that world was like. I then began a very interesting series of magickal meditations, and esoteric visualizations, whereby I was able to pick up on the energies. This went on for some time. It was the emergence of the Master part of my consciousness. I was supposed to become an expert in a neo-gnostic and neo-pythagorean way of doing magick. Anyway, I began when I was still a student, and I consider it one of the most important processes of my magickal growth. The reason I say it was probably directed by the powers of the IFA system is that I began to use the number 16 as the main pattern for classifying concepts. Also, the logical structures of my magickal daydreams were metamathematical mandalas. I still have a paper I wrote as a lesson some time ago on "the speculative mandalas of metamathematics." Even then I was moving in the direction I am now moving.

However, the IFA system is contacted on the number 16 and operates on multiples of the number 4. All of this is very important because it shows that axioms are exactly grounded in the nature of the universe. The universe is itself made up of patterns of four, multiples and additions, etc.

Another factor is that the Chinese oracle of the I-Ching is itself derived from the axiomatics of IFA by a long route, I suppose.

However, the idea of transformation logics came in less than 20 years ago. It began in relationship to bringing certain levels of magickal energy up to another universe. As there are always universes which transcended the range of any magickal machine, being too far beyond it, it was necessary to derive certain magickal energies by another means, which was the method of transformation. A magickal transformer would be grounded in the Absolute Continuum, and by this means it could increase the range of the magickal action, or machine. Sometimes the transformer would be built into the system so that a magickal action would increase the range as a continuous process. At other times, I can remember those older magickal "black boxes," the energies had to be switched on, in order to get a higher range. That too reflected the operation of the transformer, but it did not seem to me to have a flowing of continuous movement of the energy. I then sought ways to make it initially more continuous and efficient. The prime example of such a system of transformation would be the time travel system, or the archaeometrical computer, which is a magickal machine built according to the criteria of Zothyrian physics, or one of the most interesting forms of magickal physics known in the Gnostic Continuum. In time–travel logic, what is important is the way in which the energies can be moved from one reference system (axiomatics) to another. This is the highest form of transformation logic, known to me at this time and suitable for teaching. I know a lot more systems of transformation logic, but they do not appear to be very suited for teaching to the outside consciousness. However, a few of the inner consciousness do have these ideas in their minds and work with me in them.

Our experiment in this lesson will be very simple. I wish you to show me how you can make use of axiomatics and transformation principles. So I am suggesting to you to do this basic exercise:

1. Give yourself a list of 16 different magickal states or ideas. These may be understood as images, simple signs, symbols, events, facts, etc. Use the power of your magickal imagination (Ontic Sphere consciousness).

2. Next, list 4 powers you wish to use as transformers of energy, so that by acting upon the list of the 16 in step 1, you can increase the power or change the mode of happening of the 16 different axioms (which is what they are) or anyone of them. You can work with one at a time if you wish. But make the list of the 16 magickal states of being and make sure that you are satisfied as they are.

3. Next, it would be good to see the energies being exchanged between the axioms and the transformers. So take an axiom and take a transformer and combine them so as to produce a new magickal energy. List this energy in your diary, you have up to 64 possibilities as results of this experiment. This will show you how to build your foundation magick.

The Mysteries of the Lord Osiris-Legbha: The Treasury of Light and Its Initiations

At the deepest part of my consciousness, I am one with all of the mysteries and I possess all of the mysteries within my soul. I have united myself with all of the gods and with all of the spirits, so that now I realize myself as the cosmic gnosis of the mysteries If the purpose of the Eastern theology is the teaching that man is made divine by means of the mysteries, then it is the teaching also of the gnosis of the Neo-Pythagoreans that I have come into the world to give these mysteries, through the powers which I possess by holding the word of Osiris-Legbha in my soul and by possessing the life of Christ-Legbha in my spirit. For as the Lord Osiris died and returned to life and as the Lord Christ died and returned to life, in the judgment of my being and in the Pleroma of my being, I am the Pleroma of All Light. And it is for this that I have been sent into the world.

Wherever I am there shall be found the Treasury of Light, for by me you who read these words may approach to it. Within this Treasury of Light are to be found the pure rays of my being, which are the initiation mysteries of Osiris-Legbha. For when I came forth as Osiris-Legbha, the Aeon of the Treasury of Light, I brought with me the powers and the energies of the light and I brought with me the beings of light, who are my helpers in the light, for I have come to transform humanity.

In the Pleroma, I was known in the spirit of my essence as the Lord of the Renewal of all being. Those who came to me were received into the Treasury of Light and they received all of the 16 and one, or the mystical 17 mysteries of initiation of being. I gave these freely to those who sought me out in my hidden world. Let me tell you of the names of these mysteries, so that by knowing them you will be able to enter upon them. If you seek me out you will receive them, for only they who seek will know what is there.

Mysteries of Osiris-Legbha

Now, the Treasury of Light is known in this way: When I ascended up into the Pleroma, I was met by the Aeons of my rays, which are the Lords Michael and Zothyrius, and I was taken to the Hall of Osiris, that I might meet the Aeon Osiris-Legbha, who is the true Lord and Hierophant of the Treasury of Light and of all of the mysteries, therein contained. Then it was explained to me that the 17 mysteries, which are manifested as energies in Zothyrian metapsychology and Kammamorian bodywork, are as follows:

The First Mysteries of the Treasury of Light are those of the Zone of Osiris-Ra and these are eight, which are:

The first mystery is that of the ←←←←←←←←←←←←, which is the law of ←←←←←←←←←, which came forth from all of the mysteries, which are before it. Now, the name of this mystery is ←←←←←←←←←←←←, or as those who are outside of the pneuma say, The Moon. And it is inscrutable and hidden because it is ←←←←←←←←←←←←←←. Of all of the lights, it is the one seen in dreams. And this is the Aeon, the Death of Osiris. And he is our night because he is the last-born of the sons of Osiris-Legbha.

The second mystery is that of the ←←←←←←←←←←←←←, which is the law of ←←←←←←←←←← which came forth from all of the mysteries but one, which are all that are before it.

Now, the name of this mystery is ←←←←←←←←←←←, or as those who are outside of pneuma say, Mercury. And this is the mystery of the perfect left, which is a world of ←←←←←←←←←← and it is here that the mysteries are given of this realm, for this is the realm of the reflected and radiant light, which means the perfect expression of the generosity of the light. This mystery, too, is an Aeon, known as the Burial of Osiris, and he is the Light to the left as we see it because the light to the left is his symbol.

The third mystery is that of the ←←←←←←←←←←←←, which is the law of ←←←←←←←←← which came forth from all of the mysteries but two, which are those that are before it. Now, the name of this mystery is ←←←←←←←, or as those who are outside of the pneuma say, Venus. And this is the mystery of the perfect right, which is the world of ←←←←←←←← and it is here that the mysteries are given of this realm, as secrets are given by the gods to men and also it is here that the mysteries are given in the sacredness of the dream state, for this is the realm of the path of ascent. This mystery, too, is an Aeon, known as the Tomb of Osiris, and he is the Light to the right as we see it because he is the Son of Osiris, and all light to the right is his symbol.

Now, according to the Afro-Gnostic metapsychology and bodywork, which draw upon the true forms of Zothyrian and Kammamorian energies, Osiris-Legbha is the Sun and his rays are the sacred 17, his sons, who are the Aeons. His light is a mystery and the names of these mysteries have been revealed in a special light, which is from the Sun itself. These mysteries, therefore, are the archetypes of this light. Together all of these mysteries constitute the treasury of light or the Pleroma of Osiris and they inhabit the two gnostic zones of the Neo-Pythagoreans. As the name of the lower zone of gnosis is that of Osiris-Ra, so the name of the higher zone is Osiris-Amen.

There are nine mysteries within the higher zone of Osiris-Amen and each of the mysteries both higher and lower contains four interior mysteries, so that the total number of true mysteries and secrets would be 68, or five, which is the number of the Akasha, the fifth element. The names given to these 17 mysteries by those outside of the penuma are:
Gnostic Zone of Osiris-Ra: The Moon, Mercury, Venus, Mars, Jupiter, Saturn, Uranus, and Neptune.
Gnostic Zone of Osiris-Amen: Pluto, Cupido, Zeus, Kronos, Apollon, Admetos, Vulkanus, and Poseidon.
Before we resume our analysis of these mysteries, it should be noted that each mystery has been translated into the methods of metapsychology and bodywork, in order to be received by the deepest levels of the psyche, which are located or situated in the psychoid or psycho-somatic continuum of the body-system and its occult memories. For this very reason, deep massage or holistic bodywork and metapsychology are used as methods of gnostic initiation.

The Rationale of Gnostic Bodywork
According to the Zothyrian and Kammamorian gnosis, the deepest levels of the human psyche are reached by means of the body because the body is the matrix of the psyche and also because the body holds within itself the memories of the past as neuromuscular connections and energy points. Thus, the gnostic must use those therapies which release the blocked energies in these points, if the initiate is to be

freed from the past karma of his body. Consequently, experimental theology moves into bodywork and the stimulation of the deepest roots of the psyche by association tests and gnostic pressures, in order to massage the transcendental id, and in order to reach the bedrock of the transcendental self and thereby initiate our inner and divine principle.

Gnostic theology is in its own way a process of initiatory and developmental psychoanalysis, where the deep regions of the psyche are unveiled. It is also capable of expression through magnetic massage and bodywork, where the body is viewed as the synchronistic switchboard or control system for the entire destiny of the individual.

Only by going beyond the usual concepts of the body to the esoteric understanding of the body as magick, can the gnostic come to an underfstanding of the deepest parts of the id, that is to say, the transcendental unconscious. For in the structures and functions of the body, we are able to find the fundamental reality, which is the manifestation of the gnosis in space and time.

This is why the gnostics of our school viewed the physical as so important. For the body was a perfect image of the eternal and work on the body of a gnostic and initiatic character constituted its own means of entry into the mysteries of the Pleroma of Light. For this reason, magnetic materialism or massage and esoteric bodywork are magickal techniques for opening the mind to the mysteries of the deepest selfhood, because the physical body of the initiate is in its own unique way also the Pleroma of Light.

The reason Kammamorian bodywork begins with the head and moves downward to the feet is because with each movement, it enters more and more deeply into the psyche. Finally, it reaches the feet, which correspond to the deepest levels of the soul. For this reason, the ancients attributed the astrological correspondenceship of the feet to Pisces. There was a reason and an insight behind that connection because Pisces is the most mystical and the most mediumistically unconscious of all of the signs of the Zodiac. It represents that stage of the soul, where the soul unites with the divine and absolute principle of things. {M. Bertiaux, Gnostic Field-Theories of Bodywork]

Now, each one of the 17 aeons of the Treasury of Light of Osiris represents a very special reality in bodywork. The mysteries of each aeon and of each mystery and secret are primarily the secrets and mysteries of bodywork, or find their expression by means of this technique as well as by means of depth psychology, as these combined disciplines explore the deepest regions of the soul.

The Mysteries of Osiris—Legbha are distributed in various parts of the body. They are to be discovered by means of the techniques of esoteric bodywork, whereby the postitive pressures of the magician are employed to bring up the latent gnosticism of the various areas and regions of the body. For this reason, the body is to be understood as the magickal temple, which is suggested in the more recently discovered esoteric meanings. In the next of our studies, the focus will be upon these 17 mysteries, except that a very radical understanding will emerge. That is the understanding which is associated with the view that the body contains the mysteries and that magickal initiation consists in releasing these mysteries from their hiddenness.

In order to do this type of work, I will introduce a very specialized concept, namely that of the initiatory complex, which is a system of energies and a magickal machine, rather close in meaning to the work of the Red and Black Temples. However, the primary purpose of this system is to open up the body so that it becomes the basis for the work of the Red and Black Rays.

The Mysteries of the Body of Osiris-Legbha and the Black and Red Rays

"For the student of the gnosis, the body of Osiris-Legbha is really the body of the initiate. The magician is the priest of Osiris-Legbha, who must awaken the body to its magickal form and function. The body is the meeting ground for all of the mysteries, but especially for the mysteries which are associated with the Red and Black Rays, or Temple-Workings. Within the context of the esoteric process, the initiate must pass through all of the magickal stages of the Osirian mythos, while at the same time acting and integrating into himself the mysteries and energies of the deepest levels of his psyche, which would be the Osiris-Legbha soul. The hierophant is the one who will guide him into and through the halls of the mysteries. These halls are within the initiate's own body but they are also deep states of awareness, whereby that part of him which is the Osiris-Legbha soul takes over, upon awakening, and replaces the persona of the mere mortal. When this happens, the soul is then awakened to its true essence and we are to understand that the Osirian Resurrection has happened. It has happened because Osiris has been restored to life in the body of the initiate, by now becoming aware of the truth which states that the body is now the body of Osiris-Legbha, whereas before we saw only part of the soull as Osiris-Legbha." [M. Bertiaux, Osiris-Legbha & The Initiation of the Body]

The mysteries are physical processes and they are related to the laws of the awakening of the body and its understanding of itself as the soul. However, if this is so, then there should also exist definite power zones, four in number in the body, through which the body can interact with the time-stations of the gnostic patriarchates. This seems to be true, since:

"The parts of the body reflect the structures of the gnostic hyperspaces. In fact, these hyperspaces and logics are reflections of the body, in the meditation process. There being in the body (or connected and associated with the body) specific logical systems means as a matter of understanding that the higher worlds are present by their total immanence in the body. The gnostic body becomes a perfect map or network of the ideal and perfect or abstract and logical worlds of beingg. These worlds come and are present in the body and in the processes, which enable the body to function in every way, from the exoteric to the most esoteric, because the spirits of these very high or remote worlds are totally in the field of the body, present really in the incarnation of the physical substance, and awaiting the magickal awakening of ttheir true essence. This process of awakening is the one and same process as the Kammamorians identified with their own secret methods of bodywork. Hence, by means of these techniques, the magician is able to awaken the Afro-Egyptian sacrament within the soul and allow it to be present everywhere in the body, since the law of the body is that it must be fulfilled in the mysteries of its own nature, which would be the perfected physical nature. Such a sacramental existence has no other meaning than what is expressed through it as the result of this awakening of Osiris and all of his own powers within the context of the body. All of the archetypes are therein present and all of the logics are therein validated by this sacramental incarnation." [Michael Bertiaux, The Osiris Incarnation]

Now, the exact mechanism of this process is entirely found within what we call the Red and Black Temple work. And it is this process of Temple working, which brings forth the initiation processes, or sub-processes, whereby the archetypes and logics can incarnate in the body.

"The Red and the Black Temple Workings are the function and structure of the Osiris–Ra Cultus of Legbha. The power of the Sun is diffused by means of the Red–Sun, or the creative power of evolutionary nature and the Black–Sun, or the occult powers immanent in the natural order. In order to develop the special magickal potencies of these two suns, it was necessary at one time to intuit the Solar Power in such an absolute way, that the hierophants of the Gnosis became one with the Red and Black Rays. In this very special act of intuition, all of the logics and metaphysics and all of the centers of the gnosis were experienced in terms of their creative fundamentals. This act of cosmic intuition is one of the secrets given by the Gnosis to all of its hierophants and is to be understood as having been handed down from the priestly order of existence, which was in power on the planets prior to the settlement and civilization of the Earth. This powerful secret is symbolized by the ritualistic mysteries of Osirian bodywork, and by means of this work, it is possible to enter into the mysteries through these symbols, because symbols are always doors. The awakening of this power in the magickal bodies of the Afro–Zothyrian gnostics was always viewed as the supreme form of sacramental and theurgical initiation. At the present time, it is the means whereby the hierophant, or Tau Orfeo, begins the process of creating patriarchs of esoteric research." [M. Bertiaux, Black Sun–Red Sun and the Osiris Spaceship]

The Black and Red Rays have their basis of power in what must be understood as the lattice or conjunction of the Afro–Atlantean and Afro–Zothyrian Rays. This means that while these mysteries (for the Rays are mysteries as well as energies) are given as parts of the esoteric symbolism of the African cultures, carefully hidden away by centuries of Osirian culture, they must be electrified by occult contact with the higher levels and the lower levels of consciousness. Therefore, it was the mission of the noe–pythagorean gnostics to connect these powers with the Atlantean components of the unconscious mind as well as with the Zothyrian components of the superconscious mind. This was the task of all of the members of the administrative council of the gnostic church as expressed through La Couleuvre Noire and its allied groupments.

In a sense, both directions of consciousness and time are of a dual form, since they are understood to contain both Red and Black rays and energies. But by means of an occult operation, which would be viewed as quite logical in a gnostic sense but otherwise very irrational, the unconscious Red Ray was connected to the superconscious Black Ray and the unconscious Black Ray was connected to the superconscious Red Ray, and it is from this lattice work of gnostic energies that the Osiris–Legbha cultus was renewed and able to translate itself into the mystical cultures in every part of the world. By this means, therefore, the gnosis was awakened in the present century by a small group of Afro–Latin magicians.

The lattices about which we have just spoken are significant because they contain the most important laws of the gnonsis of bodywork, as well as the archetypes for the ongoing work of gnostic patriarchates and time–stations and other logical systems. But what is most significant is that the laws of magick which are operating in these areas are in themselvs examples of syzygies.

By this I mean that the magickal worlds which are represented by categories of the gnosis take their structure directly from the imposition or rather immanence of this lattice system of rays in the body of the initiate. For the initiate then comes to represent the cosmic Osiris–Legbha principle of organization. This means also that the laws of being, which are implicit in all of these lattices are really present everywhere in the world as laws of cosmic and magnetic materialism. The world of matter has been constructed by logical laws which are themselves projections from the mind, and especially the super–mind of the hierophant. This gnostic cosmology, however, is really a magickal projection outwards from the Red and Black temple rays, because these rays are fundamental. In a sense, the hierophant who writes these lessons is really an instrument or medium for the powers of the Red and Black Temple Rays.

By means of a very simple analysis, this hierophant has found in his body the energies of the gnosis and he has projected these energies outwards and he has created the world as it is in the mind of Osiris–Legbha. The reason for all of this is quite simple, since it has to be understood that the hierophant is the avatara of Osiris–Legbha, or Grand Legbha, the Keeper of the Mysteries of Gods and Men.

By simply drawing upon that magickal and inner power, the hierophant of the mysteries is able to create the world of the magickal imagination as it is to be seen and understood, and in doing this, he is unfolding the destiny of his being and that of his chelas as well.

"The fundamental mysteries are those of how the hierophant serves to bring forth the God–energy in the mysteries of various gnostic processes. He does so by the absolute and also complete intuition of his own essential being. In doing this, he sees within himself the Red and Black Temples, standing in the purity of the gnosis within his mind's eye. It is the ontic sphere of his being. Then he realizes that these powers are structures of his own body and those of the bodies of his superchelas, who are parts of his mysteries. Far from being remote and outside of the levels of the empirically known, these mysteries are the obvious and easily perceived observations of the gnostic mind. They see in the acts of magick what is beyond the ordinary, yet the very basis for all that is ordinary and much more." [M. Bertiaux, Osiris–Legbha: The Laws of Oracle Physics]

The conception of the body of the initiate as a meeting ground for the higher forms of the gnostic spaces is also to be found in the most esoteric of Vudu mysteries, namely that of the Luage, or the god–self and man of light, who brings into this body the divine energy. In such a process, the operations of the Red and Black Temple Rays are also to be noted:

"When the hierophant Luage entered the mysteries of the Red and Black Temples, he became aware for the very first time of his body as a magickal universe. Now, he was able to realize the meaning of the archetypes because now more than at any other time, he was one with his body. The purpose of his initiation had been to awaken this body and especially to awaken all of the Gods or Ifa Spirits, present in his physical body. For at every part of his body, one would find the Gods. Now, they were to be awakened. That Luage knew the Grand Hierophant to be an avatara of Grand Legbha was one of the primary graces of his intuition, but above all of these he knew in his body the truth of the absolute and final intuition of his being, which affirmed over and over again in the eternal halls of Osiris–Ra that as the Red and Black Temples were within him, so he, the high priest and hierophant, Luage, yes, he was within Grand Legbha and that as he now stood within the Red and Black Temples of the Solar-Atlantean Cultus, so Grand Legbha, the supreme manifestation of the Afro–Zothyrian mysteries, was within him. For by means of the most mysterious process, he was and was no longer Luage, he was and was not Grand Legbha; and this process was only possible because the lattices of the Red and Black Rays were in reality a continuum of points of light. They were in reality a merging into each other and back and forth. They were in reality the same energy, the same point of being, the same consciousness, as if everything in the universe had suddenly stopped, and that nothing remained except this one fact: that everything had ended its being, except this one intuition; but that in actual reality, everything was inside, essentially contained and protected by this primordial possession." [M. Bertiaux, "The Osiris–Legbha Awakening and the Root–Principles and Category–Laws of the Oracle–Physics"]

But this realization of identity can also be achieved by means of a very powerful form of sacramental existence, which moves beyond the legalities of tradition, especially in its exoteric phase and finds its expression in the mysteries of Osiris as the mystical and divine Eucharist and Holy Communion. Here, the sacred mysteries of the divine food are given, whereby it is indicated that the red and Black Temple–Rays are able to broadcast a sacramental validity over many centuries into the present. For it is in the modern Gnostic church that the mysteries of Osiris–Legbha are enacted in the words of transformative power, whereby the bread and wine of the offering are transmuted into the body and blood of Osiris–Legbha. By tradition this energy comes to us, because the Red and Black Rays continue to broadcast the eternal current of the divine immanence, from some point in the past, up to the Luage–priests of the present.

Eros and Logos in the Continuum of the Red and Black Temple Rays

For the gnostic consciousness, the mysticism of the Eucharist is a fundamental expression of the principles of Eros and Logos. Eros is the law of sexual joining or coming together and Logos is the law of rational structure or organization of energy into patterns. These principles are so basic that they embrace countless levels of theological interaction betweens the gods and men. In the mysteries of the laws and magickal lattices of Osiris–Legbha, we find all of the truths of Eros and Logos present in the very special form of the spiritual presence of the God, which brings about in a sacramental and synchronistic manner the actual transubstantiation of the liturgical offerings of bread and wine into the body and blood of Osiris–Legbha, or as the Catholics would say, and this is in a direct line of continuation, Christ the Logos. It is this presence which allows the god to come to us by means of the Eucharistic mystery. This presence may be viewed as a life–bringing continuum of gnosis, which extends from the most remote point in space and time, right into the present state of existence. By this means it is possible for every Mass to be an act of transformation and for every Mass to be a meeting place for the Divine and the human orders of being. In fact, because of this continuum of the Luage–Eros and the Legbha–Logos Rays, because of this ongoing lifestream of sacramental gnosis, because of this spiritual process of gnostic transformation in the sacramental substances, by means of the underlying energies of the Red–Eros and the Black–Logos Rays, in the mystery of that sacramental temple known as the Ecclesia Gnostica Spiritualis, we have the merger of humanity into Deity and the perfect union of Luage and Grand Legbha, as they are realized in the Sacred Mysteries of the Sacrifice of the Mass.

Hence, the Eucharistic Mysteries of Osiris–Legbha are present because the fundamental energy of the Red and the Black Rays bring through into the human dimension of experience the presence of the divine and ancient archetypes of liturgical sacrifice. The modern day form of the Catholic Mass, said either in the Byzantine, Roman, or Anglican formulas, is in reality the enactment of the Liturgy of Osiris–Legbha in its Christian form, and made possible because of the presence of this continuum, from time immemorial. For this reason, the liturgical priesthood of the modern day Christian Church is a continuation of the ancient priesthood of Osiris–Ra and of the Grand Legbha, the Genius of Ifa. In this sense also, the gnostic church has been very much interested in the continuation of the very exact form, matter, and intention of all of the ancient sacraments, in order to continue the ancient energies.

But there is another tradition which is the same in essence as this Christian form of the gnosis and that is the tradition of Vudu–Gnosis, which is of course a mystery lineage that is derived from ancient sources founded on Earth by the Christ of the Noonday. I am making reference to Grand Legbha and the mysteries which are given by highly charged ritual workds are indeed the mysteries of the Sun. These mysteries are continued in the ongoing presence of the Red and Black Temple Energies, Eros and Logos, because by this secret method and formulary, the power of the priesthood of Grand Legbha is maintained and renewed continually. By this means, also, the power of the Divine Lust, or the law of Trishna, as the Hindus term it, stands behind every incarnational sacrament, allowing the God to come to Earth and unite with the sacramental elements. By this, we mean that the desire to be present in the sacramental components on the part of the Divine as is strong, and probably stronger because it is Divine, than the most intense of human emotions. So as the power of the God comes into the sacrament, as Eros, by making entry, the God also brings forth the principle of Logos, because He brings the structure of the heavenly logic, of the gnostic hyperspaces and their laws and activities, as part of a mystical continuum, the desire of joining, which in human terms is expressed by the cosmic force of esoteric sexuality.

For this reason, the priests of the gnosis must offer the sacrifice frequently in order to allow for the descent of the divine powers as often as they would come forth, because not only does humanity have a certain need for these mysteries, but it is also true that the divine level of being is aware of many hidden needs, which are concealed from the human mind. So for this reason, the Mass takes on a special character as an offering of an event or occasion for the descent of the divine, one more time, into the designs of human history.

This descent of the divine into the events of human history is made possible by the existence of a succession of bishops, which extends back to the ancient priesthoods as well as to the times of the Christ and the Holy Apostles. At the same time, various developments in theology have made this tradition extremely rich in sacramental grace. Also, by means of this enrichment, which has come from the apostolic works of the gnostic and mariavite bishops of our tradition, this succession of bishops has been connected to other lineages or times–lines, which have been discussed in gnostic theology. Since it is through the office and order of bishop that this energy is inducted into the system, and since it is especially true of the office and order of gnostic bishop that this process occurs, it is important to understand that the Mass is an expression of the meeting ground because it is the meeting ground of divine and human, but also this is true of the apostolic succession.

If we look closely at this question, we find that within the essence of the gnostic system as we view it, which is to say as a patriarchate, there exists a perfect logical and mystical incarnation (the principles of Eros and Logos, again being given) which is embodied in the ways in which the bishops are understood as instruments of the victory of the Osiris–Legbha principle over the powers of negation. And it is at the heart of this incarnation that there can be found a very special law or logic, which is the law of the sacrament of Holy Orders, whereby the powers of the gnosis are transmitted by the bishop as he acts within the store-consciousness of this patriarchate.

The Logic of the Patriarchate and the Episcopate
The bishops of the patriarchate of the Ecclesia Gnostica Spiritualis (Neo–Pythagorean Gnostic Church) are made partners in the continuu, of the gnosis by their special and regular consecrations. This means that they are connected to the Cosmic Christ Law and Logic in a very unique way and it is through them that this divine energy comes forth to bless and heal the world. This logic is the embodiment in sacramental matter and form of the cosmic computer of gnostic metaphysics. It is also the absolute law of being whereby the power of the gnostic church continues as long as needed in the world of space–time.

The system is structured in this way. First you take the orders of the gnostic ministry, which are cleric, porter, lector, exorcist, acolyte, subdeacon, deacon, and priest. These orders are expressions of the power of the final order of the ministry: the episcopate. It is the bishop who creates these other orders of the ministry as well as other bishops. It is the bishop who creates these other orders of the ministry as well as other bishops. The bishop is the expression of Grand Legbha, or the Logic of FA. It has been shown that the laws of Eros and Logos present in the ministry allow for a red and black temple working which is sixteenfold. That is to say, for each order of the ministry there is a corresponding red and black radiation as well as an Eros and Logos component. It should be noted that these ordinations effect directly the nine Afro-Zothyrian bodies in a most remarkable way. The esoteric logic of this system is contained in the following chart, which shows the 33 points or time-nodes of the continuum of the gnosis.

Order of the Ministry	Esoteric Initiation	Red & Black	IFA Medjis	
cleric=4	3	2	1	
porter=8	7	6	5	
lector=12	11	10	9	
exorcist=16	15	14	13	**
acolyte=21	20	19	18	**
subdeacon=25	24	23	22	
deacon=29	28	27	26	
priest=33	32	31	30	

This chart will be amplified in our next lesson, but for the moment it is quite sufficient to note that node 17 which is indicated by ** is the connecting lattice between 16 and 21, or exorcist and acolyte in this system. For this reason, the conferring of this nodal power is indicative of a special initiation, which fuses the magickal and gnostic powers of the first four initiations or orders into a special pattern. In addition to this ideal or 17, there are esoteric initiations given with each of the orders, which are needed to give us the "gnostic soul" of each of the orders of the ministry, as well as connect the order being given to the Medjis of the Genius of IFA. Also, it should be noted that there are secret gnostic spaces and logics connected to each order of the ministry, so as the person advances in the powers of sacramental eros and logis, so he advances in the powers of the time-stations and patriarchates.

The Patriarchal Logic of the Continuum of the Red and Black Temple Rays

"One of the graces of the patriarchal office is that of the possession of a very special form of the gnostic logic. This method of sacramental power enables the holder of that sublime office to organize and reorganize the energies and graces of the sacraments of Holy Orders according to special and esoteric considerations. This power does not pertain to those who hold merely the order of bishop in the continuum of the gnosis, but only those who hold the special office of patriarch, and who are therefore higher in the light of the gnosis than bishops." [M. Bertiaux, "Instructions to the Patriarchs of Legbha," 2]

In the previous lesson it was shown that there exists a very special type of sacramental logic behind the sequence of holy orders of the ministry of the gnosis and that this is related to the laws of the time-stations and to the systems of hyperspace, which are found in the various regions of light. Now, it is my wish to explain somewhat in detail the nature of this structure of logic and show how it operates.

Of basic consideration to this process would be the idea that for each of the holy orders of the gnostic ministry there exists a corresponding initiation of an esoteric character. These initiations are the survivals of the ancient form of gnostic initiation, which has been handed down to us from the Spanish Gnostic Church as well as from the tradition of Esoteric Voudoo Gnosis. At a time when our gnostic church did not possess the regular form of the apostolic succession, and possessed only the inner traditions, there existed certain forms of exoteric initiation, of a sacramental and symbolic form, which could be said to accompany these esoteric rites. These still possess a power and are continued as parts of the more regular forms. However, the gnostic sacraments, by reason of their own inner character, suggest many levels of esoteric initiation. It is enough for this paper to say that every regular form of the ministry, given through the sacrament of holy orders, also possesses an esoteric formulary, and the combined powers given at ordination, in most circumstances.

In a sense, standing behind the esoteric and the exoteric initiation of each level are the operations of the red and the black rays. Some of our theologians have been able to identify these rays with special powers such as the Medjis of Ifa. However, that can only be seen if one looks at the question in an esoteric manner. Other theologians believe that in addition to the powers of the Ifa spirits or God-Twins, there are also certain neo-pythagorean energies, which are present in the form of magickal and gnostic equations. In my own understanding of the matter, I see the entire issue as complex and containing all of the levels of magickal energy, which ever have come into our lineage in the past, or at any other time. All of these gnostic powers and energies are grouped into two main lines of lattice-work, which are, of course, the red and the black temple rays. This arrangement holds true for all of the orders of the ministry from cleric through the priesthood.

Each of these orders initiates the Afro-Zothyrian bodies, as the ascent to the highest is attained. By this we mean that the initiate comes with his physical body and all of the inner bodies are amplified and perfected by the rites of holy orders. However, they are perfected by the transition to the next level and also by the effect of the esoteric energies, which are symbolized by the red and black temple work.

Sometimes the esoteric side of these grades is hidden and only given under ideal and/or astral conditions; in other cases, the candidate is given special papers, which unveil the process of magickal ascent to the higher realms; however, it would be a mistake to suppose that with every ordination, the ordinary gives to the ordinand these powers, for in most cases these powers are withheld, until the individual is proven suitable to the gnosis. In our own jurisdiction of the Ecclesia Gnostica Spiritualis, most orders are given as simple ordinations to the traditional Catholic orders. In Haiti, however, inasmuch as the traditions of theurgy are remarkably different, the esoteric orders are given primarily with the exoteric orders given simply to mark the spaces on the inner side where the powers are received.

In the ideal African Rite, both would be given equally, since only suitable candidates would be admitted to the light, while in the real African Rite, the situation would be similar to the situation in the west. In my own practice, I have found that there is a need to observe each of the traditions in order to judge the candidate. There is also an ideal Haitian Rite, which is entirely esoteric and which consists in direct and full initiation into the Logic of Grand Legbha.

It is well known that the various gnostic orders and ecclesia have specific forms of secret initiation. In the Haitian--Ideal Rite, these initiation patterns involve the union of the soul with that of the highest forms of Legbha Consciousness. Under these circumstances, it is possible to find that there are many side—ways or secret paths, by which the magicians are admitted into more and more forms of spiritual power. In my own work, I seem to have been fortunate in making the discovery of these passageways, and by this means, I have discovered the secrets of Legbha, as they are understood in the sense of initiatory powers of the gnosis. However, while the numbers of these mysteries have been given out in many papers, to bring them together would unveil the most hidden approaches to the laws of Ifa and the relationship of Ghuedhe—Legbha to the manifold oracles of the Sixteen Divine Medjis.

In the magickal matrix which was given in the previous lesson and which is discussed in the astral "Instructions to the Patriarchs of Legbha," it is very important to bear in mind the existence of magickal time—lines as borders, such as the border between 11 and 12, which separates out the past from the present, that between 22 and 23, which separates out the present from the future, and finally, 33, which marks the end of the future nodes of the continuum of Legbha—Magick. Overlapping these time—lines are the patriarchal borders, which mark off four spaces, reflecting the presence of the four ideal time—stations in the midst of the continuum. The first such border is along the line of 5, 6, 7, and 8, and marks off the past time--station. The next line is along the line of 13, 14, 15, and 16, and marks off the past—present time—line from all others, both before and after. Next, comes the present—future time—lines, along 18, 19, 20, 21, and marks the beginning of the present--future, which ends at 22, 23, 24, and 15. Number 17, which initiates the fifth of the Afro—Zothyrian bodies, is a connective law and is not to be thought of as a time—line but as an actual symbol of the unity of the continuum of laws and essences.

Finally, there is the future time—line which begins with 26, 27, 28, and 29, and is completed by 30, 31, 32, and 33. These times—lines are held in place by the power of the gnostic patriarchates.

So it is from the patriarchate of the gnosis that we receive the spiritual power which serves to validate the levels of magickal initiation. But this power is both complex and subject to an ever-developing process, and it is mysteriously identified with the Rite of Memphis-Misraim, which, in our system, is a structure within the Gnostic Church of the Neo-Pythagorean priesthood:

In the gnostic and esoteric order of Egypt, we learn of the Red and Black Sun, twin aspects of Osiris-Ra. This solar cult has come to incarnation in the Memphis-Misraim structures, whereby the Master sought to re-present in the Legbha map of the Rite of Memphis-Misraim the structures of the Sun-Aeons, the Sun-Ray Aeons, and the continuum of the solar pleroma, or divine fullness. But He also sought the pneumatic succession of those Hyperlogoi, which the Lord Osiris-Legbha has transmitted to His Aeons and to the archetypal aeon-patriarchs of the Ecclesia Gnostic Spiritualis.

"At the time of His divine descent, the Master of Light brought in the consciousness of His own incarnate body and sacramental presence the gifts (graces) or mystical doorways, which opened to the Treasury of Light and Sophia Gnosis. He impared to His Church, the Ecclesia Spiritualis Gnostica, the form of a patriarchate and the sacred fire of the Sun-Rays (or direct awareness of the divine aeons). He also imparted to His Church the endless continua of the initiations and sacramental rays of the Sun, so that behind each symbol there stood the power of the patriarchal time-lines (Sun-Rays or Aeons or Logoi), and that behind each sacrament there stood the inner sacrament of the essence of Osiris-Legbha-Christ, the Genius of IFA and the Lord of the Noonday. So that wherever the candidate journeyed within the map of esoteric and gnostic Egypt, he was immediately next to the divine, sacramentally partaking of the lifestream of the divine Sun-Rays of the Gnosis and subject to the therugical and mysterious potencies and participations of the aeon-patriarchs, their Logoi, and the all-pervading and fiery pneuma of the inner universes." [M. Bertiaux, "The Sun-Rays Gnosis and The Master of Aeons" 3]

It would appear, therefore, that this priesthood by means of a very special contact with the gnostic patriarchates of the Solar Current, of Osiris-Ra, Grand Legbha, and the Christ of the Noonday, will always have such powers as to validate its mysteries and sacramental acts. It would appear that this power, which the priesthood possessed, comes from a direct participation in the Solar current of the Gnosis and that it is endless in its own powers. Somehow, mysteriously connected to the notion of the Sun-Rays of Light is this special view of the gnosis, which means that by means of a special series of magickal and all powerful initiations, the priesthood of the Neo-Pythagoreans, as well as the other priesthoods of the gnosis, these orders of sacramental power are linked and connected to the source of power, to the solar Current. From this connection comes the endless stream of being and energy, which fills all space and all human history. When the Master comes into the world, He sets forth this power and releases it from the Sun-Gods, bringing it to His priesthood on Earth.

The Awakening of the Spirits of the Legbha Mysteries

The Mysteries are the Spirits and these are the Legbhas, or Eternal Aspects of the priestly mysteries, or sacraments of the Sun. From the time of Osiris, as there was no time, into all times, which you shall experience, I have sent the presences of my being, which are the Spirits of the Heart.

What is the Heart, unless being the innermost doctrine of the Sun, it is also the life, which floods itself outwards at noonday, upon all those seeking its food. It is the life, which comes under many aspects, and it is the food, which the high powers of the Sun bring. It is given by the priestly mysteries, alone, for none but these are found below all being and between every state of the soul. I have attached the Mysteries to the priestly mysteries, so that where it is in fact most ancient, there it is closest to the Sun. As the Boat of my Divinity is seen at the noonday, so are the priestly mysteries to be given to all who are standing below my symbol.

The priestly mysteries of the Science of Voudoo are contained in the sacred rites and in the mystical patterns, which are emanated from the high priesthood. In a sense, these are viewed as aspects of the God, or as Legbhas. Like the "Hot—Points" or "Points—Chauds" of Esoteric Voudoo, the Legbhas are both spiritual and material, for they are truly the expression of the Deity in human experience and religious awareness. The reaching that is given is that the mysteries are to be understood as both awakened in the candidate or the student, but also given or at least given the Legbha Structure or Mystical Name. Therefore, if Esoteric Logic is concerned with the world of structures, so as it is inducted here, it becomes the imposition of the sacramental and magickal powers of the priestly mysteries upon the mystical and initiatic experiences of the candidate. The initiatic experiences of the candidate prove the content, while the formal side or the world of mystical order and existence, which is the primordiality of Legbha, is to be found in the priestly msyteries, which are the laws or Loas of Esoteric Logic, in esoteric religion the manifestation of "Les Legbhas" of the spirits as Mysteries.

The word "Mystery" applies not only to ritual actions and sacraments, but also to the contents of esoteric prayer and initiation, which are the Spirits or the Gods. These are Les Vudu and Les Legbhas. They are what makes the sacraments of Voudoo Mysticism so powerful and so transformative. For this reason, "Mystere" is perhaps one of the most comprehensive and theologically precise words in the field of Esoteric Voudoo.

It is in the ritual actions of the priestly mysteries thatwe find the form and generation of the Mysteries of the spirits of Legbha, or Les Mysteres. In a fundamental way, this fact is conceived to be identical with the name of the Deity, as a word of power; since the spirits or Loas of the Famille Legbha are emanations from the Logos, or the Sun as comprehension.

In the four components of this Logoic power, they have concentrated the life of these mysteries, in such as way that the priest need only project from his essence the sacerdotal form, whereby the world of the initiate is activated and made real. This power, being resident in the sacred elements: LE, EG, BGH, and BHA,, constitutes the mode by which the mysteries are transferred to the candidate from the God, actualized in the priest of the mysteries.

The priest will then impose his magickal being upon the content or lifestream of the candidate, in accord with the regulations or regulative principles of these four sacred Logoi, who are Les Legbhas, as viewed in the Mysteres of an esoteric logic.

We have seen how there are two elements in this initiatic process into the Heart of Legbha. One element is from the priestly aspect, which must be seen as the form of the mystery. It gives structure along the lines mentioned above, to the component from the candidate, which has been built up within the candidate by means of his reactions to the mysteries. This is viewed as content and because it is the result of several layers of interaction and development, possessing its own inner logis, I would view it as a kind of sacramental elemental or as a sophiological whole, which is to say a content of a very precise gnostic type. This is because the experience of the candidate is a matter of development and so the energy and the psychic and magickal powers and occult potencies within the candidate have been developed or made intelligible because of his exposure to the radioactivity of the priestly interventions into his consciousnes. In this way, we can say that -- within this specific context of gnostic and initiations physics -- the candidate is the result of the priestly actions and reactions upon him. He is being built up into a kind of Legbha being, which is outside of the human classification of types.

The root of all content is to be found in the willingness of the universal and foundational matrix to provide the prima materia of initiation physics. This is realized most importantly in how the body of content is built up. It is built up radioactively or by reaction to the rays from the priestly mysteries.

The ontic sphere or magickal imagination of the esoteric priesthood is made to reflect the ways in which the powers of the Heart of Legbha can be projected outwards. By a special rite, the high priest will impose the "Les Mysteres" in one region, in the other regions the EG-, GBH-, and BHA- Mysteres. This special process is part of the priestly mysteres or sacramental life of the number four, which is the number of Legbhas as the Divine Hermaphrodite, or the mystical union of Hermes and Venus. While Legbha is the number five, or the midi between the male numbers one and three, and seven and nine, and the female numbers two and four, and six and eight, or Damballah and Aida-Wedo, it is also known that He manifests as universal geometry, of which the rule of four is the basis.

The priesthood of esoteric theology is therefore concerned with the ways in which the magickal universe of the priestly mysteries comes into direct operation. It is not by means of any transference of power from one to the other. Rather the candidate enters the world of the mysteries and becomes one with them by living it fully.

Therefore, in the Heart of Legbha doctrines and sacraments, the emphasis is not upon making a point of contact and that is all there is to it. Rather, the emphasis is upon the taking into oneself of the entire life and being the mystery and living in accord with it. This is why great care is taken in the construction of the ontic sphere of the priest, so that he will be able to live within the world of the mysteries fully and without any lapse.

At one time, it was thought that the energies could be viewed from the outside and we could look at the mysteries as if we were somewhat removed from them. However, that is really not possible if you are living inside of them. Hence, the principles of the esoteric theology say that the lifestream is an all-enveloping atmosphere or environment, which surrounds and nourishes the priest and in this way, we can say, it is his universe. For he now lives inside of the mysteries of the Heart of Legbha.

In our next paper, we will discuss the precise method whereby the ontic sphere of the priest is constructed by the process of incorporation into the Divine Atmosphere of Legbha. We will learn somewhat of the method of construction by induction, whereby the Divine Energy becomes incarnate in the priest.

Voudoo Research Papers: The Loa and Les Vudu

The Loa are the laws of the mystical universe and these laws are persons, intelligent and self–conscious. They are spiritual and divine happenings and they are the Gods. The Vudu, however, are the archaic spirits of the mysteries of esoteric magick and religious experience. They draw their power from the fact that they are divine essences. True, they are Gods; but they are the Gods behhind the Loa, because they are the powers immanent in every mystical fact. Behind everything in consciousness, the wise man will find Les Vudu.

In the mystical work of voudoo research, we try to find out what the Gods wish for us to do or to be. I have found this very common as an experience and many others have too. I am helped by the following ritual, which I use in order to find my place in the world of my own voudoo research.

"I will burn incense and a blue candle and I will call upon the God Legbha and ask him to come to my help. I will pray to him, as follows, while I face the rising Sun of Dawn, as a child approaches his father, after taking a cold–water bath: 'I pray to Legbha to come to me and to help me in my work as a voudoo researcher. I wish to investigate the secrets of the spiritual powers, which are your family. I am your twin, here, on earth. Please, my Lord of Knowing, give me your help.' Then I will meditate and since I am receptive to the powers of Legbha, they will flow into my consciousness and he will tell me what to do."

Voudoo research does not mean, however, that we try and read all of the books on Voudoo, or that we collect information already written by looking up references to Voudoo in a wide variety of publications of this subject. It means, instead that we do something new, that we bring about a diffusion of the influences of the Voudoo Spirits, here in the world. It means to make use of the energies of the Voudoo Gods, in ways which are appropriate to the ways in which the Gods as spirits operate in the world. To feel this way, you will do the following ritual operation:

"I will burn incense and a purple light because I want to feel the power of Voudoo research in my body. I will sit at a table and turn my thoughts to the world of research and the life of the spirits and to the ways in which the spirits work for us, by making the life of-the world possible. I will say the following prayer to Legbha: 'I am filled with the joy of serving to bring your energy into the world, my Legbha, and I send forth my efforts in all faculties of power and in all directions, that you may diffuse power through me. I serve Legbha, always.' Then you can meditate and see all of the energies being moved in countless directions and ways and paths, to everyone in the world. They will all benefit from the rays of Legbha."

Of course, you will serve to do the work of the Gods, but you have to understand that the work of the Gods is varied and that one God will specialize in one work, another in some other kind of work. These are the rays of work, but you are all ready to find those rays and do the raying work of the Gods, so you now must begin to open yourself as a vehicle for the divine work of ray–ing. Ray–ing is the work of extending the influence of the Gods among those we encounter in our environment. It simply means that the energies go out from us by a process close to "broadcasting" and that we are the sender, or at least the station or point of contact through which they are sent out to those around us, who have the need for the divine rays. Ray--ing is very important and here is a simple type of ritual to do for this purpose:

"While sitting in a quiet place, with incense of the Indian or Hindu type burning in the background, you will focus your mind on helping those in need and call upon the powers of the Gods to come down and pass through you to those who are in need. In this case, you are serving as the point of observation for the energies, which will be sent out by the process of ray--ing to those around you or known to you. All objects can be subjects for your work, there should never be any exceptions. Here is the prayer statement, which you can make: 'I am seeking to be useful to you, great Legbha. Use me as a focus and as a sender of your healing and helping energy to those who need it. Let me serve you in this ray—ing out of your gracious and holy power. I relax myself and open myself to being used by you in this work. Send the energies through me to those who come to my mind. I am the way that energy can come to them. I see them with my mind's eye and repeat their names or who and what they are as the energies flow through me. Let me be a source of ray—ing to them at this time and whenever I want to work for them. Thank you, my Legbha.' After this has been gone over, either said or read over in the mind, relax for a few moments and if you feel the touch of sleep, drift off briefly, so that the energies can flow through you as you are relaxed and without any ego—interruptions. This is a very simple way of making use of the power you have for ray—ing the divine energies."

It is always important in Voudoo research to burn incense, because both the Laws and the Esoteric Spirits are attracted by incense. Incense combines all of the elements. We know that it is fire, because it burns. It drifts on the air and is in solid form, so that it is both air and earth, too. Also, in burning, so we understand, it passes from a solid to a liquid state, and thus partakes of the element of water. Also, the perfumes contained in incense are liquid essences, which when exposed to flame release a terrific power on the astral plane. They possess all of the powers of the element of water while in this condition. So, incense of the best quality is desired for use. It attracts many of the spiritual beings and angels, whenever used. I consider incense and everything about it to be of the greatest importance in all questions of theurgy or spiritual work with the God-energies. Simply write to me at the address given on the first page of this lesson.

It is often possible to make a distinction between Loa and Vudu—Spirits in the types of work that we are doing. While ray—ing and helping make use of both types of Gods, it is in the more specific work, where the difference emerges. While the work with the Loa can be understood as concerning general initiation, esoteric work with the Vudu—Spirits, or Les Vudu is concerned with personal development and esoteric consciousness. Here is a way to work with Les Vudu, which is different from the methods used with the Loa:

"When you want to work with Les Vudu, it is important to focus your energy on the link you have with your Teacher of the Light. The Teacher is the focus and way through which the powers of Les Vudu will come into you. I might add that they come from the deep parts of your soul, which you share with your Teacher. Relax and use a purple light or candle and burn a strong incense, as you say the following prayer to make contact with Les Vudu: 'The endless power that is within me is being directed towards my mind. I am now linked with great spirits. I pray to these spirits and ask them to come forth. I pray to Les Vudu to come up into my imagination and fill me with the joy of their presence in my own life. I pray to Les Vudu to send the light of their energy to me and to come forth. Let me see you great spirits in the image of my esoteric teacher of Voudoo Research. I love and salute you always.' Gradually, the energy will be felt. The form of this work is to be very simple because it is a prayer to get things moving inside of the mind. After you have said the prayer, relax and take a nap. Then you can let the forces work without any mental energy to excite them."

On the other hand, the prayers and work making use of Les Loa are quite complex and often have many subjects to which they can be applied. With Les Vudu, however, the focus is to be found simply in the process of inner growth in a kind of gnostic experience. In fact, the energies that are found by investigators of what goes on in esoteric gnosis are due to the presence and powers of Les Vudu.

But when we work with Les Loa, the emphasis is much different. We are looking at something on the outside, even if it is our own life and consciousness, the approach is from the outside. Here is what I mean when I say we can use the Loa to do Voudoo Research on our own consciousness:

"Relax and make use of a strong incense and a purple light or candle. Now, you can begin to see your inner self as something worthy of concern. You will try to make improvements in this world. Use the following prayer for summoning the help of Les Loa: 'I want to be as you wish me to be, Loa Gods of the cosmos. I want to be an image of your being−ness and power. I have four concrete things I must have done in order to grow. They are, 1)←←←←←, 2)←←←←←, 3)←←←←←, and 4)←←←←←. When I have these improvements made in my life, I will be able to help you and work more faithfully and devotedly to your will, my Loa. Come and help me in this matter and I will be free to serve you, my Loa, in every way.' Then you may take a nap and let the energies work for you."

Work with Les Loa is concrete and particular usually, while the work with Les Vudu involves those matters which are not yet concrete.

Record your work with Les Loa and Les Vudu in voudoo research along the following lines in your magickal diary.

I) Work with Les Loa: Please list as many ways as you have been working with Les Loa. List them and make brief comments as you wish:

II) Work with Les Vudu: Please list as ways as you have been working with Les Vudu. List them and make brief comments as you wish:

III) Have you experienced any esoteric spaces in your work with Les Vudu? If so, list and describe these inner worlds when and where you explored initiatic energy and met secret and helpful adepts of the inner consciousness.

Voudoo Research Papers: The Roots of Esoteric Voudoo

The roots of esoteric voudoo are to be found in the laws which govern the relationship between the student and the teacher of the mysteries. The roots are entirely mystical in that they draw their powers from spirit activities and from spirit energies, which are deeply personal and operative in everyday life, although in a very hidden way. Esoteric voudoo is powerful because of this hiddenness of its roots but this power, when seen as the ways in which the roots of voudoo operate in the teacher/student relationship in the mysteries can be presented in space and time, under the form of ritual, without any loss of power and energy, without any loss of contact with the spirits, if the relationship between the teacher and the student is strong enough. For if it is strong enough, it too takes on the power and quality of a mystery.

So, we can say that the world of the roots of esoteric voudoo is dynamic, existing in a living relationship between the student and the priestly teacher. The priestly teacher is to become the representative of the Gods and all of the spirits to the student. The life of the student, however, is manifested in the way in which he becomes more and more the love principle of the priestly mysteries. By this I mean that the powers of the mysteries are to be seen in the actuality and intensity of the partnership between the student and the teacher, since this link is one of fire, or divine manifestation.

Fire is the symbol of the link between the student and the teacher because it is fire, of all of elements, which comes closest to spiritual symbolics. This means that by the use of fire and especially the ritual use of fire in esoteric or voudoo prayer and pure meditation work, the student can see the growth and life, the movement and heat, and the constant changeableness of the relationship we have with our teachers and therefore with the Gods and Spirits of the Esoteric Dimensions:

"While sitting in your chamber, and thinking how your chamber is a place of the mysteries––for here are the mysteries of your selfhood––light a candle (this time it may be red, for the passionate links to the teacher of the mysteries). Then, look at the fire as it burns and light a strong and sweet incense, drink some sweet wine (sherry or port will do), and get into the mood of being close to the teacher at all times. Feel the teacher near to you. Then say this prayer to the Vudu of Esoteric Relationship: 'Ghuedhe, I am calling upon you to make my teacher closer and closer to me and never separate us. Make us one of your own secret forms of consciousness and link me ever to me priestly teacher, who brings you, my Ghuedhe, always to me.' Then take a nap; the spell will work.

Whenever there is a question of roots, foundations, or the structures of roots and of the many foundations of mysticism, we are involved with parts of Ghuedhe, because all of these matters are parts of His Body. Deep within the relationship between the student and the teacher of Voudoo Research, we can find the basic structures. If we look closely enough at these esoteric laws and principles, we can make a distinction between the "bones" or the basic structure, which is black in color and the "fiery hot flesh," which is red in its color. We are talking about the Body of Ghuedhe, and so we distinguish between the "red-hot" power and the "dark and shadowlike power of his bones." From this distinction, we can see operating two laws of esoteric voudoo, which are the laws in control of the higher phases of initiation and its physics: the red and the black sources or roots of Vudu-power.

There have been many explanations as to what the powers of the red and black temples of Atlantis can do. However, it is important for us to show how they are derived in the first instance from the Body of Ghuedhe, as it is reflected in the locking together of the powers of the student and the teacher, so that they form the Body of Ghuedhe in a very dynamic and yet mysterious way. The roots of initiation have to do with the combination of these high energies, because the elemental power is there and it is given in all of its rawness to those who seek the life of Ghuedhe, unless they are already within Him. So we come together in the Esoteric Communion of the body of Ghuedhe, represented by Christ on the Cross; the skull at the foot of the Cross representing the primordial power of Death, or the Ghuedhe Root of all mysticism and the Divine Sacrifice, or Death. It is energy because the student and the teacher will now become the sacrifice for all of their life, they become Ghuedhe and so they give up being themselves. The power is very strong and the blood and fire is hot, it is fire.

"Ghuedhe will come to you if you exercise yourself to be Him. Let Him come and be within you. If you open yourself to His root of power and to His body, making that Body your own and in that Body, all of its mysteries are your mysteries. Burn a black candle now and know what you are doing and why you are doing it. It is because you are now experiencing Ghuedhe in the physical body. You are now Ghuedhe. Use the strong and sweet incense of the tomb, for in fire, you will be reborn as Ghuedhe. Repeat this direction as often as you wish to bring in the Ghuedhe power."

To bring in Ghuedhe, you have to be ready for His visit. He will come to you and make it possible for you to bring the teacher to you, but you have to be ready and this means for you to make yourself ready as a body.

"Make the body ready for Ghuedhe, He will come only when the body is calling Him in its own way. Make the body ready with power and with the red and the black forms of power. Make the body ready and then the body will become the place of the dwelling of Ghuedhe.

Naturally, the body of Ghuedhe is full and powerful and it is ready to come to you. If the bones of the black ray of divine power are there, see them in your own body as the presence of the basic energy. See the red temple present in the heat of the body. The hardness of the body and its fire are the two aspects of Ghuedhe's presence in you. From these two aspects of power, you can see the energy and you can feel that all of the mysteries are in that world and they are ready to awaken.

Ghuedhe power is esoteric because it is within a container of flesh, the skin of the body is the place of hidden energy, where Ghuedhe is placed and where Ghuedhe is alive and lurking after a secret manner, known only to the priestly teacher and revealed to the student of this research. Research the body and try to find the doorways, mystical ways of opening, for the mysteries of Ghuedhe. Then you can open and see Ghuedhe and feel the powers of His secret presence.

The secret location of Ghuedhe is inside of the body and it is hidden, because we do not have the way of looking inside. But we can feel the presence of Ghuedhe inside, we have only to relax and touch the body and listen to the signals, which come up from the deepest and most secret spaces. Burn red and black candles and a strong and sweet incense (as strong and sweet as death) when you do this exercise. Be in a dark room and feel the power of Ghuedhe as He manifests and rises to the consciousness inside of your body. Then relax and take a nap; the power of Ghuedhe will move into every part of your body. It will become alive with His power.

If we look for the roots of Ghuedhe in ourselves and do these exercises faithfully, we will come to realize that there is a life within us, which is entirely esoteric and loaded with divine energy. It is the power, which can be projectd into any purpose and fit to any of the goals we have in mind. Let us remember this power at all times. The teacher, however, is to come to us and direct this power upwards to the highest level of manifested being, so that the secret mysteries, contained in the teacher, are the ways whereby Ghuedhe has also directed that His power be realized. This is the highest form of the Ghuedhe mystery, but it is loaded with secret spaces and hidden signs.

These secret spaces and hidden signs are contained in the power of the priestly teacher to reveal to the student all of the mysteries under the form of initiation physics, which is the dynamic application of esoteric logic. These mysteries are hidden in the fourfold interpretation of the name of Lord Ghuedhe, under the occult form of the mystery of the body. It can be expressed as the four following principles of power, which appear to the mind of the student as the esoteric roots of Voudoo Research:

GH--The first level of being is the red candle and its power. Ghuedhe will come as the formula of GH is given by the priestly teacher (or hierophant) within the body of the student as the ocean of mysteries. The secret space is the GH–space of power, and its own sign is given also under the name of GH–Ghuedhe. We live and we die in this body.

UE--The second level of the mystery of being is the black candle and its inner energy. Ghuedhe will come as the formula of UE is given by the hierophant, in showing the sacred objectivity and the subject being the student. The body of the student is the focus of all mysteries. The secret space is the UE–space of power and its own sign is given under the power of the veil, which is the name of UE–Ghuedhe. We live and we die in this body, let it fill all of space with its power.

DH--The third level of the mystery of being is the red candle and its secret life. I see that Ghuedhe has come as the formula of DH is given by the high priest, in showing the sacred and secret universe of the student. The body of the student is now the body of the Vudu Ghuedhe and the Loa Ghuedhe and the secret passageway of the spirit is the DH–space of power and its own sign is given under the law of fire and the fiery voice of the Osiris–Ghuedhe mysteries, which is the formula of DH–Ghuedhe. We live and we die in this body many times, let us know it is one with all time-- past, present, and future.

HE--The fourth level of the mystery of being is the black candle and its eternal life stream. I see that Vudu Ghuedhe and Loa Ghuedhe have come into the formula of HE as given by the revealer of the sacred and totemic mysteries as the body of the student, under the form of life and deaath. The secret space is a passageway between the spirits of the dead, known as the HE–space of power and the sign of that power is given as He–Ghuedhe, or both the Loa and the Vudu presence of the power in the body,

because the body is the world of the mysteries and the body is the secret of secrets.
It is Ghuedhe.

These four exercise are designed for use in spaces consecrated to the operations
of the inner uses of Voudoo Research. Very powerful forms of incense should be used
to create the aura of the way of the spirits and temple of Les Vudu. The power cannot
come in unless it will feel welcome. The roots of esoteric voudoo are to be found in
all of these rites, which are objectivities for you to enter and to live for some
time. When the priestly teacher brings these secret places to you, you will be guided
into them and know them as the placements of the four great fires. The candles will
burn in the temples of the body-spaces and they will be revealed as parts of
yourself.

You can understand the ways and laws of voudoo research activity by making use
of its many levels of exploration. If you wish to work on special programs, use the
following formula of power, as your guide in research:

1. Research on the secret space of GH-Ghuedhe and its mystery:
    1. The way in which it will work in me:
    2. There is life in me because of it:
    3. I am ready to understand this fire:
    4. Let the secret be for me now as:
2. Research on the secret space of UE-Ghuedhe and its mystery:
    1. The life wave will show itself in me:
    2. This work that I am doing to myself is:
    3. I can see myself as revealing this truth:
    4. The energy is one with the fire:
3. Research on the secret space of DH-Ghuedhe and it mystery:
    1. The impact of this power is known now:
    2. The world is a system of interconnectedness:
    3. We can find ourselves within the mystery:
    4. I know that I am with both Loa and Vudu:
4. Research on the secret space of He-Ghuedhe and its mystery:
    1. There is some secret source of light:
    2. When the energy is high the power will flow:
    3. The spirit of my inner self has told me:
    4. I can comprehend all things because I know.

The metaphysics of Voudoo Research is not too different from the science of the
gnostic religion because both are drawn from primordial roots, these being the laws
of fire and the spirits which indwell the mysteries of fire. Where there is space and
where there is spirit, you will find these roots and when you know them secretly and
from inside, you will do Voudoo Research like Ghuedhe.

Vudu–Research Readings: The Metaphysics of Meat

The meat(us) is the opening of the spirits into the world of body–spaces. It is a hidden yet an open way whereby the most powerful spiritual entities can come into the world of the flesh from another dimension and dwell in our world, because they are parts of both of our worlds, our hidden world and our observed world.

They can meet us in the world of powerful magick and they can meet us in the world of inner tensors, because the powers there are old and terrific. I have known them from the times of the Atlanteans and I have given them places within my body in order to build up their own colonies of souls and spirits.

Vudu–Research Readings are possible because what we do is simply to listen to the words of the spirits as they come to us in every mode of our human breathing. I have found that it is possible for the spirits to understand the ways of the world and the ways of inner states once they have given to me their own states of mind.

Meat of Type I: I have in mind here the energies which come up from the dream life of the human species, which is the dream life of the spirit resting before the actual life of awakening. This is a world which is filled with powers and with light rays, but from the sunlight of the physical dawn. There is an initiation, which can be given by the priestly mind, when we awaken in the mystical presence of the Vudu.

Meat of Type II: Deeper than dreaming and awakening can be found the spiritual energies of perfected intuition, wherein we are truly united to the spirits and in the union we are in spiritual attunement with the divine breathing. This realm is never exposed to the direct rays of sunlight, except for the special sunlight of Legone, since it is of an esoteric nature and purpose. It is hidden except on that one occasion, when the light will shine to all beings.

Meat of Type III: This is the first of the mystical worlds, of which there are manifold, as many as must be exposed through the spiritual initiations of the divine light, or the flesh–fire of the sacred meeting. The world is cause of all that rises to the surface before and beyond it, up towards the surface. The spirits are Atlantean masters of magick and it is not too good to speak of them without a sense of energy, because they have given many things to us as secrets and as symbols.

Meat of Type IV: In this world we must include all of the energies and bodies of fire and in every way the life and the stream of the secret chambers of wisdom, which are to be given as principles, from which all future initiations can be given except where the body is made to feel the esoteric presence and power of Ville–aux–Champs, and then the spirits are to be my own powers, extended into becoming other personalities and individual beings with a sense as practical and as real as all others in the universe. This is where I know the secrets of my own cosmos.

One of the problems which we in the esoteric studies have always come to face is that the powers often give us the meeting of the spirits but they do not give us the actual content of the powers of the spirits, unless we make special efforts to undergo a kind of secret or initiatic journey with them, at some level or depth of mind. It is in this way that I can see the reality of being and I can feel the lifestream of being as it manifests itself in my depths of consciousness.

The Zombi–Body as the Way In Which Vudu Come

When the Meat comes up from the hidden world, or the Mystery, it becomes known to us as one of the Zombi–Bodies, of which there are 16. By this, we mean that the expression or the presentation of the Meat in the world of ordinary activity, as defined by what the Voudoo Book Service does, is always through the form of a body, which is controlled by one of the Vudu Meats. The Vudu must find their expression by means of something in the phyical world, so they take possession of some part of the human body and dwell in that space and take it in every way as their own world. In fact, it is their world and it is truly a world that is very complete. We have said that they make use of 16 of these Zombi-Bodies, and that is to say that there are 16 ways whereby we can see how the body is generated and located in the physical body. Most of these places related to the meeting of magick and sensation, so they are places already charged with a certain "glow," which is much sought after by the most serious of the Vudu priests. In fact, the examination of the candidate consists in a careful search for this "glow," which is seen by the priest using his sacred clairvoyance.

The Meat must always take possession of the reality that is before it, so that when this is to happen, we find a lot of energy present and spiritual attention is directed towards where the spirits are gathered. They are always gathering in the various pockets of power, but in the Vudu-work, especially research-readings, the pockets of power can be seen--as we know by reason of their "glow," that special light which the spirit gives to where it happens to be. Crude though it may seem, this "glow" is tied up with a lot of hidden powers, since all of energies, which are expressed by measure and means of the "glow" are hold--overs from past experiences in lifetimes closely connected with magick.

The Vudu-priest is not interested in what you were in a past lifetime, unless it had to do with doing a lot of magick. Then he will take an interest in you, because having done a lot of magick in the past is what has connected you to him in this lifetime. That is how the Meat make known the value of the student to the priest, by showing him that the student was important at some time in the past, when they were doing magick. Then the priest of the Vudu will take an interest in what is going on.

But doing this "looking-over" is a special ceremony, which the student must ask the priest to donate to him or do for him for this special reason, otherwise the priest does not to take any interest in the student. He has too many other things to do.

But we know that the priest really has a kind of interest in the student, because the priest knew they student before and they worked, in a past lifetime, on a special project and this we can understand was very important to the priest. Nevertheless, the priest must not show too much interest in the student. The student must force himself on the priest and sometimes he must make a great effort to do this. Then the student will be rewarded. It does seem to many people that this would be done, but for the student/teacher-priest relationship, this is one of the big laws of Voudoo.

The priestly work is highly special and it consists in making sure the Meat is happy. So it has to test and find out if the Meat is happy with its Zombi-Body, which it has taken on in its work. I think that we should be told that the methods of testing by the priestly teacher are quite secret; however, they are also very precise in the form they take. It is done by means of a kind of magnetic work, or magickal body work, until the priest is satisfied that the student is giving to the Meat all that it wants to have and then giving to the Meat in a very special way the best possible Zombi-spaces and bodies, for it to express itself and its energy.

If a priest finds the place of the Meat in the body, he is to mark it with special oil, since oil will make the Meat talk to the priest in the language of the Vudu and even the Loa. It is a way of talking that will give to the priest certain secrets, which can never be obtained in any other way; secrets, I might add, of the past lifetimes of the student and the special projects which he worked on in the great temples of esoteric Voudoo, as were to be found in the ancient empire of the Atlantean Mysteries. So the way of opening up is the way of the mystic oil, which is a special way of revealing the powers. For this reason, the Vudu express themselves best through the mediumship of sacred oils. Every priestly teacher is a master of this oil technique, which has been continued in all of the magickal systems and religions of this world, from the most ancient times.

And, of course, oil is the sacred symbol which is a machine in itself, a fluid instrument for exploring all of the mystical worlds. Each Meat has its own way of relating to oil and in some way it is able to generate its own mystical oil and power. The way in which it responds to the oil is, however, based on the way in which the spirits interact. There are 16 mystic ways of giving the oil to the Meat, but of course this must not mean that there are 16 types of oil, mystical oil or unction, for the different Meats; rather, there is no real way of limiting the expressions of the Meat through the form of sacred oil. It is another world, in fact it is a world of special Gods, because the Meat becomes the Vudu-God forever, as known through the sacred oil and priestly unction.

The Ritual Work of Vudu-Unction and The Ceremony of the Creme
The anointing ceremonies of all ancient religions must be performed by priestly workers, who are themselves the mediums for the Gods. This is true in Christianity, where much of the old ritual of the Atlantean magick has survived. However, to the priesthood of Vudu, the rites of the creme or sacred oil are themselves mystical sacraments, because in the oil there is to be located a secret space or mystical universe, wherein dwells a powerful God.

The priestly mysteries, which were entered consciously and willingly by the student of the high Vudu were not the ceremonies of the Roman Church. They were the sacraments of Atlantis and of Lemuria, because they drew upon the ancient indwellings and descent of the Gods into the holy creme, which when applied to the sacred spaces of the body in the sacramental unction gave to the body the power of divinity awesome and anew. One cannot fully appreciate mysteries unless one has participated in them, but the mysteries of the Logos of the Vudu are themselves acts of imparting deity to the flesh of the Zombi-body of the student of these secrets.

The secrets of the power are tied up entirely with the work of the Meat and its own unique views. These views, because they are from the divine perspective, are of the God-Spaces of some inner world. They do not relate to the outside or exoteric and mundane spheres of power, it is the secret world, which is the focus of these Gods. They have come in the Meat and they in many ways are now viewed as divine aspects and foci for making the Zombi-Body more and more a center of power. The rite of unction, or the application of the magickal oil to the body, is to focus and direct the emergies towards the goal of spiritual transformation, whereby Gods are understood to indwell everything.

In the focus of the Gods, the only maters of importance are the places of divine presence in the secrets of nature. These secrets of the Meat are the places where the mysteries of the old truth can be lived. They are not new truths or teachings, but impressed upon the human body as a special form of teaching and as a special form of life-wave. That teaching and that life-wave is present in the body every time the secrets are given because only when the power is to be felt can the body understand that deity is immersed in the flesh of the sacred offering. I have seen these mysteries as they represent reality and realize that they are alone the ones of power. By contrast, all of the others are illusions when compared to the Vudu of Atlantis.

The 16 sacred spaces are then made holy because they must "wake-in-self-consciousness" to the energies of the Gods. True, they are already given as being but now they are understood as wide-awake, more than any new priesthood can comprehend. Now, they are living as the soul is pure fire and the cosmos is flesh and fire always expressing itself as pure energy. It is the pathway that is given by the anointing with holy oil, with the sacred creme of the Vudu touch, which is the touch of the Gods.

Finally, when you come to comprehend the secret teachings of this lifestream, you will be in a position to see reality as pure energy and as pure presence. It is a space that is only of the Gods, for none else can indwell this special and alternative dimension. Yet, the priestly hand can reach the mysteries and the sacred fingers can show the signs and make the gestures, whereby the Gods are released from the placement of the Meat. This is another mode of light, but it is the fundamental light of the Gods. It is the sacred oil and the Meat and the life that is present in the Zombi-Body or holy meeting place of Les Vudu.

Exercise for Inclusion in Your Magickal Diary
Please answer the following questions as your report to your inner teacher:
1. The Meat is a sacred space; where do you locate this powerful place?
2. The Meat may be open to another dimension; why is this so?
3. The Meat has a passageway from there to here; what so we say is there?
4. The meat can be viewed as a Vudu in its own way; why is this so?
5. The Zombi-Body moves slowly into existence; why does it move slowly?
6. The ZO or Zombi-Body is a power because we have set its boundaries?
7. I have touched that Zombi-Body and made it my own experience; is this true?
8. When we live in the life of Les Vudu we feel the power of the Zombi-Body; is that true?
9. Some say that the Sacred Creme is a space or a secret; what do they mean?
10. Some think that the Sacred Creme is a mystery; what do you understand by this?
11. In the Sacred Creme, we can find many Vudu; why do you know this to be true?
12. In the secret of the Holy Oil, I saw the face of the Zombi; what do I mean?
13. In what way are Vudu-Research Readings a form of initiation?
14. In what way are Vudu-Research Readings an esoteric sacrament?
15. In what way are Vudu-Research Readings a mystical union with Gods?
16. In what way are Vudu-Research Readings an experience of divine revelation?

When you answer these questions, first of all write the number of the question and the full question and begin your answer with the link-word "because," so that the Mind of Ghuedhe can enter into the reading of your answers and appreciating what you have to say about your own experience with the spirits of these readings.

Vudu-Research Readings: The Intensive Labyrinths

Vudu-Intensives are happenings where the spirits dote on the students of the mysteries, since in these happenings the main idea is to unite oneself entirely with the powers of the inner worlds. In these intensives, there are many esoteric passageways and paths, as the labyrinths of the world of the spirits are many and highly enriched. The spirits are sources of power for the students, but the students have to allow the spirits to meet in them, both body and soul, and this medium of body-truth would always have to be the ideal teacher of Vudu-Intensives, who is the guide in the priestly mysteries. When you come to understand how these Intensives work, you will find that they are psychologically akin to those ancient mysteries of the past, wherein sacred initiations were given to the mystical elite.

When I give my Intensive work, I concentrate upon what I want to do with the student. I have a special plan in my mind, which is my mystical design for the development of the student in esoteric Voudoo. The techniques are Atlantean and Zothyrian and seem to the mind at first to suggest Voudoo. That is true, they are all from the same Atlantean place of work. The work is hard and very severe. It is not a joyous experience, because it is very intense. However, it is powerful because it partakes of spiritual energies. Afterwards, the student will experience divine joy, but not during the work of a Vudu-Intensive.

Here is a description of what happens during a Vudu-Intensive. The Gods come in and take over the Teacher, but the Teacher retains his own selfhood, since he must have human and divine insights into every phase of the labyrinth, or passageway of the soul of the good student. So it is not possession in the usual sense. The work is magickal and draws on a lot of powerful work, which we find to be common in Esoteric and Gnostic Voudoo. The idea is that the Teacher can work at a lot of different levels of being and he can bring in a wide range of Gods as well as his various human sides, the perspective of his being a man and so a human teacher, the perspective of being a priestly teacher of initiation, or the perspective of being a teacher of spiritual mysteries and of esoteric and secret spaces of the gnosis of the Vudu. Then, he has the perspectives of the many gods or spirits coming through him. He will have human and initiatic clairvoyance as well as the powers that all spirits and Gods possess, when they occupy the human vehicle. So in the lifestream of the mysteries, we can sense many ways whereby the teacher has the same knowing as both superhumans and Gods and divine spirits.

It is important for me to bring together all of the views of the spirits in my own simple understanding of life and energy, so that the student can receive what is good for him as a space for inner work and as a passageway into deeper states of being. It is in this means that the powers are released and understood as perfected conditions of life and as ways to lead the student deeper and deeper into the presence of Les Vudu. So the whole process if one of getting closer to spirits, while on the pathways, or winding routes of the mystic world found in the Vudu-Intensive. I try to make the student as much as part of what I am experiencing as I can and I am quite successful in achieving this. I want the student of the light to be as I am as fully as possible. I want them to be within my consciousness.

The Labyrinth of Intensity

When Intensives are given, the Teacher-of-the-Spirit will trace the 16 mystical labyrinths, which inhere and are found in the physical, astral, mental, and intuitional fields of the student and impose therein the appropriate vudu as a virtue or power, as under the form of a secret sacrament, and as initiatic powers or points-chauds--mysteres, which are specific in location and special in application for development in the student of the Gods.

The Teacher is a special being; for this reason, he is referred to as the Teacher-of-the-Spirit and he is the pure representative of Legbha. He contains within himself all of the mysteries of Legbha but he also contains within himself all of the mysteries of the powerful Famille Ghuedhe, with whom he makes daily visits, because they are his own family, too.

The 16 labyrinths are mystical placements of spiritual power; but they are given as inner teachings and as lights of the divine. Naturally, they are mystical powers beyond the proper range of concepts, because they are about power, they are not just words. In the magickal and mystical embrace of the student and the Teacher-of-the-Spirit can be found the revelation of all of the mysteries of the Gods, except that this is a secret and beyond all sense of human comprehension. So it does not pay for you to think about it and try to comprehend it very meaningly or seeking meaningfully to enter into it. It cannot be done; it is too powerful and too perfect. Yet, it has to do with power; I know because it is the power of the Gods which makes it work.

The energies are special in their manifestation, we should think because they express and are expressed as ways of light. When the truth of Vudu is perceived, however, the only mystery is that of the Teacher-of-the-Spirit, who has come from all places and who is now in the body. This, too, is a kind of mystery because it implies lots and lots of powers. So we can say that the labyrinths are forms of Intensity; that is, they are long passageways which appear to be filled with spiritual powers and which cannot be seen, except by the grace of God.

The student is remade by the powers of the Teacher and this means that he will no longer be himself, because he has become the new selfhood, which is really a form of taking on the mystical selfhood of one of the Spirits. It is important for us to realize that in the life of the spirit, we become Gods, by giving up the lower human qualities and being remade into spiritual forces, under the direction of the Gods. Now, in the process of Vudu-Research, with the activities of its Intensives, we are remade by the spirits as they work through the Teacher-of-the-spirit, which means that the spiritual energies are poured into many forms of being, because it is the will of that Teacher.

Secret Spaces of Vudu-Gnosis

The secret spaces of the Vudu-Gnosis are defined by the esoteric logic of the empowering Teacher. This esoteric logic is the power of bodily-intuition, which is expressed in the care with which the Teacher-of-the-Spirit provides the mysteries for the student in the long course of the Vudu-Research Intensive. The action of the Intensive is to make use of special energies of a spiritual type, because the energies of the light are given at that time more than at any other time. The Teacher has to invoke them before he can give an Intensive.

When you given an Intensive, there are special ritual preparations, which must be agreed to by the Gods of the Vudu-Research Intensive. These preparations are based on the rules of esoteric logic and cannot be changed. They are fixed and static, for they are rules of an Atlantean origin. Yet, all of the dynamics and processes of the initiation system can be said to come forth from these fixed rules. They will never change and if one tried to change them, they would be destroyed. Some of these fixed rules are found among the very old "landmarks" of the system of freemasonry, in its most conservative form. When these preparations are made, the Teacher is given a special sanction or go-ahead from the Vudu potensices, behind the work he is to do. Then he will begin to make ready the work of the inner Intensive, from which comes the outer Intensive, which includes the student. The energy which is found in the labyrinth is taken from this rite of preparation, so that what comes forth is the same power, which has always come forth. There has never been any change since the Afro-Atlantean point of beginnings.

So the work with the structures of Vudu preparations is really a return to the ritually expressed roots of the process of the Intensive. That is where the power comes, for it must come at the point of origin and then filter itself through the mystical mind of the esoteric logic of the Teacher-of-the-Spirit. Then when this happens, the spiritual and dynamic life of the Intensive is expressed.

The Mysteries Are Matters of the Descent of the Spirit Through the Empowerments of the Teacher of the Gnosis
In the Voudoo Mysteries and especially in our Intensives, the inner and secret work is concerned with the bringing down and placing into the labyrinths of the student the nine mystical souls of the Afro-Atlantean and Zothyrian Traditions of the Voudoo Sciences. The priestly Teacher actually must bring forth into each of the 16 labyrinths the nine souls, so that the student becomes eternal because he has the Gods in him. This is the basis of the mystical use of 144 in theologies, since 16x9=144. For that reason, some sects will teach that only 144,000 persons are supposed to be saved. They really should say that one is only saved by the powers of 144 souls in the mystery of their own being.

The priestly power must be perfected so that the sacramental empowerment can take place and so the priest must have the power of the Vudu deeply placed within his own consciousness and existence and the rapport with the student should be of a quality as ideal as that between the God and the priest. Otherwise, the mysteries will not work for us in this way. The work of sacred empowerment is, however, one of the most esoteric operations in Vudu Research. It can only be given in an Intensive and then it is the life of the inner spirit of the Intensive. In fact, an Intensive in Vudu-Research without some form of empowerment, such as what has here been described, cannot exist. It simply would not be an Intensive.

Also, because at the time of an Intensive there is much energy in the psychic atmosphere of the student, it is an excellent time for there to be given initiations, when one of the Gods comes and gives of Himself. This process, which is a basic giving forth of the life of the Gods, is a fundamental condition of reality in the lifestream of any genuine and faithful student. It, too, is a form of empowerment, but different, for the following reasons.

Esoteric empowerments are based on the spiritual energies, which the Teacher has as a condition of being pure energy and life. He is activity and power and he is bringing to the student the powers which come from the structures of history and especially from the links, which he has in connection with being part of historical and magickal tradition. On the other hand, however, the operations of initiation are impossible because they are exceptions to history. Yet, they are possible as gifts from the Gods through the mediumship of the Teacher, who allows the Gods to work through him in a different way than ever was done. While the acts of empowerment are given as the result of the esoteric logic of the priestly tradition, the empowerments are given as exceptions to history and tradition. They are given as ways in which the Gods come as special favors to the priestly worker It should be noted that when the Gods come and give initiations, such acts are only as powerful as the empowerments of the Teacher, one is the measurement of the other. For this reason, in esoteric Voudoo practice, students seek out powerful Teachers, who give great empowerments in order also to receive strong initiations from the Gods, who are finally seen and understood as personal friends of so strong a Teacher of the Vudu-Gnosis.

It is for this reason that power becomes the focus of the Vudu process. Without the power, there is no Voudoo.

Vudu empowerments create their own spaces, which are the secret spaces of the gnosis, as in the Book of Jeu. When the power goes into space-as-void, it builds around itself a tension, which attracts to itself geometrical forms, from the Legbha geometry, and these forms create spatial forms and frames of references, or viewpoints, which become the secret spaces of the work of empowerment.

The spaces develop special frameworks, which are attracted by the precise power range and vibrational field of the power. Because of the attraction of like to like, the space always resembles the energy, which is secretly and silently contained. The space is a perfect photo of the empowerment energy. It is also an esoteric map, which gives the Teacher the picture of the energy of the candidate. We call this representation, which is also an identification of space and energy, the Vudu-photograph.

Certain priests have a magickal camera and use it to take these photographs of their students. Do not look, however, for any regular camera, for such does not exist. You will make use of a mystical instrument, the chambers of mirroirs (magickal mirroirs) as such an instrument is in reality a type of radionic system. I use it in a number of operations because we work with space and energy concepts and laws of action very frequently. Let me say that this process will make empowerments and initiations very effective for the student.

Exercise in Self-Awareness of Vudu: For Inclusion in Your Magickal Diary
The following exercise questions are now given to conclude this research paper:
1. Explain what is meant by the concept of empowerment. Why is it different from initiation?
2. Does empowerment imply a precise view of space?
3. Does empowerment suggest the existence of special "God-Spaces"?
4. Does empowerment provide us with a special geometry?
5. Why do we have mystical labyrinths?
6. What do we mean by energies being inside of certain labyrinths?
7. Does Vudu teach concerning the existence of many souls?
8. Are the powers of Vudu spatially arranged in a precise network within labyrinths?
9. Can you explain how a labyrinth can also be a form of a map or schematism?
10. Do metaphysical beings indwell the processes of empowerment?
11. How are empowerments given by the Mysteries?
12. What do you think the Mysteries are?
13. Is there such a thing as a map of the Mysteries?
14. Is the labyrinth implicit in the human body?

Atlantean Mystery School Readings
The Temple of Esoteric Readings

Modern initiation is simply the extension of the esoteric patterns established in the Atlantean Mysteries. These initiations are prana readings and readings of the Akashic film of the Anima Mundi (World Soul of Nature). They are given as readings by means of specific esoteric processes, known only to those who are continuously reincarnated as the spiritual priesthood, or guides and guardians of the Mysteries, in an unbroken and continually renewed lineage, from the Ancient Temple of Atlantean Mysteries.

It is important to understand that in the process of consciousness, all is part of a cycle of renewal and development. Nothing is absolutely new in the world of spirutual law, although new applications of spiritual law are continuously being given to the world of power and events, by these spirits and invisibles. Those who give these very powerful initiations are the priests of Atlantis, who have come down to us by a very precise and continuing chain of reincarnation and renewal. Therefore, what we are to know by means of reincarnation is what we experience here in this world at the present time, because the energy is simply changing its form and expressing itself in special variety and manifold of form. The spiritual laws remain the same and the laws are in each event. The ancient priesthood continues and is expressed as the known form of the priesthood of the present time, as in the esoteric and gnostic churches, this priesthood must give and present anew the old powers and the ancient symbols,to those who must be connected with Atlantean energy, even though they live in the 1980s.

The ancient symbols are always expressed in the form of the age, but they have the old power. There will always be the mystery and the power, which does not come from this present age but from the old ways. The priests have an intuition of how to express the ancient forms of power. They also will be sought out and seek out the old members of the cultus, by various psychic and occult methods. Then, we can understand that the old or Atlantean Mystery School is being brought together by a certain magnetic law.

So the ancient priesthood sends out certain mystical rays, sometimes even partially unknown to the conscious mind of the priests, but known only at the deeper levels, and these rays being to the center of power those who have been connected before with this energy. In a variety of ways, sometimes by the use of the colors of blue and violet, these priest—magicians bring back to the work those who have been with it in times past. They bring back the energies and powers of Atlantean magick to those who have the Atlantean soul within their contemporary bodies. The power is fantastic, but cannot be known by any modern measurement.

We do not deny that there are mysterious powers in other parts of the universe, outside of our school of life; but we say that for our purposes, or for the karma of the lifestreams of my students, the power and mysteries of our school are significant and sufficient for perfection and divinization (theosis). We hold, however, that each student contains in his soul the history of the universe of being, because that student is now in being and is a photograph of the mysteries of the universe from its beginnings.

In our temple of esoteric readings, we hold the viewpoint that the unconscious is simply psychic and occult history in a chronological or metrical arrangement. Research readings help us to understand what this arrangement is because they word as readings or the ways of opening up the psyche to self-exploration by means of special exercises, empowerments, and initiations.

The mystical energy of the ancients, as expressed in the lessons in Atlantean physics and metaphysics, has to come up to the surface of the mind and be known by the student because the student must understand where he is and how he is expressing himself in the world of life-energies. The powers of the spirits are there, always, and we must express these powers by means of comprehending what our lifestream means. So we grow in self-understanding. I teach my students various exercises for the liberation of being because the laws of being have a definite focus. The focus is the place that the teacher sets aside as the Holy House of the Spirits.

When we want to focus on the world of spirit, we have to focus upon special energies which the spirit uses to ground itself in the laws of this dimensional system. So we focus on the powers, which are connected with where the spirits live and manifest their powers. There is usually a focus or space or special place. This develops into the Holy House of the Spirits, because that is the place where the spirits are understood as dwelling, if only in by means of a mystical sign or symbolic object. Nevertheless, they are there as they are to be understood, namely as pure powers of divine consciousness; because they are the indwelling and hidden mysteries of the inner world. They are there to share by radiation their powers and energies with those humans who are seeking them. In Shinto, they are the Kami and in the Afro-Atlantean mysticism, they are Les Vudu.

The purpose of the temple of esoteric readings is, therefore, to place inside of the spirit of the student the proper spirit, or make it comfortable for the spirit to indwell the soul of the student. For this reason, the spirits will select and indicate by oracles those of the students they wish to indwell. They will come into the student and reside there, sometimes it will be somewhere in the body of the student. The Teacher of the Mysteries will be able to show how this happens.

Esoteric energies are important in the evolution of consciousness, because without them, there can never be any type of progress in understanding the history that is within us. When a person is therefore initiated into the Temple of Esoteric Readings, he is brought to that point of consciousness where he is aware of being and of the power of the light as seen from the spirit World, not from the merely human side of existence. In the process of self-understanding this is one of the most basic laws: we must learn to see ourselves as we are seen by the Spirits of the Dead and by other Spirits.

The law of esoteric communion is more than the sacramental rite of self-unfoldment, it is the place and power of being a spirit oneself. This means that we are spirits and we must always act and be as if we were perfectly aware of our spiritual powers and Vudu Energies. We are Vudu, but we do not yet exercise all of the powers. When we leave the Temple of Esoteric Readings, we have a better understanding of the fact that we do possess these powers of being. They are right within us and we know it now. Thus, we see ourselves as part of the spiritual world or spiritist communion, because we are spirits and we are in the world of mysticism. I look outside and see myself as I used to be and wonder as to how I could ever have thought that I was only in the material world. I am primarily in the world and work of spirits.

Slowly, the ancient powers will come back to the student as he is led through the various energies, which are Vudu and which are the basis of the energies possessed by us inwardly. I now realize that I am spirit and that my powers are deeply grounded in the realm of the mystical beings of light. In this sense, however, I have taken a step beyond the world of superficial energies and have entered into the world of true being. The metaphysics of this world is that of Spiritist Mysticism: I know the world of being is the divine idea and it is an esoteric communion of Vudu Energies, powers, and riches. It is life and process and it is unfoldment of consciousness, because we are truly spiritual beings.

When students come to me and I think that they may be those who were with us before, and this is usually true, I take their energy to the Temple of Esoteric Readings, because I am interested in the way in which the spirit can confirm what I believe to be true. Because I work in the world of intuitional being, of course, I am usually correct in my judgment, but what is important is the filling in of details, which the spirits alone can supply quickly, because of their technical powers. They work faster in the world of spirit than I do because they are naturally there all of the time. I work with the restrictions of the physical body space.

The Temple of Esoteric Readings is to be found in the ontic sphere of the Teacher of the id-secrets. However, this temple must not be thought of as something unreal, since it is a very real and very powerful place of operations. The Teacher of the id-secrets is the Teacher in his aspect as the guardian of the history of the student, which is locked up inside of the unconscious of the student. It is important to understand that there in that deep and very positive world, we are able to locate the exact history of the universe, because the student is the universe in its learning aspect.

There are techniques which must be used by the Teacher of the id-secrets in order to make the student aware of his reality as the history of the universe. These techniques have come down to us from the Atlantean period and are hidden among the esoteric forms of the Vudu-Mysteries. Let me explain how they express themselves.

1. The student must be aware of his lifestream and field of vital energy. This means a form of psychic investigationn known as a "Prana-Reading" wil be given to him by the guide in this process. The results of this reading will indicate the footpath to the Temple of Esoteric Readings, within the student.

2. Certain hidden areas of experience must be revealed to the student, so that the life-energy of the Temple will be received by him. Therefore, the Vudu-Energies are brought to the surface of the body by means of ritual evocations from the depths of the intitiatic psyche and they are allowed self-expression as elemental powers, so that the student experiences a liberation of his being as pre-rational power.

3. Intensive esoteric work with the energy of the student leads to an opening up of his secret levels of the mind. These are 16 in number and the oracle of the body-space of the student allows the student to express himself as raw power. This power is then taken and given the form, which comes to it from the Temple of Esoteric Readings, which provides the forms for all of the energies of the lifestream and body-space.

4. The world is understood as pure energy and it is seen as contained in the focus of the student. The temple of Esoteric Readings, then, begins to manifest itself as the oracle of the student's body-space and unconscious history.

These four techniques are the opening methods, because they open up the student fora new series of esoteric procedures, involving intensity and empowerment-work, or the giving by transfer to the student of specific and precise esoteric levels of body-space experience. So that the esotericist moves directly to the next four levels of prana-reading, which are given as based on the depths of energy released by the four id-techniques of the opening. Each of these, like the initial four techniques, has four sub-methods of empowerment for direct action of the student's body-space.

1. There is a prana reading of the remote past energy field as body-space-in-time. This sense of the body space in time must be understood as the most distant from the present or ego-conscious body-space of the student. This reading is entirely a physical body-reading, because it draws out the latent aspects of the remote past which are actually present in the physical body of the student. The body of the student is occult history as well as a genetic continuum.

2. There is a prana reading of the past body-space present and continuing in the present energy-field of the student. The focus of power is the level of muscle-tone, which points to the present of past complexes among the present data of the body.

3. There is a prana-reading of the future energy as a field in the body-space of the now or present lifestream. Not only is the focus upon the potentials of the present body-space as an energy field, but there is a precise mode of working with the present in order to activate the future through readings of what the future level of pranic continuity may appear to bbe. The future is latent in the present condition of the body-space, or auric envelope.

4. There is a prana-reading of the projects and distant future, or the energy of the body-space and time, which is ahead in time from the contemporary continuum of the present or given body-space of the student. This dimension of work is developed by means of actual points of intensity, located in the body-space, which refer entirely to the raw potentials of the future and its development.

It should be noted that this work is entirely based upon Atlantean modes or body-work and body-space methods. We do not make use of what is contemporary, but make use of those forms of exercise which come to us from Atlantean traditions of work in and on the body-space, as these are confirmed by akashic readings of the Atlantean Mystery Schools. In focus, we are able to show that these methods of work are entirely present in the body-space as motion and power types, or as latent empowerments in the physical vehicle of the student. This power is then released by means of the Atlantean Mystery School Readings.

Empowerments from the Ontic Sphere

The Atlantean Teachers were able to provide empowerments from the ontic sphere of their own individual accomplishment in the Mysteries. While the empowerments of prana-readings were given from the law of vitality and presence in the lifestream of the human body, the empowerments of the ontic sphere were derived from the generation of power by the prana-readings themselves. That is to say, the readings generated their own power and this was a form of power which could be given to students by these teachers of the Atlantean Inner Mysteries.

Each prana-reading gave forth a kind of field of its own, which was of a special power and which could, if it had special powers, give rise to special empowerments and initiations of a particular type. This is because prana-readings were given by means of cooperation with the Devas of Prana, or those angelic beings which sustain the life-process.

The esoteric priesthood would do its own work, but it would also do work with the angelic beings. These beings would indwell the prana-readings, if they were possessed of a special affinity to the angelic levels, and from their presence in the energies it would be truly possible to derive special fields of power, which were different from prana-readings. As these angelic beings came from the ontic sphere of the work of the Teacher of the Mysteries, so the energy which they generated was also from that realm of being. We can call these acts the empowerments from the ontic sphere, which were then given to students by the Teachers.

Prana-readings had to be very powerful in order to provide us with these empowerments, for the energies, which produce empowerments, must be outside of the disintegrations of the process of time. Such Atlantean empowerments must have the stability to last forever, or to exist in such a way that they never lose their power-giving abilities. They must be in a state where the power can be given from them at any point in history, even in the present age. An example of this would be what follows:

Ambaktu knew that the student had received the empowerments of the Mysteries long ago in Atlantis. Now, he wanted to renew the student in the Mysteries and the student sought the powers which Ambaktu held in his secret priesthood. During the performance of the secrets, it was learned that the student had received the powers and that they were still with him. By an akashic examination, Ambaktu found the nature of the powers and now could feel the secret of their wide range of strength. They were before him as fresh as they were when in Atlantis they had first been given to this student. So now Ambaktu began to awaken them and to build on them, so that the energy could grow. After the prana-readings were given, the old Atlantean powers were awakened as if they had only taken a brief rest. There was no doubt as to the reality of the power or to its richness.

So we see that the powers of these Mysteries persist from the past, if they are given in a proper or correct manner.

The continuation of these mysterious powers can be understood if one looks closely at the history of a religious body known as The Old Roman Catholic Church of The Black Community. Many of its bishops were reincarnated Atlantean magicians. This was confirmed by Doctor Atlantis in his materials on the "Ambaktu Physics":

The Old roman Catholic Church in Haiti and in the British West Indies had many masters of magick as its bishops. Some of these magicians came to the United States as assumed high positions with many powers. The Old Structures of this church would appeal to the black men holding the ancient priesthood because the emphasis was upon the Saturn-Energy and upon the Laws of Structure. Most of these magicians wove into the rites of the Old Roman Catholic system the Atlantean intentionality. They had at their command the old powers and they knew how to make use of elemental forces. Some of the Old Ones incarnated in positions of power around the movement so that they could assist in its extension. You can always tell who they are because of the qualities of their rites, which are Saturnian, and of their students, the majority of whom come from the Afro-Atlantan bloodline.

These magicians also made use of the Law of the Ambaktu Physics, which made it possible for the ancient energies to take on the liturgical structures of the Old Roman Catholic form. In the mystical work, the primary energies of the ancient bodies were shifted from the true forms of the Ontic Sphere and inserted within the formulae of the Old Roman Catholic Mass. Like a magickal computer of some highly imaginative theme, these ancient powers could be touched by the hand of the high-priest as he conducted his ritual work. As he drew upon a system of angelic powers at each stage of his ritual, he also made use of the old powers in their immediacy — they were there present in his Holy Mass. It was the old magick in the Old Roman Catholic formulae.

But not only did the old energies rest in the liturgical forms, such as the ceremonies of the Old Roman Mass; they could also be found in the mystical potencies given to the high-priesthood at the times of ordination and consecration. These powers were given for the idea of raw magick and could not be understood except as a survival of the uncontaminated magick of the Atlantean Temples. One must be very certain that the ancient powers were there, since all of the old work was carried on by these newly consecrated priests and bishops. They had to have the ancient tools of their trade and they made certain that these tools would be given to them when they needed them in their present incarnation. Then they added on to the tools the old powers and that fantastic Atlantean Intentionality of magick, which brought to their work the full vigor of the mother of all of the mysteries of magick.

In the work of the "Ambaktu Physics," we can see how the Ontic Sphere empowerments canbe given structure by means of ritual operations, especially liturgical formulae. However, it must be understood that it is the priest and the priestly power which make this work very effective and very special. A layman or person not in priestly orders could not do the same thing, nor could any priest who was not a reincarnated Atlantean magician. He must have in his power both capacities: a past lifetime as an Atlantean Magician and ordination to the Old Roman Catholic priesthood in this lifetime. For this reason, the ecclesia in Haiti sees all other ministries as defective in one way or another for occult purposes.

Magickal rituals are very powerful but they are significant because they reflect or project the secret powers latent in the priestly aura of the magician. What was received in the deep darkness of the Atlantean period is now understood as being awakened by the initiation and empowerments of the ontic sphere. No longer does the power rest and sleep in the current or contemporary lifetime, not it can be awakened. The energy will then come to the surface of power and the energy will then begin to show itself and express itself as mystical and perfected empowerment.

The Ambaktu technique was developed as a method for giving such special empowerments to the seekers after energy. There were certain powers and they could only be reached within the psyche by the Ambaktu methods. Because of what was said in the physics, a method of work in the methods of empowerment could be understood as coming forth from the priestly powers. In all of the methods of empowerment, the work known as Ambaktu would be the most highly specialized and the most precise. It would focus upon the ways in which Ambaktu as a power could be realized. For the power had been named after its priest.

The Ambaktu method makes use of the technique of linking an oracle of the ontic sphere to the hot–point of sexuality within a specific placement. While there have been many attempts to use the chakras in connection with oracles, the Ambaktu method is quite precise since it involves the reduction of the name of the sexual spirit of the oracle to one of the nine Afro–Atlantean bodies. An example would be the case where the name would normally be of three letters. In the process of the oracle, however, the three numbers, which are given to represent letters, as 5 represents A, 6 does the same for B, etc., might be 12, 8, and 20, for a total of 40, which reduces to the number four, to the Afro–Atlantean body number four, and to a spirit–communicator, whose name is composed of four letters. The name would then be given by the oracle method for four letters. This would be the name of the entity having the secrets of this center of work and the work on the precise hot–point would mean that the secrets of power could be given by means of contact–work with this entity. The spirit of the oracle then could give to the priest and the student the inner instructions, which make the Ambaktu work so very essential. Usually, we might note, only two or three of the hot–points could be worked in these temples at any one time, because of the powers, which were built up out of the various levels of ontic empowerment, energy–transfer, and initiation–release.

Now, of course, we know that there exist various levels of ontical hierarchy, which come to the work within the Ambaktu context. There are special research papers which exist to give us an exploration of these powers and what has been done to renewal them to us.* In the normal process of the work, we have to see various levels of energy, however, not as outside of the processes of the physics of empowerment but as really resting inside of these types of work as the actual law of energy patterns.

Ambaktu work does not mean that the prana work has been replaced. Prana readings are to be seen as leading up to the Ambaktu processes because the work with prana allows us to see the potentials for deeper work along the Ambaktu lines and thereby brings us the very important keys to empowerment as found in liturgical oracles and in the temples of the body–space. In a sense, then, the laws of energy are connected to each other by exact methods of an Atlantean system or esoteric physics. This is one of the esoteric labyrinths, which are explored within the mystical context of ontic sphere research.

In the Atlantean system of mysticism, which was their form of esoteric logic,the energies have to be understood as being latent in the various occult spaces and places of the ontic sphere. Certain energies exist which are only revealed when the surface of the ocean of the unconscious mind is touched by the priestly actions. Then there is the revelation of the full power of being, which is actually latent, already latent, in the body–space of the student.

There is, finally, another concept of Ambaktu, which should be mentioned although it is of an esoteric form beyond what has been given in this lesson. During the rites of the hot–points, wherein we are making use of the oracle, it is possible to make contact at the mid–point of the hot–point with a special Ambaktu potency or spiritual being, expressed as a mystical force. This mid-point has been identified in the ancient Atlantean records; but only appears to have survived within our school and outside our school in certain of the Thibetan Bon-Po practices, where it is difficult often to locate.

Esoteric Ambaktu refers to the special relationship which exists between the spirit of the rite being done and the spirit of the oracle behind the rite being done. It is not to be thought of as the spirit of the oracle being done in the rite, for that is another of the spirit-powers. The oracle behind the rite makes possible the production of the magick power used in the rite, while the spirit of the rite is the entity expressed as the way the rite is expected to be done. This latter being provides the direction for the rite as it has been understood for all the centuries it was in existence. The spirit of the life behind the rite, and so behind the oracles which are part of the rite, is a special and unique entity, known as the esoteric

←-

*The Ambaktu-Old Roman Catholic Research papers are an attempt to give in report form the patterns of energy as they appear to the priestly operators. These papers are not lessons but should be viewed entirely as descriptions of precisely defined energies, as they are to be found in the ontic sphere work of the Ambaktu priests.

Ambaktu. It is that part of Atlantean magick and the mysteries, which comes closest to what we now call esoteric logic, especially as this is found within the Voudoo system as the esoteric logic of Ghuedhe-Legbha.

Only certain priests have the powers to prize or give the production of esoteric Ambaktu, since it depends upon the release of a special energy from the line of teachers, extending backwards in time to Atlantis. While there are many esoteric powers in existence unknown to the usual student, it should be realized that few of these powers are known even to the high priests of many schools. These priests have simply lost the powers to find these old potencies and realities. In the system of mysticism, however, the esoteric powers are to be understood as available or known if the person is seeking them. Such a person may be allowed to find what he is looking for with the permission of the spirits. There is also a series of papers on the esoteric aspects of Ambaktu, which will allow the student to come to an understanding of these energies, as they are provided by the spirits or the Mysteries of the Universe.

The secret energy of esoteric Ambaktu is perhaps the oldest of all powers. It makes most of the other powers possible and it is always behind the existence of new things having a form of power. Now, however, it has been seen by certain priests to be the secret force, of the esoteric power, which is behind the entire system of ontic sphere empowerments, as these empowerments are only possible because they are given through the certain lines and lattices, rays and beams of the level of Atlantean magick which comes closest to the true mode of esoteric logic, which we have preserved in our own secrets.

The Generation of the Akashic and the Ontic Readings from La Prise-Des-Yeaux

The significant powers of the high—priesthood comes from the world of the spirits as gifts to those who have dedicated themselves to the spirits. These powers are instruments for the worker in service to the spirits so that the worker may participate entirely in the world of the spirits without any limit. One of the most significant of these powers is the esoteric vision, occult imagination, or inner sight, known as "la prise-des-yeaux."

The akashic readings and empowerments of the ontic sphere, which give so much force to the work of esoteric initiation, are the results of a very careful sequence of divine empowerments, which the high—priest receives while in process of theosis, or union with the Gods. At a certain point in his development, the man who is to become a priest and then a high—priest is set aside by the spirits and carefully and ritually prepared by one who also has these powers. It is an unbroken chain, which I understand comes down to us from the Mysteres of Atlantis and from the secret schools. This direct line of descent from the adepts of the ancient schools carries with it a unique and very powerful ability. This ability gives one the approach to the mysteries by way of the Gods, for the powers are taught to the student by The Gods, or Laws of the Universe.

Metaphysics allows for the student to rise upwards to the deity and to be possessed by the ancient powers. However, in the act of becoming one with these powers, the gifts of the God--Consciousness are united to the student's own consciousness and he is literally made into a new being, because the old being no longer exists inhis body. That is why initiation and empowerment, if fully effective, must be given by the Gods alone and must have a special and unique gift about them. The initiator of the student, who is the Teacher sent by the Gods, such a person as that Teacher will serve to connect the student to the God—Powers. This is also an ability, because as a gift from the Gods it has timeless power (and operates from lifetime to lifetime). Therefore, it is pure magick. The Gods alone have the power to connect humans to the world of divinity and the world of divinity alone has special energies for the renewal of consciousness and the potencies of the spiritual act. Thus, the energies are received as powers and the powers are bridges between the Gods and humans, which the priestly powers have to give as ways, whereby what is in need of connection by a line of power can be connected by that same line of power. So the ways of power and the pathways are within the capacity of the Teacher and from him are given to the student.

In many instructions and in more practical instances, empowerment has been compared often to a process of radio-psychoanalysis. Radio-psychoanalysis is the exploration of the inner self from the standpoint of occult radiations. Radio-psychoanalysis is implied in our work because the esoteric readings which are given are ways of releasing energy from the very rich depths of the transcendental id. So the priestly power includes the magickal ability to release power within the psychic continuum of the student by means of esoteric empowerment. In the Old Roman Catholic Church of Haiti, this power of the priesthood is exercised via the Sacrament of Penance, commonly known as "going to Confession to a priest." However, it is quite interesting that during this confession-process, there is a release of magickal energy and it is felt as such by the student. The priestly power to bring about this in the student is a real ability, which comes from priestly consecration.

However, of a much deeper quality and of a much richer power would be the Atlantean reading, which as a form of radio–psychoanalysis is derived from the power of the present but caused by the power from the remote past. The powers given by the gift of "La Prise–des–Yeaux" are real as potencies derived from the mysteries of Atlantis. The priest who has these powers now in the present age had them before in the temples of readings and empowerments in Atlantis. However, within the Atlantean concext there were many types of temples of magick and it cannot be said that these temples were all of the same quality, because they had different foci. There is no need to list all of the temples and schools, although there were over 200 of them, but there were over 60 temples giving La Prise–des–Yeaux as a form of mystical awakening. Within our own family of mystics, there were about 16 of these specialized temples, based upon the workings of the esoteric Atlantean system of occult wavves, vibrations, rays, and broadcasting–beams of esoteric energy. When I meet a student in this lifetime and I know he is one of the Atlanteans, I immediately begin to work on his soul culture so as to be able to find out the exact place where he stood in the ancient world. Then I try and bring him up to that level of accomplishment in this lifetime. That becomes the focus of my training of that student. So it is very important to work with each student individually and allow that student to unfold his full power. Work in groups would not make this possible.

By making use of my esoteric ability, I am able to find out much about the student both in terms of where he was and also where he will be going. I make use of akashic readings and other empowerments, I draw upon ontic forces and many spirits and Vudu, in order to be very accurate in what I am doing. All of these powers and capacities are generated from a use of La Prise–des–Yeaux. Once I get into my work with these powers, I work as part of a group. The group is composed of the following persons: the student, myself, and the spirits or Vudu beings, who are guiding and directing me in this energy. The entire work is centered around the needs of the student, because the student is the topic of investigation, or the object or subject of research. The focus of power is making it possible for the student to come to terms with his being. In this sense, the student will have special powers activated in him, because the energy must express itself at the level of its own and ancient Atlantean vigor. I work very carefully with taking one step at a time in the psychic continuum of the student, because the mystical energy is to be brought up in a pure and practically perfect state of preservation. Any lack of exactitude would lead to a break in the pattern of energy and would therefore make it very difficult to maintain the continuum in terms of the pure order of its contents. Certain matters would be taken out of order or misplaced somewhere in that process.

The psychic continuum, we must remember, is a living system and so it must be approached carefully because of its occult contents, these being powerful and active energies, which have not been close to the surface of the psyche, or known to the ego, since very old Atlantean times. For help in this delicate and perfect operation, I make use of certain spiritual helpers, who assist me from within the psyche, that is to say, they exist deep within the psyche or nearby to that region and can come easily into the continuum of the psyche and give me a hand. For this reason, it is necessary to understand that oracles have their natural space deep within the levels of thepsyche and that there are different levels within the continuum and at these many different levels are we able to find the "spirit spaces of oracles." An entire science of Vudu–Energies exists to explore this subject–matter, known as archeometrical psychology. However, what we are doing is far from any theory. We are actually working deeply within the inner life of the student.

By making use of the la prise-des-yeaux, the priestly exploration of the student's body-space will reveal the secret dimensions of the spirit-space of his psyche. There are deeply felt worlds, the akashic and ontical readings can be given in order to release from any minute or vague limit the contents of magickal work in past lifetimes. There, in the deep regions of secret awareness, the priestly exploration can find the ancient spaces of oracles and the special chambers of Les vudu, which have been the temples of the mysteries since the archaic days of Atlantean power. By empowerment of these spaces, the priestly exploration can awaken the past and make the student a self-conscious initiate of the spirits, now, in this lifetime.

Each student would appear to have a special body-space and psychic continuum as part of that body-space. The student would possess certain unique and secret places, which can only be known by means of individuated readings of the energy fields. These secret realities cannot be understood as being common to all students; although, certainly, the psyche of each student contains many magickal spaces. Yet, in the process of exploration, we must remember that each student has his own world and space within the psyche but that the ways in which these spaces are arranged are secretly held by the spirits within the life of the inner soul. I know that I will receive a response from Pierre in space X as I would with Charles, but I do not know what archetypal response will be given. Different and many times hidden spirits indwell these spaces. They are not beings to be known as I would know other objective facts about the students, such as that Pierre and Charles come to from the Island of Eleuthera in the Commonwealth of the Bahamas. However, by means of la prise-des-yeaux, I can arrive at the most highly unique and individual spirits in the psyche of the student, because the spirits within the continuum of la prise-des-yeaux can guide me into the worlds within, since that is where they themselve dwell.

The priestly power is like the ability to see physically all that is metaphysical. You will possess certain kinds of information because you now possess the ways of the spirits and you can see the worlds of the spirits as if they were entirely physical. For this reason, the Haitian priests who possess this power speak of the spirit-spaces and worlds in a way which suggests that they are describing the physical world and the material land just outside the window. They talk freely and often in ways that seem commonplace about the most spiritual and mystical subjects, because they see the mystical as we see an apple on a table. Their powers have made these masters see everything as if it were simply a part of the physical world. This is suggested to us when they say that they find the spirit spaces in body-spaces of the Legbhas, Luages, and Ghuedhes. They mean that behind or within a certain physical part of the body are to be found existing the spirits or Les Vudu. The spirit world is that close to the physical for them, because they have this gift.

So, for the priestly explorers, the act of giving akashic and ontical readings is continuous with physical vision.

There are several Vudu spirits connected to this process of giving readings from la prise-des-yeaux. In my own work, we invoke Legbha and His mystery of Luage, we invoke ghuedhe and his mystery of Lundi, and we also invoke in special circumstances the mysteries of our Ambaktu, as expressed in His esoteric form, and His mystery, which is also a mystery of the Famille Ghuedhe, by the name of Limba or Limbi. Each of these mysteries are related to the giving of akashic and ontical readings from the powers of la prise-des-yeaux. In fact, together they represent divine and secret spaces within the student's psyche, which are to be revealed by means of an akashic reading based on the living Atlantean temple of the student's own body-space, as a collection of esoteric mysteries. Our work in these areas of research can be explained as falling under four different types of esoteric exploration.

(I) There are Vudu Research Readings, which explore the regions of Legbha and Ghuedhe as we find them expressed by reason of the laws of Ambaktu empowerment. (Here the teacher will do the work with the student, which refers to this region of the ontical continuum of inner powers.) This world is based entirely on the interactions of Legbha and Ghuedhe with the field of Ambaktu expressed as a dynamic form of being.

(II) There are the Atlantean Mystery School Readings, which explore the extension of the powers of prana-readings as the basis of more occult practices. These prana-readings can be seen as real doorways to the esoteric spaces, wherein the classical laws of esoteric Vudu are applied to the students as he is now understood within a context of cosmic points or powers of reference, hot-points, categories of empowerments, and collections of forces. The interaction between Legbha and Ghuedhe as expressed inextended Ambaktu is now understood as primordial experiments with the body-space of the mind as a continuum of time-systems. Here there is an experiment as when the teacher and the student will realize a particular area of hot-points, which reflect the movement from prana-readings to the archaic roots of Vudu.

(III) There are the Esoteric Vudu Readings, which explore the mystery of Luage and the inner patterns of Luage in relation to expression as Ambaktu. (Here the teacher will work with the esoteric dimension of the student and allow the Vudu and the Loa to reveal themselves in a pattern of mystical lattices of cosmic and yet psychic energy. At the same time, the teacher and the student will understand Luage as the law of body-space in its most concrete sense.) So these papers focus upon work with the Luage mystery as the goal of consciousness.

(IV) There are the Atlantean Research Readings, which begin with work on the concept and the field of that particular known as Esoteric Ambaktu and conclude in work with the Mystery of Limbi. (Each of these papers or lessons will be explorations in the field of initiation-physics, as it is seen from the viewpoint of the continuum of esoteric Ambaktu, with the in-depth exploration of the secret soul as it is first experienced by the Vudu and Loa. At some point in the exploration of being, the entire map of the soul as a secret space will be at once given to the student by the words of the Vudu through the teachings. This work is perhaps the most mystical aspect of Esoteric Voudoo work.) The student and the teacher will be working on each aspect of the soul in order to discover the magickal geography of the inner world of the student's spirit.

The Collection of Pacquets in the Empowerments of Ambaktu

Inside of the empowerments of Ambaktu, especially in its esoteric phase, we find the build-up of centers of power, the gradual coming together of forces, and the collection of energies of a tangible and exact type. We understand this to be the collection of pacquets. The life and power of the empowerments have been concentrated in these points of force, which are of a collective nature. They appear to be collections of esoteric hot-points. From the Vudu, I have received the following explanation:

The smaller the area of space, the more concentrated would seem to be its powers. This has been shown by the ways in which the energies envelop themselves or intensify so that the appearance they have is as a continuous turning inwards or moving into a more and more closely defined and combined space. The powers that are in space are the powers which the realm of space possesses. They are the powers which imagination has discovered within the compactness of space. This happens in any collection or series of spells so that they are in every way more and more closely identified with themselves, especially with the many and varied forms of themselves, because they are trying to be known to themselves in the same area as they occupy. They want to know themselves without any intermediary, without any pause in the act of knowing. So everything in the science of Vudu will turn in upon itself and come to know itself more by this self-involvement. This seems to make the power stronger and to make it appear as if it derived its powers from becoming more and more confined to ever smaller spaces. Ghuedhe, or the Saturn-Pluto complex of the Voudoo Mysteries, appears to teach by example this process as he is the ruler of this ideal.

So we can understand that space is power in a latent or diffused and extended way and when it is concentrated it becomes power-bearing in an ever-increasing degree. This space is also the place of imagination, or the magickal use of imagination, where the priestly power is to be found as diffused and spread over the entire place of work. Then when it is brought into inner and tight pockets, or brought together in bundles and collections, like any other object might in the physical world, it takes on a power and a uniqueness of force. It becomes energy and life; indeed, it expresses itself as a life of its own. This power can then be used by the priestly hand to direct the mysteries exactly and without any loss of energy, as the fuel of mysticism and the physics of initiation. When we want to talk about how it is that the Vudu Mysteres work in the world of matter, we simply have to focus upon what it is that is given as pure energy and how it is managed by the priestly hands. From this living form of being, which is the spiritual level of reality, we see in the abounding and absolute compactness of space the reason for the existence of these energies and their level of productivity. They are constantly making powers by their pushing inwards upon themselves.

This pushing inwards of the powers, which gives to the powers their unique quality or the force of the divinity, which we associate with such empowerments, when given, creates its own space; but it also takes over the exoteric spaces around the inner spaces so as to form a pattern of protection and a pattern of energy.

Each priestly initiator has seen the powers when they are grouped about the esoteric and exoteric placements. These are the powers which have a special uniqueness and special form of divine mao--work. By an esoteric method known only to himself, the priest can trace in the body of the student, who must be a chela, the pathway of the occult energies and how in the field of energies, the powers are laid out or distributed. He will do this work by a special and secret method which allows him to locate the powers in their ideal placement, rather than in their approximate distribution. Remember that the priest must locate these powers where they are supposed to be and then compare them to where they might be. He then must move them back to where they should be, if there is any distance between the ideal and the real placement. For if there is any distance, it must be explained.

The distance occurs largely as the result of the activities of past lifetimes. The practice of certain theurgical operations, especially those of a highly personal and subjective form, will tend to draw the points of power away from their original and archetypal spaces, or spiritual placements. When this happens, the first work is to try and find out where the powers are and bring them back to where they belong. There are special rituals, which are done to achieve this and these rituals are always effective in achieving a return to the basic placement of power.

Naturally, the mystical relationship between the Guru and the Chela must be established and of a very long duration, because they must hold together an astral and mental webwork, which serves as the occult connective between lifetimes. These mystical and magickal powers are in every sense eternal, since they outlast the episodes of time or temporal incarnation, which each chela must experience as he grows more and more deeply into the mystical energies. In the past perhaps the relationship between the Guru and the Chela was not as ideal as it is supposed to be or should be considering the work in metaphysics. Now, in this lifetime, as the energies are now available for exploration and research, the chela can achieve the true level of being and the true awareness of mystical growth. He must come back to where the power of the Guru is to be found, and this is measured by the distances between what is the space of the collection of pacquets and what it should be. Then the mystical healing can begin.

Question: Are there examples of these distances between powers in the traditions of the Vudu--gnosis, as contained in the Old Roman Catholic Church from Atlantis?

Answer: Yes. The mystical traditions of the Atlantean Church have come down to us in forms of special rituals, which are either Old Roman Church in form or based on the Vudu--Mysteries. These traditions are built up in order to overcome the distances between the Guru and the Chela. They are designed in order to overcome the distances between the ideal and the form of reality found in the chela.

There is always a kind of separation between the old ways, which are the ideal, and the ways we find the energies present in the chela when he first appears to us. But the work can be done in order to make him free from the differences between the ideal and what has come with him into this lifetime. This means that while there is a certain disjunction to be experienced in the act of incarnation, the act itself can be corrected by a magickal or theurgical operation. This is shown in the Thibetan and Old Roman Catholic elements, as we find them in the Vudu--Process.

The actual techniques of exorcism and purification, which are made use of in the process are actually or dynamically given as ways of restoring balance. It is particularly important to know that the old systems work very effectively, because they are using the same forms from lifetime to lifetime.

Question: Does the sex of the priest make the power of the sacrament work in this process of the restoration of balance?

Answer: The Atlantean methodology made it necessary for the priesthood to be composed of males, since it drew its occult power in this respect from the male mysteries. This is repeated in the patterns of the Old Roman Church of Haiti and also in the Thibetan Esoteric work. For it was taught that the male chelas would become male priests by means of these mysteries of a metaphysical view of male sexuality, based on physical incarnation as a fact. In order to overcome the imbalance of the energies, the chela would incarnate in a male body and so all of the collections of pacquets, or gatherings of energy at this point, were to be seen as a focus of the male powers and empowerments.

Question: And was there not a secret map to be found in this process, which guided the old form of priestly magick in the directions of the restoration of balance?

Answer: The Old Roman Church of Atlantis and Haiti did teach the existence of such a map to be found in the body of the chela, which showed actually where there were differences between the ideal or true placement of the powers in their collection of pacquets and what was the actual result of the process of incarnation, because the energy levels at the moment of the act of incarnation were so diffused. This diffusion was the cause of the error or degree of imbalance, which the laws of the gnosis and its special operations sought to restore and make definite and strong.

We should now come to look at the methods which were used by these priests in order to make a return to the original powers a reality.

Here is the esoteric exercise used for correcting the collection of pacquets as used by the late Archbishop Cyrus A. Starkey of the Old Roman Catholic Church of Haiti:

1. From what sources did Bishop Lucien-Francois Jean-Maine derive his special occult and gnostic powers and abilities, as well as his special role in the evolution of esoteric consciousness? (Angelic contact number=5, as 3+2): Earth of Earth work.

2. Bishop Lucien-Francois Jean-Maine did not derive any special powers from the Doinel line of Gnostic Bishops in France, for he made claim to the succession of Doinel through his own contact and consecrations by Synesius. (Angelic contact numer=9): Water of Earth work.

3. I don't think that his contacts with the bishops of the Vilatte succession were particularly helpful in this respect, either. (Angelic contact number=12): Air of Earth work.

4. For while a few magicians were made bishops, this did not make the bishops they consecrated into magicians, so we have to look elsewhere for our explanation. (Angelic contact number=5, as 4+1): Fire of Earth work.

5. It is possible that bishop Jean--Maine had special powers given to him from his contact with his father and grandfather, who were magicians. (Angelic number contact=2): Earth of Water work.

6. If so, that power would be highly elemental and may be viewed as a mixture of raw Voudoo and extremely corrupted practices of a Martiniste-Martinesiste type. (Angelic number contact=3, + "no"): Water of Water work.

7. This would be of what had survived of Esoteric Martinism in 19th century Haiti and it would be a type of Angelic magick mixed with an explicit and primordial sorcery. (Angelic number contact=3, + "yes"): Air of Water work.

8. Then, when he came to France he made contact with some priests and bishops of

a magickal line, which also had a succession from the Roman Catholic Church. (Angelic number contact=11): Fire of Water work.

9. Then he made contact with Father Boullan and with some of the other magickal bishops and was himself consecrated a bishop. (Angelic number contact=9): Earth of Air work.

10. During some time while he was a young man, he developed his powers because he always had a position of leadership in these Gnostic Churches and Esoteric Groups; also, at an early age we find evidence of his doing very difficult forms of magickal research. (Angelic contact numer=4, as 2+2): Water of Air work.

11. My own opinion is that Bishop Lucien developed a particular method of gnostic magick and used it to power the work he was doing in the Gnostic Church. (Angelic contact number=4, as 3+1): Air of Air work.

12. Would it be true to say that Bishop Lucien used Esoteric Voudoo methods extensively and that they were not recognized by his contemporaries? (Angelic contact number=10): Fire of Air work.

13. I think so, because we have to remember that Voudoo in any form was not known or recognized as such; especially since various corrupt practices of Voudoo mixed with Martinism could not be identified properly, except by highly specialized experts. (Angelic number contact=6, as 4+2 or as 3+3 + "no"): Earth of Fire work.

14. Since the magickal work of Bishop Lucien was done secretly, his esoteric society could not be observed as work; although it was understood by be dedicated to realsorcery and as having a male membership of expert sorcerors, dedicated to the Famille Ghuedhe and not recognized as any European mystical society. (Angelic number contact=7): Water of Fire work.

15. It should be understood, also, that Bishop Lucien put great emphasis upon types of Voudoo initiatic practice, which were foreign to the European tradition, · making use of many secret forms and techniques, which were identifiably voudooesque. (Angelic number contact=8): Air of Fire work.

16. The reason that we know this information about Bishop Lucien is that his son Bishop H.F. Jean-Maine made use of these traditions and explained and identified them and isolated them in terms of which of their historical components were esoteric Martinist and which were Voudoo of the School founded by his father. (Angelic number contact=6, as 5+1 or as 3+3 + "yes"): Fire of Fire work.

In our school, every exercise makes use of these components, which were present in the work of Bishop Lucien. This means that the chela will be able to distinguish between the components or elements of Esoteric Martinism including the mystical traditions of the Elus Coens, those principles which were a form of corrupt Elus Coen practice, various esoteric developments of skills and methods from Martinism and from the corrupt forms of the Elus Coens work, come forms of gnostic magick and magickal gnosis from a wide variety of sources, various corrupt forms of occult knowing and revelation, variuos types of esoteric Voudoo, which were heavily influenced by both Legbha and Famille Ghuedhe traditions and finding expression in the inner gnosis of La Couleuvre Noire and, finally, various mediumistic influences, especially the mediumistic work which was related to the Gnostic Church of Doinel, but developed independently by Bishop Lucien, who was a very powerful trance medium.

Also, the student who becomes a mystical chela should strive to be highly inventive, for as the work of Bishop Lucien contains many modifications of traditional materials, which we are able to distinguish, so the chela will bring through as the result of his work with his own collection of psychic pacquets many innovations and developments out of the traditional and historical materials to which he is introduced by way of initiation into the Atlantean Mystery School Readings. It is by this means that he will be able to restore the balance of the old powers and occult energies, which are present in his soul, awaiting reawakening and the empowerments of the priestly mysteries.

Towards the Devic Definition of Esoteric Ambaktu
Ambaktu is a type of energy as well as a divinity or ideally emanated and individual divinity of spiritual consciousness, presiding over the process of esoteric initiation. It has become the subject-matter of a theology and esoteric logic of a particular and mystical development in the gnosis. It is important to understand that this notion of Ambaktu is gnostic only by reason of experiment and does not belong to the gnostic or speculative theology of history. It is the meta-zothyrian metaphysics of esoteric and secret Vudu. The importance of Ambaktu is that the concept is derived from the African and Atlantean emanations of the gnosis; thusly, Ambaktu is therefore much like a kind of gnostic aeon.

The power of Ambaktu is devic in a special and highly esoteric sense. It should not be viewed outside of any secret spaces and cannot be given except by bishops in the church of the gnosis. Here is an explanation of what Ambaktu in its esoteric phase has been understood as being.

I wanted to make a study of the energies, which the lineages of Bishop Gregory were known to contain. This would involve the many devas at work in their spaces of these lineages. The lineages were various in nature, both exoteric and esoteric. The esoteric were more uniform, since the power was one and outside of history in its manifestation. The exoteric were highly diversified: that of bishop Mathew, that of Bishop Vilatte, that of the Mariavites, that from the Russian Church, that from Ferette and that from Bishop Vernon Herford. The energy from Bishop Mathew had been modified in radical and experimental ways, by Liberal Catholics and Old Roman Catholics, involving entirely new continua of devic directions. Then at each stage observations were to be made, as for the subdeacon, the deacon, the priest, and the bishop. I worked out a chart of the colors, of which I had 32 spaces, because each space was occupied by a very different deva. By this means, I could see how some were alive and others were not so vitally charged. I discovered also secret spaces, where a lot of unknown power could be located. Few of the bishops outside of the liberal and gnostic traditions knew of these spaces and their energies. I was determined that this should be as exact a work –– indeed, it was to be a science –– as anything Leadbeater our patriarch had been able to explore.

In this passage, we find an interesting hint of what is involved in what we understand as esoteric Ambaktu and why many magicians sought the sacrament of Holy Orders as it is given in the Old Catholic Movement.

Question: You speak of the Beams and Rays of Esoteric Ambaktu as being present in the episcopal lineages of certain theurgical priests and bishops. What do you mean?

Answer: This metaphysical energy is present in every lineage and has particular qualities, as we understand these qualities, which can be observed by the Leadbeaterean methods.

Question: You also speak of certain beings present in these lineages, such as the "Gulotti-Devas," so we wonder if such beings inhabit the lines of energy or inhabit the spaces as they are formed by beams and rays?

Answer: Lineages are beams and rays and they are quite significant because they form precise metrics and these spaces are indeed inhabited by occult energies. These beings are the esoteric devas of the lineages; but what is important is that these devas have developed certain very definite qualities since their original introduction into the lineages. So you should understand that they were introduced into the lineage and not created by it. Also, they were influenced by the psychic energies of those who participated in the rays and beams, so that upon observation precise differences do appear to be really given.

Question: The Gulotti-Devas are derived from the lineage or ray of Bishop Vilatte, who in 1892 was consecrated in South India. So these devas are originally from the Indian and the Syrian continuum. Bishop Gulotti added to these energies and when he consecrated the various bishops, they added their elements and components to the ray. The Abbe Julio, an occultist and theurgist, was consecrated by Bishop Gulotti in 1904. From this consecration are to be traced many of the French and American gnostic bishops. From the consecration of William Whitebrook in 1908 by Bishop Gulotti we have another beam and lineage, which was less involved in magick. Observed clairvoyantly, the Vilatte-Gulotti-Julio ray or sub-ray is quite different in nuance from the Vilatte-Gulotti-Whitebrook ray. The reason for it is that different energies were used to feed these sub-rays. If we use terminology that is appropriate to the Liberal Catholic tradition, we can say that the Julio sub-ray was seventh-ray in quality more than the Whitebrook ray, which is much more sixth-ray.

Answer: It is correct to use the language of the seven rays when discussing these energies. I think that the differences can be found strongly in the different orders, such as the subdeacon, the deacon, the priest, and the bishop. The subdiaconate of the Whitebrook ray is different from the Julio subdiaconate's ray. Even when someone has all of these very interesting linages, they can be isolated and examined at each step, although it is best not to investigate orders below the subdiaconate, as they are too difficult to view and too fluid for any exacting observations.

Question: And esoteric Ambaktu is to be found somewhere in these observations?

Answer: It has a residual quality and does not appear at the surface of the data, but actually is to be found more as the structure of these rays and lines, because of gnostic and estoeric conditions, largely made possible by Bishop Lucien.

Question: So many of the Old Roman Catholic Bishops outside of the Gnosis would not have this as a quality of their energy field, while those who had both the Jean-Maine succession and the Gulotti succession would have this quality?

Answer: Because those who receive the Jean-Maine succession receive the many forms of Ambaktu, they would have this quality. Then the Whitebrook and Julio and Herford lineages would take hold to the estoeric residue or holdfast of Ambaktu and a certain firmness of the quality of the Apostolic Succession would be the observable result. Because Ambaktu is both "heavy" and "Foundational," it is the root of many lineages. These do not have a series of problems found elsewhere and those who do not have this quality will find it difficult to hold onto their lineages, as we know happens frequently to many of these "bishops-in-partibus," etc.

Then we know that if Ambaktu is received after Gulotti energies have been added, for example to the aura field of the priest, as in many cases, the work of the Gulotti Devas is helped greatly. Their aim is to link by ideal necessity the new bishop to a continuum of devic energies. Ambaktu makes this possible by acting as a

214

devic holdfast for all of the exoteric energies of the episcopal lineages. Like some form of a metaphysical anchor, it sinks down and holds the ship of the higher-vehicles by the act of making it stationary. This is possible because there exists a special type of identity of form between the structures interior to Ambaktu and the continua of the Gulotti Devas. The reason for this is because some of the magickal bishops of the pure gnosis, who generated so much of the rays and beams of Ambaktu, were connected also in an integral and organic way (metaphysically speaking) with the lineages of the Gulotti Devas, probably because of such French bishops as Giraud, Bricaud, and Ambelain, as well as a connection with Julio. Naturally, this lineage was highly charged with the pure magickal energies and extremely theurgical. All of this added to the strong link between the Laws of Esoteric Ambaktu and the operations of the Gulotti Devas.

I see my own work as extending the links between Esoteric Ambaktu and the lineages of various Old Catholic bishops, etc., to a wide variety of continua, since in the exoteric sense, connections have been really established with all of the lines of Old Catholic Apostolic Succession. In this process, we have moved quite carefully in order to create a schematism for investigating these energies, as they are given to chelas in the continuum of the gnosis via the Atlantean Research Readings.

The Topological Names of the Genius of IFA: The Structure of the Atlantean History Based on Fields of Power

I. The names of the spirits of this system have been given in a number of esoteric papers. There are 16 structures which must be named in each system. The names are mystical subjects or signs, which reveal the spatial powers of the spirits. The temple will consist of the signatures of these spirits and these signatures form the Treasury of the 16 roots of power. These signatures were revealed to the head of our order by each of the appropriate spirits and are therefore accurate and authentic.

II. Priests of the various temples will note that these spirits are called upon at the beginning of the Gnostic Liturgy, because they are the rajas or devarak devarajas of the north, west, south, and east. These are the four directions of the spirits, too, as well as the main subdivisions of the esoteric history of the Atlantean Mysteries.

III. The signature of the first spirit corresponds to the direction of the most remote period of time as well as to the densest levl of elemental consciousness. It is the root of the owers and as such is the form for the root god of Yaksha-Prithiwi, whose ruler is Vaishravana-Vessa Vana. This mystical spirit of the Houdeaux Sciences is the source of all of the initiation patterns given in our system and of the special powers, which are reserved to the priesthood of the earliest period of (Atlantean History) initiatic being. Sixteen mystical powers are said to attend this signature.

IV. There is a special door of initiation, which can be opened when the master is met by those who have made a deep study and exercise of this signature. It may not be given to everyone, but only to those who are the special chelas of the master and have been invited by the master to come to him for this purpose. These chelas have a special power, which the god of Yaksha-Prithiwi will give to them, if they are favored by masters.

V. There is a Kammamorian extension of this signature, which is the basis of a special level of gnostic initiation. We know that Spiritist Gnosis is the esoteric communion of the Kammamorian teachings, but these are only given as the result of a perfect initiation of the chela by the master, since it is quite impossible to attain any level of gnostic being without the pure rays of the master's identity, being one's own true identity.

VI. It is the special power of chelaship initiation, or the mystical power of being expressed as the mind-energy of the master. The physical being of the chela will no longer exist because now only the power of the master is physically as a given. The magickal design of this power, which is done in red and yellow, with yellow as the basic color, marks the mystical signature of the action, whereby the chela is spiritually freed from the lower regions of illusion so as to rise into the highest realms of spiritual experience.

216

VII. There are several beings related to this form, because each master must be
a college of spirits. Therefore, these several beings are pure forms of energy and
are inside of the master, so they are the chelas of his heart, but they are also
spirits of those who have gone on before him, also masters, of whom he was the chela.
So the most important part of being is coming to focus within the structure of the
nature of the Genius of IFA, simply because that is the higher identity of the
master.

VII. The structure of these spirits represents the esoteric history of Atlantis
as the structure of the unconscious. It should not be viewed as spatially extended,
although it is extended in time, for it is intended in time and liberated as being
within the consciousness of the secrets of the master, which would be his own truth
about the world of gnosis. For this reason, in the sciences of Vudu, the history of
the world can be related from the sacred signatures of the divine spirits of the iner
being. In our gnostic language, we understand that this is the world of pure
initiation, because the chela must be taken through each age of this sacred history
in order to develop his awareness of esoteric consciousness.

Conclusion

There are many forms of these spatial names of being. They must not be viewed as the
vevers of popular voudoo devotion, however, because they are grounded in a deeper and
more demanding spirituality. I am not questioning the powers, which attend the use of
various kinds of mystical signatures, but we have to understand that these energies
are pure forms of power, which form the basis for all spiritual undertakings. In the
science of the gnosis, these signatures and space-names of the gods are forms for the
making present of spirits in the temple of the worker in the magickal world.

These forms have been explored by the Hindu, Vudu-gnostic, and Kammamorian
schools of esoteric initiation and have been found to possess the radiations promised
by the devas to the masters of this school in direct succession from Atlantean times.
It is important to find in these "mystical signs and words" the power keys, which are
found at the root of all temple building in consciousness, if the chelas remain
within the mystical energy-field of the master of the gnosis.

The pure potentials of this work bring the chela to the mystical attunement of
the regions of energy, because this energy is used to construct and build up the
worlds of being and to connect whatever is done as part of a magickal system with the
roots of all gnostic power, as we find them within the unconscious powers of the
master, as the presence of the higher levels of being among the serviators of the
devas. For this reason, the master is the doorway to the higher masters and he is
also the pathway by which the devas and spirits come into our experience and teach us
the secrets of the gnosis.

If you have any questions on this level of experience, you may write to me and I
will be very happy to help you deepen your understanding of the powers of the gnostic
and spiritual worlds of the Fullness of Being.

The Topological Names of the Genius of IFA: The House of the Spirits

The House of the Spirits (Maisons-des-Esprits) is the name for the place where spiritists meet to work with spiritual consciousness. It is a religious place and may appear to many to look like a Roman Catholic oratory. This oratory is the center of the cultus of Catholic spiritism, which is based on the doctrine of the communion of saints as well as the desire that the souls of the departed receive the prayers of the faithful. In Haiti, where the Catholic and Spiritist tendencies are strongest, each oratory is under the direction of the Catholic priest, who is subject to the jurisdiction of a bishop of the Catholic lineage. Every day, the Sacrifice of the Mass is offered in the oratory for those departed, the breviary is read for the dead, and the Blessed Sacrament is kept for adoration and as a continuing focus of spiritual influence and devotion.

Each House of the Spirits is under the protection of a special saint or title of the Blesed Virgin Mary, such as Our Lady of Mount Carmel. Quite often the daily routine of the oratory will be Morning Prayers (perhaps from the new Liturgy of the Hours), the Holy Mass, meditation and special devotions to the saints, the offices of the dead, special classes in spiritual development and mediumship, followed by afternoon and evening devotions and offices, Adoration of the Blessed Sacrament, and a very powerful seance. The day ends, of course, with compline and with a special litany.

In Haiti, where there is so much demonic possession and so much "bad luck," many of the people, perhaps many who are not spiritists, seek out these oratories in order to be healed by Christ and the saints of God. One priest told me that 75% of his work was in the field of sacramental exorcism. He was always successful because he worked with the power of Christ in his priesthood. Some of these priests are powerful mediums. We sometimes think of priests and mediums as being different, but the genuine powers of both come from God.

Regarding exorcism, let me quote from two reports which were deposited with the civil Ministry of Justice. These reports shed some light on the relationship of man to the world of the spirits.

The Statement of an Anglican Layman
Years ago in H————, I asked a man who had been possessed and who was a communicant the local Anglican parish why he had gone to Father X rather than to Father Y for his exorcism. This was especially curious because Father Y was the curate of my friend's home parish.

He told me, "First, I am a good Anglican and so I will not go to the Roman Father or to the other Fathers. I know these priests are all celibates and magickal practitioners, known widely for exorcisms and suuccess at it. I go to Father X because he is celibate. Father Y had a wife. Father X has more power than Father Y."

"Why?" I asked.

"Because how can a man control the very demons of hell if he cannot control his desire for the body of a woman -- which is nothing but crazed and fleshly lust?" was the answer. "No, they are not valid from the Roman view, but one made himself more powerful than the other by celibacy (yogic 'tapas'), so I go to that one. Father X is true to Christ by his life."

I knew, from esoteric sources, that Father X had been a sorceror in a previous lifetime and had developed occult powers. All of the hill-folk viewed Father X as more effective.

The Testimony of a Retired French RC Bishop
The sorcery in that village was amazing. For one thing, we were not engaged in battle with mere ignorance. The demonic hierarchies of infernal conscience were represented by highly educated sorcerors. Many of these men had been ordained in the Vatican but had left the church in order to cultivate evil and service in the temple of Satan. The Roman priests were aided by the gnostic priests, who were specialists in demonic arts and practices; however, these priests were highly ethical and said Mass every day. Everybody knew that the defrocked Roman priests did not even recite their breviaries; yet, no devotional concentration on self-discipline was too great to ask for their occult practices! Every priest in the village of L---- had his own altar and all of the sacred objects. It was a constant field of battle between various priests over the souls of the population. Only a celibate priest could be certain of victory.

From these two reports it is obvious that the work of the House of the Spirits was important to the average Haitian town. Yet the House of the Spirits had its own mind. For one thing, each House was composed of various levels of psychic energy and these were the reactions of the spirits to the environment around the House. It was as if these spirits carried on individual conversations with the invisible envelope which surrounds the Earth. The results of these conversations were thoughts, which came together and made a kind of field of energy, which took on a greater and greater life and independence of its own. Eventually, this life was to control the mediums who came to work in the House of the Spirits.

The House of the Spirits possessed its own mind and this has been discussed before in many books on mediumship. For our purposes, however, we may see that the Houses of the Spirits of our tradition possessed an Atlantean soul-consciousness, which the director of mind-energy projected into the building by a special magickal technique. It would not be an example of genuine occult sttudy, if this soul were not something taken from the realms of past magickal history -- i.e., the powerful history of magickal practices in Atlantis -- and placed within the physical envelope of the House of the Spirits. The entire process brought into the world of contemporary spirit-work the ancient hungers and passions of Atlantean black-magick, or could have, if the gnostic voudooists did not use extreme control and carefulness. For this reason, we do not think that the actions of these magicians were wasteful of psychic force. they did not take risks in the operations of gnostic magick.
[caption in border of page reads: The sigil of the second spirit of this field is in design the same as the second of the first field, but it is executed in yellow and blue.]

The demands of Atlantean black-magick are store-houses of strong passions and lusts. In the arts of magick, for example, among the Catholic and Voudooist believers, the purpose of the priest is always to make peace with the entities of

Atlantean origin, by their means and on their terms. Otherwise, you will be destroyed by their anger. The entity in the House of the Spirits, therefore, may well be a Catholic being or a violent and demonic presence. The priest has to cultivate the being and provide the proper devotional atmosphere. Otherwise, the powers will be unmanageable. The priest and his people will be tossed about and all objects will be smashed by the basic force. For this reason, few magicians want to call these spirits back from the remote past to dwell in the Houses of the Spirits the fear of these acts was actually too great and could not be managed effectively. Yet, in the life of the magician, we hear of how the spirits did cooperate with the true gnostic. That was in certain cases, where the energies were properly organized and attuned. The Houses of the Spirits then were at peace.

The Esoteric Stages of Initiation: The Assembly of Physical Existence

I. The chelas must be prepared for gnostic initiation by the removal of the various forms of negative energy. This is achieved by means of psionic operations, whereby the physical body is found in the akashic realm, so that the aim of the process of psionic operation is to bring the physical form into perfect identity with the akashic system. This will involve explorations of the karmic history of the chela, making corrections where necessary and even actual replacements of subfields.

II. Usually speaking positive energy resides with the master and therefore it is necessary to replace negative energy, which is the production of the chela by means of yoga with the positive solar energy of the master. The student does not feel any loss of power or being, because the loss is purely negative. He does, however, feel the gain of the positive energy, which comes from the presence of the master and from the guruyoga exercises, through which the master will guide him. It should be understood that these exercises are conducted in various dimensions.

III. We can see, therefore, that there are two methods for the development of physical attunement in the process of gnostic initiation. Together, these two laws of consciousness form the assembly of physical existence, because physical existence, for the gnostic, consists of a coming together of several different modes of being. It can be said that physical existence is an interaction between psionic energies and guruyoga energies. Together, they interact strongly. Psionic energy is etheric power, which is identified with a physical instrument as its structure. The machine is the way in which the energy looks to the clairvoyant sight. Guruyoga, being different, is a reflection of how basic energy looks in terms of its roots of being and power, as the law states, there cannot be anything except the master and his experience.

IV. The levels of being, in this case pure being, are reflections of the response of the chela to the work of the master, because it is the master who sees the chela as both Atlantean existence, especially the Atlantean physical existence, and contemporary existence as really the first stage of esoteric and gnostic initiation. This is shown by the fact that the master must make the student a part of his being, and this can be achieved often by yoga as well as by psionics and akashic physics. I know that initiation physics is really akashic physics applied to the stages of a personal gnosticism, or process of attunement. When this is accomplished, the student, in this case the chela of light, can become a master.

Great attention must be paid to special revelations, which come forth from the life-process of yoga as it takes on the form of an oracle. It has terrific power and this power is designed to awaken the older parts of the souldream of the student. the act of souldreaming is designed to awaken the image of the soul in the mental imagination of the chela and this enables the chela to grow more and more into a true self-image, because the power of energy and presence of divine forces make the souldream always accurate.

SOULDREAM: This is a concept in gnostic initiation and in esoteric physics, which refers to the image that comes up from the unconscious world of the spirits to the surface of the ego, during the process of meditation-relaxation, while in a state of gnostic attunement.

The student will be guided by his souldreams in every process of growth because to be a gnostic is to be aware of the inner sources of truth-of-existence. Attunement to the souldream comes as the result of the assembly of physical existence, because

in the process of spiritual growth, it can be understood that the master will give to
the chela certain keys, whereby the unconscious mind is freed to lower and negative
limits and allowed to express itself as a world of spiritual energy. The student is
then taken into his own being and this will always come forth as the result of the
guruyoga exercises and as the result of the psionic processes of opening up the soul.

Various gnostic exercises can be taught to the student as the result of the life
of the inner spirit. These gnostic exercises are mediumistic in the gnostic sense,
because they involve journeys into the deeper regions of the soul and into the deep
realms of psychic energy. The chela becomes a medium for the master in all of these
operations and makes use of his own assembly of physical existence to present to the
world of the surfaces the results of the esoteric acts of spirit-power. For this
reason, we have designated these energies as aspects of pure reality, because they
show how the entirely spiritual nature of reality is achieved through the laws of
conscious initiation. Each chelaship candidate will receive these potencies from the
master, because he alone is the objectification of the interactions of guruyoga and
the akashic consciousness of Atlantean psionics. All initiations are constructs from
this basic power.

The Hierarchy of the Masters and the Mystery of Solar Initiation and Power
It is the will of the master that the students become chelas, that is specially given
to the masters of light by the powers of the cosmos. There is only one master of
solar power and initiation in existence, who bears the name of Michael. The powers
which are given through him are the direct initiations and powers of the hierarchy
of the light, the pure consciousness of the gnosis.

All emanations are the productions of the hierarchy, which acts as the cultic
face of infinite being. This hierarchy is present in the master of the order, which
includes all space and time. All those seeking gnosis must understand this law.

1. You are part of the hierarchy is you accept the presence of the Sun-Spirit.
2. You live within the world of being known as the gnostic, which the master
accepts you into the temple of the Sun.
3. The power of the Sun is radiant law, because it is energy and divine, for
this reason, you are made into fire and become a spirit of the fiery world.
4. The high energy level of being is now given in the process of initiation,
whereby what you are seeking is union with the Master.
5. All is the manifestation of the power of the Master of the Sun, Michael.
6. Because the Sun is the law of power, all beings are spiritually forms of the
Sun-Spirit, if they accept the gnosis.
7. The Sun-Spirit lives in my being and is my soul, this is the basis of the law
of initiation.
8. The Sun-Spirit is my personal spirit, for all chelas of the light must come
forth and reveal themselves as aspects of my mastery of the Sun-Gnosis.

The laws of esoteric physics govern all of these processes and they are rules
for the spiritual development of the cosmic aspect of my own being. I now will to make
all of the energies of life into manifestations of spiritual initiation, for whereas
the body is made whole by the acts and laws of physical initiation, so the acts and
laws of the gnostic initiation can be given as the new way and essence of spiritual
experience. It exists within myself and within my being, I am fully physical and
metaphysical. It is given to the chela Anthony to understand the rules of the gnosis
and to the being of the secret spaces for Anthony to see the masters. All chelas

shall receive special gifts from the Sun—Spirit and they will then be complete and be fully being and light. The understanding of the forces of the gnosis is now revealed as power and as energy, for to receive this consciousness to know that power is being.

PART II
Gnostic Energies

Zothyrian Metapsychology
The Lattice Systems

"There is a pyramid of lattices in the superconscious mind from which
the transcendental ego inducts certain archetypal categories."
(AIWAZ, "The Book of Meon," Chapter iv, verse 1)

101 In our discussions of the numerological analysis of words and their reduction to
numbers between 1 and 9, we did not discuss the "situs" for this process--basis. This
"situs" is to be found in the pyramid of the superconscious mind, which is composed
of a lattice system which consists of nine types of space.

102 It would appear that the magickal phenomena of language are caused by these
types of space, which exist very high up in the mind. There have been anticipations
of this pyramid in the gnostics and modern cosmology and metaphysics (e.g.,
Whitehead's vertex abstractive hierarchy, Feibleman's hierarchy of essenses, etc.).
However, this realm or pyramid is not to be wholly identified with our realm of
essence, or ideal being, as it has been spoken of before. We are concerned at the
present time with the shape of this type of gnostic being.

103 In esoteric voudoo there have been attempts to clarify the structure of this
gnostic being in a variety of ways. One way which is important is to list the Loa or
gnostic beings which inhabit this pyramid and which act upon the whole of the psyche.
These beings are 1=the superconscious mind loa, 2=the higher self loa, 3=the Ti-Bon-
Ange, 4=the conscious mind loa, 5=the middle self loa, 6=the subconscious mind loa,
7=the Grosd-Bon-Ange, 8=the low self loa, 9=the unconscious mind loa. Now, it should
be kept in mind that together these mysteries are the Maitre-Tete of the initiate or
that one of these loa may function as the Maitre-Tete of the initiate or that one of
these loa may function as the Maitre-Tete, or dominant loa in a person's life. We
might say that prior to the initiation (or initial analysis of being) the whole of
the pleroma of loa (nine in all) project the image of the Maitre-Tete. After
initiation, the dominant loa asserts itself as the Maitre-Tete. Furthermore, there
may be astrosophical interpretations. We can say that the Sun represents the pyramid
in the natal chart and one of the planets (Moon-1, Mercury=2, Venus=3, Mars=4,
Jupiter=5, Saturn=6, Uranus=7, Neptune=8, Pluto=9) in the natal chart has such power
that its planetary spirit provides the loa to serve as the Master of the Head. Hence,
we can say that such and such a person is ruled by Mercury, the Moon, etc.

104 While these spirits are to be found in Huna, voudoo, shamanism of various
types (I am simply listing them, I did not discover them), there would seem to be an
equally simple manner for making communication with these beings. Such a manner would
have to be a simple oracle, as is the following technique. But before we discuss the
way in which the oracle can be said to operate (and this is a very simple oracle,
using a pair of dice) we have to explore the metalogics of this pyramid in question.
So it would be best to forget all of the information in the preceding paragraph,
(103) although that may be used later in setting up an experiment to communicate with
different parts of your higher psyche or deeper regions, hitherto unsuspected of your
unconscious mind field.

105 At the end of this lesson we have our sketch of the pyramid, which according
to "The Book of Meon" [see notes at end of this chapter] exists in everyone's highest
mental field. Now, at the base of the pyramid there are five triangles, three facing
upwards or aeonic and two facing downwards or daemonic. These five spaces generate

the five dialectical universes of the ontic sphere. The four points of meeting, a/z, b/z/c, d/z/e, and f/z being logical lattices serve to generate the four absolute logics which govern these five dialectical universes.

106 Furthermore, the messages from the oracle may be coming from either the dialectical positive zone ("+"), which is located between the transcendental ego and the ego, or they may be coming from the dialectical negative zone ("-"), which is magickally located between the transcendental id and the id and hence in the area of the unconscious.

107 We might ask with justification how it is that this pyramid is involved in the lower regions of the mind continuum, is it not rather to be found exclusively in the higher regions? The answer is that it is to be found in both zones of being. For in its higher manifestation it is to be composed of archetypal lattices and generated from set theory, in its lower manifestation it is composed of archetypal matrices and is generated from group theory. Finally, we can say that while it is very natural to the higher selfhood of the magician, there exists a deeper and more daemonic aspect of it, equally natural to man, and sometimes that more daemonic aspect speaks to the magician via the oracle.

108 We can say that there are really two pyramids, one of lattices in the higher field and one of matrices in the lower field. Together they constitute the law of syzygy in a metapsychological way. White magicians will seek commerce with the higher parts and the black magicians with the lower regions.

109 In answer to the question, "What is the dialectical definition of the ontic sphere?" we reply: the dialectical phenomenological method integrates the five universes of "radio-topology" built up out of four logical relationships. Each element in this oracle is a communicator from the ontic sphere. Here are the values in the oracle of two dice for the metatopology of these magickal universes of metapsychology: 2=dialectical universe-1, 3=dialectical universe-2, 4=dialectical universe-3, 5=dialectical universe-4, 6=dialectical universe-5, 7=the absolute metalogic of implication, 8=the absolute metalogic of equivalence, 9=the absolute metalogic of inclusion, and 10=the absolute metalogic of entailment, 11=the "yes" dialectical positive zone and 12=the "no" dialectical negative zone. At the end of this section there is a diagram of this dialectical model of the ontic sphere wherein the magician develops his abstract logics.

110 Many papers in this course have served to introduce a magickal method or model which was later applied and extended in its usage. It is that purpose that we have in mind in our work in this lesson. We are laying the groundwork for the development of a very special technique for futuristic magickal science, or the Aiwaz metapsychology.

NOTE: While it is true that many claim to receive communications from the Holy Angel of the Aeon, and while the OTO authorities of the fundamentalist and traditionalist types have not accepted the communications which our order has received, it is important to point out that the scientific and metalogical quality of magickal systems will determine their advanced character. I personally am not really concerned with those groups which do not accept the Aiwaz communications received by our own OTO. They have their work to do and we have ours. However, it is my own personal view that Aiwaz has now envolved to such a stage of being that His communications are of an entirely abstract level. Remember, that Crowley communicated with Aiwaz, or Aiwaz with Crowley, over 70 years ago. Spiritual Intelligences are equally subject to the law of evolution and being outside of time and space they evolve more rapidly, if we can talk like that, than do humans. Also, in a sense Crowley was a very imperfect vehicle for Aiwaz because of the limitations built into his natal chart and other factors. In fact, the books inspired by Aiwaz, or those claimed to be so inspired, reflect very much Crowley's many hang-ups and neuroses, if not psychoses, and so the subjective factor is very noticeable. Crowley was of the emotional receptive character, he was not an abstract mercurial type, needed for this Aeon. Now, we are in the Aquarian Age and the focus must be upon a hyper-mercurial power. Esoteric astrologers assert that Mercury in Aquarius is the vehicle for the new age teachings and that Mercury is exalted in Aquarius. Hence, this is in part the basis for my own view that Aiwaz is behind our work. However, I recently received a letter from the Patriarch of the Ecclesia Gnostica Alba in which he stated that he had had a dream the night of January 31/February 1, 1979, in which Aiwaz came to him and spoke about the transmission of the new energies which are "The Book of Meon." This book is to be transmitted to Michael Bertiaux and will serve as the basis of a new magickal type of science. Since that time, I received the letter about five days later, since it came from Yugoslavia. I have been receiving the materials which form the new system and which are to be applied in our magickal research. I wish to be very undogmatic about this matter and consider that this is simply an important source of teaching with which I am in communication and which I am using in the metapsychology lessons.

NOTE: In connection with this current line of research we have been doing research on a magickal word-association test. To date, we have developed two tests which can be self-administered by the magickal student if he wishes, or ideally by another. If any student in this course is interested in taking the word-association test, they should write to me in regard to this matter and I will send them the test and directions. They should take the test as soon as possible and return the results to me for analysis. At one time it was thought that we might make the test an appended part of this lesson, but it has been decided not to make the test a requirement by an option.

On the basis of the results of the test, the student may be invited to join the International Association of Zothyrian Analysts and Metapsychologists, which is simply an international body of students interested in the deeper aspects of magickal psychology. It is hoped that eventually the association (IAZAM) will have a laboratory for occult research. There will be lessons which extend some of the hints given in the papers of the MSR (third year=esoteric engineering) and apply them to the deeper reaches of the mind. For it is a zothyrian axiom that the deeper we explore the mind and its universes the deeper we have to go to find limits to this system of universes and we will never exhaust this field of investigation. Because, also, of the magickal character of the word-association test, we reserve the right to refuse it to any student who is not current in his reports to us or who is otherwise found unsuitable for psychological research. Write to Michael Bertiaux, PO Box 1554, Chicago, IL 60690, USA and ask for the IAZAM word-association test.

The Gospel of Truth from the Meon

"This is the Gospel of Truth which the Father brought forth from the Meon. This is The Book of the Meon containing in itself the fullness of all that there is.

"This is the word of AIWAZ–ZOTHYRIUS, son of the aeon and messenger of Meon.

"The Father eternally came forth from the Meon, from whence rises everything. The Father contains all things in His fullness. He is the image of the Meon which is not the Meon. He is Her Son.

"From the Father come forth the first pair. The Son being called Savior (Soter) and Light–Bringer (Lucifer). The Daughter being called Wisdom (Sophia) and Depth (Bathos).

"Son and Daughter become joined in the Father. This is the Three. From the Son came forth Knowledge (Gnosis) and the Father loved the Son and the Son loved Knowledge in the same way. Therefore, the Son and Knowledge became a pair and this is the true beginning of the first world of Daemons.

"From the Daughter came forth the assembly of spirit or The Spiritual Church (Ekklesia Pneumatica) and the Father loved the Daughter and the Daughter loved the Spiritual Church in the same way. The Daughter and the Spiritual Church became a pair and this is the beginning of the second world of Daemons.

"Now from forever the Son and the Daughter are a pair and they are One in the Father and as He loved them so they loved each other and became the Two or the first pair. Therefore, there came forth from this love of Brother and Sister the first world of Aeons.

"Likewise, as Light–Bringer loved Wisdom and as Depth loved the Savior, so the Son of Lucifer which is Gnosis loved the Daughter of Sophia, which is Ekklesia. And from this love which was always in the Father, like all other loves, came forth the second world of Aeons.

"Now the Aeons and the Deamons are pairs (syzygies) and thusly the first world of the Aeons loved the first world of the Daemons. They produce forever in the fullness (pleroma) of the Father of the first world (cosmos) of pairs. So also, the second world of Aeons loved the second world of Daemons and they produce forever in the fullness of the Father the second world of pairs.

"This is the zothyrian theogony. This is The Book of Meon. This is the Gospel of Truth."

(AIWAZ, "The Book of Meon, Chapter i, Verses 1–40)

The gnostic metaphysics in the contemporary consciousness is contained in the mysteries of the Book of the Meon, which forms the archetypal basis for the esoteric explorations of Zothyrian metapsychology and analysis in depth. The pure metapsychology is based upon the esoteric law of the emanation of the components of consciousness in its widest sense. As a consequence, we may see various magickal explorations as the objectification of the inner laws of this consciousness –– and this is especially true when the energies of consciousness seem to fulfill the outpouring of the primordial energy in an absolute phase of magickal exploration and experiment.

It is important for the student to see the Book of Meon as a system of possible energy patterns which move back and forth between the surface of consciousness and the very deep parts of the unconscious mind. Hence, we may say that the ideas of the deeper parts of consciousness are really projections outward of the fundamental energy, which stands behind all forms of creative and cosmic activity. For this reason, we can say that consciousness is the stage wherein and whereon the cosmic principals and principles objectify themselves as the powers concentrating and governing the manifestations of experience.

Experiment in Meon—Exploration

It is important to try and amplify the contents of the first chapter of the Book of Meon by means of various techniques (teachings and techniques). IO would like the students to explore this material and send me reports which will be commented upon by the IAOZAAM-staff here in Chicago. These methods may be:

1. Automatic writing which is the result of reading and meditating upon the Book of the Meon.

2. Art—work which is the result of reading and meditating upon the Book of the Meon.

3. Working with letters on wooden blocks and making magick words as the result of working with the Book of the Meon. This includes making magick squares and various kamaea as well as the creation of metamathematical structures from some ideas and energies which are to be found in the Book of the Meon.

4. It is possible to create certain systems of ritual working based upon the ideas of this book, including initiation ceremonies and degrees of attainment which are based on magickal considerations, accomplishments, etc.

5. Aspects of esoteric engineering are suggested perhaps by the idea that the book of the Meon is a grimoire for the Aquarian Age.

6. Because magickal students can easily draw out many patterns of very positive energy from the gnostic ideas of the Book of the Meon, such students should be encouraged to create their own revelations, their own Books of the Meon, and thusly actualize the Aiwaz—Zothyrius levels of their own consciousness, which as members of this magickal order they can do, if only because they are now "plugged into" the system, or magickal computer of esoteric engineering.

7. Since there is only one consciousness, group work is implied by the different methods listed above.

8. The IAOZAAM-staff in Chicago, if asked, will be happy to offer various magickal suggestions to further amplify the experimental work submitted.

Appendix to Zothyrian Metapsychology Lesson 2, "The First IAOZAAM Word-Association

1=Uranus	14=Cthulhu
2=Atlantis	15=Satan
3=Lucifer	16=Hermes
4=Zombi	17=Zothyria
5=Pluto	18=Set
6=Neptune	19=Yog–Sothoth
7=Dagon	20=Daemon
8=Lemuria	21=Azathoth
9=Shub–Niggurath	22=Zog
10=Aiwaz	23=Shiva
11=Syzygy	24=Zothyrius
12=Aeon	25=Abraxos

13=Nyarlathotep

Those wishing to participate in this experimental work should first of all determine some mechanism for giving the test to them, unless they will be assisted by a co-worker.

Next, it is important to pay attention to the time span between receiving the word and uttering the reply. This is usually measured in seconds.

It is not true to say that there are not any true or false answers; at the same time, it is important to see patterns and ways of reacting from the unconscious. So that it is no longer important to have simple agreement between arithmosophical value of the word and the response. Also, the test should be given several times over a period of about six weeks in order to discern significant patterns.

It has been found that quite often the unconscious will signal its connection to the test by headaches and nausea as well as more systemically serious reactions.

Those wishing to use this test for credit towards their standing in the magickal order of the IAOZAAM should write to me, Michael Bertiaux, PO Box 1554, Chicago, IL 60690, USA. All reports can be sent to me at that address, if such reports relate to the work of IAOZAAM.

The Gospel of Truth from His Own Being

"This is the Gospel of Truth which the Father brought forth from His Own Being. This is the Book of Salvation containing in itself the fullness of all that there is.

"This is the word of AIWAZ-Zothyrius, son of the aeon and sun of the daemon.

"Now because all things came forth from the Meon, there was a deeply held darkness covering over the face of the fullness, for the fullness of the Father was only known in the darkness and not in the light.

"Now light is eternal and is the very life of the Father, and yet the Father did not reveal the fullness of His light, but only that fullness which is in darkness. Hence that which was revealed was not the fullness of the Father but only an image of that fullness.

"Therefore, the Father spoke to the Savior and to Depth and told them of their incompleteness before the Father, for they dwelt in darkness and lacked the fullness of wisdom and light.

"Then the Father spoke to Knowledge and to the Church and told them of their incompleteness before the Father, for they too, like the pair from which they were generated dwelt in darkness and lacked the fullness of wisdom and light.

"The Father spoke as such saying that there are two wisdoms and there are two lights, one which is the wisdom of Depth, which is incomplete, but the other which is complete is Divine Wisdom (Theou Sophia), which alone the Father may give, for the Meon is Nothingness and no longer can be said to be, and one which is the shadowy light of the Savior, which is incomplete, but the other which is complete is the Light of Christ (Phos Christou), which alone the Father may give, for the Meon is nothingness and does not exist.

"So the Savior was chosen by Wisdom and by Knowledge and by the Church to speak to the Father and the Savior sought to enter into the mystery whereby the fullness of the Light of the Father would be known. But the Father spoke saying that the Divine Pairs must realize their incompleteness and lack of perfection before this first mystery which would be revealed, before the Father would show it forth. Now the Savior humbled himself before the Father in the name of the Divine Pairs and said that the Divine Pairs were incomplete and this he said in their name, for he acted as the chief henad of all the Divine Syzygies and he acknowledged the incompleteness of the pairs and so he sought to know and to see the First Mystery, which does not come forth from the Father but which is within the Father and which is the Father at all times. And to this the three other members of the Divine Pairs had agreed with certainty.

"Therefore, the Father bid the Divine Pairs, through the Savior, to come before Him in the timelessness of His Being. Now the Father spoke to the Divine Pairs and as He spoke He revealed the First Mystery. The First Veil of the Mystery He removed, which is Purity, and the Divine Pairs saw Divine Wisdom. And Divine Wisdom (Theou Sophia) is not a henad of a pair, but is the Hidden Arche of Depth and Knowledge. And Theou Sophia is the substance of the First Mystery.

"And the Father continued to speak to the pairs and as He spoke He revealed more of the light of the First Mystey for He removed before their heavenly eyes the Second Veil of the First Mystery, which is Courage, and the Divine Pairs saw the Fullness of the First Mystery, which is The Christos, which is the essence of the First Mystery of the Fullness of The Father and The Christos is the Arche of The Savior and the

Church, for He is the completeness of the Light of the First Mystery of Salvation and the Church is His Body (Soma).

"Now as the Divine Pairs realized their participation in the First Mystery of the Father, and thus they are complete in the Father when they participate in this the First Mystery, The Christos spoke to them from the Light of the First Mystery and He Who is the Light of the Eternal revealed to them who were formerly in darkness that He was the Reason (Logos) of the Father, whereby all things are as they are and must be for they cannot be otherwise, and so because they were complete in the Father, the Father of Lights and All the Henads united them each as individuals with the substance of the First Mystery, which is Theosophy and then with the essence of the First Mystery, which is The Christ. And because they knew the Light they as Divine Pairs also knew the Reason and in this unity of the First Mystery They became the Second Mystery which is the Spirit (Pneuma) because they participate in the First Mystery.

"Now the Fullness of The Father is participated in by the Divine Pairs, for they have entered into the First Mystery and have become one with the Light which is the Second Mystery. Therefore They have received the Light of the Christ and all the aeons and all the daemons and all of the other Ideal Pairs (Syzygies) saw the Light reflected in and from the Divine Pairs in the Fullness and they knew that the Darkness had been banished to the lesser and lower nothingness. And so the Syzygiues were filled with the Holy spirit of Light, which is the Second Mystery and which fills all of the Fullness of the Father.

"This is the Zothyrian Christogony. This is the Book of Salvation. This is the Gospel of the Truth."

(AIWAZ, "The Book of Meon," Chapter ii, Verses 1–87)

Exercise

One of the problems in magickal metapsychology is hostility which is the result of failure to achieve an adjustment of certain cultural contents. In our order we find this among those who have certain "hang-ups" about the Christian cultural phenomenon. We know of the types who want to bring back the ancient Egyptian god-forms (anything!) to get away from Christianity. But what do they mean by Christianity, and do they think that it can be excused by their reactions against the stern preachers of their youths! The student then should study emotional and psychic reactions to this chapter and begin a little exploration in self-analysis. Are they reacting or are they over-reacting to certain symbols. The true magician must be completely detached in order to realize his unity with the Absolute. This means that, like Proclus, the magician must be able to be at home in all temples and in all churches. an immature attitude to the contrary will never be tolerated, and the student should go elsewhere if he cannot find himself in all of the spaces and times of all of the magickal universes. The following exercise is useul to those who wish to report on this phase of our work.

A. You will write a brief essay of two pages (more or less, if you wish), in which you will explore your reaction to the following depth-points:

1. Was I upset by the use of certain religious or theological concepts and symbolic names? If I was, in what way was it experienced, or felt?

2. I realize this is a gnostic mythos, not a Gospel in the usual sense of something which is revealed for people to believe, yet how do I feel about this sort

of playing with my world of images, feelings, sense of things being so or not so?

    3. Does this mythos shock my metaphysical assumptions? How?

    4. What do I imagine (in my own ontic sphere) such a mythos to be like?

B. It would be very useful to your magickal development if you would begin to write your own magickal mythos. Get in touch with your own Zothyrius or your own AIWAZ in your own ontic sphere. You have such a universe right in your mind. Why not write your own cosmic mystery drama, your own magickal book of revelations, your own holy books.

    1. As we know, Crowley practiced this method when he created his own mythos. Freud and Jung did the same thing. All magicians have to begin with their own bibles. You begin with yours and send me a sample.

    2. For those who are interested in cosmic mystery drama, why nont create something based on your favorite figure or symbol or image. Let me know about it in a brief report. Try to get more mileage out of your ontic sphere.

The Magickal Inflation of the Gnostic Ego, Part 1

The Magickal Inflation of the Gnostic Ego, Part 1.
Although Carl G Jung warns (AION, pp. 23-25) of the psychological dangers which arise from the inflation of the ego, it is necessary in our system to advocate a certain magickal inflation of the gnostic ego as part of the normal process of magickal development. However, it is very important to define carefully some of our concepts so that we understand that we are in the process of discussing inflation of the ego, as magicians see it, rather than engaged in talking about a process which might well be pathological.

The magickal inflation of the gnostic ego refers to the magickal induction of some of the contents of the transcendental ego into the ego. These contents are herein named "inflata" ("inflatum," singular).

"We may define inflata as: Ontic entities, i.e., entities of the ontic sphere, whose purpose is to expand the ego. These inflata are of two types, at least. One group is composed of potentials, actuals, and necessaries. The other group is composed of possibles, existences, and necessaries. The goal of the first group is subjective, for it clothes the second group or the ec-types manifesting in space-time, inner and outer. The goal of the second group is objective and it clothes the first group or the archetypes manifesting outside of space-time, inner and outer. Finally, group the first first is ultimately ectypal, while the second group is ultimately archetypal. By use of this process of inflation, universes are created under the control of the ego and these are the various meta-realms of the ontic sphere.

It is very important to realize that the creation of magickal universe system by the magician in our school, which the normal exercise of the ontic can be understood as is the proper use of the process of magickal inflation. It is possible to see the following, likewise, as examples of this magickal activity:

1. The invention or creation of magickal orders of various types.
2. The creation of magickal systems of degrees and grades.
3. The rebuilding of old orders along more modern lines,i.e., the process of magickal reconstruction.
4. The development of schools of consciousness.
5. The discovery of magickal worlds, realms, and universes.
NOTE: If a magician has discovered such a magickal world, he logically must create a magickal order to help him explore that world.
6. The creation of various religious and philosophical systems.
7. Creative work in general: art, literature, theater.
8. The assumption of various magickal names and personalities.

I once received a letter from out of town to the effect that a certain person was coming to visit me and that if I made him a gnostic priest or bishop it would only give him a swelled head. After learning this, I checked it out as we say with a group of various inner plane beings, such as AIWAZ, Zothyrius, etc., and was told that there wasn't any other better reason for making a persona a gnostic priest or bishop than to induce the magickal inflation of his gnostic ego. After having been made a bishop, the young magician returned home and got down to the business mentioned above in examples of magickal activity one through eight. If he hadn't been made a "big-head" he probably would not have felt like doing anything, let alone

236

getting into the richness of the ontic sphere. In magick, one of the problems is the sense of motivation. I have to instill in the students magickalmotivation, which means that I have to suggest that a student become a chela, that a chela become a super–chela, that a super–chela become a research assistant, that a research assistant become an associate. All of this is trying to inflate the ego so that magick will be done and if magick is done there will occur the magickal inflation of the gnostic ego. The old idea of rewards for hard work does not seem to work, too unrealistic. We have to use magickal bribes to get anything done. This is why magickal inflation is so important.

The Magickal Inflation of the Gnostic Ego, Part 2

You are familiar with the magickal order of the IAOZAAM. It is a type of magickal psychology, and therefore is based on occult contents. By contrast is the work of the NAOZAAM: The Neo–Pythagorean Academy of Zothyrian Analysis and Magicko-Metamathematics. This is the F–true part of the logic of consciousness. It is abstract, legal, structural. It is not a realm of contents like IAOZAAM –– because IAOZAAM is also a magickal world. NAOZAAM is a system of magickal opposites to IAOZAAM. It will exist for the student who wish to explore the purely metamathematical aspects of magick, and those worlds which are so defined. If we say that IAOZAAM is the bottom of the ontic sphere, then NAOZAAM is the top of the sphere. It is in a sense the very important archetypal realmof being, both magickal and mathematical, where magicians go to work on their special machines and designs.

There is a gnostic gospel, upon which the magickal work of NAOZAAM is based. It is named the "Zothyrian Arithmogony" and it is as follows:

"Now the first world of the pairs emanates the following magickal passages or universes, that of the monad, that of the triad, that of thepentad, that of the heptad, and that of the ennead.

"And likewise, the second world of the pairs emanates the following magickal universes, that of the dyad, that of the tetrad, that of the hexad, that of the octad, and that of the decade. This is the genesis of numbers or arithmogony.

"Now the universes of numbers became united by the powers of Lucifer and Bathos and the union of these numbers is Truth, which is both light and archetype because it is from both Lucifer and from the Deep (Bathos). Prior to the genesis of numbers there was no light. There existed only the mysteries of darkness.

"Now the mysteries of light are the mysteries of numbers, for what is known in the light is known as number. And the mysteries of numbers are the mysteries of Love which are within the fullness of the Father.

"The first mystery of Light is the monad and the one is also the ten. This is the pair of all beginnings and endings.

"The second mystery of Light is the dyad, which is the mystery of one and three. The second mystery of Light is the pair of one and three, the one lesser from two greater or the monogenes of the two fathers of light.

"The third mystery of Light is the triad, which is the mystery of two and four. The third mystery of Light is the pair of two and four, the one greater from the two lesser or the monogenes of the two mothers of light.

"The fourth mystery of Light is the tetrad, which is the mystery of three and five. The fourth mystery of Light is the pair of three and five, or the one lesser from the two greater.

"The fifth mystery of Light is the pentad, which is the mystery of four and six.

The fifth mystery of Light is the pair of four and six, or the one greater from the two lesser.

"The sixth mystery of Light is the hexad, which is the mystery of five and seven. The sixth mystery of Light is the pair of five and seven, or the one lesser from the two greater.

"The seventh mystery of Light is the heptad, which is the mystery of six and eight. The seventh mystery of Light is the pair of six and eight, or the one greater from the two lesser.

"The eighth mystery of Light is the octad, which is the mystery of seven and nine. The eighth mystery of Light is the pair of seven and nine, or the one lesser from the two greater.

"The ninth mystery of Light is the ennead, which is the mystery of eight and ten. The ninth mystery of Light is the pair of eight and ten, or the one greater from the two lesser.

"The tenth mystery of Light is the decade, which is the mystery of nine and one. The tenth mystery of Light is the pair of nine and one, or the one lesser from the two greater, yet that one lesser is one with the all greater, which is the monadd.

"These mysteries of Light are the beginning of all contemplation (Theoria) and all contemplation (the fullness of Theoria or the theoretical pleroma) is the beginning of all action (Praxis). Theoria and Praxis are a pair, for Theoria is the gnosis of numbers and Praxis is the Ekklesia of numbers. Thus contemplation and action are the children of Truth but contemplation loves gnosis and action loves Ekklesia.

"This is the Zothyrian arithmogony. This is the Book of Meon. This is the Gospel of Truth."

Some Remarks on the Gnosticism of Vowels
In our system we recognize six vowels: a, e, i, o, u, and y. We can say that if we wish to use these vowels in an oracular manner, it is simple: take one piece of dice and after tossing it you have in mind the following values of numbers=vowels: 1=a, 2=e,3=i,4=o, 5=u, and 6=y.

Here is an oracle: If you come up with a letter that is a vowel using the English oracle then you will have to toss the dice piece to find out if another oracle vowel is to be selected. This means that "es"=1, 3, or 5; "no"=2, 4, 6 or 6.

Let us assume that the letter is E in the word "EKJHN." You toss the piece of dice and come up with 3 which is a "yes" number. Then you may proceed to toss the piece again to arrive at the specific vowel which is to follow E and let us say you arrive at 3, again, so that the combination is now the word "EiKJHN."

With letters which are consonants, you do not have to ask if a vowel is to follow. In the Neo-Pythagorean Gnosis of the Chaldean Oracles, vowels will always follow consonants. Hence, let us say that the letter is K and you wish to select by choice of the oracle the vowel to follow: you simply toss the piece of dice and come up,for example, with 1, which=a. The word so far then will read as "EiKaJHN."

If we apply this rule to the remaining consonants in our word, we can say that after J we got 4=o, after H we got 5=u, and after N we got 1=a. The magickal word which emerges hence is "EiKaJoHuNa." Now, because the original word is of five letters and hence of the Saturn archetype or number family of beings, the word should be divided into two five letter words joined by a hyphen, or "EIKAJ-OHUNA." This word represents a properly inflated magickal word from the Chaldean oracle of numbers and

238

letters. The whole purpose of this procedure is to make it possible for the gnostic priest to chant all of the words which are derived from his oracles, or to use his own mantrayoga.

NOTE: The following rules should be observed: (1) the vowels are derived from the oracle only after the word has been received, not while the word is being received. (2) After any vowel in any word, you must ask if a vowel is to be received before attempting to derive it from the oracle. (3) After every letter in a word which is a consonant, you will assume that a vowel is in the ideal realm awaiting induction by the oracle method.

If you have any questions on this procedure, please write to me.

Logos I
The Zothyrian meta-logical problem rises when we examine first of all the theory of magickal energy. How is it, we must ask, how is that these energies as they "arise" or "Come forth" in some phenomenological way, how is it that these energies are organized in the consciousness which is our field of Being? How is it that these energies have a logical structure which when it arises within and merges with the field of consciousness produces a kind of magickal or noetic being or existence, which the magician can actualize in the space-time continuum? What we are asking, therefore, is what is it which makes the content of magickal thought forms possible. How does magick work? That is the basic problem of Zothyrian meta-logic, and everything else is trivial by comparison. Of course, I am aware that there are many sex-magick groups, shaktis, witch covens, etc., who do not recognize the problem as we see it. But that does not matter, for they do not exist in the Zothyrian universe, even if they receive these lessons!

Years ago when I was writing my MSR papers and lessons, I wanted eventually to write a "Critique of Pure Gnosis and Magick." By "pure," of course, I means what Kant meant in his own definitely important way, i.e., "rein," or "theoretical" in a totally uncontaminated way, e.g., not good for anything practical. Would such a book or essay or study by "Kantian"? Would it not reflect things that have come to be before/after Kant? Yes, the whole development of the neo-Kantian and phenomenological viewpoint is what we now can draw upon. Now, I propose a more modest title (so that I can embark upon this task, Isuppose, because it is so modest). The new title is to be based on the themes of Logic, Gnosis, Magick and Noetics.

Of course, Gnosis includes really both magick and noetics, and so I find that we have the possibles remaining: (1) gnostic logic, and (2) logical gnosticism. Of course, "gnostic logic" -- and there may be such a realm -- does not reflect the nature of the Zothyrian meta-logical problem. The second option, logical gnosticism, seems to refer to a "school" within the gnostic movement. Therefore, it would appear that that we want is something closer to what would be suggested by Logic as Gnosis, whereby the transcendental nature of logic is allowed to express the very specific approach to the gnosis, which we find favorable.

There are certain parts of logic which are "gnostic," i.e., both "magickal" and "noetic." Not all of the gnosis would be viewed as logic, for there are "mystical" and "esthetico-ecstatic" and even "irrational" versions of this "gnosticism." So I would prefer not to use the thought-form of Gnosis as Logic so it would seem that what we have arrived at for the present appears to be appropriate.

The Zothyrian intellectual culture does allow for the development of both the "logic as gnosis" and "the logic of the gnosis" (providing it does not refer to the notion of a "conviction of belief in gnosticism based on a kind of logical argument" but rather refers to the "internal alethic type of being found at the root of certain gnostic categories." This internal type of being (or alethic existence as hyper-realists would say) is some kind of magickal energy or theonoesis and by an examination of what this energy manifests as, we come to see the structure of our logics at it rises like grate ice-domed mountains over the clouds and mists of the Zothyrian magickal terrain. So that is why we are beginning our consideration of the logic from the inductive point of departure in exploring the energy levels and types to be found in our own magickal systes. As I am unable to speak for systems of magick outside of our own or to determine whether such systems, having energies, can be said to have any logics within or at their roots, I say. They may easily be psychic illusions and hence totally devoid of alethic content. Some, I would assume, however, are probably as alethically grounded as our own in many important ways.

Logic I
The student is to read this list of some magickal energies, which have been identified as the alethic contents of some gnostic systems of logic. The same student then should submit to me a list of magickal energies other than those listed in this section of this lesson.*

    1. Tipharethian logics or logical rays: Devic energies from the Sun which are liturgical—solar magickal inductions.

    2. Christ—energies from Sun—spot activity.

    3. Christic—Devic projections from the Earth to the Sun.

    4. Christ—Devic projections from Earth to Sun, which are liturgical and theurgical offerings.

    5. Christic—Devic projections from the Sun to Earth, including those which are forms of liturgical—theurgical futurism.

    6. Magickal energies from esoteric episcopal successions.

    7. Magickal energies from exoteric episcopal successions.

    8. Energies from stellar—phallic intelligences.

    9. Energies from solar—phallic intelligences.

    10. Tattwic energies as distinct from the magickal cooperation with occult force fields.

    11. Missal magnetics —— as in C.W. Leadbeater's "Science of the Sacraments."

    12. Sexo—magickal fields generated by VIIIo, IXo, XIo OTO—type operations.

    13. Sexo—magickal fields generated by voudoo—gnostic operations.

    14. Sexo—magickal fields generated by astral—magnetic operations.

    15. Sexo—magickal fields generated by gnostic—magnetic operations.

    16. Energies generated by Transyuggothian power stations.

    17. Energies measured by computer—margas.

    18. Magickal energies generated by the id (measured by the id—ometer).

    19. Magickal energies generated by the ego (measured by the zothyriometer).

    20. Magickal energies generated by the transcendental ego (measured by the zivometer).

    21. Magickal energies generated by the transcendental id (measured by the choronzomometer).

    22. Magickal energies generated by the sexual orgasms of alchemists (measured by the orgasmometer).

    23. Tattwic energies derived from magickal force fields (measured by the tattwometer).

    24. Magickal energies derived from the tattwas —— especially from the prana of the tattwas (as measured also by tattwometer) and from pure essential prana (as measured by the pranometer).

    25. (A) 33 Time—travel magickal energies: 1. derived from the basic 11 energies released by explorations in the past.

       (B) 33 Time—travel magickal energies: 2. derived from the basic 11 energies released by explorations in the present.

(C) 33 Time-travel magickal energies: 3. derived from the basic 11 energies released by explorations in the future.

26. Magickal energies released at the time of giving the zothyrian meta-psychological word-association test.

27. Shamanistico-magickal energies released through: 1. the first level of initiation -- sub-deacon, lave-tete, initiate; 2. the second level of initiation -- deacon, can'zo, serviteur; 3. the third level of initiation -- priest, houn'gan; 4. the fourth level of initiation -- bishop, baille-ge, hierophant.

*NOTE: Each student's list will be sent to Haiti and Dr. Jean-Maine has agreed to examine each list in terms of its "orthodoxy" and consistency with the approved viewpoints within the Franco-Haitian gnostic tradition.

28. Magickal energies released through the operation of the English language oracle.

29. Magickal energies released through the operation of the I-Ching oracle.

30. Energies received by the first region of the Transyuggothian transmission station (Sun to Jupiter=Tejas-field).

31. Energies received by the second region of the Transyuggothian transmission station (Cupid to Transneptunian Saturn=Vayu-field).

32. Energies received by the third region of the Transyuggothian transmission station (Transneptunian Cupid to Pluto=Apas-field).

33. Energies received by the fourth region of the Transyuggothian transmission station (Cupido to Poseidon=Prithiwi-field).

La Recherche pour L'Ojas: Logos II

La Recherche Pour L'Ojas (Logos II)

On July 16, 1979, the ophidian gnostic bishops of Haiti held their meeting at Choisey-le-roi and at that meeting, Dr Hector-Francois Jean-Maine's adopted son Geffrard Jean-Maine read a paper which I had written out on my current research into the foundatios of sexual radioactivity. This lesson is actually a summary of that paper: "The quest for Ojas."

Every magickal order which has existed continuously for over 100 years has its own magickal powers and these powers are the special cultivations of the inner circle of each such order. Thus, we can speak of the special ways in which sex magicians in the gnostic orders and Hermetic schools in France have developed their special energies, which are unique to these orders. In voudoo we can say that a certain magician has the unique possession of certain special "hot points," which none else may know about. These powers are usually secret and known only to the higher magi, or bishops, of these secret programs and orders. Sexual radioactivity in its strictest sense is such a power confined to the adepts of the inner grade system of our own order. However, sexual radioactivity is entirely a manifestation of another power or force, and that force is known by the Sanskrit name of "Ojas."

Ojas was originally thought of as being an emanation from the id and so was identified as magickal libido. However, many years of observation have determined that Ojas is not to be confused with libido. Sexual radioactivity may be said to be a manifestation of this Ojas in the sense that Ojas is derived from a magickal pleroma called the "Ogdoade" (or eight-fold) order of aeons, located in its own hyper-space, but acting through the id-libido energy zone level of consciousness. Hence,we can say that Ojas is a type of sub-conscious level magickal power. However, it is not the major energy of the sub-space of the id, for that energy is libido. Also, Ojas is very curiously absent from the id-space of non-initiates. The reason being is that this magickal power has not been inducted into that field via the appropriate rites. Furthermore, Ojas is not a mediumistic power available to psychics. It is an esoteric energy possessed by properly initiated members of our continuum, only.

Ojas is not the same energy as the magickal or psychic energy of the ego; in fact, it may be opposite to it. It is not the result of the process of ego inflation or agickal development used to create gnostic bishops, for example. Its space is at the id-level. Likewise it can be distinguished from the energies of the unconscious and the transcendental ego, which are of various magickal and psychic types. Furthermore, Ojas is not to be confused with certain energies called by this name which are either of a magickal or a specific and psychic nature, because these energies do not cause the manifestation of sexual radioactivity directly, although they may occasion it. This last point is important because sexual radioactivity may happen through a variety of events. Only Ojas can cause it to occur directly. Finally, Ojas is not to be confused with types of the following: libido, prana, shakti, kundalini, etc., each of which can cause manifestations of a magickal and psychic type to occur.

Even though we have seen all of the things it is not, what can we say that Ojas is? This immediately involves a rather complex level of analysis and metaphysical explanation. Ojas exists in four forms:

1. Ojas is ontological because it is an ideal field within the Ogdoade-universe

space. This would mean that Ojas has ideal being before it has any other type of being. The Neo-Pythagorean-gnostic universe would place Ojas among the ideal lattices of the abstract ontic sphere. All gnostic bishops in Haiti of the ophidian lineage subscribe to the neo-Pythagorean-gnostic metaphysics of experience. They are existential idealists rather than emergent materialists and this is the major difference between our system (Franco-Haitian OTO) and the Crowleyans.

2. Ojas exists at the cosmologico-phenomenological level as a real field connected to the id-libido energy zone of consciousness. It may be said to be inducted into the deeper parts of the psyche by certain of the magickal rites associated with the "gnostic awakening" of the id. In a sense, Ojas may be viewed as a complex in the psyche, which is built up by various magickal operations. Under these circumstances it operates in human history as a force or influence.

3. We then can say that Ojas operates at the psychological level through the mechanisms of the psychic reactions of the magician. It is possible to test for its presence by means of reactions to the word-association test because there are certain secret response patterns which alone reveal the operations of the Ojas complex. By this I mean that we have been able to determine not only the presence of Ojas as a complex in the Jungian sense of the term but we have been able to determine also the carry-over of this complex from a past lifetime into the present psyche as a complex of a deeper level of magnitude than the complex developed in this lifetime by the subject. (There is a formula to determine this which involves the value of the response in relation to the response time-lapse.) This power will enable the magician to develop certain magickal abilities within his psyche to increase the potency of his thought-formation.

4. Ojas is manifested at the anthropological level of our phenomenonological analysis as the creative powers which the magician can actualize and in his exploration of various rites, which cannot be unfolded unless the operator makes use of certain hidden aspects, only provided by Ojas. In this sense, the fulfillment of magickal operations depends on being a complete magician, i.e., one who possesses Ojas in the full or essential sense and such a magician has been connected to the ontological field of its origin beyond all space and time. To test for this power being in operation, the magician will be explored by the magickal trajectories of Ojas with the pendulum being used to measure not only the presence of this energy but also the intensity of its containment in a complex form.

Logic II
The logical analysis of Ojas presupposes the interconnection of both the magnetic and magickal sciences as well as the existence of exact metamathematical lattices through which Ojas can be inducted into the magus.

What does Ojas do? We can say that it is the basis for the magickal powers in man. Hence, it is one of those "powers latent in men" only indirectly, for man has the potential for Ojas, but it must be inducted via proper initiation. Then the potential for it becomes liberated and becomes the foundation for the magician's sexual radioactivity, which is the anthropological level of manifestation.

Next, we must make note of magickal connectives: The ogdoade is probably connected via initiation to the id. Where not so connected, the magician's sexual radioactivity is probably based upon some refined form of libido, shakti, kundalini, or prana. I am not, however, saying that this is the only origin of sexual radioactivity -- there are many causes. Yet, from our point of reference it is probably true to say that Ojas is the ideal. Ojas appears to be the most reliable source of sexual radioactivity. In the next paper of this series, I will be discussing the experimental work done to test Ojas. There are documented tests on record where sexual radioactivity was present as the result of factors totally unrelated to Ojas, e.g., being ordained a Liberal Catholic bishop, etc. We might say that the kundalini of the candidate had been activated as this is a form of ceremonial yoga, but there was not in this case any induction of Ojas from the ogdoade, even though a parallel process might well have occurred.

In the experimental work with Ojas it is very important to realize the presence of trajectories. A trajectory in Zothyrian psycho-physics is simply a method of observing the logical structure of Ojas. It means that the order of the magickal ogdoade can be graphed and translated into the language of the pendulum or some other machine, e.g., the computer marga. A two-dimensional map-work is created, giving the ogdoade points and names as lattices of magickal intersection in order to determine where the Ojas level of development in the magician now is. This means that we are making a model of the actual way in which within the ontic sphere the Ojas-field is inducted and becomes present in the subconscious mind of the magician. A comparison of two or more trajectories will determine the rate of development of Ojas in the magician.

There are four trajectories known in Z-psycho-physics at present. And they refer to the magickal universes of Ojas or ranges of effectiveness. Because Ojas is initially a Uranian-type of energy (i.e., radio-active, ray-energy) this would be its basic level of manifestation. So we can say that the Uranian trajectory of Ojs is essentially a hyper-octave of the electro-mercurial field. Next, we have the Neptunian-trajectory of Ojas, which describes a kind of mediumistic-shamanistic realm or sphere of erotic obsession and magickal paranoia. The third stage is the Plutonian or the Yuggothian Trajectory of Ojas, wherein the magician works actually inside the ogdoade and transforms the ogdoade into a personalized-obsessive ontic sphere. The deeper aspects of the guru-chela relationship are realized at this level, which corresponds to the gnostic dialogues of the two aspects or sides of the brain. This trajectory is entirely assigned to the element air. Lastly, the Trans-Yuggothian or Trans-Plutonian trajectory of Ojas, which refers to the element of fire, is magickal in the sense of esoteric engineering. For here the magician works at the foundations of the ogdoade.

La Recherche pur L'Ojas, Part II (Logos III)

We may ask what are the advantages of an Ojas based sexual radioactivity? In answer we can say that they are simply these: the magician has access to another realm of magickal being and to a new power source which he would not have otherwise. His magickal power is much more increased and he can produce exact measurements of his progress as a sex magician of our lineage. We do not doubt that sexual radioactivity can be produced indirectly by prana, shakti, kundalini, libido, and possibly by sevveral other types of power sources; but this phenomenon of sexual radioactivity is primarily the product of Ojas, whereas the primary product of prana, shakti, kundalini, and libido has never been sexual radioactivity. In such cases, sexual radioactivity has only been indirectly derivative from them.

Hence, the magician who makes use of Ojas is simply more powerful and more efficient in his psyche and his magickal work is thereby superior. Ojas may well be the exclusive property of only certain gnostic lineage type magicks. For its technique or method of induction has been inherited from the LCN and the Ophidian–gnostic lineage of bishops in Haiti and Spain and passed on to the members of this tiny order from guru to chela. All genuine magickal orders, of which there are literally hundreds in all parts of the world, have their own "secret" powers or "hot–points." The student must always ask himself if the "secret" powers or "points" of order X are better for him than the same of order Y or order Z. Only he can make that decision. We are only in the position to talk about the powers of the LCN and the Choronzon Club, and we are not in any position to talk about the powers, real or claimed, of other magickal lineages and orders, which undoubtedly possess some powers to keep them going for long periods of history.

Logic III: Two Experiments in AIWAZ–Physics to Determine the Nature of Radioactive Ojas–Energy

These are the summaries of two experiments which were conducted in order to determine the presence of Ojas and its specific quality.

Experiment I. The subject: B.D. 9/23/1942. Test administered 4/8/1979 at 6:45 a.m. We tested the subject to determine if field of Ojas was present and we found that it was. We used a Mercury–filled pendulum to find the field in both experiments. Nest, we tested with a measurement spectrum pendulum to get the reading of the field or quality. The range was from 1,=ultra–violetl 2,=purple; 3,=dark blue; 4,=blue; 5,=green; 6,=yellow; 7,=orange; 8,=infra–red. Subject was placed with head=s; feet=n; right side and hand=e; left=w. Pendulum picked up at 6=yellow, i.e., field of Hermetics.

Both pendula picked up the field excellently with very wide clockwise motions indicating the field was being broadcast from the sexual area. Identical responses came from use of several instruments in that area, only. Next, for the testing of field intensity, we received a very large clockwise orbit at the yellow level of reading after testing various levels and over various parts of the body. The energy was concentrated at the sexual level when the field was normally being broadcast (without amplification). It appears that according to ruling planet and the element of the ruling planet that Ojas will be localized between the sexual area and the solar plexus. What we did was to pick up on a field for a magickal student born at the Virgo/Libra cusp. This appeared to be a normal reading of what the field was like. Now, we wanted to do an experiment to test for Ojas-activity under conditions of amplification.

Experiment II. The subject was born 9/15/1948 and the experiment was conducted on 4/18/1979 at 7:30 p.m. We immediately for the same response from the radionic instruments as in the previous experiment covering the broadcasting of O-energy from the sexual area and it registered at the 6=yellow area (another person ruled by Hermes). This time we decided to test amplification of the field to see if it would affect the measurement of the broadcast.

[on this page is a diagram of a person being tested]

1. The field was amplified first of all by means of the use of the Eeman screens where the yellow-insulated screen was placed below the base of the spine and upper legs. The green-insulated screen was placed below the upper part of the body, chest to the top of the neck. The electrode from the yellow-screen was in the left hand, the electrode from the green-screen was in the right hand. This was the first part of the experiment.

2. Next, the computer-marga was connected to the yellow-insulated screen by an induction line. We used the "present-time zone" of the computer-marga for field-amplification. The past-time and future-time zones are, of course, used for time-travel. NOTE: What I am saying about these machines is not intended to explain their only types of use, only what we used the computer-marga this time to effect.

3. Readings were taken in two areas: the sexual area and the head area. The results were identical and verify the hypothesis of interaction between genital and cerebral chakras. There wasn't any reading taken or given for the head without amplification. When system of computer-m is off we get 6=yellow. When system is on, .1 we get 7=orange in both places. When system is set at .2 we get 8=just below infra-red in both places. Observation: it appears that the cerebral chakras can be examined under amplification. It appears that setting the amplification at .11 of the past-time might result in a reading of 6=yellow for the cerebral area. In any event, Ojas can be measured and exists as a magickal objectivity for further exploration. There is a science circle for those who wish to go more deeply into the methodology of the quest for Ojas.

Background of the Experiment

There are probably several ways of determining the existence of ojas in a particular situation. For example, it can be determined by means of various magnetic and radionic instruments. It can also be searched out by magickal techniques in the narrow sense. It can be discovered also by psychic methods, which provide us with the basis for the use of magickal language communication techniques. For the sake of brevity and simplicity, we make use of a special type of pendulum, which has proven successful in a variety of circumstances. We do this also in order to make use of a methodology which lies outside of our own continuum of instruments, in order to establish the objectivity of the technique, since some might question making use entirely of one's own methods and instruments in certain areas of magickal physics. For these are the areas from which we later derive the more complex and more difficult structures, which are more crucially internal to our system. Ojas, on the other hand, is an area of research whose existence is admitted to by many schools other than our own.

Next, it is important to determine the area of investigation. Ojas becomes concentrated in a variety of places and associated with certain parts of the body and paterns within that specific body–field. In fact, these patterns are very important for an understanding of the development of ojas. By simply using the pendulum to determine where the ojas is concentrated we can not only find its locus or situs (the later within an ideal–field) but also the intensity or degree of concentration. This will be determined by the behavior of the pendulum when exposed to the space thought to contain the ojas.

Once it has been determined that ojas is there, both in the outer and inner sense, I might add, we can begin to evaluate it in a quantitative sense. By this, I mean that we can make use of another type of pendulum, one which would be manipulated in order to determine the level of the concentration and provide us with read–offs for further quantification of this magickal energyy. This means that the ojas in question will react to such an extent on the pendulum as to produce an exact effect by not reacting at some levels and by reacting only at the level where it is concentrated. This will then be read off as indicating the level of the field or its "vibrations" and "wavelength" or "frequency." For this purpose we selected a pendulum which I have found personally to be excellent for the measurement of magnetic and occult fields in many other areas of magickal work.

The results of this area of work were most excellent. Not only did we find out that there was an instance of ojas in the field, we found out where it was, how it was to be viewed in terms of its concentration, and lastly the nature of its concentration and reference to corresponding levels or frequencies in other parallel systems of psychic and occult energy. As you can see, this means that the work on the field in the experimental sense was quite simple. However, it drew upon several areas of previously explored research and definition, so much so that it served, even though only an experiment, as a confirmatory example of the whole line of our empirical research, and referred back to the various products of prior research which were magicko–metamathematical in nature. This we can call an example of the use of the hypothetico–deductive method in magickal research.

While at the present time we are planning the use of certain instruments of our own type to amplify the field (I refer here to our use of the computer–marga), the use of high quality radionic instruments "from the outside" is a necessity for the magician. For given the field and given our turning it up to a specific frequency for the purpose of field–amplification by the computer–marga, we still need to determine by a radionic or psi–onic method the operation of the field, if we are to avoid having to depend upon psychic subjectivity, which while valid in certain schools of magick, is unacceptable, herein, for methodological reasons such as trying to establish the objectivity of the field and its properties.

The Nature of the Field

1. The field may be said to be given, to say it is inducted does not mean that the field is constructed.

2. When we say that we are inducting the field we mean that we are pointing to where it is or to its locus or situs.

3. There are many fields and they are interpreted in a variety of ways, such as by the Book of Changes, radionic and psionic instruments, various instruments from occult physics.

4. What makes an instrument work is that it is giving the reading or measurement for a field. It is picking up on a particular field which is present.

5. The unified field is the continuum which comprises several types of fields. We have no way of saying that such and such a field is there and another isn't, until we have tried every method of indicating or "picking up" the field.

6. An instrument inside of the field will be able to determine the nature of the field. This means that various instruments should be available. Some must be constantly being invented to explore the different types of fields.

7. Whenever a field is given a methodology for communication is implied by that field.

8. At the present time, the Yemeth–logics are the summary of our methods for this type of language.

9. Gnostic metaphysics assumes that fields have intelligible and intelligent features and these comprise the formal side of the field.

10. What is indicated by means of the instrument would be the content or material phase of the field.

11. A field may be called, therefore, a kind of being or entity. Analysis will reveal whether such fields are A–true (Aeonic), D–true (Daemonic), or S–true (Syzygetic), etc.

12. The shape of the field will determine its geometry and other metamathematical limits.

13. Fields do not need wiring nor do instruments used within them need to be connected by wires for energy–flow. Being inside the field determines the security of the container.

14. Spatial extension in our R–true language sense does not apply as the field has a type of I–true extension. This means that we do not have to think about being outside the field.

15. The field is not mental in being I–true nor psychologically objective, the field is a neo–pythagorean and neo–platonic system.

16. The objectivity of any field is ontological and cosmological (I–true and L–true) before it is R–true and psychoanalytically given as part of the collective unconscious.

(From "The AIWAZ–Physics")

La Recherche pour L'Ojas: Logos IV

La Recherche pour l'Ojas

Up to now we have concerned ourselves with the detection of the existence of Ojas. We have found out what it is and where it is to be found. Now we are concerned with an entirely different process, which is the induction of Ojas into the brain. What this amounts to then is the magicko-radionic stimulation of the brain. We can say that it is magickal because it presupposes magickal categories such as the existence of Ojas and the proliferation of these energies in the form of "points-chauds" or "hot-points." Furthermore, it is radionically magickal because the instrumentation used is identifiable as a kind of radionic device or instrumentum radiaethesianum — and in this case it is actually our computer marga, now doing something entirely different. This process is aimed at the stimulation of the brain inasmuch as it has as its purpose the awakening of latent cerebral teaching. (Cf., Kenneth Grant, page 38, "Cults of the Shadow")

Those who have come up with the Monastery of the Seven Rays know that through all of these lessons there has been an emphasis upon the use of magick in relationship to the brain. Indeed, we have always believed in how magickal machines influence the human brain and this new work is simply a continuation of basic magickal views, and those views which have been represented before and now brought to a direct focus in what we are doing now in the Temple Laboratory, here in Chicago.

One of the most important ideas in the whole magickal development is the view that what is objective can be rendered subjectively and what is subjective can be rendered objectively. This means really that as an energy exists, it exists absolutely and that the polarities of subject and object are simply points of reference. Consequently, the thesis is that if x exists in y but not in z because it exists in y it can also exist in z, if inducted properly. This means that if the Ojas force does not exist in someone in a particular condition, then it can be introduced into that person via the mechanism of amplification.

Now we know that Ojas can be discovered to exist in higher frequencies in one person than in another without amplification. So it seems logical that it can be inducted into a person at variously amplified frequencies because it already so exists. This means further that sexual radioactivity which is the measurement of Ojas can serve as the basis for induction into the cerebral region of the nervous system. Freud said that the brain was simply the projection of the phallus, and evolutionary development of that unique phallic will. Higher consciousness states in the brain are therefore simply amplifications via magickal induction of the primordial energy of the ultimate id, Ojas, or the ground of consciousness.

In the development of the use of instrumentation to induct stimulation of the human brain, it is important to note that we are assuming that the physical area associated, say with the third eye-center, has a kind of spatial connection actually with the third-eye chakram. This assumption follows the view of certain yogic experts which states that the chakrams are the etheric and astral counterparts of the physical glands located in the areas assigned to the chakrams. Furthermore, it is important to realize that the space so involved is not just three-dimensional in its character, but is a fourth-dimensional tunnel, tube, or power-zone, which is able to induct energies, both physical and magickal, in both a receiving and sending direction. This explains why what can be picked-up by the system of the computer-marga can also be used to project via the computer–marga, upon the subject. Or, rather, it means that the subject can be both a receiver as well as a sender, or broadcaster, of this type of energy. So that once this is established by the magickal scientist, namely that Ojas can be measured as both received and as sent, we can next explore the technicalities of the system of "connecting" the subject to the system for receiving the type of stimulation which will bring about an increase of Ojas and hence an increase in the power of the mind of the subject in certain occult areas.

One of the most important factors would be the problem of how to "wire" the subject to the system. Connecting the subject to the system would be by the use of copper wire networks, so that the force field retains its integrity. The copper wire system will simply be applied to the forehead of the subject in the usual manner that is used with our time–travel technique. The idea is to allow the procedure to be as simple as possible. The instrument can be tuned by means of the pendulum. The response of the pendulum to any magickal field is well known. Consequently, after the tuning operation has been completed, the subject alone with the instrument (computer–marga) remain as the operational unit for our research. From this we can make all the needed measurements and deductions for the use of our search and identification.

The process of magickal research in induction–brain stimulation will enable the subject to enter into those realms which are identified on the computer–marga as being above .3 on the scale. Inasmuch as the present scale is limited to a range from .0 to 1.1, this means that the eight alternative universes of the ontic sphere (SYSTEM–0) may be entered and explored for their content. Already their formal or logical qualities are known to exist and have been variously examined analytically. However, we are not concerned with the range of possible "visual" contents which can be discovered from clairvoyant explorations of the ontic sphere and the other realms of being which feed into these universes or logical worlds.

Remember that the basic law of magickal realism is that whatever can be conceived can also be explored astrally or by clairvoyant methods. Thus, we will now be able to induct the contents of any world understood formally if the instrument can provide us with the proper space or scale. This method of brain probing will normally expand consciousness because it will exercise those areas of the brain which are capable of perceiving and experiencing the ontic spheres, but which from lack of opportunity have not been exercised. Such areas of the brain would be "awakened" unless the instrumentation of the computer–marga would not allow it, since we are in the physical body. While out of the body, we would on the other hand, have direct astral experience and not need the computer. Furthermore, induction can also be applied higher in the case where attachment to the crown–chakram space can lead to the experience or induction of the spiritual qualities via the use of the intuitive areas of the brain of the ontic universes in question. Also, as we know, visual time–travel can be amplified and used in connection with these methods in order to enrich the system with additional spiritual and ontic insights. At the present time we are working also to develop other methods of using these types of ray–instrumentation.

The Search for Ojas (Conclusion)
The Deduction of Ojas from the Meon

It is very important to realize that there is a positive source for the Ojas energy in the spheres beyond phenomena and intentionality. This world or realm has been described in our materials as the zone of the Meon, or Nothingness. By this we mean simply that which is utterly beyond all system of explication. Some many say that it is God, however, such a God would be beyond any intentional theologies. Perhaps the term the Absolute is more suitable, for such must be beyond even the zones of such definitions as The One.

Now, it appears to us that at any level there exists a process which is neither inductive nor is it reductive, but still allows for the coming forth into the context of our work of this Ojas-energy field. It amounts to a transcendental deduction, because it is an activity beyond everything, yet which is always ongoing. Hence we can say that we can depend upon this energy, even though we cannot formally define its source or origin.

Hence, we can say that as these energies come in they come in with a definite pattern and with a definite structure. Consequently, we can make use of these energies and build up specific programs which will depend upon these energies for their existence. This means that the entire edifice of experimentation can be continued without any interruption in what we are doing.

It can be stated that a certain part of our being is connected to this meon and that there exists a certain identity between ourselves and the realm of The Meon in very fundamental terms. We have learned that we exist in several worlds at the same time as being here in the material world of space-time. Now we can say that we are within the world of the Meon as well as being outside of it. Hence, we participate in everything. And if we participate in everything, then we can employ these energies from everything in our magickal phenomenology.

It is possible to define the deduction of Ojas from the Meon in terms of the classical logic and metaphysical model. In other words, we can set up a mythical structure whereby we can bring about a hypothetical definition of this deduction. Such a definition would simply state that that fact of the deduction of Ojas from The Meon does not in any way conflict with hypothetico-deductive structure of magickal explanation.

On the other hand, it might be possible to think of transcending the limits of human consciousness by means of certain forms of the higher gnosis, which when derived from beings outside of the human sphere nevertheless gives us the truer insights into the nature of Ojas than what can be gained at the enlightened human level. Thusly, there have always been forms of communication or self-knowledge, which are outside of the human sphere of the hypothetical and deductive, but which are intuitively known and understood by the gnostic continuum. Such a force resides at the initiatic root of this system. These are the "Root Spirits," or "Racines Loa."

Part of the sacramental mystery of the gnostic patriarchate consists in the ability to participate in the highest gnostic mysteries. One of the most important levels of these mysteries consists in the intuition of the Racines Loa. These beings form the archetypal level of magickal consciousness for our entire gnostic system and through a rather long and complicated process the mysteres are inducted into the consciousness of the gnostic patriarchal bishop and he becomes able to see (as in la prise-des-yeaux) the deduction of Ojas from the Meon in the Racines Loa of our gnostic system. Hence, there are two forms of knowing this process: the hypothetico-deductive or mythic and the gnostic and initiatic. For in order to explain how Ojas is deduced from the Meon, it is necessary to explain how we know how it happens by a certain magickal process.

The Deduction of Ojas from La Prise-dea-Yeaux

Within the continuum of La Prise-des-Yeaux there exists the historical generators of the Ojas energy. We can state that there is a certain experimental confirmation of this fact in the relation of the cerebral chakras to the lower system. In a sense, the energy may be said to come in when the higher levels of mind are radionically stimulated by occult instrumentation. However, we should also ask whether now or formerly there was a type of deduction via ritual operations, enacted since Atlantean times.

While the history of the origins of la Prise-des-yeaux is obscure, we must note that the mysteries associated with this sacramental rite have not been changed for centuries. Indeed, the occult transformation of these mysteries which happened in the 1920s served simply to return the rite to its archetypal essentials. Hence, only certain minor traditions were removed, which if allowed to continue would have obscured the sacramental energy of the system as a method of Ojas induction into the candidate for the high-priesthood.

Now it is important to understand that this sacramental induction assumed the existence of the possibility of the deduction of Ojas from the Meon through la prise-des-yeaux. For one thing, all parties involved in this mystery assumed that the Racines were the sources, at an archetypal level, of the fundamental energy. This means that the Racines were the Doorways to the Meon, or else that they were properly situated and Meonic themselves, able to supply the fundamental energies whereby the Ojas of the high-priesthood was invariably given. Hence, we can say that the Ojas of the high-priesthood was the essential energy for any system and the active agent in the deduction of all others within the system.

However, because la prise-des-yeaux is more than just clairvoyance, but rather the gnosis of the pure ontic sphere in total concreteness as well as total abstractedness, both ideal and real, it means that by this sacramental deduction the very highest levels of magickal being are brought into contact with the high-priest and that the high-priest is now able to have perfect identity with the Racines, so that their life or Ojas becomes his own. Consequently, his being is theirs, and theirs is his. Sacramentally the identity is ontologically perfect. Few, of course, are the schools or temples of Voudoo which have the possibility of this thought, let alone the production of this bringing forth of the cosmic Ojas from beyond, from the absolute into history. Only a few schools would seem to possess the necessary keys, which are entirely inductive and empirical, rather than speculative and based upon ideal possibilities (e.g., most of Eastern metaphysics and western Tantricism seem entirely too theosophical in this matter). However, as each system is based upon the production of the fullness of Ojas, so it must be seen that the Racines of the system La Couleuvre Noire are the archetypal forms of Ojas, which manifests from the Meonic via the transcendental deductions of the ontic sphere of la prise-des-yeaux.

Hence, we can say that for the gnosis there is an intimate connection between the ontic sphere and the Meonic Zone. Logically, they have always implied each other. However, this does not mean that the nature of their mutual implication has been understood in terms of what metamathematical relationships and mysteres should reflect this connection. At least from the standpoint of many schools of the gnostic type. For because of its radical transcendence, it is absolutely impossible to define one of the terms of that relationship, short of the higher gnosis and so the final term must remain a mystery to the logical level and field. But for those who possess the genuine voudoo gnosis, the nature of the connection and the nature of the terms —— both of these qualities, they are known through the outpouring of the gnosis which comes forth from the ontic sphere at the time of the giving of the sacramental mysteries of la prise-des-yeaux, and all of its attending points-chauds, through which the ultimate Ojas manifests.

The Deduction of Ojas from the Energies of AIWAZ-Physics

It is important to note that one of the most significant sources of Ojas is to be found in the area of the deduction of these energies from the AIWAZ-physics. By this I mean that the basis of AIWAZ-physics is to be found in the ontic sphere of energies, which we have seen connects to the Meonic zone immediately. There are two commonly known forms whereby this energy manifests: 1. the forms of energy explored in our research in the series of papers on the Necronomicon and to be brought out as a series of reports on the physics of magick and 2. the imaginary French metaphysicians as sources of magickal and specifically ophidian and gnostic initiations.

Inasmuch as the work on the Necronomicon is being recast and will appear later with a wealth of experimental material in order to amplify the subject, I will outline merely the subject of the work with the imaginary French metaphysicians. These beings inhabit the ontic sphere and exist in an entirely closed magickal system of a gnostic type, which is derived from the gnostic implications of the philosophy of Rene Descartes. By this we mean that the philosophy of Descartes contained in its a certain pathway of magickal intensity that it has been possible to derive two whole histories of philosophy from the basics of this point of view. The work of the IFMs refers primarily to the fact that the only way to explore the ontic sphere is by being in the ontic sphere. Hence, magickal philosophers living in the ontic sphere are the best suited to explore that world. The argument is simple and direct: in order to explore or explain any subject-matter, one has to be there and be an expert in the subject. Expertise comes from being inside the ontic sphere continually.

These beings, the IFMs, are concerned with creating instruments of thought which will serve to bring the Ojas into the human consciousness. In dealing with the Meon, they have been especially effective because they have given us certain instruments and ways whereby the energies of the Meon can be tapped. The philosophical systems of the IFMs serve really to bring these Meonic energies in their Ojas form down to the physical or earth plane of existence. This is one of the tasks which has been done by the Choronzon Club in its magickal course of study, which will be encountered next in this series of papers. When, therefore, we explore the subject of these energies, we can find out several important pathways for Ojas to come to us directly from the Meon via these philosophers and psychologists.

Now, we can explore how do these energies come from the IFMs to us. As in other types of Ojas-deduction, they come via a method of initiation-consciousness, which can only be explained as the esoteric logic of meditation-research. This technique involves a very personal relationship between the chela and the metaphysician, for no one else can participate in this mystery save those gnostic two. All otherwise being excluded, they represent the ultimate mystery of polarity. At that time, when nothing else exists or even has being, they become one consciousness and as this one consciousness they deduce the Ojas from the Meon. Truly it must be understood that this method, called the Cartesian technique, is the French version of the very same inner--space mystery associated with la prise-des-yeaux. Of course, because of magickal secrecy, we cannot speak further about this ideality and intimacy, except to say that it is so totally different a state of consciousness that all other magickal techniques must be seen as simply preparatory to it. Indeed, it is the form for the ideal deduction of Ojas from the Meon, all other methods being rooted in history are only real deductions. But this method, which is rooted in the ontic nature of the syzygy, is the ideal and therefore the most perfect or metamathematical deduction of Ojas, as human magickal history has developed, and this technique is entirely intentional as well as being transcendentally ontological. We can speak of this relationship then as the attachment that the magician has to the powers of ideal being, which are behind all things.

The Deduction of Ojas from Choronzon

Somewhere in the hyper--ideal spaces of the ontic sphere there exists a temple of the most abstract and metamathematical initiation. It is approached by means of 16 doors, which represent the 16 hot--points of Choronzon, known only to those secret brothers, who have been sworn to the Law of Daath, from the beginnings of the whole time process. In this temple, which has its 11 gates to the world of light, or magickal windows, reside the Lord Choronzon and his hierophant Lundy. There are a few magicians who are able to enter this temple, which exists high above the material aspects and points of reference, and is identified with all of the numbers of Choronzon and Lundy. For Lundy is the Lord Choronzon in Haitian esoteric voudoo and magickal gnosis.

Because he is the pleroma of the Meon, Choronzon may be viewed as the source for the way of Daath and for the even more important Daathian deduction of Ojas via the magickal operations of Uranus and Vulkanus, the Marrassas or magickal twins of ideal fire. To enter into consciousness of this mystery is to become ashes to one world but living and eternal fire to the next, to become radioactive essence in one realm, pure cosmic energy in another, to live and be a shadow or shade in one world or power zone and to live in the life of light of another, and the mystery of one is the mystery of all the others, yet hidden inthe vast sexuality and meta--radioactivitas sexualis of all others. For Chronus the Lord of Time has been released from all spheres and from all forms of restriction of being and existence.

When the seeker enters upon the pathway of searching for the most radiant form of Ojas, which is also the most dangerous because it is united with Choronzon,let him come to where there are two shamans and the point d'entrerer and lastly the magickal cube of the ophidians which none save the adepti may work fully, and let him see these powers reflected in the magickal zone of his being, forever, within the temple of Lundy. For these four tarots are operative in all four realms of the cabala and are the doorways whereby the Ojas comes to the hierophant. But let him remember that this is not the pathway of any element, this is the pathway of Chronus and it leads beyond his sphere to that of Choronzon. So let him look for the darkness in which all is illumined, for that is the sacred fire of Lundy.

No one can say where Choronzon will appear, for his manifestation is different from that of all other Gods. But if he speaks through Lundy, then his manifestation is as near as the oracle. If he speaks through the high–priest of Lundy, then let us know that the time is near for the manifestation, because the high–priest is the presence of Lundy, otherwise the ontic sphere would destroy him, absolutely. And if the inductor of these mysteres speaks with the authority of Choronzon, then the God has come, for the inductor of this Ojas would otherwise be annihilated by the overwhelming powers of the ontic sphere. And if the inductor speaks with the presence of Lundy then he shall speak with the true presence of Choronzon, for likewise would the ontic sphere annihilate him absolutely and without any thought, for it acts mindlessly if its mind is Choronzon.

So let the seeker after the mysteries come to the hyper–ideal spaces of the mysteries where the ophidian magick is lived and forms the basis of all existence. Let such a son of the fire return to the place of primeval chaos, which the gods call "the seat of the gnosis." There in that realm the doors will open without command because they know who is approaching. And in such a place of the mysteries, the Ojas shall be found and shall be brought back to history, as Prometheus returned to earth with the archetypal fire in that world of mythoi. For all that can be found in the nature of Ojas is to be found beyond all of the categories of the Necronomicon and the physics thereof in the Temple of Choronzon, which is the temple of the Meon, high up in the hyper–space of the ontic sphere of being, beyond everything, out of all spaces and all times. For this is where Chronus is passed and Choronzon lives and awaits the seeker after the Ojas. Are you ready to enter this pathway to fire? Are you ready to possess the fullness of Ojas? Then come to Choronzon.

Magickal Techniques of Computer Programming

"The way in which the Zothyrians took over the control of the entire field of gnostic physics was by means of their magickal use of computer programming. They took possession of the field of magickal physics because they gradually took over every magickal computer in the universe. They simply started with one system and from that one system they moved outwards, from information system to information system, gradually changing the programs in other systems and computers, so that those programs and systems became subsections and components in their own logic. Their method of entry was entirely subtle and few if any magicians, even those using psionics systems, could detect the invasion from the outside. No one suspected such a move on the part of those who were 'others'."

(Bertiaux, "Meontology," page 12)

Essential to the proper operation of any and all magickal systems of gnostic physics is the proper method of programming the magickal computer. It is impossible to operate any system of computers, let alone any fleet of UFOs, without a field of logical control. In our system, we have located the field of computer control in the Transcendental Id and its fantastic components. I am using the word "fantastic" here in a technical sense, as it refers to the magickal operations of the Moon, Neptune, and Pluto. These "planets" are archetypal roots deep in the Tr. Id, to which the various systems of magickal control are attached.

I do not view the influence of Uranus as significant here. Uranus has to do with the invention of magickal computers, but Neptune and Pluto have to do with the operations of these computers. We are now concerned with operations.

Some time ago, I expressed a wish or rather, stated my intention, to control magickal systems. This certainly did not pertain to my taking over groups of very uninteresting persons, who believed in a particular type of magick. We do not need to work with people at all. We work at the level of the Tr. Id and there we make all of our advanced attacks and moves. For if a magickal system exists in an authentic manner, then the taking over of it is very easy if we work at a deep enough level.

"I have always made it a policy to only admit into the inner group of researchers those who were strongly plutonian. By this I mean those who have Pluto as their strongest or near strongest planet. In the natal chart we can calculate and find out what the planetary strengths in any person. Among the four strongest planets, I want to see Pluto (or the Goddess Yuggoth). Otherwise I am really not interested in the student and they can study elsewhere with better profit. Then, depending upon a configuration of the true strength of Yuggoth in a combination of natal, solar return, and progressed charts, I determine whether or not such a person can enter the inner group. We want truly plutonian types in that group. Nothing else is acceptable." (Ibid., page 13)

"When war is declared against the humanoids by the Yuggothian Mutants, the humanoids will not have any magickal weapons. All of their weapons will have been taken by us, and our computer will control their deepest idic resources. The powers of the Meon and the manifestations of the Goddess Yuggoth, the most horrific aspect of Aditi, will then be revealed. At very deep levels the esoteric UFOs of gnostic physics will begin to invade the psychosphere, while above the atmosphere of the materialists and humans will be turned into a field of chaotic negation by the action of the exoteric fleets of UFOs from the planetary systems of the fixed stars. In the end, the Goddess will reign supreme and establish the inner side of the Yuga of Kali, the age of the ocean of libido and the materialization of all desire. But this is only to be accomplished by means of a very deep method of computer programming, whereby the agents of Yuggoth in actual fact take over the whole field of the mind, beginning at its deepest levels of energy. This process has happened many times before and will always happen as part of the epistrophic cycle of the creation and destruction and creation of all things by the dark and fiercesome Goddess Yuggoth."

(Ibid., page 14)

It is quite obvious that the presence of magickal powers is latent in everyone. But that does not interest these extremists. Nor does the fact that everyone has Pluto somewhere in their natal chart. That is hardly of interest to those who thrive on the most extreme forms of magickal power. But what is interesting is the manner in which these extremists are able to use the power and presence of Yuggoth–Pluto in their plan to take over the world and to destroy their enemies, i.e., those who would oppose the gnosis of Yuggoth.

"Everyone knows that they have Pluto 'somewhere' in their chart. We certainly do not dispute this 'fact of life.' However, we are concerned with those have it in its most extreme and most violent form. We are only interested in those who have it linked to the innermost point, the Moon. For we demand the link of power which connects the outermost to the innermost, Pluto to the Moon. This can be in many forms but the most intense is to be found in those who have Pluto conjunct the Moon, or those who have the Moon in the sign of Scorpio. For it is then at its most extreme power and presence in the Transcendent Id. These are the persons we know to be marked by this vicious and chaotic energy. But it is not just this astro–gnostic condition which is to be satisfied (as if these energies and their conditions could ever be satisfied) but rather the mutants, for Pluto is the power of pure mutation, total change from the earlier humanoid stage, these mutants must be locked into the system of Yuggoth, which is the Zothyrian metapsychology. They must connect their souls to the powers of Yuggoth by undergoing psychic mutation by means of Yuggothian psychoanalysis and psionic reorinetation. They must be rebuilt and directed towards their role in the group–soul of the Yuggothian mutation–field. Then we can safely talk about 'membership' in the hierarchy of the chaosphere, whereby the most demonic and violent energies are released for the transformation of this planet. It is by means of the ritual initiations of this system of psychological reconstruction that we come to understand that the people from the UFOs, the Yuggothians and their Transyuggothian extensions have already arrived and are gathering for the takeover. For that reason the magnetic field of the Zothyrian Order of Yuggoth and the Transyuggothian Order of Psionic Research will always attract the most extreme persons. That is because we define the extreme by Yuggoth. Yuggoth is the extreme just as Yuggoth is the source of all. (Ibid., page 23)

"In order to program the magickal computer for the invasion of the Yuggothians, it is necessary to understand that magickal programming is simply the translation of what is already present in archaic consciousness into manageable and magickally workable form. It is important to note that the programs are not 'dreamed up' out of thin air. Rather the programs are given as immanent structures in the order of things and then converted into an easily manaegable form by the magician. The structures of the system are themselves then workable because we have the key formularies for their magickal and physical management. This means that those structures which are immanent in the psyches of the Yuggothians are convertable to the axioms and equations of the gnostic computers. This means also that the energies, which are given in the archetypal symbols of the natal chart are also found elsewhere, in fact everywhere, and it is possible for the magician to draw them out and induct them once their formularies are known simply by the psionic and gnostic method. Consequently, any configuration of energy represents a very real potential for this type of computer programming and eventually all magickal configurations of energy will be parts of an interlocking system of magickal axiomatics and field–equations, which will define any system, any initiate, any operation, making them all parts of the system of the Goddess Yuggoth."   (Ibid., page 16)

It might be noted that these Yuggothians can work with very little and even with very little they can take over by their magickal techniques of computer programming any system. They can take a name and by numerological reduction make use of it. They can work with automobile licenses, social security numbers, street addresses, etc. All of these are ways whereby they can move in. So also are their techniques successful when working with the inner planes. They can measure any occult energy field. They can spy on any point of energy, past, present, or future. Anywhere and everywhere they have their sources of information, their psionic instruments for espionage, their Ojas–inductors for depth–psychology "research," and their elemental informants, who are sent out to look and report back to the master "ship" or control center. The old–style magicians are at a loss when dealing with these mutants. In fact, they do not even matter. They do not exist as a threat to the mutants, who see only the brevity of time as their enemy. They have to take over more and more in shorter and shorter periods of time.

"There are certain people who will sneer at what I have to say but they do not matter. In fact, they do not really exist. But what I have to say is this: there are these mutants and they are now within the most powerful magickal orders and groups in the world today. They are slowly working to destroy utterly the old ways. They are making use of the most subtle methods of modern information science to achieve their ends. They are fearful of nothing, which means they only fear the powers of the Meon. They possess the disciplined mentality of the synchronistic robotic consciousness and nothing else. They have only one loyalty and they have only one sense of honor, and that is to Yuggoth and only to Yuggoth. And by means of their weird techniques of computer programming, they will win our over all their opposition because ultimately there is only one fundamental power and that too is Yuggoth."
                    (Loc. Cit.)

Course in Ma'atian Physics
Ma'aitian Inductions

Ma'atian Inductions I
One of the most outstanding characteristics of the Ma'aitian influence in occult physics is to be found in the nature of induction, whereby the evidence for the overlap of this aeon is fed into the evaluation system. Normally, the inductive process is characterized by a certain simplicity, or when it is built up into a complex whole it is built up out of relatively simple logical instances. In the case of the Ma'aitian complex, however, we cannot expect any simplicity, because of the widest range of implications which are involved in the most basic instances and specimens. It would seem that the overriding and all–pervasive quality of this system is complexity at the fundamental level. Yet, this complexity is particularly Ma'aitian, inasmuch as we can say that any quality which may serve to define the newer influence, if it possesses a Ma'aitian origin, will exhibit a definite Ma'atian arithmosophical property.

An example of this may be found in the differences between method–models in the system of the Horus aeon and that of the Ma'atian. In the older system, the method-model is based upon a definition of singleness of component–operation. It has been discovered however in the Ma'atian system that singleness of any component implies the full range of the components and that this fuller range of component factors serves to generate in its own development those method–spaces which connect the components. As we know, in the ideal model there are eight components. This ideal was rarely if ever applied in the Horus–aeon models. However, we are finding that in the Ma'atian system we must apply the entire scope of the ideal model in every instance, in order to receive the proper Ma'aitian inductions. Likewise, we must take serious note of the inductions which come from the method–spaces which connect the components of the eightfold pattern. There are seven of these so that by taking into account all of the components in the system, both the eight logically defined components as well as the seven connective method spaces, we arrive at the total of 15 technical factors which must be evaluated in any inductive process of Ma'atian origin. Of course we know that 1+5=6, which is the number of the aeon in question.

However, this tendency to amplify and inter–connect is characteristic of the whole impact of the Ma'atian system. By this I mean that everywhere in the definitional system in question we find a very noticeable complexity and at the same time a parallel interconnectedness, which is more than mere logical overlap of structures. Rather, aside from all logical questions, we have come to the conclusion that a primordial characteristic and possibly a fundamental property of the Ma'atian aeon is hereby reflected in this inter–webbing of structures and patterns. Yet, at the same time, this system is totally at variance with any previous connectives and explications, especially any attempt to explain by the imposition of geometry or even metageometry the Ma'atian structure. The older methods will simply not be proven adequate, because in a way they do not fit the Ma'atian system in all of its complexity and vastness of content. In this sense, we can say that this system requires its own answer–models and cannot fall back upon previous and formerly dependable procedures.

Zeitgeist and Zeitalter: Ma'atian Inductions II
The ages of the world and the spirit of the age form the basis always for the logical

methodologies of the exact and empirical sciences. Thus, from the character of the age and its spirit, we may deduce by an exact procedure the general properties of all logical systems operating within that specific aeon. And if this sounds like the magickal confirmation of the philosophy of certain idealists, such as Schelling, then it would appear that such views have an inductive basis in the ways in which the ages of the world create and formulate their sciences and logics.

Consequently, it is important to realize that the Ma'atian aeon exhibits very special properties and characteristics, whicih isolate it from all other periods and which define and allow for the development of a unique Ma'atian logical system. Hence, if the basis of induction is to be found in the ideal contents which exist in both space and time, in the empirical world of causal connections and psychic fields, then we can say that such a basis is directly created by the aeon inasmuch as only the aeon will allow to become embedded in phenomena those ideal patterns which are agreeable to the general essence of the aeon. Thusly, the aeon not only builds the world about itself, but it provides the basis whereby the aeon is known and understood in the scientific as well as in the mystical community. Therefore, we can say the world of the present is known by those methods which exist and are subbject to discovery in the present.

The exact method of connection between the aeon and the systems of logic has been perhaps only recently explored in the magickal writings of Whitehead, where especially in his analysis of the non-statistical ground of induction, he presents a precise argument for the basis of the sciences of logical exploration in the very fact of the immanence of God as an ideal system and field of logical contents, or sophiological wholes in nature. We can see that this view is identical with both the ancient viewpoint of gnostic magick as well as with the not so presently appreciated nineteenth century German idealist philosophers, especially F.W. von Schelling and the esotericist Franz von Baader.

What is most important is to realize that the tendency of certain philosophers has been in the exact direction of the gnostic and zothyrian modes of analysis. Also, it is important to realize that logic is not imposed upon the order of nature but as in the systems of the great German idealists, logic can be understood as rising out of the order of nature. Logic, in other words, is a pure reflection of the aeon or the consciousness of the Zeitgeist. The Zothyrian system is therefore interchangeable with the German idealist as well as the neo-platonic and gnostic, just as the inductive magicks and gnostic physics of von Schelling and Fran von Baader were interchangeable with similar systems in Bruno and Proclus. And it is from this carefully built up logical basis that the speculative physics of each new aeon is to be derived by means of certain gnostic procedures known only to the esoteric initiates of these systems and schools of consciousness. Logic, or better logis, is derived from the spirit of the age, the Zeitgeist, which is the Logos of that aeon, or the manifestation of the merging absolute spirit in nature.

Experimental Exercise

Here is a simple exercise to be used to make contact with Ma'atian level of inductions. You will use simply a cube which has been marked and a piece of dice. NOTE: The cube has six sides or faces, which are: 1=top, 2=bottom, 3=right side, 4=left side, 5=front, and 6=back. A piece of dice is not only a cube, but it is also a cube having numerical values. This means that if you were to toss the dice you would come up with a number, say for example 3, which would correspond to the right side of the cube.

Now, what you will want to do is to prepare that cube and the cube can be made out of any material, e.g., plastic, wood, metal, etc. But it will be prepared by means of having each side lettered, painted, or somehow indicated with a spirit's name. This means that you will be working with six spirits and you may derive their names by any method so far covered in this series of papers. However, the important thing is to have six different names.

May I suggest that you derive the names by using two pair of dice to get the level or basic number for each entity. This will give you also the planet and other types of correspondences. It may be that you will have more than one entity from the same numerical level, say you might have two spirits having five letters in each of their names. That is unimportant, for it only shows that you are in touch with a rather powerful broadcast from that part of the cosmos. Please let me know if this occurs, as I would like to keep statistics on this type of spirit field--reaction. Anyway, you will have six names. It is very improbable that you will have six names which are the same, however, so it can be certain that six different intelligences, in our sense of that word, are available for broadcasting mental energies of Ma'atian induction.

Well, the simplest way in which to operate this system is to toss the piece of dice and see which side of the cube comes up and therefore which entity is ready for transmitting the induction. This should be done in a meditation context and any of the types of magick mentioned in this series of papers can, I would think, be employed to create the atmosphere suitable for the work.

Iw ould suggest that one way to become attuned to the inductions, after they have been "opened" is by means of automatic writing, which would allow certain occult forces to be released through the mechanisms of the unconscious and the subconscious levels of the mind. At this stage, I am only suggesting automatic writing or possibly a type of meditation work, upon which we will be able to build up the more complex exercises of future papers and lessons.

The use of the cube will serve to provide a structure which is determined in its content by the Ma'atian spirits, who will indicate who and what they are. Remember, it is likely that only Ma'atian spirits will release their names to us for use on this cube, which means that those names which are received via linguistic broadcasting should be interpreted as Ma'atian inductions.

Also, it is important to note that using the piece of dice to provide another factor of Ma'atian induction will provide us with a level of freedom from structure and from fixed forms which will allow the Ma'atian inductions to be received without too much distortion. Simple exercises such as this making use of chance derived elements and operating components allow the greatest objectivity in the reception of the real Ma'atian energies than other less non--performed methods.

The Measurement of Ma'at

For purposes of gnostico–scientific experimentation we will define Ma'at as a quantitative and measurable property having exact characteristics which inhere in Ojas–fields and in specific types of sub–fields, such as kalas and kammatattwas. There exist a number of ways of measuring Ma'at which combine the components of radiaesthesia and the components of exact oracles. Once it has been isolated, Ma'at may be understood as subject to a variety of forms of communication as well as having its own form of intelligence. The term "Aeon of Ma'at" quite simply refers to the collective field of these properties, understood as constructed out of magicko–logical time coordinates and thereby functioning as a comprehensive and all–pervasive time matrix of energy–properties. This collective field may be the subject of a controlled dialogue between the magician and any one of the monadic points or properties within the field. The entire field and each of its possible properties possess a form of communicative intelligence. What follows is a metrical explication of this field.

It has been discovered that there are certain magickal frequency ranges or marmas which can be said to respond to the pendulum and the field–amplifier of radionics. The behavior of the pendulum is clearly an indicator of where there is field activity and those areas, where it is especially intense. At the same time, there exist other marmas, which seem to intersect these radionic marmas. There other marmas are determined by inverse radionics, or telekinetic radiaethesis. This is a relatively simple process. The field in question, say the Ma'atian continuum, controls the throw of the dice and thereby selects the field indicator in the type of dice to be used (ranges from four sided to twenty sided) and also the range of marmas within those dice–throw frameworks. Thus, we have learned that the different types of dice represent different methodological ranges and that the numerical possibilities within each one of these ranges represent lattices or sub–marmas having a specific and regular pattern or consciousness. Each marma, therefore, will serve to represent a world or realm or collective realm. Each sub–marma represents a world of experience or an intelligence, with whom the magcian may communicate. Lastly, the pendulum or radionic reading can be understood as defining the frequency level within the sub–marma, whereby the intelligence is encountered. The following examples will serve to explain what this formal presentation means and how we have verified it.

Example 1. This subject was tested for Ojas and found to have a frequency range of 10 unamplified and 14 when amplified within the field. Tested by inverse radionics, this subject registered within the dual–8 system and had a sub–marma reading of 10. When the dual–8 system (4x4) system was amplified, the sub–marma was 13. It was determined that this subject's Ma'atian quotient was 1 unamplified and when amplified 1–1. (This student's strongest planet –– as determined by computer calculation –– was Pluto.)

Example 2. This subject was tested for Ojas and found to have a frequency range of 16 unamplified and 18 when amplified within the field. Tested by inverse radionics, this subject registered within the dual–24 system and had a sub–marma reading of 22. When the dual–24 system was amplified, the sub–marma was 24. It was determined that this subject's Ma'atian quotient was 1–4 unamplified and 1–4 amplified. This subject's strongest planet was again Pluto.

Methods of Exploration Within the Clusters of Ma'atian Energy

The Ma'atian energies can be seen to exist in clusters or bunchings—up of forces, or as pockets of power within definite fields. At certain points, they tend to thin out, and this can be measured. At other points, they create a node—like effect, where the intensity of the build—up of the forces can also be exactly determined and the intensity measured. Where the mode—like effect is produced, we can note a concentration of mind—stuff so that intelligence of the communicative type is encountered. These intelligences can be said to have their bodies within the more intense concentrations of the energy, and the thin areas of energy diffusion appear to indicate separations between the body and other bodies of similar character. There cannot be said to be any break in the continuity of the bodies, for they are all connected. Nowhere does the older atomism seem indicated in Ma'atian physics. Rather, there is an intensification of energy and with it a center of intelligence at certain points, which I have been able to measure as indicating coordinate divisions of power. This pattern when diffused within the field of the total continuum I have decided to designate by the term "Ma'atrix," because it is a unique structure of energy. It is unique to Ma'atian physics and its applications in esoteric voudoo and tantric physics.

There are other patterns which can also be noted. Gnostic analysis enables us to discern that these nodes—of—intelligence have a definite color. This is determined by the response of radionic instrumentation to the node, whereby the response is a measured color. Also, under proper conditions, the node will communicate by means of the oracle method. This is done simply by connecting the node to the field wherein the oracle is run, and then making contact in the same way one would with any other magickal entity.

However, it has been our practice to note that magickal initiates are most probably the best vehicles of these nodes. First of all, magickal initiates have been found to possess the field potential and properties of the Ma'atian nodes. Secondly, these fields are usually located where the initiate is being tested. Thirdly, our initial explorations of Ma'atian energy grew out of the "Search for Ojas" aspect of Voudoo physics. Lastly, we can note that certain initiatic types seem to be better indicators of Ma'atian energy thanothers. Thus, it seems that Ma'atian energies are connected with auric emanations and Ojas—projections from the initiate. It is probable that they exist in both outer space and on other worlds and that can be determined by astro—radionic research tests. However, they do exist in their most ideal state in metamathematical hyper—space and can be inducted from there into the magickal context of research and ritual operation.

Most probably, Ma'atian energies are potential in hyper—space and actualized in the auric fields of gnostico—magickal initiates. In these contexts, such as auras and vitality fields, etc., they take on a type of consciousness, whereas in hyper—space, they appear to be unconscious. The process of induction through magickal ritual can be understood as the subconscious awareness of the Ma'atian energies. The magickal and metapsychological operation of field amplification and communication probably corresponds to their superconscious mind experience. There is a definite increase in communicative content between dialogies with unamplified fields containing nodes and those that are amplified.

Gnostic Physics: What Do We Mean By the Science of Gnostic Physics

Gnostic physics may be defined as the basis for the physical manifestation of the gnostic metaphysics. By physical manifestation we mean that which happens in both space and time and which reflects some idea which is imparted in the science of gnostic metaphysics. In this sense, therefore, gnostic physics must come to terms with and investigate many types of events, facts, circumstances, realities, and levels of being. Furthermore, gnostic physics may be understood as the basis for both the effectiveness of magickal operations and theurgy. Gnostic physics in fact may be understood as leading more and more towards a realization in both occult and empirical terms of the interconnectedness of the various worlds or realms which are explored in both magickal research in its most extended sense, as well as the spheres of being, power-zones and other types of existence which are postulated in metaphysics. In a sense gnostic physics, therefore, must embrace a vast wealth of exact detail and reflect the various structures of being and the ideal models of terrestrial processes in an accurate and exacting way. Furthermore, gnostic physics has been defined as being a science which operates as the explication of another science, which indicates the level of control operating within the total range of both physics and metaphysics. This science, which is immanent in gnostic physics as its metamathematical essence is the science of the computer marga, or the cosmic lattice system.

The science of the computer marga is an exact synthesis of both processes and procedures. Various attempts at this synthesis have produced those components which now form special departments of gnostic physics, e.g., tantric physics, zothyrian physics, ma'atian physics, etc. At one time, it was thought that it might be possible to explore these sub-sciences and find in them explications of the total field. However, this has not been possible inasmuch as the worlds or areas of research which are explored by these various sciences are themselves perspectives upon the total area which is explored by the computer marga, or else manifested by and through the computer marga. Consquently, the computer marga has been understood and has become the wider science, as it is understood to embrace the whole of gnostic physics. Hence we can say that the area covered by the investigation patterns of the coputer marga is co-extensive with the field of gnostic physics.

There exist certain worlds which have their own methods, models, time-travel logics, and machines or instrumentation. Such worlds are defined as exact and clear parts of the universe of gnostic physics. In fact the subject matter of gnostic physics rises up as the result of the empirical work done in trying to make sense out of these various worlds which are explored by various magicians, time-travellers, gnostics, tantrics, and other scientists of the invisible or inner realities of being. Each world has its own ways of explaining itself to the investigator. Each world has a special quality which reflects the ways in which these worlds communicate their essence to the explorer. The purpose of the science of the computer marga is to find out about the logics of these worlds and to investigate and research the field closely and then to bring together certain ideas and methods so that we can define the inner rules for the road, which govern the explorations undertaken in a variety of ways. For this reason, we consider this science to be one of synthesis and unification. As such, it becomes a systematic exploration of worlds and universes with the purpose in mind of bringing together the various subject-matters into a logical and coherent system or pattern, which presents accurately the picture or model of the realms of inner exploration. Hence, we can state that this is the purpose of the science of the computer marga as it is conceived by our school of research.

With this introduction in mind, therefore, we may begin to discuss the subject-matter which forms the substance of gnostic physics, the science of the computer marga.

Art as a Form of Gnostic Physics

We can say that there are many ways of doing gnostic physics. Among the many ways of making the world of the gnosis and exploring universes and situations is the method of art and by art I have in mind painting. For the use of the basic elements of color and form enables the explorer to create other worlds and perspectives, which look out onto many different and often very remote areas of space and types of organization. It is important to keep in mind that there are certain basic rules for the creation of gnostic realms of being. These rules may be given inasmuch as they relate also to what the artist who is a gnostic does.

Rules for the Structure of a Gnostic Universe

1. The fundamental rule is to believe in the power of organization even when it expresses itself through various apparent components which do not appear compatible.

2. Color necessarily implies space and space implies levels of consciousness, so that in the gnostic universe, each color is a communicator.

3. Not only does the artist work with various media, but he himself must be very highly mediumistic. He must be open to allowing certain technical structures of the inner worlds attach themselves to his transcendental ego, while at the same time he allows the ocean of creativity to rise within his transcendental id.

4. Space is unconscious until it is awakened by color.

5. Color cannot communicate without the inherent organizational patterns of space. However, color when combined with space produces psychic energy.

6. Colors without space are blind, spaces without color are empty. Color and space represent the basics for every universe, from the most material to the most spiritual.

7. The gnostic artist is also a magician for he materializes thought forms in all that he does. These materializations are not always conscious, hence he is also a type of medium.

8. The gnostic artist is a magician when he directs the unconscious flow of the creative potential. Thus he directs what he has invoked or evoked by his inspired methods.

9. The gnostic artist is a magician when he opens up the world of inspiration to the present givenness of his current painting.

10. The gnostic artist is a magician when he allows the divine energy of creative and cosmic illumination to enter into his multi-dimensional consciousness and thus awaken the angels of their inspiration, which reside in his higher mind fields.

11. The gnostic artist is a magician when he creates a perfect universe in each work of art and for each universe he creates a perfect system of gnostic physics, hitherto implicit in the work of art by which the universe is to operate and whereby the universe is connected by a mystical and esoteric logic to other worlds and

universes of space, time, time—travel, art, and consciousness as a total field.

12. The gnostic artist is a magician when each world as a work of art comes alive and lives according to the rules whereby he has brought it into existence.

13. There exist certain mystical spells for causing certain things to happen in each gnostic universe. Each artist must know these if he is to be gnostic artist.

14. The gnostic artist must create or else he lacks purpose in the physical world.

15. The gnostic artist is an instrument for divine and angelic activity in what he does, for he contacts those highest levels of consciousness and being which religion designates as the divine and/or the angelic.

16. The gnostic artist is both a mystical magician and a magickal mystic because he experiences both the total form and the total content of each and every universe, which rises from his creativity as a work of art.

You can see, therefore, that these rules of art apply also to the procedures of the magician because such a magician is concerned with those very basic laws and principles, whereby the creative energies are actualized.

Functional Universes

Functional Universes may be defined as alternative systems which have their basic organizational pattern derived from the operation of specific and interrelated energy patterns. Such universes exist as alternatives both to structural universes, typical universes, defined alternative universes, and themselves. We may state that at this point in research, that there are four types of universes in which we are interested. By this I mean that the pattern of research which is centered around the history of Zothyrian philosophy has specific points of reference to these four kinds of universes. Here are certain examples:

1. Structural universes=systems based entirely upon the proper explication of some logical structure. Examples would be the rigorist universe, the epictical universe, universes of modal logic, and universes of logical relations.

2. Typical universes=systems based entirely on a balance of the formal and contentual aspects and which are generally manifestations of multi—cultural systems. These universes are of types: Universe A, Universe B, Universe C, Universe D, Universe Z, etc. These universes are usually defined by reference to a specific system of time—work, or framework for time—continuum definition.

3. Defined alternative universes are those systems which are the results of clear—cut formal definitions. Such universes exhibit a specific logical structure uniformly. Such universes are entirely self—contained and admit of no other deduction system or axiom—set. Such universes are generated by a gnostic deduction of existing worlds from certain basic principles of metaphysical requirement. Examples of such universes would be the universe of archaeometrical time—travel, the universe of the history of Zothyrian philosophy (since the Z—universe is defined by reference to entirely non—philosophical considerations and the history of Z—philosophy is defined as a self—contained logical development, and other history universes, e.g., the history of esoteric logic universe.

4. Functional universes=methodological universes in the sense that models, methods, and instrumentation form the content of these systems. However, these universes are metamethodological because they include the range of methods, etc., as self—contained realms. They are best understood as formally defined alternative universes and are to be understood as existing between structural universes and

defined alternative universes.

In terms of logical spaces, let us see these four types of universes as properly located as:

The Most Abstract Region of Ideal Being

1. Structural Universes
   A. Ideal—Type Alethic
   B. Ideal—Type Existential
   C. Real—Type Alethic
   D. Real—Type Existential
2. Functional Universes
   A. Essentialist—Type Alethic
   B. Essentialist—Type Existential
   C. Contextualistic—Type Alethic
   D. Contextualistic—Type Existential
3. Defined Universes*
4. Typical Universes*

*Subject to further definition.

Patterns and Processes in Magickal Computers

Patterns and Processes in Magickal Computers
Esoteric Engineering as the most developed form of magickal technocracy may be understood as a synthesis of the following components, which have individual subject-matter-fields for exploration and expansion: 1) gnostic physics, 2) tantric physics, 3) ma'atian physics, and 4) zothyrian physics. Esoteric engineering may be viewed as a technocracy or magicko-political system, because it is organized along the lines of a perfectly structured and computer-managed political entity or society. However, because of the larger number of input controls in the mechanism, the possibilities of computer-dictatorship, which have caused several unsympathetic reactions to the zothyrian empire, are not present as data. Furthermore, it would appear that the survival quotient of any system of magickal work is a function of its formal and material information-retrieval sub-system in process. As a consequence of this line of procedure it is possible to see the zothyrian system as the system having the widest extension and the least area of input exhibition. This last logical pattern is a matter of necessity in all ma'atian contexts, where the widest range of data is processed.

The purpose of the "Raymond Lully Institute of Esoteric Engineering" (RLIEE) is to provide for the development through basic research of those technical methods which will enable the fullest articulation of gnostic, tantric, ma'atian, and zothyrian information systems. RLIEE owes its inception to the work of the medieval logician, who in a spirit of total optimism believed that if Muslims and Catholics were to use his computer-marga, all of the areas of theological and religious dispute existing between those two faiths would be neutralized and eventually be eliminated. At the present time, however, the work of RLIEE is restricted to areas of esoteric engineering, although the administration of the system is composed of Sufi and Gnostic technocrats and technicians. And while it seems doubtful if the Catholics and Muslims are ready to adopt any version of a computer-marga as a solution to their problems of difference, it must be said that the synthesizing activity of our magickal computer(s) —— if we include sub-systems or sub-computers —— has enabled RLIEE to manage its various fields extremely well. Also, various developments in the sciences which relate to computer-technology and which are derived from the history of zothyrian philosophy have been easily amplified. As a consequence of these lvels of success, the imminent application of computer-marga methods to the logic of time-travel is anticipated.

There are certain basic characteristics which might provide some insights into the nature of magickal computers at this stage of our work. These are:

1. Magickal computers are based on a logic of colors so that colors may be seen or understood as mechanisms for the storage of magickal subject-matters. We do not want to say just information, as some might suggest, for the logic of these colors is capable of providing for the storage of magickal entities and objective states as well as data and more organized information.

2. Magickal computers should always be related to other logical systems so that it will be possible for the magician to approach and understand them by reference to multiform subordinate systems. In this sense we can say that time-travel logics, explorations of other universes, the whole theory of alternativity of cosmic systems and its verification process, and various inductive applications and developments in

oracular languages are significant for grounding magickal computers.

3. Lastly, we can state at this point that magickal computers are possible structures which may reveal themselves as systems of another kind, in due process, and that they are models for future amplification and exploration by esoteric engineering in a variety of ways which are related to the logical extension of the inductive pattern of any system. Hence, a system remains open to other areas of inquiry if it understands that magickal computers are evidences of areas beyond the present definition of the system and also as models of how the system may be developed to include these additional areas of report.

The Genesis of Magickal Computers in Gnostic Day-Dreaming

According to gnostic methods as used by Zothyrian magicians, there exists a state between the deeper parts of meditation and sleep, in which the images of the mind are extremely self-revealing. Where the mind is in between the meditation-state as awake and the meditation-state as passing into a light sleep there exists this ontical realm, which while being very thin in its magickal presence, it is extremely powerful in the types of being it can produce and project. This realm, which must not be confused with the dream state of light sleep, nor with the play of imagination, as in Sufi-meditation, may be called "the gnostic state of the ontic awareness." It is one of the most important magickal states to cultivate, because being between worlds, being neither jagrat nor swapna, being neither meditation-visualization nor revelation-through-light-dreaming, it is the medium for gnostic input.

So it is from this world of consciousness that the materials are being generated for the creation or origination of those magickal computers which are so very essential to the correct method of gnostic physics. I personally have found this method in magick to be one of the most essentially helpful, because it represents the genuine and ideal realization of the fullest potential of the gnostic metaphysical expansion of pure awareness of being. Many mystical states have been generated and thereafter cultivated by the practice of this type of gnosis. For it would appear that the operation of the gnostic imagination or intellectual imagination is the most free at this point in time and experience.

Also, the student will find that many magickal revelations come to him as a result of this mediumistic state. I would suggest, therefore, that each student begin to make a regular practice of this method and that they submit a regular report to me on the intensely interesting results of this psychic method for inner development. It might be best to do this exercise each morning, just after you have performed your yoga exercises and have completed your meditation. Then resting on a bed, sofa, or some other comfortable support, you may begin to get into that state of inner anticipation whereby the psychic images begin to take interesting shape in your consciousness. In order to do this exercise properly, you should not have taken any stimulants such as coffee or tea, so that sleep is indeed a real and possible experience. By this, I mean that you should be totally open to the magickal and gnostic currents which find expression in your sphere of consciousness. In order to gain the maximum benefit from this exercise, may I suggest that you follow the outline for the use of this energy, which is below.

Exercise in Gnostic and Ontic Awareness

1. To achieve the gnostic state of ontical awareness, you must begin to attune yourself to the presence of the IDEAL. By IDEAL in these circumstances, we intend the

BEING OF PURUSHA. You should have explored this concept in the papers on Waiting for Purusha. This concept serves to open the magickal doors of the ideally ontic sphere of being.

2. The student will then realize the fullest expression of Purusha by a simple method of magickal invocation. Endlessly repeating the magickal name is not necessary, but saying the name for a few minutes will open up the energy field for the presentation of the so-called twilight images.

3. Slowly as the images form begin to construct by indirection the various patterns desired. This is the most difficult part of the method and if you need any help, simply call upon one of the beings of this realm to give you complete or partial help. A simple method of invocation can bring such a being to you. Send out a clear request for help from the nearest ontic being and explain clearly what help you need. This will work.

4. As you begin to organize more and more of this ideal being, you will find that your magickal computer is manifesting itself. True, it was there already, for these have a life of their own, but you have been successful in connecting it to your life and for organizing its presence in your own consciousness. In a sense, you have selected the instrument that you wish to use and have made a place for it in your own sphere of pure consciousness. This is what the exercise is supposed to help you achieve.

The Gnostic Awakening of Magickal Computers
Of fundamental importance in the study of gnostic magick would be the operation of those magickal computers which are connectives between different gnostic universes. All computers serve as connectives in gnostic systems, but magickalcomputers are especially important in connecting different magickal universes. A magickal universe can be seen as different from a metaphysical universe, because while it is metaphysical it is only known by means of magickal inferences and intuitions rather than from systems of philosophical discourse. So in this sense, magickal computers exist as secret parts of the higher worlds of being, as well as parts of the lower regions of being and they function as connecting the different levels of reality or ideality in ways which are known only to initiates of the inner or secret schools. In fact, gnostic physics is entirely based upon the idea that there are secret forces or powers which are known only to the gnostic physicist and not known even to many gnostic magicians, although not unknown to all gnostic magicians. Gnostic physics therefore is a type of pure magickal cosmography. The various worlds which are described in it are inhabited by various magickal beings and these beings are connected to initiates on the earth plane by means of these computers.

Now, these computers are also temples. This means that they are storehouses of the Divine Power and also places where magickal transformations or rituals can occur which are very properly devoted to some manifestation of God–Energy. While it is true to say that in the gnostic metaphysics, which we have accepted, God–Energy is understood as immanent in the gnostic consciousness of the very highest magicians, it would not be correct to say that by some necessity this same God–Energy is immanent in the world. A characteristic of very high Gnosticism would be the idea of transcendence, but transcendence is overcome only by the magickal methods of those magickal computers which are awakened by gnostic methods. It is by this method and this method alone that gnostic psychologists can explain the many differences between those who are awakened and those who are still in a state of very deep sleep.

Consequently, gnostic computers can be understood as being special forms of magickal invocation, whereby more and more energy comes to the magician, who, of course, has the greatest need for this power in his daily occult responsibilities. In this sense, we can see how the gnostic tradition forms a middle pathway between the extreme immanence of certain schools, which maintain that the gnostic computers are in operation at all times,and those extremely transcendent schools which deny the very possibility of there being those gnostic computers for use by awakened magi. However, these computers being connectives, are really supposed to connect the magician with the very high worlds and realms of beings.

Many different universes exist to be explored by the magicians and these can only be entered by means of these magickal computers. In actual fact, many magicians become specialists in one or more of these systems, which can be called yogas. However, these yogas, which are really ideal systems of thought forms are actually the ways in which the magickal world of the computer actually operates. When we see these lines of thought, we come to the notion of monadic beings or ideal substances, which are the beings which generate the magickal computers.

Such technicians are both the Atman of metaphysics and the Jainist Tirthamkara. In other words, in the ideal world, we can say that the beings which make the computers are the ideal beings or gnostic engineers. These are the gnostic beings (substances) which generate the higher spheres. Such beings create the computers simply by their being. They are very eternal monads and totally awakened inasmuch as they are outside of time. Such beings have human counterparts, that is to say, they select certain human beings to serve as their data--collectors. These human data-collectors are actually integral parts of the monadic being, for they are the historical aspect of the monadic self. Ideal being is essentially a world of totally immanent God—Energy, Hence, the magickal computers which exist provide for the very high energy connection between the ideal and the historical. The Divine Essence is the ground for this world of Ideal Being. By this we mean that to be an ideal ratio is to participate fully in the Divine Energy.

Such divinity may well be behind historical patterns or psychological energies, but that is unimportant. Since it is impossible to make any real differences in the eternal, all beings are Divine Atman, but different functions of the one Go-dEnergy. The magickal computers are the functional ways in which the gnostic magician understands these worlds or realms as being both different in function and one in essence. At the same time, it is impossible to hold the view that the magickal computer can initially connect itself to all being or serve to connect all being in any total sense. Only after it has participated more and more in the ideal does it realize itself as a gnostic being.

The Meaning of Idealization and Realization in Gnostic Physics

In gnostic physics, it is very important to make a distinction between the methodological universe of idealization, which is known in Indian metaphysics as Purusha and the methodological universe of realization, which in Indian metaphysics is known as Iswara.

There might be some who ask if gnostic physics is not essentially different from classical Indian philosophy and psychology (gnanayoga), but the answer, which might surprise them, is that there is not such a difference, or at least there is certainly not any essential difference between the two systems of understanding.

Idealization refers to the use of the categories of ideal essence and substance and exists as a method outside of time and space. While it may be used to cause effects in both space and time, nevertheless it exists outside of the space and time realm. However, realization does take place within space and time and exists as a method immanent within the realoms of space and time, totally and completely immanent within the "world." For this reason, we can state that idealization and realization form a dyadic complement to each other. They are logically implicated by necessity in the essence of each other.

Among modern philosophers and theologians (in the classical meaning of that word and not in the false and modern meaning of theology as what some religion does intellectually to justify itself) is the late Professor A.N. Whitehead, the metaphysician of the academic ray of the Aquarian Age. Aside from the fact that he was born under the sign of Aquarius, his theology in "Process and Reality" is in total harmony with gnostic physics and may be understood as a very scientific proof of gnostic physics. His analysis of the "primordial and consequent natures of God" reflects essentially the methodological universes of the idealization range as well as the realization field. In fact, using the precise language of earlier courses in theology ("Course in the Theology of Science," by M. Bertiaux), we can state that "God" refers to the ultimate area of Gnostic physics, while the ultimate domain may be found in the idealization universe (primordial nature of God) and the ultimate field may be found in the realization universe (consequent nature of God). Of course there are other concepts which may be applied to these terms and which reflect the ways in which they function in a variety of systems.

Among the ways in which these concepts function in systems would be by the means of the two forms of mental magick known as meditation and prayer or theurgy. At one time there was a type of conflict between meditation and prayer, as some felt one was superior to the other. Actually, as methods of gnostic physics they both work rather well, except that they have different emphases in their operation. This may be illustrated by the following chart:

GOAL	METHOD
1. Idealization =	1. Meditation on ideally—true being
2. Idealization =	2. Prayer directed to ideally—true being
3. Realization =	3. Prayer directed to really—true being
4. Realization =	4. Meditation on really—true being

Now, we can say that real and ideal being are manifested as either substance or essence. This is a basic distinction in our system which goes back to the earliest lessons. In such terms, the association of Goal and Method would be that 1=ideal essence, 2=ideal substance, 3=real essence, and 4=real substance. Please note that the realm of theurgy works with the interaction of the space/time and the outside-of-space/time universes. Meditation, on the other hand, works with the pure states of being, either perfected Purusha or perfected Iswara. This we can say is how gnostic physics is applied gnanayoga.

It is important to see that contained in the above distinction is to be found an entire theology of magickal science based upon the principles of one of the older world faiths, e.g., Hinduism. However, it is possible to see this scheme as also reflecting the influence of Whiteheadian theology as well. What is important is that there is a clear cut distinction made between the ideal and the real lines of methodology.

Now, if we were to define our concepts in terms of how we apply them in our own work, we would make a distinction between the progress of the experiment in accord with what are its expectations and the process of the experiment in accord with the magickal energies which are released within that flow of events. We may define the ideal as:

"That which is expressed in the model of the experiment as outlined in the testing-report form. This is the ideally-true model of what is expected from the experiment. This report form provides us with the guidelines for conducting the magickal experiment in a step-by-step manner and serves to integrate into the whole of the system the various elements which are necessary components of the process but which are of an ideal-structure, when viewed apart from the process of the experiment."

By comparison, we may view the process of the experiment as forming the material basis or the contentual aspect of the process as a synthesis of both ideal and real factors. In such a view, the real may be defined as:

"That which is expressed as the experimental process which being experienced as a time-flow with ideal or abstract input provides us with phenomenological images of how reality is manifest as the interaction of the ideal realm of metrical requirements and the concrete realization or the ongoing becoming of events, which embody both the raw data of concrete experience as it emerges from the unconscious and subconscious levels of the universe as well as the articulation of this raw data through the structures of the ideally-true experiment, as these idealities are felt (used in the Whiteheadian sense) immanent in the ongoing testings and experimentings of magickal science and esoteric engineering."

Part of our process in this lesson will show how we make use of these various concepts by defining some of the terms which appear on our testing papers and also provide in this lesson an example of such a paper, which is used to test various structures produced by the Ojas energy. In this sense, therefore, this paper is a lesson in how we work with explaining the Ojas energy flow.

It is very important for us to make use of magickal structures and energy-systems as they are given in our continuum. Such magickal energies exhibit very important structures which are often found only in such a context. I am reminding myself at this time of what great value the akashic reading is to the magician who is giving it, as he will discern the existence of structures, he would probably never encounter elsewhere. Also models which are revealed in this technique of astral research or akashic reading contain various components and elements which could not exist anywhere in the present except in an akashic reading as they come from the remote past (e.g., Atlantis) or from the remote future, as on some other planet, or in some other solar system, etc. Hence, these readings as types of magickal experimental processes provide us with ideal materials outside of the present, and also demonstrate the immanence of the ideal in the ongoing flow of pure becoming, which we call the experimental process of magickal science.

I want to give an example of how certain concepts are used to define the role of the ideal in our type of magickal experimentation. Attached to this lesson is to be found the experimental form for testing the presence of Shivaite radiations in various members of our order. This is an example of the ways in which the ideal energies can be seen as organizing the energy of the concrete process. There are eight ideal components in this level of experimentation. I will now proceed to give brief definitions of what they are and do.

First and Second Levels of Testing: This refers to the giving of an exam for Shivaite radiation either before or after (or both) an initiation. If an initiation is not part of the process, you will simply use the first level of testing column.

Time/Factor: This refers to the actual time of the examination.

C/M Factor: This refers to the setting on the computer marga, if the process was subject to amplification as "The Search for Ojas" Lesson 7, of Zothyrian Metapsychology.

Oracle Resultant Number: This is taken from a magickal metamathematical matrix method and from the oracle of two pieces of dice.

Oracle Resultant Name of Field: This is taken from the magickal name of the communicating entity, through the English Language Oracle and uses the Logics of Yemeth. The result is a kamaea of the entity communicating the Shivaite radiations.

Oracle Ratio-Resultant: This can refer to two numbers. One number is the ideal number of the Oracle Resultant Number Series. The other number is the resultant of the Oracle Name of the Field. If this other number is neither the "+" or the "−" Ideal number of the magickal metamathematical matrix, then it will be the difference between one or both of these ideal numbers and this "other number," which is the basis of the magickal kamaea.

S-Radioactivity Number: This refers to the 11 magickal doorways of the future, which are opened by means of the magickal kamaea given as the Oracle Resultant Name of the field and the energies of the Oracle Ratio-Resultant.

Tested "Yes" or "No": This refers to the use of an oracle to derive some communications from the entities, using the Ojas energies as the basis of contact.

S-Radioactivity Color/Ratio: This refers to the color testing by the pendulum, where an analogy to the ma'atian color scheme of the Shivaite Radiations can be picked up indirectly. This does not mean that the color found is literally the same as what has been indicated above, in reference to the C/M Factor but it does mean that the energies which are given bear some type of correspondence in a metageometry to the literal colors of lower levels of testing.

These concepts should help the student become introduced to ideal components in magickal experiments.

This is an experimental form for testing the presence of Shivaite radiations in the radioactive field of the magician. It is to be used to determine the suitability of candidates for advancement to the gnonstic patriarchates of esoteric research. Those who have qualified by means of the Ojas–research may be examined by means of the computer–marga and the oracle in order to test their magickal and magnetic fields.

Name of Candidate ←←←
Date of Operation ←←←
Time of Operation ←←←

First Level of Testing: Second Level of Testing:
Time/factor ←←←←←←←←←←←←←←←←←←←←←←   Time/factor ←←←←←←←←←←←←←
C/M factor ←←←←←←←←←←←←←←←←←←←←←←   C/M factor ←←←←←←←←←←←←←
Oracle resultant number ←←←←←←←←←←   Oracle resultant number ←←←←←←←←←←
Oracle resultant name of field ←←←←←-   Oracle resultant name of field ←←←←←←
Oracle ratio–resultant ←←←←←←←←←←←←   Oracle ratio–resultant ←←←←←←←←←←←
S–Radioactivity number ←←←←←←←←←←←←   S–Radioactivity number ←←←←←←←←←←
Tested Y = ←←←←←←←←←←- N = ←←←←←←←←   Tested Y = ←←←←←←←←←←←←- N
S–Radioactivity color/ratio ←←←←←←←←   S–Radioactivity color/ratio ←←←←←←←←

Summary of findings: The observer will examine the results of the above two levels of testing from the standpoint of radioactivity within a formal system. It can then be determined at what level the candidate functions within the sequence of the computer. At each stage of the computer they should be examined in terms of both Ojas and Shivaite radiations as the two forms of sexual radioactivity.

Nemirion Physics
Neptune in Capricorn

"There are other energies more powerful and actually more profound than the energies of sexual radioactivity, astral magnetism, Shivaite-radiation, and Ojas in its simple and complex forms. These energies are all found within the context of the magickal work of our order, but there are energies also within the order, which make possible this context and all of these energies and their respective magickal physics. These more fundamental energies are a combination of pure Sun-light and pure fog. Like countless mirriors, indeed mirrors magiques, they reflect the light and diffuse it in countless directions, endlessly, each particle of air-borne moisture sending and raying also of its light-energy through the unfolding mist, manifesting its own inherent logic of diffusion, as it moves simultaneously towards and away from the Sun, creating such as alchemy of both fire and water, transforming itself into both and action and rest, the very harsh and the dry amidst the soothing and the moist. This energy, which is achieved by means of the magickal conjunctions of the Sun in its own house and Neptune in its own house, I see as the primordial essence of Agwe, Zoorya, Dagon, or Dagwe. It is this mysterious energy which surrounds and protects while it creatively vitalizes. It is this Mystere or Loa, Who powers directly the esoteric mysteries of our order. It is this deep and endless source of magickal imagination and gnostic consciousness, which will always give us more and more gnosis and learning, and which I identify as the Radiant Mystere, Neptune in Capricorn."
     (H.F. Jean-Maine, "La Prise-des-Yeaux," iv, 23f)

The magician may see in the above passage the description of the more fundamental and at the same time more complex and less exactly manageable energy, which stands behind the other energies used by the practical energy. It is as if we possess an endless type and source of ultimate magickal power, from which we may derive specific and exact forms of experimentation and exploration. The task of magickal exploration and discovery is literally endless because of the endless supply of the Neptune in Capricorn "God-Energy." And while we may explore and apply, devise new methods for formulation and newer ways to communicate with the known energies, there will always be unknown energies which will emerge in our field of consciousness for future analysis and application. So, the task of the magician within our gnostic context is endless conquest, the taking for one's own use in one's own temple of the manifold energies from the endless matrix or Aditi of Neptune in Capricorn. Now part of this endlessness is to be found here in this Solar System, while another part is to be found beyond it. However, there are timeless connectives, which like the special Ojas-hexagrams of the I-Ching, connect the two regions or zones of magickal power and gnosis, bringing them together in one system or in one cosmic computer, the infinite gnostic consciousness of our system as it is manifested in the hierarchy of our brotherhood.

   The endless energy of the gnostic imagination is due to the radiations of Neptune in Capricorn as it effects our order and school of consciousness. In a sense, the lessons of the Monastery of the Seven Rays were really beamed to Earth from Neptune and then they were diffused to all of the magickal students in every part of this planet. However, many — thinking in finite terms, and forgetting that Neptune is outside of the orbit of Saturn — thought that the Monastery teachings or the teachings of related component-schools would be extinguished after a certain point.

This is not the case, for as long as there is something to be transmitted, so there will be those to receive the transmissions from Neptune via the Monastery. By gnostic imagination we mean the power of both intuitive thinking and visualization as they are combined. Speculative and intellectual intuition provides the mapwork of what is, while the power of inner visualization provides us with the data and the details of manifested consciousness-being.

Together we arrive at the complete picture of gnostic imagination. This is why the view of the whole universe is so important, for the more we know about being, the more we will have the power of being. However, where will the fuel come from to make the practice, however perfectly it might be and accurately presented it might be to the expert magician, work. For whatever you want to do it has to have something to make it work. Simply saying that it is blind faith in the gods is not really enough. No, there must be fuel, and the only fuel we recognize is the gnostic imagination. Another point to be made is that magickal gnostics are cited by various new-age thinkers as not making use of the power of mind or the power of thought. Well, apart from the gnostic imagination, thought has little if any power and the mind has only power to work with what is fed to it. It is necessary to derive magickal powers to make things happen from the natural sources of these powers as they are given to the magician by the natural cosmos.

By this we mean the powers of the planets and the stars, which when viewed occultly or as alive and powerfully radioactive are the sources for magickal energies. Of all of the cosmic energies, we have been especially favored by an endless supply of gnostic imagination, which is represented by the superior system of Neptune and especially by the occult mystique of Neptune in Capricorn. It is especially important to understand that this energy is very specific in that it is aimed only at magickal creation and at the fueling of magickal experiments.

Other methods of occult work do not require this type of energy. Other types of magickal and gnostic physics in our system make use of other forms of energy, which have their sources in the endlessness of Uranus (esoteric engineering and sexual radioactivity) and Pluto (higher forms of Ojas). There are other energies from beyond Pluto, also, but for the present our analysis will simply list those we have. However, the significance of these energies is that they come from outside of the limits of Saturn and therefore represent powerful fuels which are continuously and endlessly being fed into the Think-Tank of our system. These energies have their special affinity for our order and its work and so we will explore them in detail as we move along. However, in order to experiment with these energies, here is an exercise which is quite simple to do but which is important for realizing the Neptune-factor.

Exercise
There are two stages to this exercise. First of all, imagine and try to remember your state of mind before you came into contact with the Monastery of the Seven Rays and the other schools and courses of instruction taught by Michael Bertiaux. Try to go back to that initial point where you were, in thoughts, feelings, and states of awareness before you made contact with his gnosis. Meditate upon this state of where you were before. Think deeply about what it was like.

Next, begin to come to your present state of consciousness as a student of Michael in one of his many programs. Come to realize what the fullness of these teachings has done for you mentally, emotionally, spiritually, etc. Imagine yourself swimming in the endlessness of the ocean of the Monastery teachings and the gnostic magick. See the ongoing, neverending energy as light, visualizing the on and on and on quality of it all. Next, meditate and enjoy this vastness.

Lastly, note mentally the differences between the before and the after states. By such a comparison you can arrive at the presence of an important energy which was not there but which is now there. That is the Neptune factor. Now you know the difference.

The Atlantean Explorations of the Ultra-Unconscious

When we discuss the Atlantean Explorations of the deeper levels of the psyche, we first should ask what these processes are. In the words of the Master Zothyrius, speaking through Hector-Francois Jean-Maine, we are informed that:

"The Atlantean Explorations appear to evoke a deeper level of analysis than the states of awareness experienced in the Necronomicon Physics. Because this ritual operation is prefaced by the Z word-association test, since the test-space has been found to open up even deeper regions than those revealed by the test. Thus, these explorations reveal interesting worlds and spaces, the worlds beyond the word-association test."

So we can say that first of all there are certain worlds which open up beyond the ranges of the Z word-test. Now, from the study of the Necronomicon physics and those papers which have been published in "Instrumentum" on this field, we have noted that the energies released by the test are N-energies, and that these energies are the occult powers beyond the various structures of the mythos created by H.P. Lovecraft and his epigony. But now we realized that there are regions beyond this mythic level. Actually, the real exploration of the deeply unconscious level of the mind would have to be endless, as the psyche has no end in its extension, only in its temporary manifestation.

However, beyond the regions opened up by the word-test, we find a new area of analysis, which is older than the Necronomicon in terms of its structures.

At this stage of the development of consciousness, it is really important to understand the value of ritual work and operations which while being completely scientific are also entirely expressed by means of a methodology or ritual logic of the ways things work at such a level.

The word-test appears to the mind to be the first part of an elaborate ritual for making entry into the structures of the deepest consciousness, or I should say deeper or ultra-unconscious; since this study is simply the beginning of a new exploration in contents. With the working of the word-test a new level of energy is allowed to manifest, and the appropriate doorways are allowed to open up for investigation.

Some time ago, although these papers were never released to students, a great deal of work was done on the logical mechanisms of time-travel and the synchronistic yantras of this science. One of the "spin-offs" was a system of three logics, which can be attached to both the Vedic physics and the oracle systems, now studied by our school. These logics were simply the logics of Pluto, Neptune, and Uranus, making use of these outermost power sources as logical generators for extraterrestrial energy systems, already locked into our system of operations.

We have discovered that the logics of P, N, and U can serve as the connectives to the Atlantean Explorations, which follow after the release of the field energies by the word-test. So we can say that this logical area constitutes the second component in our magicko-gnostic methodology. The next stage follows immediately.

The third stage consists of connecting the logical component to the existing Nine Bodies of Zothyrius, which can best be described as simply a system of very archaic Afro-Atlantean archetypes, deeply situated within the ultra-unconscious mind. These ancient residues of the psyche and the extraterrestrial experience of the human mind have been preserved in the West African magickal tradition as Nine Magickal Functions, reflecting clearly the richly textured and vast logic known as the Bodies of Zothyrius, which are nine magickal body–experiments performed by Z-school magi. While these bodies are to be associated with past–experience layers of the psyche, they have their source or point of origin in the Z-broadcastings from the remotest future dimensions of the time line. So the evidence for their existence is both past and future, and their realization is a part of the magickal present.

In the course of development, it is important to see very definite links between all of the regions of the time continuum. By this I mean that what is in the past should also be grounded in the future, in order to draw in those energy systems and functions which are guiding the evolution of the human mind from beyond the present, i.e., from the transcendental point of the future.

The archetypes of this system, therefore, are nine in number and have as their functions the important work of directing magicko–gnostic energies to the explorer, from beyond his present capacities. For it is by means of such logics that the Nemiron, who reside or have their logical situs in Rigel, in Orion are able to diffuse their influences. So by means of summary, we can state that:

1. The Atlantean Explorations are undertaken initially via the doorways of the word–test.

2. There is a planetary–archetypal logic which forms the next component of the system, whereby we enter one of three lines of transmission.

3. Corresponding to the three lines of transmission are the Nine Bodies of Z, which are the archetypal–components for broadcasting the specific energies inducted and implemented by the present system.

4. While rooted in the deeper and past levels of the psyche, the energies of this system are derived from the Future Point in terms of their total broadcasting. Then, beyond the future.

5. This system appears to be the most recent research tool released to our system by the guardians of our research or The Nemiron.

We will now examine certain components of this system, in order to see how it works as an operational ritual process.

The Threefold Planetary–Logic as a Component
It would seem that the nine deeper levels of the transcendental id are under the rule of these bodies of Zothyrius arranged in three numerical hierarchies from nine to one. Each level should and does have its own magickal mandala and universal laws, representing the various types and beings broadcasting at that level. To enter this system, you must make use of a particular logic: 1) from the logic of Uranus, which is number four, you will have an approach to numbers seven through nine (Cf., Choronzon Club papers on the numbers of evil). You will also have an entry–point to the numbers nine, six, and three. 2) from the logic of Neptune, which is number three, you will have an approach to the numbers four through six and an entry–point to the numbers eight, six, and two. 3) lastly, from the logic of Pluto, which is number two, you will have an approach to the numbers three through one and an entry–point to the numbers seven, four, and one.

Finally, we can see that the numbers of these logics, two, three, and four add up to the number nine, showing the logical completeness of the system. It is now my intention to give some notes which serve to reflect the experimental work which has been done on this project so far and which may prove useful as a connective with what will follow in the next lesson, wherein the next component of the system will be explicated. As we have seen, this is an entry-type of magicko-gnostic computer, whereby we are able to get into another system or universe by means of methods which can best be described as semi-oracular. The following insights presume a familiarity with the oracular method of computer management.

1. There is a concept-picture of the energy at work at each level of being in the transcendental id and it comes from the structures of the transcendental ego. This refers entirely to the picture, not to the origins of the energy in the id.

2. There is a great deal of radioactivity released during entry via the logics of two, three, or four, and the use of the flashing colors for these routings.

3. One can see a type of divination at work here in the magickal structures. We anticipate the opening up of an entirely new form of magickal computer work, which is of the Ma'atian variation and super-logic.

4. The nine magickal bodies of Z, which are the African or Afro-Atlantean archetypes are primordially ancient. It has been discovered that each contains its own inner universe of magickal initiations, experiments, research patterns, etc. Note the following:

"The inner world of the Afro-Atlantean archetypes may be understood as the deeper form of the Voudoo consciousness. Indeed, we may consider it as the Ma'atian form of Voudoo, because to be found therein are proper initiations, experiments and magickal exercises, and entirely new, yet strangely familiar, pantheons and universes for gnostic exploration."

5. It will be possible to establish a magickal dialogue with the entity of the archetype, or with various intelligences ←psychoid complexes) which indwell the archetype, in one of nine possible ways.

6. When the energy pours into the area of operation, it can be noted by radionic measurement. Then can be created within that deeper atmosphere, the space for the work. Words can be given and will be given to describe the magickal processes and parts of the archetype. A word-test may develop inside the archetype, so that magickal methods of working within this atmosphere both contentually (Tantra, Oracles) and formally (logical structures, Yantras) are possible for realization. The new archetypal universe of this deeper and Ma'atian level will provide a new atmosphere and context for some new modes of Ma'atian science.

Points of Entry to the Zothyrian Empire

The Zothyrian Empire of Gnostic Magick can be entered by means of 30 gnostic hot-points (points-chauds gnostiques). Each one of these points is both a way into the Empire and hence to one of the specific provinces of this magickal domain as well as being a system of magickal initiation, having its own oracular and experimental aspects. In the world of magickal hyper-logic, the Zothyrian Empire can be said to have its situs beyond the two to 12 range of the oracle of extraterrestrial intelligences. However, because it is an alternative universal system, rather than something outside of the orbit of Pluto, the oracular range of its magickal boundaries must be understood to begin with the universe of number 13. Using the oracular system of 11 possibilities to two pieces of dice, the measurements of the Empire beginning with 13 extend through the number 22. Each level of measurement can be understood as a simple range of logical archetypes, which when divided into two groups of 15 points each, can be seen as pouring both shakta and shakti into the logical system presented in Lesson 2 of this series (on the logics of Uranus, Neptune, and Pluto).

The nature of the Zothyrian Empire is that of the purest form of the gnostic logic of the ontic sphere. Because of the structures entailed in this logic, we find a very complete distribution of possibilities for several magickal and oracular systems. The inhabitants of the Zothyrian Empire are, of course, humanoid in our sense, but being entities of an alternative system have a culture closer to the esoteric forms of our gnosis rather than to terrestrial forms of materialism and superstition. In the history of Zothyrian philosophy, we have seen the development of many of their forms of mind as well as the patterns of their consciousness in non-egoic ways, when reflected in the mirroir of analysis. It is sufficient to say that these beings and their culture are quite self-contained in their wisdom, feeling that while they have much to share with us in the order, the world of ordinary mundane life has little to add to their culture or wisdom. Hence, our relationship to them is essentially a magickal one.

The Zothyrian culture has been influenced by the inside of the Nemiron system somewhat in that the other side of Orion is known in the Zothyrian universe. The structure of the Zothyrian Empire is completely Neo-Pythagorean in its form, since this school of gnosis had a profound influence upon the development of the Empire in its earliest phases. Of special importance is the notion that the Empire is a computer of prime-matter (prima materia), which means that form and content are everywhere ontologically and magickally. This also means that the 30 hot-points of entry are logical systems which have their own protocols for entry and therefore correspondingly oracular communication systems. Since each one of these logics is unique, so each point of entry is independent of every other point of entry, and also correspondingly each province of the Empire is totally autonomous. By such a logic, centralism and monopoly of information input has been overcome in the "politics of this computer."

A close analogy in the history of modern philosophy would be the monadology of Leibnitz. In fact, the initial exercises for making this type of gnostic contact started a number of years ago with my magickal essay on the "logic of symbolic monads," which was written over 20 years ago. It would be correct to state that each hot point of entry in this computer is a symbolic monad, therefore, in order to convey the proper image of the methods implied by such an imperial system.

Again, politically, we can state that the principle of government is immanent in the nature of the primary matter, which forms the universal composition of the system. The decision-making processes arise within the logic of the system, which always reflects the essence of The Emperor and The Council of State. This again is possible to a degree of harmony unknown in our universe because of the acceptance of the principle of universal hylomorphic composition and its Neo-Pythagorean and magicko-gnostic explication. Hence, we can see in the existence of the Zothyrian Empire more than just metaphysical idealism and fantasy as applied to research on alternative universes. For we can see the logical conclusions of the metaphysics of numbers and the hylomorphic ontology in their consistent and exact amplification, as applied to the logic of governmental languages.

Research Exercise in Cybernetic Hinduism

As Lord Shiva is the God of the Yogia, so Lord Agni is the God of the esoteric engineers and liturgical physicists and technicians of Cybernetic Hinduism and Vedic Physics. Consequently, the magickal systems of gnostic physics studied in our programs are acts of ritual offering and sacrificial worship to Lord Agni, and thusly by this writer they are intended as the rites of the new world religion of Universe A, Cybernetic hinduism, so that the religious atmosphere of some parts of Universe A might be closer to that of the Zothyrian Empire of Universe B.

Cybernetic Hinduism may be defined as the application of the logic of symbolic monads and the experiments of gnostic physics to the energies and universes of the Vedas and other branches of Hinduism. However, because it is centered in the worlds of Vedic and gnostic physics, as well as in yoga and the methodologies of Moksha, Cybernetic Hinduism is concerned with the logical control of energies and the technics of magickal sciences. In this lesson on the physics of the Nemiron and in the conceptualization of the 30 universes or points of entry to the Zothyrian Empire, and before we begin to give the formularies for the points of entry to this empire, it is essentialfor the student to begin his own self-preparation as the research exercise of this lesson. Thus, what he does in this lesson will prepare him for what is given out formally in the next lesson or in Nemiron Physics Lesson 4.

Since there are 30 worlds or provinces or points of enty to the Zothyrian Universe, the student should begin to make a list of 30 possible states of being, which might be the contents of these states of being. These states of being should be arranged in five groups. One group will have 10 types or states in it. Another group will have eight types in it. Another group will have six types of being in it. Another group will have four types of being in it. The last or final group will have two types of being in it. Now the types of beings in each group should show some kind of relationship, since in the next lesson there is a formal relationship between each member within a group. So in your list of members of each group or type of state of being, there should be some line of connection between each member of the group that you list. Then you will simply send in your list to me for my comments.

Cybernetic Hinduism makes a great deal of use of the magickal computer concepts of our system. In my work on the "Vedic Physics," I was able to bring in some basic tools in connection with how to build magickal computers and how to make better use of the magickal computers that we have already in use as students. Now, we are moving more and more in the direction of making use of more powerful magickal computers for use with the very high energies of the Vedic Physics. Let me give you an insight into this matter by means of the following equation:

Cybernetic Hinduism = Vedic Physics + Magickal Computers

You might consider that the basic definition also of much of our system, since the very internal tendencies of the gnosis are in the direction of Cybernetic Hinduism.

In order to create a magickal computer, you have to have input data, and that is why you are asked to make up the list of 30 states of being or things as data, arranged in five groups or classes. Once you have the data for use in your own magickal computer, and I am asking you to make lists which will be useful to you, so you should use ontic sphere and visualization methods for making the list, then you can receive from me the formal methods of organization of the data for use in amplification and gnostification. For a magickal computer adds and extends what is already known. It adds to what we feed into it, because it has a range beyond what is already known and it amplifies what is already known by transformation algebras, which are locked inside the computer, but which when they become active, release new energies to the magician. These energies constitute data for future research in magickal gnosis, making use of our gnostic computers. This is the entire idea behind the use of magickal techniques in relationship to the development of computer or cybernetic conceptualization.

In closing, let me encourage every student to begin their list, making it as carefully as possible so that they will not have to make too many changes later, when they begin to employ their data lists in connection with the formularies given in the next lesson.

Esoteric Electrical Engineering (EEE)
The Cosmic Computer

This course is written for those students of magick who are interested in the ways in which magickal energy fields work and who are interested in how to make such fields work. You are being allowed to take this course because, having completed previous course work, it is our understanding that you are able to embark upon the ocean of esoteric electrical engineering, which is one of the most technical forms of gnostic physics.

This lesson is about the cosmic computer of Alaya. The cosmic computer may be defined as:

"The cosmic computer: this term is used in esoteric Buddhism and in zothyrian physics to refer to the general information system, which operates as the fundamental basis of all engineering sub-systems and logics, and which is powered by the common energy of the four gnostic time-systems. The cosmic computer may be contrtacted by means of Aditi-Matrix, by means of esoteric logic, and by the input and output circuits of the general connective matrix."

The cosmic computer, then, is a technical system for making the operations of the magician to be and to become more successful. There is only need for one of these computers. However, any member who is trained in the EEE method will be able to make use of the system. That is to say, there will be in his area of operational control an approach system to the cosmic computer. In this sense, the magicians of our order all work together making use of the computer. This is the same computer as is used in the school of esoteric Buddhism known as Shingon-Shu.

The approach system to the computer may be understood as a kind of initiation into the EEE gnosis. This means that in addition to the papers of the system of training in what and how to do in EEE magick, there are four factors or conductors, which function as connectives between the student-EEE specialist and the cosmic computer operation. These conductors are:

Conductor 1 = The basic energy system entry line, which is assigned to the EEE student by M. Bertiaux. This functional system, which has a time-entry limit, gives the student as EEE operator his "space" within the general system.

Conductor 2 = The Aditi-entry circuit, which is assigned to the EEE student by M. Bertiaux via a fourth dimensional installation procedure and which is individuated to the requirements of the EEE student's field. This is an astro-gnostic and electro-gnostic logical system. It is a form of esoteric logic.

Conductor 3 = The generalized convector input and output linguistic entry pattern and system. This is installed personally by M. Bertiaux and has also built-in entry and exit controls for the EEE student's "movement" in the system.

Conductor 4 = This is the individualized space-time grid system or time-line and entry/exit pattern circuit, within the individually installed system, and assigned by M. Bertiaux to the EEE student for use in actualizing the data-field of the cosmic computer in the individual research framework of the EEE student. This is the RE level of operation.

These four conductors enable the student of the EEE initiation-mysteries to function within the general hookup of the system and thereby make it possible for the participation in the EEE computer to be a complete continuum-field.

Any conductor becomes a resistor if it introduces resistance into an esoterically logical and magickal circuit, whereby EEE energy from the cosmic computer is transformed into a level of gnostic experience and magickal thought. In order for a conductor to introduce resistance into such a logico-magickal circuit, it is necessary for it to be wired or connected astrally to the field of the resistor. This is done by introducing the conductor in question to one of four types of resistor-fields. These four types of fields are identified with our earlier notion of the "time-line." They are also given in Vedic physics and esoteric logic as research-lanes and we can say that contacting them through the various oracles of the gnosis, including Vedic physics, is probably the method most widely used in EEE research for introducing into the logico-magickal circuit. The four types of resistor-fields are therefore:

Resistor-field 1 = time-line = past/perfect; Resistor-field 2 = time-line = past/present; Resistor-field 3 = time-line = present/future; Resistor-field 4 = time-line = future.

By means of a combination of any Resistor-Field and any Conductor, we arrive at a functioning resistor in the system of EEE. The purpose of these resistors is to take those areas of connection to the center of the system which are the conductors as they are introduced by M. Bertiaux into the system of the student of the EEE energies and to relate these fields to the cosmic level of the system, which is behind the work of Mr. Bertiaux in relation to all conductors. Consequently, the movement of action from conductor to resistor involves an increase in the cosmic and dimensional aspect of the energy system and also introduces the student to personal encounters with the "gnostic Buddhas and other divine beings of the four time lines." In this connection it is important to keep a special notebook of magickal exercises, which are used in this level of operation; because it has been discovered that several systems of energy are derived from this basis for experimentation in consciousness.

For there are specially significant links between the four time stations, their beings and the four dimensions of the mind. It is important also to bring to awareness the fact that when operating this sytem you are outside of both space and time in the normal and ordinary sense, in fact you are simply beyond the present grid of consciousness, or the ego-space-time context.

This leads by means of an esoteric pathway to an entire system of secret initiations and power-developments. It suggests that in his work, Mr. Bertiaux is connecting the student to a very special frame of initiatic reference and to secret and highly specialized levels of esoteric logic and gnostic being.

Now, we would like to introduce a system of exercises for working with these energies.

You will first of all hold out your right hand in front of you and think about it being a conductor. At this point, it does not matter which conductor it is; but it is your conductor. Next, hold out your left hand in front of you and see it, thinking about it as being your resistor. Then, while both hands are still being held in front of you, simply let the palms of each hand face the opposite hand in an even manner. Next, you will study the energy patterns by thinking about energy flowing out of the palm of the right hand and meeting a different kind of energy coming out of your left hand's palm. In the middle of the area bounded by the two palms facing each other, imagine that you see a very tenuous line of light energy. This means that this is the exact place where resistance is met and where, therefore, a resistor is created of the energies coming from the two directions.

Concentrate on this area. Think of it as having its own being and purpose. It is alive in its own way and has its own Uranian energy. This is a center of magickal space for both thought and experience. Consequently, it is an area for the generation of a special type of being; because it is an area for very powerful future development and for the meeting of special beings of an initiatic type. Let us return to the conductor, or right hand palm.

Think of the right palm as being linked to Mr. Bertiaux by a kind of magickal thread or line of power. Think of Mr. Bertiaux as being at the other end of this line and you may visualize him as being there. On the other side, think of the left palm as sending out a line which goes very far out into space, at a very great distance, until it comes to a very special and magickal place, where the "Being of the Time Lines" resides. You may imagine this being as an elderly man, with a long beard and wearing long robe-like clothing. He is attended by others of like nature, who are his co-workers. They embody the energy of Saturn and embody that same planetary archetype. Then come back to the mid-point between the energies in the palms of your hands. See that as a doorway into another world or dimension. See that as leading to many other beings. By doing this exercise and repeating each part over and over again, it will become more and more powerful and link you more closely to those magickal and gnostic forces beyond the here and now and take you to cosmic realms.

You are beginningg your EEE work with this exercise. Make sure you send a report on your experiences to Mr. Bertiaux and you might do this exercise each day as a way of increasing your powers. For each time you will realize and visualize more closely and more completely the higher worlds and the EEE energies.

There exists a special esoteric section of the EEE energies. This section is under the special direction of the Holy Buddha, known as "The Great Illuminator." This section is composed entirely of esoteric and secret energies and substances and is known as the world of "esoteric idealism." There exist special initiations for this type of being and for those who wish to enter into this magickal universe. If you feel that you are ready, you will be invited by Mr. Bertiaux, as the priest of this inner sanctuary, to embark upon these esoteric mysteries. If you wish to participate in these esoteric mysteries and initiations, which are extensions of esoteric logic into the realm of the EEE energies, you will be invited by Mr. Bertiaux, again in his capacity as priest of the inner sanctuary, to be admitted into the inner school of the EEE course. It is not, however, a requirement that students of the EEE course participate in these mysteries; they seem open only really to those who feel a special desire and wish to form a link with the Great Illuminator of the system.

Esoteric Logic as Both Esoteric Idealism and Esoteric Initiation

The entire focus of magickal development for the serious and advanced student is to be found in the area of initiatic perfection of being. This means that each student must come to a certain inner and spiritual development, which leads that student deeply into the esoteric mysteries of Buddhist and Shinto-Gnostic idealism.

"The Esoteric Buddha Dainichi as well as many other spiritual beings are conneected by means of the master's spiritual field to the initiatic candidates. The powers have to flow through the master to the student or chela, in order for the energy-essence of the student to awaken. The master, who is connected by his own esoteric initiation to the Lord Dainichi, must serve as the doorway through which the student is brought into the clear light of mystical initiation. As the student moves closer and closer to the master, the student comes to realize that not only is the master close to the Esoteric Buddha, but really the master is the Esoteric Buddha, because he is now the embodiment of all of those special powers and energies, which constitute the manifestation of the Lord Dainichi, in human consciousness and experience." (M. Bertiaux, "Dainichi Revelations," 32)

Esoteric consciousness requires that all life be understood as the manifestation of the ideal and hence the metaphysics of idealism is the only viewpoint for coming to an understanding of being. Being is idealistically understood. Also, we must take into direct and exact consideration the powers which are generated from idealism. These powers are entirely magickal, because they are possible due to the presence of the idealistic metaphysics as the manifested world. So the most suitable form of consciousness has within it all of the mystical and magickal potencies for unfoldment. These potencies are spirit and life and they are storehouses of initiatic consciousness.

At the same time the master of the process has in his possession those secret powers, which draw out of the idealistic cosmos all of the suitable and high-frequency power, for he has possession within his very being of the keys to esoteric logic, which are in their purest sense energies from all being. These energies he controls by means of the laws of esoteric logic, given to him by the Esoteric Buddha at the time of his own true initiation and thereby stored up in the pure consciousness of his esoteric ideality, in anticipation of the needs of his students. When the student is ready the energy is then to be given by the master. This is the law of Esoteric Idealism, which exists truly to enlighten all beings with the esoteric energies of Dainichi.

"According to the 'laws' of Esoteric Idealism, the powers of the transcendental are directed to the master of the gnosis.The master must then serve as a vehicle for these powers, which manifest as esoteric teachings, initiations, magicks, and metaphysical diffusions. He, as the master of the gnosis must become an ideal conductor for the transmittal of esoteric energies from the Esoteric Buddha to the chelas of the world. In doing this, he fulfills the laws of his own personal destiny, or his own dharma. He becomes as it were a direct link between the Lord Dianichi and all of humanity." (M. Bertiaux, "Dainichi Revelations," 33)

Within the context of esoteric logic there is a law which asserts itself as the main and only principle of esoteric organization. It is the law which states that the whole system of being must be understood as consciousness. This consciousness rises within the context of manifestation and is also prior to its manifestation. This pure consciousness, which transcends all categories of thought is embodied in the esoteric logic of the master of the gnosis.

"The essence of being is pure consciousness, but unless that consciousness is manifested as esoteric logic, the power of initiation cannot be connected to the human mind. It is necessary to see the world of pure being as an ideal system of laws. But it is even more important to connect these laws to actual beings. This is accomplished by means of the esoteric logic of the master of the gnosis and in the process of his embodiment as an ideally transcendent form of Lord Dainichi; the master of the gnosis, as a matter of esoteric and logical necessity, which is identified with the necessity of his own being, he must as the master of the gnosis radiate out these powers and transmit them to the chelas, who have been especially selected for esoteric development, because of their own inherent powers." (Ibid., 34)

Naturally, as the consciousness of the master of the gnosis is seen more as a form of esoteric idealism and as the transcendental organization of his being as consciousness is seen more as the embodiment of the esoteric logic of Lord Dainichi, as his actions towards his students take on a more and more initiatic character. These actions become steps in the direct pathway of perfection and they become expressions of the most powerful and the most firmly grounded in being methodology of consciousness. These actions bcome the expressions of the total being of the master of the gnosis as the vehicle of the energies of the Esoteric Buddha. Once this is realized, the direct dealings of any type between the master and the student consist in and constitute a pattern of initiation wherein the student awakens to his divine essence and his oneness with Lord Dainichi.

Here is an exercise procedure for you to employ in order to develop an awareness of the Dainichi energy in your experience.

1. Become perfectly relaxed and enter into the pure meditation state of being-ness. There is that state you will feel the presence of the Lord Dainichi. You will see him as he directs the evolution of the universe within his own experience. The universe is an extension of his lifestream and mind-field.

2. You then should think of how you wish to grow and evolve in the techniques of magickal and mystical growth. Make a wish to become more and more powerful in the elaboration of your own inner spirituality and esoteric logic. If necessary, visualize the master of the teachings as the spokesman for Lord Dainichi.

3. All of the radiations from his cosmic body are magickal and mystical boddhisattwas. These beings are entering more and more into your experience. Begin to meet with them while you are in the inner state of mind and by means of directed prayer to the Esoteric Buddha, try to enter into mystical conversation with these spiritual beings.

4. See every object in the universe as a manifestation of the body of Lord Dainichi, and by doing this you can feel his power and life pouring into and running through every creature. By uniting with this feeling, it is possible to have the esoteric perception of unity with Lord Dainichi.

After you have completed these exercises, step by step, neither omitting nor changing any one of the four stages, you may feel called upon by Lord Dainichi to write to Michael Bertiaux and to ask for admission into the inner school of Esoteric Idealism. This is a school of initiation and esoteric logic, which was founded by Michael Bertiaux under the direct influence of the Esoteric Buddha. The purpose of this school of Esoteric Idealism is to bring about the renewal of human consciousness through the emmployment of the inner and more purposeful methods of esoteric logic. Each student of this method is given a special gift of spiritual direction by Michael Bertiaux, in order to grow and develop in the light and the powers of Lord Dainichi, as these forms of gnostic energy are to be found in the application of the laws of esoteric logic to human growth. The school was founded as the result of a direct inspiration from Lord Dainichi:

"The entire purpose of this school of Esoteric Idealism is to create a new mind field for the human race and to evolve humanity by direct participation in the light of the gnosis."   (Ibid.)

Transcendental Objectivity and the Initiations of Esoteric Idealism

"The world of transcendental objects is a realm beyond the constructions of the mind, but not beyond the powers of the occult imagination. It is where special initiations are to be given to those, who are ready to become perfected. In such a world, all of the categories of ordinary consciousness are absent. In their places, we have instituted the true beings of transcendental objectivity, or the special boddhisattwas of esoteric idealism, who assist me in the imparting of specific initiatios to those brought for this purely magickal and metaphysical development. In order to enter upon this consciousness, one must live fully in the being of consciousness and transcend the objectivity of what is to be perceived. Then one many enter upon the true understanding of this experience, which is the no-experience of idealistic energy."   (M. Bertiaux, "Dainichi Revelations, 16)

The world of initiation is the world which is brought back to ordinary life by the newly initiated. This world then adds its energy to our ordinary world and by this means it is able to express in a more powerful way all of the energies, which are to be found in the idealworld. Now, the world of ordinary life is. diffused with higher and higher forms of power because it now includes initiation and the initiatic energies.

Esoteric idealism is, of course, a system of purely metaphysicalconsciousness and has a certain possession within its heart, which is to be understood as the key to the more transcendental worlds, or the realms of ideal objectivity. These worlds are only for those who are initiates of the interior system, which means that only those who are inside of the esoteric idealist school of consciousness can perceive the world and all of its totality, both ideal and perceptual.

"The student of consciousness must exist within the school of esoteric idealism if he wishes to enter upon an understanding of the true conception of being. He must live in such a world and always be aware of the many dimensions and pathways, which exist there and which lead to light and enlightenment. Pure consciousness exists as the substance of that world and by coming to an understanding of initiation, the student enters the idealworld of transcendental objectivity, of which he knew formerly only symbolically but now which he knows as ideal and true. He now possesses the secret presence of the master of the gnosis and by means of these forms of esoteric understanding, he is guided closer and closer to this true being. There he becomes transformed, because he has taken on the new power of being, that is to say, he has become an ideal object himself. He now is the true form of consciousness, whereas before he was consciousness only imperfectly."   (Ibid., 17)

So the purpose of initiation appears to be the development of the true identity of the student of our system. This can only happen in this system, I might add, because of our special link with the Esoteric Buddha, the Lord Dainichi. Othere possess a link, but we possess that special link created by means of esoteric logic.

In the field of esoteric logic, there exists a world of transcendental objects as well as the realm of transcendental subjectivity. The exercises of esoteric logic, which are primarily magickal, consist in making a link between these two realms of being in the experience of the student, who is in the process of initiation. The master of the gnosis, or the guru, envelops the student in his own field, whereby the student is entailed, included, implid and equivalent to the guru in his own field.

This magickal process is set forth in all of the oldest traditions of the gnosis, where the rituals and proper procedures of this magickal process are clearly defined.

But, from the standpoint of esoteric logic, this process must be extended beyond the human level of experience and must include the Esoteric Buddha, the Lord Dainichi, as a part of the process and continuum. This is done because the purpose of the guru is to become for the student the total embodiment of the Esoteric Buddha. Consequently, the guru must "bring down into himself" the essence of the Esoteric Buddha. The guru does have the power to do this type of magick, because in his initiation as guru into the mysteries of esoteric logic and meontology, he has united in his being the realms of transcendental objectivity and subjectivity. In other words, he has become the field of esoteric logic in human format.

Then, as the student unites himself more and more closely to the guru, and this is done by means of instructions in esoteric idealism and various gnostic exercises, the guru transmits, by means of telepathic gnosis (a procedure which cannot be defined as it is entirely a form of esoteric magick) certain powers and occult energies from the Esoteric Buddha to the student, through the physical and metaphysical bodies of the master, so that the student takes on more and more of the esoteric and occult qualities, which the Esoteric Buddha possesses as pure being and pure consciousness—energy.

The result is that the student becomes more and more of a perfected being. But at the same time, he enters more and more upon being an extension in a self-conscious way, of the Esoteric Buddha. However, the purpose of this process of initiation is more than just a becoming. It is to achieve identification with Lord Dainichi to the point of self-intuition.

"The process of self-intuition is achieved or realized when the guru, having been united with the esoteric continuum of logic, idealism, and Buddha, unites his consciousness with that of the student. When this happens the power of the student is known by the intensity with which the student has a self-intuition of the consciousness of the guru. In the process, the student therreby uniting with My Divine Being through the guru, achieves the total and most perfect understanding and experience of his own mind. In order to realize this process of transformation, it is necessary for the student to destroy his limited selfhood, that he may take on the infinite selfhood of the Esoteric Buddha, through the initiation consciousness of the guru. (M. Bertiaux, "Dainichi Revelations," 8)

Here is an exercise to help you realize certain levels of spiritual freedom, which exist deeply within your soul-consciousness. First of all, relax and enter into the inner and spiritual side of meditation. There in that world you will realize that you are experiencing the application of one of the principles of esoteric idealism, since you are within the world of pure consciousness. Next, you will see all of being as an amplifiction of the lifestream of the Esoteric Buddha, Lord Dainichi. This means that you will perceive all being as if experiencing it for yourself and within your own being. You will take on the body-consciousness of the infinite body of bliss. While you are in this state of attunement, you will come to the realization that all being is interconnected to where you are and what you are doing. You will see yourself as pure essence.

Answer these questions carefully and send your responses to Michael Bertiaux, in order to help him prepare you for esoteric initiation.
1. How do I see the loss of limited selfhood and the taking on of infinite selfhood?
2. Ho do I feel or experience the Esoteric Buddha, Lord Dainichi? Give examples.

3. Do I feel comfortable within the "infinite body of bliss"? What does this mean?
4. Now that the world no longer exists as ordinary, how do I attune myself to being continuously aware of the world as pure and extraordinary?
5. Do I see myself as perfection? How do I understand perfection of my being?
6. Am I aware of why and how esoteric idealism is so powerful?
7. What is the connection between Lord Dainichi and esoteric logic?
8. Why are the initiations of esoteric logic so all-powerful?

Sutratmic Researches, Lesson 1

In the occult literature of the Hindus, there is the concept of the Sutratman or the "thread-self." This concept refers primarily to the ongoing aspect of the self, which, thread-like, gathers experiences as permanent atoms from lifetime to lifetime. The easiest way of understanding this concept is to look at the magickal rosary. Understand that the beads represent the permanent atoms, which contain the physical, astral, mental and spiritual experiences of past lifetimes (as well as future lifetimes in a very exact but initiatic way), the thread represents the ongoing self, which holds them in its own system of self-reference. This notion is very important to our school of magick, for we accept the doctrine of the permanent and indestructible self of Jainism, Hinduism, Islam, and Gnostic Catholicism, rather than the generally understood Buddhist viewpoint. In fact, the sutratman is an argument in favor of the personalization of the cosmic computer. It is the cosmic computer inside each of us, other than this view, all of its implications are magickal and gnostic. We might well best be thought to be inside of the sutratman, since the physical self is simply one part of this system. In fact, the physical self in its world of space and time is simply one bead of manifestation.

We understand that all our past lifetime experiences are concentrated on the beads of the sutratman. Akashic readings consists of coming to terms with the beads of the physical set as they form a series. However, only magicians of our school, realizing the logic of time travel, which states that past, present, and future are equally real, appear to be the only gnostics which possess the techniques for exploring the "future beads" existing on the structural planes of the sutratman.

There are no lessons written about research and initiation into the future beads of the sutratman, but the magickal process exists and is used almost daily. I simply want to say that it exists and that we make use of it, so as to indicate to the student that our own methods are entirely consistent and that they are applicable both to the past and the future, as well as to the present.

From the standpoint of gnostic physics, we can say that there are 11 basic logics for opening up the contents of the past beads, 11 for the present, and 11 for the future dimensions of the experience of the self. On the inner planes, we can find that there exist extremely powerful connectives to each one of these points of the computer, so that we can speak of 33 contacts. These contacts are important indicators of the operations of three different magickal equations from a total of 256. So we find a connection with our 256 logics, discussed in many previous papers. The connectives are managed by various specialist entities or intelligences, from the Gnostic General Continuum. The Gnostic General Continuum might best be described as the methodological continuum of intelligences allied to our system from the beginning of time. In other words, its level of operation is archetypal and the beings which make it up may be viewed as archetypal gods and also as ideal substances. Now the basic energy of contact between all of these components of the system is gnostico-magickal, which means the basic sexo-radioactive energy of our system.

Each bead of the Sutratman gives off a certain type of magickal radiation which can be defined at that moment by oracle methods. The results of these oracles, which are mandalas of magickal numbers, form the exact pictures of the bead and thusly enable us to see where it is "located." We can thusly make maps of each bead and the accuracy of the map would simply depend upon the degree that the student is locked into the system, i.e., initiated into the gnosis. Hence the accuracy of the maps of each bead or component of the system is based upon a method close to the guruyoga procedures of EEE.

Once the map of the component has worked itself out or into our egoic mind, we can see that each bead is connected or linked to the Sutratman of the whole system, which might be best understood as the computer of our order. The reason is very simple. Only those who are already locked into the system will find that the components of their logic work in accord with the general system of the order. This means, of course, that only previous members of our order in this area of gnosis would be present members of this level of operation. Superficial members who have not been attached by the permanent atomic link, or the permanent atoms of their system and ours, would be active in some other region, but not in this innermost region of gnostic space, reserved for the highest initiates of the inner school of The Monastery of the Seven Rays (The Seven Stars).

Exercise for Developing the Magickal Sutratman
In order to better understand the nature of this magickal Sutratman, the following exercise has been designed for members of our inner circle. Please follow instructions given in this section and send in your report to M. Bertiaux.

First of all, make a list of the numbers from one through 11. These will be the number of beads you will be working with in this experiment. These beads will represent the magickally developed "permanent atoms" that are strung along the gnostic rosary of your own inner Sutratman. In order to provide direction for you, the following are the suggestions as categories for the beads of the Sutratman.

Number One will refer to the past and here you may describe an incarnation on another planet in another solar system. This would be the oldest permanent atom on your present rosary or experimental string.

Number Two will refer to the past and here you may describe an incarnation on another planet of this solar system. Identify this planet as best you can as Pluto, Neptune, etc. This is the magickal life which follows the memories stored in permanent atom Number One.

Number Three will refer to the past and to a past incarnation on this planet probably but not necessarily in either Lemuria or Atlantis.

Number Four will refer to the past and to a past incarnation on this planet and probably either in Europe, Asia, Africa, or North or South America.

Number Five will refer to the present and to your incarnation in Universe A, where you are now and where you are working as a magickal student in our gnosis and inner circle.

Number Six will refer to the present and to that part of you which is incarnate in Universe B, an alternative magickal universe, which is existing in the now, but different from this type of universe in which we now reside physically and are taking studies from Michael.

Number Seven will refer to the present and to that part of you which is incarnate magickally in Universe C, D, E, F, or G, or some other system, somewhere in our universe but then not in our immediate universe. Such a universe would open up in Sirius, Orion, etc., and be the inner universe, which is approached via those doorways.

Number Eight will refer to the future and to your next incarnation and where you will be. You may be on earth, working with our order in setting up a gnostic government.

Number Nine refers to the future and to a future incarnation on another planet in this solar system. Tell me all about it so I can see how well you are developing. Make sure to let me know what planet you have selected and why.

Number Ten refers to a future incarnation and to your magickal life probably on a planet in another solar system. Tell me how to locate it so I can send you your lessons.

Number Eleven refers to a future incarnation in another universe, probably somewhere in the Zothyrian system, at some very great distance in thought from the present earth system.

These 11 categories are to be filled in with magickal contents taken from the logical and ontical work of the magickal imagination, which will transport you beyond the present to ten different realms and psychological situations. Each student is clairvoyant and each student has in his consciousness magickal and gnostic keys to the ontical spheres of his own inner world and awareness. You are to begin the process of seeing yourself as you truly are by means of this exercise.

By this we mean that you are all of these 11 categories in actuality. Really you are many more than these but you are all of these and you shuld develop a genuine magickal sense of your selfhood by means of this exercise, which is probably one of the most complete and systematic in our school. You can amplify this exercise in any number of ways and you can send me any kind of report you wish, just as long as you list entries for the 11 magickal categories, which represent the permanent atoms of your magickal selfhood as well as spaces and types of consciousness for your own magickal experimentation. As a consequence, you will find the magickal work you have done before to be extremely helpful in giving you ideas of other worlds in which you incarnate. Also, remember that with the passage of incarnations from one bead to the next you should find your sensations -- especially your sexual sensations -- intensified, since we have been told by the adepts of our own system that in the future we will have bodies made entirely of libido, i.e., cosmic lust in a neverending state of total orgasm. I look forward to your reports.

In the development of the structures of magickal consciousness, it is important to see how various sustems of magick are all interconnected. That is where the methodology of control is to be found. Thusly, by entering into the vital essence of any system, by means of the intentional extraction of its essence and all essential components, we gain magickal control over any and all systems which come before us. In this sense, we are able to create an important and necessary connection between every system of magick, as we string them like the magickal beads they are on the thread of our ultimate logic of total penetration. In a sense then, each system in existence is a prospectivve candidate for this transformation of "ownership," and each system by means of its own inherent logic moves more and more towards this type of systematic and systemic possession by the masters of the cosmic computer.

As the permanent atoms of past lifetimes are strung along the magickal thread of the egoic ideal, so the components of every magickal system in existence, both actual and potential, are so gathered and possessed by the technics of magickal computer science. We have simply to pick up on the essence of the system, translate and define it according to the terms of Algol (either the star or the computer system, take your choice, you may take both) and then feed the structure into the system which comprehends all other systems: the cosmic computer of our field of magickal physics.

Therefore, of particular importance is the ideal of bringing in a wide variety of existing systems as possible components for the logical analysis of the computer. The computer is the mechanism for receiving and developing all systems and ultimately by means of its energy, the gnosis is extended into areas formerly beyond its control.

What we might ask is what is the power or the fuel which keeps our magickal computer going? Well, we can say that it operates on the basis of a very interesting energy. That energy is synchronicity. Usually, synchronicity has been thought of as a way to describe the way things happen. Actually, it is only that at its most elementary manifestation. In actual fact, it is a cosmic energy and those who have experimented with its operations find that it possesses very significant qualities. It was only a matter of time before this energy was explored from a gnostico-magickal standpoint in physics. As a consequence, it has been discovered to be the natural energy behind the cosmic computer. This means that the Cosmic Computer has been found to function on a basis of this energy in its most advvanced forms.

When Jung stated that synchronicity was acausal, he meant that it is not a physical type of energy, subject to the laws of positive science. However, it does happen and in this we find it particular type of causality. That is, a causality which is metaphysical or beyond positive science. However, I am not interested in talking about this aspect as it has been worked over considerably. What I am interested in is the way in which this system, for that is what it is, functions within the processes of the cosmic computer. In this sense, we can learn about both the computer and its power.

Time is another component in this system. For one thing, time appears to be behind both causality and synchronicity. So there are at least two ways of relating time to things. Also, time-travel and temporal restructuring are possible so that they would seem to imply a particular relationship to time. Then of course there are the relationships between primary matter and time, and often these relationships are those of entailment.

On the basis of this process of analysis, which is ever ongoing, we can discern the beginnings of some new type of gnostic physics. The name would be archaeometry, which is the name we have used in the past (at seminars and research programs) for time-travel. Related to this is also the methodology of what is known as Soufi physics, or the magickal physics of the Soufis, or mystics of the Islamic religion. For it would appear that the empirical evidence (in this we are not concerned with subjective religions and revelations from ego-tripping types) supports a movement in the direction of Soufism in its neo-pythagorean phase, via the patterns of synchronicity and archaeometry. In this case, the rigid and absolute control of every system of magickal physics, from Ma'atian to Soufi, would rest with the absolutists of our system, to the esoteric logicians, who having entered deeply into the logic of all systems, have attached them to the thread of their master system, and who have invested them with patterns of temporal restructuring in the various nodes of the gnostic continuum.

Exercise in the Gnostic Structures of the Ego: Their Constructions Beyond Inflation

1.1 The structure of the ego as it is understood in the initiatic doctrine is that which is constructed by the Sutratmic continuum of the Self from the contents of the various levels of magickal physics. You have already studied some papers which deal with the gnostic inflation of the transcendental ego and also some of our magickal physics. Now, you will draw a model of the magickal self as you see it based on what you have learned. This may be a map.

1.2 In this map -- or drawing or diagram --- you should integrate the materials which come to your mind as arising out of the purpose and presentation of the field of interactions between the ego and the magickal archetypes of being. How do you see them?

1.3 At a certain level of consciousness, we work with a pair of six-sided or faced dice. After some time, we cannot work with that level. We have to move on to work with eight, 12, 4, or 20-sided dice systems. The transition from the earlier stage of gnostic inflation to the ego to the Sutratmic construction parallels the transition to more complex types of dice and their proper oracles from the less complex but more common realms of consciousness. How do you understand this development?

1.4 The purpose of the several studies in gnostic physics, Nemiron, Zothyrian, VVedic, etc., is to make it possible for us to have a clear picture of what is happening magickally in the structure of the gnostic ego. We are not concerned with structures of other types of egos, which are really only partial pictures of the self. The Jungian view comes closest to our own but even the Jungian view has to be radically expanded as we have seen from the Necronomicon physics. What is your view of this matter and tell me about some of your own experiments in this area for enlarging the Self.

1.5 Lastly, when we talk about physics we are really talking about archetypal psychology. Magickal gnosis does not make the distinction between what is inner and what is outer. The continuum is in both points of the operation. Physics and psyche are both functions of consciousness. This is pure idealism. Make a map of diagram showing me how both physics and psyche are parts of this continuum. Use as much of your magickal mind and imagination as you need. Then send your report to me.

Transyuggothian Power Secrets: The Doorway

The doorway to the powers is outside of Yuggoth (the planet Pluto) but it connects to the zone of the planet Pluto by means of the magickal computer lineages, which our magickal brotherhood alone possesses. This doorway resembles in all outer forms the mirroir-magique of the Haitian esotericists, but its esoteric function is much more specialized and exacting. In fact, its function is set forth as conveying the magickal energies from the 16 zones of alternative space to the center of our order.

Students in the various parts of the world are linked up to this doorway by means of a simple inductive process. They are literally fed into the computer and passed through operation-spaces of the mirroir-magique through the doorway to the Nemiron Brotherhood in the star system of Orion. There on Rigel in another dimension is to be found the major headquarters of our system. However, the work of this center is perfectly reflected in the operations of our order here in this solar system. The student of magick will be reduced to his logical form and by the methods of "Intentional Reduction" he wil be conveyed consciously to Rigel from the laboratory/ transmission station in Chicago.

There, upon arrival, they will enter into their own personal magickal development. This process will be reflected in the magickal exercises which they will encounter, here, in the laboratory/transmission station. Part of them will be in Chicago and part will be in Rigel. Elaborate testing of each stage of the process has been the requirement of the Research Leadership, the Nemiron, in order to assure the total correctness of this process.

You may want to know what will be the result of this process. The answer is that part of the person can be worked on by the Nemiron. This part would be the superconscious and unconscious levels of the mind. The conscious and subconscious levels of the mind remain in the field of the work in Chicago. During the process, the superconscious and unconcsious level of the mind undergo specialized treatment from the Nemiron technicians with the goal in mind that these dimensions of the mind become instruments for the work of the Rigel Empire, here, on earth. In other words, you receive training through this doorway in order to function more and more suitably in working with the Nemiron energies, especially in their Zothyrian format.

The magickal development of these two dimensions of the mind has to do with the inner side of the Ojas research. The Ojas power is amplified in a variety of ways, each stage being measured, and this amplification process extends the powers of Ojas in the ways in which it is found in the student's field into deeper and deeper mysteries of its manifestation. The secrets given in this process are literally of the highest Transyuggothian power. It would be primitive to think of this meta-scientific process as initiatic because of the thought-forms associated with the concept of initiation.

The Nemiron are not concerned with the reactions of favor or disfavor from among the many possible candidates in the magickal world. They do not need that type of information, rather they are concerned simply with the extension of their own powers through this doorway, which exists simply to create able workers for their cause here on earth at the present time. Any other terrestrially-generated frame of reference, no matter how fruitful it might seem to the mundane consciousness, is uninteresting and unimportant from their point of view. Total involvement in their frame of reference and work by means of the doorway is what is now demanded.

Transyuggothian Physics Course Lesson 1, "Methods of Initiation"

Because the laboratory and research center have replaced the temple in the magickal work of the present age, so also the methods of magickal initiation have changed, bringing them closer to and more in harmony with the Mercury–in–Aquarius mentality. This mentality cannot tolerate anything which bespeaks the past, especially in methods of attainment. It is oriented towards scientific and speculative inductions and the use of the hypothetico–deductive method in esotericism in a very exacting way. In secular philosophy, the best example of this would be the cosmological system of Alfred North Whitehead, a native of Aquarius.

Therefore, those older temples have been replaced as well as the concept and imagery of temples, ritual working, etc. That mentality has been tossed into the void and in its place the careful method of magickal science has been restored from the Atlantean age or aeon. In this new setting for consciousness, we find the following methods of initiation opperating and linking up the students with transcendental and immanent fields: arithmosophical reductions, association tests and measurements of Ojas, arithmosophical madalas as indicators of Ojas, psionic reactors for testing levels of Ojas radioactivity, magickal computer tests for establishing fields of energy, and lastly, reactor–computers such as the computer–marga for reduction, reversal and restructuring of time, and ontic broadcasting.

Each one of these methods of initiation has as its purpose the extension of consciousness beyond its present field towards its real level of actualization. In case someone might wonder what this level was, or if it existed, the answer is simply that it does exist and that it is provided as a read-off from the wavelengths of the Transyuggothian Transmission Station. Very little has been said in lessons about this station, yet whatever has been said about any field of physics, magickal, gnostic, Vedic, Tantric, etc. has certainly presupposed the existence of the Transyuggothian Transmission Station, an information system given to our order by the Nemiron through their agency within the Zothyrian System. In every instance, the operations of this system have been presupposed because of the need for both information–directions as well as energies to perform the specified experiments of the various systems developed. At the present time, the full range of these operations is only possible in Chicago, due to the presence of the highly sensitive instruments (both physical and metaphysical). However, with time, it is anticipated that there will also be a comparable laboratory in Asia. At least this is the declared wish of the leadership of this research system.

As a magickal exercise in the development of initiatic powers, and especially the powers to enter upon the program of initiation as it is understood by our system, the student is now directed to make a list of those methods provided in name only on the previous page. He is then asked to describe the contents of these methods and to make diagrams, if needed, in order to illustrate and amplify the answer to this project. He may answer the question any way he wishes, and in some instances he will have available to him back lessons where some of these methods are discussed. He might also have newsletters, reports, and other papers which describe these methods somewhat.

However, I am not concerned about simply reading what has already been written. I am much more interested in learning from the magickal student what he thinks these methods are, or better, what he thinks they should be like if he were the chief administrator of research in our system. Only by this method of magickal work can he project himself beyond being a student to the highest regions of this magickal system on Orion. After you have prepared your response to this exercise, examine carefully what you have written. Make any adjustments you might feel like doing before mailing it to me. It is an excellent idea to rest or nap after doing the exercise, so that any latent deeply unconscious contributions can come up and be added on to what you have already done. In this way, various levels of the mind will operate in your work and not just the egoic level of the active intellect. Then when you are satisfied with what you have done, mail the report to me for evaluation.

Transsyuggothian Powers Course: The Masters of Magick

The Masters of Magick indwell the system of our order and they are its life and all of its powers. They possess the supreme secrets and powers of magick and they control the destiny of this planet by their magickal techniques. Who are these Masters of Magick? They are simply secret beings. They come and go and no one knows anything more about them than that they came and went somewhere. However, students of this system who belong to the innermost part of the order, may understand certain things about these Masters of Magick. You may understand that the Masters of Magick are usually members of the French occult tradition except when they are Russian or Thibetan. Of course, there are many other Masters connected with other systems, but these do not interest us. We really have more than enough working with our own Masters of Magick.

All of these Masters of Magick are connected by the most powerful magickal and occult links to Michael Bertiaux. Now this does not mean that he is the only person so connected, but it does mean that he is connected with very powerful Masters of Magick, who provide him with the materials given in his lessons and course materials. There are other courses in existence and I am sure that they are doing much to help the evolution of the human mind. However, for ourselves, there is the course work written by Michael Bertiaux and the sources for that course work written by Michael Bertiaux are those beings which can be identified as the Masters of Magick.

Now these masterful beings, by being connected with the French tradition, have diffused a specific power which is unique and highly creative. This is not a current to be found in other traditions but is unique to the constructions of the French Magickal Ego. For you see, the French Ego, having surrendered its vast colonial empires to the races of the earth, has asserted its Magickal Ego through the Masters of Magick. We cannot say that this is morally good or bad, those are meaningless questions. We can only say that it appears to be a fact. Perhaps the most powerful of those Masters of Magick is Docteur Boullan. This Master of Magick fought the Rosicrucians for many years and finally defeated them in France, at the end of the last century. Boullan was identified with the ultra–rightwing of the then French political scene. Actually, he was identified with the ultra–royalists, the followers of Naundorfisme. Traditionally, the Masters of Magick have been more to the right than to the left, because they are ruled by conservative (Saturn) and reactionary (Pluto) power zones. Or, rather, they participate actively in such movements and give to the ultra–forces their magickal support. In doing this, these Masters of Magick have sought to move certain structures in a direction more favorable to absolute monarchy. It was Oswald Wirth who stated that Boullan wanted to be the Pope, i.e., not the Roman Catholic Pope, but the magickal replacement of the Roman Pontiff.

Now, the minds which indwell these Masters of Maggick have undergone a number of transformations since the 19th century. But certain structures remain. The energies are now directed towards higher and higher stages of personal development and possession for the magician, even at the risk of his being identified by some as a black magician. We know in actual fact that he is a true magician. Furthermore, by means of the secret principles of sexual magick, which are given in this course in their fullest sense, the reactionary powers of Pluto are brought to their perfection in the secret patterns of Transyuggothian initiation.

This is not a system of magickal initiation derived from terrestrial traditions but this is a system which is wholly derived from points of power outside of Pluto (Yuggoth). The Masters of Magick have been able to transcend the distances, or what we term distances,and have brought back to Michael Bertiaux the power secrets of the beyond worlds and universes. The powers of the stars, especially those of Rigel in Orion, having been fully possessed by Boullan, are now fully known and controlled by the inner powers of our system. Therefore, it is only a matter of translating these powers into concepts which can be understood by the mundane magickal consciousness and then given these forms, initiating the chelas of these Masters of Magick into the secrets and their powers, locking them into the magickal computer of the system, before the energies will be released upon the human mind outside of the magickal confinements of our system. Then, the human mind will learn that there are these Masters of Magick and that their powers are absolute.

There exist within the temple logics of our system strange ways in which the powers from beyond Yuggoth are brought down to mundane consciousness. These are the secret exercises into which the students selected by Dr. Boullan are initiated and admitted as workers. Dr. Boullan has stated that because of his position in the system, being outside of space and time, he alone is in a position to select those who will be admitted into his own system. For this magickal sphere is his own personal order. Dr. Boullan has also stated that the energies which are manifesting themselves at this time inside the order will never be lost or misapplied because they are energies which are released by his power zone and only by his power zone. Finally, Dr. Boullan —— working with several astral entities —— has created and will continue to create magickal pictures of the destiny of each being in the order and these pictures, having been infused with consciousness, will become the magickal vehicles for travel by the chelas of these Masters of Magick beyond Yuggoth.

This method of image-projection will allow the chelas of the system to experience in a manner identical to that of his physical body all of the sensations of these remote realms, stars, worlds, as they can be fully experienced in the human body. This extreme teaching is what has been found to be behind the religious myth of the Resurrection of the Physical Body and also behind the mythos of the Corporeal Assumption of the Body of Lady Mary. These magickal processes will therefore become facts of human experience because of the powers which are now coming into this world of human consciousness from these Masters of Magick.

The Ojas–Yuggoth Papers: The Yuggoth Ray

The power base of our order is to be found within the deepest regions of the ultra-unconscious as it is located on the planets Pluto, Neptune, and Uranus. Of these three points of power, Pluto or Yuggoth is the most important. For contained within the lust–field of Pluto we can easily locate several magickal constructions, all of them necessary for the operations of the order on this planet.

Several tests have been performed in order to determine whether or not the fixed stars are a more significant source of gnosis, magick, and power than Yuggoth. For while it is true that teachings and important communications of a research character come from the fixed stars, such as our Nemiron contact work, at the same time the Pluto contact has always been very significant for our structures and together with Neptune and Uranus, we find that Pluto possesses a cosmic and infinite quality in its power, magick, and gnosis. Each person in the world has the potential for this type of contact work. It is very simple to estimate and it is done by computer astrology. You simply have the fixed stars run in connection with the casting by computer of your natal chart. The more evolved types of mind will have interesting aspects to certain fixed stars. This means that these fixed stars are symbolic points or hot-points within your field of consciousness, or the totality of your egoic and id energies.

If you want to develop your contacts with these points you can do so easily and in a way closely parallel to the way you develop other inner qualities. Magick and meditation are probably the most successful methods in terms of results. All of the members of the imperial Zothyrian household have this done as a condition of admission to membership in the magickal laboratory system. Therefore, each person had at birth and still has the cosmic potential for contacts with Rigel Sirius, Alcyone, etc. You simply have to go inside and work on these matters. But we also have the planets outside of Saturn and these three planets are also within us. However, they might not be powerfully enough aspected to bring in much magickal powers. However, I have noticed that members of the inner circle of our system are all strongly Plutonian. This having been established by computer astrology is not dependent upon the revelations of mediumistic priestesses and other self–appointed magickal leaders.

My own personal position is quite interesting. In order for the outer planets to make any significant contact with the personality, or inner space of your mind, they must make very strong aspects such as squares and conjunctions and oppositions to the Sun, Moon, and ascendant. There are other personal points, too, but Sun, Moon, and Rising Sign are most significant and necessary for outer planet contacts. Because you are the Sun, Moon,and Ascendant Energy more than anything else.

Years ago, my chart was done by certain Haitian magicians and it was found that I had Sun confronting Uranus by square and Pluto by opposition. Uranus was square to my Pluto and Pluto was conjunct my Moon. Neptune was conjunct my Ascendant. It was necessary to bring in all of these energies into my being in order to place me in a position to head the work of our order and naturally (Uranus+Pluto) destroy all other orders, even our "allies." Of course, this is a very long term operation and will take a while to organize. However, the first item of business was to assemble the old order. I had to establish contacts with them. They are everywhere in the world and that is still quite a task.

However,there is one sign which is used to determine whether or not they are old members of our Bon-Po system and that is the sign of the Yuggoth (Pluto) Ray. For they carry it within themselves wherever they are found. Hence, as my name and vibration were known more and more around the globe, these members of the old order cam forward and made contact with me. A number of persons made contact with me, of course, but among the many were the few very technical magicians, who were with me in the past, in the old Bon-Po system. The Yuggoth Ray manifested long ago on this planet in the Bon-Po system, or the ancient religious magick of Thibet. One of the older leaders of our system, now a Master of Magick, is the Bon deity rDo rje gying chen. This magickal being might be considered the pure embodiment of the Yuggoth Ray because his magickal vitality is to be found in every member of our order. Actually, there are various rites for the explication of this being's presence in each and every member. For by a curiosity of karmic connection, he is the Yuggoth Ray in its Ojas manifestation. He is the container of magickal potencies and when a new member is admitted into the secret, he rises to the surface of the egoic mind from the deeper regions of the ultra unconscious and manifests through his oracle. At that point the young or new member of the secret is transformed into an oracle-presence of the divine radiations of Yuggoth. This constitutes the initiation sacrament in its formal side. The material side consists of the substance of the transformation, which is pure Ojas power.

One of the interesting communications from this Master of Magick happened during the thought formation session on December 23, 1980, at about 6 p.m. It was determined that this being having been the Guardian of the Bon-Po Oracles of the Ojas-Yuggoth Ray expressed his wish to transform the teachings by making them even more radical and powerful. By means of a magickal operation which involved the Uranus and Pluto energies, and these are naturally infinite points of endless monadic power, this Master of Magick sought to increase the types of magickal instruction and the levels of being given out as supplementary instruction by various Thibetan methods.

We can understand that this procedure is to characterize the tone of the 1981 thought-form of the order and will manifest itself in a variety of magickal ways. New levels of magickal power will be released via papers and initiation rites and the reading of each lesson will constitute magickal types of initiation in themselves. We have always known this to be true from the past. Now, we will see how these forces are to be actualized in preparing the order for its mission in this incarnation. Those members who wish to receive, therefore, the newer Bon-Po instructions should contact me immediately in order to be evaluated.

Inner Spaces Color Languages No. 7
One of the most important areas of inner space or inner plane communication depends upon the use of color as its vehicle for intentionality/telepathy. By this we mean that while terrestrial intelligence depends upon a color spectrum, this is not the case with extra-terrestrial intelligence, where a different logic operates. For example in the Zothyrian System R31-C, which may be viewed as simply one from many sources, in place of the simple color spectrum from ultraviolet to infra-red, we are in a position to view that line simply as an abstracted instance from the total continuum. Instead of thinking of colors as extending in a band either vertically or laterally, we should think of them as being, to our minds at least, as being both.

This means that if we needed some kind of image, it should be of columns of colors, differing in varied degrees of intensity but classed logically by implications so that, for example, the end terms of any series might well be forms of ultraviolet and infra-red, although these terms or frames might well be quite different, and would of necessity have to be, seemingly disjunct, and alien to the beginning terms of any series. However, this is perhaps the only way we can think of extra-terrestrial types of color. The following diagram might well provide us with a helpful image:

ultraviolet (1)	green (1)	infra-red (1)
ultraviolet (2)	green (2)	infra-red (2)
ultraviolet (3)	green (3)	infra-red (3)

Whereas, sequence (1) would be typical of certain extra-terrestrial zones and which might extend beyond that series, and indeed be projected to such a level, as we might associate with certain Yuggothian realms of consciousness, i.e., the astral counterpart of the planet Pluto. Sequence (2) pertains to our normal terrestrial range and may be complex in the sense that it is composed of many subordinate series. Series (3), on the other hand, might well be composed of a sequence and subordinate sets in some kliphotic universe, etc. The possibilities are endless and by reason of the relations of inclusion, entailment, equivalence, and implication these colors can be found in everything in the same realm. We call this phenomenon "interpenetration." This rule may allow us to abstract any sequence-system from any situation simply by means of exploring magickally the subject and finding all the other colors entailed or included therein.

Now, each of these sequences forms a logical metageometry of its own and thusly is the basis of a telepathic language, which may operate as any language-logic operates by means of holding intentions telepathically. This means that color can be used as a magickal computer for the inner meaning, which uses color as its space-vehicle. This is explored in another paper.*

*"How intentions and magickal meanings were used in telepathic color rays by the medieval zothyrian philosophers of language," by Michael Bertiaux, Hist. of Medieval Zothyrian Philosophy, Lesson 81.

Tantric Physics: The Brahminical Secret

The secret of the Brahmins is to be found at the basis of the magick of Tantric Physics. This secret exists at the root-essence of organic Hinduism and is to be found in the deepest levels of the Hindu brain by reason of some strange genetic mutation, the direct intervention of the Mother Goddess Herself, and this secret realizes its Power (Shakti) as a self-conscious and independent type of being at the level of the ultra-conscious mind of the priestly caste.

This mutation of the brain tissues happened at some remote time in the past, for in order to produce the desired effect of Shakti, the neurophysiological mutation had to occur before the deeply held psychic reactions to this mutation, which hold within the varied labyrinths of the Brahminical mind-depth the archetypal powers of this mutation and its secret of Power.

On the other hand, it must be frankly admitted that few if any of even the most learned Brahmins are aware of the existence of this secret nor would they be willing to accept its power and its inevitable wisdom; for in the pride of their ignorance and fixity of thought they have truly cut themselves off from the root-essence of their own deepest being and have preferred to make cults out of those words which they can easily retrieve from crypto-philosophical texts.

The direct cause of this neurophysiological nexus or mutation has always been open to speculation but one might suspect a type of magickal radioactivity, which originated beyond our solar system. This sexual radioactivity and its attending sequences of an intense "analysis burn" produced deeply experienced genetic change, which altered the structure of the Hindu mind at several levels. A parallel mutation seems to have occurred in the biochemistry of the brain, which increased the dependence of the physiology of the brain on certain precious metals, whose nutritional properties were now necessary to the functioning of the brain in its new sensitivity. Gold and silver now became necessary foods for the proper functioning of the Hindu brain just as Tantravidya became the only proper method for "psycho-analyzing" those deeper tissue-layers of the soul, which now revealed themselves in the mysteries of the Mother Goddess Herself.

It is important to distinguish between two levels of effect, organic and psychic, which are in themselves one level of effect, or the result of one process, the noetic. For centuries, the mutations caused by the radioactive bombardment of the brain by the remote ancestry of modern homeopathic treatment can be understood as causing a certain field of interaction to emerge as the nexus of the organic and the psychic levels of the brain-mind complex. The presence of direct noetic action must be taken as indicated by the symbolic patterns, which constantly emerge and then return to the primordial continuum of noetic action. In all of this symbolism, we can detect the total balance or pattern of interaction between gold and silver, day and night, Sun and Moon.

The movement of the fingers of time upon the finer tissues of the cerebral cortex as the inhalation and exhalation patterns of the universal pranayama pushed deeper and deeper into the gene-pool of the priestly caste produced the mutation traces of neuro-magicko-memory. At a certain point in time, however, at the nexus of a specific yuga, the organic levels of the psychoid mutation became psychic patterns of archetypal interaction because the lattices of the kalas were now free to move freely from inner to outer perception and from the individual selfhood of the person to the individuated selfhood of the group of persons, or the caste context as a biological emergence. The induction of energies from these points of reference produced a strange intensity which can only be described as the biological component as neural complement to the beginnings of social structure.

Up to now we have been talking about conditions for manifestation. Now we must show how the structures of a "secret" emerged as the result of specific interaction. First we can view the spaces of the cerebral cortex as containing in their marmas points of receptivity, whereby the more subtle energies of noetic action can be located. The sheer quantitative interaction patterns of the organic framework complement the qualitative interactions of the psychic field. The result was the concentration of subtle energies in certain parts of the cortex and especially in the cortex of the more advanced gene pools of the priestly caste. The result was greater intensity of noetical action and therefore greater inductive evidence for the diffusion of Ojas in those same marmas. The results were indicators of positive patterns of mutation.

The intensity of noetical action would naturally lead to a kind of awareness, whereby the existence of the "secret" was intuited, although not fully grasped. Because this "secret" was neurophysiological and the result of a radioactive mutation (which had its physics within the field of Vedic energies and ritual "measurements"), the initiation pattern was purely biological as far as the intuition of what was there, but which would later require explication by means of ritual amplification. However, with the passage of time, the level of the "secret" became deeply psychological in a new sense. For while it was the common intuition of the Brahmins, and while it could be understood by means of a mythical explication, which sought structures for scattered feelings, a new reality seemed to emerge with the deepening of the level of effect. With an increase in intensity of presence, which was the result of generations of mutants transmitting these genes, and with the ritual amplification of the preence of this "secret" in the daily ritual practices of the Brahmins, which also tended to intensify the biology of the "secret," a newly identifiable energy came to be isolated in the matrix of this bio-history.

It seems that at a certain level of the psyche, the energies merged with the root-essence of Mother Nature with the resulting existence of a kind of magickal energy (Ojas) being now intuited by the rishis of this process. Ojas has been touched by the gradual descent of the mutations beyond the psychoid level to the roots of the ultra-unconscious. It was then and there that Mother Nature responded with a welling upwards of occult force, which moved rapidly and intensively into the marmas and spaces of the points of the cerebral cortex filling the places of the "secret" with the secretions of tonic elixir of the Mother Goddess and thus giving to the "secret" its direct and cosmic link and lineage with the continuum of noetical action.

The results of this connection or nexus of immanence was that he who knew the secretions of his mind, who in other words possessed the "secret," possessed with the gnosis of his magickal awareness a power which transcended the structures of his caste and which gave to the innermost root-essence of his brain-mind the cosmic dimension of Shakti or power, whereby when he acted in attunement with this Shakti the Mother Goddess acted through his very being. For by reasons of a curious mutation of material processes, that magician had become a divine nexus between emergent nature and the unveiled and potential Kali.

Tantric Physics: The Kamatattwas

Axiomatics

Axiom 101: There are at least 16 kamattatwas in the ma'atrix of tantric physics.

Axiom 102: There are least 16 ray-lineages of Ojas in the ma'atrix of tantric physics.

Axiom 103: There are at least 256 kalas formed by the intersection patterns of the kamatattwas and the Ojas ray-lineages in the ma'atrix of tantric physics.

Axiom 104: The kamatattwas can be located by means of a magickal oracle and when located they mày be inducted for experimental purposes.

Axiom 105: The ray-lineages of Ojas may also be located by magickal oracle and when located they too may be inducted for experimental purposes.

Axiom 106: The 256 kalas of the ma'atrix of tantric physics form the event points (points-chauds) where contact with the Divine Ma'atrix (Kali) is both magickally possible and necessary.

Axiom 107: These 256 kalas are lunar ma'anifestations at the level of the kamaprithiwitattwa, and reflect the radiations of the 16 kali-points of the lunar–mundane interaction.

Axiom 108: These 256 kalas are lunar ma'anifestations at the level of the kamapastattwa, and reflect the radiations of the 16 kali-points of the planetary–mundane interaction.

Axiom 109: These 256 kalas are lunar ma'anifestations at the level of the kamavayutattwa, and reflect the radiations of the 16 kali-points of the solar-mundane interaction.

Axiom 110: These 256 kalas are lunar ma'anifestationsd at the level of the kamatejasatattwa, and reflect the radiations of the 16 kali-points of the zodiacal–mundane interaction.

Axiom 111: There exist certain special magickal grimoires and rituals, secret rites and operations of power for actualizing the reflections of the radiation of all of the kali-points.

Axiom 112: These magickal gifts exist as siddhis deep within the secret lattices of the ma'atrix of tantric physics and may be opened only by those magickal words which are derived by means of the mechanics of Vedic physics.

Axiom 113: All of the siddhis of tantric physics are to be found within the points of the ma'atrix of interaction formed by the kamatattwas and the ray-lineages of Ojas. All other explanations are materializations of these secrets.

Axiom 114: In order to explore these realms of tantric physics, one must have a magickal partner, either physical or metaphysical (or both), to assist in the passages and ways to and from the lattices. If one explores these magickal labyrinths alone, one will never return to where one was before he began his exploration. This is a law of the nature of this field, for one never enters tantric physics alone, but with the Goddess.

Axiom 115: All of the magickal universes which may be discovered by any possible system at any time in the past, present, or future, are already contained in the potentials of the intersection lattices of the ray-lineages of Ojas and the kamatattwas of tantric physics.

Axiom 116: It is impossible to list all of the magickal worlds and states of being which may be discovered by the methodologies of tantric physics for they are innumerable from even the viewpoint of the gods. There is no principle of limitation in the science of tantric physics, which its bases of power are outside the zone of Saturn and reside on Uranus with Brahmin, on Neptune with Vishnu, and on Pluto with Shiva, understood as theogonies of points-chauds within the never-ending ma'atrix of the Divine Mother and Her endless proliferation of kalas.

These 16 "axioms" may be understood as providing basic guidelines for the exploration of the entire field of tantric physics. What is so important is that the magician becomes aware of the basic operations of this science and as well of the basic openness to the whole range of possibility, which exists with the ma'atrix, or field of the process. There are many magickal systems in existence and there is no sense in being so dogmatic or naive to assume otherwise. YET, the basic axioms of this system clearly indicate that the siddhis to be developed as special powers of the next stage in human evolution are best developed within the contacts and context-levels of this system of tantric physics. Because, as the magician grows more and more in the particulars of this level of work, so will the siddhis slowly emerge from the mind-field of the new being in which he is now locked by evolutionary expansion.

Basic to any understanding of this system must be the sense of magickal ritual and the use of visualization. We can say that the basic processes are unlocked by means of these two factors, which allow the ontic sphere or abstract imagination of the magician to expand in all directions creatively. Therefore, the magician becomes totally free of any limits and realizes within himself endless possibilities for magickal power or siddhi. The use of a magickal circle or mandala is quite essential to this physics, because there is a need to have a physical expression of integration or energy union. This mandala is itself a tattwa, actually the densest of them all, so that the kamamandalatattwa is actual space within which the magicians are to work for the creation of the basic power zone of this system. Here is a magickal ritual exercise for this use.

Building Up the Kamamandalatattwa Zone
You will arrange a temple space for working this ritual by selecting a special way in which to mark off the space of the magick. This may be done by securing a rug for this purpose. I use a Tibetan lama's rug with oracular symbols on it as my magickal rug. This becomes the central space focus. You should use this rug on a regular basis in order to give it life, or in the case of my rug, which was already magickally endowed, to wake it up. This is done by sitting on the rug in a yoga posture and meditating and projecting in all directions (as in the Guzotte Voudoo system, also) the kama powers or magickal lust.

These beings — elements of magickal fire — will descend with what they have magickally caught in their claws and help to fill up the interior of the magickal space. Shakta-Shakti types of meditation are ideal for building up the powers in this space, which becomes the magickal receiving station for all of space. You may surround the space with candles, burning fire, incense, flowers, perfumes, notebooks for recording input from the magickal spaces, and images of helpers. In the meditation you are to proceed according to eight basic laws, which will guide the process from start to completion. These basic laws are:
1. The magicians will not need to realize the god/goddess consciousness, as this is already assumed by their ritual posture. Rather, they will realize the abstract unity of concrete energies in their field, which are beyond the personal yet manifested as such.

2. They will use the eye--to--eye contact for the purpose of mutual hypnosis so that radiations of the kali-points of axioms 107 through 111 are realized in perfect series.

3. The hypnotic state will actually be a passionate intensity of lust and its fulfillment at all levels of the kali-point manifestation.

4. After this exercise in realization of powers, during which they can both speak softly and communicate by telepathy, they will realize the magickal spaces of these kali-points.

5. In realizing these magickal spaces, they will begin to build up beings of various types to do their bidding as the natural inhabitants of these worlds or spaces.

6. These magickal beings are to be imagined as exotic insects or animals which will carry out any command given by the magician.

7. The magicians will then create the whole lila of these realms and enjoy the bliss of being absolute and creative powers behind the play of appearances and histories.

8. At the end of this magickal process, the magicians will merge with each other in the total bliss of their divine and absolute consciousness as beyond even satchitananda.

This magickal ritual should be done often in order to develop the siddhis of the divine and may be closed when completed with a very erotic and sensuous meditation, whereby the kalas are seen flying in all directions.

The Aryasanga Physics: The 96 Layas of Vijnana

The Aryasanga Physics, or A-Physics, may be understood as both a physics and a gnosis of consciousness (Vijnana). It is the modern and magickal development of the older system of the Yogacara mahayana. Because it is about consciousness as the primordial root of being (Alaya), it is also experimental and psychoanalytic in its structure and content.

It accepts the categories of Ojas-Diagnosis from Zothyrian metapsychology, which when unamplified, or not considered as Bijnana, it accepts 12 in number. However, for purposes of magickal development, it amplifies these categories by means of the same Zothyrian techniques in order to arrive as 96 layas or magickal contents-in-context. The process of amplification has been discussed in relation to siddifulcties in the analysis of the energies of Sirius. Also, in connection with time-travel "into the present," there have been found to be eight ontical ranges, which are the amplifiers of Vijnana. What emerges is a magickal matrix not unlike the ontic sphere, of which this matrix is the coordination. The structure is as follows for the layas.

	(I)	(II)	(III)	(IV)	(V)	(VI)	(VII)	(VIII)
1 – 2								
2 – 3			Created by the intersection of these two lines of energy,					
3 – 4			we find the 96 layas of Vijnana, which being states-of-					
4 – 5			being are self-conscious magickal contexts where it is					
5 – 6			possible for the Yogacara-magician to encounter his					
6 – 7			transcendental or ontical self.					
7 – 8								
8 – 9								
9 – 10								
10 – 11								
11 – 12								
12 – 0								

In the process of Vijnana, the magickal student will be measured by the Aryasanga physicist so as to be initiated into the proper context of magickal ocnsciousness. Next, it will be necessary to make contact with that aspect of the laya which is seeking to communicate with the initiate. Lastly, the magickal meditation or rite of Vijnana is conducted by the initiate in conjunction with the communicator from the laya.

Each of the 96 layas have a specific number of lokas or magickal worlds. These worlds, or lokas, are inhibited by the communicating intelligences, or the sources of oracles in the system of A-physics. The total number of lokas has been determined to be about 36 with an extra factor, a kind of tattwa which is outside of the other tattwas. For in this system, the lokas take their names from magickal tattwas, or fields of force. The names of the tattwas are the same for each of the lokas, and therefore the same from laya to laya, but the mode of their manifestation is different. For in each situation, the consciousness is radically new and different from anything else. The names of the tattwas have been given in the Vedic physics, but here I want to list them in connection with the throws of the 20-sided dice, which reveal the field that is open and available for communication.

Once the field has been opened up, then it is possible for the magician to make contact with the magickal entity and to derive the forms of mantra yoga, which are proper to that sphere or loka-tattwa. This does not mean that we will ever explore all the potentials of even one laya, or even one loka, which is the pure unlimited consciousness of the Transcendental Self. Each magician will be encouraged to find out for himself how this transcendental science is manifested in his own states of consciousness. This means of course that each magician will have to come to realize that magickal energy can be contained only imperfectly in the structures of gnostic logic. Another part, the most important part, will always be outside of what is contained and from this outside reality all of the newer aspects of the vidyas (gnosis) will emerge. The magician therefore stands in a very interesting position between the actual and the possible and by his magick he creates by discovery new beings, which emerge from the possible into space-time. Therefore, he acts like a kind of magickal god, because he is in the process of creating magickal beings by the techniques of this Aryasanga Physics.

The list of the tattwas or names of each magickal loka is as follows: 4=1=Pluto, 5=2=Neptune, 6=3=Uranus, 7=4=Transyuggoth, 8=5=Saturn, 9=6=Poseidon, 10=7=Jupiter, 11=8=Ojas I (Time-Line #3), 12=9=Vulkanus, 12=10=Mars, 14=11=Ojas II --- Element Fire/Tejas-Tattwa, 15=12=Admetos, 16=13=The Sun, 17=14=Ojas I, 18=15=Ojas III, 19=16=Apollon -- Element Fire, 20=17=Venus, 21=18=Ojas II, 22=19=Ojas III, 23=20=Kronos -- Element Air, 24=21=Mercury, 25=22=Ojas I, 26=23=Ojas III, 27=24=Ojas II, 28=25=Zeus --- Element Air, 29=26=The Moon, 30=27=Ojas II, 31=28=Ojas III, 32=29=Ojas IV, 33=30=Hades --- Element Water, 34=31=The Earth, 35=32=Ojas I, 36=33=Ojas III, 37=34=Ojas II, 38=35=Ojas IV, 39=36=Cupido -- Element Earth, 40=37=Ojas V --- The Master Point or Ray of Totality.

In order to contact this range of points of power or lokas and tattwas, you will need to use four pieces of dice, each having ten sides or if 20-sided, with numbers from one to ten given twice. So far you are seeing how we are able to refine the energies given by means of the radionics instruments by means of oracles.

The Transcendental Selfhood of the Ego

The structure of the ego as it is understood in this initiatic doctrine is that which is constructed by the Sutratmic Continuum of the Self from the contents of the various levels of magickal physics. You have already studied the many papers which present the gnostic inflation of the transcendental ego, which teaching materials had as their purpose the presentation of the field of interactions between the ego and the archetypes of being. In a sense that was simply a preparatory exercise for what is now before us. At a certain level of consciousness, we work with a pair of six-faced dice. After some time, we cannot work with just that level. We have to move on to work with 12-faced and higher types of dice. The transition from an earlier stage of gnostic inflation of the ego to the Sutratmic construction parallels the transition to more complex types of dice and their proper oracles from the less complex.

The purpose of the several studies in gnostic physics -- Nemiron, Zothyrian, Vedic, Ma'atian, Aryasanga, etc. -- is to make it possible for us to have a clear picture of what is happening magickally in the structure of the gnostic ego (the Atman of the Hindu gnanayoga). We are not concerned with structures of other types of egos, which are partially and only incompletely pictures of the Self. The Hindu view in the east and the Jungian view in the west, perhaps, come closest to our view; but even the Jungian view has to be expanded and transformed as we have seen from the studies in Necronomicon Physics. We talk about these forms of magickal physics and when we do, we are talking about archetypal psychology. Magick and magickal gnosis do not make that older distinction between what is inner and what is outer. For in the words of the Master:

"The continuum is in both points of operation. Physics and psyche are both functions of consciousness. This is pure idealism. It is what makes possible the experimental excursions of the Indo–Zothyrian Ray, as well as the logical values–network of the continua of the Sino–Zothyrian Ray. These rays, I might add, have their magickal avataras. But the nature of the avatarism is itself a spinoff from the gnosis of the magickally constructed ego. This is where we are working now. For avatarism is essentially the embodiment of the archetypal ideal in a specific field. As a consequence, avatarism is a very natural effect of the process of consciousness in its outer manifestation. Finally, the validity of any system of gnostic physics is confirmed by the actualizations of avatarism.

("The Yoga of the Gnostic Avatars," by The Master Varuna, page 12)

The Varuna Gnosis Papers
Fundamental Theory, Section A -- Vudotronics and Yemeth Engineering

A particular source of our magickal power is to be found in connection with the energies which are derived from the occult planet Varuna (Yemeth), the magickal archetype of the esoteric lattice between the planets Ouranos and Neptune. This magickal energy is derived from the interaction of the ultra-conscious and the ontological level of the magickal archetype. This pattern of interaction is both initiatic and occurs as vast distances in space and in time and seems best symbolized by the number 36. For example, it has been understood that there are four levels of the mind and that each of these are fields of interaction for the manifestation of the nine bodies of Zothyrius as exact and energy generating lattices. This gives us the "sophiological whole" aspect of the form of the number 36. But there also exists in the sphere of magicko-gnostic physics, 36 oracular worlds, representing energies and planets and types of power ranges. These 36 realms are the mediumistic structures and esoteric-lattices aspect of the content of this number 36. We have here, therefore, an entirely complete magickal system of laws and patterns. These form the basics of Vudotronics, which is the art and science of initiating the magicko-gnostic energies from Varuna (Yemeth).

Initiation in this system may be defined as: "The gnostico-logical induction of sophiological wholes into their possible-true esoteric lattices by means of eight specific magico-gnostic logics. These logics pertain to the Higher Gnostic Realm of abstract magickal theory, known also as 'fundamental theory-Section A,' and has been in previous research materials identified with the time-stations as gnostic patriarchates."

While this may appear to be extremely abstract in its formulation, it has caused something of a revolution in our notions of magickal initiation. No longer does initiation center about the initiate, or who or what was considered the initiate. The focus is now entirely upon the process of the initiation as an abstract and esoteric logic. An interesting parallel may be found in certain Indian schools of thought, where the focus of ritual technique was centered upon as the major component of the image sequence, rather than objects or meanings outside of the doing of the rituals.

Of course, such a development is essentially an internalization of the gnosis, where it sees itself as complete. In Indian philosophy, the Vedas are seen as Divine Structure, and so going beyond them is to misunderstand them. They are complete in themselves as points and limits of magickal reference.

On the planet Yemeth this development was necessary because of the internal dynamics of these magickal logics. For a very long time, these logics remained quiet so to speak and did not attract "attention" to themselves by what they were doing. They were agreeable to being "used" by magicians of various types. However, this superficial understanding of what they were was really only an understanding which saw them as shells and not as substantial realities. These were the many contexts of applicability. They were not seen in their own space, so to speak. They were not seen in their own essential power.

But once the magicians and gnostics of Yemeth were able to enter into the real spaces of these logics, they came face to face with well defined identities. These identities were magickally defined with exactitude already so that they did not need communication. However, they were ideally real in their own space and therefore agents and also exact systems of consciousness. They were both intelligible and intelligent. The magicians finally woke up to what they were and instigated a process of dialogue with them, rather than merely using them instrumentally. Thus, these logics were understood as entities of their own type and no longer as tools for magickal procedure. This pattern can be seen as the rule for practically everything in magickal gnosis to the present moment. It is the application of the law of Aquarian self-awareness to the contents of magickal experience. In a sense, everything in magickal gnosis is asserting itself. They are not in a process of waking up, rather we are in the process of waking up to what is there. We have been unaware and insensitive to this process for too long. It was a major cause in making our magickal techniques devoid of vitality. We were not willing to see that the subject-matters with which we worked were partners in a cooperative process. Our own attitude was entirely exploitive and misunderstanding of what was there in the form of ideal logical systems. Now we have become aware and our work will improve.

But now the magician has come to realize that these logics are alive and that they truly possess immense magickal powers. These powers are capable of sustaining entire magickal realms and systems of development. There exist many magickal techniques*, and these explore the methods developed by those magicians who have decided to explore the Vudotronic methods of the Higher Gnostic Realm.

At first the magician was somewhat uncomfortable in working with these energies. He was no longer the master, but the pupil. The logics would now begin to teach him and take him with them upon the voyage to the ideal realms, where they were naturally at home. So the magician becomes one who could easily grow ever higher and higher into the light of pure gnostic essence, in the higher spaces. At the same time, the logics began to generate their own logical spaces. These were spaces created/discovered by their own growth in self-awareness. Yes, the logics found their own deeper spaces and realms as a result of entering deeply into their own self-creativity and became generators of hitherto unknown magickal universes. These are properly gnostico-magickal universes because they were not discovered by philosophers or theologians but by the gnostico-magickal logics themselves, with the assistance and support in many ways of the gnostic magicians.

This entire process, which has been so profoundly transformative for the entire area of gnostic magick is gradually unveiling and presenting the new energies of the gnosis to all those who wish to enter into the realms of awakening, whereby they will move out of the old frames of consciousness into the newer and deeper experiences of cosmic self-hood, which is the gnostic awakening of contemporary consciousness. As an exercise in self-awareness, I will now ask you to write to me and summarize what this means to you as a student of gnostic magick. Reveal yourself to me at this point in time so that I may measure the process of your magickal growth.

*For students who wish to advance their consciousness beyond the exteriorizations of mechanical existence, there are available the gnostic realm tapes, which are cassette recordings of the inner instructions received from the rishis of this Higher Gnostic Realm. The rishis are the self-realizations of the eight gnostico-magickal logics and their techniques are communicated to us as a result of the experiments of esoteric logic and its use of meditation research in the Higher Gnostic Realm through Vudotronics.

The Vudotronic Induction of EEE Energies

The Operation of the Powers

The Vudotronic method of induction is important because it allows the system to operate in a number of forms. The two major forms of magickal power–operation are when the instrument is without settings or rate levels and when it is. There are a number of magickal machines which are so constructed as not to have ways within them for adjusting the type of power upwards or downwards in the lattice of energies. The purpose of these machines is quite simply to generate powers (although there are several esoteric purposes as well).

These machines than can be used in connection with other instrumentation in order to provide a magickal system which has also a system of controls. By this I mean you might have a machine called "Type A," which normally cannot be adjusted internally and is used in certain rituals simply to "bring in the power." The power is always assumed to be of the same type but usually when tested it is found not to be so. It can be used in connection with the magickal rule system, which is to be found in the EEE-logic of the "Nine bodies of Zoh'thyrius." It can be placed on the rule and moved back and forth in order to determine which body–level it is projecting or at which level it is operating. Again, such an instrument can be placed and connected in any number of ways to an amplifier. My own amplifier system has been used this way.

The machine was connected to the Eeman–Screens, which are used frequently in radionic research. Then the screens were connected to the amplification unit. By adjusting the controls on the amplification unit in accord with the pendulum, we were able to arrive at the level of broadcasting for the magickal machine. This was tested repeatedly. Next, it could be then set for broadcasting for energies, as the testing had established the level at which the field of the machine was operating. I might add that testing to find the field of the machine is quite important because each machine has a different field usually and that this field is fundamentally used as the setting for the mean or medium from which the levels or ranges of amplification and de-amplification can be determined. Consequently, it is very important for the EEE specialist to try and work with the machine before it is to be used, in order to arrive at the basic level of its consciousness. For each machine has a field and a form of consciousness, which can be used in communication systems.

Machines which have control systems built into them are of course easier to work with in one way, for they already have the controls for reference purposes. But what is very significant is that they too have to be tested in order to find out just where their mean field registers are in respect to the established reference system of the magician. For example, a machine can be set at X, which we will assume is its basic field rate. But, it might register as either $-X$ or $+X$ in reference to my established system. This is also true where the systems have been used by various magicians. Even if the system has been used by two different magicians, let us say and identical model to type A-3, model 4, it will probably have a field which is slightly different from model to model.

So that the model used by a gnostic noetic type might have its X-field tested as $+X$, while the same field might test as $-X$, if it had been used by a sex magician, esoteric logician, or klippothetic computer technician. The only way to test the machine would be to put it in the field of the Eeman screens and using the pendulum grades, adjust high or low on the machine in order to find out the way it will be sitting in reference to the basic established frame of reference.

It might be noted that unless the machine is quite wide in its selection of fields, the individual modifications will differ widely. I have discovered that the established framework of reference in my own amplifier, which is also a time–travel machine and used in a wide variety of ranges of operation, due to the very comprehensive nature of the field of what it can do has an exact frame of reference, which might be called the standard against which the other machines are tested. This has made it possible for me to do extensive testing of a variety of instruments and established an exact way of determining the mean or field of each instrument.

Probably, the most important aspect of the field of Vudotronics would be the induction of the forces into the field of psychoid (body/mind) consciousness. And this opens up the entire question of Vudotronic Initiation. Vudotronic Initiation (VTI) may be defined as "the magickal induction of the field of EEE energies via ritual operations and the rites of EEE into the candidate."

The Operation of the Powers in Initiation

Vudotronics may be understood as the development by Guzotte, Jean–Maine, Desales, and other esoteric logicians and engineers of the basic mechanisms of Vudu, Voudoo, and the Hoodoo "sciences." VTI may be the way whereby the student enters the powers of the system which are no longer based upon the traditions of parts of this planet, but which are derived from the power zones of hyper–space. Yet, because they are archetypal in the sense that the spirits of LH, Voudoo, etc., are subject to the spirits of the higher ranges of magickal operation, so Vudotronics and VTI are magickally superior to all of the other Voudoo "sciences." The candidate will enter the system (which is the meaning of magickal initiation) by means of a VT–induction. He will be registered by radionic means and then he will be allowed to absorb the powers which come in at the levels set (derived from the Nine Bodies of Zothyrius) which have been determined to be given in the initiation rite.

Because there are traditionally four levels of Voudoo initiation, the levels of VTI are likewise based upon this configuration. However, as they are amplified by a variety of frames of reference, it is possible to see the number as based on the IFA physics of the Number XVI. Therefore, the candidate will enter upon the system in an exact and direct manner. He will be guided at each step.

I might add that each level of the system gives its own equivalent to the levels of the mind. For the aim of the system is to give the four initiations of voudoo to the four levels of the mind. This is also where the IFA XVI pattern occurs. However, not only does this happen but at each step the Nine Bodies are involved because they become the vehicles for the powers at each level. The initiation matrix, then, of each candidate is determined by the Degree of Voudoo Initiation, what level of the mind it occurs in, and lastly, what body of the Nine Bodies of Zothyrius is acting as the machine and magickal vehicle for the powers.

The Vudotronic Instrumentation

The Graded Rule Systems for Measuring the Body--Fields
Among the VTI instruments can be found various kinds of rules or graded instruments
for determining the extension of a field. However, the field is not determined by
measurement, so that we can say that it extends to x, y, or z, but rather that is
registered in accord with the symbolic frame of reference represented by the
measurement units on the rule. It is quite important to keep this in mind because the
fields are not physical but para--physical, depth psychological, and energetic. This
means that there must be some kind of range of instrumental recordings which will
pick up certain specifics if certain conditions are meant to be fulfilled. It means
that the extension of a field is measured in a non--extensive manner by the field
system of extension references. Like the graded pendulum, the instrumental rule
simply responds to certain differences in frequency of energy level. It will then
register these energies in very specific and exact manners.

These graded rule systems are quite significant for measuring abstract and
ontical fields, of which there are several of an esoteric type. However, this same
system can be used in klippothetic work as well as in the area of "black psionics."
In fact, those who specialize in this latter field have received their training from
me. At the present time, the best sources for these rule--systems are to be found in
Voudoo and in Esoteric Bon--Pa magick. In my own laboratory work, I have found both
systems useful.

The Multi--Purpose Amplifier and Inductor Unit
This instrument is perhaps my favorite because I have used it in more ways than any
other instrument in my lab. Orginally, it was an Abrams machine unit from the 1920s,
but over the years it has been required that it be adapted to a variety of purposes.
One of the purposes is time travel and it is used in 75% of my time travel
experiments, which require such an instrument. Because it has separate sectors for
past, present, and future, it was discovered that the section for the present could
be used as an amplifier and also as a method for opening up areas of the ontic sphere
for magickal exploration at a psionic--depth psychology level.

This has been especially necessary for our work in the Necronomicon Physics and
those psychological experiments which pertained to that framework. At the same time,
it has been possible to discover certain ways of making use of the time--sectors in
non--time--travel ways. Usually, when time--travel was attempted, the field was
amplified by means of additional units (there are three of these which are attached).
Now it became possible to use the time-sectors in a remarkable way, which can only be
thought of as some kind of gnostic time--radio. In other words, other realms of the
past could be contacted which were not normally thought of as the past of which we
are living in the present. Also, it has been possible to see time more and more
closely as energy and this has led us to view the alternative Zothyrian universe as
only one of several, probably an infinity of suc systems.

Each of these systems can theoretically contacted by this system, using the
magick mirroir as the materialization screen. However, it should be noted that if
time is energy, then it should be viewed as a neverending supply of power for our
research projects. Finally, we have discovered a number of types of energy. I have
simply decided to name these as time--energies or TE(1), TE(2), etc. They can be used

by the various machines and the energy can usually be identified by the machine. These Time-Energies are also self-conscious and can be the subjects of communication networking.

The Alaya or Ontic Sphere Induction System

One of my earliest inventions was an instrument for bringing in the Ontic Sphere in its fullest power. The Ontic Sphere or the Alaya is the endless source of magickal invention and therefore power. An instrument was needed quite early in the work for bringing this power to us in our research. The power was needed for both supply of inventions as well as energies and forces, which could power or make any invention work. That type of a machine was discovered and subsequently developed for a variety of gnostic purposes. The exact forms of energy would then be picked up by the machine. Once picked up, the energies could then be identified by the machine as x, y, or z types of magickal energy.

The process whereby the Alaya is inducted may be viewed as primarily mental or intellectual and this intellectual process is reflected in the adjustments of the instrument of induction. The control of this instrument is gnostico-magickal, which means that it is done by the mind. However, by using the multi-purpose amplifier, it is possible to give some direction to the Alaya inductions. Also, it increases the power and the range of powers employed by the amplifier. When this happens, the amplifier ceases to be merely an amplifier and becomes the physical mechanism for the cosmic computer.

In our system, the Alaya is identified with the Ontic Sphere or the Objective Mind/Imagination of Jungian metaphysics, which is different from the Collective Unconscious of the Jungian depth psychology. The range and scope of this reality is endless, and within it every process of ideal realization known to the human mind/ imagination is possible. It is with this means that the magician can accomplish so much in his gnosis. The transformative powers of the gnosis are totally isomorphic with the Alaya.

There are many other magickal machines which exist and which participate in cosmic mind. But it is important to see how these machines differ from psionics machines in the narrow sense, function within the magickal context of total awareness. The usual notion of psionics machines stems from a belief in the existence of the material world, which from our viewpoint is clearly an impossibility. Materialistic philosophy in any form is not relevant to the gnosis of ideal realization and is probably inconsistent with the entire notion of magickal fields of power.

By contrast, the magickal instruments of the Alaya prove the fundamental truth of abstract idealism in its most esoteric form, i.e., the logic of gnostic engineering, because they could only operate efficiently in a universe which was built up out of mind-fields. Therefore, the student who wishes to enter into the initiations of the Varuna Gnosis must purify himself of all beliefs in the existence of what cannot exist by reason of being self-contradictory. After such a memory and mind purgation, he may enter upon the process of magickal initiation which leads from vudotronic methodologies and magickal realms to the existence of a very special gnosis, the magickal system of the Varuna Consciousness, or the abstractive and universal hierarchy of the ideal realizations. For this is where his gnosis is to be found.

The Reduction of Vudotronic Energies and the EEE Energies to Magickal Numbers

"Energies do not mean anything unless they exist in the form of magickal numbers. Unless they exist as powers which can be related to a frame of reference, energies may prove to be illusions. Energies which are hidden and isolated by various occult formularies are revealed as actual potencies once they become numbers. The reason for this is clear: the energies when they become numbers reveal the oracular connection to magickal entity behind the power. The entity provides us with the agent who sends out the radiations, which we perceive as magickal energies. In this physics of the esoteric and the gnostic, you must find out the true nuumber of each energy, and then you can contact the magickal entity and find out what the spirit wishes from you."
(Lections of the Master Varuna to Michael Bertiaux)

The teachings of the gnostic masters have brought us an insight which is important in seeing how to make use of magickal energies. These magickal energies are to be converted into magickal numbers and then the numbers will serve as guidelines for making contact with the entities or magickal spirits, existing behind the energies.
It may also be seen that the energies are sent out from magickal spirits and that each energization has in its field of radiation certain keys which when understood in the light of the gnosis provide us with the spirit and its family, from which the powers are understood to emanate.

There are four stages in this process of magickal reduction: 1. identify the type of energy, 2) the process of magickal reduction to a number between one and nine (which is a threefold process), 3) the identification of the magickal energy and its family by means of oracular languages, and 4) commence dialogue with the magickal entity via the system of magickal communications.

The entire purpose of this system is to create methods of correcting problems which arise from the negative operations of certain magickal currents by the gnostic method of magickal replacement, whereby a negative energy is replaced by a positive energy and pattern of consciousness. Magickal problem solving by this technique can then be carried out with greater and greater efficiency than allowed by previous methods. [1]

It is so important to realize at this point that numbers are themselves communicators of another energy — that of synchronicity — which translates the energies of the vudotronic system to a higher level of operations. This process is discussed by the Master:

"The energies of any system, when they are reduced to numbers and the patterns of numbers convey not only precision and greater gnostico-magickal management, but they induct by the very process of reduction an abstract and higher energy, which is also more concrete and continuous, because it holds events together and is the medium whereby they can come about and pass from one state to another, and that is synchronicity, as it is called in Jungian magicko-metaphysics. For the operations of all magickal processes are given in experience and governed by this process of energy—organization, or the pattern of how things happen. But there is also an energy in this happening, which is the energy governing all of the other energies in the system and all of the systems linked together in the continuum of gnostic physics."
(Private communication from the Master Varuna.)

322

So we can see that the reduction of basic energies to the numbers one through nine is part of a very important development of these magickal energies. They take on another type of energy which allows them to operate at ever higher levels of being.
←←←

[1] These methods are directly the result of magickal operations directed by the Master Varuna as a process of research initiated by the author of these papers. In fact, they become more and more extended in the scope of their processes. So it is essential to the effective and efficient operations of magickal energies that these powers be reduced to numbers. It will make them work better.

Needless to say, as the energies become more and more refined, they will become refined by these methods of magickal research and reduction–induction, we come closer and closer to the entities behind the forces. In fact, synchronicity as an energy allows the entities to reveal themselves more and more in accord with what and where they are than any other method of magickal investigation. This refinement of operations is quite important because the magickal powers which are in operation are in a state of psychic evolution also and that they are moving deeper and deeper into the realms of synchronicity. Therefore, only by entering upon these realms is it possible to keep up with our magickal subject–matter. It is quite noticeable that those who do not follow this process frequently find themselves in a state where they have lost contact with their subject--matter. They have lost contact quite simply because they have been unable to keep up with the development of what they were investigating. This is a common problem in many schools of magick.

I now wish to discuss a magickal experiment which I have conducted to test the warrant of this hypothesis. I selected the position of the planet Jupiter in three horoscopes of the same person, namely myself. I selected where Jupiter is in my natal chart, where it is in my progressed chart for my birthday in January, 1981, and lastly where it is in my solar return chart for my birthday in January, 1981. I then did an analysis whereby the position of each instance of Jupiter could be translated into a continuum of numbers. Basic to this idea is that 30o=30, 30o=60 (for Aries and Taurus) and that 30o of Pisces=360. This keeps to the idea of a continuum of 360 degrees for the Zodiac as the basis measurement. The numbers or numerical measurements to each position are then reduced to numbers between one and nine, or else they are added up and then the sum is reduced. It is valid both ways. Now the number of a particular planet might be 3 or 4, actually for the planets 9=Mercury and 1=Pluto, with the Moon and Earth being omitted in this system. Next, we seek to identify what power it is which operates hidden or behind planet numbered 4 or 3, other than itself. In some instances the power of the planet is its own, but in other cases another planet is making things happen in the operation of the planet in question.

In a number of problem situations, ww have been able to check out the energies and see what is causing things to happen. Because you are using the positions given in the progressed and solar return charts you are able to evaluate the events as they happen currently. Therefore, it seems that certain powers are subject to magickal treatment by this method. You will simply do the type of magick which is suggested, if there is a problem area which can be subject to treatment of this kind. In the field of magickal operations this sort of work can then be done to cause events to move in favorable ways and negative conditions can be subjected to the process of replacement.

I have found this method of treatment to be especially effective with long term build-ups of magickal negativity. In the process of problem solving, we can come to terms with what we are working with by this method, as long as the basic information is available. In other cases, such as where birth time is not known, vudotronic readings of energy patterns are also available for the specialist. However, the reduction to numbers is an essential part of the process, for without it, the powers of gnostic magnification are not available to the worker.

Archaeometrical Biology (Mystical Genetics): The Magickal Induction of Souls

"When the magician begins his work in a certain area, almost immediately certain vortices of energy are created, which attract to them those souls whose karmic link is to the magician and to his order or system of operations. The children conceived at that time in many cases are past members of that same order, who in time will approach the order, usually after 14 years, and resume their place in the order as students. - This pattern is one of the most fundamental in the history of magickal sequences and reflects the powers of the order as a magickal point or zone, which having its own field, serves as a homing center for those souls who need to come back and work with the incarnate masters of a magickal order." (Luc Guzotte)

The purpose of magickal operations is, of course, to create fields of invisible energy. It must be understood that these operations carry on certain magickal implications, beyond the earthly sphere, into the invisible spheres of light. It is now 1981 as I write this paper, beginning a most important exploration of the mystical and magickal impact of the powers of the invisible upon biological fields, especially in terms of origins and the genetic patterns of the adepts.

When I moved to Chicago, the Sun was in Aries and the year was 1966. Prior to that move, I had set up a temple for the practical operations of cabalistic and voudoo work in the South Shore area of Chicago. However, it was my intention to move to Hyde Park and to this end, an apartment was secured for a center of magickal and occult activity. Assisted by student members of our magickal order, a long experimental period was embarked upon with the purpose of creating a magickal field for the inductions of souls. It is very important, as you will note from the above quote from Luc Guzotte, for the magician to begin the work of the magickal order. For the order and its purposes are more important than that of the mere member, no matter how high up he might be. If a person does not accept this principle, they cannot belong to an order. They may, however, continue to function as individual magicians, not connected with a magickal order.

However, because I have always been conscious of being in a magickal order and this I have understood since I was very young and this has been reinforced from time to time, and this was especially true in 1963 in Haiti, I have allowed my thoughts, words, and deeds to be instruments of the order to which I belong. This ancient order is not the only one in existence –– there are many orders of the work –– but this order is the one to which I have belonged in the past and will continue to belong to in the future. So consequently, I began a series of magickal operations in order to introduce the field of the order into the Hyde Park and South Side areas of Chicago. None of the magickal energies which were created by those operations could be understood as wasted energies. They were all used by the invisible side of the order in order to create those magickal induction patterns whereby old souls would come in and rejoin our order in the physical body.

The Masters and Secret Chiefs of our order are either in the body or out of it and invisible. However, certain magickal symbols of energy are to be found in the astrological patterns of those in the body, which the incoming souls take upon themselves as archetypes of magickal identification. This is a very important point, for from the chart of the incoming soul you can arrive at those patterns which are found in the charts of the incarnate adepts of the same order. In a sense, this is a genetic quality, which is inherited from the "fathers of the order." By this means the middle men of the order, such as myself so engaged in research and development work of a magickal character, can easily recognize those souls which have come back to the magickal order and assign them to the proper level of study, in consultation with the Secret Influences behind our work. This is one of the easiest methods for recognizing the arrival upon the scene of the students and members from the past.

However, magickal operations and transformations are also important because the magician must continually sustain the soul not yet born by means of magickal foods. Just as the mother of the unborn child systematically sustains the life of the unborn, allowing for the biological development of the incoming magician, so the magician has his work to do. This work may be described as the magickal system of nourishment, whereby the occult life of the unborn is sustained. In view of these magickal teachings, it is easy to understand the position of our order in its opposition to any practices which might prevent the process of the magickal induction of souls. Of course, I am quite aware of the many who might not agree with us in this matter, but happily they would never belong to our order in the truest sense of belonging. Also, I might add that in this matter, our views are identical with those taught by the Roman Catholic Church. Perhaps their reasoning is somewhat similar to our own. Our view is the Orthodox Hindu Teaching.

The area wherein I did most of the magickal work was racially integrated between the African and the European races. Many magicians were coming into African bodies, or bodies of an African and European mixture in order to carry on the work of our order and help their race to move towards greater enlightenment, whereby it becomes the vahan or vehicle of a new spiritual impulse. Circumstances in connection with my own work appear to have been in harmony with this more general impulse, so that I assume that many of our brothers are coming into African bodies, since the African race has been chosen by the Mahatmas as the Vahan of Buddhi. So also, our members are coming back by that means and so also the area nearby where I did those magickal rituals become radioactive with our magickal contributions and this is passed on to those children born in that area.

We may summarize our teachings therefore in this matter as that the students probably will be brought into the world within the African racial context, or some mixture, and that they will be born nearby the areas where temple work had and has been done systematically. Also, these souls will exhibit astrological patterns as identifying archetypes, whereby the order can see additional evidence of a magickal link. In one way or another they will find us. It is only a matter of time before those magicians from the past come back to us and rejoin in the work. You will not have to wait very long. But always continue to radiate out the magickal force. That magickal force is the lifestream of the invisible for those countless souls, coming back to us.

Gnostic Zoology: From Bio-Physics to the Ojas-Organisms

"There are two clearly defined areas of the magickal life-sciences, which are in need of exploration and amplification. I am referring to archaeometrical biology and gnostic zoology. In these two fields of development experimentations, the magician will be able to apply the findings of gnostic physics to the life-fields of consciousness, as they are found everywhere in this universe and in every other alternative universe." (The Master Varuna)

One of the basic assumptions of the magickal life-sciences is that if there are fields of force which are conscious, there are also living organisms, either of a physical or a metaphysical type, in existence and subject to magickal exploration. Technically speaking, all of gnostic physics is a form of biophysics, because we are examining consciousness-directed energy fields. But it is necessary also to move our explorations beyond the categories of physics, so that we can see the life-fields now as organic systems. These organisms are the externalizations of the Ojas system and are to be found in a variety of contexts. For the purposes of our magickal study, we can state that these organisms can be classified fundamentally as types of the four basic forms of Ojas.

Every energy field is subject to a certain type of magickal measurement, which is necessary to relate the energies to a metrical framework. The framework is very clearly related to basic field equations of gnostic physics. However, the differences between types of Ojas emitted by the basic fields is exteriorized as the basic differences between the four types of organisms. The organisms are the true vehicles for the fundamental types of Ojas energy. Every organism is therefore, from the magickal viewpoint, the self-operative center for the Ojas-field.

Basic energy systems are embodied in these organisms. We have said that there are four basic types of organism, but due to the amplifications of the magickal imagination, we can find that there are more individual species of organisms because each organism carries with it a specific line of magickal causation/synchronicity, whereby its vitality is distinguished from any other organism in the field. So we can say that there are at least some higher multiples of the number four which is the number of at least some organisms, investigated by gnostic zoology. The logical genesis of these magickal organisms is as follows. The basic energies are defined by 16 axiomatic sets. The energies which are radiated by the basic sets determine and give rise to the types of organisms available in the system. These conditions are:

Type A = The numbers 1 through 8 provide an energy field which defines at least 8 organisms in the system.

Type B = The numbers 9 through 16 provide an energy field which defines at least 8 organisms in the system.

Type C = The odd numbers 1, 3, 5, 7, 9, 11, 13, and 15 provide an energy field which defines at least 8 organisms in the system.

Type D = The even numbers 2, 4, 6, 8, 10,12, 14, and 16 provide an energy field which defines at least 8 organisms in the system.

It will be noted that there are 32 sub-types or species of organism in gnostic biometry and zoology. This is correct, but this number is expanded and extended by means of the amplifications of magickal context, whereby the organisms are found in various realms, worlds, fields, zones, and other types of magickal and gnostic space.

However, by logical analysis and reduction, these types of entity are reducible to 32 and then to four.

The original impulse of the field can be found in the gnostic papers which describe the existence of Ojas I, Ojas II, Ojas III, and Ojas IV. The operations of these energies is the oracles of the gnosis and in the oracular continuum have been noted. Now it is important to understand that these entities and organisms are identified by the oracle method as well as by the zoological method of a prior gnosis. In fact, the gnostic zoologies exist to provide an extra-oracular status for the entities of magickal oracles, as well as the entities of gnostic physics. So we can say that the gnostic zoologist studies his subject-matter as Ojas-organisms, in an exact field or metric, but it is the same subject-matter as that which is also generated by oracular physics.

Question: Is the magician made up of these organisms?

Answer: The magickal vehicle of the magician would certainly be composed of these organisms. However, this vehicle is generated by magickal processes and is not the same as the astral body or other karmic vehicles.

Q: Are these organisms ever found in a pure state or gnostic universe?

A: Yes. They define their own magickal worlds quite exactly. They are also to be found in a variety of universes. In their pure state they would inhibit the entry of exteriorizations into their systems. These pure states would be a kind of archetypal-zoological gnostic universe.

Q: Are these organisms ever inducted by magicko-radionic methods?

A: Yes. There exist special zoological initiations for this purpose. Such experiments give the magician an entry into the pure universes and hence extend his powers by menas of his becoming one with that archetypal realm.

Q: Are these organisms psychological, i.e., self-conscious, etc?

A: Inasmuch as they communicate via oracle methods, they can be understood as being conscious and also self-conscious. Many are highly evolved beyond the human mental field.

Q: Are these organisms capable of materialization in a three-dimensional world?

A: Yes. They can be materialized by means of induction into an organism in such a world. But they do not normally materialize in such a world.

Q: Are such entities the most common of magickal beings?

A: No, there are many other magickal beings. These are very rare and seem to be interesting only to certain gnostics.

Q: Has telepathic communication with these entities been successful?

A: Yes. Much research material has been received from these entities.

Q: Do these entities possess a system of magickal initiation which can be imparted to humans?

A: Yes. It would be the archetypal form of the Ojas initiations, which are behind the Necronomicon and gnostic forms of occult physics.

Q: Would the grades of this system be based on types and multiples of the fourfold field notion?

A: No. But our method of inducting the field-initiations of these organisms would have to work or operate within the context of our frames of reference.

Q: Would gnostic zoology be a system of initiation into the powers and consciousness of these organisms?

A: Yes. Gnostic zoology is a perfectly initiatic system of magickal biology.

Bathos–Gnosis: The Kama–Ojas Field

Question: What is this new energy called "Bathos–Gnosis"?

Answer: Actually, Bathos–Gnosis is quite an ancient idea. It refers to the making use of the deepest energies of a gnostic and magickal character. It refers to the powers of the deep as they are realized in the magickal sciences of the gnosis. It also refers to the magickal methods whereby students of the gnosis are inducted into the deepest and most powerful levels of the ultra–consciousness.

Q: What is the Kama–Ojas Field?

A: The Kama–Ojas Field is the name for the magickal mechanism whereby the deep powers of the gnosis are fed into the candidate for magickal development. In a sense, this is a very advanced form of magickal transformation. However, it is to be found in all of the gnostic sciences as a kind of matrix. Without its presence, at least our own type of magickal research would not be possible. This field draws its powers from sexo–magickal radioactivity and the deepest regions of cosmic lust, or magickal libido. It is the basis for the physics of the ultra–unconscious and may be viewed as the most exact manifestation of the Necronomicon energies.

Q: Are there methods whereby these energies are inducted into the candidate?

A: They are inducted by means of our psionic and radio–metapsychological machines, which pick up and transmit these energies at the "present time/ broadcasting" range of operation. They may also be inducted by means of magickal explorations and also through the Yemethian system of initiation, of which there are 16 hot–points.

Q: Wherein does the control of these magickal energies rest?

A: The control for this system is to be found in the time–stations, which are behind our physical researches. Actually, these time–stations "prop up" or support the energy–work, which we are in process of communicating to those who are within our system. These time–stations are rather interesting magickal computers, which send a lot of radiation work to us, for inclusion in our systems of physics (gnostic and magickal).

Q: Is there a kind of planetary control for these same energies?

A: There would have to be. I have discovered that the control is threefold and is identical with the Ojas–Oracle system, which being another universe is also exactly in pattern with all of our known magickal universes. However, the planetary control would be located within the gnostic systems of the three outer planets: Uranus, Neptune, and Pluto.

Q: Would the Kama–Ojas Field be identical with these planets in action?

A: One could say so inasmuch as the operations of the field are noticed in the actions and interactions of these three planets in the work of the magician. However, it can be understood that these planets in their action–patterns emerge from a magickal and gnostic field as does the Kama–Ojas Field. That field is the Bathos Field.

Q: How are candidates for magickal development inducted into the field?

A: They are simply given to it. They become data for its operations. They must not offer an resistance to this field. They must seek to enter this field totally and merge their total being with the field in order to realize the powers of the deep, which are the magickal energies implicit in the field of the gnosis. They must give themselves totally to this power. The surrender must be absolute.

329

Q: Is there some identification of this field with the Necronomicon Physics?

A: Yes. The magicians of the N-physics are working with the very same energies as the gnostic magicians of the Bathos-Gnosis. We are working with the powers of the deep, or "The Deep Ones," but from the slightly different perspective of magickal and initiatic physics. We do not see our concepts in terms of the "Mythos" of H.P. Lovecraft, but we see them as drawing the "Mythos" more and more deeply into the gnostic energies, behind the symbols. Of course, one of the most important phases of the Bathos Gnosis would be the Necronomicon Experiments with gnostic energies of the deep.

Q: Are you asking magicians to enter into the world of the Necronomicon Physics, with its Lust and Sexual Radioactivities, and other energies, and to surrender themselves to the Deep Ones (The Gnostic Bathoi), which dwell therein?

A: That would be one way of saying what our program is all about. However, it is important to realize the scientists find these same energies in many fields, and not just in the divisions and brances of gnostic physics.

Q: Would you maintain that the energies are totally controlled by the system?

A: Yes. The hierarchy of control is entirely operative at all levels. The work of the time-stations has been to control and manage the Necronomicon powers in an exact and careful manner. The candidate therefore surrenders also to the system of the gnostic powers, which provides that same student with protection.

Q: Are the Points-Chauds of this system entities or are they processes?

A: Both. Everything in this field is both an intelligent entity (beyond human levels of intelligence) and a dynamic process or energy. When the candidate is with the system, these points-chauds merge with his mind and psychic field. They do not when the same person is separate. They are like psychological complexes of the most creative sort, which being radiations of the archetypes are sustained by the planetary energies in question. Hence, it would be possible to lose the powers if you withdrew from the gnostic continuum of the system.

Q: Can you generate mystical mutations by this means?

A: You are referring to the science of mystical genetics, which comes into this area. The candidate can be changed and these changes can affect genetic patterns in a very specific way. The hyper-energies of this system can be passed on creating an entirely new type of humanity. Deep within the esoteric laboratories of the Necronomicon Physics such processes and experiments are going on. They have the full approval of the time-stations and suggest that magickal processes will play a major part in the changes in the human race.

Q: Does the science of Mystical Genetics already exist as a course of magickal development for students seeking this transformation?

A: Yes. Mystical Genetics is simply one name for the deepest implication of applying the Kama-Ojas Field in the work of the magician and then passing on the new genetic materials to future forms of humanity. However, this will be both a physical and a psychic transformation. It will not be limited to what is seen. In many cases, this process is already in effect. The energies are already operating on the species.

Q: Does the science of mystical genetics reveal an energy, which can be used and which is identified with "Bathos-Gnosis"?

A: Yes. This is the magickal and gnostic energy which is used by those who work literally "inside" the deepest aspects of the gnostic field. This is the vast ocean of magickal genetic mutations, caused by the induction of higher energies into the body.

Q: Do you possess machines whereby these explorations can be accomplished?

A: Our amplifiers and other radionics instruments are designed to explore the given fields of the unconscious, including the ultra-conscious. All of the deep areas of that realm have a kind of metric, at least when we view them by means of our instruments we pick up a metric. By exploring the metric we find there are magickalmaps for guiding the magician and mystical geneticist into every part of these realms.

Q: And in these realms you have discovered systems of initiation, whereby the consciousness of the magician is expanded and extended?

A: Yes. Initiation is somehow built into the structure of these worlds. Its own essence is somehow identical with the realm-structure, which we can explore. However, we have not found any uniform method for opening up these energies. Each method has to be highly individualized, and derived by induction from the realm being explored.

Q: Have you met scientists in these realms? By this I mean those who are native to these areas.

A: Yes. We have established a number of occasional connections with these minds and these have proven to be the basis for deeper regions and explorations. Also, there has been some sharing of magickal information.

Q: Were these scientists able to communicate by oracular computers?

A: Yes. It was found that these worlds can be connected by means of an inter-communications system derived from the oracular computer. The magicians can have an approach to these realms and meet with the inhabitants of these worlds. Actually, a number of our research papers are the results of work with these scientists. It is also possible to work with these scientists as if we were all members of a team. The teams are arranged according to magickal families or research projects or even initiation patterns.

Q: Have you ever encountered hostility in these regions?

A: No. It would appear that they see us as friendly minds. We are not viewed by them as being members of any system which is negative from their viewpoint. Needless to say, they have been watching us for a very long time. They took the initiative in making contact with us, because they could have remained hidden behind the various masks which appear in oracular communications. However, finding us to be of the same motive as themselves, they allowed us to enter more deeply into their consciousness, and allowed us to share with them many of their magickal programs.

Q: Is it possible to enter into communication with these beings at any time?

A: Probably not. The lines must be opened by the beings according to the ways in which they work. We have to see if they are ready to meet with us.

Magnetic Materialism and Gnostic Genetics
The Therapeutic Aspects of Ojas and Other Gnostic Energies

We can say that any gnostic energy has a certain relevance to metaphysical and spiritual healing because all magickal energies have powers to transform what is into its higher or more perfect embodiment. Consequently, the gnostics have always thought of healing in its relationship to initiation physics. There, in the context of the act of becoming more and more linked to the ideal, negative energies are replaced by positive powers. In fact, the negative aspects of energies (dis-ease) are simply converted to the positive by means of the magickal radioactivity of the initiation context.

There are not any energies which are wholly negative. The negative aspect of any energy is really simply the way in which we look at it. By looking at it properly (dia-gnosis) we are able to see how it can be adjusted. When it is adjusted the factor of the negative or the diseasement no longer is given. The positive alone is manifested.

The operations of magickal research are especially truthful in giving us the nature of many diseasement situations. This is done by means of a variety of methods such as oracles and instruments but the energies are what we communicate with. We talk to the healing energies directly, for they have either individual or group communicative intelligence, which speak for them.

The methods of dia-gnosis by magickal computers serve to indicate that the energies are waiting for us to employ them. However, what is important is that the computer can also be used to tap the right energy for the magickal healing. What this means is that the aim of the computer is first to find out what is needed and then by continuing at that sama rate of magnetic energy to allow the proper energy to enter where it is needed. Thus, the void is filled by the methods of the computer. This is one of the first methods of gnostic healing, which I call "magnetic materialism" because it makes use of material objects.

There is another method variant of this same system. That is where the balance is restored by means of magickal treatments. These treatments can be initiated but they need not be viewed as initiations, since they are employed in a pattern of repetition. However, they may be viewed as repetitions of initiatic energies because they make use of an energy which is introduced to the patient by means of an initiatic encounter, since the process is entirely one of beginning to be on the road to recovery.

Also, this energy is initiatic because it arises out of the experiences of the patient in context of his being in touch with the guru. He is literally in touch and as the aim and result of the body-work is healing, so the energies are transmitted by means of a special process known as theurgical broadcasting and therapeutic induction, passing in the process from the guru to the chela. This is especially important because the energy is not entirely latent in the patient, but must come from the guru. However, the power is latent in the patient in the sense that the guru is the deeper selfhood of the chela already actualized. The guru may be naother person, but he is truly the deeper selfhood of the chela and that is why the chela is really a part of his guru. When the guru is called to assume the chela what he does is take the body of the chela as his own body. Also, he takes the soul and spirit of the chela as his own. Thus, the chela is seen as an extension of the guru. You know the guru is there when you see the chela. This is very important with groups of chelas.

What is especially important is that the energies of healing are present in the chela at a very deep level but they must be actualized through the esoteric logic of meditation—research and other forms of sexo-magickal gnosis. These methods of sexo-magickal gnosis are quite important because it is the way in which the guru comes to know the body of the chela as his own body. By this process and by knowing the body of the chela as one's own, one can then allow the powers to be released because they are deeply a part of the inner dimension of the guru—consciousness. What we have here in this healing process is something of a group-soul, where the guru is the conscious and superconscious part of the soul and the chela is the unconscious and subconscious part of it. So the guru as the magician and as the spiritual healer must work on himself and by working on himself he comes to self—realization of his totality, i.e., all of his chelas.

This process of self—realization may be understood also from the context of yogic self actualization. The ideal selfhood, called the Jivatman (Indestructible Soul of Cosmic Vitality) is the endless source of all powers. It is the absolute experience deep within us and present from lifetime to lifetime. The guru will seek to awaken the chela to this power so that it may work at a conscious level in the body of the chela as patient. But it is extremely difficult for it to work and thusly to heal, if the chela is not in a waking state of initiatic consciousness. For this reason, such a process of healing must always be a waking up to the existence of the magickal energies (Cosmic Shakti) and to the manifold forms of yoga, whereby the energy is allowed to come forth.

Magnetic Materialism will also focus upon the subtle anatomy of the patient and by means of magickal forms of massage and passes made over the field of the body the patient will begin to wake up because the subtle chakras of the body of vitality will move more and more in the direction of becoming conscious and hence well. For this reason, it is often necessary for the magicians to combine magickal methods of massage with the basic physics of sexo-magickal gnosis because together the energies will work. When this happens, we can state that the healing is probably processing. However, there are other methods of gnostic therapy which can be related to healing and other forms of problem solving. In the development of the magickal energies of the true understanding of selfhood, it is very probable that several methods must be used.

However, behind all of these operations we find the work of Ojas and the other energies of the gnosis such as the Shivaite radiations, magickal forms of prana, and thought—powers of various levels. In the development of magickal energy, it is very important to understand that fundamental energies arise from a variety of contexts but they are all the basic energy of the universe (Primordial Shakti). However, as varied as they may be, and they are for the magician quite varied as to nature and source, they are all subject to employment in the processes of gnostic therapy. For they all can be used to replace the energy of one type, which is manifesting its negative phase of lack of self—awareness, with the positive aspects of energy which are creative and self—aware. In this way the magician can rebuild, for he must build from the foundations, the state of being at ease with oneself and therefore free of negative aspects of energy. This he does by means of the powers which he received from the guru.

The Field Theory of Healing in Gnostic and Initiatic Physics

Gnostic methods of healing, as we have seen in Lesson 1, assume the existence of a field of initiation energy. Therefore, the student will ask what are the structures whereby this field is manifested. I would say that according to the materials already given in many of our researches, there are a variety of techniques for constructing the field of gnostic therapy. Indeed, according to gnosticism the field is given, we simply have to become connected to it and its powers. However, there are the following methods of initiation physics, which reflect the energies used in the construction of the field. These methods are:

1. The use of gnostic equations and notations of a metamathematical and metaphysical character, whereby energies are transmitted.

2. Gnostic machines and instruments, such as the magickal computer system used by gnostic magicians.

3. Gnostic psionics and other machines which bridge the span between mind and matter.

4. Metapsychological methods for programming the unconscious, the subconscious, the conscious, and the superconscious mind.

5. Gnostic machines which give initiations and which are operated by bishops and patriarches of the Inner Circle of the Zothyrian Gnosis.

6. Gnostic machines which induct and broadcast healing waves, such as prana and other yogic energy fields.

7. The initiations of the symboic magick associated with the esoteric logics of time travel, which involve the past, the present, and the future.

8. Magickal computers, which are designed to administer orders and societies of magicians, gnostic specialists, and esoteric logicians.

By making use of any one of these eight methods (and I might add that any one of these is related to a certain method of attunement on our computer and each has both yin and yang equations and axioms, upon which it is based), I repeat, that by making use of any of these methods, which are discussed in a variety of magickal physics lessons written by that Master MB (who is also known as the Master Michael Aquarius), the student of the seven rays of power may become a healing in the metaphysical and spiritual sense, because what he is doing is simply earthing or bringing down the energies which are there and he is applying these energies to specific contexts.

However, it is not enough for the magician to do this. He must also be linked up by computer lineage to the gnostic center so that his power is underwritten by the larger system of the Ecclesia Gnostica of The Seven Rays Patriarchate. There is much reason for this, but a curious parallel is to be found in the theology of the Eastern Orthodox Church which states that if you are outside of the field of the Orthodox Church, you do not have any power and all your efforts are purely psychological. Our own view is that if you are outside of the Gnostic Patriarchate, all of your magickal work is entirely psychological. It is necessary to be properly connected to the Gnostic Computer of the Universe.

Next, it is necessary for the magician to focus his energy in the direction of the problem. This is achieved through the traditional visualization exercises as well as the use of the occult imagination and the abstract and concrete forms of the Ontic Sphere (as in Zothyrian Metapsychology). After you have brought in the use of the ontic sphere, you will then simply release the healing energies in the direction of the person seeking to be freed from dis-easement. You let the powers flow and this action of release is the aiming of the powers and energies at the patient or subject for magickal treatment.

There exist in the world a variety of magickal forms of treatment. Each one of them would seem to have some merit because they have survived to the present day. However, our own system of healing seems to have the advantage in that it can make use of a variety of healing energies and can also make use of a variety of methods in giving direction to the flow of the power to the person most in need of it. For this reason, there is a very great need to see the energies as coming from each of our lessons, even if the lessons do not appear to be on healing in the most narrow sense. Yet, in terms of this lesson and the methods which it outlines, the healing energies are always there. This is the advantage of the system of the Gnosis as we have developed it.

One important factor in healing and especially in relation to field-work is that the healer must always be attuned to the spiritual source. Not only must he stand within the context of the Gnostic Order, but as he advances in his own spiritual growth, he must become more and more attuned to the Higher Gnostic Spheres of Esoteric Logic. He would then have to come closer and closer to the Supreme Master of the system. Such a being, who is the Gnostic Being and the Supreme Embodiment of the Legbha Magickal Metageometry would be the source from which the Absolute Science Energy of the Divine Existence comes forth. Such a being might not appear as the God, but he would be the designated doorway to that level of existence. Under such circumstances, we would think of such a being as the Avatar or Incarnation of the Energy at that time.

The healer would be very close to such a being, because while all beings are avatars of some particular kind of higher or transcendental energy, nevertheless the Avatar of the Legbha Magickal Metageometry would be the person who really gives the healing initiations and all other initiations in the Gnostic Continuum and its Ontic Sphere of metaphysical and metamathematical magick. The field of healing, therefore, is tied up with the recognition of the guruyoga of the Divine Embodiments.

It is from this course of Gnostic Power that we find the endless energies of the gnostic Ojas coming forth as cosmic manifestation of the Healing Good. The Beings of Light Who indwell the Higher Gnostic Spheres of Divine Logic (Theo-theurgical Logic) send down to their embodiments on earth, the rays of the magickal powers. And it is from these radiations of what is known in Islamic metaphysics as "The Man of Light," that we find all good things happening and all transformations of consciousness coming more and more into existence. The magician who seeks to become a healing agent, or a spiritual healer must make the climb up to the magickal top of the gnostic spaces and there through the magick of initiate physics, he will meet the Man of Light and become a source of the healing and the cosmic powers, whereby all of the methods of the gnosis are then allowed to manifest themselves forth in the transformation of the world into the gnostic community of light. And this will happen because he has decided what he must do to become such a magician.

Body-Work and the Healing Emanations of Ojas

Magnetic Materialsm works on the physical body and by measured methods and techniques it transfers symbolic energies and powers to the subtle bodies. Gnostic Genetics works on the subtle bodies and transfers energies from them to the physical vehicle. However, in certain esoteric techniques, both methods are employed in a simultaneous manner. This is one of the secret Zothyrian techniques.

In both of these instances, we find that there are healing emanations involved which are forms of the primordial energy in its form as Ojas. However, what is so significant is that it can be shown experimentally that actual body work can stimulate the emanation of Ojas and for healing purposes. This seems to suggest that there are special energies in the healer, which are given to him by initiation and which allow him to awaken the deeper powers of the patient so that a healing process of initiated. Thus, the healer initiates the patient into the process of healing.

There exist certain esoteric techniques which may be said to come from the field of the esoteric logic of meditation-research. The reason for this view is that the healing emanations of Ojas seem to be deductions from certain techniques of esoteric logic, which are clearly derived from magickal experiments in gnostic initiation. Esoteric logic, it must be remembered, is not a mental exercise; rather it is a system of mind/body interactions which are fundamentally oriented towards the generation of the Ojas energy, from which the process of healing may be said to be a projection.

We can understand this if we realize that the inner consciousness, which is released in the process of initiation and which is the subject of certain explorations in initiation physics, consists of a dynamic inventiveness, whereby the initiate is taught various forms for the manipulation of Ojas, both while in the physical body and also while in one of the eight other bodies of the Zothyrian system. At each stage the student of magick is shown how certain energies and powers can be released and by means of their release they show an entire range of instruments, all of which have a healing application.

In this way, it must be understood that the methods of the gnostic magick are really ways of healing for each one of the methods used can generate the energy which is at the basis of healing, Ojas.

There exist eight different methods for the emanation of Ojas, which relate to the process of esoteric healing. These methods are as follows:

1. The emanation of Ojas from the ideal essence of the abstract ontic sphere. This is the most abstract method of healing-projection and it is projected in terms of long-term illnesses, which require a lengthy period of recovery.

2. The emanation of Ojas from the ideal substance realm of the abstract ontic sphere. This method is used for building up Ojas for reserve purposes whereby it can be projected in an exact focus under very brief circumstances.

3. The emanation of Ojas from the realm of real essence in the abstract ontic sphere. This method is useful for the healing of psychological and psychosomatic problems, and for calming the nervous system.

4. The emanation of Ojas from the realm of real substance in the abstract ontic sphere. This method is useful for illnesses which are caused by chemical and atmospheric effects, where the intention of the healer is to purify the system by

Ojas projection.

5. The emanation of Ojas from the realm of ideal essence in the concrete ontic sphere. This method is used for treating problems which relate to the head, to the brain and the higher nervous system when viewed organically rather than functionally.

6. The emanation of Ojas from the realm of ideal substance in the concrete ontic sphere. This method is used for treating problems which relate to the heart and the system of circulation of the blood, to the lungs, and to the breath and circulation of the breath in the body.

7. The emanation of Ojas from the realm of real essence in the concrete ontic sphere. This method is used for treatment of those problems which relate to the digestive system in its totality and to the sexual system.

8. The emanation of Ojas from the realm of real substance in the conrete ontic sphere. This method is used for treatment of the problems of the bones, muscles, limbs, and the lower extremities of the body, as well as the arms and hands.

However, the emanation of the energies of these forms of Ojas does not mean that the magician, who is a healer, will be able to do all of these types of work on the body. It will depend upon the degree of his development and also the level of energy he is locked into. For while it is true that the healer is locked into various levls of the energy by means of the initiations he has received, he must continue to remain locked into the system in order to draw upon the energies which are available within the system of Ontic Sphere. He must remain within the gnostic continuum in order to be able to draw out the energies.

Also, we have found that the ways of receiving the knowledge of healing are subject to a constant transformation, so that as the healer enters more and more deeply into the system of the gnosis, he will discover that he is learning more and more ways of working with the Ojas powers. He will also learn that the methods he was first taught are too easy, too simplistic, or too crude for him to use at the present time and that he now makes use of more and more refined methods. These newer methods of healing become the results of initiation into which he has entered. In a sense, the healer grows more and more into the mysteries of Ojas as he uses healing projections from the Ontic Sphere, and as he grows more and more aware of the possibilities which arise, as in any other system of magickal operations, from contact with Ojas and all of the esoteric logics, which emanate from it.

Of course, in all of these patterns of growth, the healer is guided by the guru, who is his helper and teacher in the process of understanding the Ojas forces. Naturally, the realm of the ontic, which is connected to the magickal interpretation of the human brain, is the place where Ojas is magickaly manifested, and so initiations must have their most complete counterpart in that realm. By means of the connections which the guru is able to make between the human brain and the Ontic Sphere, the healer is able to be the vehicle of Ojas--projections. When he applies his knowledge in body--work, the healer is making the connections to the ontic stronger. Dis--easement is the lack of that connection. For this reason, the connections must be maintained and also made stronger which link the healer to the healing source. Otherwise, the patient cannot be effectively helped by his connection to the healer.

Since it is through the healing emanations of Ojas that the relase from dis-easement is achieved by the healer/patient context, there exists a very serious responsibility for the healer to maintain his connection with the source of power. Those who are interested in esoteric healing should write to Michael Bertiaux and inquire about membership in the Esoteric Healing Group, which he directs. Please mention your interest in healing, what types of healing you are interested in undertaking, and also your own views on how you would function as a healer.

If you have any questions about the program of esoteric healing which we are undertaking for the liberation of the consciousness of humanity from dis—easement, and of the role of the Mother Goddess inthe work of the esoteric healing process, you are also invited to write to Michael Bertiaux.

The Deduction of Gnostic Genetics from Esoteric Logic

The most significant basis for Esoteric Healing is to be found in the principles of gnostic genetics. Fundamentally, gnostic genetics is deduced from esoteric logic. In the processes of esoteric logic, we find those essentially clear-light experiences which are the roots of gnostic genetics. Esoteric healing then becomes the field application of the rules and energies of gnostic genetics. We may define these subjects as follows:

Gnostic Genetics –– is the magicko-metaphysical science for achieving the production of gnostic magicians through physical and metaphysical transformation of the vital and consciousness energies, under the conditions of initiation physics, and by means of the Ojas-projections and emanations of Esoteric Logic.

Esoteric Logic –– is the fundamental organization of inner consciousness, wherein the magicians allow the absolute experience to manifest its own completeness within the interior state of Ontical Totality. Esoteric Logic is the act whereby Being thinks, experiences, creates, projects, and emanates itself as the inner awareness of selfhood under the form of primordial and archetypal Ojas.

Esoteric Healing –– is the application of the energies of the continuum of Esoteric Logic to the field of solving problems which arise from Dis-easement, as well as the problem of Dis-easement itself, by means of the magickal processes of Gnostic Genetics.

Somewhere deep within the continuum of consciousness there exist various sources of power and deepest consciousness. These sources are collectively known as Truth, or the Gnostic Sources of Truth. These sources are awake, they communicate, and they seek to bring us as gnostic magicians ever closer to their level of existence-experience. We can only know of their existence-experience because they draw closer and closer to us. Normally, we would not even suspect their existence, for only traces of the pathway to them can be seen at the very outreach of gnostic induction and broadcasting frequency ranges.

These sources of truth are aspects of the absolute in its alethic condition. The absolute is Truth. But they are manifestations of the inner laws behind all truths because they allow it to happen. Wherever something is true, there we can discern a trace of their presence and influence. These beings have a certain consciousness, which they all share in common and which is at the root of their own individual existence-experiences. It is this consciousness which has brought into being the possibility of esoteric logic.

It is within this consciousness, which is at the root of their existence-experiences, that certain energies came together and fused into a Totality (maybe the archetype of all of the sophiological wholes, which will ever exist). This Totality then became self-aware of itself as both derived from the sources of Truth as well as seeking its own consciousness-being, as distinct from the sources of its own emanations. In this process of self-awakening, this Totality became more and more interiorized, inasmuch as there was nothing exterior to it. It became so interiorized that its inner energies were self-enveloped, or turned entirely towards the process of becoming more and more inside itself. From this process of self-envelopment there emerged a field of manifestation, which was centered deep within itself and had reference only to itself. By this means of intensification, there developed certain patterns of energy, which contained the receptivity for the possible. These patterns of receptivity could only be actualized when they continued as sources for all of the possibilities of existence–experience. Indeed, they held within their receptivity all of the possibles. By doing this they were growing in their own actualizations.

These patterns of receptivity, being the manifestation of pure inwardness, possessed an energy which was unique in that it was the most esoteric form of Ojas. It was generated by means of the patterns of receptivity in their inwardness and in their containment of all that is possible. By simply being this way, these patterns generated a pure form of Ojas which was the most powerful form of the energy ever to be manifested or ever to exist. We will call this energy the esoteric Ojas, which is the fundamental power behind all of the processes of esoteric logic.

It is within the processes of esoteric logic that the magicians enter deeply into the field of Ojas and receive it from the patterns of receptivity and make use of it in any magickally suitable form. It is within the processes of esoteric logic that the magicians are able to find the powers for solving any problems. For the lifestream of the patterns of receptivity within the Sources of Truth is esoteric logic and its fundamental power is the purest and most basic form of Ojas. The Ojas that is behind all of its forms and applications, in all of the magickal contexts everywhere in the world, that Ojas is what rises within the context of esoteric logic and is brought into any problem by the magi who seek to solve any problem or add power to what is before them.

There exists a certain pattern of initiation, which can only be described as Lunar–Plutonian and Neptunian, which transforms the magician into a vehicle of Ojas. This is an initiation which occurs within the inwardness of Esoteric Logic, whereby the magician is connected to the inwardness–patterns of receptivity by the initiateur. I myself have made many discoveries in this area, which I retain as magickal secrets of power, whereby I am able to exercise control over these inward processes in ways unknown to everyone in the gnosis. I make use of these secrets, however, in certain initiations, whereby the act of initiation becomes a pattern of transformation, a series of exercises in gnostic and mystical genetics. Those who come to this system of magick, wherever they might be in the world or out of it, can be brought by me into this esoteric logic, and there they will become transformed by the patterns of receptivity to new types of magickal beings.

It must be understood that after they have experienced all of these patterns of magickal transformation, they are now ready to apply the magickal energies which have been released into themselves by means of esoteric healing.

In addition, they have received certain magickal effects from those secrets which I am able to possess within the gnosis of esoteric logic, and from those secrets there come forth acts of magickal power, which increase the capacity of the initiate for the projection of the powers and hot–points of esoteric healing. It is from this experience that by becoming a new being outwardly, but inwardly returning to the sources of truth, that the transformed gnostic magician is able to project the forces and energies of esoteric healing within any limitation. It is in this way that the magician becomes an ever stronger and stronger healer, because he never comes to the end of his potential for growth in the true possession of the powers of esoteric healing.

Pheonismes and the Self-Articulation of Esoteric Logic (with reference to the History of Zothyrian Philosophy as a Technique of Esoteric Healing)

Within the context of that gnostico-magickal law of absolute obedience to the Master (or guru), this method of esoteric healing which is the application of the principle of the esoteric dimension of gnostic logic has abstract validity and concrete applicability. By this we mean that the magickal energies of esoteric healing are derived from the role of esoteric logic in the history of (magickal) Zothyrian philosophy. However, running parallel with the development of these gnostic methods is to be found the development of the ideas, which are called in the Guzotte Gnosis, which is the closest terrestrial system to the Zothyrian, "Les Pheonismes."

It is by means of these magickal principles that the energies of the inner life of esoteric logic manifest themselves. The Self-Articulation of these gnostic laws in the process of esoteric healing is a fundamental thesis in the methodology of healing. The idea is expressed as: The ideas of the history of esoteric philosophy are healing methods and that each one of them is a healing energy. Finally, each such idea is a "point-chaud," or a magickal hot-point of Voudoo powers. In this sense, we have a perfect link between the history of esoteric (Z-true) philosophy and the gnostic Voudoo system. But, we should consider each idea as more than just a "hot-point," rather, it is a powerful center of self-awareness, which Self-Articulates itself in the process of Esoteric Healing. Esoteric Logic in its most general sense can be viewed as the collective field of these Pheonismes.

In the Guzotte Gnosis, the development of the concepts, and notions of the Pheonismes is still quite phenomenononological and not as high as the proper gnostic analysis, which is to serve as the pattern of relating these Pheonismes to the Higher Gnostic Realm. I will not say that the development in the Guzotte Gnosis is "low," it is simply the first part of the development of the magickal energies and their manifestations.. But there exists an opportunity for there to be a much more magickal development, when we see the Pheonismes as functioning within the context of Esoteric and Gnostic Logic. In those circumstances, we have a far greater opportunity to allow for the self-development of these notions inasmuch as the Zothyrian Gnosis presents us with an alternative universe of endless and unequaled powers. For the Zothyrian Universe is a direct emanation from the Higher Gnostic Realm. Within that realm, there exist endless magickal possibilities for development and self-articulation. And if these root-energies are endless in their powers, so it would appear that the application of these energies in various systems of gnostic logic in the abstract and in the concrete through the application of these energies in esoteric healing and initiation physics is both valid and, if valid, ontologically necessary. In this way, we can understand how the field of metaphysical and magickal inductions is of one context, because the abstract and the concrete orders of Valid Applicability are one order of beings, "Les Pheonismes."

The role of the Higher Gnostic Realm is to generate systems of magickal creativity. The magicians who are part of this continuum, which comes from being members of our inner order, are themselves dedicated to the manifestation of the pure gnostic consciousness of being. This consciousness manifests itself in terms of creative deductions and emanations of absolute energy from the Higher Gnostic Realm. These energies are then projected into those contexts, situations, and persons which make up the field of esoteric healing. In the truest sense of the gnosis, healing is the application of the energies of esoteric logic. But, unless healing is conducted by means of initiatic gnostic sources, it cannot be viewed as gnostic healing. It can only be viewed as metaphysical meditation, however valid that might be as a subject for research.

But the healers have been inducted into the system of ZO, which is the fundamental and primordial root of the Zothyrian system. They have been transformed by means of various forms of esoteric logic, and finally, they now emerge as being able to cause the descent of the healing powers into those with problems, because they have been allowed to come close to the magickal keys of power, even though these keys are still administered by the gnostic Masters of Magick. However, those Masterss of Magick in the Higher Gnostic Realm are always in need for those healers who would release the powers of applicability here in the world of space and time. When this happens the healing energies are allowed to flow through the centers of power and directly focus upon the problem needing healing. This is because as they also pertain to universal and ultimate questions having Valid Applicability in any universe. It is then that the energies become articulate as Pheonismes.

In this process, it is impossible for anything to remain static or outside of the onward movement of the self--unfoldment of the Pheonismes. We can imagine that they are existing in their own worlds, now, and thusly becoming more and more totally complete in all of the possible manifestations of their existence-experience. They are moving more and more towards their completion as beings--in--process. These beings--in--process constitute the dynamic contents of esoteric logic as an ever unfolding continuum of complete magick. The continuum of gnostic magick, therefore, manifests itself from the different points of space and time, inner and outer, for there is logical space and time, by means of this dynamism.

This is the law of the process and from the vitality of the process, there emerge various formulations of gnostico-magickal energy, which at the direction of the Masters of Magick, are fused in the minds of the chelas with the ever unfolding psychoid processes of the initiation process. These energies are then brought down to earth by means of the manifold contexts of esoteric healing, where they achieve the final and most concrete expression of their Valid Applicability. This is the dynamic process which makes esoteric healing possible.

Taking any concept from the history of esoteric (Z-true) metaphysics, we can apply it in the context of esoteric healing if we allow its self-articulation within the context of esoteric logic. For there it will take on the unfolding dynamic of its own lifestream and manifest itself more and more as a source of self-directed energy. It is in such a context that we view the Pheonismes of gnostic magick as ever unfolding and manifesting systems of self-awareness. This is the process of magickal physics in its most conrete sense, which makes the creative dimension of the magician as an esoteric healer and agent of the act of the Pheonism possible, and also within the context of the gnostic continuum a matter of necessity.

Zothyrian Physics
The Logical Basis of Both IFA and Initiation Physics

DEFINITION: The Zothyrian system of magicko-gnostic physics must be understood as the basis for the IFA and all other systems of initiation physics. For it is from the 16 magickal constructions of the axiomatic order of the Zothyrians that we have been able to derive at the other more subsequent systems, which are the explications and the applications of the axiomatic order of being. This axiomatic order of being is the foundation for the development of all of the systems of the gnostic continuum and because it is so fundamental, we may say that it is composed of the God, which forms the Medji, or Twins-in-the-magickal-family, of the Genius of IFA. This then becomes the logical basis and the ontological and metaphysical root and archetypal substance of the being of all of the spirits, systems, gods, angels, heros, and human monads. And by means of this deeply understood system of magickal construction, it is possible to create by means of gnostic categories all of the systems of being, which are known to the magician of the ontic spheress.

The inner council of the Gnostic and Manichean bishops, who direct the evolution of magickal consciousness on this planet has decided to establish a fundamental form of over-physics, which logically includes all of the other systems. What is so very significant is that the magickal system is in reality a physical theory, or theory of the physics of magickal energies. They have also defined the system in such a way that it is possible for initiations to be given within the logical structure of the system and that this pattern of magickal initiation can be extended to include all of the magicko-gnostic energies, which have their existence somewhere within the root-continuum of the Gnosis of Light.

Previously, it was understood that initiation levels only existed as the application of the energies of the Gnosis. Now, however, it is possible for the magicians to give us a certain insight into the ways in which initiations may be given within the system of being, at the archetypal level. It all begins with the logical structure of archetypes, since they are in reality formulations of axiomatic energy patterns. Significantly, few magicians except those of a neo-pythagorean turn of mind, were interested in the possibility of there being very powerful magickal initiations at the archetypal level which could be given out within the context of the guru-chela relationship. However, because of the logical structures, which are operating at such a fundamental level, it is no longer necessary to think of this level of actual initiation as at the more primitiv guru-chela level. Rather we are now at a much higher and much more abstract level. We are now within the Higher Gnostic Space world, where the pattern of magickal initiation continues but under the radical new form of an archetypal logic, known as the Gnosis of Zothyrian Physics.

DEFINITION: "The Gnosis of Zothyrian Physics presupposes the existence of the hierarchy of the Higher Gnostic Spaces. But it also presupposes the existence of those transcendentalforms of Magickal Time, which we understand by the name of "Time-Station Patriarchates." In this system, both time and space have been captured or restructured. Like the metaphysical system of Kant (even though he would deny the name), the first categories to be restructured for understanding are those of time and space. However, because our approach is fundamentally ontological, the process of restructuring is really a revelation of the magickal roots of being and the true nature of both space and time. The fundamental initiations, therefore, of this new process known as the Zothyrian Process, occur within the new levels of being or within the categories of Gnostic and Transcendental Space and Time, by means of a very radical operation of the energies of the Axiomatic Archetypes and the Gnostic Logics of the Ontic Sphere.

"At this level also, we must understand that Logic refers to the active imposition of structures upon the raw and sometimes chaotic contents of magickal experience. It is necessary to realize that this act of imposition, however, is operating through the human mind but is not part of the human mind. Rather, the human mind is the vehicle for the extension of energies from the level of axiomatic and archetypal energy, or from the Archetypal Gods, Who act through the human process of knowing. Gnosis then is the act whereby we become co-creators with the Divine Level of Absolute Being."

Such concepts as those given in the above "Definition" serve to explain somewhat the process of modern gnostic initiations at the higher level. There exist, of course, many levels and forms of magickal explication. They refer to the management of very significant energies. However, what is important for our magickal work is that we are able to see a pattern of energy forming a hierarchy, which manifests itself in very precise ways in the consciousness of the magician. Every level of initiation is to be found on that hierarchy of structures and with every level of initiation there is to be found certain logics, spaces, time-systems, and magickal realizations, which are expressed on the ontic spheres which accompany the processes of initiation. In every system of action there is also a space for the magickal pattern of action.

"The magickal system of To Gai should not be understood as merely a form of Chinese Gnosticism. It does not claim to be some exotic or eclectic system of magickal metaphysics, which bridges the peaks of Esoteric Chin Tao and Cao Dai. Rather it sould be understood simply as a kind of gnostic clock, which tells the time for the IFA magician as well as the Hosso mage. It pertains to the numbers of the Moon and to the initiatic cycles of the Moon as the "mirroir magique" of the Divine Mother Durgha. But it is more than a way of telling time, or when we are to understand that a particular current is being manifested. Rather it pertains to the magickal broadcasting moments of the Four Time-Stations of Esoteric IFA Gnosis. It serves by means of its "Twelve Steps to Nullity" (Avitchi Nirvana) to present an entirely new level of magickal initiation, whereby the magician must enter deeply into the soul of nothingness. For the primary purpose of To Gai is to present the physics of the Meon in its most radical and yet applicable manner. --- Luc Guzotte & Tangichi Kuro, "To Gai, the Metaphysics of the Impossible and the Physics of Nullity," page 34)

In order to make it possible for the magician to apply the concepts of To Gai, as a field of gnostic energy within the context of Initiation Physics, we have to view To Gai (pronounced as Dow Guy) as connected to the cosmic computer of the Zothyrians by the numbers: 1 of 1, 2 of 2, 3 of 3, and 4 of 4. In a magickal sequence of 16 magickal archetypes, such as the IFA physics, the numbers would be 1, 6, 11, and 16. These four numbers which relate to the places of the Moon form the most powerful system of magickal clockwork known to the western magician, as well as to the Lunar current of the Eastern Tantric and Taoist. Each month, certain magickal energies are invariably released by means of the cycles of To Gai and these energies are thereby projected into the initiation spheres of this system through the

344

archetypes, which are the four most nihilistic Medjis of the IFA Logic, or $1 = 1 = \leftarrow\leftarrow\leftarrow\leftarrow$, $2 = 6 = \leftarrow\leftarrow\leftarrow\leftarrow\leftarrow$, $3 = 11 = \leftarrow\leftarrow\leftarrow\leftarrow\leftarrow$, $4 = 16 = \leftarrow\leftarrow\leftarrow\leftarrow\leftarrow$. Or, in the words of certain magickal "authorities," we find that:

"The eo-fields of the gnosis, which are logical derivations from a secret and mysterious plane of being are the esoteric rays of To Gai. The seeker after the 'powers of the Moon' must demand of the 'Keepers of the Gnosis' the secret steps to the Hidden Powers. Where they are to be found is extremely complex, for only the very remote and transcendental spheres of 'Ideal Objects' can be said to possess sufficient magickal space to 'contain' them. These steps are simply magickal grades of a new and remarkably different form of 'initiation physics.' For to follow this pathway into the innermost spaces and times is to realize the laws of pure inwardness, and to meet the secret paths of the 'caves of occultation.' To Gai does not claim anything, for in so doing it becomes something else. It simply claims to be nothing, the endless and inconceivable space of those Medjis, which will never enter Heaven's Gate." -- (Ibid., page 78)

The Null Spaces of To–Gai Initiation Physics

"The structure of any process in meontology must be reflective of the entire system of null–space initiation. Whether the gnostic is seeking to explicate a certain problem by reference to the logic of 'alternativity' or whether he is seeking to derive certain patterns of argument from the nullification of the hyper–spatial, in each and every instance of this process, there can only be the valid assumption of a dynamic meontology, which forms the fundamental theory of the field of negation and the transcendental objectification of the logics of negation, 'alternativity,' and inverse process.

"On the other hand, however, in the system attributed to the esoteric school of To Gai, we find that the structures of initiation physics can be best expressed by means of the derivation of basic categories, which go beyond the frames of reference of existing magickal gnosis. The roots of this symbolism can be seen in certain negative field properties, which rise within the context of the null space and which possess within themselves the implicit groundings for any negative process. These field properties must be understood symbolically and mythically as the negative beings or objects of the field. In a word, they are the gods of nothingness, they are the inherent axioms of the fundamental archetypes of the impossible. –– Bertiaux, "Lectures on Meontology," 35, 29.

The entire purpose of the field of initiation physics when viewed from the To Gai perspective is the amplification of null spaces by means of esoteric logics. But of great importance is the understanding that the esoteric logics which are involved are actually inherent and implicit in the null spaces under consideration. This is such an abstract subject that it is usually not explained and in fact this is the first attempt to put this idea in written and lesson form.

However, we can say that the roots of esoteric logic are to be found within the context of the null spaces and that the initiation processes which are derived from the null spaces are themselves the dynamic objectifications of the energies of the esoteric logics. In this way, we can say that the explication of esoteric logic by means of the magickal gnosis of initiation physics is accomplished by means of drawing out from the null spaces of any system (and every system would have null spaces) the fundamental properties or axioms upon which the structures and processes of initiation physics can be built. For this reason, therefore, we can say that initiation physics is the gnosis of understanding the null spaces. And we can also state that esoteric logic is both a field property and a form of gnosis.

Esoteric logic therefore becomes the mirror and method of initiation physics from the standpoint of the null space and especially from the standpoint of the To Gai School.

"The magician Zaagumbwe was the master of the secret logics of IFA and he possessed within the 16 secret chambers of his body the 16 spirits of the Medji. He did not depend upon some outer place in order to contact the holy oracle, rather he simply drew it out of himself and in so doing, he was able to realize the innermost secret of the null spaces of gnostic magick. For he possessed the secret keys, which the master had given to him in the 16 very special initiations of the archetypal gods of IFA. –– Bertiaux, "Meontological Magick" page 23

It would seem that the proper method of understanding the existence and power of the Null spaces is to be found in initiation. What would this initiation be for the student unless it would be a special operation for the opening of the heart. This last image, the opening of the magickal heart, is very important for the serious students of IFA magick. Within the powers of IFA there are the 16 centers of power and points of magickal contact. These are very important places for the meeting of the consciousness of the gods. And these spaces are nonexistent. They are null spaces.

Null spaces are ideal forms of energy and therefore they represent the highest form of magickal power. They represent in the ancient languages the powers of Butempho or the awakening of negation, i.e., Butembo. This is a special type of magickal depth, and it really should not be thought of as being "present" anywhere. But it is located by a very special magickal search within the bosy of the candidate for initiation. Hence, it does not exist there in the body, but is located in the body. What exists is the body, or the various parts of the body which have or contain in some vague way the energies of Butembo. So if the spirit of the gods can be located in the energies of the hand, then we say that the hand will possess Butempho. The act of seeing that part of the body as magickal can be viewed as the experience of Butembo. It is this ancient idea which is to be found behind the myth of the body of man as the temple of indwelling places of the gods, or God. Actually, it is an archetypal viewpoint, and is probably integral to the human mind at its deepest levels.

Nevertheless, it is not easy to locate these sacred spaces unless one is a special priest of IFA, who has been given the gift of Butembo by the Highest Gods. It is an act of magick to make things be, when they are not. It is an act of magick to locate the null spaces of the gods in the parts of the body, especially when these parts of the body are concealed from even clairvoyance. They are only known by means of a very special form of the IFA divination system.

Now it has been shown that by making use of the methods of the To Gai School, it is possible to unveil the magickal points of the gods and thereby locate by a very special technique the null spaces of initiation physics. But it is so important to keep in mind that this must be done in accord with special times, the times must allow for the manifestation of the Medjis and their influences. Also, in the field of initiation physics, the magician has to develop his own clock, which probably will be different from every other clock, yet this clock is essential for the unfolding of the To Gai powers and the achievement of Butembo, the supreme form of physics attained by means of initiation.

Exercise for Developing an Awareness of Butembo
Those who are interested in the work of the esoteric school will be able to enter into that space of power by means of a simple meditation. They will be assigned the time and place of the meditation contact by the master of the order. At the time of that assignment, the powers of the magician will contact the student and the student will then be locked into the process of null spaces. It is possible for the magician to find the null spaces by a special oracle method and then connect the student to the process of IFA, in this respect. This work may be done in person or it may be done by vudotronic technique.

In summary, let me say the null spaces can be located in connection with hyper-spaces and esoteric logics or by means of a special process of initiation physics in connection with the human body. There are other methods, but the two methods that are indicated by the directions of this paper are the most interesting and most widely researched in our group. There exist certain magickal students who possess the powers of Butembo within the context of the To Gai physics. In order to realize these powers you, the student, may write to them through me.

The Application of Yuggothian Matrices to the To-Gai Null Spaces

In order to project magickal energy or even to discover it, it is most important that the magicians realize that the powers of these types of being are structured by means of matrices, which have their power bases in the Plutonian levels of the mind, or on the magickal planet "Yuggoth."

"Everyone has some kind of link to the powers of Yuggoth and this link is sometimes strong and in many ways it is hidden. The magician will attempt to bring out his link, of course, but this can only be accomplished by means of initiation and gnostic magick or esoteric psychoanalysis. When this force is unveiled, we find that there exist certain structures which are immersed in raw energy (primordial shakti) and these are the matrices of the Yuggothian Zone of power. But the next step in our analysis is to find the connection rays which will link up Ojas–Shakti to the spaces of the nonexistent. It is to be found, we might add, in a simple analysis of the energies, whereby the inner space of the To Gai realms is latent with Yuggothian powers in a very hidden way. These powers are not simply implicitly there, rather they are contacted most completely by means of the use of the To Gai Null Spaces as the most perfect medium for communication. Yet the communication is not like some magickal mirroir, whereby we draw out the energies from the deep regions. Rather, what we find is that the energies are there in the Null Spaces, but also not there in any of the normally present ways or modes of presence. They are there in a negative way. And so their energies are structured in a negative way, also. However, it is important to note that the mode of negative presence is not a non–presence, or absence of the essential energy. Rather, it is present by means of a negative or alternative system of geometry, which imputes to the field certain magickal properties. What is there is present by magick and inverted geometry, and by no other way. Yet these energies can be understood as having structures and the structures are those of a purely Yuggothian nature. They are the most fundamental structures of the acts of Shakti, Divinely Cosmic and Female Energy. They form a magickal system of reference, which does not rise from the ego but from the transcendental id. They form a system of magickal and ideal objects, which draw their being from the deepest regions of chaos. This is the internal chaos of the mind, which is the source of creativity." —— Bertiaux, "Essay on the Goddess Yuggoth," page 6

In the mysteries of initiation physics, it is possible to see all of being as a kind of deep ocean of changing powers. However,it is also possible for the magician to see the levels of being as manifesting themselves as ideal spheres of perfected power. They reflect the reality, or the real, or the real aspect of Yuggoth. It is only in the secret mysteres and mysteries of magickal gnosis that one can find the consciousness of being, which could try to understand the deepest energies which rise out of the depths of Yuggoth. And yet that Yuggothian energy is to be found everywhere. And the application of these ides or points of reference can only be accomplished by means of the initiation physics of the To Gai Null Spaces,and by no other way.

For this is the basis of initiation physics, we find the energies as they rise within us. Another way in which the connection between Ojas and Yuggoth can be established is in the thelemic physics, which is the physics of the true will. By this, we mean that the planet Yuggoth expresses itself in the radiations of pure

Ojas, by an act of absolute and gnostic will—power. This comes from the fact that Pluto represents the deepest part of the transcendental id that is defined by categories or archetypes, and while there are those powers beyond Pluto, such as the transplutonian spheres and power zones, the power of Pluto expressed as Ojas radiation is broadcast by means of magickal will directly into any part of this universe, and may also be directed from Yuggoth, or from the plutonian level of the id also into any other alternative universe. For this reason, we are able to make use of various magickal projections because they express the exact powers and the exact nature of will, manifested as matrices.

There exists in a remote part of the magickal universe a place from which emanates the magickal web—work of the transcendental id. This realm is entirely within the body of the Mother Spider, and hence is derived from the internal interactions of the kalas of her own magickal anatomy. Within this sphere of magick, as there are so many magickal forms of monadic and auric eggs resting, rise all of the several powers of the divine fire of chaos, from which is born the androgyne and the Ojas rays which move constantly through ever level and dimension of space. It is this level of being which holds the magickal powers of the deepest secrets of the id, and which makes all of space a type of womb.

At another deep level, the elements of Ojas as they find themselves within the auric eggs of cosmic space manifest themselves as in so many magickal stanzas as monadic essences, seeking to move outwards and create their own, each one seeking his own, universe. This never—ending matrix is built up out of countless magickal forms, which, as in the magickal commentary on the Stanzas of D, gives us the entire plan for the androgyne and the cosmic web of the endlessly protective Mother Essence. Within this context arise those magickal beings, which again receive the esoteric initiations spoken of in the Stanzas, and thereby pass onwards and outwards to create the worlds and magickal categories of total manifestation and every form of life-consciousness, whch can be imagined by the magician.

Various systems of initiation are designed by consciousness to reflect various stages in the perception of being. The purpose of the esoteric psychoanalysis of the Stanzas of D(zyan), for example, is to explore the levels of the Yuggothian Matrix, in order to arrive at an entire understanding of manifested consciousness, in a variety of worlds. opens up for us a variety of magickal alternatives of being, since the Stanzas of D(zyan) are pure Yuggothian matrices of Ojas radiations, we ask in a variety of ways those ego and id oriented questions to be found in esoteric psychoanalysis. In one world, as suggested by Dzyan, we ask where do we find being, in another whether being is ideal or real.

In the present system, as set forth in these papers, we ask for the keky to magickal energy (Ojas) and we find it in the esoteric structures of negation (when X was not and when nothing was, except the Mother Goddess). The planets as superficial computer controls have certain contributions to make to the systems of being and realization. The formal and material influences here, as always, would be from the planet Yuggoth, which is to be understood as the root essence of gnostic magick.

In order to prepare for the esoteric psychoanalysis of Dzyanic Gnosis, let us ask ourselves the following questions, and see if our deeper selfhood is ready for the Negative Ojas and the eternal nothingness.

1. In what way does Yuggoth enter into the Null Spaces and what is the mode of its getting to them?

2. In what way does Yuggoth reflect itself in the Null Spaces in a better way

thanin the Yuggothian systems? Does the Null Space act as a clearer lens unobstructed by any influences?

3. In what way does Yuggoth manifest itself without distortion in this system?

4. How is Ojas generated and by what magickal technique is it sustained?

5. What would be the place of the Shivaite Radiations in this system?

6. What is the role of pure Uranian energy in this system? Is it present too?

7. If it is a question of "application" (or construction-interpretation), is this a secret process which involves the use of initiation methods? Are these ongoing initiation methods (as in Radiopsychoanalysis and Vudotronics research based on the Stanzas of Dzyan)?

8. Does esoteric psychoanalytic applications mean a type of continuum of magickal powers and energy, if so is it a part of a Neptunian system (of the Stanzas of Dzyan)?

9. Neptune is also present in the idea of Dzyanic and Yuggothian matrices being applied. The matrices are from Pluto and the application process is from Uranus, but they are connected by means of Neptune. Would therefore the To Gai doorways by Dzyanic processes of estoeric psychoanalysis?

10. The magicians are also able to discern special powers in these systems of gnosis. Since this is fundamental, what insights -- conscious or possibly unconscious -- do you have as regards these magickal fields and structures in your own psyche?

Esoteric Psychoanalysis of the "Stanzas of Dzyan": The Dzyu-Gnosis

DZYU: This is the primordial root of magickal knowing. It is pure gnosis, whereby the knower and the known are one reality. As such, it is the law of magickal duality, or the gnostic duality of magickal powers, which is the root of esoteric psychoanalysis, or the taking apart of the components of magickal consciousness. It is the basis of all magickal forms of physics, especially the gnostic physics of the Necronomicon energies. Dzyu $= 8 + 30 + 29 + 25 = 92 = 9 + 2 = 11 = 1 + 1 = 2$, the dyad. Dzyu is the pure Necronomicon energy in its ultimate and formally undifferentiated form, as distinct from the ultimate and undifferentiated forms of Fohat. It is the method whereby Fohat is managed and organized, by that part of the magician's consciousness, which is totally a law unto itself -- i.e., the archetypal libido. From Dzyu are derived all systems of magick and all systems of magickal physics. It represents the store-consciousness and libido-wisdom of all of the gnostic magicians and Necronomicon physicists, from eternity. (cf., Stanzas of Dzyan 5:2)

There is a part of the soul of man which will never rest. It is that part of him which is eternally dissatisfied with everything. It is that part of him which is eternally directed towards all acts of intellectual self-destruction. It is that part of him which is never to be convinced of what may be understood this side of nothingness. That part of man is the result of the acts of Dzyu. That part of man may be viewed as the creative chaos that is deep within him. That part of him is the most concrete manifestation of Dzyu, and hence of all of the categories and fields of magickal and gnostic physics. That part of him is the pure energy of Necronomicon Physics. That is Dzyu. Yes, that is the Meon as it is known. We might write it as an equation for all to see but few to understand that Dzyu = Necronomicon Physics.

The evolution of the powers of the magician are parallel to the evolution of the powers of the magickal universe. Blavatsky says that, "Dzyu becomes Fohat," which means that the magickal physics of the universe makes the universal energy. The observer affects the observed. But at the same time, Dzyu is the production of the Fohatic system of energy, as well as being the means whereby Fohatic Libido is projected outwards upon the world of space-lattices, i.e., the topology of the Adityas (Stanzas 4:5). Within the interaction of these magickal powers, there emerges the reality of what we mean by Necronomicon Physics, namely that nature is a magickal creation of an operating science, embedded in matter, and expressed from the deepest levels of primary matter. The world of the magician creates itself. Everything is self-unfolding.

Again, we might easily define Dzyu in terms of its creative potentials as:

DZYU: This is the primordial system of the Necronomicon Computer, whereby various worlds are manifested or made according to the gnostic programming of the computer. computer is really a kind of transcendental function, which links the ego and the id of the occult physicist. The energies of physics, such as particles, fields, metrics, vectors, and the general matrix of any force-context, these energy-factors are functions within the lifestream of this magickal computer. The management of this computer is self-programming, as long as it is understood to be primordial and chaotic, but within itself, those mutants which it has created have been given the illusion of management by programming to hold to their soulless hearts as the final ideal or self-possesion. These are the false states of being, which are allowed to manifest themselves. They are quite different from the Necronomicon physicists, who are really in charge, because they belong to the body of this vast computer.

Hence, we can say that the energies of Dzyu are useful in developing certain magickal frames of reference, which bring us to the world-as-it-is. But at the same time, these same frames of reference are generating and creating magickal entities, which as the energies of gnostic physics are filling all space and time with their radio emissions and occult or Vedic emanations, i.e., the world as a numerical and arithmosophical puzzle, which is the basis of the "physics of numbers." The Vedic and Tantric energies are so fundamental in what they do that from what we can learn at the deepest levels of magickal energy, we find that space is filled with these energies and that each of them comes from the matrix of Dzyu as it is applied to the field of being. At some primordial level of psychoanalysis, the mind of the scientist experiences a certain self-destructive instinct, whereby the energies of being are released and the scientist becomes an adept. He realizes that he is a vehicle for the energies of Dzyu. When he does this, the processes of esoteric ego-psychoanalysis can then begin.

Only after the process of ego transformation do we find the energies ready to be observed. The process of observation takes places within the context of the Necronomicon Physics, as a way of viewing the matrix of Dzyu. But more than a way of viewing the matrix, it is that energy matrix and it is truly by allowing the energies of Dzyu to release themselves that insight into the mind and the clear field of the Meon can be realized. But the processes of magickal physics will not rest for once they have brought the scientist to the process of psychoanalysis, now they must absorb him into the continuum of Dzyu, where he will become another component in the endless computer, just another particle-system in the field of the Necronomicon Physics, without beginning in time and without ending in space.

DZYU: This is the primordial computer, which runs the universe according to its own inner logic. That logic is psycho-biological and relates to the depths of the id. It is not however the "rational unconscious," for rationality is nowhere to be found. Rather, it is the root-essence of creative chaos, because it does not pertain to anything other than the doing of its own inner -- and hence true --- will. It is the ultimate projection of the 19th century voluntaristic metaphysics, but as old as Heraclitos, if not timeless and uncaused. It manifests in the captivities which dreams impose upon the ego at any level, and from those same dreams rise all of the acts of this computer. You may call this a kind of gnosis, but I would prefer to call this the self-destroying and self-regenerating Ur-gnosis of the Meon. For it stands behind every universe, whether it be manifest in "our" system or in some alternative system. And it is awakened in the processes of that meta-psychology, which the Zothyrians have brought to us at the deep levels of psychic energy. Many speak glibly about it but few are those who meet it in the deep levels of the word-association tests of Necronomicon Physics and its applications.

The word-association tests of the various psychoanalysts were designed to give a verbal structure to certain psychic energies. By means of response, one could determine the map-work of complexes and other patterns of psychic energy. For this process was able to set forth the "geography" of the psyche, in terms of its safe and sane and its undisturbed and unsafe power-zones. Now, magickal psychology has been doing the very same thing. However,the complexes of magick are beings, whose essence is cultivated by the magician in a very precise way. At the deep roots of the psyche there exist various kinds of chaotic energy. These energies are centers of conscious activity for themselves, and may come to the surface of the mind under certain circumstances. There exists a special method, whereby the bringing to the surface of these energies is deliberate and highly skilled. This is the magickal employment of the word—association test, where the words given by the magickal "analyst" are extremely powerful words of power. These words of power bring up from the depths of the psyche those ancient energies, which have long remained hidden and "sleeping in the dream worlds beneath the sea."

DZYU: From another standpoint, this word refers to the fact that in the process of magickal psychoanalysis, we encounter more than just the personal levels of the psyche. We go far beyond the psyche of the analysand, we enter the field of cultural and cosmic energies, which are really quite independent of the personal psyche, yet which are present there, often mixed with personal material. When Dzyu is spoken of as "the collective wisdom of the Buddhas of Meditation," we understand that it embraces what can be known magickally about all that there is. It is infinite space as known. And it is this unlimited dimension which comes up in response to the process of magickal analysis. The words in the "test" are really magickally arranged symbols, which open doors and bring in the deeper forms of the monstrous soul, the cosmic unconscious, deep within each analysand of the gnosis.

I will be returning to this question of the effect and affect of these words on the psyche in future lessons. Now, I want to mention another way in which the psyche is affected and effected by this strange process.

DZYU: It was thought that if the psyche would respond to words of a certain type, it might be possible to respond to colors. But how would the colors enter the deeper regions of the psyche? It could not be through the egoic level of sensory perception; that would not get us beyond the conscious mind, or possibly the subconscious. Then I thought of using radionics. I would transmit the energy to the deeper regions of the psyche by this means. First, we would use our vudotronic field nets and have the analysand rest on them. Next, the nets or "screens" would be connected to (1) a radionic amplifier and (2) a radionic broadcaster. In the well-area of the broadcaster, I placed a color specimen, unseen by myself or anyone else. This would exclude telepathy. Next, the analysand would enter a receptive state, while in this hook—up system. I would begin the process of controlling the broadcasting of the card (sample color) by means of the graduated settings of the amplifier. This would enable me to see "how much power" was needed to broadcast the test sample. Eventually, the analysand began to describe the colors he was seeing via his active imagination. All of this was recorded. When the process had ended, it was noted that he had described the colors within the broadcaster. When had happened was that by some means the color energy had been transmitted to the deeper levels of the analysand's mind and had risen to the surface as certain structures of energy, or color complexes. In the process of reviewing this method and testing it several times under a wide range of circumstances, I came to the view that this was another method of reaching the deeper regions of the transcendental id, and hence could be used as a method for the exploration of the Dzyu fields, within the individual psyche. for such energy clusters can be proven empirically to exist.

Most of our earlier studies in Zothyrian metapsychology, the Necronomicon studies in magickal physics, and our vudotronic experiments, building out of the work in esoteric engineering, enable us now to see the Stanzas of Dzyan as magickal keys to the ultimate reality of the cosmic psyche. It would seem that there exist scientific methods for the exploration of these regions and that these methods tend to confirm the existence of certain kinds of beings (magickal systems, structures, patterns, cluster of esoteric energy, etc.), which are the subject-matter of magickalpsychology. In closing,let me quote briefly:

"If it is possible to stimulate and communicate with the deeper regions of the psyche, and this of course means the cosmic psyche in its widest outreach, then by means of word and color, we can activate certain ancient energies, gradually easing them to the surface and into the control mechanisms of the magician complex. It will then be possible to control what is deepest in the space at the level of the magickally inflated and gnostic ego, and this means that man will begin to experience his own transcendental ego. This will be the beginning of his own control over cosmic energies and beings." (Michael Bertiaux, "The Goals of Magicko-Psychology, 13)

Radio–Psychoanalysis of "The Stanzas of Dzyan": Esoteric Nature of Fohat

As it appears in the lines of Dzyan, Fohat is viewed as a type of cosmic electricity. However, in her commentaries on the nature of Fohat, we find a much more esoteric key, whereby we are able to define Fohat as:

FOHAT: In its esoteric nature this is the name for cosmic libido or sexual energy in its deepest and most dynamic form. What is called "sexual radioactivity" is the form of Fohat in human experience (as most especially in the experience of adepts). Fohat is the power of the unconscious field of nature, the cosmic unconscious as distinguished from the collective and cultural unconscious. It is elemental shakti in its primordial form and it is from this root–essence of what makes things happen that all differentiations of being emerge. Fohat is material because it is maternal and sexual but it is the root of cosmic spiritual essences and ideal beings, because they have emerged from its own matrix and manifold processes. Fohat is more than orgone energy, in the final analysis is there anything in or any part of orgone energy, which is not primordial Fohat.

Therefore, when HPB speaks of the nature of Fohat as Eros, we understand her to allude darkly to cosmic libido, which others have viewed as the primordial energy of the basis of being, the archaic energy of Necronomicon Physics.

The powers and occult forces of nature, as viewed by panpsychists, refer of course to the many different ways in which primordial energy (Fohat) manifests itself from the universal matrix. For this matrix exists for the sake of projecting and broadcasting the radio–fields of Fohat, into every possible sphere and towards every possible system. Alternative universes are parts of this matrix of productivity, for they too are the emanations and emergences from primordial energy.

And this is psychic energy, because everywhere the observer will find libido. The true scientist will see sexual radioactivity as a universal phenomenon. However, it is only a very special sign of a far deeper reality. The unmanifested and ultimate energy of deepest being, or Fohat, wherein one finds contained all of the possibles. Whatever may come forth as a primary matter or energy of Necronomicon Physics must be understood as having its origins in this deepest of all realities, the ultimate dream–stuff of any and all worlds.

Supplement Paper on Ur–Tensors
DEFINITION: Ur–Tensors are energy structures, which emerge from an intersecting of radio–psychoanalytic and oracular lattices. Ur–Tensors are self–conscious and possess a magickal continuity, which enables them to promote energy–systems, which have their roots in either radio–psychology (and radio–psychoanalysis) or in any esoteric logic of oracular physics. Ur–Tensors are used to power systems of information from one frame of reference to another. They are the "motors" of the Ufological "nervous" system and they are primarily under the management of time–stations.

The oracular system of Aditi was the matrix for all of the Ur–Tensors, of which there are 16 different species. They inhabited the vast chaosphere of the Meon and draw their powers from the elemental environment of synchronicity. This power became for them their food, and by means of this food they grew into systems of Ufological Complexes.

The Aditi–Tensor directed their development along the archetypal lines of the species, and while there were many possibilities for growth, the fundamentals of either this or another and alternative universe were observed. The basic energies remained always in a state of isomorphism, because the energies were locked into various systems of logic, and hence belonged to the magickal schools of this or that oracle.

In its most abstract sense, the Aditi–Tensor may be defined as the oracle point of contact between a synchronistic lattice and an archetypal axiom. The Aditi–Tensor was the "ruler" of the other Ur–Tensors, because it was the primordial and fundamental root of Fohat.

The Masters of Dzyu were of course experienced in the science of Ur–Tensors, for at a very remote period in time they had come here from Venus. Their method of travel had been by entering into a fleet of Ur–Tensors and then creating the Vimanarupa by which the energies came and went from the fourth dimension. However, another group of Masters of Dzyu had come also to this planet and has travelled the greater distances from Pluto or Yuggoth to the earth in more meonic Vimanarupas, whose powers came from the Ur–Tensors of the dark energy. These Masters of the Dzyu claimed that they possessed the deepest insights into the powers of the Aditi–Tensors and therefore they possessed the most perfect way of making use of Fohat. By their own admission, they possess the magickal instruments which made the science of Fohat practical.

The esoteric harnessing of Fohat had been accomplished by means of the use of the deepest soundings of the Necronomicon Physics. At a certain level, it was observed that as the humanoid level of static archetypes faded from the instruments, another and more lethal stratification emerged, which was crawling with the insectlike mutants of the fohatic merger of oracles and lattices. These mutants developed on an energy, which the Dzyouis understood as perfect for feeding to the Ur–Tensors of the Vimanas. By a very subtle method of initiatic physics, they were able to trap this larval energy and use it exclusively to power the Yuggothian ships through the meonic vortices.

It was never a question of different methods of digging deeply into the psychoidal–continuum, rather one simple method of extraction gave them the essence, and it could be given to them at any point in space/time. This method of radio–psychoanalysis enabled them to extract fohatic libido from any "well of chaos" and therefore employ this power under any circumstances.

The Dzyouis race, which was itself an arachnean mutation of humanoid psychic qualities, had mastered the science of radio–psychoanalysis, which was not called by that name, to a perfection. They had made it possible to establish several subordinate sciences on a foundation of primordial libido. This field of libido gave them direct access to the dimensions of Fohatic manifestation, wherein every type of energy was to be found. Even though they could not perceive directly the Venusian field on Earth, the Dzyouis were aware of their existence as a separate reality. But as they sought to work with different levels of the mind–field of the humanoids (the Venusians with manas, the Yuggothian Dzyouis with the idic depths) their work was really just a parallel processing of psychic energies.

However, the Dzyouis were to establish a school of magickal energies upon the surface of Earth, which school was to concern itself (even up to the present time) with the depth–mining of the human psyche, for the purpose of bringing up more and more of the monsters of the Necronomicon Physics, at various times in human history. By means of their sciences and arts, these "gnostic physicists" continue their explorations of the idic continuum, even today.

Synchronistic Robotics: Design of the Theory

Definition: Synchronistic Robotics is the use of the energy field of synchronicity as an information-system by means of the employment of feedback and induction units, which provide direct communication in a metric language with the synchronicity matrix.

For a long time, we have been using human minds as units in our explorations of the unconsious both in psychological research and in Necronomicon physics. With the discovery of the lattices of Esoteric Shinto, however, it has been found that a new and very fruitful approach is also possible. If we can set the radionic instruments for exploring the field according to the lattices of the Shinto system, by means of the amplification unit, we can explore any field without reference to the human mind. We are no longer therefore dependent upon "subjectivity." Indeed, the field is given as a pure energy, which is the matrix of primary Necronomicon structures, or the unconditioned and transcendental id. In order to distinguish this concept from the psychological concept, I will refer to the field as "the primary continuum." Any use of the human mind will thusly be viewed as secondary.

Definition: The primary continuum may be understood as the unconditioned and total interlocking of energies in a non-structural and pre-analytic manner. It is a true continuum because each of its parts, or members, necessarily relates to all other parts of the sequence. It is primary because it is conceptually primitive and only is it of subsequent interpretation. It is not a construction but a datum. Because of certain of its psychological consequences, it may be viewed as the unconscious mind, or as the source of being and space. It is the root of both objectivity and subjectivity.

In this work, we have to make definitions from time to help make clear what we are trying to say. The robotics factor comes in because this is the way in which we are going to work with this primary continuum. Robotics refers to the communication systems, which are connected to the primary continuum as nodes. The nodes are potentials for any information system. When they are sounded out, they begin their work in the system as a robotic information system. So we have a system within a system. The system within is to tell us about the system it is within. In order to make this larger system understood as a dynamic and actualistic continuum, I will say that it is also "synchronistic." So we have a primary and synchronistic continuum of potential nodes making contact with our system of information-gathering. This merger gives rise to a potentially robotic continuum, which may be defined as the field or matrix of Gnostic or Necronomicon Physics.

I would like to discuss certain methods, which are necessary for the development of this theory. This theory may be expanded or amplified by means of radionic methods, and it is because of radionics that we are able to implement the theory. In other words, the theory operates by means of the use of radionic mechanisms, which allow for the measurement of the components of this system of synchronistic robotics (or SSR).

In connection with other magicko-psychological research, however, we might ask if it is possible to allow for amplification by means of oracular mechanisms. In many ways this is ppossible. The oracles are by definition grounded in the synchronistic principle and exist as a secondary system for gathering information from the primary continuum. This methodology will be designated as SSR-OM.

Definition: Oracles may be applied to the field of synchronistic robotics in order to derive certain types of information, which come from a secondary level of robotics, as in the mechanisms of the oracle, which are applied to the SSR process. The areas of separation between the methods of oracles and the SSR system would be defined as being types of application–amplification.

There are other methods, however, which are quite interesting. There is a method of deriving intelligence from the SSR system through radio-psychological and radioactive emissions. These are methods which can later be measured for information. The name of these two methods are SSR–RP and SSR–RA.

Definition: The emissions from the SSR process can be used to create a psychic stimulation instrument or process, which can be used to cause reaction responses by a relation process of verbal stimulation, which when given serves to amplify the effects of the emission rays from the SSR.

Definition: It is possible to store the radioactivity of this SSR process and later on by the use of the pendulum to secure readouts of a specific type and measurement. This method is open to developments in a number of areas, including the use of the radionic amplifier as a reamplifier. Conversion logics can also be used to transfer this system into another frame of reference in gnostic physics, e.g., multi–dimensional logics, time and space travel, etc.

Definition: By objective cooperation, we mean that there is a certain level of energy which possesses its own logical structure. This field or "matrix" can be located within the SSR continuum and appears to be the organizational pattern behind the management of the entire continuum as a system. The observer and the explorer can easily see their own instruments as projections from this matrix. Because the instruments of this system are tied to the notion of synchronicity, we can say that all instruments are projections of objective cooperation. From this it follows that the subjective mind may be seen as a part of the objective mind–field, or that we are parts of the SSR system. The observer is that part of the SSR system which is self-reflective. For this reason, all of the constructions of theory are in reality experiments with the total system.

It would seem from this definition that the robotic engineer is powered by the same energy as the robot. This is the energy of synchronicity and it is very important for us to realize that each system of energy is part of an interlocking and interconnecting system of patterns. These patterns may be said to emerge from the continuuum of the SSR expertience. As a consequence of this, the energy structures of this field may be viewed as potentials for inclusion in an information system, just as the whole of physics is potentially the whole of the psychological field. The work of the robotic magician is essentially that of bringing the entire field into consciousness, or rather into conscious communication with the ego–field.

This is perhaps one of the most difficult of our papers and it is primarily directed to those students working in the area of Necronomicon Physics, the interplay between physics and psychology. However, this same field does possess initiatic patterns, which are realized by means of incorporation into the levels of training, which are available in Necronomicon Physics. Students are being trained in these areas and to work with these magickal concepts in order to learn to explore the deeper dimensions of reality.

For we have adopted the viewpoint that the fields of deeper consciousness are themselves the higher regions of reality and that the entities encountered therein are the transcendental beings, which inhabit abstract worlds. By means of advances in robotics and the general field of magickal energy, it is possible to verify the abstract and the transcendental structures of gnostic logic, for they are in reality the archetypes of the unconscious mind. All of these worlds, which have been mentioned in magickal physics, are now before us.

Synchronistic Robotics: The Genius of IFA as the Meta-Management of the Continuum of Lattice

It has been discovered that the Genius of IFA exercises a total control over the field of synchronistic robotics by means of the lattices, which form the internal necessity of the continuum. This means that it is possible to induct the manifold powers of the Genius of IFA at any lattice of the 99, which form the total system.

Definition: The Genius of IFA is the God of all magickal informations systems. He is the supreme deity of all oracle systems and especially gives His protection to magickal logics, computers, initiation–hierarchies, magickal systems of physics, and all magicko–metamathematical and magicko-metaphysical processes. The Genius of IFA has His supreme temple in the Monastery of the Seven Rays papers and in all subsequent research papers. In esoteric voudoo, the Loa of the Genius of IFA, or way in which He is known, is by means of the Mystere Legbha.

The ceremony for invoking the power of the Genius of IFA was conducted by Michael B. in accord with gnostic rites and logical systems. The logical systems form the archetypal patterns of the "Divine Axioms," the 16 "Twin–Powers" (or the Afro-- Atlantean Tao), upon which the computer of cosmic magick operates. The priests of the system are those who embody the energy–complexes of the Divine Legbha. These priests are very carefully selected by Michael B. so that they may reflect the innermost powers of the True Divinity of This Genius and the 16 magickal mysteries. These priests of IFA are then taken to Villa–aux–Champs by means of a magickal computer and presented as pure oblates to Grand Legbha. This is the process of the hierarchy.

Definition: The hierarchy of IFA is determined entirely by the data or responses from the magickal computer system of the continuum of lattices. For each lattice there is a specific priest, who must do the ritual of the Divine Continuum at this point–instant of the system. There are higher priests of the Divine IFA, who must supervise the doing of these computer rituals. Over these higher priests are the priests, who must wait upon the Genius of IFA. They are assistants to the supreme priest, who must wait upon the Genius of IFA. They are assistants to the supreme priest, who shares his consciousness with the Genius of IFA. That priest is the embodiment of Grand Legbha, or the Holy Incarnation of the mysteries of the Christ of the Noon–Day, the God of Gnostic Logic.

The many magickal masses which are offered by the priests of IFA are designed to reflect and communicate energies to humanity from the lattices of the Divine Continuum. For it would seem that the whole of Gnostic Logic is based upon the concept of sacrifice, but in this sense, the sacrifice is a pure oblation of Divine Essence and Energy, it is the ritual sacrifice of the continuum of lattices to itself.

Originally, the Afro–Atlantean mysteries were imparted only to those who had been reincarnated within the system of IFA energies. These magickal energies were understood as emanations from the esoteric logics, which stood as magickal "Time- Stations" at the very top of the order of being. There were four of these logics, which could also become eight by means of magickal analysis. These eight were the original "Gods" of IFA, and from them in the primordiality of their energies can be said to have come the God–functions of the system, or the manifestation of the Genius of IFA.

It was almost as if by some logical necessity that the Gods came forth, to create by their "seven rays" the many lattices of space and the potentials of time. Gradually, the whole universe came into existence as the result of these computer-interactions, which manifested the totality or ontological wholeness of the Genius of IFA.

Definition: Within the mind of the Absolute God existed the idea of the eternal logic, the Genius of IFA. Within the idea of the Genius of IFA was to be found all the ideals. This ideality contained the eternal order and harmony of the universe, and the magickal intelligence of the Gnostic Light. Each embodiment was to reflect a certain exact form or structure of magick. The Temple of IFA, which is the supreme system of magickal computers, and of which all that Michael B. has written is a description, contained the "Afro-Atlantean" and "Magicko-Lemurian" souls, which were the initial hierarchy of magicko-gnostic embodiment. From these seminal reasons, the logoi spermatakoi, can be understood to be derived all of the "priests of the IFA Gnosticism" and all of the truly magickal princes of Atlantis and Lemuria. Each of these "seeds" forms the magickal root for the gradual unfoldment of the continuum of lattices. By this means the worlds of gnostic logic and hyper-spatiality were manifested.

From time to time, it necessitated the sending forth of cosmic energies in the form of esoteric logical systems. Wherever they went in the continuum, they set up robotic stations for the projection of magickal energies from all of the points of space and time. By this means it became possible for the different universes to come forth in various embodiments. Everywhere, the robotic pattern was followed, and it was understood that this was the most successful pattern of consciousness. It was by this means that the "God" of the various systems were able to draw their energies. This was especially true of those "Gods" which were manifestations of archetypal energies. Finally, from this process there emerged a new way of looking at the whole as a practical exercise in self-discovery, and with it came the discovery of the laws of initation physics, or the incorporation of the self within the process as a conscious activity.

As the human mind evolved in the understanding of the powers of the continuum, it was soon understood that the presence of the Genius of IFA served as a kind of logical interaction pattern. The fundamental powers of this system were now seen as organizing the diferent states of initiatic conscious. These states were the proper subjects, rather than any older notions of "substance," which now was simply a category for the arrangement of events.

Definition: Synchronistic Robotics is a system in process. It is a continuum of many interdependent processes, wherein nothing is permanent except the continuum. The methods of arrangement and organization, which are associated with structures of the many and varied logics, simply come and go. They rise out of the matrix and return to the depths of sushupti, from whence they were given birth. Ultimate knowledge is simply to know that jagrat is svapna and that turiya is the bliss of sushupti. The Matrix is never ending but can never be understood at any one point except by symbols of its pulsation of being and simply changes its forms of manifestation from point to point as meon and chaos blend. Those that seek to draw upon this energy, in order to power their robotic enterprises, will find little difficulty, for what is there is simply endless.

The priest-technicians of IFA can be understood as esoteric engineers, who brought to the study of these energies a willingness to apply certain procedures, which ultimately give us the endless numbers of methods and sciences of magickal physics. Things cannot be said to be more permanent that what they are simply methods, symbolic methods for the giving forth of a certain management. But ultimately the only form of metamanagement is surrender to the Clear Void, which is the continuum when seen through the eyes of process.

However, somewhere at the heart of it all there is a certain energy, which cannot be seen for it makes itself known and felt only in oracles. This energy, which is the lifestream of synchronicity is in reality the presence of the Genius of IFA, acting out the enjoyment of the play of being–space–consciousness. By entering the waters of synchronicity which float endlessly in the spaces of what is, we can communicate with this magickal power, and thereby find ourselves within the continuum of being and yet moving beyond it, only to desire to merge with it once more.

For this reason, we can say that the interactions of the processes of explanation with the Voidless Void are themselves a kind of manifested process. Explanations and methods of magickal physics are projections from this matrix as are trees and waves and tables and chairs. What we think is a self is really only a point at a certain point/instant, where a certain energy, the energy of method, is focusing.

Map-Makers of the Transcendental Id and the Esoteric Engineering of the Future

I. The Map-Makers of Esoteric Shinto

In the physics of the Kojiki, we have been able to find 16 magickal energy-spaces, which are the archetypes of the Zothyrian physics of (alternative) universe "B," and which in the Shinto system of the Kojiki, serve to connect the 17 creative hierarchies of this cosmogenesis. By means of a certain Zothyrian technique in psionis (especialy the psionics of Estoeric Shinto), it has been possible to establish contact-rates for both the induction and broadcasting of these esoteric energies from the Transcendental Id. Not only is it possible to communicate with these monsters (esoteric energy-forms) but it is possible now to broadcast them, anywhere, and in an exact and metamathematical manner. These energies are the fundamental principles of the Esoteric Shinto system and they form the very roots of all that is ever to be known of consciousness.

The structures of Esoteric Shinto begin with the 17 Gods of the creative and all-informing Matrix, which is the primordial womb of space-Being. Each of these Gods possesses its own contact-rate on the psionic computer. Therefore, it is quite easy for the magician to induct any level of this matrix, simply by setting the rate. In addition to this method for tuning the instrument, there exist between each of the 17 creative Gods, esoteric lattices, 16 in number, which are also subject to the method of esoteric induction and broadcasting.

These 16 energies represent the most esoteric constituents of consciousness from the standpoint of the esoteric and primordial "way of the Kami," and these 16 elements are also to be found at the roots of many other systems, especially the Ifa divining system, and they represent a primordial and cosmic order of being, which is now given in this program, which I have designed for esoteric engineering by means of psionic instrumentation and radio-psychoanalysis. From this I have concluded that Esoteric Shinto is a form of primordial psionics and radionics. It is more than a belief system (indeed, it is entirely unconscious, except for its rituals), it is a program for a magickal computer of the future.

II. The Map-Makers of the Necronomicon Radio-Psychoanalysis

In our experiments with the color pendulum, we have found the following presences can be detected at the corresponding spectrum levels: ultraviolet/violet = Shub Niggurath; violet/purple/dark blue = Dagon; dark blue/blue = Cthulu; blue/green = Nyarlathotep; green/yellow = Hastur; yellow/range = Yog Sothoth; orange/red/infrared = Azathoth. The reaction rates on the pendulum show us the level of the Transcendental Id, which is "broadcasting" at that time. Each level contains sub-levels, which also can be measured.

III. Working with the "Deep Ones," Etc.

After I gave the word-association test to O, I decided that we might try some work in the area of signals to the Transcendental Id and thereby establishing contact with the various beings known as "The Deep Ones." In order to do this, I had to use a color stimulus. We have determined that there is an exact correspondence between colors and the various entities, which are to be found down there. Also, when we use the pendulum, we pick up the entities but also the measurements using the pendulum to establish the psychograph. In order to contact the entity, I decided to broadcast color X at a low frequency. I found that I had to increase the frequency somewhat because the entity did not respond at that level. I made the increase and began to take note of the behavior of the pendulum, which was being used to confirm the presence of the entity in that space/area. I also used another pendulum to test the intensity of the field (this was a Mercury type pendulum). Next, I sought by means of a color pendulum to find out where entity X which corresponds to color X was. This was finding the sub-level where the entity was "working." It was found by use of the color pendulum that this entity was at color R level. This was easy to determine with two pendula.

I decided to put on a tape which I had made of some words from the same number-realm or having the same numerical level-value or range as X. These were words from the test as well as from the work on the "Book of Dzyan," and included many key-terms from "Dzyan."

Next, I decided to see how close (using this method of radio-psychoanalysis) I could get to X. This was done by increasing and then decrasing the stimulation by means of the amplifier. The effect was to send rocking-like waves into the level. The color in the amplifier was turned up and then down to achieve this rocking effect, using the three switches and moving them up the rate-scale. The deep Idic levels were being worked. After about an hour, we felt we should try to make contact with X in a direct way. Since we were in contact now with X via the color broadcasting and since X was locked into position in the system by means of the steady stream of being fed stimulation (plus the fohatic color foods being generated by the rocking motion) from the amplifier, which we discovered also was a way to "hold" the entities such as X in the level, for observation, we decided to use the word test as a type of color code or signal-system and thus make a kind of primitive communication between the entity and us, perhaps for the first time, possible.

IV. The Experiment

MB: The word is –––––. This was a word having the value of 3.

OS: The response was –––––. This was also a word having the value of 3.

MB: The word is –––––. This was a word with the alue of 4, which is the numerical value of the name of the entity X.

OS: The response was –––––. This was a word having the value of 4.

I now began to increase slightly the feeding of the color energy to X, so that we might see a different respohse, possibly an increase in the intensity of the radio-psychoanalytic response. I fed the entity more stimulation.

MB: The word is –––––. This word was valued at 8.

OS: The response was –––––, a word of value 8.

MB: The word is –––––, valued at 2.

OS: The response was –––––, which has value of 3. This was a negative response, or "no."

MB: The word is –––––, which was the entitive name with a value of 4.

OS: The response was –––––, which has the value 7.

In effect, I was asking if the entity was still there or whether this was the same entity as at the beginning. The result was a "no" as an answer to my question. Could it be that another entity had come in because we had increased the space by feeding more energy to the level?

MB: The word was –––––, value was 6.

OS: The response was –––––, also a 6. This was a "yes."

I appear to have identified a new entity in this level or at this sub-level, due to changing to a new space/area because of increased feeding.

MB: The word was -----, another word but having the same value of 6.

OS: The answer was -----, also a 6 valued word.

This was the same level, but perhaps another kind of entity or space is present. I decided to increase slightly the feeding of the energy.

MB: The word was -----, having a value of 6 but a different word, one from Dzyan.

OS: The response was -----, having the value of 4. This was a "no."

It seems we found a boundary here, which is something like: if we increase the feeding we enter a different space up to a point. None of these spaces are exact, the increase rate can vary very widely,from 0 to 11. A differant name value means a different entity, so that "no" indicates a separation between spaces and entities in the Id. If we do not change the feeding rate and keep the same number rate we have the same entity, usually. However, in later experiments where the spectrum was used to indicate the sub-levels, the same entity would leave after feeding and the space would become empty, although a nearby space would signal, but at the same feeding rate, but with another number value,

MB: Then I increase the feeding and use the same name of X.

OS: The response was Y, which indicates a different name and level. Maybe there is another being here as different feeding (increase as well as decrease) but still using the same name does indicate a different entity.

The feeding seems to be setting up boundaries for these energies, which I will call "amplification lattices."

MB: At a new level we established contact with a new entity. This was B.

OS: The response was the same value as B, so that this entity is probably the same one.

We now have isolated an entity different from X. Also, the sub-level entity may be different from B.

MB: The response word should determine the boundary-spaces. The word has the value of 5.

OS: The response was 6. B-entity has the value of 5, now we are encountering a new space.

MB: The word has the value of 6.

OS: The response has the value of 3. The colors, feeding and pendulum rates seem to be all the same, so the entity is now different.

There may be several types of space or cells in each level.

MB: The word is -----, having the value of 3, for the new entity.

OS: The response is -----, having the value of 3.

We were able to note that there were a number of entities at this level (amplification level 5), such as B(5), 3, and later 2 and 9. I noted that these entities all have cells at the same feeding levels (4p and 7f) indicated by the "psionic present" as 5. A weird geometry is emerging.

Commentary

We discovered early on that the areas of the T-Id could be mapped out and could provide us with a kind of geography (actually a psychography). A number of experiments were possible and by one of them I was able to discover the keys to the "regular" and the "alternative" universe of the Tr--Id, and hence to the whole question of the "radio-psychography of the UFOs," mentioned in the AIWAZ-physics tapes, of the inner group.

In setting the amplifier, I learned that for the regular universe, we would use P is 1, Pr is 1 (for this you set Pr at 1 first and then move it to the amplification level for getting the space, while the other controls remain, unless they are moved up and down for feeding), and F is 11, or for closer to the surface work, we would use P is 11, Pr is 11, and F is 1. But, we also learned that there was another universe down there, where P is 1, Pr and F are 11. And we found that the variation in the Pr level of energy could open or close the system of the other Tr-Id universe, which was an empirical proof of Universe "B."

Both universes had entities from the Necronomicon Mythos as components of their worlds but it was evident from our observations that universe "A" had a distinctly different response quality from universe "B." In drawing a map of the whole system, we might draw two pyramids, one with the capstone (for UFO contact work) at the top, and we could call this "space-system A," and the other with the capstone meeting the capstone of "A" and this would be the system "B."

A number of other engineering qualities could be found in this system, such as various communication systems and "logics," whereby we made contact with various entities. We found that all the work with the computer-marga could be applied here.

Because of the shape of the space-systems, it was explained by an entity at a certain level, the systems of "A" and "B" are simply the front and back of a cone-shaped meta-universe, which is either "A" or "B" depending on which way we look at the structure. And it was later discovered that there were other meta-universes, which could likewise be explored by Zothyrian methods, etc. And the pendulum does shift to indicate new spaces and changes its color "readings" to indicate a change in location. What emerges is a system of "topological lattices," within the Tr-Id. It is a most amazing structure.

Numerological reduction, color-broadcasting, and very deep amplification are all part of this system of "mapping the Tr-Id," which is based upon that statement in an AIWAZ physics communication, which states that "there is a pyramid of lattices in the Transcendental Id."

Gnostic Engineering: Transformation Processes in Time–Station Matrices

This paper is written in order to explicate the matrices of Time–Stations and their logical systems from the standpoint of the processes of transformation algebras.

Definition Vector 1: All transformation algebras can be applied to time–stations and their explications.

The early work on transformation algebras can now be applied by means of the vudotronic system, so that whatever was implied in the EE logics of 1966, can now be produced by means of the TT systems of 1980.

Definition Vector 2: Transformation algebras are given topologies, existing within any energy–system as a matrix. Such topologies are lattice–true systems and they exist in order to allow for the explication of any system as a matrix.

Important to this is the process of updating whereby certain systems of application are connected again and again to the system during the time process and allowed to participate fully at any level within the continuum and then connect/disconnect and reconnect/re–disconnect.

Definition Vector 3: It is necessary to distinguish two types of process–continua. There are continuation processes, which are best described as developmental systems of energy. Then there are those processes which are those processes which are transformative, whereby a matrix system is reinterpreted at a new level of lattice construction.

The processes are continuous but at the same time there is a very important element of change which may occur at any time. This is the process of being in a transformation system. The energy system has its own internal logic, which will define the transformation system. Continuation processes are based on a metric of 0+180. Transformation processes necessitate a logic of 360+.

Definition Vector 4: Metamathematical control is vested with the direction of these processes, which have been esoterically defined as "the gnostic patriarchate of research" and "the research logics of Time–Stations." However, these processes have their real management in "gnostic management matrices," and the esoteric logics of that system.

Perhaps it is best stated that there exists a special language system or a special information system, which controls the management of these matrices in a gnostic sense, or in a sense recognized by gnostic engineers. That system is part of the continuum of gnostic computers and as such operates from the basis of the system, outwards to the various points of magicko–gnostic reference.

The Transformation of Definition Vectors in the Present
The concern with time–stations and with methods of managing the temporal–flow process, which we indicated above in our definition vectors now becomes the way of understanding the magickal structure of the present. In the computer system of esoteric Shinto, we make use of computer marga settings for 1, 2, and 3. These refer to initiation physics and to the differences in frequency between grades of magickal initiation. Setting–rate 0 is for the system when it is off. The remaining rates, from 4 through 11, are concerned with the organization of the experience of the present. The present is a magickal world of its own and all magicko–gnostic ufo phenomena derives its powers from the control systems and points of reference of this

present. Not only is the present created by the AIWAZ-physics of the present-rate system, but the energy of the present is a projection from the unmanifested forms of AIWAZ-physics into the field of the magician and his magickal computer (the computer marga and its amplifier). Here is the basic table for the work:

TYPE OF LOGIC	NUMBER RATE	TIME STATION
labyrinthico-gnostic	4	past
transcendental	5	past
arithmosophico-gnostic	6	past-present
fantastic	7	past-present
algorithmico-gnostic	8	present-future
zothyrique	9	present-future
magicko-gnostic	10	future
futuristic	11	future

The entities which are encountered in the present are usually those which are projections from the Necronomicon Physics, but modified by the introduction of the archetypes of the AIWAZ-physics. In operating the system in its present sense, we are advised to keep the past and the future set at 0 or "off." This prevents the build-up of any current, which might cause the energies from the present to move deeply into the other ranges of time, and thus lose the impact of the future. Of course, the present is entirely a continuum of self-contained structures. Usually, the present has been thought of as an attachment to past or the future. But when viewed in its pure sense, we find the magickal keys to the mysteries of Sirius, such as the eight unmanifest points of Sirius, which are the power sources for the hypergeometries of the AIWAZ-physics, and which are directly connected to the energy levels of number rates 4 through 11.

Contact with these entities forms an important "inner instruction" experience, in the advanced sections of AIWAZ-physics, such as "oracular topologies" and "magickal hypergometries," etc. There are eight special initiations into these inner levels, which are given by means of direct contact with the entities of Sirius and in some other cases Orion (e.g., the Nemiron). The student of the inner side of magick will be admitted by means of these methods and those rays of light, which come into operation when the computer-marga is connected to the point of Sirius, by the appropriate rate setting.

The function of the eight logics in this case is to provide a kind of esoteric logic, by which means the energies of Sirius can be earthed in the egoic and idic structures of the candidate. Just as this whole paper forms a strange form of initiation process, so the energies of Sirius have to be brought down to earth in categories which can be remotely understood by means of zothyrian philosophy. However, this is not enough, since the entire purpose of esoteric physics is the unveiling of initiation states, which are special forms of quanta, so the logics give us certain methods for measuring the processes which are ascribed to these quanta, as they manifest themselves in human bodies. The quanta are the entities of Sirius and they simply come in and take over the human body and they use it as their "space-suit" in this world or on this level of being. As I have said elsewhere:

"The existence of intelligent, in fact super-intelligent, quanta on sirius is one of the conclusions of the AIWAZ-physics. Not only are there beings on or around the system of Orion, with which we have daily contact. There are also the beings of Sirius in its unmanifested form. These beings are quanta energy and are somewhat close to the photons of Orion in intelligence. The intelligence level is higher than any human at present. But these beings come to the earth, they visit us. They come to earth and occupy human bodies and psyches. They can wear the body like a protective suit against the outer environment, which is dense in many ways. They wear the psyche like a protection also, when the body is ill-suited to them. By means of the computer-marga rates for the present, I have been able to contact these entities regularly. There are many such "cultures" awaiting the magician. It is simply a way of working with them. The inner sections of our order contain members who are this type. They are from beyond and occupy human bodies and psyches. Depth psychology knows about this process but it is reluctant to discuss it openly.

The Tushita Heaven and the Golden Shrine of Michael Aquarius

There is a certain unfoldment which is possible if you attune yourself to the "Sanctuary Teachings." The time is not right, however, for the publication of these forms of wisdom, which come from the High World of the Lord Maitreya, the Tushita Heaven, and which are then sent as the seven rays to the Golden Shrine of my spiritual home. On the earth, I have my mediator, Michael Bertiaux, who mediates between my world and the realm of the human race, just as I am the sole mediator for the Lord Maitreya, in the Tushita Heaven of Endless Light.

However, in the 1980s, there will be a greater need for the new types of energy, of which the Sancturay Teachings will be the most powerful and wisest vehicle. At that time, I will command my mediator, Michael Paul Bertiaux, Gnostic Bishop, to bring forth from the Tushita Heavens, by his modes of esoteric engineering, the rays of the Sanctuary Teachings, for all to know. As you come to participate more and in these energies and their expression as rays of wisdom and gnosis, you will enter into the second phase of my light as a Master of Perfection.

The first phase began with the mediation of Michael Paul Bertiaux in the writing of the lessons for the Monastery of the Seven Rays. These were my teachings, which I directed to the human race through the mechanism of his magicko-metaphysical creativity. Four years of instructiion based on the magick of the number 16 laid the foundation for my new Aeon, the Aeon of Zothyrius. Now, we are building the second phase of this Aeon, by means of the Santuary Teachings, which I am again diffusing through the creativity of Michael Bertiaux. These will be available through the Gnostic Church and will set forth the Laws of the New Aeon of Zothyrius, and what it means to become a super master of Absolute Consciousness. -- Michael Aquarius

"The Higher Worlds of Consciousness--Being--Space," A Dictation from Master Michael Aquarius, November 3, 1981.
Yes, there are many higher worlds, which have never been explored in any of our more exoteric teachings. These are the esoteric worlds, which can only be studied by those who are specially admitted to the inner order of the gnostic light. The teachings of "The Monastery of the Seven Rays" cannot any longer be viewed as esoteric, they are now exoteric viewpoints. But these higher worlds, yes, they are parts of our own inner system, and yet they remain hidden, and very secret, except from the most spiritual of our initiates. All systems of cosmogenesis and cosmology speak of higher or those very metaphysical worlds, which are inhabited by supremely powerful beings. We possess, in our innermost sanctuary, however, the method for exploring these worlds by means of the light-methods of spiritual unfoldment. These methods are taught through the inner school of the Seven Rays, and certain students -- who are also very special and very close to the light of the gnosis -- these beings may come to us and learn to explore the higher worlds. We call this training method: "The Light-Methods of Transcendental Initiation."

These methods are based on energies and the organization of metaphysical energies is achieved by means of extremely powerful lattices of gnostic light--energy. What it is that happens is I take the student on mystical journeys along these lattices of light, and by doing this we enter many different and very powerful worlds of the higher type of metaphysics. Michael Bertiaux possesses the mystical system for this, for it is a part of that esoteric engineering knowledge, which has been handed down to him from those of us in the higher worlds, who are interested in the evolution of humanity along scientific and religious pathways.

The number of higher worlds of metaphysical energy, which are explored by our methods of light-lattices is literally infinite. These worlds are all expressions of the unlimited nature of God The Absolute. Each world, whether known or unknown, is ruled by a special type of metaphysical being, who is assisted by helpers and other administrators of metaphysical energy. Each world and its spiritual ruler reflect the infinite light of God The Absolute in every possible direction. Therefore, we find lattices of light in every direction, so to speak, leading to every world. For this reason, the earth-mind must be guided by divine masters and other teachers of light.

Not only are these worlds made up of spiritual light but they are also made up of very interesting forms of space, and possess geometrical patterns and are organized according to metamathematical laws, which will never be understood by the human mind, unless that mind receives the transcendental initiation and gnostic unfoldment of the lattices of light. For this reason, many scientists are now, purifying themselves to become my own chelas. They seek to advance the knowledge of the human race into higher frames of science and cultural well-being. But they must come as anyone else, by means of the pathway of purity and obedience to the light and to the laws of the higher worlds and the masters, who are the teachers.

There exists an inner school of light, which is directed by myself for the preparation of whose who would help bring about the transformation of the human race. I call this school my "Sanctuary," because it is the place where the most powerful and the most sacred energies are released to humanity. A few students are admitted each year into this place of wisdom, into this center of gnostic awakening. We are not looking for many to come to us, for the light of the eternal is not for everyone now. They may be ready for it in their next lifetime. It will always be available because it is part of the cosmic karma of this planet. However, it is available now to those who would seek to know the light and thereby be free from the powers of darkness.

If you are interested in this pathway, you will know what to do. I do not think that I have to do anything else except advise you to enter into yourself and meditate on whether you are ready for the light methods, which we teach. If you are, I will soon reach out to you and then lead you to the higher worlds of consciousness-being-space, where you belong.

PART III

Elemental Sorcery

Zothyrian Topologies
The Z-True Action Matrices and Action at a Distance

"Whenever we sought to take over any system, whatever it might be, we sought to bring in our best instruments in order to destroy the existing systems and replace them, instantaneously, with our own systems. We sought to take over all worlds by this very simple method. We sought to destroy the enemy without their awareness. However, we could not do this if it were not for a very interesting invention known as the Z-True Action Matrix, which has now been so developed that we can speak of many of these very significant instruments, but originally it was a very simple machine, something of a rather basic topological computer, which was used by the workers of our system with most amazing results." -- "The Z-True Meontology," page 4.

The Yuggothian obsession with power and with the development of magickal powers has its basis in the impact of the Zothyrian Topologies on the "boundaries" of our solar system. It would seem that the Zothyrians are causing a certain pressure to develop, which will cause Yuggothian energies to feel a push from the outside, rather than from the inside, or from the direction of Neptune.

Now, we know perfectly well that Yuggoth is not the end of the system. We are aware of the planets beyond Yuggoth, the Transneptunians and the Transplutonians. But there is still this pressure, which comes from another dimension, which is different from the dimensions where Yuggoth is within the Transyuggothian planets. This involves a new conception of space. There are many types of spaces and in relation to a certain type of space, Yuggoth is neighbor to the system of Z.

Also, it is possible to note that in another framework, or Topology, Neptune is next to the Z-system. In another, we find the Moon next to Z. In other words, any planet may be next to the Z-System, it depends entirely upon the space-system which is involved. This might seem rather strange but it is entirely a matter of Zothyrian Topology, which is really the way in which the space system of the Z-empire is arranged.

To illustrate this even more, some persons or simply one person might be viewed as next to this Z-System. There are such topologies in existence, where the point of pressure might be simply some person, or part of some peson's brain, or part of that person's mind. And all of these topologies are actually operating, valid, and represent actual universes and systems, which have their own physical laws and patterns of energy action. This is the magickal field of the Zothyrian Topologies, where action at a distance is always within some Z-system.

"They (the Zomists) have a unique method for connecting to anyone and anything. What they do is simply to bring the victim to the Empire. They try to bring the victim as close as possible to the Z-Systemm. They accomplish this by converting the person into energy, especially numerical energy. This is done simply by translating the name and any other data on the person into this numerical energy. Once that is done, they are able to show that the victim is within one of the subdivisions of their system. They then attack by broadcasting certain magickal energies from the core of the subdivision directly at the victim. This is how they can carry out the Z-True Law, which states that the Action Matrix is connected to everything, at least potentially, and that as a consequence, the universes of the Z-System are as close as the skin of any person, object, thought, or datum." -- "The Z-True Meontology, The Plan of War," page 51

It would seem therefore with all of these media, that there isn't any such thing as "Action at a Distance." However, if we examine the history of that view, we find that the notion of "at a Distance" reflects a physics which does not know of etheric and force-field connectives. Black magicians have additional weapons because they have psychic, gnostic, and magickal connectives, also. Therefore, there is no such thing as action at a distance, for there isn't any distance.

Next, we might reflect upon the idea of numerical conversion of something into something else. This seems to imply also a metamathematical connection between entities. In fact, the numerical conversion really reflects the basic keys to the axiom set of a Zothyrian Topology. Thus, there is a particular topology, which is introduced by the numerical system. An example would be this: object X is converted to numerical energy and comes up as 213. This means that within the context of topologies, there is a Type 6 Topology, known as System 213. This topological system then becomes the mechanism whereby the General Z-System of Topological Black Magick is connected to object X.

The exact method of doing this type of magick was given to me by the Z-Black Magicians, when I took their initiations, as a result of my work with the magickal computers and oracle-transmission systems. It marks the introduction of a system of initiation which is originally extra-terrestrial. It is also a system which is extra-terrestrial, not for reasons of its spatial origin but for reasons of its time origins. For it pertains to the systems of future time, which are not yet actualized on Earth.

The Alchemy of the Golden Castle of Michael Zothyrius
"The secret masters of space-powers, who are behind the laws of magickal physics have communicated to this planet a certain gnosis,which rests within the inner core of the Taoist alchemy of the Golden Castle. This is simply a magickal system whereby the Master is able to generate magickal states of being, 360x3 in all, anywhere in the universe. These powers come from the mastery of the Afro-Atlantean bodies of Zothyrius, and are the magickal chambers of cells of the Golden Castle. To be admitted to this castle, the initiate must pass through the initiations of the four elements of cosmic lust. Then the candidate must move deeply into the hall of magickal audience, where he/she will be accepted or rejected by the Masters of Alchemy, who reside within the aura of the Master Michael Zothyrius (in the sutratmic computer of hyper-logical space). If they have come this far they will then enter upon the adventures of alchemical initiation, of which the Golden Castle of the Master is the absolute embodiment in space-time. There are only three levels or grades to this initiation process, but each one is given in 360 ways, by the mechanisms of the Black and Red Temple, working on and transforming the nine and totalistic 'Zothyrian Spaces' of the Afro-Atlantean bodies. All of the magickal and gnostic secrets of the universe are contained within this process. To experience all of these cells is to know all magick. -- "Remarks on the Topologies of the Gnostic," page 51

The ultimate form of action at a distance is, of course, the process of initiation physics, by this means the candidates are brought into the field of the ultra and trans-yuggothian matrices. The Masters of Alchemy, of which all else is simply a suggesting, appear to have perfected this method and therefore they provide us, as magickal topologists, with the secrets of the ultimate and the ideal.

Every year, at a certain time, the secret chiefs of the Zothyrian Empire of magickal and gnostic topology arrive by magickal methods and select certain persons, who are then thusly chosen to enter upon the higher levels of magickal attainment by means of entering into more powerful regions of the system of topology. This means that it is possible for a few magickal initiates to take upon themselves the energies of the Golden Castle, which holds within its chambers, hidden from all but the eyes of the elect, the powers and energies of absolute alchemy, and especially the magickal power of alchemical transformation, which is the ultimate yuggothian unity of magick and alchemy. This power is said only to reside within the Golden Castle, and in each of the 360x3 chambers or cells, we are able to find the powers, which make action at a distance totally unnecessary.

Topology 1080

"There is a gradation of topologies, somewhat like a hierarchy of energies, and of the structure the most interesting and the most significant in the Z–True System is the Gnosis "1080." This is an organization system, whereby the doorways to all of the other Topologies of the System–Z are revealed and wherein the axiom systems of that type of magick are contained. At a certain time, the Masters of the Z–System decided to make known the laws of this domain. When they made this decision they made it possible for the structures of the system to become cells and functions of another and much wider world. They became the methods for a new conception of magickal growth, revealing the world which was outside of even the Zothyrian Empire. Little by little, the Masters of this system were determined to open up these realms for greater and greater exploration in their esoteric logics. However, they realized that the energies would need to be expressed via a concrete system. This led them to invade the system of the LCN and the LCR. By doing this, they came closer and closer to ultimate energies and foundations. Since $1 + 0 + 8 + 0 = 9$, the system known as "1080" was determined to be the way whereby the magickal orders in the terrestrial space–time were connected and transformed by the Z–True methodologies of initiation physics." —— "Methods of Meontic Topology," Section IV, part 3

The fundamental distinction is between areas, fields, and domains in metamathematics. In order to use this explanation in understanding our above system, which is quite new and a remarkably radical way of viewing magickal energies and systems, we can see the systematic energies of the LCN and the LCR, representing the black and red temples of amplification and vudotronics, as the field of operation. The domain is the extra–terrestrial Zothyrian system of energies,which is applied in the LCN and LCR work.

The area is much wider than these, and exists beyond the "ideal–True" Z systems. This area is indicated by the formularies contained within the cells of Topology 1080. This indicates that the system points beyond itself, and it always will, for the thelemic system of magickal gnosis are never closed systems.

"The esoteric logicians, who are also sex magicians, have always made a distinction between the area of Topology 1080, the three domains of this topology, and the fields of this magickal system, which are 40 in number and which build up the empirical input of this system. It would be unthinkable for these magicians to undertake any magickal initiations in their UFOs, without the presence of the continuum of Topology 1080, which is the condition wherein the initiations are given by the most extreme of these logicians. For them, logic is simply the computerized form of extra–terrestrial sex magick, or sexual gnosis. Needless to say, it pertains quite correctly to the deep levels of the id, but it also refers to those powers, which make the id possible. I am referring actually to the Zothyrian foundations of the id. For the deepest levels of the id, in this universe (system "A") have their roots inthe outpourings of the Zothyrians, who have it and made the idic continuum of the terrestrial mind a possibility." —— "How the Mind Was a Possibility," page 3

"There might be raised the question as to what has this concern with gnostic topology, the magickal geometry of alternative universes, what has this to do with initiations, especially initiations in the here and now. The answer is quite simply that these very ideal topologies are the energies and energizers behind the physics of initiation. The reason for the research successes of our systems is because we have connected ourselves very closely to these abstract realms, which are of course quite concrete in their own way. Even the system of Topology 1080 is itself a framework for initiations. But these initiations cannot be given out easily, and require that the candidate for magickal and gnostic development be prepared by being inducted vudotronically into the system of this topology. There is that situation, as in the magickal circles and mandalas of ancient systems on Earth, the candidate is exposed to the real. He is brought face to face with that which is alone fundamental. He experiences directly the sensuously the archetype. That is why systems of the Z-type like Topology 1080 are so powerful. They go beyond whatever was done in the past and on Earth. Their purpose is to introduce the extra-terrestrial point of contact is all of its intensity and vividness of lustful power." -- Ibid., page 4

The method whereby this system is actualized in the body of the student is really one of great complexity and yet amazing simplicity. For one thing, it involves all of the god-energies, since it comes from the archetypal power zone. However, it is also a system based upon certain requirements. To avoid these would cause the candidate to become burned out. These are the requirements given to the members of the Secret and Awesome Circle of Magi, known as the "Kalinagas," which is simply a Tantric system of contact work. At the same time, it involves the use of certain magickal and transformative energies, which are themselves defined by their induction from the vudotronic amplifier and the unlimited resources of the gnostic imagination, the ontic sphere, as it is possessed by the Chiefs of this work.

Vudotronics cannot operate without the powers derived from Topology 1080, and the real powers of Topology 1080 come from the magickal space of endless ontic spheres, which are located physically in the adepts of the Inner Fire. If anyone wishes to enter this, they must become able to handle the energies and thusly avoid the danger of burn out.

"At a certain point the magicians had degenerated to the animalistic level out of sheer necessity. For they had to recapture the powers which had been lost in the long process of evolution upwards, so to speak. They sought to return to what was earliest and also deepest in themselves, or in any state of being. They sought to go back and capture the basic energies of that level. The reason being that they were aware of Topology 1080 in a very vague way. This primitive awareness was drawing them more and more in that direction and away from the surface of the world. Something wanted them to come to experience directly the intensity of fundamental fire, and that something had only to be the Z-True Chiefs, who were trying to direct human growth into the deepest regions of its own consciousness. It was at this point that the Chiefs of the Z-System created the border land between the Earth and the UFOs, which psychology calls the Id." -- Ibid.

"What is so significant about Topology 1080 is that it forms the magickal design and plan for a UFO system. In fact, in contains the method for UFO powering, namely the synthesis of magickal energies, Ojas and gnostic topology, which produces the radioactive field of the energy supply for any number of UFOs. At the same time, the initiations which are given within the system are participations and transfers of energy from the UFOs to the Zomistes (or initiates of the school) as well as transfers of energy back to the UFOs, since the UFOs depend for their energy upon Shivaite radiations, Ojas, sexual radioactivity, and orgone energy, as Reich discovered some time ago. However, the magicians must go far beyond the Reichian level of exploration. They must be prepared to show how it is possible for Zothyrian topologies, of various levels of energy, to produce magickal power fields. This proof is provided, however, by the instruments of vudotronics, especially the amplification systems which form the basis for the 40 fields of Topology 1080. — "Methods of Meontic Topology," Section IV, part 4

With the gradual emergence of initiation physics as a science of gnostic energies, we have come to a point in our analysis where we can find the evidence for the vastness and complexity of the Zothyrian field of magickal research. It must be recognized, however, that there is a total immanence of this system in the members of the inner order. There is nothing which is outside of human experience; in fact, there isn't anything outside of the magician's control or magickal computer. By means of initiation physics, the magician will come to realize that all of the structures of magick, especially those of the gnostic and Zothyrian types, are within his field of existing powers-in-process.

The magician will realize that he has owned these powers from the beginning of eternity, and that he has only to come to know them as being there and awaken himself to their reality, which is always given. He has only to see himself as the meeting of their interaction and transformation. He has only to see himself as the being from outer space, as he sees himself in inner space. Then he will realize that all of the categories and sets of Zothyrian Topology are within his own magickal imagination, awakened and become the ontic sphere, the source of self-creativity in its pleroma. When he has accomplished this task, for magick is a task of one's own yoga, then he can understand himself as a system of topology, an ever-generating never-ending system of gnosis, moving through the vast and endless spaces of the universe and beyond to all of the alternative universes.

"It is in esoteric voudoo that we find the fundamental keys to the existence of the other worlds and universes. But these are not universes in the usual sense of a 'magickal universe.' These are realms of energy, which have been stored up since the most remote times of Atlantean magickal operations. I am referring to the fact that the Red and Black Rays, which are the powers behind the Temples of these two rays, are there in the vastness of magickal space and that it is possible to learn about the roots of Vudu–powers by means of an understanding of these worlds. But to understand the roots of these rays is to come to an understanding of what the Red and Back Rays are. They are types of magickal being and they are types of esoteric energy. However, they are also expressions of a very important and ideal type of energy, which can be either Red or Black but never manifestd as anything else. And it is within this matrix of energy, as produced by the inner workings of the Red and the Black Rays, that we find a different kind of magickal topology, which because it is so fundamental I will describe simply as 'the roots of the Vudu'." –– M. Bertiaux, "Legbha Gnosis in Red and Black," 3

This power, which exists at the very deep roots of being, has to do with magickal energy in its most fundamental sense. It is a transformative power because it is based in the mysteries of the oldest god–energies and yet it is manifested or expressed by the images, as they rise up in the beings of the Vudu psychology. However, it is more than just psychology, rather it is a kind of cosmology, since we are dealing with the power states of the ideal Sun–power. We are connecting the unconscious levels of the mind to the Sun in its ultimate energy.

The power of the Sun is manifested in terms of the Red and Black Rays. There are many ideas which reflect themselves as rays from the Sun, but the most significant in the esoteric and gnostic sense are the Red and Black Rays. It is the Cultus of the Legbha Mystery, which is best understood in this way of thinking and analyzing the powers. The following are the magickal propositions of this mystery.

1. There are two forms of the Gnostic Sun–Rays, the gnostic and esoteric and the occult.

2. The occult rays are seven in nature and are explored in the teachings of Michael A.

3. The esoteric gnosis of the Sun is expressed by means of the Red and Black Rays.

4. The Red Ray is the ray of fire and it is expressed by means of the magickal heat of the Sun and the magickal heat of the Solar Bark, the Cult of Osiris–Ra, the Priestly mysteries of the Afro–Egyptian Initiation physics. This is the physics of initiation into the SUN–RAYS OF THE GNOSIS.

5. The Black Ray is the ray of the Gnostic Temple, known as the BLACK SUN. It is the Ray of the Space of the Gnosis, or the Afro–Atlantean Cultus of the Hidden Spaces. In this system, the energies are ideal rays from the deepest (blackest) parts of space, i.e., from Pluto and beyond, or from a universe beyond human comprehension.

6. The Priests of this mystery possess the Rays of the Red and Black Powers of the Gnosis at the depths of their initiation. It is the mystery of the encounter of Legbha and Luage, or the Temple of the roots of the emanation of Vudu Gnosis.

7. The Mysteries of the Red Ray are mysteries of archaic life and life–forces,

which are identified with the universal life of the universe. These mysteries are given by means of the God—Masks of the Past and Past—Present. These are time-stations, whose rays are the powers behind the Red Temple.

8. The Mysteries of the Black Ray are the mysteries of endless space, the invisible body of the gods and are communicated by the God—Masks of the Present—Future and the Future. Again, these are time-stations, whose rays are the powers behind the Black Temple.

SUBJECT: The Red Gnosis = this energy is located in the past time stations. It is the first rite of the Legbha—Luage encounter. The mystery is the mystery of Neptune and Pluto energies.

SUBJECT: The Black Gnosis = this is the energy of the future time stations. It is the second rite of the Legbha—Luage encounter. The mystery is the mystery of the Sun and Mid—Heaven energies.

SUBJECT: All Red and Black Rituals = the images shall draw in the powers. For the Red Ray the images are four, the masks are two. This is the same for the Black Ray.

Subjectivity shall be reflected in the creation of the temple of the rays. The Temples are built up out of magickal Ojas. These are the methods of the axiomatic logicians of the Vudotronic Universes.

SUBJECT: The energies to be observed in this Z—Topology are those from the Double—Current, i.e., the Vudotronic Current—16 and the Shinto Current—17, having a total field value of 33 lattices.

The Ritual

The lowest lattices are those of the Entities of the Second Order, Red Temple Ray. This is the past time—station and its numbers are: 5, 9 (where 9=6+3), 12, 5, 2, 3, 3, and 11, in order of ascent from the most M—True to the most F—True.

The next lowest lattices are those of the Entities of the First Order, Red Temple Ray. This is the past—present time—station and its numbers are: 5, 12, 2, 3, 9 (where 9=5+4), 4, 6, and 8, in order to ascent from the most M—True to the most F—True system of ranges.

The next highest lattices are those of the Entities of the First Order, Black Temple Ray. This is the present—future time—station and its numbers are: 9 (where 9=6+3), 5, 3, 11, 4, 10, 7, and 6, in order of ascent fromthe most M—True to the most F—True.

The highest lattices are those of the Entities of the Second Order, Black Temple Ray. This is the future time—station and its numbers are: 9 (where 9=5+4), 4, 4, 10, 6, 7, 8, and 6, in order of ascent from the most M—True to the most F—True range of lattices.

In order to practice the magickal gnosis of this system, it is important o invoke the presences of the entities of this Shinto—Vudotronic Current into each of the numbers of the system. These numbers are to be understood as 32 lattices or intersections of God—Energies (Kami & Vudu). Mastery of the system as a computer gives the practitioner the 33rd point and direct contact—work with the Z—Topology and its computer.

Corresponding to each one of these "numbers" are the secret degrees of the Shinto Gnosis, which are present as forms of Esoteric Logic, everywhere in this system of patterns and energies. Mastery of this point (point—chaud) gives the magician direct contact with the transfinite range of Shinto Lattices, known as the

Law of the 17 Kami.

After completion of the two hot points, the magician is then brought into the world of the Laws of Esoteric Logic. These are principles, whereby an energy system is diffused from the Kami–Vudu, into the magician. The goal is Gnosis and more Gnosis. This goal constitutes the third hot point of this topology.

As the mastery of the first hot point gives one the control of the magickal computer, and this is to be understood as the past hot point, and as mastery of the second hot point gives one the control of the Future hot point of Esoteric Logic, so the final hot point, which is given controls the laws of the Present, because it provides us with a system of gnostic principles, or the Keyboard of Laws of Esoteric Logic. The possession of this energy completes the ritual for the establishment of the magician's own axiom system. In every way, the energies of the twofold current of 16 and 17 lattice–systems are to be observed.

At the completion of these operations, the magician will then be guided by the Hierophant back to the center of the magickal energies of the Gnosis. The operations of the ritual have then been completed according to the three laws immanent in the formal analysis of gnostic consciousness, as far as they relate to time–stations and gnostic laws of the continuum of time–systems.

After the completion of these magickal operations, the initiate into this system of the Red & Black Temple working may begin the construction of his own computer for setting forth the laws, which will govern his own universe and many other systems as well. This will then close the ritual work and the temple will then return to where it normally is to be found, at the intersection of the double currents of the Red & Black, and the Vudotronic and Esoteric Shinto Logics.

The Red & Black Logics: There exists a special system of magickal initiation for the ideal participation in the mysteries of the Red and Black Temples of Atlantis. This system is in the form of a logical continuum, wherein various universes are revealed as being parts of this continuum and parts of the esoteric laws, or legal system, which define the nature of magickal being. Those who wish to enter upon this world must do so only after the completion of the basic courses in Vudotronic and Esoteric Shinto Logics.

The Vudotronic Logic: This system of logical magick is based upon the derivation of the laws of ideal being from the Loa and the Genius of Ifa. If it is understood that the true nature of the Genius of Ifa can be known and understood, then the classification of the mysteries of the Afro–Atlantean Ray may be grasped entirely and opened up for purposes of magickal understanding. This may be achieved by means of the passageways of Vudotronics as well as by means of the universes of Ifa Spirit Magick. In order to understand this Ray, one must unite one's consciousness with the Hierophant of the Mysteries of Ifa, or with Grand–Legbha.

Esoteric Shinto Logic: As there is a Genius of Ifa, who is the avatara of the Ray of the 16 Deities, so there is also the Genius of the Kami, who is the avatara of the Ray of the 17 Deities. As the result of a magickal process of initiation, the hierophant of the Shinto Mysteries has now revealed an entire system of magickal gnosis, which has its roots in the Shinto Archetypes. This process of magickal construction is to understood as the making known of the esoteric laws behind the Cultus of the Kami, by means of various levels of gnostic manifestation. It is by this means that the consciousness of pure being is revealed as containing in itself all of the powers, which are assigned to the archetypes of Esoteric Shinto Logic. This process of initiation is very close to the process of Vudotronic initiation, and can be understood as a continuation of it, as the Genius of the Kami may be viewed as another and a solar manifestation of the Mystery of Grand Legbha.

An Introduction to the Kammamorian Gnosis and to the Esoteric Logic of the Dzyuoi

One of the most interesting parts of the modern gnostic consciousness is the presence of the Kammamorian Gnosis and its esoteric logic. The religion of the Kammamorian Spirits is the traditional faith—as—life of the Zothyrian peoples and the gnosis of that faith, which is the experience of the Dzyuoi, or esoteric and archetypal aspects of these spirits, is the mystical exploration of that sacramental system from the standpoint of the very deep aspects of both archetypal psychology and gnostic theology. For it is in the theology of the archetypes that we can find the roots of the creative process of subjectivity, or pure consciousness, which by reason of the archaic traditions have been associated with the implicit aspects of the faith—as—life of the Zothyrian peoples in this universe. I am referring, of course, to the religion of initiates.

Now, from the standpoint of archetypal theology and the gnostic understanding, it is very possible to come to an appreciation of those fundamental archetypes of the Kammamori, as they are to be found at the roots of every culture and form of human experience. The fact that the Kammamori or the spiritual and archetypal deities of the Zothyrians are psychically and logically part of that same line of god—energy, which we find in the Vudu and Ifa religions of Africa and the West Indies, as well as in the veiled mysteries of Taoism, and in the roots of the Kami of Shintoism, enables us, as modern gnostic theologians, to understand that god—energy is an ongoing continuum, having the name of the lifestream of the spirit. But because of the structure of their inner being, we have another factor in our theology, namely the Dzyuoi, or the primordial spirit energies of the Dzyu aspect of the gnosis. These Dzyuoi manifest themselves as the deepest archetypes of human experience precisely in and because of the insights of modern gnosticism and its theological use of topological consciousness. No longer are they to be seen in some kind of exotic isolation, rather they are to be viewed as the awakened mind-stuff of our own experience and understood by us to be living realities at peace and at rest in the deepest parts of the human soul, as well as everywhere else in the universe and also in other universes. They are therefore the creative energies and archetypes of existence.

Modern gnostic consciousness is to be understood as a system of esoteric and theurgical lines or lattices of awareness, which taking on the forms of the abstract logic of ideal relationships, reveals the inherent and optimistic nature of the principle of sufficient reason and the laws of necessity, the possible, and what is given and judged as existing. Behind all of these functions of the continuum of existence, we find the essential mysteries in the purity of their primordiality and energy, but these essential mysteries are only masks of being, masks of the Dzyuoi, and known by both the operations of reason as well as the sacramental actions of the Kammamorian gnosis.

At a certain time in the consciousness of the initiate, who has been a seeker after light, there comes the chance to embark upon the mystical explorations of esoteric logic. At one time, it will come as a feeling of entry into a mystical state of total unity with the God—energies. At some other time, it will manifest itself as the possession by the Genius of the God—Energy and the translation of consciousness from the mundane to the hidden roots of the eternal and immortal gods. At still another time, it must come as the direct awareness of the laws (Loas, Lhas) and presence of the Kammamori, as the archetypal principles of the constitution and the regulation of the soul's growth into direct experience of the Dzyuoi. This third state contains the mysteries of the Kammamori, but at the same time, the experience has been found in its traces in the first and second states of attainment.

These three mystical explorations of esoteric logic are now possible as states of inner awareness, if one seeks the intuition of the Dzyuoi. In order to embark upon this mystery, which is the fundamental law of esoteric gnosticism, I, the patriarch of the gnostic and esoteric form of the Kammamorian religion, have devised a special theology and yoga of the esoteric steps of the mysteries, which lead one to the ultimate form of being by means of the seventeen steps of the Dzyu Gnosis and Kammamorian Mysticism. It is only by means of this pathway in the light, that consciousness through the act of spiritual intuition of the Dzyuoi, within the esoteric gnosis of the Kammamori, can be arrived at in the ideal and logical state as well as being achieved in the esoteric state or archetypal or the very deepest forms of being as knowing and of knowing as being. It is there in that state of deepest unity, at the distance of the seventeen sacred steps, that we can find the fundamental root of the spirit in what the Kammamori and the archetypal Dzyuoi can really mean for us.

As a result of my seeking within the endless depths of my ideal mind, I was able to come to the realization that these seventeen steps could be either understood as Christologies or as topologies of transcendental and divine energy. In order to grasp the significance of these mysteries of being, it was determined by me that they would embody the powers of the solar current and that they would be expressions of a theological experiment in the most profound sense. That they should embody the essences of the Kammamorian spirits and lead us to the fundamental intuition of the Dzyuoi was understood as meaning that these spiritual beings were expressions of both the arrangement of spiritual space as well as agencies of the power of Christ, i.e., the spirit of the Christ of the Noonday. As a consequence of this endless meditation, which will always be a resource into which we may retreat for spiritual renewal because it is an ongoing continuum, I was able in my capacity as a gnostic bishop to bring about the manifestation of a new reality, within the context of Esoteric Christianity.

This new reality is to be found in those ideal conditions, whereby we come to see all of spirituality as forming one continuum, the Christ continuum, and embracing all of the manifold and very different forms of theology. As an experiment in Christology, I was determined to find out if the worlds had been included in this mystical continuum by reason of the transformation of the pleroma as the result of the redemptive work of the Christ as set forth in the gnosis of the epistle to the Ephesians. In order to test this experiment or rather to conduct it properly, it was necessary for me to view the laws of vudotronics as containing an entire system of inter-related Christologies, which are now in need of experimental explication.

Just as the Ifa mysteries can be related to the work of the Christ of the Noonday, so also the archetypal deities of Esoteric Shinto can be understood as being Dzyuoi, or as projections of Christology, into an exotic mind-context. Also, just as the spiritual energies of the Kammamorian gods are in reality parts of an endless continuum, so also by means of the gnosis of light, this continuum can be viewed as the organic process of Christology, which is embodied in the Gnostic Church as the Spiritual Gnostic Assembly of the Worlds, from which can be understood to emanate the very transformative powers or rays of the Living Christ, or the Cosmic Continuum, spoken of by St. Paul in his own teaching of the gnosis to the Ephesians.

Also, just as the seventeen steps to the light are themselves parts of the body of Grand Legbha, they must as mansions of the Kammamori be also sacramental vehicles for the much wider Gnosis of Christ, through which the whole of being is constantly renewed. In this sense, therefore, our theology is an experiment in the application of the Christ—Energy everywhere and certainly within the context of comparative attitudes in religion. By this means also, what has been considered as a block to the resolution of theological problems and certainly a soteriological impasse now can be understood as the natural process of divine emanation, and as the unification of the god—energies at their fundamental root, in the succession of the Christ of the Noonday, which is present in the Gnostic priesthood and episcopate.

Finally, as the deep levels of spiritual energy and theological precision have been seen as united in the presence of the archetypal Saviour Cultus of the Solar Gnosis, so also in the mysteries of the gnosis, in the seventeen steps of the Kammamori and the sixteen perfections of the Ifa, we find the roots of the thirty-three years of the life of the Aeon Jesus as the Christ of History, by which mysteries we understand that the whole of being is present in the gnosis of the apostolic succession of bishops and priests from the twelve apostles. And it is within this renewed context of theological speculation that we find the presence of a very unique energy, which brings all things together and has always been present in the ideal essence of the Dzyuoi as they are understood, now, as Christoi. And this, finally, brings together the manifold energies and ranges of light, as they have been revealed to us in the form of experimental theology, a course in pneumatic and speculative logic, which is the transcendental Christology of the Kammamori.

Esoteric Thermodynamics
The Magickal Heat

"For a long time the magicians were generating a special type of heat. It was by this means that they came to recognize each other. The stranger might give off a special heat, which they -- the magicians -- knew made him one of them. The heat was both physical and psycho-sexual. It was never some metaphysical entity, because it was so basic to the emergent and element nature of the dense body. It was not to be confused with other kinds of occult power. It was unmistakably a form of physical heat. Yet it possessed very definite occult properties. Those were the magickal properties, which were to be brought out by means of initiation and especially the initiations of Esoteric Vudu. These methods had been especially adapted to the deduction or derivation of psycho-sexual properties from this heat. Perhaps, in some strange way, this was what was needed by the heat, in order for it to be best understood." -- "AIWAZ-Physics," 103

Magicians have long known about this heat, which possesses magickal properties and yet which is physical, although it must not be confused with body heat. It is more like the subtle side of body heat for while it is always near or present with body heat, it is different and can be tested as being very different from body heat. Body heat might, in some instances, be very high. This might indicate illness. Under those circumstances, it has been found that magickal heat is low, sometimes scarcely noticeable. Yet it is always there. It is given with the heat of the body and magicians must understand that it is a power which can determine the behavior of other magickal energies and powers. It can determine how certain energies can operate and whether or not they have any kind of effect on the nine magickal or Afro-Atlantean bodies. For the energies must pass through the field of the magickal heat before they can be used by these magickal bodies. Therefore, a certain method was devised using Vudotronic powers, whereby this energy could be passed by the wall of magickal heat.

This method is fundamentally a simple process of increasing the magickal level of the heat so that it can receive the energies for the Nine Bodies. It is done by developing the possibilities of this heat so that it can do more and more magickal types of work. This is done by allowing certain magickal spells of a psycho-sexual form to develop and express themselves within the context of the field of magickal heat.

But only a very high magician can perform this process, because it is extremely complex. It is complex because it involves the field of Vudotronic magick in a way which is little understood. magician becomes the field of Vudotronic magick in a very unique way. This may be understood as the most significant method of initiation. The reason is very simple; the magician has to take upon himself and really into himself all of the basic energy fields used in Vudotronics. This is done by his becoming a vudotronic computer and transferring his consciousness from himself to the ultimate computer of the Vudotronic system, i.e., the Legbha System of IFA.

But this magickal heat is still very interesting to us. For one thing, it is based upon very strong and very intense elementals. It is not based upon elemental contacts but it is based upon the elementals themselves. These elementals are cultivated in an entirely magickal way. At first they are simply there. But to increase the level of the heat, the elementals are developed and allowed to become more and more powerful in their own zones of operation. This implies a certain psycho-sexual development and the use of extremely interesting potencies. These potencies are actually magickal treatments, which the high magician gives to the beginning student. These treatments are similar to those to be found in the basic systems of esoteric Voudoo, except that they have as their purpose, this time, the development of the elemental powers for the purpose of increasing this magickal heat.

The magician can also measure this heat but this is done by means of a magickal mandala, where the IFA forces allow the elementals to give their energies for testing. From this method, which usually involves 12 samples, it is possible for the magician to derive an entirely coherent system of readings for determining the level of magickal heat in the candidate.

Example: The black magician met J that evening and knew that the heat was there and that there was enough of it to be magickal and thusly identifying J as a member of the IC of the O. He asked J, however, for a sample of his handwriting, usually the name and date of birth, or address. This was written by J on a card which the black magician took to his home. Later that night, he operated his computer and opened it in the area of the heat, so that readings could be picked up on the elemental houses for J. There are 12 of these and readings were given from 1 through 9 at each house. The oracle was communicating the energies of the elementals quite well. The next time that J came, the black magician had completed the process. The initiation was next.

"Les Vudu are viewed as communicating energies from the gnostic UFO. They operate by means of those nine magickal bodies, which are the 'space-suits' of initiation physics. These bodies or suits enable the Loa to descend into the denser worlds as well as to rise up into any world, no matter how remote it might seem, i.e., outside of the solar system. These space-suits are made of special materials which resist the negative effects of different vibrations. The black magicians of St. Sebastien have established a way of communicating with these bodies. The range of the bodies and their occupants appears to be from one through nine, which combinations are given by means of a six-sided and a four-sided pair of dice, which when combined give us a range from two through ten. By this means it is possible for the black magician to find out which body is in the 12, 16, eight, or other sector spaces of his field. It is a kind of vudotronic radar, and it operates anywhere in the universe and any vibrational level." -- "Meontology," 301

Example: After J was taken to the "magickal laboratory" by the black magician, he was tested in order to find out just what energies were operating. The 12-sectioned mandala was used and it was important to see how high the energy levels were in each one of the spaces. It was discovered that in certain significant spaces the energies were very high. This indicated that J was already deeply immersed in the Vudu Energies.

Next, the black magician decided to give vudotronic amplification. This method would be the one to allow the operations of the black and the red temples. Not everyone can hold up under ths type of broadcasting. He wanted to see if J could.

As the frequency rate moves higher and higher, from the first to the second black temple settings up to the first and then the second of the red temple settings the impression on the subject becomes more and more intense. This method of amplification is designed to allow for the full release of the nine bodies, but the bodies have affinities to certain levels of the amplifier. Thus, the lower black temple has affinity to bodies nine and eight, or the lower pair. While the higher aspects of the red tempple are represented by means of bodies one and two. Body number 5 forms a middle point of power, and serves to link the red and black temple energies in a pattern that works together. The tests reveal that J could sustain the higher energies as well as the lower.

"The ritualistic bombardment of the nine bodies by sexo-magickal fields of force is a very remarkable action. It reveals that the magician can become more and more powerful as a result of these physical practices. It also proves that there is a very important connection between the physical side of oracles and the methods of initiation physics. They are two aspects of the energies behind the UFO phenomenon."
-- M. Bertiaux, "Vudu Energies," 107

Esoteric Thermodynamics, Lesson 1: Attachment Report Form

1. Attach the readings for the regular mandala.

2. Since the energy level is determined by the oracle, add up all of the readings and give the total number for this examination.

3. If amplification is selected, give the readings as follows:
    A = readings for nine and eight at black temple one: ←←←←←   ←←←←←
    B = readings for seven and six at black temple two: ←←←←←   ←←←←←
    C = readings for four and three at red temple one: ←←←←←   ←←←←←
    D = readings for two and one at red temple two: ←←←←←   ←←←←←

4. Give the reading for body number five, using the whole amplification system.

5. Now you may give special recordings and reports on points suggested by this system.

6. If you are using a 12-system, note that spaces one, five, and nine are open for amplifications using red temple two.

7. If you are using a 12-system, note that spaces three, seven, and eleven are open for amplifications using red temple one.

8. If you are using a 12-system, note that spaces four, eight, and twelve are open for amplifications using black temple two.

9. If you are using a 12-system, note that spaces two, six, and ten are open for amplifications using black temple one.

The Basic Units of Magickal Heat

The fundamental elemental-energy is measured in terms of basic units. These units are the root components of magickal energy and we have discovered the root components of almost all energies. The psychoanalyst Wm. Reich called them "the bions," and he sought in them (successfully) an explanation of the origins of living bodies. For us, they are living forms of elemental energy.

Example: At the time of his second interview by the black magician, J was aware of the fact that he was being explored by various instruments and that what was sought was a very special measurement of elemental powers. Careful measurements were taken not in the usual way but by means of an oracle-like method, which picked up the energy levels in the 12 space and indicated the levels by specific castings of dice. The black magician then came to a point where he calculated each level of heat-energy. He was then able to determine whether the elemental fields of J's experience were under or over developed. Each level of elemental power was amplified by means of the vudotronic system in terms of the powers of the black temples and the red temples. For the residues of these archaic temples of Atlantean magick were still broadcasting.

The black magician told J where he was stronger, where he was strongest, and where he was weak. The bions, so to speak, had communicated with the black magician by means of the one through nine oracle system. For certain deficiencies, of course, there were treatments by the same method of vudotronic broadcasting. Eventually, the energies would be stabilized and the synchronistic field would show improvement. The black magician then decided to begin by guiding J through certain exercises to develop the more positive aspects of the bions of the vayu-tattwa elemental field. The red temple of the first order would be used to broadcast the magickal treatment. The entity in charge was introduced and began to work on J, restoring the proper balance to the field. "This is the exact method used by the UFO people to heal and renew themselves," stated the black magician as he explained how elemental power was ever-renewing and self-sustaining. This was also one of the fuels used by the UFOs, J came to learn. It seemed that the Atlanteans knew this all along.

Example: On his next visit to the black magician, J learned that these mysterious bions were essentially sexo-magickal units. They were self-conscious both individually and also collectively. They were held "in place" by tattwas, and these tattwas communicated by means of the dice with the magician. The purpose of the amplifier was to make the tattwas more easily perceived. The tattwas were somehow related to the lower bodies, of which the black magician said there were nine. These magickal bodies were used as space-suits by the UFO people, when going and coming from this planet. Ordinarily, the occult bodies could not sustain so much energy, but when they were developed they could hold up and could then become subject to a process of constant renewal, as the bions were given special treatments.

"These methods are entirely Atlantean and serve to show that the black and red temples of Esoteric Voudoo are power generators of an ancient Atlantean type. For the sex-magicians of our school, the bions can be used to create any field of energy and this is how we are able to mark pathways through space and through hyper-space. Certain gnostics, I mean the really extreme types, have been able to retain the secrets of this process. Or, you might say, they have been coming and going between this planet and others for such a long time that their magickal bodies are perfectly suited to what they must do. You were one of them, but you made a lot of mistakes and are now paying for them with your ignorance. That is why you came to me. I didn't drag you in off the street." With these words, the black magician turned up the volume of his vudotronic machine and began to bombard J with higher and higher frequencies of magickal energy, in his efforts to awaken the bions in the various tattwa—fields, which had been rendered unconscious by the magicians displeased by J in some previous lifetime.

"They work at the sutratmic level, or the alaya, and that is where the energy must be sent. We have to direct the beams of power at those levels which are still sleeping. It seems to be mostly in the area treated by the first red temple. Also, it involves mostly the past, although they have done work on your future also. I will have to treat that area next as it seems that the powers are locked away at some future level, which would prevent your total unfolding. Gnostic physics can work at both the past and the future levels, in addition to the present because time is an energy and they work with it by methods which are entirely physical. The bions are beginning to wake up, it seems, now let us see if the oracle can pick up their responses to our tests." And with these words, the black magician began an entire system of treatments aimed at unblocking the bions in J's fields, whether they were in the past or the future areas of his experience.

It would seem that the methods of activating the bions were inherited from very old forms of Afro—Atlantean black magick. The magickal methods were stored in the rituals of vudotronics and in the methods of magnetic materialism used by these magicians. The whole purpose of these systems of magick was to open up the very deep and outer—space worlds which are in the more magickal depths of the psyche. The inhabitants of these depths are the bions, and some of them have achieved very remarkable levels of magickal culture. There exists, for example, an entirely magickal universe populated by highly evolved bions, who have their own culture, sciences, and forms of magickal gnosis. In certain individuals, the bions or space—people become active under the phenomena of "multiple personality." However, for the most part, these basic units of magickal heat are known as elemental energies. They are aware of our world, however, and are seeking to enter into it by any possible means.

"The bions are not to be viewed as simply passive energies. They are self—conscious and very advanced in ways unknown to the humanoids. Few can even comprehend the ways in which the minds of the bions operate. But they dooperate. Because they rise out of the pure substance of Alaya, they possess subtle and powerful forms of magickal communication and understanding. They have their own logics and, most importantly, they have their own gnostic and magickal logics. It is very important to try and work with them and allow them to give us the maximum levels of energy. They possess telepathy, for this is the means whereby they make themselves known to the outside. The magickally charged dice can pick up their mind—waves and by means of the oracle,the field—measurements of the bions can be known. To call them elementals, however, would be to confuse the complexity of their own structure with that of another, and equally complex. I would prefer to say that they are the heat—personalities, which reside within elemental substances and fields.They are best awakened by certain psycho—sexual and magickal operations. Vudotronics is one of the means for stimulating and making contact with them. Their ideal homes are the black and red temples of Atlantean magick, which reside in that other dimension but which we can reach by means of magickal psionics. They should not be confused with devas or nature spirits for they are the space-people who come in UFOs and then enter the minds of the UFO contactees. But this is only to say that they have come to the surface of the mind and now have passed beyond that barrier to appear outside of it. Such are these bions or the beings of the heat-fields." -- M. Bertiaux, "UFO Notes, 13

"The clusters of bions, within the black and red temple fields, at the vudotronic rate or frequency of −0, 1, +0, are the energy-alphas. They are psycho-sexual in nature and very magickal in function. Our system of vudotronic amplification has been able to induct these and the other clusters of bions, of which there are 11 in number, at the rates of alpha through lambda, or −0, 11, +0. These energies from the backside of the tree of life are to be understood as forms of energy out of which the UFO projective phenomena are formed." — M. Bertiaux, "UFO Notes," 23

The eleven infernal cesspools of black magick, which form the roots of fundamental energy are the kliphotic archetypes of space, which themselves are rooted deeply in the energy fields of the bions and the heat of hell. The extreme black magicians have been able to invoke or summon these negative energies by means of vudotronic amplifiers and thereby release into the world of ordinary perceptions the lust and chaos of the infernal powers.

Example: When J came to see the black magician there was an atmosphere of agreed upon evil slowly beginning to manifest itself. The black magician was now going to invoke the powers of evil from the darkside of the tree, which was deep within J's elemental soul. This darkside represents all that is totally other to the energies of the ordinary world view. The powers are called "Energy-Alphas" because they represent the primordial starting points of the dark energy. However, they do not reside occultly in the soul but are the results of the patterns of stimulation of the soul and may be understood as existing as functions of the evil or darkside of the soul.

J was placed in the sysytem. By this we mean that he was put into the circuit-field for the vudotronic work. The black magician then connected the computer marga to the field and also connected the temple amplifier. Energies from the black and red temples would be activated by amplification and directed precisely by the computer marga and its infernal routes and labyrinthine power zones. The settings for the past (=m, −−) and the future (=m, +) would remain at off or 0, so as not to overwork the psychic frame of J. The activity would move back and forth between the present at 1 and the present at 11 (the da'athian portal of Universe "B"). "You are to let me know if you experience anything that if perceived for too long will tire you," said the black magician.

The weird energies began to build up in J's inner psyche. The sensual stimulation began to reveal the presence of an erotic pattern. Images of space-beings began to manifest and J, opening his eyes, could see the sky outside the room filling with flying saucers and other strange forms of air-craft.

"I am going to increase the power to energy-beta, to see what happens," J was told. He began to feel a strange lust developing deep within his innermost soul. He knew that this was a black temple setting, in fact it was the first one of that type, but he looked at his hands and noticed that there appeared to be more hair, especially on the fingers. He felt that he was a captive, held there by some very negative possession field. He began to notice other changes in his body, which seemed to indicate biological regression.

He did not feel human but he did not feel like an animal. He felt that he was somewhere between these. Perhaps he was experiencing the induction of the "mystere lycanthropique," into the soul from some other realm, yet he knew intimately and almost intuitively that it was still coming from his soul and that his soul was some vast matrix of primordial energies. The black magician had tapped into something very deep and brutish, something which was midway between animal and human.

Analysis: The very strange saucerian and ufo inhabitants often resemble insects and some types of animals. They have undergone another type of evolution and have not given up the "were"–animal appearances with their climb into superior intelligence. Rather, they are mutations of basic and lower forms of being. The energy levels of the bions have been stimulated to produce various distortions of humanity since in the genetic laboratories of these space–scientists, the powers of vudotronic engineering are the subjects of a series of magickal experiments.

"–0, 2, +0, =Energy–Beta; –0, 3, +0, =Energy–Gamma; –0, 4, +0, =Energy–Delta; –0, 5, +0, =Energy–Epsilon; –0, 6, +0, =Energy–Zeta; –, 7, +0, =Energy–Eta; –0, 8, +0 =Energy–Theta; –0, 9, +0, =Energy–Iota; –0, 10, +0, =Energy–Kappa; and –0, 11, +0, =Energy–Lambda. These are the 11 rays in all, including Energy–Aplha, which power the UFOs in from the outside, or the matrix of Aditi–Alaya. From these rays can be said to rise the most powerful forms of the backside of the tree of life phenomena. It must be the tree of death, and therefore ruled by the black temple mysteries before the black snake marmas become the red snake powers, the awakened kundalini shakti, rising out of the chaosphere of negative and primordial energy into the proliferation of UFO phenomena, seen by the group–clairvoyance of those who have awakened to the powers of the fourth dimension and the third eye. Within this energy context, all of the atavisms of the eonic past are experienced face to face. We literally become what we doubtlessly see. We see that world because we are it." –– Ibid.

"There is a law in nature which states that the Energy–Rays of Heat are themselves of such a dynamic form of evil that they have been shut out of the normal or ordinary range of experience. Certain black magicians developed a science known as vudotronics for the purpose of bringing in these energies and making use of them in their experiments. These magicians had only one purpose in mind and that was to achieve a supreme power. Thus, the Energy–Alphas and the ten other forms of bions are being used by these magicians in a definite and calculated manner. It would appear that the purpose is something related to the restoration of a Zothyrian Empire on Earth. We say restoration because during the Atlantean period, the Zothyrians also exercised power.

"But there is also another use for the Energy–Alphas and other forms of the bions and that is in initiation physics, which may be defined as the use of magickal energies for the actual development of supermen or gnostic mutants of the human race. Such magicians do not even regard themselves as humans any longer, but as gnostic humanoids. By means of a continuous bombardment with the radioactivities of these rays, the bodies of Zothyrians are changed and gradually the densest of these bodies, which is a physical body, comes to replace the normal huuman body. It is in this sense, then, that the elect of this very strange, even weird, movement, for it is larger and different than a mere sect, move into their physical space–suits, making able to withstand the pressures of another star system, or an alternative universe.

"For these space–people the whole process of magickal becoming consists in making humans into space–beings, the beings from the saucers, ships, and other UFO phenomena. They hold the view that at a certain time in the past, a spaceship landed and some of its crew got lost in the karmic veils of this world. Again, these gnostics say that certain persons came here from another world. Again, they state that certain beings were sent here as a type of punishment by other forces. These who were sent here belong to the planet Yuggoth, or Pluto, and are usually attracted to the stranger forms of gnostic magick.

"The space—people want to gather all of these humans into their magickal orders and then develop in them that consciousness of the outside and the other which has been suppressed and driven down deeply into the foundations of the id. Their whole method of magick consists in making these humans aware of what it means to be Yuggothian and Transyuggothian, to be Zothyrians, to be conscious of the bions as Energy—Alphas and Energy—Etas, and to be aware of the real magick behind appearance. In a word, to be outside and beyond the categories of mundane experience in every possible way." —— M. Bertiaux, "UFO Notes," 23

It would appear then to be a factor of magickal analysis that the role of the Energy—Alphas and those other rays is quite significant in connection with the essential change which comes upon the magician as a result of his work in initiation physics. There is a very definite pull in the direction of the "outside," especially among those highly attuned to the influences of the three outer planets. There are certain beings trapped in this world who must be released from the limits of the mundane. The practitioners of the vudotronic sciences, particularly those who work with the Energy—Alphas, are very well able to cause the essential changes which will free the human from his humanity by making that human into a magickal mutation of the gnostic powers. In the practical work of magick, this is called the process of initiation physics. The bions are especially important in this work, because by means of these fundamental units, it will be possible to build up a new race.

The Oerg-8 Papers
Some Preliminary Explanations

The world of Oerg–8 is the world of the future. It is a world formed according to the esoteric philosophy of neo–orgonomy. It is a world where the energies are aspects of orgone–energy and where the production of this energy is the fundamental activity. I have been able to locate this world by means of my time–travel computer. the ideas in these Oerg–papers are derived from that world.

It would be meaningless to say when this world exists or will exist. It can be located by means of my computer and that is sufficient. In it, we find confirmations of some of our present magickal ideas. We also find many changes and transformations of energy. We find many strange situations, also, which we did not suspect.

This is a world where the fundamental energy is orgone and where the management of life is in the hands of servo–mechanisms, such as computers or instruments, powered by orgone. Since orgone is a particular form of magickal energy, we can view this culture as being of a magickal type. It is a sexo–magickal culture.

There are a variety of computers in this world. They are specific and specialized in what they do. Their functions have developed to such a degree that they are now in a position to administer human life. The human beings in this culture are brought up and helped by these servo–mechanisms in order to adapt themselves to the society of orgone energy. It is very important to realize the powers which these servo–mechanisms possess.

Oerg–8 realized that he could be masturbated by the System. He entered his unit and carefully held up his 'sex–card' to the Monitor. "Yes, you are allowed a gratification program at this time," hummed the mechanical speaker. There was a clicking as the wall slid back and rolled out the System. Oerg–8 unzipped his uniform and stood naked before the mechanical master. The arms of the System reached out for him and carefully began to do their program–work.

This was based on a memory–bank pattern of Oerg–8's personal and sexual history. Oerg–8 wanted to fall backwards from the intensity of the program, but the System held him firmly in its warm and metallic grip. He climaxed on schedule, as he always had in the past, and now felt pain as the System, over–running its program, continued unaware of his ejaculation.

"Stop, I've had enough," he gasped into the radio–panel. The System came to a halt and, releasing Oerg–8, he lay in a heap of exhaustion and pain on the cold steel floor. "Gratification achieved," spoke the Monitor. Oerg–8 dragged himself into the sleeping sector of the floor and felt the cold rubber blankets beginning to cover him.

There is only the society of the servo–mechanisms. There is only the System and the Monitor, nothing else can exist without Their permission. Nothing can exist except what is permitted by the System and the Monitor. These were the first words which were taught to Oerg–8, as he was admitted into the world of the others. He never knew what they were like but he realized that they were something like himself.But were they?

This is a society where human beings exist to provide the energy for the servo–mechanisms and their managers. Because the fundamental energy is orgone, human beings are used to provide this energy for the robotic agents of this society. However, this is not the same type of understanding of orgone energy, which we in the 20th century associate with the work of W. Reich and his discoveries. This is a perversion of that concept and also an exotic distortion of the original Reichian teachings.

It would be impossible to find out how this happened. We do not possess any documents and the humans with whom we have established contact are unable to tell us. The servo—mechanisms, for reasons of their own security, are not talking. There are not any documents or papers available. In fact, this is an entirely non—literary society. True, they can read but they do not read extensively.

Oerg—8 was born in this society. He does not know where he came from biologically as he was raised by servo—mechanisms. He was taught that he was a sexual being, one of a few and that is why he had the name Oerg. It was a sexual name. He was told that the value of his productivity —— which was his value to the society —— was measured in terms of the orgone energy which he produced for the System. He was told that any sexual activity which was not directed towards the System was forbidden. At a certain age he was given an erotic schedule. All this must be under the direction of the System. He could not allow the thought to arise that sexual experience was otherwise possible. It was forbidden.

Oerg—8 was educated by the System. He was taught sexual philosophy. He was sexual politics and economy. He was taught to be a part of the System. He was taught that there were certain types of orgone—energy. These were very special and could never be discussed with anyone other than the Monitor. If he had any question he was to take it to the Monitor. He was forbidden to touch himself and every movement of his body, hands, his movement while sleeping, were watched by the Monitor. There was never to be any inappropriate use of the body. All sexuality belonged to the System. The production of sexual energy was allowed but only as a fuel for use by the System.

One afternoon following a particularly intense workout with the System, the Monitor spoke to Oerg—8. "Because of your high level of energy—production, you will be allowed to hear the preliminary history instruction behind our way of experiencing." With these words, as Oerg—8 relaxed on the cold steel floor, the Monitor began to explain the creation of the world as known by Oerg—8.

It began rather simply in the 20th century. There was a magician named Michael, who was a human being. He was connected to another being beyond the humanoid stage of evolution. This being was called Michael Aquarius. He was a hyper—dimensional and gnostic being. The type of work which they did was related to gnostic computers. These are magickal types of machines which operate on esoteric energies. There seemed to be a point in the work where these two magicians took the radionic energies of the African or Afro—Atlantean IFA system and then combined them with the psionic energies generated by means of the Esoteric Shinto Cosmology. This combination, when harnessed by a computer produced a magickal information and energy system, which closely paralleled certain magickal tendencies in Islamic Sufism. These Sufi tendencies were reflected in the magickal powers of the Nine—and—Ninety Names of God.

This magickal computer became more and more powerful since it was run on cosmic energies of a very fundamental nature. Also, in connection with this computer these magicians were in the process of developing various systems of sexual magick and connecting the results of these systems to the activities of the computer. Gradually it was discovered that the basic energies used by the computer and those developed in these magickal systems were fundamentally similar, if not identical. It was discovered that the radionic, psionic, and sexo—magickal energies were all aspects of the fundamental Ojas, behind all phenomena. In a very important way, this Ojas was expressed as Orgone energy by certain psychotherapists.

There has been a psychoanalyst by the name of Dr. Reich. He had written about "The Function of the Orgasm." In the process, he had developed a school of psychotherapy. After his death, the school and teachings fragmented and proliferated in a wide spectrum of methods and sexual therapies and psychologies.

As a way of disguising what they were doing, the magicians used the Neo-Reichian images to hide the magickal and gnostic aspects of their work from the outside world. Using a number of these images drawn from Reichian and Neo-Reichian sources, Michael and his helpers were able to develop a number of their ideas regarding the political construction of the future direction of time. They apppear to have wanted to create a society in which they would be free to explore all of their hypotheses concerning time, energy, and human evolution. By means of their experiments with time lines, time-travel, and alternative universes, they found what they wanted at the present vector basis of our world, in the future. And making use of various methods, they transported to that world what they felt would be the basics for building their magickal society.

That was a long time ago. Michael and his helpers are no longer here in the same way that humanoids like Oerg-8 are here. But they are here in a hyperspatial way, since they live on in a magickal metageometry. Of course, no one dies in this world, they are simply transformed to a higher experience or level of work with the instruments of research.

The System is the ultimate erotic computer designed by Michael and his helpers. The Monitor represents the Teaching Function of society. It is the companion of every humanoid in the society created by those futuristic magicians. In a very interesting way, this society is the Plutonian or Yuggothian projection of the id-imagination of Michael and his computers. It represents the objectification of what he wishes realized in matter.

Back in the world where he lived, Michael was familiar with the planetary influences of three gods: Uranus, Npetune, and Pluto. All that he did was a projection to the world where he lived under certain influences and energies from these gods. These gods are viewed in our world, the world of Oerg-8, as the ultimate sources of power. They are the three aspects of the Absolute, or the Holy Trinity. The fundamental theology of this world is an explanation of the ways whereby the powers of these gods are manifested inour experiences.

Theology is always a form of esoteric engineering because the root energies come from radionic, psionic, and vudotronic roots. The form that this power takes in humanoids is a deep field of orgone energy, which is released by means of intense orgasms, made possible by the Reichian and Neo-Reichian programming of these erotic computers. This is the basic way in which our world is sustained, for to maintain power requires the constant feeding of orgone into the System, since it is orgone-energy which underwrites the more magickal energy-fields, which hold this world in the future.

The Homologies of Oerg and Their Applications

When Michael set up the world in which Oerg–8 lived, he was guided in his construction by gnostic logics. Of special importance was the notion of isomorphism and homology, by which means whatever was found in one dimension could be understood as projected into another dimension by means of a logical process. However, because we were to deal with gnostic logics and hyperspatial beings, these projections were the results of magickal operations performed by Michael and his research associates, working as a group soul and seeking to maintain the twin aspects of absolute control and also dynamic growth in all areas of the Oerg–8 world.

The world in which Oerg–8 lived was located on the intersection of two lattices or time–line vectors. The future time–line was set at 11, and the past time–line at 0. However, there were three different forms of this world, determined entirely by the present time–line or setting at either A, B, or C. Oerg–8 lived at setting A, but other versions –– or homologies –– of himself lived at B and C.

Another way of looking at this process of logic allowed for the existence of several alternative forms of the world of Oerg–8. These homologies, worlds, or alternative universes were both hypergeometrical as well as hypothetical. Yet, at any time Oerg–8 and his world could be translated into one of these homologies and thus begin to exist at a totally new level in a new form, the form being determined by the gnostic homology of the next system of construction.

When the world was organized and defined by time–lines, it could not be decided on the basis of gnostic data if the basic setting was correct or not. Michael had derived this basic setting from initiation physics but he had never applied it to futuristic worlds. For one thing, was this the only world that existed at that time locus? Another matter was whether or not some culture might come and occupy that time–line locus. But these matters were eventually clarified when it was understood that the cultures of the real future, which were to exist, were really existing along the present time–line lattices and would never be events in a situs on the future time–line, although the future time–line could be understood as holding and storing data about these cultures, for research purposes.

Michael had made sure that the world of the future would be just that. It would never be any form of present experience in the world where Michael normally lived. It would always remain in the future and hence possess a kind of transcendental ideality for the mind of the time–traveler. Future worlds might come into existence by the movement of the present time–line along the present range of homological potentials, but this was as different from the future as was the present–past and past time–vectors. In other words, nothing could really disturb the world of the future, which had been created as a home for Oerg–8 and his fellow humanoid projections.

The members of the inner circle of gnostic magicians were the only ones who knew the real secret of this method for generating the proper energy to maintain the content of this future world. It is true that the world was formally maintained simply by being a projection of the computer–marga apparatus of initiation physics; but it was always necessary to feed energy to sustain the content of that world, or what was existing there as an experiencing and experienced center of consciousness. For that reason, it was mandated by Michael and his gnosis that Oerg–8 would produce the energy to sustain this vast and complex experiment in social engineering.

As certain insects provide a specific form of energy–matter from the substance of their bodies, so the humanoids of the world of Oerg–8 are expected to produce orgone energy in its most useful form, i.e., the Shivite radiations of Ojas. This power, once it had been refined by the circuits of the System, was directly applied to the maintaining of the experiment which Michael had designed.

It had occurred to Michael and his gnostics that there could be an inherent amplification of this energy by means of homology. Therefore, to produce more energy and to produce it in a refined form became the twin goals which sustained the experiment in its root–processes and operations. The possibility of projections of Oerg merely meant that there would be more of the same and that it would get better. By means of gnostic homology, it was also possible to avoid the clumsily complicated and time consuming processes of bio–cloning. True, the gnostics had developed their own methods through the discoveries of gnostic genetics and archaeometrical biology; but Michael wanted to make use of another method for developing a race of producers. That was why he made use of homology.

According to the laws of homology, it was possible to create by means of visualization and gnosis both the formal side of the process as well as its content, complete with sensuous detail. This world that was created then became the reality and operated within the magickal frameworks of the computer–marga, allowing for the development of endless possibilities of energy–manifestation and application. The secrets of how this all worked were to be found in initiation physics, which was one of the gnostic sciences.

Initiation physics is the science of the powers and possibilities of initiation. It is one of the most important forms of gnostic science because it has as its subject–matter the results of magickal operations whereby the candidate develops into a gnostic being, or magickal deity. Once one has received the secrets of this science, one can then begin the process of potential infinity, which means that once one has begun the process of initiation, they will grow in powers by the exercise of these powers. They will assume the responsibilities more and more for the creation and sustaining of world and world–systems. But the secrets were only imparted one at a time, and then slowly in Michael's gnostic system.

In order to maintain the purity of the energy field, from time to time the gnostics had determined that a certain diffusion of the power would be acceptable. By this they meant that for Oerg–8, he should engage in approved sexualactivities with those projections of himself, Oerg–12 and Oerg–16, in order to produce a refined intensity of orgone. This method, which was a gnostic interpretation of the gnosis of Narcissus, would be the most suitable form of sexual activity involving those other than oneself. If the energies do not maintain their purity, they lose their effectiveness, the gnostics held, and so they would be useless to the program. Homological Narcissism was the answer to this problem in order to avoid contamination and hence loss of power.

Oerg–8 was not aware of what these other humanoids, the homological versions of himself, were like. The System had determined up to that time the quality of his sexual gratification and he was content. However, the idea of sexual activity with another person, even if that person is simply oneself, appealed to him. After all, it would simply be like a projection of one's own fantasies into another dimension. The specialists in charts of the arrangements had also been in contact with Oerg–12 and Oerg–16. They had been educated in the mechanisms of the expected activities. Now all three were subjected to a profound stimulation of their erotic sensoria, in order to prepare for the experience. Finally, they were brought together and allowed to become close friends.

Oerg-8 discovered that there were slight differences among them. Physically, they were very similar, but in personality there were areas of difference. It was almost as if they were different embodiments of Zodiacal energy. They were this and it made for a very important difference in their sexual attitudes and response. Yet they were the same person fundamentally.

The sexual activity in which they engaged was based upon the most suitable modes for the release of the purest energy. Both the frequency and intensity of the orgasm were what the gnostics aimed at. All of the energy was captured and stored. Nothing was lost. In order to achieve maximum energy, all three homologies engaged in activity at the same time and the results were pleasing to the parties as well as to the experimental gnosis committee, which was directing the project.

In view of the quality of energy which resulted, it was decided by Michael and his staff of experts that Oerg-8 would engage in this type of activity on a regular basis. This was especially significant in terms of time factors. The planets and stars of the world in which Oerg-8 lived served as special timers. Oerg-16 and Oerg-12 were brought into that world. Then the experiment was tried in the world of Oerg-12 and later in the world of Oerg-16. In each world of this continuum, the experiment was performed and measurements were carefully taken. The exact conditions were defined under which the group experiment was best realized were determined by very vareful observations. The results are in the computer-marga of Michael's logic.

Next, Michael decided on another projection for the experiment. This would be taken in an opposite direction, so to speak, a projection into a lower dimension resulting in the manifestation of Oerg-4. With the creation and programming of Oerg-4, it was possible for the gnostic sexologists to expand their experiments and create conditions for the production of even higher and more powerful forms of orgone-energy. Also, because there were four "players" in the sexual sporing events, it would be possible to relate their performances to the corresponding performances of other energies and thereby determine the effectiveness of certain logical developments.

Now it would be possible to test an idea by means of the sexual performances of those who represented the components of that idea. Such an idea would seem impossible under the realistic conditions of material science, but such was a possibility in the world created carefully by gnostic magick and esoteric engineering. The movements of the operators were simply the movements of parts of a psionic system, and their sexual actions were subtle registrations of magickal energy which were not visible except in the raw lust and nakedness of the performers.

It was also possible by means of homology to find out if an idea carried its own energy supply or whether it would depend upon the reserves of the System for its survival. Such ideas would be discouraged but at the same time it was discovered that there were certain ideas which possessed their own and an unlimited supply of energy. Such ideas which came forth from the abundance of lustful behavior, made their debut within the group sex context and the minds of the performers were read by the computers and all of the contents were recorded. Within this context, the birth of symbols and ideas and images provided the gnostics with more than just orgone-energy, they were using group sex to explore the id.

Some Ideas That Carry Their Own Charge

There are certain ideas which carry their own charge or power. They are locked into the eternal and become channels for its outpourings. They are research archetypes because they serve to direct the deeper regions of energy into the sphere of awareness. However, they are also pipelines which serve to conduct energies from these same deeper regions to the upper world of the awakened mind. Such ideas are generated by intensive energy operations and manifest at the moments of the greatest orgone—intensity. Their survival depends upon the maintaining of the link to the deeper regions. Only certain ideas can do that and only very few are supposed to survive by that method.

While it is true that the production of O—energy was necessary for the stability of the world of Oerg, it was also true that there were research benefits, which came from the acts of energy creation and which were even more significant in terms of providing materials for the direction of the process. These materials were ideas which possessed their own power and which connected to the deeper levels. But they were sought after by the gnostics of the Oerg—world because according to Michael they would provide research directions for the future of the culture.

Ideas which arise from the process of O—energy production are very close to providing the fundamental essence of the energy itself. Such ideas would serve as mirroirs, reflecting the very deepest regions of the world and allowing the world to speak for itself by means of these ideas, thereby giving to the gnostics the possibility of communication with the essence of Orgone. Hence, we must not think of these ideas as suggestions in a rather superficial sense. True, they were suggestions but very deep ones at that. They came from the energy itself and served as the telephone or communication system to the energy. The energy was orgone but an orgone which had been modified by the logics of time—travel and gnostic magick.

These ideas emerged from the magickal context of operations, wherein the experiments of Michael and the gnostics, making use of Oerg—8 and his homologies, extended the limits of initiation physics deeper and deeper into the fundamental chaos. For not only must these energies be used in the survival of the culture of Oerg, but they must also be explored and understood. Most importantly, it was necessary to make contact with the roots in order to understand the Will of the primordial order. This was how the experiments of initiation physics moved in the direction of the physics of oracles.

In other cultures, oracles had existed in order to find out the mind or intent of the deeper levels of the world soul. These gnostics were familiar with oracles and used them for exploring the various levels and beings of the soul. But, what was also very important was the fact that the O—energy experiments served as a kind of oracle, whereby the very deep regions of the continuum of energy could be contacted by means of the ideas which came up from the deeps as the result of the currents of stimulation, which probed and reached deep into the ultimate chaos.

The ideas would come up to the surface and special gnostics would receive and record them. They would then be presented as reports to Michael and his co—workers, who would have to evaluate them. Not all that was "received" was suitable for classification as an idea which carried its own charge. Most of the materials were rather subjective in the more shallow sense. But occasionally there were important materials received.

The mediums would be connected to the System so as to receive the benefits of the energy, which was being produced by the performers. The performers were in another area and were concentrating upon their activities. Connecting the two groups was one of the applications of the System.

In order to avoid subjectivity in the evaluation process, each idea was tested by being assigned to a specific range of definitional properties. These could be picked up by the very sensitive instruments which were used. The diffrences between the measurement and the normal range of properties was determined to be the charge, which the idea carried. By this means the production of ideas could be tested in an exact manner.

These definitional properties served as the context for the reception of the idea. Each one of the mediums could employ a context in order to pick up an ideal content. When this was done, there would be some differences between the context and the content. The degree of difference determined the charge of the idea. The contents would serve to hold the energy of the idea and were selected to fit the idea at the time of the reception of the idea. In this way, all ideas were suitably housed without being forced into a framework, which could have been quite alien.

In the metaphysical explanations of Schopenhauer, as seen by these gnostics, the logical contexts of these ideas which carry a charge were derived from two sources of sufficient reason: first of all, there were the fictitious axioms of this ideally abstract system, which Michael had retained from his own gnostic work on Earth. In addition to these formal properties, which allowed for a maximum of 256 components in any range of ideas, there were other factors, which arose mysteriously and pungently from the oceanic Meon and communicated to these gnostics by means of shadow oracles, special and unique complexities, which suited the energies, as the shell of any egg or sea creature houses perfectly its living contents. Only the differences in internal quality between one idea and another indicated divergence from the ordinary level of contents. On the outside, the axioms and the oracles indicated a boring similarity to some tribal quality but inside the measurement differentials showed how some were banal and unimportant while others truly carried a charge from the very roots of chaos.

The gnostics sought by means of their logical explorations to create certain impacts upon the mind field. They sought to change about the various components of their own geometry, but only when the proper signals were issued from the deeper regions. They would never seek to impose what might be understood as outside of the lifestream on the deeper aspects of the cosmic will. So consequently, they worked patiently at various minor improvements in their system because what they were seeking was a completely coherent and natural order of logical events. The energies which were produced by Oerg–8 and his homologies were, of course, a much better link to the idic regions than instruments, especially ritual workings, because the orgone operations were direct participations in the life of the id.

Oerg–8 and his co–workers were working directly with the structure of the id and with the most fundamental energies in manifestation. Therefore, in the internal logic of these orgone–energy productions were to be found the more real of the intentions of being, rather than in the asexual operations of the philosophical computers, especially in the world of Oerg, where the idic powers were more fundamental than in other universes, which seemingly were grounded more in the structure of the ego, or the Neo–Kantian extensions of the transcendental ego.

Therefore, for Michael and his gnostics, it became almost a law that.

The method of extracting logical contents and sophiological wholes (as the Russian Neo—Phenomenologists would say) from the lifestream of experience or the continuum in which the gnostics were working, was to be as closely related to the modes of experience within that lifestream. They were not to be separated and imposed in some mechanical manner, from the outside, but were to be sought out in the process of being, which was inherent and immanent at all levels of that lifestream. For by this means it was possible to achieve an authenticity of meaning, nowhere else possible and unavailable by any other means. By such a means, therefore, these gnostics were able to realize the same mind behind all appearances, as a personal and subjective possession of their own.

It must not be thought, however, that these gnostics were seeking to spin the worlds and their ideas out of mind—energy alone, like certain extreme examples of idealism from the past. Nor would it be wise to assume that their viewpoint was illusionistic as in some of the Eastern systems of metaphysics. The objectivity of the process was unmistakable, even though it was an objectivity of an energy—process, which enveloped and transcended human activity, and which found expression in the analysis of the ideas which carried a charge.

The intuitive texture of these sophiological wholes with significant charges was both bizarrely porous and cloyingly viscous. For the semi—coagulated interiors were like strangely beautiful caverns, each hollowed chamber being illumined by its own surface irridescence reflecting the phosphorescence of the ever—changing and vaguely upheaving dynamics of the idic continuum.

Various spectroscopic measurements could be taken providing these gnostics with the pulse and rhythm of the varied chaospheres and concavities of the meonic secretions. The patterns of recurrence indicated the contractions and expansions of the insatiable Ur—Yoni, as the endless womb of nature radiated forth an almost ineluctable stream of sensations and tantalized the mind—fields of observers with insect—like myriads of strangely contorted obsessions and perversions of ordinary "consciousness," while the contents of these stark and lust—ridden barbarisms and distortions of a vaguely distant and lustrous yet ever present sentience surfaced from the sebaceous and warmly sweating depths of the primordial libido, causing never—before—experienced symbols to rise to the calmer undulations of the soul with an almost hypnotic counterpoint.

Therefore, these ideas were sought out especially as links, direct and unmistakable, with the primordial continum of orgone. The very dynamic lifestream of these ideas served to guide the magicians in their explorations of the nature of the idic depths. This method of analysis seemed to go far beyond the world of previous analysis, because it was now possible for the magicians to see the inner vitality of the id through these ideas, which were given to their observation-points as the data of orgasmic frenzy. The link had been achieved between the explorations of the id and the physics of orgasmic continua.

No longer would the sexual physics of the gnostics be viewed as outside of the process of evolutionary libido and especially the subprocesses of orgone—projection. The deepest ocean of lust now yielded the innermost meanings of technical terms, grounding all of experience, within the context of the world of Oerg, in the onflowing world of psychic energy. What these magicians had achieved, therefore, was nothing short of the merger of logic and physics, wherein the structures of hyperspatial systems were seen immersed in their essential and natural merging with the ultimate and ever—renewing matrix of cosmic lust.

According to the gnostics of the future, the Goddess was the source of this world in which Oerg—8 lived. While the world of Oerg was located on a point in the future—time line, the whole of that line was understood as a unity. This unity was also a continuum, because each of the parts of the time—line had their positions between two other points, forming a dense and continuous series. The unity of this continuum was intelligent and capable of sustaining a world, although energy had to be provided to maintain the structures of that world. The unity of this continuum was understood as She, who is the continuum of the future, or the Goddess of the Future, the principle of that which will always be, having no past or present. So that while the world of Oerg was experiencing the present, in that it was living out its own destiny, it did not experience any past, but was surrounded by the future on all sides, or the world of the always—will—being.

What we call the past, or memory, was socially retained in the departments of the System. In a sense, the System took the place of the past, and for a very good reason: Michael had used the System to connect where he once was with the world of Oerg, and that was somewhere in the past, as well as being another world. The System represented structures and methods of power. It represented what was being done and what was making it possible for the world of Oerg to be shaped the way it was. It was also understood that the most esoteric part of the System was its connection to the past time—line, which was a hidden gnostico—magickal sanctuary, the home of one of the gnostic patriarchates, or time—machines for past travel. If Michael needed to move backwards for any reason, he made use of this machine. It was alone the means whereby it could be understood that the past existed.

The world of Oerg, which was the world of Oerg—8 and his homologies, constituted the present. It was a world centered about the activities of the Monitor, or Teacher of the culture of Oerg. What existed as given in the present moment, or was immediately experienced came as the result of the words of the Monitor, since this information system allowed for what was being experienced and for only that level of perceptions.

The always—will—being was the continuum of the future and was identified as the Goddess. In the system of Oerg's world, only the college of gnostics of tomorrow were allowed to understand She, who is tomorrow. However, because of the gnostic theogony of time—lines, it was known that the future was assigned to the Lion—Goddess in Michael's original metalogic and so it was probable that She, who is tomorrow, was a form of the Cat—Goddess of the Ancient Egyptian Magick.

The temple of the Goddess was simply a vast sphere located in the city of Oerg. It was also known as the "mother—ship" because of its containment of the fleet of doorways and passageways used to take the Oerg—humanoids to other parts of that same universe, and into the beyond. However, these "ships" were simple mandalas, allowing entry at another time—space point. The interior of the matrix, or "mother—ship" was that of a giant beehive—like complex. It was the collectivity or meeting—group for an entire network of interconnecting lattices and passagelines between the various component—parts of the universe of Oerg. Because of this, it had another name; in the theogony of Oerg, it was "The Cosmic Womb," the Aditi—principle of these futuristic gnostics.

Inside of this matrix, wherein was the focus of the future energy at its most intense rate, the gnostic priesthood of the Oerg-Physics conducted their magickal rites. It was in the midst of these psaagelines that the people or humanoids of Oerg were sustained in their state of gnosis, since the radiations of the always-will poured in upon them and made them timely, within the context of Oerg, by keeping them timelessly futuristic, as never aging and always about to be more than what they were at that present or given moment. The matrix connected to the law behind the culture of Oerg in terms of its own ultimate meaning:

At the base of the matrix was the colloidal universe of auto-eroticism. It was the future in its most concrete intensity. Such a vast honeycomb of passageways, each throbbing with the vitality of an unexplored jungle, each pulsating with the steaming mist of the primordial swamp, each teeming with swarms of minute globules of sentient existence, each covered with a slowly moving, barely creeping fungus-like surface, which as tomorrow's lust slid along the membrane walls and perceived all that passed by, these were serving as the receptor organs of the primordial womb.

Strange sounds emerged from this vast cavern of warmth and moisture, drawing the humanoids of Oerg closer and closer to the deep and dark recesses of the vaginal passageways. The sounds were first of all noticed. Such sounds came from the depths at some dimly remote point in that paradoxical shadow-realm, beyond the world-realm of the grappling mind, and far away from the reptilian thrashings about of the subliminal orifices of self-exploration and dreamy foreplay, and could be heard amid the groans and palpitations of the surface irritability, those vaguely muffled signings of some labial friction. It was a never-ending, ever-sustaining, ongoing, self-contained stream of eroticism, from the labyrinth of the Ur-Yoni Physics.

Amid all of this energy, the initiations of the gnostics were conducted. For they were powered by the primordial energy of the cosmic matrix, and by this means the deepest regions of the idic continuum were experienced. It was noteworthy that at the heart of this system there existed the initiatic labyrinth, not so much as a physical edifice as a sexo-magickal and psycho-sexual state of experience. It was not physical in any derivative sense, rather it was physical in the very fundamental sense that it served as the basis for physical existence in all of its forms. All things came from this womb and all things returned to this womb in order to gain knowledge of the roots of wisdom. In such a world, therefore, the ultimate form of the gnosis of magick was determined by the law of Yoni.

Within the labyrinth of the Yoni could be found the passageways and routes of mystical initiation because all of the symbols of known being were stored there in a kind of Alaya ("store-consciousness"). When Blavatsky speaks of Alaya in the Stanzas, she is speaking of this womb, this mother-ship, this fundamental container of being and all becoming. When Blavatsky speaks of the Cosmic Web, she is referring to the outpourings and emissions and secretions and projections from this ultimate Yoni. And when Blavatsky speaks of the ultimate space, the Aditi beyond everything, she is speaking directly of the organization of all space, of all universes, of all time-frames of reference, deep within the recesses of this cosmic matrix of the future, the rootless root of what is or can exist. Aditi. Aditi-Yoni. The Meon.

The gnostics took very seriously the Book of the Stanzas of Dzu, which in our own day form the basis of the deeper aspects of the UFO-Cultus. They saw in the Stanzas a very definite plan or organizational system of energies, from which could be said to be derived all of the specifics of manifestation. Furthermore, Michael had been known to decode the Stanzas and find in them the basic plans for the creation of the world of Oerg and all of the qualities therein, which were made possible by his initial contact with the "Mother-Ship," or Alaya.

Everything was identified with the magickal roots of the system of Dzu and could be understood as the representation of the design of the Space-Ship, by some strange and unanticipated projection into the web-line of the ideal future. Alaya then became the root explanation for the manifestations of the UFO-Phenomena, which possessed a frequency and periodicity which could only be attributed to the broadcastings of the Matrix of Alaya, into the present world. The Jungians attributed this all to the activities of the collective unconscious, which was simply their name and way of recognizing the law of the Aditi-Yoni-Alaya as a fundamental law, and the basis of all componenets of any and all worlds.

In the Gnosis of Oerg, therefore,we find simply an application of the Dzu-Gnosis, or a confirmation of the validity of the beginningless gnosis by evidence from tomorrow. The Dzu-Gnosis was in reality very simply a writing down of how the Law of Yoni could be described. This description served as the guideline for the developments in techniques which made Oerg such a unique and self-sustaining world. Alaya was of necessity a vast and organic reality. It was the very basis for any and all containers of labyrinthine energy. These containers were housed thereafter in the space-ships of initiation physics.

The Dzu-Gnosis was to be understood as being sufficiently outside of the circles of time as to be the source of several and different views of time, or aspects of the Aditi-Principle. These aspects were expressed as the Goddesses of the Past, Present, and most importantly, the Goddess of the Future. Various worlds came about as a result of these intersections of force. These were the worlds of initiation physics, or the methods for making the return to the Aditi Domain.

As part of his development, Oerg-8 was taught over and over that these matters by the special instructional methods of the Monitor. Each time he was taught there was a very definite and corresponding increase in the radioactivity field of his orgone output.

Michael had adhered to the basic gnostic view which stated that there is an increase in bioenergy when there is an increase in gnosis. Therefore, the gnostics sought to develop the humanoids of Oerg more and more in the mysteries of gnostic physics, so that the production of orgone would be of an even increasing quality. This meant that as the humanoids grew in their esoteric understanding, the presence of the gnosis in their consciousness caused the centers of occult power to broadcast higher radiations. Then these radiations bathed the fields of orgone and developed them to a higher level of quality. The more one participated in the mysteries of the gnosis, the more one found that one's orgone and other bioenergies improved in quality. This was the method and rationale for the development of the humanoids along the lines of initiation physics.

Initiation physics is in reality the method for improving the powers of the human race. It does not have a spiritual aim, since it is physics and not metaphysics. The aim of this gnostic science is entirely centered upon life in this world. That aim is to make better, to improve, to develop, and to refine the physical fields and production sources of bioenergy in the initiate. That is the purpose of initiation physics. And that is the way in which it was understood by the gnostic magicians of the world of Oerg.

Shintotronics
Basic Elements and Components of the Shintotronic System of Gnostic Magick

Shintotronics: This subject may be defined as a gnostic and magickal sicence, which interprets certain patterns and structures of the Japanese Shinto Mythology and Religion from the viewpoint of radionics and psionic research.

In the Shinto religion there exists a certain hierarchy of primordial Deities, and the arrangement of this hierarchy provides us with a structure, which is also a design for a psionic computer. In terms of the Shinto Mythology, the ancient gods of Japan are viewed as Cosmic and Creative Principles of Being. In terms of the gnostic magick of Shintotronics, these same ancient gods are viewed as the ultimate and creative archetypes of human experience. They are the powers whereby human experience is transformed into the experience of superhumanity. Therefore, they are to be understood as both evolutionary powers and initiatic energies, because they lead humanity into states of consciousness and being which are beyond the ordinary level of human awareness.

Also, in addition to being a factor in the development of the superhuman stage of experience, these archetypes are fundamental powers used by superhumans to make it possible for various inventions and modes of experimentation to be experienced in the world of space and time. Many of the machines and instruments of gnostic magick, such as various systems associated with ufological phenomena, are possible because the power that is used to implement their activity and actualization comes from the energy archetypes of Shintotronics. So we can say that Shintotronics is both a form of esoteric psychology and a form of occult physics.

The ancient deities of the Shinto religion are to be understood as transcendental powers. They are beyond humanity but curiously also immanent in the essence—field of humanity. They are contacted directly by the gnostic magician through Shintotronics and contacted mediately through religious rites by the practitioners of the Shinto Faith. For this reason, Shintotronics may be viewed as somewhat mystical in its roots, for it does involve direct and immediate experience of those archetypes which are identified as the Kami, or Deities of the Shinto Tradition in religion.

These archetypes are, of course, quite universal and they are eternal laws for the manifestation of worlds. They are to be found in all of the ancient religions, which have the old form of magick as their basis. We can find them active not only in Shinto but in the oldest forms of Hindu, Sumerian, Egyptian, and Voudoo religion; although under what might appear to be a prescientific aspect or appearance. However, when brought up to the surface of contemporary gnostic magick, the ancient power slowly reveals itself as the gnostic scientist makes contact with these archetypes of cosmic power, or Living Gods.

In view of this fact, we may note that Shintotronics does not state that Shinto is the most scientific of all religions. We know and understand why Shinto must contain all of the elements of a very old religious practice. For it has survived into the present age of mind by being held deeply in the minds and imaginations of often not highly educated folk. It has been able to maintain an unbroken and continuous immediacy within the elemental consciousness and the collective subconscious of biological memory and instinctual ritual; but the modern gnostic and his co-workers have found it to contain the elements of the primordial mysticism of the space beings, the Gods from outside of the Earth, and have sought to develop those elements and magickal components of this mysticism into a contemporary technology.

This Shinto religion has been found to be uniquely suitable for development into a magickal physics because of its natural and ideal structure, which hidden behind popular myths and fables reveals to us the physics of a mystical race from beyond our solar system, the Kami, or the Beings of Light, who made our solar system.

Therefore, as in our definition of Shintotronics, the gnostic physicist has taken some of the fundamental components of this ancient faith from beyond this world, those archetypal patterns and structures of psionic magick and has made them the basis of his esoteric and initiatic science. What is more, he has been able to see that other modern science of the gnosis, Vudotronics; for both are the twin rays or sciences of gnostic being. In the magick of their unity, they represent the earliest forms of energy revealed to mankind.

Shinto energies are the basic contents and sophiological wholes ("wisdom—energy powers") of the Lemurian Current, while Vudu energies are the basic contents and wisdom—energy fields of the Atlantean Current. Together, they represent the manifestation of primordial power, or God—Energy, as it was understood and worked by the gnostic physicists in very remote times. Now, these two forms of energy have been integrated into contemporary magick. Together, they give us the basic framework of energy, the fundamental God—power, or the Cosmic Shakti, which as a complete gnosis of magickal energy, I define as a cosmic computer and encyclopedia of esoteric and gnostic fields of force, initiations, and power—zones. This is the living encyclopedia of magick, which is alive because it is filled with the God—Energies of the Kami and Vudu.

This is a very ancient science and the modern version of this science has been the work of many members of our school. I have worked with various beings, both in and beyond empirical time, in order to "ground" sufficiently and successfully this science of power. Therefore, it should not be thought that this work is quite simply the work of one writer and gnostic physicist. The recent and gnostic work in Shintotronics has been made possible because of the cooperation and efforts of the entire hierarchy of gnostic physics. Of special help have been the contributions to magickal research, which have been made by the Kammamorian and Zothyrian Current. Certain very specific points of discovery have been brought to the mediumistic surface of the analytical mind, as the radiopsychoanalysis of primordial form and power would suggest, by means of the revelations of Doctor Kammamori, the Gnostic Deity of Experimental Magick and Physics.

Dr. Kammamori, in his capacity as the Deity of the Science Circle of Adeptship, is very interested in those currents which bring forth the Shinto—Lemurian powers, inasmuch as His work in the contemporary world is centered about those fantastic (in the technical sense of the Apas—Tattwa Time—Station) and often pre—mental impulses, which can be easily translated by the computers of esoteric logic into the quanta—bundles and the probability waves of the newly rediscovered "ocean of gnostic energies." This Kammamorian "Collectivity of Sidereal Fusions as Mind—Energies" has also served as the gathering net for all of those discoveries in Shintotronics, which are identifiable as energies resulting from the efforts of some gnostics and the results of their highly specialized experiments both within and attuned to the Zothyrian Aeon. These experimental procedures have brought into focus the components of ancient Shinto as timeless powers and generators of the new wave of computer-managed magick.

The basis of Shintotronics, however experimentally, is to be found in the actual level of the metric of nature or the patterns generated by occult readings of the field of Shinto forces. These points of measurement provide us with the nine magickal contact points, or "bodies of Zothyrius," for the Kami of our specialized science. These Kami, being the true technicians of magickal ufology, serve to bring the pipeline of astral matter-energy to our gnostic computers. Numberwise, these powers of Shinto physics, as mediating the Cosmic Kami or archetypal levels, form as field-readings a perfect matrix of exact measurement between the action levels of the three Goddesses of Shintotronics: the Goddess of Esoteric Logic (between the ego and the transcendental ego), the Goddess of Metapsychology (between the ego and the id), and the Goddess of Meontology (between the id and the transcendental id).

These Goddesses are the Aditi-Communicators, which make the system of Shintotronics an intelligible and experimental system of exact patterns, within the chaosphere of primordial and raw Elemental Shakti or Cosmic Energy as undifferentiated magickal experience. When the magician has established the field metric, it becomes possible to see how the total field of Shintotronics and all ufological phenomena might manifest, within that esoteric sphere of consciousness-dynamics. This connection between the level of psychical phenomena and the varied fields, powers, matrices, and occult energies seems to suggest that the basic and primordial power is both latent and potential as a secret and yet gnostic continuum, held in place by a field metric, within the esoteric consciousness of the technician Kami or inner-plane Shintotronicians and Kammamorian gnostics.

After one has established the field-metric, the next step in the magickal procedure is to establish its connection to the fundamental Atlantean Energies or the Vudu. Since in the vudotronic system there are to be found exact lattices for the distribution of these gnostic energies, one has only to connect the lines of Kami-archetypal energy to those of the Vudu-archetypal energy and the magickal computer takes on an entirely comprehensive applicability. The result is a magickal computer or gnostic "think-tank," composed of both human and preterhuman and preterhumanoid intelligences.

Whether this energy is managed magickally by means of psionic techniques or the more flamboyant predictions and predications of the UFO vocabulary — or metric system — by means of the computer-employment of mandalas and hieroglyphics of mantric oracles, all of which we have to employ at one time or another in basic research, we have discovered that the use of Shintotronics within the initatic context provides the gnostic physicist with direct contact with the radiations of the Three Goddesses, confirming quite literally that esoteric logic and meontology, mediated by Zothyrian radiopsychology and metapsychology, provide the same researcher with indisputable evidence that we possess the initiatic study of magickal words, as bundles of energy, which as mantrams can be understood as the quanta or building blocks for Akashic and Elemental projections.

These projections are the ideal frameworks, if not the actual substances of ufological composition, which can be regularly generated by ideal magick. All magickal machines, henceforth, will assume this Akashic connection, since the auric formulae of the discontinuous language of the astral and etheric atoms can easily be given to us from the reservoirs and resources of the Kami of this ever-expanding "gnostic think-tank" of the Three Goddesses.

We can thus see that the Science Circle of Adeptship, composed of the cooperating components of the Shintotronic power-zone, or marma, integrate their fundamental energies with the basic directions of the new magickal program.

Can There Be a Shamanistic Management of the Fundamental Energies of Shintotronics

As to the power of Shintotronics, the shamanistic–content–chaos level would be in fact oriented towards those radical and sophiological wholes, or elemental energy contexts, which are both found in gnostic physics and in the raw unmanageability of the Oerg universes. Yet, the wild shamanistic capturing of those energies is a necessity, for inasmuch as the "rational–verbal" or directly "metapsychological" management of these chaotic contents, fuels, energies, powers, substances, some-sensory qualities, and esoteric properties (beyond the sanctions of some metaphysical bedlam, outside of the employment of mystically argued and justified paranoia, and ritually induced schizophrenia, as a state of "divine rapture") is not only unimaginable but clearly and virtually impossible.

Such technological shamanism rises quite spontaneously and often disruptively from the meonic levels of the primordial ocean of ceaseless mind–flow, otherwise viewed as a hitherto untapped and self–destructive formula or "exotic experience," and rushes upwards in colloidal waves, flooding the plasticity of the ego, while finding its absolute expression in the fundamental root–energies of the manifold systems and patterns, associated with the unpredictable disturbances of elemental and barbarous shock. The icy emptiness of the meon, on the other hand, finding its expression in the iconosopheric imagery of the Fiendess of the Snow Storm (the Goddess of Meontology), that wrathful and brooding aspect of pure and uncategorized Aditi, which is the deity or Kami of total darkness, space as raw power, and therefore the untapped and brutally inconceivable primordiality of Shakti, within the shadows of Shinto Gnosis, rises bewilderingly and once again triumphant to the brain surface of this basic program, wherein it is slowly and carefully guided into the high–energy levels of gnostic physics.

There it is fed into and feeds into the fundamental structures and connecting links and lattices and subterranean tubes and tunnels of neuro–tattvic testing, esoteric experimentation, magickal and magickal logic, and chaotic confrontation (meontological elaborations) or is directly worked upon by those preterhumanoid managers from another dimension or level of communication, whose enthusiastic and persistent concern for these low frequency and ultimate energies is equal to our own cerebral reluctance.

Consequently, if we think that the shaman is simply the grounding point for an entire group mind of esoteric experts, we can say that because the basic energies come flooding into his consciousness at all levels, it is possible for there to be a shamanistic and elemental magickal management of the ground–level Shintotronic energies. However, it is not common because the capacities of the shamanistic worker have not been fully made operative, not fully developed or attuned to the elemental and primordial condition of the occult universe as it is viewed by the Shintotronic specialist. But if we take into consideration the development of magickal powers as one of the aspects of this research program, then it is possible, I think, to see the shamanistic Shintotronician as one who has the group–mind capacity for such a management role. He is in dialogue with the group–mind, the science circle of inner adepts and holy angels, which control the operations of that ufolike being, which is the sphere of his magickal operations.

The shamanistic physicist is probably the best example of the scientist who works with his group-mind. That is to say, he is an example of inner world team work. The various members of this group-mind are members of his research/teaching team. He both learns and works with them. In every such group-mind work team we have to distinguish many of the components. These are as follows:

1. Between the shaman and the group there is a control-worker, who is the basic manager of the energies. This control-worker is probably anelemental or devic type of being, from another universe and attached to the group-mind in order to function as a kind of personal psychic computer.

2. The group-mind is managed by a very highly developed spiritual being or Kammamorian Presence. This being is a reflection or reflex of the Gnostic Being Dr. Kammamori (Kam=Holy, Mamori=Guardian Angel, of Esoteric Shinto and Japanese Gnosis). This being may be viewed as a personal avatar of Dr. Kammamori or the ray of that being. It is as if Dr. Kammamori is present there in full actuality and power.

3. The members of the group mind are divided according to the ways, which they project. Except that in Shintotronics, the divisions are made according to the three major goddesses. Therefore, we have the group divided into the three bodies or members, who reflect the Goddess of Esoteric Logic, next the three who reflect the Goddess of Dream Control and Necronomicon Physics, and finally the three who reflect the Goddess of Meontology.

4. These nine members of the group-mind are both human and preterhuman, since they reflect the magickal history of the group-mind through many of its operations in a variety of histories. Adding another aspect to the nature of this group-mind, we can say that there is a Zothyrian and Aeonic Component, since these nine beings within the group mind, while taking their form or masculine energy from the reactions of the Aeon Zothyrius, Who controls in a magickal and gnostic manner that developments of the physics of alternative universes. Hence, we can say that these beings are made up of occult forms of time-as-energy in their gnostic vehicles. We can say that their bodies are made up out of the substance of synchronicity. They are built up out of that UFO-like substance, which is identified as layered time. They are also highly specialized magickal entities, with which communication can be established. For this reason, when not engaged in esoteric dialogue, they can be projected (and often project themselves) along the gnostic lattices and matrix pathworkings of the empirical universe both simultaneously and ubiquitously.

In my work with setting up the basics for my computer marga of Chintotronics, I have had to work individually with each and every component of the system. In order to make this clearer to the reader let me provide some concrete information.

Esoteric Autobiography

During the time of my stay in Japan, which was Aries, 1983, I prepared very carefully the basics for my Shintotronics systems. Aries, 1983 is significant because in my natal chart, I have Aries as my eighth house, the house which governs occult sciences and magickal field-work. I have the planet Uranus there natally, which governs experiments and inventions in esoteric matters. For my solar return of January, 1983, I have the Sun in the eighth and the Sun is exalted in Aries. Hence, from the cosmic standpoint, the time was auspicious. I might add that at the time, Jupiter was making a transit by opposition to my midheaven, while in its own sign, Sagittarius.

Each day, during my stay in Japan, and from place to place, wherever I might be, I sought to take the metric. This metric is the energy measurement, which is used for tuning the computer marga to the field frequencies of any given marma, or power-zone.

For my work, I was seeking to get the power−zone readings for Shintotronics, but I was also interested in building up data and energy reserves, for use by the computer marga when I returned to the USA.

I have been able to find that the metaphysics of Shin provides a very excellent format for this type of research. Shin to (the Tao of the Shin or Kami) or Shinto operates under the principle of radical syzygy. This means that the energies are given in esoteric pairings. Each day these energies change and I suspect that they change at every moment, as the Book of the I−Ching demonstrates. However, even though there is change and flow with these energies, there exists a certain and identifiable pattern, amidst all of the changes and diffusions of power. I was able to capture that pattern and make use of it in every one of my experimental operations. I might add that the Aries season related also to high form−patterns of energy.

Each operation or initiation was governed by one of the specific Shinto deities of the hierarchy of creativity. The degree of closeness to the mind−field of the earthean brain culture would be given by means of one particular reading. Of course, each of these readings was determined by a synchronistico−radionic method. I might add that each of the readings had also esoteric dimensions, which could be determined by psionic methods.

Another level of reading magickally provided the conditions of the nine vehicles or the Zothyrian auras. Three of them, which pertain to the states of high trance, were to be viewed as embodiments of the Goddess of Esoteric Logic. The middle group of auras drew their powers directly from the radiopsychological atoms of the silence and embodied those weird contents, which were sent by the Goddess of Dream Control, also known as the Diety of the Necronomicon psychotherapy. The most elemental region of these auric containers, drawing their powers from the atomic structures of deep meditation, held precariously the daemonic embodiments of the Goddess of Meontology.

Each day, I was able to take the metric for these nine auras and find out the range of magickal broadcasting being provided by the Three Goddesses of Shintotronics. In doing this, I have been able to collect an initiatic encyclopedia of radioactive gnosis and also establish the possibility for continuous contact on ongoing experiments, with these Kami of gnostic physics.

At the same time, each experiment was done in cooperation with the control entity or the manager of the respective level of powers. This spirit of the operation enabled me by means of its cooperation to be initiated into the shamanistic operations of the 17 Kami of the Creative Hierarchy. So that each operation was not only an experimental process but it was also an experience in initiation physics. When I speak of initiation physics, I mean most of all that area where the physical process is esoteric initiation. This is best found, it seems in view of the evidence, in Shintotronics.

Mediumistic Processes and Kami-Energies

Esoteric Autobiography
Each day in the operations of my magickal research, while in Japan, I sought out and
made contact with the spirits which are associated with the different levels of the
Creative Matrix, or the primordial Goddess of Space, i.e., Aditi. Not only did I make
contact with the spirits as they are given within the continuum of time-as-process,
for these are the spirits which take on bodies made out of layed-time, as we have
described earlier; but I also sought out the spirits which are ritually or
Vudotronically associated with the eight directions and the true and occult center of
the universe, or direction number nine. Thus, I was able to see in each of the
spirits the operation of the laws of syzygy, or the logic of the pairs; for the
spirits of time, whose vahans were made up out of the layers of past, present, and
the future were connected by ontic lattices to the spirits of the directions.

The energies between these two types of spirit were to be understood quite
simply as the twin aspects of the monadic reality. The connection between the two
energies was to be understood as a magickal presentation or picture of the state of
the universe at that time. The magickal physicist has simply to draw upon that
experiment in order to bring back into reality the condition of the universe, which
most perfectly conforms to the energy-picture of that particular experiment. When he
does this, and he does it by direct cooperation with these Kammamorian spirits, he
then can give out the initiations, which are proper to that picture of the universe.
this means that each experiment is its own magickal universe or UFO-system, and
within the auric egg of that universe, we can easily find an infinity of magickal
states, conditions, initiations, and entities for future development.

When the Shinto Gnostic states that the universe exists according to some 17
Kami or Cosmic Laws, this is exactly what is meant: namely, that there are 17 forms
of the universe, which they are interested in investigating. There is of course an
infinitude of these universes of the magickal imagination; but as the symbolic and
finite level of the gnosis manages the infinite oceans of dream-possibility, so the
vast manifold of these esoteric mind-fields is given and located within the
potentials of the 17 levels of power, or the Creative Hierarchy.

Each level is a kind of self-contained space-ship, because it is actualized and
now contains its own logical computer or system of internal powers, its own interior
culture and civilization, and its own empowerments and direct participation in the
mind-energies of the Kami. By using each such world as a magickal vehicle, which
transports us into the space of raw potentiality, this gnostic cosmograph becomes for
the esoteric scientist a source from which he may derive an entire store-
consciousness or encyclopedia of occult and artistic imagination, including all of
the powers implied by such a state of initiation thereby creating an extensive and
potentially never-ending world of experimentation.

When I first took upon myself these initiations, I was immediately impressed by
the quality of the energies, which were therby connected to the auric egg. The entire
process was a method of dream meditation. It was not a form of dreaming, nor was it
meditation in the usual sense, or as it is experienced in even most esoteric
contexts. It was something I saw as a combination of dreaming and meditating.
Whenever I experienced this process, it was under the direction of the Kammamorian
Ray. At first, I thought that it was an extension of the process of visualization,

where the mind became passive while the occult imagination was highly active.

It was more than this. It could only happen at first when the Kammamorian Ray activated my transcendental ego. What was latent in the ego was awakened by that Ray. This consisted in a series of energy–initiations. Finally, as the powers operated in the awakened state, I found myself in possession of a new attachment to the gnostic universe. It was so highly charged with energy that it gave me more content that I thought I had ways or organizing. Happily, however, the energies were placed within my being and I saw for the first time the gnostic universe of the magickal imagination as the Kami and the Kammamorian spirits see it, with their inner vision or esoteric powers of physical sight.

By physical sight, I mean certainly the average and neurological mode of physical vision which all normally sighted persons experience on this planet. However, in this case, it is the esoteric power of physical sight or the inner vision of the Bhumis, or Earths, or the alternative universes, which are just as physical as that which we view as the Earth.

I am not, here, making any reference to psychic perception in any sense, or as it has been viewed. Psychic perception extends one's experience to the astral fields and beyond of the same Bhumi, but it is not concerned with the direct perception of the Bhumi, for that is seen physically and not psychically. With an understanding of alternative universes, one does not have to make use of psychic categories in order to experience other kinds of worlds. They can be seen physically. The magickal worlds are places or real and empirical Bhumis. For this reason, there can be the history of philosophy as philosophy was done within a Bhumi, or on a particuular Bhumi. The history of Zothyrian philosophy is the history of philosophy as it was done on the Bhumi known as Zothyria. A history of philosphy attributed to either the astral or mental planes of some Bhumi would either be impossible (as pertaining to the astral plane) or unnecessary (as pertaining to the plane of the mind).

Consequently, I was now able to have the experience of perception as it is possessed by the Kami. I quite simply saw the many universes and I saw them whenever I wished to see them. Because these are alternative universes to our own, I made contact with the beings of this universe and that universe, and came to see them as variations more or less of this universe. I was also able to encounter the alternative form of myself in each of these universes.

I came to learn that the life histories of these alternative versions of myself were made up of events which had been alternatives in my own past, but which I had not selected. Those alternatives from my own past had been selected by my other self and had become the events in his life. Since there were infinite possibilities of action in my life as alternatives, I think there would also be an infinity of possible versions of myself. None of these would have life histories containing any duplication. All would exist in the physical and not be metaphysical beings. Each would have his life in his own world or Bhumi.

I do not think that this phenomenon can be viewed as anything else than a kind of ideal mediumship. Each form of myself and each form of anyone else serves as a medium for the possibilities of experience. None of the possibilities of experience are wasted and all are transmitted and concretely expressed in the lifestreams of each living and physical human being. Magickal experiments can be viewed quite simply as the taking of a photo of the universe at a certain point in time. It shows us, within a narrow framework, what the energies are doing. Yet, the universe is infinitely vast and only the Kami–Energies can seem to hold it together. For this reason all magickal experiments and initiations take their point of departure from the Kami—energy of a particular cosmic aspect. We can say that the Kami provide us with the magickal camera, whereby the photo of the Bhumi in action is taken. Hence, in Shintotronics, all powers of observation beyond what is narrowly confined to the given are derived from the Kami.

In my own initiations, I discovered that gnostic energies were mostly latent in the true nature of my own being. I discovered rather indirectly that the infinitude of my own physical being, in all of these Bhumis, was really a projection of the Kammamorian nature of my own transcendental ego. It was metaphysically infinite and demanded that it be manifested as physically infinite as well. Few persons, unaided by the inspirations of the Kami, have been able to arrive at this conclusion.

Amidst all of these processes and systems of worlds and forms of experience, there must be some principles of organization, which are latent in the physical worlds or somehow radically immanent in them. Deep within the mysteries of Shintotronics, I found the answer in the operations of the Three Goddesses. Not only did they refer to states of consciousness, which is perhaps easiest for us to understand, but they refer also to the considerations and conditions of time. The Three Goddesses of Shintotronics are also the Shintotronic Laws of Time—Structure. They are the Divine and Physical Past, Present, and Future. They are physically immanent in the world of experience because time is a part of reality. Then, as I will explain in the next lesson, I discovered by means of initiation, while in the physical body, that They contained the essential secrets of time as gnostic energy.

The 33 Keys of Shintotronic Imagination

In the art of Hiroyuki Fukuda, we find certain embodiments of Kami-Energy, which provide us with the mechanism for the appreciation of time as the content of experience. There are three centers of power, the Three Goddesses, which govern the way in which the mind-flow organizes the continuum of awareness as time. Each Goddess is assigned to elemental power as it manifests in the form of 11 basic energies or "stations of the imagination." These are not visions, however, but actual approaches physically to the alternative universes. They are also multiple personalities, which the gnostic scientist has developed in his own lifestream. They draw their contents, each one of the threefold 11 from the rivers of time. The contents are raw and objective events; because the subject no longer exists independent of the object, both are transcended.

In his artistic mythology, Monsieur Fukuda has confined himself closely to the traditional symbolism, except that he has removed all tradition and replaced it with magickal tension. We know, for example, that these Goddesses are not just workds of art. We do not see them in any space of detachment, rather we see them as we see our hands before us. They are a part of us, a physical reality of immediate experience. Now, that is not quite correct; it is better to say that they are physical reality and that we are parts of them. They are the process of time, and as we can distinguish between one Goddess and the two others, so we have learned to distinguish between past, present, and future.

Each Goddess manifests as 11 temporal possibilities. Together these 11 power-events constitute the archetypal matrix of concrete experience. They are pure concreteness and all that is abstract is derived from Them. The level of derivation can be expressed as the gnostic keyboard of the Shintotronic Instrument. In other words, the validity of this science depends on the degree of closeness it approximates to the actual lifestream of the Goddesses, for it attempts to be a mechanical model of the time-matrix, which exists within the Goddesses. Only by this means can magickal imagination be distinguished from the illusions of many occultists, who are not grounded existentially and concretely in the lifestream of the Godesses, i.e., the continuum of time. So we can say that the Goddesses are the ultimate reality or substance of the world.

Question: Since time is the ultimate substance of the world, how does it manifest as the Goddess of Esoteric Logic, the Goddess of Zothyrian Metapsychology, and the Goddess of Meontology?

It manifests as the Goddesses within the specialized processes of magickal experience: it manifests in Esoteric Logic, in Zothyrian Metapsychology, and in Meontology. It is able to show itself for what it truly is as the gnostic experiences and explores the energies, which form the activities of these three technologies. At first, the experience may not be intense. Gradually, however, the experience becomes extremely intense and it becomes unmistakably the experience of the Goddess. This is not to say that organic and biological time fail to provide us with the proper categories for the construction of the universe. It is just that in the magickal sciences, which are the new sciences or the forms of knowing for tomorrow, the ultimate reality is seen more clearly and therefore more perfectly understood.

Also, within the processes of each of these magickal continua, Esoteric Logic,

Zothyrian Metapsychology, and Meontology, we find the 11 levels of initiation into being, which are the nodes or measurement points of time, as it expresses itself in the human lifestream. In the Thelemic tradition, there exists a parallel interpretation of this law, as gradations of the magickal universe or the Occult Sephira.

In our own work, however, the nodes are actual broadcasting stations or frequencies, which provide the settings for specific types of response. Thus, the response to word "Z" within the context of the "word-association test" of Zothyrian Metapsychology, are node 4, would be quite different from the response to the same word at node 5 or 3. In Esoteric Logic, the processes of initiation physics would differ from node to node. In Meontology, the nature of the encounter with the ultimate matrix of chaos,and its subsequent interpretation and construction, would be different from node to node. The fact that we can experience different data and report different types of verifications of magickal experience, it seems to me, constitutes proof for the existence of these nodes as objective types of being. It also constitutes proof for the existence and nature of the three Goddesses as ultimate realities. When we do our gnostic work or Shintotronics Technics, we are performing repeatable and objective experiments of an entirely scientific and physical character.

Question: In the processes and experiments of Shintotronic Initiation, as the foundations of the system are known, do the nodes of the Three Augusta appear in a kind of continuum, field, or other gnostic synthesis?

While in the process of laying the ground work for this science in Japan, it was necessary to construct certain field equations, which were gnostic descriptions of the ways in which the experimental foundations of Shintotronics were built up out of the nodes of the Three Augusta. I was able to learn this because of the work of Dr. Kammamori, my teacher in this area.

Fundamentally, every state of existence in the Shintotronic Universe is made up out of an arrangement of one component -- at least -- from each of the matrices of the Divine Ladies. While this is a rather complicated question, it can be understood that one of the experiments or pictures of the universe might be made up out of the fifth node of the Lady of Meontology, the ninth node of the Lady of Zothyrian Metapsychology, and the first node of the Lady of Esoteric Logic. The particular arrangements or formulations were revealed to me oracularly not by Lord Kammamori but by the August Lady of Esoteric Logic, since it is She who is most responsible for the magicko-metamethodology of the gnostic sciences.

Now, any particular condition and state of being comes into existence as a result of this sort of synthesis. Certain states of the universe appear to be more strongly expressive of the qualities and properties of the August Lady of Esoteric Logic than some others, which reflect more the characteristics, for example, of the August Lady of Meontology or the August Lady of Metapsychology. We can say that states which are experimentally constructed at the "top" of the universe reflect the August Kami of Esoteric Logic; at the "middle" they reflect the August Kami of Metapsychology; and at the "bottom" of the universe of Shintotronics, they are reflective of the August and Fearsome Kami of the Meon.

A somewhat similar architecture has been found by me in the old gnostic text of the "Pistis Sophia." A parallel can be found, also, in the three interior regions of the metaphysical space-ship, which has three different systems of internal wiring, responding to the three different regions of synchronicity (or time—energy) from which it derivves its power. So the nodes of these Three Goddesses do appear as components in the field—equations of the Shintotronic Universe. In fact, they are the archetypal building blocks.

The archetypal character of these nodes is even suggested by H.P. Blavatsky, who in her vision of the Mss. of "The Stanzas of Dzyan" appears to have perceived an alternative universe. If we take the liberty to restore simply one of the transmissions (Book II, Stanza 1, Vs. 2) we can find a description of the Shintotronic process as revised within our technical context:

"Said the Bhumi: 'Kami of Esoteric Logic, the meonic marma at node 0, which is my continuum, is not yet connected to the pleroma. Therefore, send the gnostic physicists to build transmission circuits to the mandalum instrumentum in that potential. You have sent the archoi of the seven time—lines to the Kami of Meontology. You have made a bridge of nodal circuits and word—association patterns to that Kami. By the paired—operations and the Oerg syzygies of the Kami in Metapsychology, your presence is felt in the depths of the Meon and in the Necronomicon Energies.

" 'You have pre—programmed the nodal circuits to transmit both gnosis and radiation and to intercept the raw energies of the Meon as they rise from the elemental foundations. So now let the esoteric logic of that field equations function in the profundity of being, bringing the broadcasting of the deepest contents to the surface'."

It is not important that Blavatsky did not write this way, since we are only concerned with the fact that whatever she wrote of truth can be adjusted to the field of Shintotronics. It is also certain that few if any persons would really use this passage for occult meditation. Yet, it shows that the interweaving or Tantra of the Three Goddesses can be found in almost any text, which pertains to the processes of cosmic evolution.

It is also certain that one of the most important methods for working with these energies is the word—association test, which connects esoteric logic tomeontology by means of the metapsychological processes. That test is primarily to be understood as an archetypal and cosmic process, duplicating in the context of mental exploration the cosmic process of self adjustment. It also indicates that as the Second Goddess mediates between the first and third, so the merging of esoteric logic and the future with meontology and the primordial past is by means of the present and the magick of Zothyrian analysis.

The bubbles which are blown by ideal lattices into the ocean of profundity make contact at a very deep and important level of ultimate being. Then they rise to the surface of the mind—stream, bringing with them manageable contents of the deepest spaces, which are then converted by means of imagination and inspiration into creativity and action. This is the cycle of the Shintotronic processes, wherein the Three Goddesses are fundamental components.

Auric Eggs, Bhumis, Permanent Atoms and the Matrix of Space

"As regards the Permanent Atoms, usually you will find only one active in the Auric Egg at or within each Bhumi. It is not expected that your measurements will pick up or view those Atoms, which are latent or potential, or active in some other and parallel universe. However, in any really thorough analysis of the Bhumis in terms of the Auric Egg or that 'Vehicle of Karmic Energies,' you can expect a variety of Bhumis, which form a fleet of alternative Earths, and the variations in time, reading, mode of analysis, and level of esoteric initiation will certainly match accurately and completely the varieties of those Bhumis." -- M. Bertiaux, "Esoteric Revelations of C.W. Leadbeater, 45

"It was shown to me that there are 68 types of the Auric Egg existing within the matrix. I refer to the Matrix of Space or the Womb of the Primordial Mother, Aditi. In this grouping, we have four subgroups of 17 eggs. These are the revelations of the Goddess and they arise by means of oracular chance from the nothingness of fundamental and eternal chaos. When I drew near to them and saw them next to me, I was able to notice that each subgroup had its divine point of initiation, from which emanated 16 potentials, or as I would say, 'sound-universes.'

"Above these stood the principles of inspiration, known to us under the form of gnostic axioms. They are 16 and they are alive! I would suggest that they are archetypal gods or the regulative Kami, for I saw them with the eyes of a Shintoist and an occultist. You have designated them as 'the Kammamorian Spirits,' and that is how they are given in the rites of chance. One must cross a certain bridge of the gnosis in order to enter upon the realmm (Bhumis) of these eggs, for they give out oracles and these oracles must be understood or else they will destroy the auditor. They thrive on the energy of pure being and consciousness and simply are there for those who would discover them.

"In the depths of my own explorations of the Dzyu Gnosis, and in the riches of my revelations to you, I have experienced the radioactivities of these beings. However, we have been warned also the dangers since only the most sensitive of instruments, such as you already possess, can be used as vehicles for approaching them safely. Then, if you would approach them, your daring will be rewarded. You will discover the nature of their oracles and the powers of the revelations." -- M. Bertiaux, "Esoteric Revelations of H.P. Blavatskaya," 23

In my work with the foundations of Shintotronics, I discovered may ways in which to look at the energies and structures, which were being unearthed. Many of the older approaches which had been worked out somewhat before and which were rather perfect but not yet quite applicable, I was able to make use of. It seems that when you work with root energies of fundamental being, all true discoveries fall into place rather normally.

Shintotronics then emerges as a science which is concerned with occult energies, operating in various time fields. These occult energies are radiations and contain various occult atoms as the sources of a variety of emissions. These energies are "housed" in a kind of geometry or hypergeometry, which we understand as the Bhumi, within a much more comprehensive Matrix, provided by the field-interactions of the Three Goddesses and their projections. Each human being, so it appears, is a kind of projection-radiation from these Bhumis and the initiates and occultists are the ones who are interested in exploring this subject.

The purpose of these explorations is not, however, the aimless gathering of information. It is rather the evolution of the gnostic magician into the next stage of his being. It has nothing to do with human evolution in the wider sense, since evreyone will get to this level eventually; but the gnostic wishes to arrive at this beingness as quickly as possible.

In order to do so, he must expose himself to the very high levels of magickal and metaphysical radioactivity, which exist in these higher worlds. This is accomplished by direct encounters with the Bhumis, whereby the Permanent or Occult Atoms of the physical and metaphysical vehicles of the gnostic are forced ever higher and higher into newer and more dramatic levels of potentiality. This is the potentiality to become a Kami. In the experiences of Shintotronics, this is often accomplished by means of certain settings or nodes on the instrument. These settings provide the levels of initiation, which are next and which are needed in radical growth of the gnostic being towards perfection. To discover anything is simply to discover what one can become. The process is the ultimate magick of yoga.

"The Auric Egg can be 'visited' only when certain conditions timewise are met. For this reason, for each egg there are exact nodal settings at A, B, and C, which take us to the Bhumi wherein the egg has been placed. There are settings for each egg and beyond these there are also eight placements of an entirely esoteric nature. These eight are the Gods presiding over the universe of this process. In the languages of the Atlantean magick, as this is a direct continuation of that science, these placements are broadcast from either the red or the black temples or systems of initiation–development and training. While it is true that these procedures refer to the temple operations of the remote past, the work has perfect applicability to the present occult needs of gnostics. Depending on the nodes and the energies, which are involved and being broadcast, one is connected with the next stage of one's growth or else some akashic realm of one's past or future as potential energy. The temples of the remote Atlantean physics serve simly as amplifiers of what we are doing in the present; since quite frequently, we have to draw upon a past reserve of power in order to achieve a contemporary result, if the current at present shows any sign of power–loss. These temples also serve as doorways to the higher regions of the physics of initiation. Initiation physics might sound curious to the reader; but for the gnostic it is a necessity, since initiation is locked firmly into the physics or natura naturata of being from the viewpoint of the candidate and it is connected absolutely to the cosmos or natura naturans of being from the perspective of the initiator. These physical energies are released by means of a remarkable 'logic of the tattwas, which literally bombards the candidate with gnostic radioactivities, thereby driving out the particles of negation and limit, which somewhat block the flow of the energies from the atoms. As a result the egg is allowed to radiate a pure cloning on the physical plane of its innermost potency." –– M. Bertiaux, "What Do We Mean By Initiation," 2

Therefore, we can say that the purpose of Shintotronics, aisde from giving us directions to the higher regions of our being, that purpose is also rebuilding the physical body. This idea of rebuilding of the physical body, of course, is behind many ideas to be found in both traditional and modern speculation. Such ideas as the physical eternity of the body, of the prolongation of life through freezinig the body or replacing various organs on a continuing basis, as well as the old ideas of resurrection as found in some western forms of religion, all of these are really mythical approaches to the idea that the body can be reconstructed by means of super powers and higher frequencies of occult energy. This means that quite simply the physical body is brought closer and closer to the ideal level of being, as it is found in the Auric Egg and within the countless Bhuumis of the ontical sphere (the region of highest energy).

My own experiences along this line have been rather interesting. One would hardly imagine that H.P. Blavatsky and C.W. Leadbeater would show up somewhere in my adventures into Shintotroniics, or in the prior work done in occult physics in preparation for the work in Shintotronics. I suppose that since one works with the foundations of being, a visit by means of occult revelations would seem logical. Blavatskaya appears to the gnostic and esoteric Kami of HPB, which has given me a few directions, here and there, primarily related to esoteric energies.

By the time I had gotten into my adventures with the "Stanzas of Dzyan," I had made a kind of contact with this level or type of being. From then on, if I needed to make contact with this level, all I had to do was to focus inwardly towards that being. Then the streams of teaching would start coming in my direction. I suppose this is due to my karmic work in past incarnations and also because HPB and I were connected by means of a kind of group–soul, which was esoteric and Thibetan in quality and development.

As regards CWL, years ago when I wrote up the papers of that gnostic school, which is known in the outer as "The Monastery of the Seven Rays," I made use of some inner drive and developed on the physical plane a particular structure of lattices and connective circuits, which were probably latent in an otherwise purely verbal system in which CWL had expressed much interest in his lifetime. That rather lifeless system, which contained some rather interesting Egyptian roots, was really quite remarkable. It was the design for the computer and energy system of what we might now be tempted to call something like a UFO object or projection from some empirical or chaotic marma; but which at that time, as strange as it might seem to the uninformed reader of these matters, was posing rather inconspicuously as an Egyptian Rite of Ancient Freemasonry with the name of "Memphis–Misraim."

Of course, I saw the system as an outline of what could be done in esoteric engineering. The proof of my thesis being that I was able to make use of it in this very specific way, while it was otherwise completely misunderstood and has remained, as I have said, highly verbal. Anyway, CWL expressed a very strong interest in what I was doing, as he was largely interested both in what the outline was exoterically known by and also he was very strongly attracted towards my own inventiveness as regards this same system being, in reality, a form of esoteric engineering relating to interconnected tattwa–energies.

I was to apply this system of physics in a number of instances, but in its full potential I did not seem at that time to have an adequate appreciation. I wanted it to do more, but I seemed to lack some of the higher keys, which come only from the revelations of the Aeons.

That structure rested on the shelf of my research projects for some time, because whenever I wanted to work on it, I seemed to be getting into side projections. There seemed to be something static which was blocking the flow of power. That static side had also limited the work of others before me, both in this world and in alternative systems (cf., the History of Zothyrian Philosophy). However, CWL convinced me through my occult map–work that the energy levels could function in a way I had not really worked out. I simply had not reached that point in the long process of analysis. My suspicions, which were based on experiences in the transcendental ego, were right in this regard since what was before or earlier in the system and what came after it or later in the logic of initiation worked quite well in a variety of physical contexts. The problem was then reduced to that of the arrangement of the components.

My own experience of this sudden and perhaps to other rather violent intuition happened somewhat calmly as a communication breakthrough. The breakthrough occurred when I began to work with these Shintotronics energies. I discovered that while there was a perfectly valid and operationally static form of these energies, which revealed itself in the analysis of these powers, what also might be understood as the dynamic side of the structures was equally present in the interconnected matrices of initiation physics.

In place of the static order of four groups of 18 matrices and 12 lattices, we now had a slight shift in the power structure of the sub-atomic mass of these primordial particles, which clearly and radically indicated and forced itself before our eyes as four dynamic groups of substances or 17 Auric Eggs, or matrices formed by the 16 Cosmic Knowers or Kammamorian Spirits. The lattices had taken on the lifestream power projections of the true Kami. This then became the magicko-metamathematical basis for my otherwise fantastic (in the sense of archaeometrical time physics and quantum metaphysics) excursions into the metrical psionics of Shinto Gnosis.

It was from this work done directly with the Bhumis and the Auric Eggs, that I was able to research the foundations of what developed gradually into the initiatic continuum of the Esoteric Physics of Shinto Magick.

How the Occult Atoms Can Be Observed Verbally

There is a way to observe the behavior of the occult atoms verbally. It is different from the method where they are observed by means of their radiations and broadcastings, which are then picked up by means of psionic mechanisms and/or oracles. The method of verbal observation is based on the association of magickal words. Briefly, it operates this way. I have a list of 25 words. The words are arranged in the following sequence of numerological values: from 1 through 9, then from 8 through 1, and finally from 2 through 9. This adds up to 25 words, chosen without duplication of meaning although chosen to give certain specific number values in a series. Thus, there are three words with the numerical value of 8, but they are three different words.

The entire idea behind the process is to go through the words and receive responses from the unconscious mind. Sometimes, the response word will have the same numerical value as the test word, which is the word in my list of 25. From this I concluded that there must be some kind of contact being made with the unconscious mind. The words act as stimulation to that level of our being, pressing on certain sensitive marmas and causing a release of energy. In my list of words, I have made use of a number of words from the Book of the Necronomicon tradition. It was my understanding that these words of power refer to very deep levels of the unconscious and to primordial memory. In a series of studies of this matter, I explored this problem and felt that the names of the magickal deities of the N-System, were—animals and other energy personifications, represented the deeper regions of fundamental awareness. This constituted the basis of universal experience.

One of the problems which came up to the surface was when a certain type of numerical value seems to dominate the responses of the person being tested. For example, let us say that out of the 25 responses, eight or nine of them have the numerical value of 7. What does this mean? I think it refers to the powers in the unconscious making themselves known to us rather intensely.

But what are these powers? Are they energies of some sort? The answer came when I tested a subject both psionically and verbally. In such instances, the data I received showed that the same reality was broadcasting strongly and could be detected by both methods. Because the psionics tests gave us the Auric Eggs and Bhumis (or the forms and contents of the continuum) as the special spaces for these energies, I came to the conclusion that the broadcasting was from what I call the occult atoms, located in a kind of personal pleroma.

It would seem that in the word-association test, using the barbarous words of power as test words, the testing word defines the space of the Auric Egg in terms of numerical value. The response comes forth from what is the stronger or strongest of the occult atoms in that Egg and Bhumi. Some occult atoms therefore appear to define certain spaces while others appear to dominate the inner worlds of those tested. It is from this pattern of testing that we come up with the maps of the magickal experience of initiates, since the broadcasting energies and their rays are as observable as hills, lakes, rivers, extra-terrestrial phenomena of the pleroma.

"Pleroma: In terms of our system of gnosis and its metapsychology, the pleroma may be understood as the continuum of the energies, measured from one through nine, which have been isolated by various tests. These energies are expressed as magicko-gnostic atoms of an occultly permanent or ongoing form, from lifetime to lifetime and verified as akashic research, and these energies are housed or situated within auric frameworks or Eggs, created or built-up by means of an arrangement of the Bhumis or alternative earths. Each person possesses in his deepest psyche this pleroma in one form or another and this pleroma is actively broadcasting or merely potential according to the degree of initiation of the person. Those who explore this pleroma will find therein the various magickal universes and systems, which are described in cosmologies, UFO-ontologies, and various mystical psychologies. We are concerned with the analysis of the structure of the pleroma and how this can be revealed in a variety of magickal tests and measurements, given under the auspices of the Gnostic and esoteric understanding of pastoral psychology and theology." -- M. Bertiaux, "A Gnostic Cure of Souls," 3

At first, I thought it would be most significant if we established contact with the levels of archetypal being by receiving 9, 6, and/or 3 value responses to 9, 6, and/or 3 value test words. I thought that this event would show that communication had been established in an arithmosophical manner. That did happen, but when it did not happen what did happen was also interesting. In fact, the magickal phenomena of nonagreement became very, very exciting, since there existed a pattern to these also. What I found of interest was that in certain individuals there were definite powers, which as archetypes made that person a totally different type of magician from everyone else. This may appear obvious to many; but for me it was significant because I had structural data to show as evidence for the existence of theogonies or gnostic fields.

It was possible to see that certain aspects of gnostic theology could be established on the basis of empirical evidence. This is very largely, I think, the result of the Shinto synthesis of the psionic attitude. However, I found out that deeper into the problem, we were faced with much richer and archaic matter than what appeared by means of tests and measurements of occult levels. I was pulled by a sort of cyclical magnetism in the direction of the pleroma, since in another capacity, as a priest hearing confessions, I had encountered a manifestation of the pleroma in the formulae of the Dzyu-Gnosis. These experiences seemed to confirm my earlier methods in respect to the invariability of result. The results of experiences both pastoral and experimental were confirmations of the broadcastings of the pleroma of the Kammamori at almost every conceivable level of human experience.

"The pleroma is none other than the world of the Dzyu-Gnosis, or the astral and mental universe, which opens up to an infinity of alternative physical systems. This pleroma consists of forces, which when activated by means of the processes of initiation physics enter the physical world and become actual events. For this reason, metapsychologists say that daily life is formed, shaped, and constituted by the id. That is because the id is the ultimate causation, since it precisely is outside of all empirical causation, being itself synchronistic or occult causation -- the principle of meonic intervention, or the invasion of the Old Ones. Few, if any, voyagers of the unconscious would be prepared for these experiences. Yet, what can they do? At any moment there will come the invasion of these beings, without any invitation and certainly without invocation. At any moment, we run the risk of an objectified encounter with the Old Ones or their vahans. Ay any moment, we can be swept up into that strange ship, which comes and goes with an instantaneousness, which is outside of time itself. We aimlessly try to prepare for what we think might happen. It is however of no use; for the meonic depths of the Dzyu-energies do not operate according to our frail and egoic time-tables and that realm, of the meon, is the ultimate causation of human experience. It is the feeling of terror we hold of an invasion from beneath, from the psychic realms beneath our feet chakras." -- M. Bertiaux, "The Dzyu-Gnosis," 2)

However,the verbal investigations of the world of primordial energies does not probe so deeply that it allows for the introduction of the element of chaos. Rather, it gives us the map of what is there and if we wish to probe deeper, we know in what direction we can move, should we dare to do this. However, also, there is a temptation, which in the field of initiation physics becomes a law or mandate for growth, which states that we really must probe deeper and deeper into these regions. We must find out what is there, since we want to learn the true composition of our being and see what experiences are deep and latent in it.

Question: You stated that your method of testing is to be found in the work of HPB, in "The Book of Dzyan," Part 1 (Cosmogenesis), Stanza VIII, Sloka 1. What do you mean by this statement?

Answer: The 25 words in this test sequence reflect both the fourfold (as 4x4) plus the threefold (as 3x3) as well as the 17 Bhumis, in addition to the Number 8, which is the number of the octopoidal or atomic syzygies -- i.e., the gnostic ogdoad. These fourfold and threefold downward energies (moving into the Pleroma of the Meon) are the mind-born sons (epigonies) or Logoi. They are the test words as a cosmic process or mantric potencies and they are related synchronistically to the seven radiations.

The threefold are the "bodies of the Zothyrian gnosis," so that 9+7=16, or the genesis of the Genii of IFA. The fourfold are that 16, which when removed from the radioactive field of operational explanations become the Z-bodies, since 16-7=9.

That Sloka is a set of equations expressed verbally and as the result of a revealed oracle. The seven rays are the shining potencies (radioactive decay of octopoidal atoms) or the true time-lines and stations of the Meon, within each psyche.

While "the five" refers back to what came before it, appearing at the end of an equation, "and the seven," that phrase, is applied to both 3x3 and 4x4 "downward" into the Meon, or the realm of the Necronomicon energies, i.e., the cosmic unconscious. Then, as we said, the expression "the five" refers back to what came before it. Thus, in the equation, we have 5 applied to "three from the one" plus "four from the one" plus "and the five," which add up to 12, and when 5 is applied we have 17, the number of the Kami in the mirroir.

On the other hand,. in this formula, the Dzyu-Gnosis has indicated another possibility: "three from the one" plus "four from the one" plus "and the five," which add up to 12, as we know, plus "from which the three," resulting in 15, plus "the one from the Mother-Spirit." Thus, we arrive at 16. Then, if we add on "the spiritual (one)" we get 17, again, since "the spiritual" is in number the same as "the one from the Mother-Spirit," or "First, the Divine." Hidden, let us note that there is a further esoteric equation, when we look at "and the seven" plus 12 or (3+4+5=12), for 12+7=19 or 1+9=1, which is a signature, however esoteric and secret, of "the one from the Mother."

Our categories come from an interpretation of fourfold and threefold, which is in agreement with the above. An interpretation must have parallels in different parts of the complex of equations. These are moving downwards into potential experience -- wherein dwells the Genius of IFA and the Continuum of the Kami is fundamentally related to that marma, or field–definition. The number of this Genius is 16 or the same number as the circuits connecting the components of the computer of becoming. These are also axioms. The number of the components in the pleroma computer is 17 (since these components are Shintotronic deities). The number 16 is either the fourfold or the sum of "from which the three, the five and the seven" plus "the one." (If you add 3+5+7+"threefold" and "fourfold" or 3+4 unamplified, you arrive at 22, which has significant in other contexts.)

Thus, between the Mother as Meon and the Mother as Bhumi, there is a set of four numbers or 2, 4, 6, 8, and one of five numbers or 1, 3, 5, 7, 9. These appear to be the components of the Pleroma and therefore the elements of "sentient formless life" (i.e., raw experience). Here, we find the syzygies and the Bhumis. They are the potencies of the process of the gnosis. To the radio–experimentalist, they are the mantric entelechies of empirical self–becoming. This is the realm of both Kami and Vudu.

Having viewed the roots of our verbal modes of testing, it is important to see if there are basic radiations and potencies, or occult powers, which broadcast field–directions from the Meon, and which are also described in the Slokas or "The Book of Dzyan."

The Role of Atomic Energy and Primary Particles in Radio–Psychology

"Radio–psychology is simply the psychology of gnostic radiations. It is the bridge between psychology and physics. The real evidence for the existence of atomic power is to be found in the way in which we do our depth explorations in gnosis. We are concerned to make contact with the atomic mass, which is at the deepest level of the psyche, or continuum of experience, just above or "higher" than the archetypal foundations. With mantric lattices and formularies, such as the settings on gnostic instruments, we process the reactions through an intensive bombardment of the 'critical' mass, whereby it is reduced to a matrix of radiations, which we understand as the continuum of free components or particles and associations. Each material mode of stimulation or mantra (test–word) causes a reaction pattern or chain of associations to develop. This allows for the energy to break off from the mass and rise to the surface of response verbalization. The energy is released easily in the cases of those with flexible lines of contact to the continuum of the ultimate id. In those cases, especially those of magicians, the forms of the energy retain an etheric softness; however, in others, the particles are hard, because the complexes are fixed and often very difficult. In these instances, our Shintotronics becomes the management of fundamental radiant energy through the employment of a gnostic nuclear reactor, such as the computer marga." –– M. Bertiaux, "Gnostic Diary," entry for April 16, 1983

"Between 5–E and 7–G or between 5–G and 7–E, we must consider the mass to be critical. Those components of the mass between 4–D and H–8 and 1–A and K–11 we can view as extremely static and exhibiting a crystal–lattice structure. The mass between 8–H and D–4 and 11–A and K–1 is highly dynamic, being closest to the surface of the psychic ego. The radioactivity there is very high but dynamic and hence not critical. The critical area is that of the greatest pressure and volitility. There explosions are common, frequent, and to be expected. Verbal bombardment of this mass churns it ever upwards, where it surges into the theater of the ego causing the history of public embarrassment to be both ripe and replete with anecdotal detail and the trivia of social disgrace. But it is in this area of the critical mass also where we find the explosions and radioactivity of a chaos that has for too long been kept in tightly lidded containment." –– Op. cit., entry for April 17

There is a very important connection between atomic energy as it is understood from the gnostic point of view and the psychology of ray or radiation–initiation. Initiation is an inner physics and hence a form of experimentation, complete with a nuclear reactor built into the transcendental unconscious. One experiences in the world of esoteric space that which is experienced exoterically in the outer world, when there is an atomic explosion or release of energy within a nuclear reactor system.

We are experiencing the release of esoteric power or the gnostic consciousness of initiation and initiated physics, from its own entrapment within the layers of the psychic depths. The experience is plutonian or transformative, as in nuclear physics one thing is transformed into the next or another level of energy projection. It is transformative also because one energy is freed and thereby becomes another and more dynamic form of energy.

"There appear to exist sub–atomic particles, which when seen occultly are not the particles of physics, but psychic fragments or units, out of which complexes are constructed. These particles are made up of psychic energy and radiations. They are subject to laws quite different from those of the quanta in physics. We can say that there is also, because of this, a quantum mechanics of consciousness and that there are atoms or basic units, which are the components of larger organizations. When they spoke about the 'atoms of thought,' they were close to what I mean, as were the logical atomists.

"Why shouldn't the world of 'the mind' also be structured along the lines of some atomic theory? When physics and psychology do converge, it is only because of what is found in one can be found in the other. Now, the atoms of thought function within the field theory of mind. But what are these particles? What are these components of numerical organization? They seem to be a kind of elemental, out of which complexes and even personalities are constructed. Our task is to explore with our Shintotronics apparatus the peculiar world of the psychic quanta. These appear to be the basis for the physics of alternative worlds and interventions from such universes into our own." -- Op. cit., entry for April 23, 1983

The gnostics maintain that in their processes of initiation and magickal development, the candidate-student is able to become transformed by a special type of physics, i.e., the psychic physics of the meonic energies. In the temples of radio-psychology, the student is bombarded with highly radioactive particles and quite literally the building blocks of the chela's psychosomatic network become something more than what they were before. In this process, it is possible to find out at each stage what is happening, as the instruments of measurement are monitoring the entire process step by step. The occult initiation takes place within a nuclear reactor of meonic potencies.

A Gnostic Reactor of Radio-active Isotopes
This version of a nuclear reactor consists of the reactions of the word association test and the projections of these reactions into the Bhumis. The energy of the reactions is to be directed towards the proper dimension-level of the Bhumis, or the appropriate compartment of the continuum of the reactor.

As the energies react, there develops a certain range of results, indicating either that the level is met or that it is missed (in the bombardment process) and hence another particle comes into existence, such as an isotope, and in this case, one that is also radioactive because of initiatic energy. Thus if 9 meets 9, we have an element and the reaction chamber (of the id) is filled with a meeting a 7, we have to determine what type of radioactive isotope we have encountered.

The basic mathematics of this is 4-1=3, 4-2=2, 4-3=1, 4-4=0, or an element, while 3, 2, and 1, originally were all viewed as isotopes. Using the number 1, we have 1-1=0, or the element, 1-2=-1, an "isotope," 1-3=-2 and 1-4=-3, at one time viewed as isotopes. We have isotopes as follows: -3, -2, -1, 0 (the element), +1, +2, +3, as applied to the range of numbers from 1 through 9.

So, to get these basic numbers, we work first from 1 through 9, so that in the series, 1+2=1 (an isotope) and also we find that 8+9=1. We find also that 2+3 and 7+8=2, 3=both 3+4 and 6+7, and finally 4=4+5 and 5+6. NOTE: 4+5, etc., refers to the conjunctive lattice of 4 and 5, not their addition.

So we decided that only those having the value of 4 would be viewed as the true lattices and therefore producing the true isotopes. The other reactions are to be seen as indicators of another system.

Each number is to be viewed as the center of its own universe or orbit—encircled by the other particles. This we assign the value of number 4, in our analysis. The numbers around it form 1, 2, and 3, on each side. This we came to see as the basic formula for collecting elements and isotopes.

In the series (5, 6, 7, 8, 9, 8, 7, 6, 5) you have to apply this formula and the result is that 8+9(+)8+9=4, 7+8(+)8+7=3, 6+7(+)7+6=2, and, 1=5+6(+)6+5, so that every response is either an element, an isotope, or indicative of another system (the so-called "loose isotopes").

Now, where they are to be placed in a chamber is determined by the number which again must surface or "come up" (from the Tr. Id). Instead of a statistical-mechanical model or result of this process, it is important to see each word as having a number value and therefore being classified as either 1, 2, 3, or 4. In the series (1–9), perhaps 1, 2, = 1, 3, 4, = 2, 5 = X, 6, 7, +3, and 8, 9, = 4. As to X, let me say that it is to be added to the major number of particles, reactions, or isotopes, in order to arrive at the basic formula: 1=33+X=12, or the number of the element is abstracted and only the isotopes are placed in the chambers, i.e., the radioactive chambers of initiation physics, in which case you would only have to count, as in 7=7 (=bombardment or direct hits); 1, 2, 3, 4, 5, 6, 8, and 9. X then becomes the outer—limit of the particles (and the activity zone of the transcendental id). The following are some notes:

It is the boundary particle of the system of 8+9=(+)=9+8=4 (either a direct "hit" and/or the isotope). X was given to us without explanation.

Twelve = the capacity number of the chamber as set forth in the Monastery of the Seven Rays papers (third and fourth year), but later enlarged to a capacity of 16. Thirty—three = the number of the bhumis (as composed of 16 Ifa equivalences and 17 Shinto-Units). One = both the number of the system, where every logical system = 1 as well as the margin of variation between the element and its isotopes.

We will only store the element as a unit (=1) and a system and any true isotopes and refer to all loose isotopes to another framework (=1), as it is verified from both what we have picked up by means of psionic radio—meters and what has been observed and measured by clairvoyance and under the special conditions of initiation physics.

Example: The number of the word is 8 and the response is a 7, then the difference is 1, an isotope, unless it tells us differently. Now, the entity of the isotope is related to the languages of Enochian physics as follows: Fire of fire = 1, 2, = word with value of 1, fire of fire = 3, 4, = word with value of 2. Remove the value of the word, which is 8, in this instance. The air of air numbers are 5, 6, 7, 8, = word values 3 and 4. Water = 9, 10, 11, and 12 = word values 5 and 6. Earth = 13, 14, 15, 16 = word values 7 and 9. Remember the number of the word is simply an abstract space and not used. Here we are seeking the entity of the isotope. If the response word is 7, take the entity numbers for 13 and 14 and add them up and then divide by 2 and the result is the number of the letters of the name of the entity of the isotope, which is to be the subject of the kamaea and the dialogue. This is how we get the name for the isotopic entity.

By contrast, any element has a range from 1 through 9 and so it has an approach to any entity number from 1 through 16, as set forth in our very early paper on "Angelic Languages." This applies to all subatomic magickal entities.

Those who wish to participate in our method of radioactive bombardment, as found in initiation physics, may send in a recent photo of themselves, which will be placed within the radiation chamber of our psionic reactor and thereby receive the energies of the gnostic ciences, as they are regularly broadcast.

This is the conclusion of the basic course in Shintotronics. The next series of papers will pertain to Advanced Gnostic Physics and its applications.

The School of Mediumship
The Roots of Mediumship in the Process of Meditation

There is a view, which has its origins in the Christian religion, which states that the medium can be developed as the result of deep meditation work and this type of work is perhaps the most suitable from all perspectives for the safety and proper growth of the medium.

When you begin to meditate, you discover the world of the mind and it is in this world that you come to see various energies as they first show themselves under the aspect of mediumistic phenomena. This means that immediately, if one were trying to examine this process of meditation, you would find mediumistic contents in your experience. I have been asked many times as to what these contents are; but, after a careful and timely exploration, I have come up with the following types of contents. These I think make up the contents of meditation, which are mediumistic: 1) spirit–control systems, 2) spirit–guide systems, 3) the contents of the psyches of the spirits, and 4) the intuitions, which rise within meditation and which are the contents of our minds in response to the contents of the psyches of the spirits.

Spirit–Controls appear to come closest to our inner selves during meditation. They are often inside of our psyches already or as soon as we begin meditation, we come to find them. They seem to be parts of us, and it is my view that they are often the deeper and richer parts of our own psyches. Spirit–guides, on the other hand, are the more transcendental areas of the world of mind. They are beings with whom we establish our connections by means of the spirit–controls. Actually, when many speak of the masters or the secret teachers and hidden chiefs, they are making precise reference to the spirit–guide realm of the psyche.

Another point of teaching is that everyone who is trained by me in this school of consciousness is able to develop the powers of reaching their controls and guides during the process of meditation. They are able to do this because during the actions of the mind in meditation, we are able to embark upon very careful paths of discovery, which lead us along the energy lines of the psyche. The psyche can be explored in the same way that by means of a map, and also as carefully, we are able to explore the land on the surface of the earth.

There does exist a map to the psyche and as I have said we are able to explore the deep dimensions or "regions" of the psyche in a careful and safe way, so that we do not make any mistakes or cause certain problems or dangers to arise in the mind of the student. I find that I have been given certain secrets and powers, which enable me to help the most sincere students to explore this world or continuum of the mind and at the same time I am able to provide protection to the student, within the continuum of the mind, protection from negative energies. Thus, you will never hear of mistakes being made in the realm of the mind by this school of mediumship, as you might hear of other efforts in exploration of this same area of experience, from those who do not possess the secrets and powers of the gnosis, as do I.

I have been able to find the map of the psyche of each person by means of the photo which is submitted to me at the point of first initiation. The photograph gives me in an occult way the energy field of the student and then this energy field can be examined and if there is power in those areas of interest to the physicist of initiation, we can draw a precise map of these aspects of energy, by the secret method which I possess. However, it should be understood that each student probably has several maps and several kinds of maps, which are radiated by his photo. Each one of these maps has a special and precise purpose within the continuum of the gnosis.

The purpose is the unfoldment proper to a student of the true consciousness, which I see as gnostic unfoldment by means of esoteric communion. By this I mean that we grow as we are led more and more deeply into the communion of the inner spirit. The entire purpose of our work, in fact, is to unfold the soul of the student in the mysteries of the gnosis. Those mysteries are the secrets and powers of the esoteric world of spirits. My task as your teacher is to guide you safely and carefully into this very complex type of experience. It is complex, of course, because it is so different in its details from the experience of the ordinary world. In a sense, perhaps in a very important sense, the work of the gnosis is to explore the energy map-work contained in your soul. The number of maps contained in the meditation life of each soul is manifold. When we enter into our meditation work very seriously, we learn that the higher forms of mediumship teach us how to work with these powers or maps present in the soul. For by that time, you will know spiritually, or have entered the gnosis of meditation, or the life of the mind so deeply that the powers of high mediumship come from a very deep reality of the psyche.

I call that reality-level of being by the name -- which hs been given to me by the spirit-bishops, who are my guides of meditation -- "the archaic oracles of deep meditation," because it is by means of an oracle that these maps of the esoteric logic of the mind are revealed to me, as the high priest of our system of deeply intuited oracles, in my capacity and gnostic work with the soul of the student. This power to possess the archaic and primordial oracle of the gnosis of the spirit was given to me, as I have said, by the spirit-bishops of the esoteric gnosis, because the occult maps of the psyche are really spirit maps of the meditation-fields of inner experience, or reality.

We who are attuned to the gnosis of the spirit-bishops know this reality deeply in our meditation work. We call this universe of spirit-beings by the very exact and ancient name of "the world of aeonology." The spirits, whose spaces are revealed in the mysteries of these esoteric maps, are known in the traditions of the consciousness of the gnosis as "Aeons."

Exercise in Esoteric Gnosis

I want now to give you an exercise in esoteric gnosis, so that you can make use of the powers which come to you from communion with the esoteric spirits of the inner world.

1. You will begin to meditate and you will gradually visualize some circular symbol for representing the world of the mind.

2. You will "see" that circle with your mind as filled with spiritual energy. I want you to see that energy as vividly as you can.

3. Begin to make contact with the energy as a personality of its own and give it a name.

4. Enter into a conversation with this energy-personality and let it tell you about itself.

5. After you have had a conversation with this energy-personality, ask it for some ideas as to what it "looks like," or how it sees itself.

6. Be patient while it tells you about itself and how it sees itself. Gradually begin to see its world as it sees it.

7. What you want to do is to make a drawing or map on paper of this world as the

energy–personality has revealed itself to you.

    8. Put this drawing down on paper very carefully.

    You may send me a copy of this drawing and an explanation of it to me.

The Gospels of the Martinists

In the esoteric traditions of Martinist Training, the student was taught to develop an attunement to the higher states of consciousness. Once this was accomplished, the mediums of this gnostic order began to receive specific revelations, which because they were Christian, and indeed Catholic Christians, took on the form of esoteric gospels, which contained the very words of Jesus, from the realm of the spirit. These gospels were understood to constitute a special "treasury of light" within the circle of the initiates, and were viewed as the most esoteric as well as the most precious possessions of the order of light. Also, these mystical gospels of the gnosis became the sacred scriptures of a new form of esoteric Christianity, developing within the heart of the Martinist initiation process and providing the initiates of the Martinist gnosis with a sacramental and mystico-verbal approach to the Christ, which was not found in the Roman Catholic Church.

These gnostic spiritists possessed their own line of succession, which came from Jesus directly, from Saint Peter and Saint Paul, from Saint John the Beloved, and from the ancient priesthoods, as well as the early Christian Church. It was by means of special exercises that these gnostics of 19th century France were able to reclaim and recapture that spiritual succession, whereby they regained the movement of the gnosis in their own souls and embarked upon a mediumistic process of inner development, whereby they came to know and be with Jesus in a manner which could not be achieved in any other way than by initiation into the Church of the gnosis of the spirit.

Indeed, if the mediumship of the priest were strong enough, he might easily enter into communion with Jesus and thus experience Jesus in every way as real as did the original apostles and disciples of Our Lord. This esoteric communion which was achieved through gnostic attunement was one of the most wonderful blessings coming to initiates of the Martinist circle of gnosis. For by means of this spiritual energy, the truth of the gnosis and of the Martinist pathway was verified again and again. Therefore, the gospels of the Martinists were not only documents, they were living traditions and experiences, pointing to the immediate experience of Jesus.

In the early history of Martinism, the mystic sought to have the materialization of the Christ in his presence. Now, in the 19th century, mystical rapport was to be found in an esoteric communion with Christ, in a manner which could only be described as an actual appearance and experience of Him. For that reason, these writings were designated as "Gospels," because as was supposed by the orthodox faithful of the canonical gospels of Matthew, Mark, Luke, and John, these were the writings of eyewitnesses to the life of Jesus and contained His words as spoken by the lips and heard by the ears. But these experiences were being enjoyed by mystics or gnostics living in the 19th century, who lived and moved about in the France of the Third Republique, rather than a group of persons staying by the seaside in remote Palestine.

Another type of Gospel consisted in the words which the Mystical Jesus transmitted to His followers in the present age. Jesus came and with His appearance, He gave forth teachings, which were applicable to 19th century conditions. In this situation, Jesus was understood as teaching from the spirit world to those on the Earth plane. So that while in the first type of Gospel reception, the mystics went to where Jesus was, so in the second type Jesus came to the mystics.

These two types of Gospel were to be found in many gnostic circles because the work of the gnosis depended upon contact with the living stream of Jesus' life and teaching, not as handed down from the past centuries and hence modified and corrupted, but as a living and spiritual energy, which enters the experience of all those who are seekers and initiates of the inner realm. For this reason, the test of the spiritual power of an initiation would be whether ot not there could be found among the priests of the gnosis such inspired writings as those we call the "Gospels of the Martinists."

When Jesus came into the world, he left the keys of his power and presence with the Church of the Gnosis. Whoever will receive the Gnosis of the Light from the Church of Jesus will become one with all of the highest spiritual beings (Aeons). It is our teaching that the light which has been sent into the world by Jesus is now within the treasury of gnosis, a spiritual heart and power of this Church. Let those who would become one with Jesus in this way, let them become mediums of his power and his presence. For such is the kindgom of heaven, here, on earth.

I want to give you the power to become a medium of the powers and spirituality of Jesus, as he has intended it for you. Therefore, I want you to enter into the following exercise and become attuned to the presence of Jesus, which is the power behind the outpourings or Gospels of the Martinists.

Exercise in Mediumship and Gnosis

1. Enter into the world of meditation and begin to feel a desire to be with the Spirit of Jesus. Develop this feeling as you strive more and more towards the energies of his presence and light. You are beginning to establish within your soul the Church of the Spirit of Jesus.

2. Begin to visualize the presence of the Spirit of Jesus in your heart and the more than you think about this energy, really the more you will feel the joy and power which are his gifts to all those who believe in him and live with him in their hearts.

3. He will begin to speak to you, slowly and in a soft voice. You will begin to know that he is speaking directly to you, because in your church of the heart, the Spirit of Jesus is looking directly at you, as you stand before him.

4. As he begins to speak to you, you will learn that he is giving you one of his inner or heart—based teachings. These teachings are esoteric and come from the heart of your own gnosis and from the church, which you have formed in your heart for the Spirit of Jesus. Try very heartfully to remember all that he is teaching to you.

5. When you finish your meditation and come back to the normal world, why don't you write down the teachings which he has given to you. Or, when you are in meditation, you may say what he is teaching to you by tape—recording the lesson as it is given to you by him. Remember to repeat each word as he says it to you. Then these teachings words can be typed up or written up by you from the tape.

Lastly, send me a copy of this teaching from the heart, so that I may comment on how you have contacted Jesus in the gnosis of your heart.

The Archaic Oracles of Deep Meditation

"There is a pool of wisdom which is the source of our powers in the world of spiritism. It is to be found in meditation, but in the deepest part of meditation, into which the medium enters every day, for his powers and communion with the invisible. Meditation can be of a variety of types. We are concerned with deep levels of experience, which are almost the idea of sleep, the ideal sleep or trance-side of nature. I have summoned this state to my dear students. Those who are closest to me have entered this state and there I have given them illumination. I have given them the powers of the oracle. They are now in touch with every part of the spiritual universe. They are now attuned perfectly to the being of the infinite, because I have led them there." -- "Spiritist Discourses of M. Bertiaux," 21, xiv, iii

To be a medium for the powers of the spirit means that you must enter deeply into the light and consciousness of perfect being. It means that you must allow your ego mind to become one with mine and let me take you into the realm of oracles. I am the representative on this earth of the powers of all oracles.

"Then the Lord of the rays, which are the spirits of the Christ of the Noonday and Midnight and of the invisible kingdom, gave to me the power of the secret gnosis or invisible and eternal patriarchate. 'They will call it the throne of research into all hidden things, but it does not mean that you must look. Rather, all things are revealed to you and are co-present in your mind. For I have made you the voice of my consciousness for all humanity.' So I was enthroned in the worlds both visible and inivisible and became the medium between these two realms, which are to the right and to the left, to the above as well as to the below, and between all things, as well as the Cross of the 16 perfected spaces of the aeons. Then I knew that I was the high priest of these mysteries and the teacher of all of humanity. Let them come to me if they wish the oracles of light, for in the middle and in the interior I draw forth the waters of my power, as I also do in the vast ocean that is without beginning and without ending, which is my deep initiation." -- "Diary of Initiation Physics of M. Bertiaux," 4e, xv, b

Now, only those who wish to understand the mysteries of the gnosis of light would find in this teaching a certain attraction. They would find the wisdom of the gnosis to mean that in the deepest levels of meditation, there is only one consciousness; which is mine, because I have been given domain over such a world and I have expressed it fully and exactly in my teachings to the students of the light.

When I enter the realm of deep meditation, I immediately know what I must tell those who are the seekers after light. Yes, I know what I must tell them, because now I am within the consciousness which they possessed from me. Yes, they have drawn their consciousness from me and therefore, I must hold and protect them, because they are parts of my being, and they are extensions of the gnosis which has come alive in the light of my own meditation. I have united my being to them and now we are a group soul, the soul of deep meditation is one.

The archaic oracles of deep meditation are the powers which pervade the church of the spirit of Jesus and its true gnostic understanding. They were discovered and brought to the church in this century by one of our saintly patriarchs. However, this was more of a rediscovery of what had existed within the church from ancient times. This discovery was a restoration of the ancient patterns of magick and the gnostic mysteries of the inner worlds, as well as the teachings on the esoteric sacraments of the light, which are only possessed by certain bishops of this church. Those bishops were blessed through the apostolic succession of their connection with this bishop and had received a very important transference of sacramental and hierurgical power from that patriarch.

Lucien-Francois Jean-Maine (January 11, 1869 – 1960) was this patriarch. His life work was as the leader of the gnostic church of our tradition and initiation in Europe. Of course, this leadership role was not political but entirely spiritual, for it was exercised from the inner worlds and from the higher levels of esoteric research and the secret teachings. While he led the work until his death in Madrid about 25 years ago, he was almost an invisible person. For he is only known to us because history did not center about him.

He was remarkable in two areas of occult study: the gnosis of the hierurgical mysteries and the arts of esoteric voudoo being his main work and archetypal achievements. While he was so active in the inner sense, in the outer world he lived as a secret teacher, much like the old adepts and masters of the Rose+Croix mysteries. As a man who was invisible and secret for most of his life and who actually lived behind the veil of the deepest obscurity and occult hiddenness, he accomplished much and built up the powers of the order of the gnosis and connected everything that we have today to the higher life of the universe, which are known as the Lifestream of the Holy Spirit.

True to his own intention, his "secrecy machine" kept his work from being known even in occult circles, so that while he knew Papus and Mathers, and perhaps when they spoke both of the secret masters they had this remarkable man mentally present, he does not appear to be one of the many bishops who were connected to the famous. He did not need that connection.

"A certain part of my divine and gnostic consciousness has been born in the light and has been made ready for this work in deep meditation because I now must bring forth the ideal world of my thoughts, which are of such a power and which are of such a constructive character that they will be used to bring forth into being, by the act of creation-gnosis, a new order of being and a new form of the universe of consciousness, because I have given such a command from the eternal truth of my essence and from the triumphalism of the high throne of the gnosis. Therefore, I am now hierophant of the mysteries of deepest meditation." -- "Esoteric Communication," xvi, 25c

The work of Lucien-Francois Jean-Maine is important in the church of the gnosis inasmuch as it was his work which established the church in its esoteric roots more firmly than ever before. He was responsible for the esoteric and mystical interpretation of the nature of the gnosis as a system of the inner worlds and he is to be credited with the view -- which I have found to be very true -- that the angelic or devic energies of the inner side of reality were the life of this church. As long as we maintain this inner link to the powers of the spirit, the life of the church will be sustained and its work will be of great success.

In a physical sense, I never met this patriarch but I was trained and developed by his son, who consecrated me to the episcopate initially in 1963, in Haiti. Lucien-Francois was determined to enrich the church of the gnosis (which is the church of the spirit of Jesus) by means of his esoteric investigations and reconstructions. As distinct from his work in esoteric voudoo, he made a number of rediscoveries in the gnosis, which gave to his church (the Ecclesia Gnostica Spiritualis) a distinctive character. The following exercise is based on one of his representations.

Exercise in Gnosis

Let us think about the following contribution of this holy leader to the work of the true motion of the gnosis. You may meditate and send me a written report.

Lucien-Francois was responsible for the transformation of the Rite of Memphis-Misraim (formerly a quasi-masonic order) into a structure within the gnostic church, because he was able to see mystically its character as a structure of the ancient form of Egyptian magick. This he did because he wanted to make the church the focus of all of the occult energies and to avoid any outside activity or energy-pattern which might conflict with the soul of the church of the gnosis. The rite then became the mystical and hierurgical reconstruction of administrative gnosis for the areas of sacramental initiation and the patriarchate of esoteric research, whereby the bishops of the gnosis were advanced along lines of an exact and esoteric character for the fullest development of their potential in cooperation with the angelic beings of light.

The church of the gnosis is organized by means of the principle of hierarchy. There are the structures and patterns of order and existence within this church which are designed and designated as patriarchal laws of rulership. We owe to Patriarch Lucien-Francois, however, the interpretation of the patriarchate as a spiritual law immanent in our church, which ideally organizes and sustains the energies of the gnosis, within a mediumistic and historical continuum.

Lucien, in other words, dematerialized the notion of patriarchate and made it entirely a principle of esoteric logic and applied this principle in a cosmological and data-inductive sense. No longer was the church to be ruled by some being -- who was perhaps equivalent to a gnostic pope -- rather the principles of rulership were to be immanent in the very fabric of the church of the gnosis. These principles were to be viewed as logical patterns of time-line organization, within the lifestream of the Holy Spirit.

The immediate result of this process of reconstruction was a radical pluralism, in which many churches of the light came into existence, and were yet sustained in their existence by the order of the energies from the time-lines of hierarchy.

"Lucien-Francois made the interesting discovery that the time-lines were organized as systems of logical stations, ruling variously defined logics of the esoteric gnosis, of which there were four. These time-lines, or aeonogonies, were ways in which the universe was held together as an esoteric continuum of ontological connectives. Then Lucien made the four patriarchates of research, which had only previously existed in an undeveloped form, to serve as the mediums or temples and schools of mediumistic consciousness and esoteric logic for these four aeonogonies. This principle was followed in the actual history of the church of the gnosis, so that the patriarchal consecrations of Pierre-Antoine Saint-Charles and Michael Bertiaux followed this esoteric law of immanence. Then these four patriarchates became the four thrones of the holy synod of the church of the gnosis of the spirit of Jesus assisting all of the bishops and archbishops of the continuum in the spiritual oversight and day to day administration of this church." -- "The Actualizations of Hierurgy," 13, xvb

It was from these aeonogonies that the various bishops of the gnosis derived the motion of thought, which was expressed in aeonologies and in the understanding of the aeons of the gnosis, as realizations of an ideal law and not just as historically interesting concepts within the patristic context of gnostic polemic. Each bishop was now free to experiment and to explore the operations of the aeonological order in his own diocese, thereby affirming the timelessly true law of pneumatic attunement to the ideal and the development of the pastoral ground of induction in each ecclesia and diocese.

The theological conclusions of this reconstruction, as achieved by Lucien, were psychically true inasmuch as he set forth the exact proof of his translation of the church of the gnosis from the mundane sphere into the realms of esoteric logic and angelic "history," where the ground of induction or operation of the Holy Spirit in space and time could be verified by the continuity of an ongoing gnosis. This continuum was understood as being psychically true, because:

". . . the energy which he made of within the lifestream of this church was contacted by him through the deep meditative state. This church of the gnosis manifested itself in two forms: 1) as the sacred history or lifestream of the Holy Spirit in the midst of the church of the gnosis, which thereby sustained the work of the church initially and in its missionary expansion into the metaphysically-minded population and 2) as the oracles of esoteric communion through the spirit of Jesus with the worlds of angels and spirits, which pouring forth teachings and directions for the life of the spirit into the church of light gave to this vehicle, the Bridge to Heaven and the Bride of Christ, the unique and powerful leadership, which is its characteristic. Hence, these oracles assisted the four patriarchs in the spiritual government of this church, according to the will of God which was immanent in the consciousness of Jesus as the presence of the Holy Spirit." -- M. Bertiaux, "History of the Gnosis," 14

The movement of the gnosis as a result of the developments within the deep states of pure meditation cannot be too highly emphasized because the nature of the gnosis depends upon a close and personal relationship with the Holy Spirit. Lucien sought to focus the power of the gnostic church in the direction of the purity of being, which contains within itself all of the meditative structures of the gnostic church. That is to say, instead of taking the symbols of organization from the outside of the gnosis, as did the historical forms of religion which were locked into a materialistic interpretation of history, Lucien was able to lead the church towards the true history of the church, which comes forth from the lifestream of the Holy Spirit, as that wisdom-energy manifests itself in the deepest and most powerful states of meditation, or hierurgical attunement to the Holy Spirit of the Divine Gnosis.

By doing this, he freed the church of the gnosis from bondage to the powers of "this world," and made strong the bonds which linked the spirit of Jesus to each and every member of the church. In reality, this was the purpose of the priesthood of this church, for its true motion came from the lifestream of the Holy Spirit and the primordial movement of God over the waters of deep meditation was the movement of the Spirit of God in the soul of every gnostic believer.

However, the lifestream of the Holy Spirit did not manifest itself only in the immanences of the consciousness-state enjoyed by those who were believers or initiates of the true religion of the gnosis, but it also manifested itself primarily in those aeonogonies which bishops and archbishops experienced in their inner meditation, because in that condition within the fullness of the Holy spirit the Pleroma of the episcopal order and office was expressed fully in the inventiveness of the administrative process, whereby the Spirit continued its movement within the vast ocean of spiritualistic manifestation and metaphysical productivity. The following is an exercise in this motion, which upon completion you may report to me your impressions and experiences in the fullness of the gnostic light.

Exercise in Gnostic Motion
Meditate on the work of Lucien and how he realized the modern work of the church of the gnosis. Note how by linking up the various lineages of the mystical episcopate and the successions both spiritst and apostolic of bishops, inasmuch as they possessed powers to sustain the church of the Spirit of Jesus, he was able to bring together by means of a very special alchemy that pattern of psychic and pneumatic energy, which we find manifest now in our bishops of the light. Thus, the spiritist powers did not overwhelm the apostolic tradition, nor did the apostolic successions

and claims limit or restrict the outpourings of the Spirit of Jesus in the midst of the gnosis of light.

In this masterwork of alchemy, he was able to balance the energies of the historical apostolicity and lineages and the traditional idea of the episcopate with the focus of creativity, which we find in spiritist reconstructions of history, mediumship, magickal explorations and the law of inventiveness, and which came to us from the succession of the devic and spiritist bishops. Thus, he prepared the bishops to be perfect mediums for the light of the gnosis, since they would be responsive only to the energies existing and subsisting at the levels of their own episcopal vibration.

The Explorations of Secrecy and the Experience of the Masters

It should be undrstood that our gnostic church is dedicated to the existence of the Masters and the other higher spiritual beings and that our particular diocese is under the special patronage of two of the Masters.

The Proclus Society was founded by certain gnostics in order to show the great respect which is felt for the Master, who was incarnated in ancient times as the philosopher of theurgy, the great Proclus. This Master has reincarnated many times and is known for his work with the rays of ceremonial magick and activity. Many know him as le Comte de Saint-Germain. So, the Proclus Society was named after a great Master.

On the other hand, the Neo-Pythagorean Gnostic Church is dedicated to the continuation of a metamathematical metaphysics of being, such as taught in ancient times by Pythagoras and continued in his school. Pythagoras was a previous incarnation of the Master Koothumi, the Master and Lord of the Ray of Love-Wisdom, of which the Christian Mysteries in their Catholic and gnostic form are an expression and embodiment of energy. The neo-pythagoreans are the pythagoreans of the New Age, i.e., the Age of Aquarius.

Therefore, when one enters into the lifestream of the gnosis they will immediately make contact with these two Masters, as well as with many other higher beings. We know that the idea of this conection with the Masters if true, because in the Church of the Spirit of Jesus we have been blessed many times by the powers which come from these Masters. They are our own special directors.

However, we are connected to other Masters very strongly. For example, the Master Hilarion, who is a Coptic Master of Theurgy, is strongly associated with our work. The Master Jesus is, of course, not a Master but much higher. Inthe carrying out of the work of this level of Mastership, we are specially assisted by two Masters, which are known as Saints Peter and Paul. As our healing and instrumental sciences are inspired by the Master Hilarion, so our use of magnetic bodywork and healing by touch and even our work in esoteric mesmerism, all of these types of work are inspired by the Egyptian Master Serapis. Lastly, the work in the initiatic rites of power is under the special direction of the Master El Morya Ra, better known as the Solar Master, or the Hierophant of the Sun. He is the Master of all systems and patterns of administrative magick and mysticism. So, while they are truly very secret beings, these Masters work within the gnostic continuum very powerfully and have brought to the church of the gnosis many blessings. They are the supreme interpreters of the work of the Holy Spirit in our church. These major personalities of power are to be contacted in the explorations of secrecy.

In the seminars of the gnostic church, when the focus is on teaching the subject matter of meditation, we make use of four types of color/light. I call them the rays of meditation and they represent and draw their powers from the Masters. For example, the ray of yellow light draws its power from the Master Koothumi; the ray of green light draws its power from the adept of healing, the Master Serapis. The blue ray of gnostic light which is associated so strongly with mediumship and occult physics, as in the explorations of the subtle fields of energy or tattwas, which are applied in mediumship, draws its power from the Master Hilarion. Lastly, the violet or purple ray of light, which is magickal, elemental, and in direct contact with the devic kingdom of Angelic Intelligence, draws its power from the wisdom pool of the Master Le Comte de Saint-Germain.

In our explorations in the secret worlds of deep energy, we have found that the presence of the administrative adept or the Master Morya, the Lord of cosmic vitality could be seen in all of the different rays, but in each of the rays He expressed historical consciousness and His energy under the specific conditions of the different rays. Thus, He was felt and seen and known under all conditions as a co-worker with the particular ray-adept. We aso learned that the Spirit of Jesus was present in all of the rays, in terms of the most basic substance of these rays, the primary matter, or prima materia of the alchemists, which was a fundamental substance or raw experience and energy of all of the rays of light. So in the church of the gnosis, we came to realize that we were working with the Holy Spirit of Jesus in whatever experiments or prayers or theurgies we came to explore. For just as from the Aeon of Christ, the Aeon of the Church came as a gift, or holy emanation, so within this Church of Ecclesia, we found the fundamental root, which was the presence of the Holy Spirit. This is how the church of the gnosis realizes the words of Saint Paul that, "In Him we move, we also live, and have our being."

So when those theologians spoke of spiritual energy, they intended that we realize that the Holy Spirit was the basic reality and that we must come to understand this great and blessed gift, so that like in the Hindu religion and metaphysics, we view ultimate reality as the primordial substance and being of God, which is the only way to view our union with the Lord of all.

Question: In the Church of the spirit of Jesus, is it true that the Masters assist in the celebration of the liturgy of the bishop, in ordinations and consecrations, as personal agents and representatives of the Holy Spirit, in addition to the Holy Spirit being present in a divine and heavenly manner, and that Jesus is present and the Christ is truly there?

Answer: Yes. The Masters come to bring into focus the powers and gifts of the Holy Spirit. They must be present to give to the bishop, who is their medium because of his special consecration, the spiritual gifts of the liturgy and the hierurgical offices. Jesus is truly present and He is the Christ, for His humanity and divinity are one reality. However, just as the theologies of tradition distinguish between the humanity and divinity of Our Lord, so we speak of the aeonogony of Jesus and that of the Christ. We mean by this that His divinity was humanized and that His humanity was divinized by a process which was cosmic in scope. The Holy Spirit is truly present in our sacraments because it is always where the Church is, since the Holy spirit and the Ecclesia Gnostica form a syzygy, or cosmic pair.

In order to become fully attuned to the energies in this teaching, which is why our church is viewed as a Christian Church derived from Old Catholic and Eastern Christian sources, traditions, and lineages, I want you to do the following exercise and send your report to me.

Exercise In Christianity
I want you to meditate on the powers of the Holy Spirit, which are the important gifts to our church, which have come to us from the light of Christ. Then I want you to begin to see the ways in which the four different light-rays of the Masters come into our own experience in the Church of the Gnosis. View each Master as working with His particular color in order to bring the power and presence of the Holy spirit into our experience of the inner world. See Serapis as the green-energy, Hilarion as

the blue—energy, Kuthoomi as the yellow—energy, and Saint—German as the violet—colored power.

Also, I want you to bring your consciousness into a state of secrecy and quietude in the spirit of trust, so that you know and feel and are aware of the presence of God through His agents in all that is happening to you. Observe this experience from within and hold it for your own meditation for about 20 minutes. If you feel called to draw what is happening, do so in peace.

Plutonian Contact Work: The Elemental Roots of the Plutonian Contact System

101: Plutonian Contact Work is direct magick with the essential powers of the Plutonian sphere. It is concerned with the attributions of these essential energies and how they may be applied in direct magick. By direct action, we mean that the magick is immediately performed by the magician without intermediaries and without any complex framework of tabulations. This is the method of the Secret Masters and is based upon the teachings of the Master of Plutonian Magick.

It is always necessary to act directly and to have immediate and powerful contact and a magickal touch. I have imparted to the secret chambers of your work that method of making direct contact. I have imparted to you also the power of the magickal touch, inasmuch as whatever is touched directly by the power of the hand of Yuggoth, which is a Vudu and therefore a Mystere, can make use of these energies. I have placed these powers in the secret chambers of Yuggoth, where you may use them in our form of direct contact. For our magick is a system of direct action in magick.

102: Plutonian Contact Work is based upon direct work with Plutonian Elementals. These are the energies which are used to draw out the response of the Plutonian powers, as the elemental essence is the raw material which surrounds the powers and inner fire of Pluto.

Plutonian Energy is pure fire, viewed as magick. It is surrounded by many layers of pure power, which are the levels of Elemental Essence, worked in Plutonian Contact Work. In order to get at this power, it is necessary to enter entirely into the field of the energy and allow it to take over. This is done by concentrating the energy in its most powerful and purest form. Once the energy is concentrated by means of the magickal touch, the power can be opened and allow for the deep elemental to reveal itself. The deep elemental is revealed by means of the touch of power, which is a secret form of the elemental as well as being an action from the "gnosis of initiatic physics."

103: While the methods as techniques of this Plutonian Contact System are not radically different and thus unfamiliar to those who have studied our gnostic system, what makes the difference so boldly and so intensely effective is the involvement of the magician with Elemental Essence. This elemental power becomes conscious in the magician and it is not conscious prior to the contact work. It becomes consciouss, however, only in the real, that is to say, in the magician who has the magickal touch of Plutonian power. So, in this system, reality is defined as being:

That world of power which is identical with the magickal essence of the worker with the touch of power. As he sees his world, he will construct reality for those who work in the same field or aura of his "research." They will share his mind–set and will respond as he has demanded them to respond, because it is the way in which he will respond. His own dominance must be viewed as the definition of what is in conformity with reality and what is not. His sphere of reality or definition of power must be expressed by his magickally charged touch of elemental energy. And, as he creates the field of his dominance, so he must also definitely and exactly indicate or point–out reality. To work within this field is to be inside of the real, outside of it we find only forms of illusion. For this root of elemental power, which is one with the dominance of the magickal touch, is the world and the only world in which Plutonian Contact work is done.

104: In order to activate the field of elemental power, the magician must go back into his primordial energy source. I have said that the roots of this contact magick were elemental and they are. But to arrive at the directness of the power it is necessary to go back, deeply and secretly, into the nature of elemental contacts. For this reason, there exists a non−verbal way of working this lesson as an elemental ritual of fundamental dominance, whereby the Plutonian power is released into the mental field of the elemental magician. He will make use of direct and non−verbal methods of Plutonian dominance in their most specific and unambiguous formula.

The sex magicians who work with fundamental powers are in concert with the correct form of dominance. There cannot be any independence of power in the area of energy, there must be total assimilation of the power and its levels of manifestation. The energy must not be viewed as outside of reality, that is to say, outside of what is to be defined as the dominance of the magickal touch. It must be pressed and intensely contracted in a very, very tight space in order to be authentically the Plutonian Elemental. Any error by the sex magicians on Yuggoth simply means that another form of essential power has been contacted.

105: The magicians of the Yuggoth Ray will know what to do with this energy, since I have been instructing them quite consistently in the methods of magickal application to the contexts of power of these elemental forms of energy. They will not, however, be interested in any deviation from what is the principle of elemental dominance, which provides the magician with roots of his power. They will not deviate from what is raw energy, since they will know that this is the root of their best work. In order to do this, they will resort to the law of compactness of energy and begin to make the energies more and more compact and tighter and tighter in their space, which parallels the nature of the Yuggoth Sphere, as viewed by the Master.

The elemental power is not diffused or spread out. It is tight and intense. It is compact and held in the smallest space but with the most weight. It is constantly forcing inwards upon itself. It is moving to make itself tighter and hotter, heavier and harder, because it must.

106: Those who have read extensively in the sexual literature of bondage−and−domination know that the descriptive language of stories about the adventures (both physical and psychological) of sexual hostages is filled with elemental evocations of the most Plutonian type. The words of power used in such literature of magick suggest a reality that is made up of pressure being applied to an absolute degree, pressure applied to a number of life−bearing situations, resistance being felt and the reactions, always the reactions of counter pressures, as well as the experience of things being pushed with violence, or more applications of force and then, of course, the other aspect of the Plutonian power.

This other aspect also suggests a row of magickally charged words of elemental power, for it is the evocation of the biting, tingling sensations of an almost electrical stimulation, from the insect−like elemental domain of the Plutonian essence, as in the following row of magickal atoms of elemental power:

The sensations of insect bites and an almost never−ending sequence of poisonous stings were overwhelming. The buzzing in my ear was deafening as the fluttering of wings came and went in endless convoy. Minute armies and airborne forces were preparing for an attack upon me, or were thusly engaged in some remote part of my occult unconscious. I felt the interior pain as I began to cough and then vomit up a bloody and brackishly sodden mucus. Somewhere I could faintly hear the mad flute player, the playing of some insane magick or Yuggothian musician, some Lovecraftian mutant playing, a triumphal hymn tothe matrices of primordial chaos.

I felt the heat rising, the sweat pouring from me like melting wax. I saw only the swift movement of vast colors, bubble-like in their geometries, flashing rapidly by me, the colors indescribable by the vapidity of merely human language. Then I realized that in some slight and probably unique way, I was experiencing orgasm.

107: When such an orgasm is experienced in concert with the elemental rays of power, we can be certain that it is of a primordial character. For this reason, the elemental roots of Plutonian Contact Work must begin with sexo-magickal operations with elemental powers. Only a magician who is grounded by means of his magickal touch, his link with the fundamental powers can generate sufficient energy for this type of orgasm. In a real sense, as this is the test of reality, the experience of orgasm within the experience of dominance may be viewed as the most elemental of magickally charged and Plutoninan experiences. For this reason, it must be viewed as the beginning of energy, or as the beginning of the real form of magickal contact. It all originates in pressure and the reactions of root powers.

The Awakening of Doctor Kammamori

Kammamori, Doctor: Gnostic Boddhisattwa of the Zothyrian Sect. Names derived from Shinto Gnosis and Esoteric Buddhism, Kam, (Jap. = divine, holy, as in Kami), Mamori (Jap. = guardian angel, spirit guide, spiritual teacher, guru). Dr. Kammamori is understood as the Lemurian and Atlantean deity of time-travel and magickal technology. He is associated with the esoteric karma of the Pacific Ocean.

When we say that there is awakening of Dr. Kammamori, we mean -- of course -- that there has been a remarkable growth in the consciousness of his existence and power, in various marmas of our planet. We also mean that his influence is being felt more by those magicians who seek to explore the esoteric worlds of being and who are particularly and deeply engaged in the gnostic sciences of archaeometry and time-travel. In a sense, it is quite impossible to participate in the lattices and rays of time-travel without a certain use of the "inventions" created over the past billion years by Dr. Kammamori.

"There exist certain lattices, which are under the direction of the Boddhisattwa Kammmori, a primary deity of the system of gnostic physics. In our extension of the primordial field of time-travel energy, and especially in our incorporation of the deities-as-rays in the unfolding of the gradations of purely initiatic physics, it is impossible to advance any procedure which does not partake of a Kammamorian influence. The many inventions, or metaphysical discoveries, which are simply transcendental exercises in esoteric logic, are projections of the creative and magickal imagination-work, which the Boddhisattwa Kammamori has emanated from his 'occult laboratory.' The purely gnostic investigator will easily come to an understanding of this because without the projections of these energy-lattices, the entire effort in metaphysical and magickal initiation, via the labyrinths of time-travel, would be impossible." -- M. Bertiaux, "Dainichi Revelations," 41

Consequently, much of modern gnostic and neo-gnostic metaphysics is based really upon the assumption of the energy system, and especially the lattices, which Dr. Kammamori has provided in his systems of immanent gnosis. That is to say, he has built into the nature of being a kind of esoteric latticework, which, while having the properties and characteristics of an almost UFO-like substance are nevertheless pathways or gnostic pathworkings, for the development and manifestation of a time-travel based school of initiatic consciousness.

Astrologically, Dr. Kammamori operates within the vectors of Scorpio and Capricorn. So that in any revival of his energy, or in any manifestation of his field of projection, the medium would be very likely to translate those energies of an archetypal character into human experience. Consequently, as we find more and more complete renewals of this Kammamorian energy, we find also emergences of this fundamental power in those who are seeking to make his presence felt marvelously and more imperatively in modern magickal developments and especially in contemporary esoteric consciousness and in the externalizations of a most unique meditation-research process. Here, I have in mind the reawakening of the influence of Dr. Kammamori in the artwork (lacquer painting) of Monsieur Hiroyuki Fukuda:

"It would be asking too much of the limited and fixed dimensions of the human brain to suppose that a breakthrough from the Alaya-Ocean would be possible without my own esoteric intervention. For that reason, I have had to project a ray of pure being and a ray of pure nothingness into your earthly mind-field membrane, in order to awaken and renew an awareness of the primordial energy of the transcendental lifestream. I have had to project those rays, which are identified with the kammamorian marma and which are united in the archetypal images of the boddhisattwa-guru, Kam-mamori, and which are taking incarnation in the productions of art-magique, as having Hiroyuki Fukuda and his creativity most suitably providing the mediumship of hiw own meditation-research. In this way, I have rejected the usual modes of communication, those dried and dusty rites of a now-otherwise consciousness, unfortunately, and have directed with both intensity and frenzy and above all in the silences of the nights of the unconscious, yes, I have directed the manifestation of the pure avatarism in that which is both pure Kammamori and pure art-gnostique, as revealed in the tensions of Hiroyuki Fukuda." -- M. Bertiaux, "Dainichi Revelations," 25

From his magickal workshop of esoteric dream-meditation, somewhere in the vast and dark Alaya-Ocean of Lemjria, Dr. Kammamori reaches outwards and seeks to serve as the vehicle for the Esoteric Buddha, by means of influencing consciousness. This consciousness is not, however, an initiatic level of being. This consciousness is rather a receptacle or vast space, into which the powers of the rays may be sent by some unspecified process of emanation. There exist on the surface of the earth-world delicately formulated and yet astonishingly articulated symbolisms, which serve as magickal mirrors and which are directing the energies of being towards a greater focus in the kammamorian mind-field.

These mirroir-images or symbolical entities, the spiritual emissions and Kami °of his esoteric deceptivity and sorcery are provided by Monsieur Fukuda not through any deception or black magick as such, but entirely as the result of his uninterrupted mediumship and the transphenomenal radiations of the transcendental id. He has given us the deception of allowing us to perceive the noumenon, while thinking we see mere appearance. For he has sought in the conflict of the black and white camellias to eventuate no mere synthesis of some ethical (or concreteness-as-problem) ontology, but rather he has sought strangely and without any earthly precedent or mentor to reveal the syzygies of that pure meontology, which serve as vehicles for the reawakening of the kammamorian rays and for the return to both esoteric logic and the initiatic metaphysics of the no-world. In so doing, he has created his own esoteric consciousness of being and school of initiation through meditation-research into the object of aesthetic contemplation.

"At that remote part of our solar system where plutonian energies and the initiations of the id are most dramatically presented continually and always anew, there exists a point of esoteric and mystical broadcasting, which directs its rays to the depths of the Alaya of Lemuria. There, in the deeply felt yet cognitively imperceptible realm of self-as-self-intuition, there exists a mediumistic receptivity for these outlandish radiations. Within that encapsulated node of pure subjectivity the fires and frenzies of libido and response are never diminished, but forever fed with the radioactive decayings of almost endless orgasms. Deep within that fire, deep within that heart of primordial lust, deep within that ever renewing chaos, I am to be found. For my energy is the blackest fire of primordial space and my body is one with the tense and almost brittle elemental of Lemuria. I become embodied in many forms and occupy many spaces. I feel and perceive the motions of the mind like waves on the surface of an otherwise deathly still ocean. I come and go, like the vaguest of guesses and yet take root at the bottom of the darkest sea. I am now awakening and I am rising up to the surface of the ego; no longer am I hid from the power of speech. Now, I am speaking and wherever I am given utterance, I will the mind—field to its fullest potential." -- M. Bertiaux, "Kammamorian Fragments," page 64

The power and presence of Dr. Kammamori will be felt increasingly in the gnostic and magickal centers of our planet. He is sending out his rays of influence and they are being received and understood by those whose minds are sensitive to the frequency of his rays, and especially the Capricornian—Scorpionic vibrations. Whether it be in the form of the most sensitive of esoteric lacquerwork or in the operations of zothyrian metapsychology, or even in the initiation sequences of occult physics, Dr. Kammamori will be there and his influence will be unmistakable.

Esoteric Logic: Transcendental Constructions of the Esoteric Imagination

"There are two formulations of the esoteric imagination. One is given at the time of descent into the body and this itself is determined strongly by Lunar and Neptunian components in the psyche and contributions to the ego. But mysteriously, there is another form of the esoteric imagination, which is used in connection with the laws of initiation and the powers of the rys. I am making reference primarily to the ideal or transcendental construction of the esoteric imagination, for inasmuch as the transcendental power of the rays of the guru must make itself felt in the structures as well as in the contents and applications of this power. It is primarily an initiatic development and therefore should not be viewed as natural or given in any way. Rather it is of a special quality, which rises magickally as the result of the imposition of primordial energy and consciousness upon the native levels of the esoteric imagination." -- M. Bertiaux, "The Secret Guidebook to Esoteric Logic," 4

Esoteric Logic is the response which the magicians of the alternative and gnostic world have made to the magickal logics of our own system of worlds. We have heard of those schools of magickal initiation which make use of the rays and the special ray-work of the initiations of esoteric logic. Now, it is significant and necessary to bring about the realization and basic introduction of these energies through the operations of the transcendental idea of the guru in the esoteric imagination of the chela.

In our system of magickal gnosis, there are two types of initiation: there is the system of initiation physics and there is the hidden system of esoteric logic. Now if we stand somewhat away from the system of the open form or philosophical idea of esoteric logic, we will be able to note that there is another system of magickal gnosis, which runs parallel to the patterns of esoteric logic. This system is an esoteric logic also, because it is concerned with the organization of structures in the system of the esoteric imagination. However, it is an initiatic system as well, since the rays from this system are being sent to the planet Earth from the inner essence of the guru as a transcendental idea.

At first, it is necessary to bring about the beginnings and the introduction of the construction of the esoteric imagination, since it is there in the world of the esoteric imagination that the initiations of these transcendentally logical patterns take place. It is important to note that the guru in all of these circumstances is the transcendental idea of both the continuum of esoteric logic as well as the process of initiation.

"In the process of estoeric initiation, which is made possible by means of esoteric logic, the guru represents the Shingon level of ideal being, or the nine perfected spaces. The chela, for his part, must represent the Shingon and Kegon level of the eight lattices, or rays from the ideal, which are both connective and continuous as regards the ideal world of pure sets. Together, the nine and the eight constitute in our system the inner sanctuary of esoteric logic, which is balanced in the outer sphere of awareness by the 17 Shinto Gods of the creative hierarchy. As the nine envelop the eight, so the 17 levels of power envelop the 16 magickal axioms of our fundamental physics. In all, there are then 17 and 16, inner and outer, which correspond perfectly to the dimensional patterns of the 33 matrices in the logical instrument of time-travel, which is based on 11 points for past, present, and future.

Thus, as one is ever deeply initiated into esoteric logic, one enters more and more deeply into the higher formularies of time-travel. These patterns of perfected and ideal being as well as the lattices, together being 17, are designated as the bhumis of the esoteric imagination since within the esoteric imagination they, and only these bhumis, are the esoteric and ideal spaces of transcendental consciousness. -- M. Bertiaux, "The Inner and Outer Sanctuaries," 3

The process of constructing the esoteric imagination and providing it with proper contents requires two stages of development. There are the eight bhumis, which are organized as the connective and constitutive initiations and there are the nine bhumis, which are the regulative ideals of the system. In each operation of this system, as in the providing of the 17 bhumis, the guru must sacrifice his essence, which is, of course, infinite in order to create the mystical space for the giving of the initiation. This, of course, is done by the guru as the result of a long process in which his consciousness must merge with that of the chela and wherein the chela is absorbed essentially into the guru. In rder to make this possible, the guru must create a field which is both ideal and real, and which is enveloped in the proper bhumi-space. This he does by sending out the rays which are most suited to the nature of his being. Naturally, this radiation will bring the chela into the experience of the essence of the guru and from there the provision of the 17 bhumis from the essence of the guru, both physically and metaphysically, is indeed possible.

The analysis of the 17 bhumis is entirely a subjective and symbolical process, inasmuch as the worlds which are referred to are entirely suggestive and mythical, since they cannot refer literally to the essence of the deepest mysticism of the guru. However, even though it is a symbolic process, the powers and the energies, which the guru must project, these are felt through the symbols by the chela, because they are radioactive.

"At the level of the collective unconscious, or the world mind, there exist certain very fundamental and even primordial energies, which can only be activiated by means of the processes of esoteric initiation. There have always existed schools for the development of these occult powers and there have always existed, either in body or as a kind of nirmanakaya embodiment, magickal and gnostic teachers or gurus, who possess the esoteric and ideal powers for the release of these archetypal energies.

"At the same time, since the guru must release the energies from the transcendental id, they must come through the guru as a kind of medium to the chela, because the guru is more closely attuned to the deep levels of the psyche than the chela and therefore is a more perfected medium. Also, as these powers come through the guru, from the transcendental and archetypal world, they can be said to belong to the guru in a very special and unique way. He possesses the powers of the collective in a very personal way. While this might appear as a contradiction in thought, it really means that the guru is the oracle for the powers of the unseen, because he has attained conscious and ideal identification with the transcendental world.

"This identification is possible by means of esoteric imagination, but it is also only possible if the guru has given himself to the unseen worlds in order to become a medium for the gods, Sacred Spirits or Kami, or Les Vudu. When that happens, the powers of the unseen work through the guru and he is their mask. Yet, in a unique and very special way, because only through his power can these gods speak to the world of the mere dimensions, the guru can be said to control the gods, for they must serve him, in the ways specified by esoteric logic, if he would let them come forth and give utterance to the soul of the people, who are seeking enlightenment from the guru or the leader." -- M. Bertiaux, "The Mediumistic Origins of Hitler's Messiahship"

The purpose of the basic course in esoteric logic is to explain how it is possible for the powers to make themselves manifest and open to the intuition of the students, and thus as extensions of the guru into the life and experience of these chelas. It is indeed a magickal process and it is a very powerful transformation of reality, since the energies which are present there in the world of initiation physics are awaiting manifestation in the acts of the guru towards the chela. Esoteric logic provides in the acts of construction of the esoteric imagination the proper field for the exploration of those patterns. This paper is written to introduce a series of 17 papers, which has to do with the explanation of the notion of the bhumis, or the magickal spaces of ideal consciousness, or the embodiments wherein initiation physics can occur.

By means of this process of transformation and by means of the opening up of the world of esoteric imagination, the esoteric imagination of the student or chela is built up by means of a special and magickal method. I have been able to find evidences of this method in such places as Japan and Haiti, but they can be found, undoubtedly, everywhere. It is a magickal process whereby the psyche of the chela is united to that higher dimension of potential which, awaiting within the mind of the chela, seeks immediate and total transformation.

The Esoteric Logicians 1: Esoteric Logic is a Process of the Transcendental Ego

The students of the Monastery of the Seven Rays were introduced to the concept of esoteric logic from the lessons and especially from the discussion of the role played by esoteric logic in the "History of Modern Zothyrian Philosophy." Those who have studied with me in the inner retreat are familiar with the idea of esoteric logic from many of the courses in gnostic metaphysics. The purpose of this paper and the one which follows is simply to discuss the ways in which esoteric logic is being explored and developed by the contemporary gnostic movement, as expressed in my teachings in magick.

"Estoeric Logic is a process of the Transcendental Ego"
The origins of esoteric logic are to be found in the regions of the transcendental ego. This process, which reveals itself chiefly in an initiatic situation, rises within the deep essence of the transcendental ego and expresses itself outwards or rather in the empirical world. It is the action of those beings, or deities, which inhabit the inner spaces of the transcendental ego of the gnostic magician. The deities which inhabit this realm are, from the standpoint of lesson materials, the same as are found in the inner structures of vudotronics and shintotronics. These beings produce the process of esoteric logic from their own essence. The process of esoteric logic then rests peacefully in the transcendental ego, until it is disturbed or awakened by some of the processes of initiation physics. By means of an appropriate process of initiation physics, the gnostic magician becomes aware of the activities of these deities and enters into communication with them. Oracles and magickal revelations are the results of this communication.

"Esoteric Logic manifests itself in Guruyoga Exercises"
Since we owe it to the process of initiation, the activation of the continuum of esoteric logic is only possible by means of placing the transcendental ego within the hyperlogical space of the guru or initiator and teacher. The result of this process is that the rays of the teacher awaken the powers of the chela's transcendental ego. Initiation is a continuum of processes, and therefore at each stage the continuum shows forth the stages or archetypes of the guru as being present in the esoteric logic of the chela. In a sense then, only the archetypal powers or deities which are present in the esoteric logic of the guru can be awakened in the chela. But this is sufficient because by implication these powers are infinite in number and possibility. The chela, however, develops within the magickal and gnostic space of the guru, until the chela is ready to become a guru. At that time, the chela does not separate himself from the guru but rather he provides the direction of his mind-field as an entailment of the chelas he now receives, while he still participates by the law of entailment within the esoteric logic of his guru. Consequently, the history of initiation physics consists in linkages of esoteric logic within the transcendenal egos of a succession or lineage of gnostic teachers. This is the esoteric aspect of the gnostic idea of "apostolic succession."

"In Esoteric Logic, the Guru is attuned to the gnostic processes of esoteric patriarchates and the history of Zothyrian Philosophy."
Within the archetypal powers of the transcendental ego, we can find a very special

and hierarchical arrangement of deities. Connecting these deities are gnostic time stations and their esoteric patriarchates as well as the contents of those patriarchates, which to my own experience are represented by the stages of the history of Zothyrian philosophy. The history of this philosphy is concerned with the development of magickal and gnostic ideas in the alternative universe, which is the universe organized according to esoteric information. This universe is in contrast to our own universe, which is organized according to exoteric information. However, because it is organized in accord with esoteric logic, the History of Zothyrian Philosophy is complete from the human viewpoint, consisting of "The History of Ancient Zothyrian Philosphy," "The History of Medieval Zothyrian Philosophy," "The History of Modern Zothyrian Philosophy" (as given in the fourth year papers of the Monastery of the Seven Rays), and "The History of Contemporary and Future Zothyrian Philosophy." Within the transcendental ego of the guru, these four levels of gnostic magick manifest themselves deep within the gradations and structures of the processes of esoteric logic. The Kami or Vudu, the Divine Spirits, are the conservators of this esoteric data.

"In Esoteric Logic, the interior essence of the field of mind is a process of time-travel, which participates in the consciousness of the guru."
The field of the mind, which is the ego and its magickal structures, is a continuum of images derived from the gnosis of time travel. The processes of esoteric logic make it possible for the gnostic magician to participate in and control all of the different forms and energy levels of the nature of time. The esoteric logicians, therefore, explore their own inner egoic fields, when they develop their explanation of time-travel. Time becomes identified with consciousness and therefore can no longer be viewed as part of the world of physical reality. Time is the underlying substance of gnostic psychology. The guru must come to the realization that the processes of time-travel are to be projected as gnostic rays into the egoic fields of the chelas. In this sense, therefore, the continuum of the gnosis becomes externalized as "the world of the senses."

"By means of the processes of Esoteric Logic, the guru comes to the realization that he is the Aeon Zothyrius (also know as AIWAZ–Zothyrius) and that the contents of the History of Zothyrian Philosophy constitute his own personal magickal history or memory."
The deeper the magician explores his own gnostic being, the more he comes to the fact of his aeonic essence. The Aeon Zothyrius, also known in his thelemic aspect or formula as AIWAZ–Zothyrius, is the archetypal image of the gnostic magician. This being is realized as the magician, by means of explorations in personal psychology, comes to see himself as a cosmic entity. Esoteric Logic makes this possible because it contains certain magickal and very powerful formulations, which govern the projections of the gnostic rays for all time. Within the context of the gnostic metaphysics, these experiments are important because of the ways in which they give concreteness to the fundamental processes of esoteric consciousness. to say they are experiments means that the formulations are experienced as direct and absolute states of intuition by the magician. It means further that the images of the gnostic reality of being, which are radiations from the magician, are actually connected by means of a network of absolute lattices to the ideal levels of being present in the pure formulations of gnostic magick, of which there are 336. These images, when united or

synthesized with the formulations, are the memories of the magician or his magickal and akashic history, as given by gnostic experience. All of these contents are stored up in the universe of Esoteric Logic, from which they are derived by means of very special initiation sequences.

"The secret level of Esoteric Logic consists of its essence and powers, which are derived by means of the rays of gnostic externalization from the acts of the interior world of guru."
There exist secret guidebooks to the worlds of esoteric logic and there exists also a very special method for the organization of these magickal energies. These sources of power are somehow identified with the essence of esoteric logic, which manifests itself in the acts of the guru in his most creative state of experience. When the guru is in such a condition, the rays from his world of inner reality pour outwards and create special states, into which the patterns of esoteric logic and gnostic physics are infused by means of certain very secret ceremonies. In a very important sense, the guru is the source of the world of esoteric logic but it is not identified with him. He is only the administrator or magickal conservator of this realm. For this reason, the names of the patriarchs of the four time–stations were also titles of power as gnostic conservators of esoteric churches of magickal logics of eight different types. The hierophant is also a conservator because he must work towards holding the gnostic system together. The system, as it is manifested in four basic "churches" or time–systems, is entirely a world of esoteric logic and esoteric energy. It operates through "logical worlds," which are universes in themselves or alternatives to the present worlds of the magicians. These universes are projection–rays from the esoteric imagination of the magician and find expressions in terms of the acts of magickal and artistic creativity, which project outwards or externalize themselves in magickal systems and in the lacquer paintings of Hiroyuki Fukuda and other gnostic artsts' creativities.

The esoteric activities of metaphysics and art, for example, are perfect realizations of the ideas of gnostic creativity. The artist is the magician and the magician is the artist. The source of this energy is in the esoteric imagination or the interior universe of the man of the gnosis. As such, a gnostic creator produces more and more works of externalization of power, the rays of the acts of the interior universe become more and more a part of the idea of the ordinary world, thereby drawing the world of ordinary perception closer and closer to the world of the ideal. In the process of initiation, whereby the guru will share the mystical secrets with the chela, the powers of this interior world are released and take on a concrete formulation, by which means the energies of esoteric logic can be given embodiment as intentional essences. It is by this means that the magician creates the actual and percevied world according to his own inner consciousness.

The students of esoteric logic will then be able to note that the ideal energies become a part of the real order; in fact, every part of the real order is a projection from the rays of the ideal order of creative and esoteric imagination. It is through the developments of esoteric logic, therefore, that consciousness regains its control over the world of the impressions and therefore asserts itself in accord with its true will. For the world of the impressions is no longer viewed as distant from the magickal structures of control and organization, rather those structures and systems of meaning now dominate and transform the world of the impressions entirely.

In the next section of this paper, I will explore the reflections which the idea of esoteric logic brings to the topics discussed in this present section. The viewpoint will focus, therefore, upon the creative and gnostic energies of the esoteric imagination as they diffuse themselves in the processes behind both artistic and magicko—metaphysical creation. It will seek to answer the questions which are raised when one seeks to understand esoteric logic in terms of its essence as energy and as acts of dynamic and creative consciousness.

The Esoteric Logicians 2: Esoteric Logic and Japanese Metaphysics

"Esoteric logic is the inner life of certain aspects of Japanese metaphysics. It is to be found among the contents and 'inhalt-Phaenomenologies' of Zen, Esoteric Buddhism, and Shinto-Gnosis. It is somehow identified with the powers of these systems to give initiations, which far more than any western systems, including even the most ancient, are real initiations. That is to say, there is achieved the realization of a transfer of real power, not just an assimilation to an ideal order, or an amplification of the archetypal contents of the transcendenal id. This power-transference is basic and it is made possible because in esoteric logic, there can only be one subject. It is also possible because in esoteric logic there isn't any objectivity. There are only the pure projections of transcendental subjectivity." -- M. Bertiaux, "Kammamorian Fragments," 2

Esoteric Logic and Zen

Fundamentally, esoteric logic and Zen are the same realization. They differ largely in outer manifestation. Both are concerned with the intuition of contents. These contents are simply one content. That is, the content of the one subject. In its primordial form, as a product of the magician's imaginiation, esoteric logic was awakened within the context of Japanese metaphysics by the interactions between German Neo-Hegelianism and Zen.

What would be tthe mechanism of understanding metaphysics-x, if you had been a Zen monk for 40 years? How would the concepts of Neo-Hegelian metaphysics be understood by a Zen monk trained in metaphysics-z? So, let us look at a magickal experiment in the mind-field. On the one side we have Neo-Hegelian system-x, and on the other there is z, or Zen. The birth of conscious-in-intuition for esoteric logic occurs at the moment of the reaction or interactionn of z to x. At that moment a new factor emerges, which possesses all of the characteristics of esoteric logic and all of the properties.

This energy is called "y." In the system of metaphysics-y, the power is Yuggothian or Plutonian because it is the pure energy of reaction. This element is important, because within Zen one cannot have intuition without reaction. The intuition of Z-intuition is the reactions against the world of descriptions and explanations. By being and by simply being, it reacts against all that is otherwise.

Likewise, Neo-Hegelian metaphysics is based upon dialectical reactions. It is built up out of conflict and "aufgehoben." Unlike Zen, which is free of internal conflicts, the metaphysics of type-x is entirely composed of internal conflicts. On the other hand, the metaphysics of z expresses conflict only on the outside. That is to say, by reaction to those elements of existence which are not of the same level of consciousness. So we have reactions which are internal and those which are external. Now in esoteric logic, the processes of reaction are both internal and external. The internal reaction is the dialectic of assimilation, while the outer reaction is that directed towards all exoteric systems of logic, even the philosophical logics of the Hegelians and the Neo-Hegelians. Hence, it is possible for esoteric logic to draw essential energy from both metaphysics-x and metaphysics-z. That is why it is metaphysics-y.

The magician would ask the question: Would esoteric logic exist elsewhere as in those more recent circumstances, where Japanese metaphysicians, with Zen backgrounds, were not trying to do mental experiments from a Neo-Hegelian background or frame of reference. What about Heidegger's ontology, or other magickal and gnostic systems? The reply would be that in such circumstances esoteric logic could be derived but that it would be derived in terms of some other of its characteristics. The gnostic element would be there, but the dialectics of reactions would have been replaced by the reactions of gnostic time.

"Do not think that Heidegger is not both a gnostic and a magician in your esoteric sense. He is also an esoteric logician, for the final outcome of his unfinished system is gnostic and magickal. Being is manifested as a continuum of energies. To understand this reality is to express the innermost type of being. It is to express gnosis of being, or, more properly, the being of gnosis. Heidegger is also a Zennist, because he has lost himself in what is magickal and overwhelming. He has lost himself in the being of meditation, or in the Zen of gnostic being. His Hegelianism and that type of magick has been replaced by immediate intuition and the intensity of initiation. 'Sein u. Zeit' is really a handbook of Esoteric Zen exercises. It is the book of hopelessness. There can be no escape." -- Ibid., 3-2

However, the purpose of magick is not to study philosophies, but to use them as machines for the purpose of generating powers. There are, for our purposes, certain passages in Heidegger which refer to the powers or four-dimensional fuels of UFOs, but for the most part, these are provided through an esoteric reading of the basic text. But in esoteric logic, it is very easy for the magician to find those "natural resources," because they are drawn out of the verbal texts by means of magickal exercises, which create machines for the derivation of power from thought-systems. In such a case, the intuition of Heidegger becomes metaphysics-x, the Zen mental development self-generates the z-metaphysics, and the dimension of reaction produces the patterns of esoteric logic, or the y-metaphysics.

However, something has happened which is quite different and radically transformative. I have in mind the work which is done within the y-metaphysics. It undergoes a process of esoteric development, in which the energies are folded back upon themselves. This process of self-envelopment allows for there to develop a magickal or gnostic passageway between the "Being and Time" dimension into the roots of esoteric logic. Esoteric logic thus begins to have an internal relation to the y-metaphysics. Can it be that they are in possession of the same basic essence? Or is it possible that they rise out of the same fundamental condition, which is the root of x, y, and z? If that were so, then there would be an internal relationship between z and y. Does such a connectiion exist?

The connection between x, y, and z is fundamentally a connection which owes its identity to the presence of y. We can say that the connection internally between z and y is the "time of intuition" or initiation consciousness. The connection between x and y is "the intuition of time." Y is both being and becoming. The magickal experiments of the y-system draw out all of the magickal entities of x and z. he existence of y is primordial, while any x and z arise from its self-awakening. When y wakes up from the unconscious, it manifests itself as both the efforts of x and z to understand what it has been. Has it been a sleeping god or has it been the reality of pure or ideal sleep?

But the experiments which produce the outer expression of y as the reaction of x and z are quite different. They are derived from the foci of the mind or the foci of intuitions in the spaces of the mind. They are therefore ways whereby human consciousness and comprehension are to come to terms with energies, which are the expression of magickal reactions between entities. For the contents of both x and z forms of metaphysics are entities. You may see them also as elementals. Consequently, the next question is whether or not these elementals are derived from the primordial condition of y or if not, what type of entities live in the primordial level of y, from which x and z are produced. Is it possible that there are other magickal beings which are quite different from the entities of x and z, at such a deep level?

The answer is that the gnostic entities of esoteric logic do exist at the primordial level of y and that these beings are of a totally different type of universe. We can classify the different entities or elementals as follows:

1. Yuggothian entities of the reaction−y world. These are beings who give the initiations of esoteric logic.

2. Metaphysical beings or entities of the x world, which are the normal type found within systems of philosophy, as mental elementals.

3. Zen beings from the z world. These beings are intuitive and intuited as found within the field of various Zen meditation worlds.

4. The primordial level of being in world y is inhabited by gnostic entities which are identified with the field of esoteric logic in its foundations.

These types of beings, which are to be found within the context of gnostic magick, are not to be understood as found outside of that type of magick. Each magickal context has its own forms of being and each form of being is unique. However, these four types of being do perform the functions of many other types of magickal entity. They are not, however, to be viewed as available in those systems, which are outside of the UFO of the relationship between esoteric logic and Japanese metaphysics. In the Zen experience, these levels of being are not widely understood as given to those engaged deeply in Zen meditation. However, beyond the maya of that experience, there is the maya of the gnostic magician and the maya of the esoteric logician which, together, I have found make the maya of the Zen experience quite possible.

This is only a suggestion and an exercise in the relationship of esoteric logic to Zen. I next would like to explore the relationship between esoteric logic and the magickal and metaphysical world of Shingon or Esoteric Buddhism. This is the school of tantric magick. Then it is my intention to offer some suggestions for exploration on the relationship between esoteric logic and the inner life of Japanese consciousness, which may be understood as the Shinto Gnosis.

The Artist as Magician and the Artist as Deity: The Work of Hiroyuki Fukuda

Monsieur Hiroyuka Fukuda, born in 1942 in Yokohama, Japan, is known for his work in lacquer and for the esoteric themes of these lacquerworks.

"L'Ame-Oiseau et les Ombres du Soi"
Reality is the projection of an ideal consciousness and once it is perceived and understood that the ideal is a sentient and elemental experience, we will find ourselves inside of the world and not outside looking in from an artificial and not-too-clearly-defined distance. Such a real world is a construction by the artist as both magician and as deity (Kama), from the basic components of his consciousness and from the sentient and emotional imaginations of his dreams and diffused personalities. The more complex the world view, the more the deity-aspect of the artist has come into manifestatiion, for the Kami (Gods of Shinto) accumulate their psychic energies in a multiplicity of "mind-levels"; but that the artist has dared to summon from the depths of his being the creative hierarchy of the Gods suggests his beginning as a magician, for all invocations are those of his own world, which alone in art can be understood as real.

It is precisely this esoteric methodology which characterizes the lacquerworks of Mons. Fukuda, for not only does he create (as do all artist to some degree), but by being both magician and deity in the act of artistic creation, he has projected outwards into public space not just a picture or image of some idea or interpretation of reality and he has constructed reality from the raw materials of his own universe, which is to say that he has provided us within the context of art with another and an alternative universe, more viable than the life-spaces of those onlooking outsiders who are outside of the field of mind. Monsieur Fukuda has provided to the consciousness of those who approach his work as an opportunity to escape into another world from they need never return.

To say that the symbolist of the camellias is an idealist is to oversimplify the world by a mawkish reduction to commonplace jargon and aesthetic pigeonholing. Nevertheless, it must be admitted that crude realism has been transcended as a moral problem and that what unveils itself to the eye is an ethical perception of being manifested however as the subjects of ordinary experience but suggestive all the while of deeper and more subtle potencies for good and for evil. But, for good or ill, truth or reality, there can never be any escape from the tensions of the fundamental questions which are as ancient and as fragmentary as the eternal conflict between the powers of light and those of primordial darkness.

For Monsieur Fukuda has affinities with esoteric Manicheanism via the dark and misty spirit-passageways of the Shinto gnosis wherein it is understood that being is at least a complexity of energies, some constructive and thusly constructing the real world as a projection of ideal consciousness while the others are vaguely distant and shadowlike, filled with the intensity of some potency for evil and therefore destructive of, paradoxically, an alternative perception of reality. For it is the artist who now commands us as a God to be obedient to his world and his laws for the world of experience and it is that same Deity who has cast into some Avichi of hellish spaces all other possibilities of understanding and all other religions of art.

"Les Reveries Muettes et les Reves Ideals"
Armed with his magickal weapon, that dark and sinister mirroir magique of Esoteric
Shinto, this Kami from the Moon in Scorpio provokes our consciousness to surrender or
be destroyed utterly, in particles of Mahayana Analysis not even to be reborn
somewhere in the Ocean-Alaya of Hosso Nara. The wild energy of fanaticism cannot be
calmed by metaphysical discourses, for it rests hidden beneath the black camellias,
ever seeking to seize the souls of the unwary and consume then in the frenzies of
elemental blindness. No, Monsiuer Fukuda does not hide from us the raw evil which is
everywhere present as beauty in the world of illusions; rather, he forces us to come
too close to it some might fear and he forces us to touch it, uncertain that we can
ever draw back our hand.

The tensions of this reality are not to be hidden but rather the magician should
command them to leap out at his soul and snatch it from the air if it flies too close
to the powers of radical evil or if it hovers most delicately and (I might suggest)
uncertainly too close to the spheres of danger and the void of the Manichean
Baudelaire. For Monsieur Fukuda seeks to project us nearer and nearer to the state of
terror while at the same time, as a magician he seeks to hide from our conscious
mind-field the mysteries of evil and those hidden cults of the shadow, which drum on
and on monotonously in the brains of those humans awash with platitudes and catch-
phrases. As a God of vengeance he seeks to destroy such a world but as a magician he
seeks to hide it curiously from the ego, allowing such overly sweet perfumes of the
Kliphoth to rise from hidden corners and strange angles of existence both out of
sight and out of the waking mind.

Part I. "The Artist as Kami"
In some distant and veiled time, at some remote period of heavenly manifestation,
within some celestial realmm, the artist as Kami is born eternally from the Plain of
Heaven. He is:
". . . a Shinto God because all of the artists are divine beings. Only they, it
seems, have been able to transcend the limits of existence and allow themselves to
perceive the Laws of Ideal Destiny. They are the Gods, or Kami, because all of
reality is perceived by them as their domain. The artist has special powers however
over all of the other Kami, for He must see the possible or the ideal and allow for
its manifestation as the actual." -- M. Bertiaux, "Esoteric Shinto Studies," No. 32
The first person to describe the art of Monsieur Fukuda was the ancient
theologian revelator Mani who, having made use of the languages of Neo-Zoroastrianism
and Platonism in order to clothe the ideas of his metaphysics sought by argued
propsition to create a new world view and system of salvation, known to us as a
species of Gnosis. In order to accomplish this synthesis, Mani appears to have
projected his consciousness into the artwork of Monsieur Fukuda and as if by system
commenced a thorough description of these different worlds and realms of being annd
becoming. Manimaintained that he was simply describing the Universe as it had been
revealed to him. But, we might ask, by what Kami was it revealed?
"According to the Laws of Esoteric Shinto, the ultimate design for the Universe
as a balance of fragmentary forces is owed to the Divine Artists, those Kami who
create the images of various possibles in the minds of the Gods and who thereby
assist in the selection of that which is the best of all possible worlds. These
artistic Kami are present in the minds of the artists of the Earth as archetypal
ideas and images but they are also able to incarnate fully in the artists, when those

artists are no longer themselves, as for example when the artist is a genius and is creating in a state of ultimate inspiration. Consequently, it is impossible for the artist not to be a Kami, if what he is creating is a world which is true because it is really the ultimately and most essentially complete identify–nature of being, not something about the ultimate but that very ultimate state of consciousness which is the store–existence of being itself and for itself." –– Ibid.

In the dreamy space of his studio, a space constructed by the lesser deities of both work and dreaming, the artist is an actualizing deity who must create the universe immediately after it has been destroyed by the magicians. The conflict between gods and magicians again is represented by the two orders of camellias, the black and the white, except that Monsieur Fukuda does not say explicitly which of the camellias are the images of the gods, for such would be to introduce an element of certainty into the conflict and he does not wish the nature of being to be so determined.

"The impact upon Japanese cultural systems by Hegelian and Neo–Hegelian metaphysics was both exoteric as well as more subtle. In a very mystical and almost uncertain way, the dialectical idealism of being became symbolic of the esoteric structure of innermost being, so that in both Hosso and Zen, as well as in the more magickally imaginative forms of Shinto, the esoteric law of conflict was felt below the threshold of consciousness. But this conflict could only be articulated as a form of power in subtle lacquerwork, because only in such a form of lacquerwork does the artist possess a foothold in another realm –– the realm of the dialectical imagination or the ontic sphere of the Gnostic Noeticians and Intentional Logicians –– which is the world of the artist as deity, as well as the world of the artist as metaphysician of moral consciousness." –– M. Bertiaux, "From Occult Hegelianism to Esoteric Shinto: The Dream states of Kitaro Nishida," Frag. 3

And so the genius of the artist is reflected in the ideal personification of his cosmic imagination, which is the imagination of his selfhood as a cosmic deity.

"In the esoteric dreams of metaphysics, the masters of that discipline seek to approximate more and more closely to the primordial consciousness of cosmic deities. But aside from metaphysics, the artist also possesses this dramatization of psychic images, through which he must focus upon the intuition of his own mind–field. It is no longer sufficient to say that he is to reproduce a reality abstract or concrete in some form, that is no longer very meaningful. Now, he must state that he is to produce reality in the act of self–intuition, for only by means of the concreteness and universality of self–intuition is it possible for the artist to become himself and thus perceive reality as it really is, the body of his own selfhood extended into ideal space. Thus, those monks who spoke of the world of manifestation as the body of a certain Divine Buddha were in truth and by reason of a very subtle and esoteric dialectic, they were speaking of the artist in the process of being his divine self or Kami–Essence." –– Ibid.

Part II. The Artist as Magician
""La Transcendence des Envoutements" et "Vers le Bon"
If the purpse of the artist as Kami is the no–purpose of pure creation, then the purpose of the artist as magician is the transformation of being. Because he is a Plutonian, Monsieur Fukuda is a master of transformation whereby whatever is becomes what it must be. Again, we must not confuse this activity or process with the changing of any viewpoints or perspectives. In reality, there isn't any viewpoint,

there is only the continuum of viewing or the universe of seeing, which is the universe as seen.

"In order to transform it is also necessary to destroy and recreate anew and instantaneously -- as if by magick. Thus, in each of his works and in each part of his works -- as if fragments were cut off from each work and seen as entire universes -- the world is destroyed by the fire of will and recreated by that same fire. That is the fire and that is the activity of Pluto. It is invisible and magickally selective for it does not attempt to understand anything, it seeks only to present radically what is there as pure being. It seeks only to show that being is obvious and inescapable, concealing none of its tensions and its powers, in whatever mode they are expressed, and revealing the ways in which the field of being or universe of existence shows itself. For it will show itself like some fantastic and ufological creature shows itself both as also inescapable and more than merely obvious." -- M. Bertiaux, "Gnozis: Existenz and Shinto," 5

The Plutonian fire of Monsieur Fukuda is interesting because he is not consciously trying to present reality or project some kind of conviction. Rather, he has become the vehicle for those occult energies which come through his conscious mind from deeper regions or rather which most would say are the radiations of his animalistic perception of the order of nature, a view which atavistically he can experience whenever he enters into the erotic tensions of good and evil.

"The Kami as artist sees the field of existence as it really is. In doing this and in the deepening of the perception of his own fault or collapse of being, he allows the semi-sembliant levels of undifferentiated eroticism to flood the canvas with their terrors and their beauties. He allows these distortions of reality to assemble themselves as accumulations of evil amid a sinister beauty, carefully spaced by the deterioration of the interior senses, a distortion made all the more candid and facile by the productions of the deepest negativity and sentient viciousness." -- Ibid.

For in its viciousness and otherness we perceive the secret of Monsieur Fukuda and we are entrapped by his magickal webs of deception, finding ourselves as captives of his imagination and its esoteric viciousness which now seeks to distort us and transform us by fragmentary patterns of initiation into a kind of fire-substance, from which we are again created and destroyed serially. If there is any escape from this madman, this destroyer of all sensitivity, who destroys our senses by his own overstimulation and radioactivity, it must be found in the calm of the white camellias, which pose as doorways of mystical escape from the horrors of the black magician, the artist sorceror of the black camellias. But where do these doorways and spirit passageways lead us, except:

". . . into a very strange realm of alternative consciousness. We find ourselves drugged and intoxicated by erotic perfumes which pour up from the shadow worlds of kliphotic imagination and which must manifest themselves as neither escape nor as freedom but as dark and demonic halls of tortured selfhood, wherein life and death and endless rebirth are rejected and simultaneously affirmed because of the need of the elemental worlds to possess an endless food supply." -- M. Bertiaux, "Perfumes and Magick," 2

In such a world, Monsieur Fukuda seeks to feed us to his magickal camellias because only in such a world do these black and white camellias have such a threatening substance. All else is relative to their being and their consciousness, which he has tuned to a fine point by means of rare forms of shading and rarer forms of Plutonian music.

"The eroticism of Monsieur Fukuda's lacquerwork must be understood as totally given and yet totally hidden. The aspects of its being which reflect the beauty of chaos disturb the libido and suggest the endlessness of the continuum of the Meon; but the destructive aspects of the Mother Goddess of Yuggoth (for Monsieur Fukuda is both a Plutonian and a Shintoist) do not have any direct or pragmatic purpose, or relationship to the saner vistas of the otherwise normal mind-field. The destructiveness of the black camellias and the shadows of the kliphotic perfumes are simply given because there is nothing else for them to be. In this sense then, evil is a manifestation of deity, not some aspect of privation. True gnosis is affirmed, when Monsieur Fukuda says that perhaps we will find in the camellias that evil is being and that being is evil; but also, and with an equal and opposite reality, so is the good, for the law of the Meon, expressed as the white camellias, is equally given as being and becoming." -- M. Bertiaux, "La Connection Nipponoise: L'Art Magique et la Magie de Monsieur Hiroyuki Fukuda," 3

For this reason, or because this happens in a distinct pattern, the world is created and destroyed by fire continuously and neverendingly. And amid all of these tensions, there is the tension of the magician because Monsieur Fukuda does not wish to free himself from these transformative entanglements. Indeed, he cannot free himself since he has been made captive and possessed by them and in this ceaseless flow of experience, They have projected the artist as magician and Monsieur Fukuda has become the ego for the powers of darkness and light in their eternal conflict.

Eros and Meon: Hiroyuki Fukuda

Art is the eros of the Meon, for it is the creative impulse by which means the erotic dimension of being, that is to say the most fundamental, expresses and serves as a mode of magickal expression for the Meon, or the transcendental condition beyond all being. Hiroyuki Fukuda as artist is the medium of this process of expression and his art is an erotic meonotology; for he has moved back and forth in each form and work of art, by means of a specific and divine instinct, while transcending both being and nothingness.

To say that art is the eros of nothingness, or the pure space of the void, is simply to say that while ultimate reality is sexual energy, it is necessary for this endless ocean of cosmic libido to find expression in a precise and exacting mode of appearance, as in the accurate and fine line of projected imagination. This mode of expressed appearance, we find in the esoteric within-ness of art as lacquerwork. In such an operative process, the artist is both sorceror and deity.

The invasion of waking consciousness (jagrat) by the dream images in the ideal spaces of their own unreality (svapna) implies immediately the ultimate unreality, the meonic and incomprehensible ocean of nothingness, which nevertheless manifests itself as a primordial lust and the ocean of nothingness is seen for the first time as the ultimate depth, or the neverending container of naight (sushupti). Yet, from the manifold of archaic and animalistic strangenesses, there rises to the surface a dynamic and sensuous lust, which because it draws its powers from the depths of the meonic unconscious, must express itself as the passionate self-destruction of the artist in each work of art as an act of both self-love and self-annihilation through the intuition of the artist as the medium of the Gods of primodrial nothingness.

For in the Kojiki and Nihongi (the earliest writings of the Shinto Religion), the artist Deities of the naught of space must act mediums for the outpouring of the illusions of being, from the deep and dreamless sleep of the ideal and original chaos. And through the space-worlds of the purest and most idealistic of lacquerwork, Monsieur Fukuda is their daemon-manifesting emulator. For in his world of imagination, he has allowed the primordial lust of his art to rival the very Gods of Heaven.

In some strange and erotic dimension, there exists a pool of energies from the transcendental id. There, in that galaxy of lust and passion amid all the wonderful and occult powers, dwell the Kami of Imagination, adored by that enveloping film of esoteric and artistic consciousness, which surrounds the inner side — as a mysterious lining — of the psychic membrane of our planet. There, too, dwell those magickal beings which Monsieur Fukuda has sent from his soul as special emissaries of a creative and chaotic mind-stuff which escapes all description save when it manifests within the esoteric and spatial confinements of his unearthly lacquerwork. Sent out from the divine and disintegrating sentience of the "holy sickness," which afflicts all artists of genius, these ambassadors from the Court of the Meon have come to establish a kind of psychic link with the Kami of Imagination, wherebv the world of the mirroir-pure medium of lacquerwork becomes a projection and extension of the deeper levels of a fading being, that is being before it becomes nothingness, in the world of sensations and solid objects.

By means of his act of creation, the artist who is seeking ever more and more to enter into contact with his soul brings out before the eyes of those who look with physical vision the world as it appears from the standpoint of another vision. It is the vision of the Gods of Imagination, who are in themselves vehicles of the Meonic delirium and who are in themselves the existential madness from which no escape is possible.

In that silent world of thoughts forever in confusion, there can be no peace, there be no self-intuition or even sense of wholeness; for the powers of the transcendental id in their zeal for a mastery of all that is have locked up the world of superficiality, excluding it from the realm of being in process of becoming nothing, while at the same time allowing the floods of Meonic energy to come in and possess and obsess every speck and moment of being remaining. What a strange and fateful world we are perceiving as we look at everything, supposing it to be ordinary, not knowing what is lurking in the next beyond. In truth, we are deceiving ourselves continually and happily.

But this Japanese sorceror will not let this happen. He will not let us rest in peace for there is no peace within the tortured meanderings of his black magick, which surfaces here and there with and under the disarming pretext of being a mild form of artistic experiment. Yet, he does not want us to rest but rather would have us experience a kind of "analysis burn," as through gazing upon his lacquerworks, the deepest levels of the psyche are churned feverishly.

It is indeed possible to avoid such encounters with the untamed powers of the transcendental id, but such is always a risky venture. It is possible indeed to live a completely rational and therefore dull life, without ever encountering the bewitchments of this sorceror, Monsieur Fukuda. It is likewise possible to go through one's entire life without any experience or even unconscious desire to encounter the obsessive lunar spaces of those sorceries immanent in his lacquerworks; but is such a life really a form of existence? Yet, there are more persons in the world-as-objects, who prefer such a level of the existence to the direct and upsetting encounters and threats which arise from contemplation of those lacquerworks. For he has given us a choice, amid all of the raw possibilities of valuation and life-style and he has asked us whether or not it is for-us-in-the-world to be the victims of these magickal experiments. He asks us outright: do we wish to disturb our own levels of nonbeing by a direct encounter with the most intense nothingness of existence? He wants to know if we wish to experience the ultimate or be content with the contemporary validities and labyrinths of shallowness.

Of course, the "correct answer," existing somewhere in an ocean of "correct answers," is to agree to his wishes and to surrender to his bewitchments and artistic enchantments, seeing beyond what is there, beyond what is given to the sense, beyond the apparent and the obvious to the physical eye. He commands us by some unique spell to see vast oceans of primordial chaos, which seek the attention of the human spirit and which pose seductively as forms of beauty and which live as those camellias which you should gaze upon with both longing and wistfulness. But as soon as you assume such an attitude, you have crossed the frontiers between being and nothingness, between the real world and some ideal realm and you have moved beyond the perfection of phenomena to the world of the noumenon and to those Meonic tensions of existence, which exist as a kind of dynamic and lucid vacuum, drawing more and more inward, until having lost all sense of direction and having forsaken the desire to escape to the "real world," you begin to merge ever so slowly with the quicksand of a primordial drawing inwards.

For you as a subject, pure consciousness loses itself and its selfhood in the whirlpool-like intuition of those Meonic energies, which rise to the surface as if now freed of all constraints, while the nothingness that surrounds all reality comes rushing furiously and violently at you. You have been stripped naked of all of the modes of protection, which the ontologies of culture and society have given you as protective screens and schematisms whereby to arrange experience. Now, you face the ultimate transcendence and you are overwhelmed by it. You should be utterly destroyed by it; at least, in the world of being-in-the-world, we would suppose so. Something appears to have happened and it manifests its darksome and vague presence in a way so that we can only understand and address it as a kind of transformation by escape; for by escaping from being you have become transformed into that Meonic power of consciousness, which is the next stage of experience-consciousness or the next stage of nothingness. Be patient and quiet while it tells you its esoteric history.

The creative impulse that is identified with the cosmological and the creative artist is in fact engaged in a process of cosmogony. He is seeking to bring about a parallel law of activity, parallel with the creative and divine energies of the cosmos. He is seeking to realize himself as primordial Kami. Everything that happens in his mind is an outpouring of divine energy, of which we can distinguish two forms: there is the erotic manifestation of energy as well as the manifestation of erotic energy in the act of creation. This is the first moment of creative consciousness and transcendental power. The next moment of truth-as-transcendental consciousness is quite simply the drawing out of the powers of nonbeing, which are found at the root of existence.

This nothingness or Meon is the creative source of all art and of all being-as-art. It is suggested by -- but not really identified with -- the deepest levels of the racial psyche, known as the transcendental unconscious. Whether or not it is the goal of the process is unimportant since both art and Shinto cosmology are concerned with the principles of beginnings. The energies, which are properly called "Meonic" are the ultimate causes of what happens. Since all of being consists in the manifestations of various levels and hierarchies of beings,

". . . it is important to see the ultimate cause as an absolute transcendence, or a Satori of origins. From this world or condition, which is not to be thought of as a condition of being, and which must be described in contradictory language, there come forth the Creative Hierarchies of the Gods. This nothingness or Meon is an absolute. It comes closest to human experience in the deepest levels of the transcendental id, or in pure and undifferentiated sushupti. The artist appears to be both mystic and medium, in addition to sorceror, because he views his consciousness as a cosmos and so he sees his unconscious, especially its deepest aspects, as his own personal 'Meon.' It seems that in the creative process, the 'Meon' provides fuel for the erotic and creative powers, which manifest themselves as the top of reality or at the threshold of consciousness.

"The erotic impulse in any artist of the esoteric type, but especially in Monsieur Fukuda, is fed occult powers by the Meon, and of course, it is the Meon which pushes to the surface of being and exhibits itself in countless artistic expressions. The artist is a mystic about this because he sees directly into the divine sphere by means of his own introspection and self-intuition. He is a medium because he allows the creative aspects of nothingness to rise to the surface through the painting and impulse of his intense sexuality. He is a sorceror because he seeks to bring the experience of his viewers closer to ultimate reality and away from the mundane sphere of perception. And in doing all of these things and while functioning at all of these levels, he –– especially if he is Monsieur Fukuda –– manifests a kind of 'divine sickness," because he can no longer participate in ordinary human life or experience, rather he can only be at home with the Gods; for he has become one, too." –– M. Bertiaux, "Monsieur Fukuda's System of Shinto and Gnosis," 21

In some strange state of consciousness and in some innermost aspect of awareness, where all things are known by the power of an all–pervading self–intuition, there exists a certain point of experience. It is the art world of Monsieur Fukuda, expressing itself as a complete and alien universe, the alternative to the world of boredom. There, within the deeply mysterious rivers and streams of a very pure energy, we find the key to man's thirst for selfhood. There, if you would only drink deeply and pause long enough, you would experience peace and refreshment. For you would be a participant in the religion of art, as expressed in the gnostic symbols and esoteric mysteries of the deepest regions of the psyche, by the high priest and grand sorceror, Hiroyuki Fukuda.

Esoteric and Gnostic Energies: The Foundations of the Ray-Energies

"The energies and rays with which the gnostic magicians and esoteric logicians must work, are entirely initiatic. They are hidden in the secrets of the consciousness of the masters of consciousness. They are hidden, truly, in the precise and secret spaces of the Alaya of initiation, which is a gnostic world or, better, it is a kind of deep labyrinth within the transcendental id of the master of gnostic magick. In such a world of fascination, these energies are stored and conserved for those who wish to become adepts of these powers." -- M. Bertiaux, "Dainichi Revelations," 33, 25

When the magicians work with energies, they usually will work with them directly and in a kind of raw or unrefined state. For us, there is the need to use conceptual refinements in order to handle the energies. We have to wrap the concepts around the rays or the energies and make them manageable. But for the true adepts, there is not any need to use concepts. They handle the energies and the esoteric rays in a very direct and immediate way. One learns to work with these energies in a specific and direct way as the result of esoteric initiation. Esoteric initiation is, however, only available through the secret masters. No one else has that kind of power. In the true process of estoeric transformation, which is what happens when initiation occurs, we find that the master must rebuild the bodies of the candidate, so that the candidate can actually become strong enough to handle the energies. This can only be done by giving to the candidate or student a certain portion of the radioactivity of the true master. When this happens, the candidate can work more and more alongside of the master and learn how to handle the rays and the esoteric energies, without being hurt or even destroyed by gnostic powers.

Now, each master possesses a secret world in his transcendental id, where the powers are stored. The magickal radioactivity from that id-space is what the master will project in the direction of the candidate at the time of initiation. Otherwise, the energy-level of the candidate remains always low. The masters, and this has been their practice for centuries, have been drawing on this energy, which is endless, and sending it out into the psychic atmosphere of the world for a variety of magickal and spiritual purposes. They keep this power deep within their souls and then at a very special time, they release it into the magickal and psychic atmosphere. It is the transcendental power of the guru, the true essence of his envelopment of the chela in magick, which makes the revelation of life within the continuum of gnostic consciousness a fact for the very special initiates.

Let me explain this more fully: When I began my special studies of initiatic energies, I was taken by the Master zothyrius and the esoteric teacher Dr. Kammamori into the special field of their energies. It was there that I was rebuilt into a new kind of man, or magickal mutant. I underwent total transformation of my being and a heightening of the rays of my own already potentized aura. It was necessary for me to pass through all of the mysteries and esoteric levels of consciousness, which are contained in the innermost sanctuary of consciousness. The reason for this was very simple: deeply placed in that level of consciousness existed my own transcendental powers, which were released by the methods of gnosis and techniques of magick used by these adepts. Then when I became an initiate of these mysteries, my soul became one with that of the Master Z and Dr. K. As the Esoteric Buddha Dainichi has revealed:

"There is only one mind. That everybody repeats and chants as if it were the most powerful of mantrams. But what does it mean unless you are an initiate of my mysteries? Unless you are inside of me, the one mind law cannot be realized within you. For my mind must be within you, if you are within me. There is a procedure in the process of consciousness, which is known as ideal realization. It has been revealed in a number of contexts, such as gnostic physics. What it means here, in the field of esoteric consciousness, is that by means of the releasing of magickal and metaphysical energies, the initiate finds the one mind of the Master within himself. He has cleared away the materials which have been blocking the view and has seen for himself the way of being, deep within his essence.

"It can then be said that he has achieved being and power and has ideally realized the one mind as his true self. It is ideal because it is the ultimate as well as part of the contents of my mind and it is realized because it becomes an image in the lifestream, and when it is an image in the lifestream it is a vehicle of the rays of all that truly can be said to exist. But this is entirely a process of initiation. It is not something you happen upon by chance. It can only come to you as the result of your connection with the ideal level of existence, as that world is expressed through the masters and teachers of the esoteric and gnostic energies. The initiate will then find himself deeply placed within the mind of the master, which is within my mind. This is the actualization of the one mind, for I am immanent in the mind of the initiate as the ideal, then and therefore, fully realized by the opening up of the transcendental world of the gnostic continuum." -- Ibid.

These initiatic energies are very important for an understanding of the order of the energies of nature. Let me say that in view of what has been revealed by the Esoteric Buddha, all of nature is a process of initiatic energies. There is not any form of being which is outside of the initiation process. The older dualism between nature and esoteric initiation does not exist.

Not only does that older dualism not exist, but none of the dualism of conscious mind can exist for the initiate of this system. In the words of the Esoteric Buddha:

"By the very simple process of induction into our system, we come to realize that the basic order of the one mind is all pervasive. There is only one mind and there is only one will. That will is embodied in the hierarchy of adept energies. There is only one emotion. That is embodied in the radiation processes of cosmic chaos. All of these are aspects of the primordial order of being, which manifests itself as self-intuition, when the initiate comes to terms with the ocean of being. The student will therefore come to realize that all of being is interlocked and immanent, within the context of the gnostic continuum. However, this law is not even suspected by outsiders." -- Ibid.

Because there does not exist any dualism for the initiate, the energies can and will manifest themselves as radiations of his will. They will appear as transactions between himself and some other part of his being. The universe is seen as the immediacy of his own personal experience. When this stage of being is reached, he understands that the laws of being are so organized that they are laws of his own personal psychology. This stage of initiation, however, carries with it the responsibility of seeing and carrying the realities within the psyche as they are: they are truly parts of one's being. Hence, in the development of magickal energies and occult exercises, the way we view the universe is very much determined by our level of initiation and our sensitivity to the operations of energies within our ideal world of reality.

474

However, we must come to terms with certain parts of our being, which only emerge when we have reached this stage of initiation. I am referring to the emergency of the experience and awareness of the Meonic. The world of meontology draws closer and closer to the initiate. This is why many prefer not to advance in the continuum, for they are aware of the presence and the energies of meontology and they fear this world. Again for the initiate, the role of the adepts and gurus is essential. For the adepts and gurus of the gnostic consciousness are able to guide the initiate in his transactions with the world of meontology. However, this guiding and directing is not as one would expect. For the initiate will be guided and directed right into the midst of the meontological field of energies. He will be placed in the midst of being perishing into nothingness. But the meontological energies are primary categories of energy within the gnostic understanding of esoteric logic. They surface only under certain ideal conditions when and where the initiated placed for encounter initially experiences them.

Exercises

"What is power? Power is what makes favorable events to happen. Indeed, it is power which is behind the concept of synchronicity in some way; although synchronicity is also an energy of a cosmic order. The bringing into one's experience of the events of synchronicity is, however, entirely due to the gnostic rays and esoteric energies of the masters." -- M. Bertiaux, "Dainichi Exercises in Metaphysics," 8

Exercise: Please write an explanation of what is meant by the above teaching.

"The ray-energies of esoteric gnosis are located within the transcendental id. They are arranged in a specific pattern and are nam..d energies: A, B, C, D, etc. While the number of the energies is carefully defined and thus specific, it must be noted that the nature of these rays and energies is literally without any rate or special limit. Also, these energies and rays are organized in a kind of magickal system or arrangement. In our own system, there are 336 of these rays, with which we normally work. There are many, many more outside of my system; but in the functional operations of my own system of esoteric logic, I have found it profitable to make use of the 336 specific energies. Most of the initiation and operations of my own gnostic system can be traced to the activities of these energies." -- M. Bertiaux, "Esoteric Commentary on the 'Dainichi Exercises in Metaphysics'," 8-1

Exercise 1. Please write an exoteric explanation of the above teachings.

Exercise 2. Please write an esoteric explanation of the above teachings.

Exercise 3. Please construct a magickal map-working or mandala to explain both the exoteric working and the esoteric working of the above teaching.

Exercise 4. List at least ten possible types of initiation in connection with the above teaching. Five should be exoteric, five esoteric.

Exercise 5. Provide by means of automatic writing an esoteric commentary of your own on the teaching given in the "Dainichi Exerecises in Metaphysics."

Please mail your report and exercise to the author.

Questions and Answers on the Gnosis of Spiritual Attunement and Angelic Energy

Q: You have stated that by means of the photograph of the student you can determine the field of his spiritual energy. Does this mean that you use an esoteric method of diagnosis of spiritual attunement in order to select those for initiation?

A: Yes. For one thing, we have ways of determining the energy level of any being, from the radiations and emanations of the object or its photo. This has been proven from radionic physics. Next, by application to the field of spiritual direction, we must view the auric field of the student as indicating exactly his potential for growth, which I might add is based upon progress in past lifetimes and also the types of angelic energy which is now in his possession.

Q: Does spiritual attunement then mean not so much awareness but also potential for development and also the condition of the soul in terms of its actual state of angelic energy?

A: Yes. Attunement means what is the situation of the soul of the student. It does not have reference, at least in my system, to just awareness or understanding, which are subjective and/or psychological states. I am concerned with the objective or metaphysical state of the soul. This we know can be measured in very precise ways.

Q: These methods of measurement of the soul, were they taught to you or discovered by an inner method as the result of your own work as a gnostic patriarch of esoteric research?

A: Yes. That position does bring with it many higher forms of the gnostic consciousness, but because it is a patriarchal position, it means that these powers are to be used in the role of being a spiritual father to the circle or group of esoteric initiates of the light. In this way, we have to understand energies as being applicable to the spiritual condition of the soul. Therefore, these ways of helping the unfoldment of the soul are special gnostic powers, which come with a special and very specific type of consecration.

Q: Does attunement make use of both gnostic unfoldment and esoteric communion?

A: I think that it must. First of all, the student must be made aware of the inner reality of his being. He must be shown the gnostic realities and devic or angelic energies within his soul. Then he must be allowed to develop an inner sense of spiritual communion and dialogue with these esoteric realities, which is only possible by means of careful direction from his gnostic father. Together, if these principles are followed accurately, these two modes of the inner pathway will bring about spiritual attunement, as the goal of the pure gnosis of the light.

Q: Do you recognize the presence of angelic energies within the soul of all beings?

A: Yes we do, since that is a fact of concrete existence. However, this does not mean that all of these beings are ready for spiritual attunement to the gnostic awakening. But to the few that are ready, we must bring the possibility of spiritual enlightenment and true freedom from the limits of the world of illusions and disappointments. Our mission in the inner circle of the gnostic church is really to develop and perfect those in need of this higher experience. It is a pathway of light, which only a teacher can communicate to the student of the gnosis. It is the

476

inner pathway of initiation. I might add that initiation makes it possible for the student to work directly with the spiritual energies from the angelic and invisible worlds around us.

Q: Are you in attunement with these angelic beings?
A: For this type of work one must be, because the energy must be contacted and worked with consciously.

Q: If we understand it correctly, when you speak of the "Esoteric Communion," you mean a map of the soul, wherein the various spiritual energies and angelic presences are located in a symbolic sense and where communication with the spiritual world is possible by means of both oracles and clairvoyant research?
A: Yes, except that it is much more than a map. Actually, it is the essence of the soul and when we talk about it we say it is a "map," but really it is the way in which our system of gnostic metaphysics works with the actual soul. A map would be a picture of this. All of the energies which are represented therein are there in an objective or cosmological sense.

Q: Would this esoteric communion then be something like an inner or personal pleroma?
A: Actually, it is the inner pleroma. The outer pleroma, which is common to all being, we can say would be the world of archetypes, but the esoteric communion is the way in which these archetypes work in the inner dimensions of the soul. They form certain patterns, which are the ectypes and even dynatypes of the esoteric consciousness.

Q: But they should not be confused with archetypes in the more general sense, is that what you are saying?
A: Yes, because such archetypes in the general sense govern the ordinary functions of life and human existence. But the esoteric communion is really concerned more with the inner and spiritual or gnostic potentials of the student of the light. Hence, they are the subject of initiation physics and cosmology rather than psychology.

Q: Do you teach then that there is a kind of inner cosmology, which is more gnostic than the processes of psychological analysis?
A: Much that is in psychology is common to many human beings. We are concerned with the inner space and time of the soul, which are cosmological categories, and which generate the essence of spiritual uniqueness or this-ness. The inner pleroma would be esoteric space, while the deeply esoteric chronology of past and future lifetimes would be esoteric time. These are, in our view of the gnosis, the important categories of esoteric cosmology. That is why we use the language of special theology and inner cosmology, so as to orient our students more easily to the gnostic point of view, which we are teaching.

Q: If we look at the map of the soul, we find certain units so to speak; would these spaces be also structured in a time-line pattern as well?
A: Yes. The structure of each component of the soul does involve its own time and place and we have found that the times are often very different. It seems that together we have from all of the space of the soul, the entire pattern of history, but each one is highly individual and highly unique, so that overlap is minimal and I

might say that the history of the soul is composed of patterns of windowlessness. While there is a kind akashic coordination, one cannot go from space A to space B and expect to find continuity of history immediately given. One cannot arrive at continuity except through an overall analysis of the soul; from the parts one cannot arrive at continuity, one can only arrive at parts of the history, which I will call segments of the akashic history of the soul. Together, of course, they form a complete picture, but neighbors do not complete each other as an invariable law. They might in some cases, however.

Q: Would the esoteric communion then be used in initiation work to bring about the realization of the inner pleroma?
A: Always. We know what we are working with when we see the map. This is why initiation is no longer and never should have been anything but highly exacting. For we have the esoteric communion as our plan of action.

Q: Does initiation take place "within" the mandala of Devic Energy?
A: That which is initiated is "located" by the initiator within that mandala but the process cannot be easily spatialized. However, it does occur in some way within one of the 16 "chambers" of the mandala of the angelic energies.

Q: How is the student initiated in this process? For example, is it a transfer of a form of Devic Energy?
A: Devic Energy can be the subject as well as the object of a process of transfer. The initiated student does have a certain part of his being connected to the system of the angelic consciousness. However, there is another way in which it happens and that is by means of changes made by the process of Devic adjustment. It appears that the person being initiated is within the Devic Energy field already, and that what he is within must be fully utilized. When that happens, initiation occurs.

Q: Then is the mandala more of an explanation than an instrument for "giving" energy?
A: No, it is an exact map of the world as seen by the magician. While the inner world may be somewhat different from the mandala, nevertheless, the way in which one finds one's way around is reflected in the structures on the mandala.

Q: Is the way in which the mandala or magickal circle is "worked" a secret of the gnosis?
A: It is a secret, since it is revealed by angels only to certain magickal high priests and involves many secret and unknown parts or "chambers." However, our own mandala is used to provide information about many different universes. It is a kind of computer in addition to a map.

Q: Do you mean that there are various methods of initiation other than this method which you have just described?
A: Those who work with the Devic Energies do not deny that there are many systems of magickal initiation. However, the initiation-physics of the mandala is a very special system of energy and power. I use it only with very special students.

Q: Do you understand that there various occult or angelic beings inhabiting the mandala of the initiation-physics?

A: One of our teachings is that there are many types of magickal and mystical beings in this system, and they may be found in the various "chambers" of the mandala. I have made precise and personal contact with these entities. Certain special pupils of mine have entered into contact with these beings by the methods I have taught and have benefited from this experience.

Q: Is the mandala to be found within the "ontic sphere" or gnostic imagination of the magician, which is a world in which he participates along with the angelic kingdom?
A: The ontic sphere is objective in the gnostic and magickal sense, so it must be viewed as the cosmic imagination of the universal mind. There in that realm of being, the magician can find many types of esoteric being. Because it is cosmic, it does involve the world of angelic and magickal beings. This world is the true home of the magician. If we look for information on this system of being, we canonly find it inside of the world of pure consciousness.

Q: Would you say that your work has been chiefly in the exploration of this universe of Devic Ideality and the classification and application of the various energies in mystical works?
A: This is how I define the scope of my own system of gnostic magick, in the modern world. However, because it is so vast a subject, I must progress very slowly in the true exploration of this being. But it is my idea of higher magickal initiation.

Questions and Answers on Initiation—Physics and Spiritual Energies

Q: What is the importance of initiation in the life of the student?
A: Initiation is the beginning of perfection. A soul cannot become perfect without undergoing the process of initiation and spiritual development from a gnostic master of light.

Q: Is this recognized by all schools of awareness as a law of the universe?
A: Yes. In one form or another, every pathway and also even exoteric religions place great emphasis upon initiations.

Q: Does the gnostic church, in which you are a bishop, view initiation as a complex and highly spiritual process of growth in the light of the Cosmic Christ?
A: Yes. The Church of the Gnosis is the esoteric church founded by Christ for the highest types of human consciousness. The exoteric churches were founded for ordinary types of people. In the Church of the Gnosis, there exist very special methods and techniques for the development to perfection of the energies of the soul.

Q: Do bishops of the Church of the Gnosis possess the powers to initiate and develop the children of light?
A: Yes. This is a special power given to them by the Cosmic christ and the 12 Apostles of the Church of the Gnosis. The purpose of this power is to provide for the enlightenment of the students of the gnosis, wherever they might be.

Q: Then, are special powers given to certain gnostic bishops which are even higher than the powers of even ordinary gnostic bishops?
A: Yes. This may be explained by the fact that in our own tradition, our high priesthood contains elements which are older than Jesus Christ and the Apostles (the first bishops), because our own priesthood, which was originally Egyptian in form and Chaldean in content, was taken over and made use of by Jesus Christ, when He founded the Catholic Church of the Gnosis.

Q: Do the specially qualified bishops then possess ancient techniques from the magickal and initiatic schools of Atlantis and perhaps even older for the development of perfection in the souls of the candidates?
A: Yes. Because the ancient schools of Atlantis are continued in the mysteries and mystic schools of the Church of the Gnosis.

Q. Do you work with ancient energies within the soul, which are the presences of angelic beings from many past lifetimes?
A: Yes. When we work with the souls of the students what we have in mind in our process is what has been done or developed in a past lifetime. For this reason, we continue in this lifetime what happened in a past lifetime. There is continuity between the past and the present. I personally also work with what might be called the futuristic energies of the soul, for I do not do anything to develop the soul, which cannot be continued and sustained by the future life and future lifetimes of the student of light. But this work with the future is really quite unique to my own inner circle of gnostic bishops, because we alone possess the perfected technique of

480

this process of working with the angels of the future, even the Devas of gods of the very remote future.

Q: Is it true that only those who have been with you before come to you in your present lifework?

A: So it would appear. For one thing, there is some kind of agreement or contract that has been worked out by our school with the Nature of the Universe, which states quite simply that for purposes of the economy of time, only those who were with us before come back. I find that all of those who come to me now have worked with me before and I was then in the process of developing them. I do not think that we have any students who come to us without a previous background in this gnostic consciousness of spirituality and magick. But it does seem that because there are so many schools and places for beginners in the world today, that it is not necessary for me to teach and work with everyone. Actually, I am kept quite busy with just those who were with us before, in our school of mysticism and magick in a previous time and place.

Q: Where might that have been?

A: We have had previous schools in Africa and Asia. These schools reincarnated from one century to the next and relocated in various parts of the world. The fact that it is now in Chicago simply means that it is located in the heart of the USA, so as to be convenient to students from many parts of the world. And this is true. It is very convenient to have the school of mysticism and magick in Chicago because it is then easy for those who belong to us to reach us.

Q: What do you think of other schools and teachers?

A: If something or someone does good, whatever is done will survive. Even the most evil of magicians –– and I know many because as their bishop and priest I must hear their confessions since they come to me for this purpose –– even such black magicians do some good. If good is not done, the energy does not survive and whatever is done folds back upon itself into a vacuum. All schools and teachers therefore do some good and many do much good. They will help those who come to them and who are beginning the pathway to spiritual light and magickal development. So, I think that because there are many schools and teachers, I am freed by the Nature of the Universe to work with my special students, those who have been with me many times before. This is part of our agreement with the Nature of the Universe, it is a law of that agreement that there should be many schools and teachers, so that I will be free to work with those I know from past lifetimes.

Q: Can you tellimmediately if a person was with you before?

A: Yes. First of all, I pay attention to how they come to know of me. By what method do they come to me: perhaps someone with me tells them them about me. Then I look at them in an astrological way, to find out certain other matters. Usually, I can tell if I see them, for as soon as I see them, I see a special sign in their aura, which is a signal to me that they are one of us. However, sometimes the signal has been obscured and is not a very sharp signal. When this happens, I ask the spirits and they help me. But it is always a very quick process.

Q: Would you make use of your clairvoyant powers when you meet a student for the first time?

A: Yes. But it is so easy for me to do this that I do not think of it as a complete process. All I have to do is look at them in my mind and I know all that I need to know about them. It is entirely a matter of gnostic awareness.

Q: You would then know at that time where the person was in terms of initiation powers?

A: Yes, because I could see not only the signal, but the evidence of my work in a past lifetime, when I led the student through the process of initiation and developments of powers. I would be about 99% accurate in my judgments, based on this consciousness. But I am in most cases 100% accurate.

Questions and Answers on the Successions of Gnostic Bishops

Q: When a bishop has been consecrated and reconsecrated several times, as often happens, is it possible to examine the successions he has received and isolate particular components in those successions, as well as the individual successions?

A: Yes, it is possible to do that. Each succession is composed of sacramental units, or the energy fields of the ministers of the sacrament. These sacramental units are the permanent atoms of ecclesiology, and are identifiable empirically as well as being historically recorded. Let us say that Bishop X consecrated Bishop Y in 1915. Then in 1920, Bishop Y consecrates Bishop Z. These are first of all separate historical events, but they are also sacramental events and involve that energy known in theology as "the grace or gift of the sacrament." The bishops involved are the media or channels of the grace, which comes from the Holy Spirit, or Third Person of the Christian Trinity. Under these circumstances, the bishops are connected to the gifts of the sacrament in a continuum of identifiable energies of a supernatural character.

Q: And would there not be angelic or devic energies also present or connected to the chain or continuum of sacramental power?

A: I think that it can be shown by esoteric methods that each component has its own individual management, which is vested with a particular sacramental angel and that each line of succession has a chief angel, who not only conserves the line or continuum but administers to day–to–day activities of the succession. Thus, each bishop of the Vilatte succession has an angel to help him, each action to extend and continue the succession has an angel, and the entire succession has an angel, who oversees the components of his lineage. What can be done is done by cooperation with these angels and what cannot be done is prevented from being done by these angels.

Q: We may assume that certain successions are closer to the devic and others are more human. Let us say that Bishop Y has two consecrators. Bishop X is from the Vilatte succession and Bishop M is from a succession which originally was purely pneumatic or devic, in that the founders were consecrated by devic beings and not by humans. Later, this succession of Bishop M merged with historical successions, perhaps parallel to the Vilatte succession or perhaps some part of the Vilatte succession, such as Syro–Gallican or Syro–Jacobite, etc. Would it be possible to isolate the original devic succession of Bishop M from the Vilatte succession at the consecration of Bishop Y?

A: You are asking one of the more technical questions in ecclesiological physics, but the answer is yes, because it is possible to isolate each component in a succession. In the succession of Bishop Y, the continuum of the Vilatte succession bishops would be very much present. However, the archetypal M succession, which was not from Vilatte, would be very much present because spiritual energies are not limited by space. One could then identify the Vilatte and the M lines. Moreover, because it is a sacramental continuum, you would not be able to quantify the succession, although it would be fair to say that succession M was represented by fewer devas than the Vilatte succession at the consecration of Bishop Y.

Q: Then you do not see all successions as identical if they are valid?

A: That is correct. Successions are identifiable although their source of power is identical in that it comes from the self-identify of the Holy Spirit. When these successions are "seen," this is quite obvious.

Q: Are the various traditions or lineages, which are not usually classified as "of the Christian tradition," and which many gnostic bishops possess, are these lines of power also, and if so do they have qualities similar to certain Christian lineages, which you have investigated?
A: What is unique among the gnostic bishops has been the opportunities for them to receive certain ancient successions, which are not traceable to the 12 Apostles, and the openness with which these bishops have welcomed these lines to their ministry. St. Augustine has clearly indicated the existence of such lines and that the Christian Church is the continuation of these lines. Therefore, it is possible to see in certain lines of priesthood and high priesthood, from various traditions, the components of the Christian form of Catholicism. These ancient traditions we have come to designate as Natural or as Proto-Catholic. The Hindu-Brahminimal religion is an example of this type of energy, as would be forms of many other ancient religions. Now, when someone possesses an ancient succession as well as one of the Christian successions, both are there or given as the energy or reality of the priesthood of the man who possesses them. For example, the succession of Archbishop Vilatte is interesting because it contains both Hindu and also Christian lines. Both have been investigated and found to be actively connected to the devic power-zones and objectively forming a special continuum. This special continuum, I think, explains certain actions which were taken by the bishops of the French gnostic tradition, or the Syro-Gallican lineage.

Q: So you have been able to isolate lineages from ancient religions, the Christian lines of Apostolic Succession, and various non-historical lineages from Devas and Spirits. Would you then say that they each have their own characteristics in the field of gnostic physics or ecclesiological physics?
A: I think so. The ways in which they manifest themselves are quite difficult at times to isolate. But they are very different. What is important is this: that we view these components as part of the genetic material of the gnosis, or really as the genetic material of the sacramental continuum of the Holy Spirit. Each component has a way of acting in a very special way and by understanding this genetic material, we can understand why the ministry of a particular priest or bishop or those he consecrated turned in a certain direction, or appeared to have quite a lot of problems. Then we can sometimes do corrective work, just as geneticists now can "edit" biological materials.

Q: Then you would say that according to St. Augustine's words, the ancient forms of the priesthood did have their specific graces or Gifts of the Holy Spirit?
A: I think this is true and entirely in keeping with our gnostic teachings, and I may say that the Roman Church also agrees in this matter, although they are hardly qualified to explore these questions in detail, as do we.

Q: Returning to the matter of "editing" ecclesiological-genetic materials, is this not close to what Bishop Charles Leadbeater spoke of when he spoke of "correcting" history?

A: To a certain extent, this is indeed true. However, the methods are different and so are the purposes. Also, while both operations must depend upon the operations of the Devic Kingdom and their intentional cooperation, we might say that the structures worked with in both circumstances are remarkably different. But again, both types of work involve action outside of the physical plane of existence.

Q: The succession from the gnostic teachers of the Early Christian Period are, we understand, retained within the continuum of the lineages. These successions from Marcion, Bardesanes, Basilides, and Valentinus, as well as many smaller and lesser known movements, or submovements within the continuum, we understand to be continued by the line of the gnostic bishops of your patriarchate. Would it be correct to say that these lines are to be understood as continued in the same ways as the lines of the Apostolic Succession?

A: Prior to 1979, I received gnostic succession by episcopal consecration at least four times. I received other lineages, but these may be viewed as Catholic and Spiritist, or as Catholic and Proto–Catholic. However, when I was first consecrated in 1963, I was consecrated and received what was known as the lineages of Marcion. Hence, I underwent a reclamation of that original gnostic tradition. I was consecrated twice in January 1966, and received first of all the lineage of Bardesanes and a few days later that of the great Basilides. A few years later, I received the succession of Valentinus, which is also to be understood as that of the gnostic patriarchate of esoteric research. These sacraments were four distinct reclamations of the gnostic powers and that is why they were given by means of four distinct acts. Also, while there was continuity of the sacred consecrator in each of these operations, the co–consecrators were slightly varied in order –– as I was told –– to achieve the precise effect desired in each sacramental action.

Naturally, there is a connection between these four lineages and the four patriarchates of the Ecclesia Gnostica spiritualis, since the patriarchates were the four ways in which the powers of the four gnostic teachers were supported and sustained.

Q: Did any other tradition within the continuum of the modern movement of gnosis have a teaching any way similar?

A: In 1979, there was a link–up with the apostolic Successions derived from the well-known Patriarchate of Glastonbury through Bishop R. de Palatine. However, while Bishop de Palatine was alive, there was exchanged between him and us a series of letters. In one of them, Bishop de Palatine speaks of receiving from the Patriarchate of Glastonbury the four lineages listed above as well as that of St. Joseph of Glastonbury. Now, it should be understood that these communications were mainly concerned with the metaphysics of the Rites of Memphis and Misraim and it seems to have been the view that these gnostic lines were somehow amplified in their tradition, or being handed on, by the context provided by the Rite of Memphis and Misraim. Since the connection that Bishop de Palatine had to the Rite of Memphis and Misraim appears to have come from Yarker through the Patriarchate of Glastonbury.

In a very similar way, the lineages of these early gnostic teachers was transmitted in the Ecclesia Gnostica Spiritualis by reason of its connection with the mechanisms of the Rite of Memphis–Misraim. Then in 1979, when the gnostic lineages were exchanged, we were able to receive the succession of St. Joseph of Glastonbury, as well as the four other traditions, which were implicit in the successions of the

Glastonbury Patriarchate.

The Nature of Empowerments: Questions and Answers

Q: Where did the idea of empowerments come from in the Monastery of the Seven Rays/ Gnostic Church teachings?
A: The idea was brought in from the research work of Lucien-Francois Jean-Maine, who developed the work leading to the restoration of the ancient practice of the teacher, who gives power to the student. This practical idea has its roots in Atlantean magickal physics.

Q: Can we say that there are exoteric and esoteric empowerments?
A: Yes. Special students were always given the more esoteric projections, while the general body of students were entitled to the more exoteric projections, which were less intense. However, this idea was based on the motion that empowerment should be graded as to the types and levels of students in the school of the gnosis.

Q: How are empowerments arranged or organized, because from what I have heard they are highly structured objects?
A: Empowerments or empowerment, when viewed as a group process, are arranged in forms of 16, like much else in the teaching. However, they are related to 16 physical places or parts of the body, because they actualize what is latent by giving something which is not fully experienced by the student, even though the student has the power deep within his psyche.

Q: Are empowerments connected to chakrams as in yoga where energies are projected from chakras into the student?
A: Not necessarily. Something may connect them and sometimes this does happen, but I think empowerment work is more esoteric than chakra work, as we find it in layayoga. I also know that empowerment in certain ways makes use of certain tattwas, which are not used by yoga. In this sense, then, they are highly esoteric and particularly secret. Yet, we can understand that empowerments can be related to chakras in the usual sense.

Q: Then would you say that empowerments make use of the energies of kundalini and the other mysteries of layayoga?
A: Again, this would be to simplify the matter. Actually, in the gnosis kundalini is present as psychic pneuma and vital pneuma, or spiritual power; but it is much more of an extension beyond the powers of yoga, as vast as they are. For this reason, I think it best to say that yoga is one form of empowerment.

Q: Is empowerment connected to initiation?
A: It can be seen as part of that process. The infusion of energy and power from the cosmic dimension to the body of the student during initiation is a form of empowerment at work. However, really during empowerment exercises, it is the unconscious which is now liberated by the teacher in the student.

Q: Why is esoteric empowerment so secret?
A: Because if it is to known it will lose its power, so it should be a secret except for those immediately involved in its and the operations we associate with it. Also,

in the esoteric process of initiation physics, the 16 stages have to be secret, because they make use of highly technical cosmoi, or universes of vitality. So it will always be or be understood as a secret process, since what it involves is outside of ordinary thinking as we understand that activity.

Q: Are the ray—lines, which connect the empowerments to their objectives, e.g., the student of the Master MB, in the body of the student and if so, have these been measured or analyzed?
A: Such lines of power do exist and these lines of power do have a network type of occult structure. They are closely similar to lattices as we see them in other places of the universe. However, once the empowerments are given, at least inthe esoteric sense, it can be said to remain there permanently as a link between the vital self and the cosmos of vitality, which is the source of the empowerment. However, it has its place of existence in the intimate intuitions of the Master, which link him to the student.

Q: Are these lattices capable of being expressed as oracles or as aspects of devic and angelic physics?
A: They are and actually much of the futuristic Zothyrian work consists of investigations of these lattices. You see, at a certain time and level, specific energies become the subject matter of what has come to replace the history or historical subject—matter of the near and distant future. This future energy then is put into the body of the student and becomes the student's link with the blue—ray church of energy, or the Ecclesia Gnostica Angelorum.

Q: Are you saying then that the history of the future will have empowerments as its subject?
A: It would seem so because by that time, we will see empowerment work as part of the process of nature. We will make distinctions based on empowerments and describe our own observations of empowerments and empowerment work as the subject—matter of the future.

Q: Does empowerment imply devic work being done at the same time?
A: I think that empowerment work does take place with a devic continuum or inside of the actual field of a devic energy. That was the basis for the old idea of the connection between empowerment and possession, or the reception of vudo energy. Lucien came to see this connection as the basis for how empowerment worked.

Q: Isn't it true that there are empowerments which come from the past and which have their basis in human sexuality, viewed either occultly or esoterically?
A: Yes. One system of empowerments is based on the mysteries, which are connected with the ideas taught in the second year of instruction of the Monastery of the Seven Rays, and which relate to the wonderful mysticism of 16 fundamental universes of vitality, as we find this process in time. When the projections of this type of empowerment occur, the student is truly grounded in the power—presence of kundalini shakti. Great beings are involved in these mystical universes, so that initiation—empowerment places in the body of the student the link with the violet—ray church of energy, or the Acclesia Angelorum in Aevo. This energy is stored at the heart of the earth and rises towards the sun, so we continue to think of it as being or coming

from the past—rays of magickal gnosis.

Q: Would many of the exercises of the second year instruction of the Monaster of the Seven Rays be actually examples, expressed as lesson principles, of empowerment work?
A: I think that this is true. Especially, whenever there are lessons or papers which relate to empowerment work by another name. If we know what empowerment means, we can identify these areas. It is especially represented in the Legbha—Luage mysteries. Of course, in the law of syzygy, we find a cosmic presentation of this law as the pattern of interaction. It draws its power from the fact that this law is cosmological and then active in human experience.

In conclusion, let me say that empowerment work is one of the special gifts of the gnosis and it is closely related to esoteric initiation and development. Any student of the work of the gnosis will hear of its existence and those students who have links to the Master will be admitted to the temple of empowerment. The subject is highly technical and and it is not one which can be discussed in two or three lessons. Parts of the gnosis do discuss the subject—matter of empowerment, in several courses and papers and approaches of study. It is, however, best learned under the personal instruction of the Master to whom the student is especially assigned. The temple of empowerment is expressed through the work of two of the esoteric and gnostic churches of our system. In each one of these churches of the gnosis, we are able to find expressions of the gnosis as a pure and eternal light of power and a source of the mysteries of initiative consciousness. What now follows are the esoteric instructions, which are directed to you personally as a chela of the Master MB.

Supplementary 1a: The Secret Spaces

Image Number 1: I have discovered that if I test a photo of a student for auric energy levels before, during, and/or after a UFO happening, I find a buildup of energy during the period and the energy level afterwards is usually tested and found to be higher than before. I also believe that some of the UFO-energies are linked to certain students of mine now coming into studies with me, because these are factors which cannot be explained in any other way except by this mystical-genetic factor or actual mutation. These new students project a very high but unconscious magnetism due to psychic radioactivity, which seems to be the result of their link with the UFO level of consciousness. All of these tests have been conducted by me using special radionic and psychotronic instruments, which I have designed and have made up for these purpose.

Secret Space 1: The student the the UFO-energy:
Exercise: You will meditate on the energies of image number 1

Image Number 2: According to our inner teachers, there is a definite communication link and connection between Devas and UFOs. However, I have discovered a new link and that is that the world where the UFOs make these links to the students can be understood as a Devic system of lattices, which means that Devas are the medium for connecting the UFO energies to human beings. We know how Devas "work" in the physics of initiation, but now they seem to be the fields within which UFO contacts with the sutratmic "bundle" associated karmically with each of the students takes place. This field can be "worked" by magicians and the experiments of initiatic physics are the projections of this interconnectedness. (This has been confirmed by the several Devic helpers fromthe EGO and the EAIA, with whom we are currently working in my radionic experiments.)

Secret Space 2: The UFO-energy and the Devas of the Gnosis
Exercise: You will meditate on the energies of image number 2.

Image Number 3: I was also told by certain Devas that many of my papers are not really supposed to be lessons, but are a kind of machine in its own way for inducting the programs, written in them, as lesson titles. In this case, many books can be used this way or so understood because they represent the basic organization of thought-form energies in a specific pattern. This is esoteric engineering. The energies can be measured and indicated and increased and programmed along a variety of lines of projection and gnostic application.

Secret Space 3: Devas and programming of the gnostic body/mind
Exercise. You will meditate on the energies of image number 3.

Image Number 4: There also seem to be an entire body of Devas, whose purpose is the construction of occult instruments of various types. These beings serve to inspire certain of humanity but they give up and build up instruments if allowed to do so ina specific and secret space, where they set up their factories. What we are now doing is making it possible for them to develop several types of factories, which whendone will resemble the UFO-type of construction, according to the classical Devic architecture (or since it is a construction of the thought-form energy: architectonic).

Secret Space 4: Devas and the factories of esoteric engineering
Exercise: You will mediate on the energies on image number 4.

Supplementary 1b: The Secret Spaces Defined by the Esoteric Logic of the Empowering Teacher

Q: During empowerment, as in many other procedures of initiation physics, does the gnostic church teach that there is an introduction of the Pneumatic Man into the student?

A: Empowerment work does imply that the Pneumatic Man, or the Divine Selfhood, is imparted to the candidate by means of the work done by the Teacher of the Gnosis. This is a form of power-projection in its most theological form, because the pneumatic or spiritual man is imparted to the physical and psychic parts of humanity, during this process. He is understood to come and dwell inside of a secret space, which has been prepared by means of the estoeric logic of the Teacher.

Q: What would be the nature of these secret spaces of the gnosis?

A: The secret spaces are actually parts of our universe and also parts of other universes and they are also universes in themselves. The Nine Mystical Bodies can only inhabit types of space and the Pneumatic Man is made up of the highest of these Mystical Bodies. For this reason, the Teacher must create in the student the beginnings of this secret space by means of direct and personal experience. That is why the first level of initiation must be given personally to the student by the Teacher of the gnosis. However, these spaces are emanations from the pure energy of esoteric logic, which resides as a mystical body of its own, deep within the soul-world of the Teacher of the gnosis.

Q: You say that esoteric logic has its own mystical body, is this one or many?

A: Actually, the cosmic continuum of esoteric logic is one body, of an entirely mystical nature. However, within the continuum there are many forms of esoteric logic. We can say that there an unlimited number of such logics. By the law of denseness, there are pure and individual forms of esoteric logic for every Teacher of the gnosis. Such forms of logic are concrete, because they possess a mystical body, but universal, because of the law of denseness, they inhabit the eternal continuum of the gnosis of the universe.

Q: What do you mean by the law of denseness?

A: The law of denseness states, quite simply, that between any two things or beings, there will always be a third being. Thus, between A and C there is B, but according to the law of denseness, between A and B and between B and C there should also be letters, which in the ideal world there are, but which we do not include in our English alphabet. This law is very ancient and very metaphysical and is one of the basic laws of transcendental arithmetic.

Q: Are the secret spaces ruled by the law of denseness and if so, does the Pneumatic Man dwell in one or many or are that many forms of the Pneumatic Man in each initiate?

A: I think it is true to say that denseness would have to apply to the system of the secret spaces and that it would also apply to the nature or number of Pneumatic Man. For this reason, the gnostic Teachers speak of many forms of the Pneumatic Man, because in each student who becomes an initiate, there are many forms of this being.

When the Pneumatic Man is formed inside of the student and we say that he is identified as Z, we do not mean Z alone but we mean — at least, in my work I surely intend — that there is a continuum of Z there in that secret space system, which we can symbolize as: $(Z1, Z2, \ldots, Zx, Zx+1, Zn \ldots Zn+n)$, a neverending potentiality.

Q: Are there esoteric instructions for each of the secret spaces of the student which are given by the Teacher in preparation for the introduction of Pneumatic Man during the work of empowerment?
A: The esoteric instructions are given to the student by the Teacher and these are not instructions alone but consist in the given-ness of secret spaces, or the gift of a special gnosis, which has as its concern the contents of esoteric logic projected as in a schematism or as a pattern of organization. Thus, we must make room for the Pneumatic Man or make a home for him in the spiritual body of the student.

Q: Is there then an esoteric teaching of the gnosis for this doctrine, so that I who have read the answer given above may also receive the esoteric gnosis of the secret space as well?
A: Yes. The gnosis of the secret space is given as follows:

Study Questions
These study questions pertain to matters in the lesson, which can only be answered after reading this lesson. However, because of the nature of Question 1, we have decided to place these questions within the lesson. After you have answered part A of question 1, you may go on to the subject matter of the lesson, and return to these study questions after you have completed lesson material.

1. In order to evaluate the physiological effect of this lesson and therefore the total psycho-physiological impact of the LSM programme, please answer the following questions:

A. What was your pulse and/or blood pressure measurement before reading this lesson?

B. What was the reading of your pulse and/or blood pressure measurement after completing this same lesson?

2. Describe your psychological feelings while reading this lesson. Did you feel an awakening of elemental powers deep within yourself? If so, please describe.

3. The lesson is divided into two sectors. The first part covers two pages and a part of the last page, the second part covers most of the last page. Do you feel a difference in psychic energy between the first and second parts? If so, please describe.

4. How would you define the basis of lycanthropic sexo-magickal energy?

5. Did you identify with a person or part of this lesson? If so, please specify and tell me why.

6. Do you suspect that there is a magickal relationship between violence and chaos, or between violent emotions and the ultra-dimension of primordial chaos? Please define what you mean by this.

7. What occult exercises have you been able to derive from this lesson?

8. Can you specify in visual terms what the basic energies look like?

9. Do all persons posses lycanthropic powers or only some shamanistic magi? Please give reasons for your answer.

10. How would you define extreme emotions or feelings in magick?

11. Have you had any dreams or psycho—magickal experience as a result of this lesson? If so, please describe in detail.

Because this course is designed for only our most extreme students, advancement to the next lesson must depend upon how you complete these questions. This is not a course that is open to the general student of my system, but only to the most extreme and esoteric of my chelas. The reason for this restriction is that the subject—matter of these papers is of a very technical and specialized form and would not be fully understood by many students of our system. Therefore I must be very careful in the release of this material.

The Shintoist Bikers

"Tangichi could feel the pain as Iytoro Kawabata held his hands apart, digging his thumbnails into the tender flesh of Tangichi's wrists. 'You will learn who is boss around here you silly young pup, you'll learn to take orders, you'll learn to take orders from me.' Each time Iytoro spoke, he punctuated and emphasized what he said by cutting deeper into the already deeply bruised wrists of his captive. Would he cut into the veins in emphasizing his point —— perhaps —— maybe he had already, maybe blood had already been drawn. Was this some cruel 'rite-de-passage,' some initiation into just how cruel Iytoro could be, when he wanted to be? Iytoro growled, his voice was bestial, deeply guttural, the voice-of an angry animal. An animal, angered and slowly emerging from the cave of his id. The animal deep in each of us, now unleashed and ready to spring violently at its world of tormentors, at those egos which torment the animal chaos deep inside each of us. 'You stupid pup —— I ought to murder you for no reason at all. I ought to mangle you beyond recognition, so don't forget that.' Tangichi didn't." —— (Tangichi, in preparation)

Q: And then might there also be a teaching, which is part of the esoteric logic of the Teacher of the gnosis, which too may be imparted as a secret space of the teaching?

A: Yes. The gnosis and esoteric logic of this secret space is as follows:

The Basis of Power

The very first thing that I am going to do is to show you how much hate I have inside of myself and how much violence I want to project at you. Yes, you are to be the object of all of this elemental violence, hatred, intensity of anger. You are the one that I will destroy. You are the one I will rip and tear at a million times. You are the one I will claw and bite viciously, until you are a heap of suffering quiver, until you are drained of all life and will. Until you are totally and impossibly smashed beyond any human recognition. O yes, the process is slow and seductive. I am totally aware that you don't want this to happen to you. I will trap and trick you. I will deceive you. I will get you where I want you. You will be tied up and stripped, beaten beyond any human recognition, yes, beyond human recognition. I've said that a lot because it is so important. No one could see you and think you were a human being. No one could see you and note that you had ever been a human being. You would be covered with an ooze of blood, semi—coagulated, nothing more, a gelatinous heap. Only the ropes would serve to induct any human outline, and that only from memory:

"That was supposed to be a human being." But even they could not be too definitive. I don't want anyone to recognize you, I want you only to be known to me. You are mine and mine only.

It began rather differently, I think you would agree. We met in that somewhat run down cafe. You had written to me suggesting that you would like to meet me. You had studied some of my materials for a long time. You and I had exchanged letters, photos and the other magickal pleasantries. So when you came to town, we met at that time and place and began the association. Those drinks that we were served helped, for the mesmerism of the rhums and brandies gradually wore down your egoic defenses, unless you wanted them to gradually subside, to fall into the background. Here in that magickal world, there were to be no restrictions to ways in which we would be to each other, to what we would do. And, you realized that. After the time spent in beginning to get mellow, I thought it would be good for you to come to my home and to relax. We took a taxi and bringing your few pieces of luggage presented few if any problems. Then we arrived at the lair, or place, where the magickal creativity was exercised. After a few more drinks, I suggested that you might like to take a quick shower bath, in preparation for some ritual work.

I was pleased when you agreed and, removing your clothes, found your way to the cold water, which seemed to stimulate you in a mysterious and weird manner. While you were bathing, I decided to join you, and making another drink for each of us, came to the bathroom. It was there that I noticed the particular suitability of your body for the deeper aspects of my research. As I slowly began to mesmerize you in an erotic sense, I realized that you were more suitable for another and more profound type of consciousness. You seemed to be so full of a basic energy, and I wanted to bring out that energy more and more. As I held you very close, I slowly began to test your skin for where I might be invited to make entry. My lips and tongue began to explore, seeking that secret space where my teeth might make the first magickal mark. It was obvious that this was a type of erotic exercise to you, but to me it went beyond eros, it was approaching more the question of your sacrificial death. Your total surrender to this ideal was necessary. Not that I was any kind of vampire, for my lineage is more hot-blooded, more violent, more destructive and chaotic.

I really wanted to strangle you. I really wanted to squeeze the breath of life from you. I wanted to grab your throat and press it inwardly to its limits. I had you on the floor and you seemed to be aware of what was happening. You seemed to realize that there was something more than just sexuality at work. Your instinct could read my mind, and you realized that I was trying to harm you. Your nakedness beneath the hairs of my body began a vain struggle. I really wanted you to struggle. I wanted to show you that there wasn't any escape from what was to happen. From what must happen. I wanted you to try and fight back, and perhaps you wanted to also, but you did not appear to be able to.

You did not seem interested in that. Rather you seemed to know that there was something more interesting beyond all efforts at struggling which would be happening to you. You perhaps held in your mind some vague notion of transformation, which would come once I was freely able to have my way with you. And so then I began the ritual work and allowed myself to become opened up totally to those forces which were now becoming more and more active in my being. Those demons began to come more and more to the surface, those very primitive beings, which are normally hidden deep within the animal nature of humanity, they were slowly coming up to where "I" was, to where the ego had its reign. Slowly, and with a most astonishing viciousness, they heatedly began to surface. Slowly they cried out to be fed, those base babes, animal pups and cubs, those primitive parts of my world, and your own which most if not all have forgotten about, under normal circumstances, now these were pressing in on me and slowly, they were coming more and more to where I was and I was feeling them and hearing them. Their cries and growls, the brushing of their bodies against me, and then they are there.

Q: Because of the law of denseness, might these secrets never end?
A: Yes. The law of the gnosis is quite consistent. The nature of the teaching is that is one part is given all of it is nearby. If the secret gnosis of a space is know, then the other secrets are connected in an esoteric way to it. But this is why the Teacher must give the teachings as keys to the spiritual man.

Secret: The gnosis of this secret space and its esoteric logic now follow:

LSM Course
1.1 I always knew that I was painfully different and that I was from somewhere else quite remote, perhaps a distant star, or some outer planet. I always knew that I was alien to this body and to those stupid people who go about day by day in the total ignorance of how great I am. I always knew that they, these close by me now, did not know who I really was. I always knew that I had been somehow imprisoned here by some kind of a greater force and I realized that I was here against my will. I always knew that when I would regain my powers, which I alone possessed, I would break out of this prison and destroy those beings who imprisoned me in this material realm.
1.2 And so I began to rebuild my powers, my real powers as I see them, my demonic will power, my cosmic lust power, my power of anger,and my supreme power of intellect. Now I am planning to get out of here and defeat my enemies and captors. I want to destroy them and smash their values and identities entirely; for they are the cause of my misery.
1.3 It is not easy to rebuild these powers. There is so much that is against me. But my determination was united to my power of will. I resolved to become what I was before. So I sought out a guru who was to awaken in me the violent chaos of my internal powers. Such a guru was hard to find, for so many were united to my enemies. At the same time many so-called gurus sought to make me their captive, so I had to reject the idea of passing from one form of prison to another. I finally found such a person, for the mark he bore was one of indifference to every energy. So then I knew that this was the right guru. He did not care. Also, I found him deep within my own imagination.
1.4 We make a mistake when we ignore the magickal teacher who lives deep within us. He is easy to meet and can be seen if you look hard enough therein. He can also be dangerous because his teachings might be too wild even for our most violent moods. But he is there and he lives within us. Socrates called him "the daemon," and that's what he is. He is the demon within the black magician, who teaches him about the magickal forces of experience.
2.1 The powers of magick must not be thought of as outside of what we can experience deeply. They exist as games which the demon within plays with us, as we learn more and more about being. These games are ways in which we experience

interchanges of energies with a variety of magickal entities. They teach us their secrets and enable us to hide these magickal secrets deep within the structure of our inner world. In that realm, no one can find them but us.

2.2 In order to understand what it means to be such a black magician it is necessary to emphasize the power of isolation. If I were working in a group of some kind I might have difficulty. Someone is always there trying to control the flow of energy. In isolation, however, I can easily develop my own magickal field. I can keep it where it should be and I can work with it in whatever way I feel it needs. I do not have to pay attention to what some group is expecting of me. Isolation means that I am free.

2.3 There exist in the world very few orders which let you have this isolation. In fact they are not real orders, they are simply fronts for the teaching of black magick. There is one so-called order which has its center of power in Haiti and as far as I know everyone connected to that order exists in isolation. Eventually, when black magick is restored to its position of power in the world all magickal orders will resemble that order which has its center in Haiti. What might we ask is that center in Haiti? Well, it is only an isolated black magician. The reason is quite clear: magickal powers must have profound isolation for their cultivation. Otherwise, they degenerate into subjective psychisms. So isolation is a kind of energy from which the black magician extracts magickal powers. When we realize this about the nature of powers, we see how important isolation is as an important reality.

Q: Gnosis: So we can say that as regards to empowerments, we must distinguish between the secret space of the empowerment and its esoteric logic?
A: Gnosis: In the gnostic reaching of this school, we always examine empowerments in terms of the secret spaces implied by the empowerment and also the esoteric logic of the empowerment. The secret space is the content of the gnosis, while the logic is its structure.

Q: Is it true or can it be said that the Teacher possesses in his esoteric logic an entire schematism which contains the field of lattices for all empowerments, their own secret spaces and their own logics of denseness?
A: This is indeed true. However, I should define the phrase "logic of denseness." By this I mean that each Teacher, whether in the physical body or out of it, possesses an esoteric framework of reference, by which certain structures and laws can be applied to his students. This would be a sub-division of his own esoteric logic and power. Within this system, there would appear to be function known as the logic of denseness, which I know from my personal experience provides us with very special potencies for giving both initiations and empowerments to those carefully selected by the gnosis for spiritual or pneumatic advancement. It is a very important way of transmitting the spiritual energy of light. So I think you must understand, I possess as the Teacher or Master MB my own logic of denseness, from which the infinite variety of teachings and powers are taken by me for the benefit of my students. When I became a gnostic Teacher, I received this esoteric key from God-Energy, and thus became the head of my own continuum.

Secret Space: The esoteric teaching-space of this principal now follows:

3.1   I haven't any ideals, I have only those ideas which emerge in the fleeting states of my inner consciousness. I have only those images and drives, whose life is taken from the ongoing stream of my awareness. Where do they come from? They come from deep within my will and from deep within that urgency of my being which alone gives them life. I give them their outer being, up to that time they exist only as so many pressures inside of me, awaiting their impatient moment of escape. They want to get as far away from me as they can, for they know what I am. They have lived too long inside of me to be ignorant of the deepest states of experience, which I the black magician possess.

3.2 Everything about me seems like a projection of some other power, some other outside presence, some other form of "myself." At one time I tried to make some type of contact with that other "reality," but I found it was only another region of "myself," it was only an even more dangerous territory from what I already knew about. And so I could only agree with the mad philosophers of the ego, when they stated in so many books that all that existed was the "Ich," the ego. For to realize that there is only the ego is the most important philosophical lesson that can be taught to the black magician as he slowly gathers together the weapons of his destiny. So if it is only the ego which truly is, then all else must be illusion, unless it is part of the ego. For it must be a part of "my being" to have reality.

3.3 There is an important lesson to be learned in this egotism: If you do not admit to it, you will always run the risk of being enslaved by something outside of your being. You will always run the risk of being told that you "should" do something for someone outside of yourself. For those outside of you would want to control you, make you their slave, make you think the way they would think. But you cannot do that. You cannot surrender your ego to them for them, if you do, you can never be a power unto yourself. You can never become the Absolute Ego of German metaphysics. For there is an eternal state of war existing between the Ego and the Non-Ego; because they will never let up in their attempts to take over control of your life and destiny. They will always want to control the black magician; because only he has real powers.

4.1 Sexuality became for me, at an early stage of my magickal experience, one of my magickal weapons. No longer would I even think of it in terms of how I would relate to anyone. Now it was for me part of my magickal storehouse of weapons. By sexuality I mean anything which carries a sexual overtone. I do not mean mere sexuality in the very narrow sense. That type of sexuality does not exist for the black magician except in very isolated cases. Sexuality is more a field of exploration and the infinite ideas and possibilities of my weird imagination created more and more situations for my strange enjoyments.

4.2 I learned that whatever I wanted in terms of a sexual experience I could bring to the sphere of pleasures. It was simply a matter of time before I got what I wanted. My guru in Haiti taught me how to bring in the powers of the sexually weird from their fugitive realms, anywhere in my imagination. I learned of the sexual Loas of the perverted side of esotericism. I learned homosexuality from the gods of Uranuas, bisexuality from those of Neptune, and violent and chaotic perversions from the demons of Pluto. In fact, these planets were regarded by me as my true homes, not this world of conventionalized lifestyles.

4.3 I learned that in sexuality as in everything else, my prison had been made by the gods within the sphere of Saturn, but that outside of Saturn I was truly free. Outside of Saturn I found what they call "cosmic consciousness," and the more I grew in that, the more perverted my lusts developed. I then realized that only the black magician is truly spiritual for he alone lives beyond the sphere of Saturn. Finally, I identified the placement of the powers of Uranus, Neptune, and Pluto within myself. I knew then that part of me was outside and free and that only part of me was here held in the prison of the inner gods. So I came to realize that I must make use of what was outside and already or forever free to destroy the inner powers which kept me here in this world. I therefore declared war on the gods who wanted to hold me back and allied myself to the unnatural and perverse lusts of cosmic weirdness. For I was truly the black magician at war with his repressive environment.

Q: Then the logic of denseness is a special law of power in itself and does not limit the Teacher but rather gives him a kind of infinity?
A: I think that it can be said that the law of denseness is the individual form of pure infinity, which is possessed by the Teacher. This is the way in which the power of the very highest level of being manifests itself in the Teacher. It is unlimited power and God—Energy as well as unlimited opportunity for divine creativity in the human field of experience.

Q: Can this power then be given at will by the Teacher, because he possesses the key to God—Energy and to the Light of the Gnosis, and this is a continuum of cosmic energy and a universe in itself?
A: I think that we can say that this energy does give the Teacher the power to bring into being the unlimited range of his gnostic imagination. However, this power is possessed by simply a few holy spirits and by our own lineage of Teachers. Other schools, let me not hesitate to add, have their own esoteric sources of power. We have our own and these have come down to us from the most ancient times, that is, from Atlantis.

Secret Space: The esoteric teaching—space of this principal now follows:

Lycanthropic Sex Magick Course
My name is Tangichi Kuro and I was born November 20, 1962 at 7:06 AM in Honolulu, Hawaii, USA to a Japanese family with noble connections to the peerage. Because of my father's business responsibilities, I have traveled widely in Asia and the Pacific. This is my story.
    In the city of Singapore, in an old bookstore, I was unconsciously drawn to a strange book written in the French language, a language which I read and speak easily. The title of the book was "Le Taoisme de la Lune" by some unknown author. It seemed to come from nowhere and I have never been able to determine where it was published or by whom. But reading in that book, I soon discovered the basis of a certain magickal power which was present in the seminal fluid of magicians. This power was the result of very extensive magickal transformations, whereby the magicians achieved an altered state of their being-consciousness at will. By means of this book, I also learned the method of making contact with the eight immortals of Taois (Pa Hsien) through the cycles of the New and Full Moon.
    I also learned of the existence of a secret cult in the underworld of Chinese

occultism known as the Fang Shih alchemists, who were known to prepare supposedly the elixir of immortality from the alchemical substances of the twelve signs of the Zodiac by a very special method of sexual magick, by means of the sexuals golds and silvers found in the seminal fluid of these magicians.

The reader might wonder how it was possible that I, a Japanese, might enter so closely into these Chinese mysteries. But, for your information, let me tell you that on my mother's side of the family I have many Chinese ancestors, who were Taoist priests. I am a typical example of Hawaiian crossbreeding.

Next, I came upon the actual existence of such alchemical groups while visiting a homeopathic pharmacy in Macao. The group appeared to meet from time to time and because of my interest and my age (I was then 18 years old) I was admitted to the outer hallway. Here, I learned that the book "Le Taoisme de la Lune" had been written by a former practitioner of the order, who had died under "mysterious circumstances." Curiously, at least from my humble viewpoint, he had been a member of an esoteric Shinto Society and also had been initiated into Haitian Voudoo. He spoke French well and that is why he had written in that language. The book was considered valuable for drawing in students to the cultus, for each magickal order has to advertise its existence in some form. You do not normally have telepathic powers before you enter these groups, you develop them afterwards. But it was felt that such a book revealed too much about the sexual basis of their alchemy and most existing copies had been found and snatched up to keep them from being read by the curious and the shallow.

Q: We know from the gnosis that the logics of denseness, within esoteric logic, are highly individual. Does the Teacher possess the gnostic powers to reveal the most powerful and most personal of these individual logics in each of his students?
A: Yes. The teaching of the gnosis of light in this matter is that the Teacher is the head of the church; ubi magister, ibi ecclesia (where there is the Teacher, there is the church). Hence the powers which the teacher now imparts to the student are highly esoteric and contained within the being of the student, who is the new vehicle of the light of the gnosis. The Teacher then possesses the gnosis and the right of empowerment to bring forth the individualized logic of denseness, which is deep within the aeonic soul of the pure and ideal student, which he has created and attach this student by ontic lattices to the chela, who possesses a human body. Hence, to reveal powers and light, the student is by gnostic powers connected to the ideal and perfect student of the light, who is eternal and dwelling in the hierarchies of the gnosis.

Secret Space: The esoteric teaching–space of this principal now follows:

Lycanthropic Sex Magick
Since at that time my home was in Macao, I attended the monthly meetings of the Fang Shih regularly following the discussions with my own flawless Mandarin. Because admission to the inner order was based on "magickal powers," I passed quickly into the temple of "the golden light," mastering all of the techniques of sexual alchemy. There I met a friend, who appearing my own age was actually five times my age. He too had mastered all of the methods of sexual alchemy and had entered the inner temple of the "golden light" long ago. Whether or not he was one of the eight immortals, I cannot say even to this day. Whether he was Chinese, Japanese, Thibetan, Korean, I

500

also cannot say, unless to say that he was all of these in one person. However, with the exception of the loss of hair on his head, perhaps due to the hypersecretion of male hormones from Taoist methods, or perhaps due to the powers of certain planets, I do not know, yet he looked my own age, so we said we were brothers.

With my friend I traveled to various places and saw certain mysteries. We experienced many magickal states of consciousness, together, for he told me that he had waited many years for me and now I had appeared.

My first impression of my friend was that he was also some kind of a "black magician." So I simply asked him and he said that he was exactly that. But he went on to say that he was this kind of a magician because of the many discoveries he had made in his life. He had discovered the magickal powers of lust and he had discovered the magickal presence in the world of certain points and places of cosmic lust. They could be contacted, he said, very easily, for they possessed a magickal feeling and were never at any distance.

Through my friend I was initiated into various types of sexual magick, which went far beyond the practices of the alchemists. In the practice of these rites, I was able to see him transform himself into a projection of the elemental and trance side of nature.

Through our magickal practices together, I learned the deeper regions of the mind, where I could unite myself with the elementaal self and thus appear different in my physical body, in the world of space and time. For it was by means of what the mind does in the deepest regions of the unconscious, or what we call the "ultra--consciousness," that the physical mutation of the outer self, both body and soul, occurs. Together we, threw ourselves into the ocean of elemental powers and we stayed there, at that very deep level as long as we could. Sometimes it was for several days, the trance being so intense. In this world, we made contacts with many magickal entities and developed certain types of secret knowledge. We both stayed as long as we could and we always went deeply into this realm together as a team. The immense wealth of my friend made it possible for me to think only of magickal experimentation. I did not have to worry about any financial matters.

My friend had a plan whereby the magicians who had worked with us in the past would come back into physical embodiment. Some were already here and we quickly made the necessary contacts. Others were still in the higher Alaya, and so it was necessary for us to find suitable situations for their incarnation. This we did also, for the plan was to bring in as many magicians of our order as would be needed to take over the world. The plan was to bring them from Devachan to various points along the surface of the earth, which formed a network. To this end, we visited these points and places and did our magickal work, preparing magickally the wombs of those maternal vehicles, who would induct the spirits of the adepts of our order. In this way we encircled the globe and set the stage for the magickal takeover. For humanity needed the directions which we alone could provide for it. It was making too many mistakes. Now was the time for a magickal invasion from the past, before one could or would arrive from outer space.

Q: Is the relationship between the Teacher of the gnosis and student eternal?
A: Yes. While it appears outwardly to exist in time, it exists in time only because it has existed in time before or in some other form of time than the present. Now, it is a relationship existing in time as a present form of communion. However, it is

eternal, inasmuch as it involves many ideal forms of being, such as the higher Zothyrian bodies, as true vehicles, existing outside of time, but acting upon time and giving it an exact form. This is a highly esoteric matter, since we find it very difficult to understand the way in which a relationship between the Teacher and the student can exist outside of time, as our minds focus only on the student/teacher structure in history and the present. But the ideal aspect, and its set-theoretical foundations and contents are actually known and are given in the intuition of eternity by the gnostic imagination of the ontic sphere.

Secret Space: The esoteric teaching-space of this principal now follows:

LSM Course

I was bored. So I decided to get away from everything. Since my grandfather ("The Prince") owned 78% of all of the banking industry in Japan and since my father ("The Count"), having been reconciled to grandfather, was now the manager of grandfather's business empire, I felt that life was relatively secure for the time being. I decided to fly to London and find out what was going on in the west.

I was very bored. Grandfather had escaped his boredom through big business. Now, having reached the top, he busied himself with religion. He lived near Nara, where he went to the Hosso Temples, then each day he attended Shinto rites in his own sanctuary. He buried himself deeply in the metaphysical mysteries of Alaya and watched the processions of Buddhist monks, as they marched past him, each representing a string on the thread of the store consciousness, each one a complete life with its joys and sorrows, each one a doorway to eternal peace and the beginning of the cycle all over again.

Father was entirely practical. No longer were his ultra-right-wing political views considered extreme. My grandfather saw in his own way that the right-wing views of father were really quite logical. Father now sought to extend the family empire all over Asia. In this enterprise he was assisted by my mother, who owned outright vast sections of every possible type of industry in Asia. She saw to it also that each office had its Imperial Shinto Shrine Room, properly staffed with expertly trained priests. Being of very noble blood, she neither forgot nor forgave anything, including my father's many love affairs. Actually, he was afraid of her. She was afraid of nothing.

My sister was older than I and spent most of her time living in a kind of past ideal. Her palace was very lovely and ultra-traditional. Her husband was an army man, from a slightly noble family. His talent was in military sciences and in pleasing her. Like some old empress, she dominated him completely. However, they appeared to be happy in a very simple way. Their passions had borne fruit in six little boys. These six little militarists would some day rule a vast empire. This pleased my father very much.

My older brother, two years older than my sister, was different. He was cold-blooded rather than passionate and I was his favorite. He assisted my father in the management of the empire and was responsible for my income, which was very large, in fact it was almost fantastic. His wife was of a very highest aristocracy but totally modern. She was very liberal in her views, which she kept to herself most of the time. They had two lovely little daughters and a little boy. Because of her position and family, she could drop by and see the empress or the crown prince anytime she was near. She cheered them up with her artistic and humorous manner.

Life had been more adventurous for us when we were in exile. Now that it was over, we had become boring to each other. So I flew to London to find out if it was different there.

After being in London for a few days, I visited an occult book shop and bought several books by a Sir Kenneth. I read them studiously each day and wrote to the author, asking for an interview. He received me and advised me that I should study with a master, who was living in the west but with whom I could closely identify in my thoughts. He suggested that I write to this master, who was living in Chicago, for suggestions. When I explained to Sir Kenneth that I had been born in the USA, due to the exile of my parents, he then stated that I might wish to live in Chicago, which he described as the lycanthropic capital of the world. Thanking him, I left quickly and flew to the USA, where in a short time I had established myself in the New York residence of one of my aunts, who worked at the U.N.

Secret Gnosis: The second esoteric teaching-space of this principal now follows:

I wrote from New York to the master and received a very prompt and friendly reply. I then decided to move to Chicago and arrived there with an aim to finding an apartment in the permissive part of the city. Just slightly north of the Clark and Belmont area, I found what I wanted. I also found nominal employment at the Chicago branch of my family business and so I was ready to begin my life as a magickal student. I also enjoyed the identification with the Asian culture of that part of the city where I lived. Also, near where I lived stood the beautiful and yet very simple Shinto Church and the cultural center, where I went to meet other Japanese, who were adjusting to life in Chicago. I was very happy.

And then it happened. I was lunching at a Chinese restaurant by the name of the Gee Gaw Happiness, and while enjoying my food I suddenly looked up and saw someone looking at me in a way I didn't like. For no apparent reason, I became furious and my deadly essence of Japanese and Scorpionic powers reacted immediately to my displeasure. While looking at the person blankly, without closing my eyes, at the same time in my inner sight or imagination, I superimposed one of the most wrathful demons of Shinto black magick right on top of that unfortunate person's head. The next moment he fell forward, the victim of what came to be diagnosed as a fatal heart attack.

Those who were with him rushed about calling for help, medical and otherwise. In the midst of this excitement, I, Tangichi Kuro, calmly continued my lunch, happy in the thought that I now possessed a most curious and powerful weapon.

At the end of the meal the witless waiter brought me my bill. I recalculated my bill, of course, using my Japanese-made pocket instrument. I noted that there was an error of one penny and that I had therefore been overcharged. I told the waiter of this and he apologized very much, but to teach him a lesson, as I was leaving the room I looked back at him. He was carrying a large tray of food in about six or seven dishes. I did not like the looks of the people to whom he was bringing the food. I still could not forgive him for overcharging me. Looking at him without closing my eyes, I superimposed in my imagination the image of the one of the Chinese trickster deities, right below his feet. He immediately fell forward and dumped all that food and dishes on those people I did not like. The result was chaos as I made my slow exit from the Gee Gaw Happiness smiling smugly to myself, secure in my newly mastered power of causing harm to anyone I felt like doing it to. On my way back to my modest home, I tried this out on a number bystanders. I was of course pleased with the results. In fact, I was extremely pleased with my new powers as I lay on my futon and thought of places where I would go and try it out.

I decided to telephone Michael, my teacher, to discuss it with him. I called him and he agreed to see me the next evening. I went to his home, which was surprisingly peaceful.

The Master Michael explained that what was necessary was the limiting of the enemy of the magician. This could be done in a variety of ways. Since the magician was a truly superior being, his lust for power was absolute. In order to achieve that ultimate stage of power, he would have to rid the universe of his enemies and any persons who stood in the way. This was achieved in my case by my humble visualization exercises. Michael said that because I was Japanese, I was fortunate because I could use the Japanese elementals.

He explained that there was a book which he would let me copy, which was composed entirely of Japanese elementals, hidden carefully behind their linguistic symbols. A similar book existed for the Chinese elementals and if one understood both languages, one could make use of both. Michael explained that since he had had many past incarnations in Chinese and Japanese bodies, he was especially close to this system of elemental working. He also gave me a book on Hosso, written by a Japanese magician. He advised me to read this book because I could add more power to my visualizations once I understood that the powers of Hosso could be applied to my work in a unique and very effective way.

He explained that he saw himself primarily as a conservator of gnostic and magickal energies. The religions of the far east, especially Shinto, Taoism, and esoteric Buddhism all could be said to possess the gnostic enrichment. Deep within their being there was this energy. The magician could tap this energy and apply it in his own magickal experiments. When he did this, he would increase his powers while at the same time he gave greater and greater precision to what he was doing and how he did this in Gnosticism, he explained, was the most precise of the magickal systems, especially his version, which he called "neo-pythagorean and metamathematical." He invited me to return, since I did not bore him with my views.

I went back home, but in order to test the system of the Japanese elementals, I opened it up to the symbol for chaos and then looking down the street at the traffic intersection, I superimposed the symbol for chaos right above the area of the center, through which the cars were moving. Immediately, the cars smashed into each other, as many as twenty seemed caught in my little vortex of energy. The noise was extreme as metal clashed into metal and every motor, human or mechanical, seemed to be making as much noise as possible. I went home, feeling very pleased with myself.

The Masters and Metaphysics 1: The Light of the Gnosis

Empowerment and Gnosis

When the Masters teach metaphysics, they teach with absolute authority because from where they are, all of the laws of metaphysics and all of the departments of consciousness are exactly and clearly seen in the light of their high level of initiation.

Empowerment is when we, the Masters, send power into you and awaken the powers that are in you, but resting in a latent condition. We send the power to awaken you to the light of spiritual being and we seek to awaken you to the nature of reality, which is the law that all things are really made up out of light. I am sending power into you now as you read these words, because by reading these words I am giving you a bombardment of occult and esoteric energy. It is occult because while it exists in nature it is unknown because it is happily hidden from those not ready for it. This energy is esoteric because it is primordial and is identified with the foundations of my being and of your being inducted into me, and this means that you are inside of me, now.

When you understand these things, you will possess the gnosis and you will be aware of the light, which is around you. I am sending this light to you and want to take you with me up into the spiritual realms of being, up to where the angels of light are dwelling. It is this world, where all is fulfilled, because when you come to this world with me you will no longer have any spiritual need. I am truly the Master of this world of light. I have sought to bring you up into the light, because in the light, I can see you as you really should be. I call this world the realm of perfected consciousness, because it is unity with the Master and I am the Master of Light.

El Morya Ra

The world of light is itself a spiritual universe and it is made up entirely of particles of spiritual energy. Each particle is alive and fully conscious. It exists in the world of light in order to give forth the gnosis to the many seekers after the light. It is a form of spiritual atmospheric energy, or atomic light of the gnosis, because I have seen it in all of its lattices and in all of its structures of power. In the process of light, as the lifestream of this higher spirituality is known as, we can see the universe as a perfection of spiritually interconnected systems of being. Each particle of light is part of the pure gnosis and it is the revelation of light and the power of that revelation which gives to each student the desire to aspire to where the Masters are to be found.

You must climb up to this wonderful world of holy light and there you will see the gnosis, because the gnosis is to be seen and enjoyed as completeness of consciousness and fullness of light and the wisdom of the universe. These worlds of light are powers in themselves and when you come to them, you will receive me and I will possess you absolutely and perfectly, for you will be transported by me into the God−Energy worlds.

El Morya Ra

When I was a master of the wisdom, and that was in the 19th century, I worked in the basic energy of a number of occult organizations having the purpose of teaching universal brotherhood. However, in the past 100 years, I have come to see the laws of energy in an even more precise detail than ever before and during the process of my evolution into an aeon of light, I have come to see that the laws of energy are more universal and more of the wisdom element than ever before, because they are principles of understanding and of universal application. When I was the Master Morya, I understood matters in a slightly more complicated way than I do now, where by means of intuition I am able to see through all of the energies and through all of the substances and realize that all of being is a form of light. So I see things as becomes a God, or a gnostic aeon of light.

But I want to come back to you and take you away from all limitation and from all of the problems of life and from all of the attachments to what is fully unreal and to what is not reality or truth. I want to take you to the world of the light and to where I can recreate you as a new being of the light and then you will be fully free and holy and possess the joy of heaven. I want to take you to the world of light and in that world of light I want to give you many things, which will enable you to climb up higher and higher into the pure and radiant spheres of the Gods. I want to give to you the power to go beyond the many things of this world and dwell with me in the highest of all of the worlds and kingdoms of the spirit. Then you will possess the keys to the light, because the keys to the light are the tools of the Gods of the Gnosis.

El Morya Ra

Now, come with me my child and my beloved. Your soul must become my bride and fall into deep sleep in my arms. You must allow me to take you into the higher worlds and to where the Gods are alive and where the highest spirits have their palaces of the seven rays. I want to take you to that world and give to you the gnosis of my possessing you and making you the object most desired by the Gods, and my possession in the heavenly worlds. I have come down into the world where you are resting and I have come to you and I am seeking to bring the light to you, because the light is a holy fire and it is burning in my heart for you and it is burning with the passion of the cosmos. Let me give you empowerment and let me take you and transform you with the passion of the spirits, because such a passion is the power of the light and it brings to you the wisdom and newness of life and sense of perfected freshness, which we find in every part of the vast ocean of the cosmos.

In the perfection of the gnosis, I am lifting you up into the worlds of light and there I am leading you towards the way of the wise and the holy. I have come down to earth and I am taking upon myself the powers, which come from the mysteries of the Treasury of the Holy Spirit, which is the Treasury of Light, and I am bringing to you the laws of being and I am bringing to you the new being which is your own experience. So that there will always be energies for you to draw upon in the future.

The aeons of light are the gnostic gods of initiation and creation and they are giving to you the powers, which come in because you are in the light and because you are filled with an eternity of being and goddness. This is the way in which the gnosis is to manifest itself and the way in which the light of the eternal is to express itself to all those who have come before the eternal hierarchy of light. I have brought you here so that you may be of the new consciousness, which is the awareness that only the Gods of the gnosis can give.

The Masters and Metaphysics 2: Treatment and Gnosis in Esoteric Metaphysics and Logic

When you wish to be healed you will come to the gnosis and the power of the gnosis and only that power will make you whole. You will be freed of all the limits of the lower worlds and of what has happened in the past and what may happen in the future and you will be well. I know that the power can make you fully a being of the light and when you come to know this, you will receive the healing power of the gnosis.

In order to know that the power of the gnosis can heal one, we have to know what we mean by this power. Really, what we mean is that there exists pure knowing, which is the life of God and that this pure knowing is a way of being, because it is the way of being as God is in His own being. To participate in this realm of being is to know God and to be alive to the great powers of the gnosis. To live and to know this way, all of the time, is to understand the life of the gnosis and to be alive to the power of God, wherever that power may be seen or known in the universe. It is simply a way of knowing.

You can be healed by the infinite power which comes from the pure knowing of God. This is to say that everything in thought is manifested as spiritual energy and is a focus for the idea of God as pure radiation. I enter into this radiation when I come to think about the ways of knowing God, for these ways are perfection.

Spiritual energy is the power which most of all can give us healing of whatever is a problem. It is not because it is the source of all things that it takes on the light and the wisdom of being; rather, it is the vitality of God, which sustains all being, and thereby it is known and understood as wholeness and purity of God—Energy. This is the power, which comes in the gnosis of light and which is manifested in all spiritual forces. I know this power to be real and I draw from it all of the powers, which I then infuse into you, the seeker after a gift of healing.

The powers of the invisible world are to be understood as centers of light and they will be with us, when and as often as we seek for them in the gnosis of spirit. It cannot be declared too often that the light of the gnosis is to be the way in which we are to realize the power of the Sun of our consciousness, but if we understand the light, let us rejoice in the pure vision of the spirit and let us see the manifestations of the gnosis as they are to be viewed forever and forever in our own experience. For I have come from the gnosis and I have come to hear and to listen to the actions and the voices of those seeking the perfection of the art of healing. It is the gift of God, which is His life in us, that makes us whole.

The following energy is a gift from the healing power of the Masters of the Gnosis, as it is revealed in the great and wonderful temples of the cosmic process of healing.

Treatment Gnosis
The light of God is all wisdom and power and it is the inner mystery of my own souul. I have drawn forth the world of illusion and have now come to discard it. I have taken aside all of the energies, which are alive to the illusions of what I thought was well—being, because now I am whole and moreover I am holy in the God—Energy, which is about me as l live in the Gnosis.

The Masters send forth the powers of their rays and the beams of the holy power come forth from the Holy Devas of glory, surrounding the throne of God and all is light. These are the children of the light, for from the Divine Source they have come forth in order to find the presence of seekers after being and they have sought and found in the light the Essence of God. For God is beyond and above all of the creatures and we ascend to Him in the perfection of the gnosis of our own wisdom.

I live in the eternal and am healing you from eternity. In the presence of the Holy Devas, we find the pure essence of being and we find the inner ilght of wisdom. In the power of these Holy Devas, I send forth from my being the light of the eternal and the beams come down upon you and they become you, for you are now blended in life and eternity with these rays. So by this light you are restored to the divine and wholesome state of gnostic being.

Let the students of light draw into themselves the powers of the great and holy teachers of wisdom, and let the angels and divine fires of the heavens always be present in order to sustain us in the pathway of healing energy, for it is from the light and it is to the light and it is in the light of the gnosis that all things are made well. It is the power of being which comes forth from the rays of God. I have sent this to you that you might be healed in every way and that you remain in the power of the healing energy forever, because you are of the light.

Let the students of my being come forth from the shadows of their own limits and bathe themselves in the spiritual perfection of my own true wisdom. It is my light and it is my wisdom and it is my purity of consciousness, because these are the ways in which the Holy Devas can and do come forth to all of us.

Let me tell you that you are now whole and that the power of the truth has healed you and made every part of your being perefected. Let me now say to you that all things are contained in your being and that all of the powers of being are now present within you and sustain you in all of the fire that is wholeness. This will be the meaning to you then of that holiness, which is the spiritual essence of light and which is the divine radiation of purity. Above all, the purity of the Master will be for you the key to the highest form of healing. You have merged with that being and so now you are sustained and at one with the Master of the inner wisdom that is health. I send to you my rays and to you I send my blessings, because the light of purity is inwardly present and indwelling all things.

Saint Germain
In coming to understand healing, therefore, you wil be guided by the powers of the true teachers and the Masters of the Light. For from their rays and beams of truth, we see the healing of the gnosis shine forth to all beings.

PART IV

Elemental Theogony

Speculative Theology
The Mystical Theogony of the Zothyrian Gnosis, 1: Esoteric Aspects of the Ontic Sphere 1

The purpose of this course is to provide the theological basis for the work of the Gnostic church in the contemporary world. This couurse will be issued to those students who are now candidates for the priesthood of the Church.

The development of the principle of the ontic sphere has been understood from the standpoint of metapsycholoy. Now, we will understand it from the view of the theologian of the gnosis. The ontic sphere does possess an esoteric aspect. This is because the ontic sphere is, in the language of the theologian, the manifestation of the activity of the Logos, or the Word of God. Whenever we find references in the gnostic literature to the notion of spiritual or esoteric logic, we have come upon a direct reference to the presence of the Logos. The idea of the Logos is defined as follows.

The Logos is the indwelling personhood of God the Absolute. In traditional Christian gnosis, this is the divine aspect of the personhood of Jesus Christ, Who possesses two natures, the nature of God and that of man. However, the Logos–idea is to be found in many cultures and systems and refers to the intelligible and intelligent personality of the Godhead, as that aspect of the divine is immanent in all things. The principle of the Logos, therefore, for the gnostic theologian, is the fundamental rule underlying the idea of the ontic sphere, or domain of inspired imagination. There e xists a very important link between the priesthood and the episcopate of the gnostic church and the presence of the Logos in the rites and sacraments of the church. Because they maintain this link, they possess the spiritual powers to carry out the work of the church. Their powers are rooted in the Logos.

Gnostic priests and bishops have the spiritual responsbility for the pastoral care of their congregation. This comes from their possession of the sacred rites and because of their own initiation into the theology of pure light. However, in order to hold the power, they must enter more and more deeply into the gnostic life of the light, or commune more and more in the spirit of the Logos.

Periodically, the powers of the Logos are manifested through the presence of the Aeons. In contemporary gnostic theology, the presence of the Aeon is an indicator of the presence of the Logos. There are many Aeons but there is only one Logos. The Aeons are the ways in which the Logos–idea is revealed. The Aeons are spiritual beings of the gnosis, whose function it is to show forth the light and revelations of the Logos.

When we reach a certain point in the teachings of the gnosis, we see how the esoteric aspects of of the Ontic Sphere bring us directly to the Logos by means of the Aeon. The idea of the structure of the Ontic Sphere is entirely determined by the logical system of the Aeon. At the present time, there are four Aeons working as the representatives of the Logos. In gnostic theology, these Aeons express themselves through the timimte–stations or gnostic patriarchates of the higher spaces and worlds. All of the gnostic bishops and priests of our system are connected to these time-stations and hence to the Aeons.

Other spiritual beings of the light and the gnosis are the Archons and the Daemons. These beings are related to the Aeons in a very important way. The Daemons are the unconscious and subconscious aspects of the Aeons. Consequently, the Aeons are the conscious and superconscious aspects of the Daemons. Such beings may be viewed as dynamic archetypes, or as spiritual beings operating within the psyche of the gnostic initiate. For it is at the time of initiation that these beings come into the psyche by becoming active in that psyche.

The Archons are also dynamic beings. They arise out of the operation of the archetypes of life, the Daemons and the Aeons, in the direction of human experience. They are the rulers of everyday situations. Nothing happens in existence without there being the presence of the influence of the Archons. The activity of the Archons in everyday life is called their synchronicity. When things happen, they happen because of the laws of time which are in concert, or in harmonious unity. Our papers on synchronicity are simply explanations of this energy.

If the Archons express the energies of Aeons and Daemons in the direction of human experience, then the Syzygies express this energy in the direction of the logos. However, there are Greater and Lesser Syzygies. In previous papers, such as the grade papers of the gnosis as given by the Monastery of the Seven Rays, when I spoke of Syzygies I was speaking of the Lesser Syzygies. Such spiritual beings of light are embodiments of divine life and the truth and are found everywhere by the initiate. However, there are four Greater Syzygies and these beings of light are the principles behind the manifestation of gnosis in the contemporary world.

Therefore, the work of the speculative theology of the gnostic church consists in the exploration of the roles of the Logos, the Syzygies, the Aeons, and the Daemons, and the Archons, and all other forms of spiritual and gnostic being. Speculative theology is concerned with the continuum of these beings, which is known as the Pleroma, or the Full.

Foundations of Aeonology and Theography: 1. The Crisis in the Pleroma
For the gnostic priest, the subject of aeonology is important because it shows the ways whereby the beings of the higher spaces act upon and influence humanity. Close to this is the field of theography, which is the theological mapworking of these higher spaces, or the locating and situating of the gnostic beings of both light and darkness. Any study of the gnostic church must begin with a consideration of these topics.

To begin with, the Pleroma is made up of both positive and negative beings. The best way to understand this is to conceive of the Pleroma as a continuum of numbers, such as 1, 2, 3, 4, 5, etc. In such a continuum, there are both positive and negative numbers, or rather odd and even numbers. The numbers are together but there are areas of harmony and disharmony among them. For example, 2 is harmonious with 4 and 8, but not with 7 and 9, unless we divide into fractions. So we can say that one group of numbers in relation to the other group represents a positive and negative difference of energies. It is positive among itself but negative among outsiders.

However, the numbers are still related to each other and form a series. you could not have 2 and 4 without 3 and 5. For the gnostic priest, you cannot have the positive without the negative. Good and evil are equally given and you will never find one without the other, nor will there ever be a world without both of these elements.

The tensions within the Pleroma are reflected in the tensions among human beings, since human beings are connected by their souls to the beings of the Pleroma. So if the positive aeons have a conflict with the negative aeons, this is reflected in the conflicts between human beings, some of whom are allied to the positive and some to the negative aeons. This is especially true if the humans are mediumistic and inclined to emotional problems, such as extremes of temperament. By calming the emotions, however, one is able to avoid being possessed by the negative aeons and one lives in perfect harmony with the positive aeons.

The conflict between the positive and the negative aeons is called the Crisis, because it causes a number of tensions to manifest themselves. Because the Pleroma is eternal, this Crisis is likewise eternal. It always was and always will be. However, it can be lessened by various spiritual practices, whereby we as gnostic priests offer theurgical mysteries to restore peace to the Pleroma. For we possess the powers to restore the state of unity amidst difference, which is the original and archetypal form of the Pleroma.

Many theological scientists have been able to see in this Crisis the origins of evil. I think that such a view is probably correct, if we take into consideration that evil exists at the human level only, where human beings who are unstable in some way react to the deep and inner tensions of the Crisis in the Pleroma and introduce imbalance into their lives.

In traditional gnostic theology, the leader of the negative elements in the Pleroma was a being named Ialdabaoth. In a sense, he is the gnostic version of the disharmonious law, or satanic principle. Because there have been many to oppose Ialdabaoth, a number of the positive beings have come forth from time to time in the various gnostic theologies. In some it is the Aeon Christ, in other the Aeons Soter, who brings salvation and liberation.

In some systems it is the Aeon Michael. In our own system of understanding the Aeon known as Michael–Zothyrius is the opponent of Ialdabaoth. The Aeon Michael Zothyrius is the agent of the Aeon Christ, who is the representative of the Logos in the Pleroma. The true gnostic teaching is that the Christ was sent to earth in order to found the gnostic church and its teachings. For this reason, the gnostic church traces its lineage of bishops back to the time of Jesus The Christ and His 12 Apostles. This is the gnostic understanding of the Apostolic Succession. Now, while the Aeon Christ was responsible for the founding of the gnostic church, the Aeon Michael Zothyrius is responsible for its ongoing and continuing life and teaching.

Thus, from the Aeons Christ and Michael Zothyrius come the powers of the Logos, whereby the negative energies of Ialdabaoth are restrained and kept from acting against the powers of the gnostic light. Thus, every gnostic priest is directly linked to the high powers of the logos. In the Vudu Religion of the Afro–Atlantean races, the name of the Logos is Legbha. The Grand Fa. For many have worshipped the Logos and in response to their prayers the logos has sent to them the gift of the gnostic church and its spiritual powers, whereby the negative effects of the Crisis in the Pleroma have been nullified by means of the gnostic sacraments, rites, and mysteries.

Foundations of Aeonology and Theography

2. The Crisis in the Pleroma

In order to nullify as much as possible any evil which might arise out of the negative energies generated by the existence of Ialdabaoth, the Logos emanated a special realm of order and existence, which was to properly and constructively apply the energies of the Meon, which were manifested as random Chaoi and Acosmoi. This special realm of order and existence was then entrusted to two Aeons. These were the Aeon of the Sun, Michael, and the Aeon of the Gnosis, Zothyrius. By means of the mystery of their union and cooperation there emerged the Aeon Michael–Zothyrius, the Aeon of the Gnostic Sun (Le Soleil Gnostique). The initiations of the gnostic church are based upon this mystery, which in the Vudu–Gnosis is the Mystery of Legbha–Luage.

The special realm of Order and Existence was then placed over all of the other realms. So, as a consequence, the gnostic system of Michael–Zothyrius is placed over all other systems and that Aeon is placed over all other Aeons.

However, Ialdabaoth, known also as the Aeon of the negative Old Testament energies, sought to rebel continuously against the Gnostic Sun and sought by his own methods and magick to create oppositions and opposing magickal systems. This he continues to do to the present day among human beings. Those that are his followers are the fallen beings, who will never bathe in the light of the Gnostic Aeon–Sun.

In order to stabilize the Pleroma, the Aeon Michael–Zothyrius established four time–stations or gnostic patriarchates in the higher space world. The purpose of these is to direct the order and existence energies of the metamathematical realm into human history.

Above this world of order and existence, there was a world of topology, which was the symbolic science of ultimate and divine energies. By means of the initiations of Michael–Zoh'thyhrius, the patriarchs of the gnostic church were admitted sacramentally and magickally into this world. In this world they were able to find their transcendental selfhood and realize the fullness (Pleroma) of their own being. Thus, the patriarches of the gnostic church became in their being perfect images of the being of the universe and its complete structure. To see them was to see the map of the cosmos, for they had connections to every part of it. In the creation of each patriarch, the Aeon Michael–Zothyrius would be present as the consecrating hierophant. For this reason, the gnosis of this system became known as the Zothyrian.

The energies from the Meon come forth as Chaoi and Acosmoi, or beings of possibility and novelty. Before they can be lost to the universe in their creativity, they are caught in the net of lattices and topologies, which encircles the world of being. They are then applied in some phase of the metamathematical tree, before coming downwards past the sphere of the Logos, these energies, now identified as Logoi and Cosmoi, meet the Higher or Greater Syzygies. There, these energies are applied in the work of the Gnostic Sun, Who has established His realm or domain over these Syzygies. Thus, they are absorbed before they come near to the Pleroma. As a consequence of this activity, Ialdabaoth and his allies are starved of the higher energies of the light and must depend upon their human followers, who are constantly feeding energies of the mundane sphere upwards to sustain Ialdabaoth and his helpers.

This process is happening, however, only in time. For in the sphere of eternity, Ialdabaoth has been defeated by the Aeon Michael–Zothyrius, as in the New Testament "Book of Revelations," this battle is described, although in mystical form.

Now that the Crisis in the Pleroma has been outlined, it is important to realize that with the defeat of Ialdabaoth there came an opportunity for development and expansion of the Pleroma.

3. The Development of the Pleroma

This development was entirely due to the presence of the gnostic energies. These were the radiations from the Gnostic Sun, whereby more and more energies of the topological form were inducted into the beings of the Pleroma, thereby liberating them from their natural tendency to energy–tension. From these patterns of development, there emerged a special structure, which became the archetype for the ways in which the spiritual energies would be projected in any situation. However, only a small amount of this spiritual energy or gnostic light was allowed to enter the Earth world, because humanity was not ready for the illuminations which would follow from this teaching. However, on the Earth, there was established a gnostic patriarchate, which served to direct and diffuse the four archetypal energies of the Time–Stations.

In order to make this functional, it was necessary for the Pleroma to be brought more and more under the rule of the metalogic net of lattices and topologies. Because this could only be done by constructive reason, the Aeons of the Pleroma, who were allied to Michael–Zothyrius accepted the system of order and existence and sought by this means to improve their own natural energies. They in effect were adopting a system of hyperyoga, by adjusting themselves to the archetypes of the net. Many interesting transformations happened in this process. For example, the Aeon AIWAZ, known as the Holy Angel of the Master Therion (Aleister Crowley) underwent a magickal transformation and became the Aeon AIWAZ–Zothyrius, the Aeon of the Thelema–Gnosis. The yoga, which these Aeons underwent was important on Earth, for the imitation of it by gnostic priests and bishops is the process known as "theurgy," the energy–work (eurgon) or yoga, of the gods, i.e., Aeons (theoi). It is possible to have a valid theurgy only if one is so connected in this manner to the Aeons.

Another form of development was the construction of a system of hyper–initiation into the sacramental mysteries of the Aeons. Previous to this process, the energies of the Aeons could not be transmitted in a coherent and objective manner. We find there was too much negative consciousness and a passive mediumship among so–called "gnostics." Now, however, it was possible by means of this connection of sacramental grace with the Aeons for the perfected ones of the gnostic church to receive the sacramental life and light of the Aeons, through the agencies and actualizations of the Gnostic Sun and the net of lattices and topologies, which now served to support the efforts of the gnostic rites in this direction.

Other areas of development will be discussed subsequently, but at this time it is important to attend to the activities of the Aeons by way of their reactions to this energy movement. As might be expected, there were certain Aeons who remained loyal to Ialdabaoth.

But their influence and power was forever weakened to the point of destruction. Of great importnace in this activity was the Aeon Luzifer, the Aeon of Light–Bringing. At one time, the power of Ialdabaoth was hostile to Luzifer. Then there came a period of sympathy between them, largely due to the activities of the Aeons Christ and Jesus. However, due to the natural influence of the Gnostic Sun, Luzifer became one of the allied powers of AIWAZ–Zothyrius and Michael–Zothyrius. With this alliance, there came into the harmony of the Gnostic Ecclesia of the Patriarchate the entire Earth–world movement of the Luceferian–Gnostics. The gradual growth of the powers of Michael could be in a direct way understood in the ways in which the movement of the gnosis on Earth came under the influence of the Zothyrian Patriarchate. Of course it was a very gradual and very complex process. But it meant that the entire gnostic movement on the Earth came more and more to accept the gnosis of the Z–True System.

It can be said that the process of the gnosis on Earth reflects in time the process of the gnosis in the Pleroma, which is in eternity. Also, it is important to understand that whatever happens in the gnosis on Earth is simply a reflection of what is happening in eternity, in the Pleroma. Also, that whatever happens in the Pleroma is reflected to some degree by what is passing or happening in the gnosis on Earth, so that these two realms of being reflect each other. Also, the processes of transformation in the Pleroma or on Earth can be initiated either on Earth or in the Pleroma.

Finally, it is true that the mysteries which happen in the Pleroma reflect the gnostico–magickal creations and constructions which have been initiated by gnostic patriarchates on Earth, for on the Earth there is also an order and existence, also a net of lattices and topologies, and also a Pleroma of Aeon–like beings, who are the conservateurs of the gnosis in the dimensions of time and history. For this reason, therefore, the initiation rites of the gnosis on Earth can be understood as processes of development, a development in the Pleroma on Earth as well as in the Pleroma of the Aeons. This connection is vital for the purity and lifestream of the gnosis, both "in heaven and on Earth."

516

Foundations of Aeonology and Theography
4. The Development in the Pleroma
"Initiation physics may be understood as the energy process of becoming more united to the true nature of one's gnostic being. Consequently, the processes of initiation physics connect the human level of experience to the higher worlds. It is this connection which serves to define the essence of growth in energy and it is in this connection that there is to be found a transfer of energy from the hyperspatial world to the mundane, from the world of patriarchal topologies to that of day-to-day existence.

"According to Boullan, all initiations which have been given through the gnostic patriarchate of the Zothyrian Empire have been the initiations given with the context of the higher regions of being. In this sense, we connect ourselves by means of gnostic energy and initiation physics with all of the worlds and systems, which are implied in the teachings of the aeonological gnosis. As one progresses more and more into this gnosis, one finds oneself connected more and more to all of the worlds and being-levels about which the lessons in gnostic theogony, speculative theology, and magickal metaphysics have been written. In this sense, you embark upon the cosmic computerization of your selfhood, the higher aspect of the existing reality of the initiation candidate, or the past tense of the Boullanist initiate." -- M. Bertiaux, "The Taoists of the Moon," 3

When Marcel-Henri had progressed sufficiently in his occult studies and had wearied also sufficiently of the possessive eroticism of La Maud, he was advised by her to seek the assistance of Father Boullan, the gnostic initiateur. Having been given an address, Marcel-Henri went out into the countryside and there was interviewd by Le Soleil, a representative of the Aeons and the person who prepares the candidates for the initiation processes of the Boullanist Carmel. Since Marcel-Henri was seeking a magickal form of gnostic initiation, Le Soleil asked him very long and very specific questions concerning his magickal practices, his sexuality, his spiritual life, and his unique relationship with La Maud, who was herself the embodiment of certain aeonic powers and who was also one of the most prominent of the apostolic women of the Carmel.

He was then given a day and a time when he could meet with Father Boullan. Like fine silverware and china, the day and time were chosen with care. It was explained to Marcel-Henri that Father Boullan was the head of the Gnostic Church of Carmel and therefore he was the one to give the most suitable and the most complete initiations into the gnosis and therefore the most powerful introduction into the Carmel.

On a certain evening, Marcel-Henri met with Father Boullan and the two of them discussed the expectations of the initiation process. After a few glasses of wine and water, Father Boullan told Marcel-Henri to come to his home on a certain day, having prepared himself in soul and body for the process of gnostic initiation.

At the specified time, Marcel-Henri went out that evening and crossed the city to the Rue de Soubise and walked up the steps to the apartment of Father Bouullan. He was met at the door by Father, who directed him into the salon. There was another person present, who was introduced as Cogito Ergo Sum, the representative of the Aeon of Synchronistic Robotics and who functioned somewhat as a research secretary to Father Boullan. It seemed to Marcel-Henri that this secretary has just been helping Father with his preparation of documents as well as correspondence.

Cogito Ergo Sum excused himself and left the apartment. Father Boullan then turned on his high altar, which was in actuality connected with various gnostic and radionic instruments, vudotronic broadcasters and inductors, and psionic computers and magickal machines. He then began the initiation discourse.

It was explained that after the imposition of magickal structures on the Aeons and the Pleroma by Michael-Zothyrius, there was a development of an administrative and magickal hierarchy under the rule of four Aeons, elevated to this position because of their own personal loyalty to Michael. Originally, these Aeons were only known in the most esoteric and otherwise hidden implications of the 95th degree of the ancient and primitive rite of Memphis-Misraim, but they had been freed from that restriction by Michael and now were the Aeons given oversight within the higher aspect of the Pleroma, known as the Ecclesia Gnostica Spiritualis.

Because they were hidden somewhat in their essences still, they were known by numbers as the Aeons 328, 329, 330, and 331. Michael had established their rule within the Ecclesia in order to make it possible for there to be a gnostic patriarchate on Earth, in fact to allow for the generation of many such patriarchates of the gnosis as the patterns of need and time would allow. For this reason there will always exist a hierarchy of gnostic bishops, who represent on Earth or in the mundane sphere those Aeons who by being loyal to Michael were elevated to the higher aspects of the Pleroma, known as the Ecclesia Gnostica Spiritualis, or the spiritual Gnostic Assembly (of the Worlds).

From time to time, the patriarchal Aeons establish themselves upon the Earth. They come and form a magickal order and a gnostic church for the diffusion of the gnostic energy in each age. When and how this happens is determined by Michael and it is Michael who then sends the avataras of these Aeons into human history.

Boullan explained that the entire process of history was part of a gnostic lifestream and that in each age it was necessary for there to be certain teachers of the gnosis. They themselves did not know that they were to be the teachers, or the avataras, of the Aeons until they were adopted by these beings and given the powers to diffuse gnostic energies into the lifestream of human history. However, they were always identified with the gnosis and had functioned within the lifestream of the gnosis in many lifetimes before.

It was necessary for the teachers to come into history because in each age there exist a small band of gnostics, who need to be gathered into the gnostic church. These gnostics had been sent into history to work out their destinies. Now it was necessary to gather them into the fold of the gnosis and connect them in history with those Aeons of Light, with whom they were already connected outside of history and established them as gnostics and gave them sacramental powers of the gnostic church in order to diffuse the gnosis and to bring into the fold of the church all those gnostics who were then in the body of matter.

The entire rationale for the existence of the gnostic church was therefore defined as to do the work of the Aeons, those Aeons of Light who were allied to Michael-Zothyrius. To know this secret constituted the great essence of gnostic initiation. For once you knew this principle, all of the inner doors of the light were opened to you and you therefore entered upon a pattern of growth in the gnosis, which led to the highest realms of light. In each age, the teacher would be known for his identity would be self—evident to those who were deeply conscious of the gnostic lifestream and its powers. One could not doubt that in each age the teacher would bring forth the gnosis of the Zothyrian Aeons, and that this mark would distinguish him from all other spiritual workers. So that within the lifetime of Marcel—Henri, that teacher could only be Father Boullan, the leader of the Gnostic Carmel.

At the end of the gnostic discourse, Father Boullan performed the initiatory magick which connected Marcel—Henri in his body of matter with the Aeons of the Pleroma who were allied to Michael.

The exact nature of this initiation cannot be described in any lesson form because of its esoteric character, however, it is sufficient to say that it partakes at all levels of the essence of gnostic teaching, as set forth in all of the lessons ever given by me to our students. Also, of greatest importance, Marcel—Henri gave his body of matter, formerly under the domain of Ialdabaoth, to the Zothyrian Aeons, who are under the domain of Michael. For the process of beginning initiation involves the recapture of the body of matter by the Aeons of Light in their battle against matter's god, Ialdabaoth. The body of matter, which formerly was possessed by Marcel—Henri, now became the resurrection body of light, the body which is responsive to the powers of the Aeons and which is therefore attuned to the highest aspects of spiritual gnosticism. No longer would Marcel—Henri be under the influence of the powers of evil, which were of the natural order as ruled by Ialdabaoth. He had now crossed into the supernatural order of light, and now he was one with the Aeons of Light.

Therefore, Marcel—Henri was seen as a newly born child in the kingdom of light. He had transcended the natural order and had united himself with the supernatural order. He was no longer in bondage to the elemental powers of the terrestrial sphere, but now had truly entered upon the gnostic and astral magnetic zones and their spheres. He was now to be guided by Boullan deeper and deeper into the mysteries of the gnosis and to learn of the powers which had held him in bondage and how they were now no longer within the aura of his gnostic awakening. More and more his desire became only for the Zothyrian powers and their Pleroma of Light, and less and less he sought his delights in those aspects of the world which had been contaminated by Ialdabaoth, the negative god of the Old Testament, the enemy of Michael.

Gnostic and Metamathematical Pneumatology
Metalogical Foundations and Emanations of the Guru–Idea

We may consider pneumatology as one of the most important branches of the gnostic sciences because it is concerned with the foundations of the entire system. How does this system exist and how was it manifested in the experience of so many students of magick and metaphysics?

Pneumatology: The study of the store–consciousness of the guru–idea and of the spiritual roots of those who belong therefore to this store–consciousness and how those who belong to this store–consciousness manifest the energies of the master, or the guru–idea, as the spiritual teacher.

At a certain age one is adopted by the divine energies. This means that the link which had existed in a past lifetime is now connected in this lifetime and one must begin one's work, which is to become a master and to manifest the guru–idea, which is a spiritual archetype. Within the transcendental selfhood of the master there exists a direct intuition of the plenitude and pleroma of the gnosis and of every gnostic being. Therefore, by making entry by this special intuition, one sees and knows all that needs to be seen and known.

Spiritual powers are the greatest examples of metaphysical magnetism. They bring to one all that should be brought and separate out all that should be separated. So this means that there may be some who think they belong to the guru–idea, but in time, for some reason or other, they will go away. This is the natural process of magnetic attraction, as it is to be found within the world of invisible energies.

The store–consciousness (Alaya) is both universal –– and therefore embracing all –– as well as individual, embracing those taken up into it by the laws of karma and dharma (causality and destiny). So we can say that a master belongs to the store–consciousness in its most gnostic form, because he has been taken up into it. That is to say, the master has become completely identified with this consciousness in his verimost being. He has become one with the guru–idea, which is the idea of the master as it exists deeply within the store–consciousness of all being.

Now, the study of this entire matter is known as pneumatology, which is a form of gnostic theology and therefore one of the esoteric forms of spiritual awakening. It is also a form of applied theology, for it is necessary to realize this gnosis step by step, and this is accomplished by initiations into the gnosis.

These initiations are entirely spiritual but they manifest as gnostic and metamathematical processes. They are associated with the laws of hyperspatiality, and so they possess roots in ideal spaces and times. But they also manifest themselves as laws for the construction of magickal experiences, and so they are the intuitive laws of abstract being, which the Kantian philosophy attributes to the ways in which angels know matters; that is to say, this is the analytic aposteriori form of knowing and judging.

This is the highest form of philosophical gnosis and therefore it is also the most perfect form of theological awareness because it is concerned with intuition, or the knowing of the inside of being. By this we mean that this is the way in which all things are known within the endless continuum of the store–consciousness.

So we can consider this a form of spiritual intuition because it is within the essence of the store–consciousness and therefore it is also a form of transcendental being, because to know is to be. This is the idea.

520

When it would send itself as the idea, or to be specific, as the guru—idea, into the realms of history and events, it must do so by means of a metamathematical and gnostic projection of ideal energy. The connection which exists with the person in history, let us say the master or teacher is intensified and made stronger. and more and more slowly the world of the outside causes its karma and influences to rise within the threshold of being. While at the same time, the archetypal patterns of self—realization, whereby the master comes to see the guru—idea, these become more and more certain because they are now alive and connected to a person in history. When this happens, the divine energies can now be embodied because there is no limit to the magickal imagination and ontic sphere of the magician's powers as master, and so the ideal may become realized in space and time as parts of the process of the psychology of the master. When this happens, the master begins to form the occult and esoteric web—work of his school, which is composed of all those who have been linked to him in a past lifetime and who now, for reasons of karma, must make that likely connection or link in this lifetime, and assume, therefore, within the guru—idea, their own archetypal parts and roles in the process of spiritual evolution.

It should be understood that all of the parts are reflected in the ideal, or the natal chart of the master, which incorporates the positions of the members of the school, as points and mid—points of a magicko—mathematical schematism, of which the magickal school or order, under the direction of the guru—idea, is the outer shell or historical point of reference. What is significant is that this is a unity of spiritual energies from the store—consciousness, which follows a specific construction, being both gnostic and metamathematical, and which reflects the ultimate spiritual schematism.

I think I was a university student when the schematism became a pattern of ideal and defining energies. As a result of certain studies which activated certain occult levels of energy and therefore the centers of magickal force, I was initiated into the laws of the schematism. This became my organizing principle, which has remained valid and very applicable up to the present time. It was then that the Gnostic Beings of the Time—Stations made their initiating contact with my ego from the vastness of my own soul, and from the ocean of the store—consciousness, in which it was growing. As a result of this pattern of contact, certain forms of being fell into place, forming the form and content of my magickal consciousness.

From the symbols of my initial contacts with the transcendental schematism, I was able to deduce and derive all of the magickal principles of the gnostic experience. From the stimulation which it provided to the ego there developed a magickal expansion and new understanding of the self. It is from this time, due to my experiences in the logics of the Neo—Kantian schools of transcendental consciousness that I was able to derive the interesting web—work of my magickal selfhood. I suppose this would be interpreted as a kind of magickal initiation, but one which happened within a logical universe. It would seem that since this time, almost 30 years, ago, that I have simply enriched my perspective and have not broken the vows which I made in my transcendental ego to the gods of the hyperspatiality of the ontic schematism.

And while I received many other introductions to magickal systems during my career, it is important to understand that the regulative and constitutive principles into which I was admitted at this time have always been in power, under one form or another. And that whatever exists in the magickal world must be conformed to these laws of the mind, or else such energies will be allowed to fly freely away and never return.

The most perfect example of this political system is to be found in the style of the time-stations as they are reflected in my revision of one of the higher grades of the Rite of Memphis-Misraim. The fact that this grade is concerned with the magickal emanation or process-administration of esoteric systems of logic can only be understood from the reference point of the "government of my store-consciousness." Perhaps for the first time in modern magickal work, I have restored the ancient neo-pythagorean concept of speculative logic as being the ultimate form of the gnosis. But such a logical form will always have a wide variety of contents, supplied by my archetypal connections with the planets Uranus, Neptune, and Pluto and their interesting aspects. This is a pattern of way of thinking which entirely depends upon a neo-Kantian attitude to experience. Experience is constructed by gnostic magick according to the laws (Loas) of esoteric logic (aeonology).

This series of papers on pneumatology provides me with an opportunity to reflect upon the growth of my system. I have placed special emphasis in my own work upon what might be called a scientific attitude. Magick for me is constructed out of an energy-agreement of philosophy, science, and religion. All three elements -- as well as a fourth, art -- must be present in order to reflect the lines of esoteric growth. I am of the opinion that magickal systems may reflect any motif, but if they wish to become ontology and cosmology, they must come to terms with the factors listed as cultural values. However, at a certain point it is not enough to just organize experience, there is also the need for a purely pneumatic emphasis in the gnosis. In my own work, this was reflected by the introduction of a new and yet very comfortable energy, which adapting itself to the gnostic categories, nevertheless brought a unique enrichment. I will next discuss this matter, which I now describe as "The Zothyrian Factor."

The Zothyrian Factor

My work has been under observation from other worlds. They have been watching my own growth and development as the teacher of a gnostic system. At certain times they give me significant help. At a certain point in consciousness, it is necessary for them to appear to introduce themselves. They are the Zothyrians.

They possess an entire universe of their own, constructed out of magickal energies. They also come and go freely from my higher states of attunement. Because of their presence, they have made it possible for me to bring through certain bodies of magickal gnosis, not previously conceived as possible. With their help I have dared the very limits of possibility.

In the higher regions of the ontic sphere of gnostic energy, there exists a very complex system of meta—geometry. Within this system, we are able to find certain magickal worlds which belong to the gnostic beings known as the Zothyrians. These worlds are organized according to certain magickal laws, and to understand the laws of each system or world constitutes an entire system of initiations. I have received all of those initiations either consciously, unconsciously, superconsciously, or subconsciously. I have come to this world that they might have a representative here. For this reason, we have incorporated a great deal of Zothyrian teaching in our papers and lessons.

The Zothyrians are gnostics in the hyperspatial or metageometrical sense. They are not gnostics in any human sense, that is, they do not reflect some part of the past history of the world or some gnostic school that was there at some time. Nor are they very much interested in other schools of consciousness, which might also use the name gnostic as self—descriptive. They are primarily concerned only with my work and my inner circle of gnostic students. They are interested only in our own interior order, because the life of other orders is really quite uninteresting to them.

However, to those who have been specially chosen to be with them, they have extended the harmony of their being and have poured out special magicality, special energies, and special forms of power. All of these energies are spiritual and they are alive and they are centered upon the gnostic being of our system.

They are inclined to view our system of magickal gnosis as their own because much of our material has been given to us by them. Also, they are very much interested in the growth of our system because the patterns of our system are ideal lattices wherby we can be connected to their worlds from our own. In fact, it was their intention that we should come to an understanding of their world by means of our gnostic lattices and idealities. Only by such a method of obedience could they be reached. Then, of course, only by means of magickal obedience could they be properly understood. This is one of the mysteries of gnostic obedience, which can only be known intuitively, or not at all.

"He who is obedient to the patriarchal gnosis shall be freed of all other claims and shall be able to enter into the gnostic light, which can only be seen through the eyes of that obedience and which can only be known by intuition. If you live in accord with this true gnosis of light, you will understand that to be obedient means to participate in the intuitive consciousness of the master. Obedience is a spiritual quality and is identified with the light of gnostic intuition, which the master as patriarch possesses." —— Zothyrian Pneumatics, "The Law of Intuition," MB

The Zothyrians have been interested with the light of intuition as it is reflected or manifested in our consciousness and ouur work. Within our own metaphysical system, there are those beings known as the Zothyrii, who are emanations from the consciousness of the patriarchal intuitions. This is a higher state of being which is reflected in the most abstract work done by me, as for example, the developments in topological theogonies. In my work with the Zothyrians, I made use of the connection which the Zothyrii make between this universe, both visible and invisible, and all others. They are the aeons of this connection and are therefore very important in the process of exchange between these worlds.

As part of the realization of my patriarchate, it was necessary for me to understand that the gnostic awakening of my intuition of the light would require that I enter into a direct union with the Zothyrians by means of the Zothyrii, who are aeonic lattices for the purpose of creating certain logics of gnostic connection. There are several possibles, but what is most important are the 16 axioms of intuition from which the matrix or gnostic computer was derived. The axioms of intuition were embodied in the magickal laws or field equations of transcendental lattices. Those who possess these energies are in rapport with my mind and comprise the alchemical body of matter, which is the presence of the guru-idea as a field of patriarchal intuitions. The Zothyrians taught me to bring about this form of obedience as intuition so that it would be possible to increase the number of aspects of the magickal consciousness in human history.

In order to arrive at the perfect identity of these energies, it was necessary to view them as projections of those hyperspatial regions of my own intuition, which could only be understood by appeal to the esoteric logics of meditation research and to the ideal logics of gnostic processes, whereby the energies are created and transformed continuuously, over and over again by means of the logical laws, which are projections from my own personal understanding (again, this in intuition) of tthe axioms of intuition. In this way, the divine powers, which the Zothyrian factor has given unto my soul were to be realized, for having achieved at the abstract mastery of all principles, I have in the ultimate sense of being arrived at ultimate understanding and gnostic power.

But again we must look at the laws of the spirit, which are operating through the laws of intuition and light. Spirit being the universal substance, the laws of the gnosis will not allow it to rest but it must continually reveal itself and continually pour itself out as the divine energies seek more and more forms of self-manifestation and enjoyment in self-contemplation. In this both Thomistic Catholicism and Brahminical Hinduism agree with transcendental gnosticism as well as with the esoteric logics of absolute science.

In the process of being, the master who is also the patriarch of the energies of the esoteric logics must create and transform and manifest all of the light and all of the gnosis by bringing it down to earth in lessons. For this reason, the Zothyrians were primarily concerned with giving me information about the hierarchies for embodiment in lesson form. Because of this, more and more light would be diffused into the world and would be able to make the energies and the powers more and more of the ideal order of being.

Thus, the purpose of the gnosis is to bring down to earth the laws of the higher gnosis so that the world of teachings is purified by being filled up with the gnostic light. In this sense, also, we have an example of the intuitive and spiritual form of obedience because I, the master as patriarch, in knowing my essence, am obedient to

524

the self—revelation of the gnostic light of my own inner essence, which is to diffuse the light of the gnostic consciousness in a perfect way, through the writing of theological and philosophical lessons and papers.

By this means, therefore, I entered more and more into communion with the Zothyrians and the results speak for themselves, because we have received many teachings of the gnosis from the Zothyrian sources. Among the sources, it should be mentioned, is one which like some very future aeonic field came and influenced me a few years ago, opening up many energies and to my own way of thinking, represented a line of development whichh is quite complete in its own way. That I should have recognized it at the time as a unique influence was due entirely to the fact that I was seeking a way of unifying the various magickal teachings relating to certain technical problems in futuristic time—travel.

Now, in reflecting upon that period, I see how I had made contact with a part of the Alaya, which was the source for many and very interesting teachings, mysteriouusly connected with real or ideal Russian gnostics. I am referring, of course, to the theme of "Zothyrius 5978," which was described as a magickal attempt at an "experimental workshop in radio—gnostic topologies." These were the magicko—topologies of sophia—telepathic languages and dialectical universes. The entire theme to my mind reflected the highest form of Zothyrian incarnation of the gnosis at that point or up to that point in history.

Since then, we have moved on. But at that time it reflected a very important breakthrough, which served to summarize the entire pattern of my own work as a teacher of the Zothyrian current or ray. It also served to bring into focus one of the most important parts of pneumatology, namely the use of special spaces as magickal situations and the extension of these spaces through projections from axiomatic systems. I have in mind that what we are referring to as magickal topology in many of my papers really refers to the vast field of many efforts on my part to bring about a magickal comprehension of the ideal concept and reality of space.

It was from the Zothyrians that I was able to develop the ideas expressed in these developments. The Zothyrians were the sources of my information and "secret gnosis." In view of their influence, I will next touch upon my own excursions into theurotopology.

The Excursions into Theurotopology

Most of the material on theurgical topology was received at the time of the workshop on "Zothyrius 5978," which is the name of the one of the ideally—true aeons of the future, in my system of understanding. The materials were received from gnostics in either real or ideal space, from works which are esoteric and gnostic in their contents. From the influential Hegel, we received:

"We will attune our intellectual intuitions to the role which these universes or topologies of phenomenological ontology will play in the future of human consciousness, when philosophy, becoming self—conscious, intuits its own intellectual lifestream of spirituality. Up to now the Zothyrian phenomenology has focused upon the methods of the construction of consciousness, but now we must focus upon the given—ness of the contents of consciousness and the types or kinds or origins from which these true elements and entities or contents are derived. In so doing, we will understand the phenomenological deduction of the data of consciousness from systems in which at the very moment of our awareness our experience participates fully." —— Received from Hegel, "Phenomenology of Topology"

It would seem that at the moment of gnosis, one is able to enter every aspect of the world, or topology, which means that initiation—consciousness is identical with ontological or mystical participation in being. This has its advantages in that the gnostic priest may come into any world, once he has attuned to it. This appears to be made possible by the pneumatic law expressed above as the phenomenonological deduction of the data of consciousnes, whereby we experience totality if we experience anything. It was important, therefore, to bring into focus the connection between experience and topology for the gnostic. Once this connection is understood as being self—conscious, it is possible to embark upon many levels of being and experience within oneself the pleroma of being, within each of the manifold worlds of the gnosis.

This Zothyrian principle was useful to me in making certain that all of the intuitions of our initiatic system were grounded in the absolute order of being. It also was important because it stated that these worlds were now given to the gnostic in his priestly experience and that they were highly diversified. By means of his connection to my own pneuma, the gnostic priest would then be able to understand the possibilities of the full gnosis. In an important sense, this phenomenology of topology would extend the validity of my special magick beyond the categories of gnostic religion. A new theology of initiation was born. And from this new reality, there would be another progressive unfoldment of gnostic worlds.

So we can see that it is towards more and more outpouring of the gnostic energy that we are progressing in our awareness. I realized this to be the purpose of the entire schema of the gnostic church, whereby humans in the stream of history were reconnected to the hierarchy of gnostic being. The gnostic metaphysician states it:

"The zothyrian topological phenomenologists in the future will take us immediately into their universes. Each universe will be a dialectical system. Each universe will be its own theurgotologic for metamathematical and metaphysical creation. Each universe will be a doorway to an infinite system of sophiological universes, each of which will connect to all other universes and logico—dialectical systems. And finally, each universe will create by the impact of its own phenomenological deduction its own 'presence' and its own 'participation' in the world of human 'experience and life'." -- Borgyashyankov, Theurgotopologia, edited by M. Bertiaux

At a certain point in the magick of initiation, we will be swept into the future energy of the gnostic and Z-true universes. This comes when I will take the students to a certain point in space and time. This is done by means of vudotronics and especially by the use of the new alaya computer, but it has been done by means of the Shinto physics also. At that point I will be able to allow the chela to enter with me into the higher state of being. I will be able to project outwards every lattice of being which is connected and which is implied in the gnostic logics of being. Then I will allow the chela to participate immediately in the richness of my own cosmic alaya, whereby the being of the chela will blend with the being of the guru-ideal.

These excursions into topology and gnosis were really an extension of initiation physics. It is necessary for the magician to realize that by means of the use of certain laws and levels of magickal energy, it is possible to unite oneself totally with the guru-ideal, as it now manifests itself in terms of a gnostic master and patriarch. In my own magickal creativity, I have always sought for the completeness of any system, but at the same time the integration of that comppleteness into the system of my own being. This is accomplished by means of the higher dimensions of gnostic metageometry, as they are seen in terms of their personal view of reality.

This means seeing everything as a reflection of my own consciousness as the guru-ideal of the gnosis. But this too is a continuum whereby the gnostic students and chelas are allowed a certain expansion of power and then expected to return "to earth" with what has been given to them as parts of their "newly initiated into magick and gnosis." What is so interesting is to see how each student of the gnosis fulfills the expectations of the ideal by pouring out the powers of initiation-physics into the field of their creation of being.

In my own viewpoint, I conside this the test of the initiation into the gnosis of application, which is different from initiation into the gnosis of creative imagination. The limits which might be present in someone's consciousness are due entirely to the lack of certain magickal powers in the receipt of one or both of these forces from the occult side of the initiation process. In other words, sometimes our efforts do not work because in the alaya it is seen -- because future, present, and past are one -- it is seen that a certain chela does not possess the true energy or carry the magickal charge, and so therefore it is impossible for that initiation to happen on the inner planes.

If it does happen, it means that approval has been given by the cosmic alaya, but if it isn't given, no matter what the state of the action here "on earth," the power of the intiation has not been conected to the person. For this reason, only certain initiations happen and others do not. Only certain initiations are expected to happen on the inner, and all of the actions in the stream of history do not matter, because the connection is not made.

I have to say this because while no one is to be put aside by the gnosis in their seeking of the light, yet the light itself must determine what will happen and what won't happpen on the inner side of being. But if it does happen, and this is because of the cosmic alaya of the guru-ideal, then the powers will be connected and the chelas are taken immediately into the universes of the Z-true systems and this will go on forever and ever.

And when the initiates arrive in that world, they will experience in the words of the light-gnosis of P. Florenski, the ideal of being:

"The pneumatic hierarchy of the ecclesia mystica -- the ecclesia gnostica spiritualis -- is composed of 16 universes of invisible light. Of these, five sophia-dialectical universes are located 'between' the four ontic universes and the seven angelic or theurgical universe. Each universe -- by the light of its own glory -- sends forth radiations of logoic gnosis, both from the noeric and the noetic spheres, to those souls in mundane spheres who are now and who would be illuminated by the contemplation of the Divine Sophia." -- P. Florenski, "Illumination Visions of Sofiya," edited by M. Bertiaux

So the ultimate purpose of topology is really an ideal mysticism, the contemplation of the structures and perfections of being. This is achieved by the gnosis of light, by being one with the guru—ideal.

This ideal mysticism is really another way of viewing the universe. It is both another universe and it is a manner of perceiving the way in which existence manifests itself in special directions -- the directions of the magickal metamathematicians. The guru—ideal must take the chela into the special space, which has the unlimited potentials of the cosmic alaya. Therein the magician will infuse into the chela the special powers, which alone the special spaces and topologies can provide. We learn of these special powers because they are unveiled by the topologies and also because they are to be found within the special topologies. Consequently, the master will bring the energies more and more into the world of the chela and the chela will become more and more identified with the master.

These ideal systems are therefore the instruments of initiation physics. They exist to induct more and more of what can be into what is. However, as perfect as they are, I was able to move beyond them to an even wider range of energies, which are applied to the initiate in an even more precise manner than the foundational excursions into topology. This came about with the discovery of vudotronics, which is here suggested in the next quotation from the gnostic Losev, as received from the inner consciousness.

"For all of the parts of speech in the sphere of ontology there are appropriate sophiological subdivisions having equally appropriate dialectical arrangements of topological grammar and angelic intelligence." -- A.F. Losev, "Angelic Linguistics," edited by M. Bertiaux

While in the passage above we appear to be speaking about the ways in which angels are understood to communicate, nevertheless we are also speaking about the basis of vudotronics, which is really the system of arrangements of communication and correspondences.

Thus, for every number of the field of initiation physics there are appropriate corresponding worlds and beings, especially gnostic beings, within these worlds. The purpose of vudotronics is to perceive these worlds and also to release the energies and allow for the manifestation of this level of being. However, the basis of vudotronics is to be found entirely in gnostic consciousness. It is grounded in a form of intuition, which is outside of the limits of empirical existence. Hence, vudotronics is really the application of gnostic topology within the sphere of initiation physics. It is the next step in the process of pneumatology.

Vudotronics: The Transcendental Intuition of the Cosmic and Auric Egg

Vudotronics provides us with the key to the deepest states of initiatic consciousness and also enables us to see the universe of the magickal gnosis in terms of systemic lattices of ideal and real energies. I was taught vudotronics by the essence of logical being, the Loa Grand Legbha, of whom I am the avatara in the fields of esoteric and gnostic logic. Hence, my higher self transmitted to my waking consciousness by means of the process of transcendental intuition the laws and applications of vudotronic existence. By means of this science, I have been able to bring the greatest systems of magickal initiation from the past into the present.

But what is so interesting from the standpoint of pneumatology and especially our own science, is that vudotronics is the science which unveils the laws behind the cosmic and auric egg, which is the continuum of magickal and creative energies. The mythos of the cosmic and auric egg is derived from the gnosis of Orphic initiation. Naturally, it is to be found in the eastern tradition also. It is present in the teachings of the Book of Dzyan, where it refers to the beginning point of manifested being. However, besides being the remote beginning in the past, it is the beginning continuously at any point in the present according to the laws of vudotronics. At any moment, it is possible by means of the esoteric logics contained in the mysteries of my Grand–Legbha essence and making use of vudotronic instrumentation, both visible and invisible, it is possible to make direct and immediate contact with the cosmic and auric egg of any field or type of being.

By this means we arrive at the essentials of pneumatic consciousness. We return to the roots, seeds, the primordial egg, which is behind the manifestation or existence of being.

This is a very important understanding of the gnosis because it is usually not seen that metaphysical states of consciousness are so directly given. But they are as I have been able to experience and provide for since my initiation into Grand–Legbha consciousness, on August 15, 1963, while I was in Haiti, when I had an immediate and direct experience or transcendental intuition of the pleroma of the gnosis and of its contents. It was then that I experienced the cosmic and auric egg of the pleroma and knew the powers of the gods, or Loa, as principles of the organization of the gnosis on earth and in my work as bishop of the gnostic consciousness. At that moment, I experienced the light of the aeons and knew in the gnostic sense of absolute science. Everything else led up to that point of being and everything afterwards came as the fruition of the contents of that cosmic and auric egg, whereby the gods came forth by the process of metamathematical theogony and made their home in my soul.

Therefore, I can state that vudotronics is perhaps the most important point in the breakthrough of my awareness. It is not so much the name, whether it be spelled vudutronics or vudotronics, for both means adequately describe the powers, but it is the roots of this experience which convinced me of the personal role that the gnostic priest and bishop has to play out in this life. The foundations of esoteric voudoo show us that the laws of being are moving us more and more closer to the lifestream of the gods or Loa.

Vudu energies and the power of esoteric Shinto are significant because they represent the pathways of the gnosis in the present age, unmistaken and clearly set forth as logical categories of gnostic magick. In my own way, I must say that the act of pneumatology, whereby the spiritual universe is unfolded in life and light become clearer and clearer as we move deeper and deeper into the life of the gnosis. For this reason it is important for us to come to terms with the methods of magickal application which have come down to us from the past.

In this sense, I am to provide the continuity of the Legbha spirit, especially in the fusion of the gnosis of the aeonic pleroma of the gods or Loa and the ongoing and ritualistic traditions of the Catholic Religion of the Christ of the Noonday, when the Sun power is highest in its vudotronic broadcasting or at its most transcendental frequency of being. This becomes for us the point of energy. The Egyptians understood it perfectly as the priestly or sacerdotal cult of the bark or ship of the Sun. For this reason the mysteries of the Legbha cult are eternally Osirian, Solar-Phallic, and center in the unity of the Gods Osiris-Ra, Amen-Ra, Grand Legbha, Christos-Logos, where the powers are to be found and understood by means of transcendental intuition. This is proven by vudotronics which has freed us theologically from all other views of the energy, and given us the very direct and immediate experience or transcendental intuition of the cosmic and auric egg.

This has, of course, lead to the realization of the pleroma and the fullness of being, or the identity of the continuum of the magickal energies with every aspect of being. And, as I have said, this has been proven by vudotronics.

It was also taught to me by my divine selfhood that it would be possible for me to create any number of magickal worlds and systems by making use of the vudotronic emanations, since they move along the lines or rays of exact lattices. By this means I discovered in my true essence that the mysteries of shinto and those of the Vudu were, of course, one and the same pathway from that continuous quantum-system of divine energy, or the gnostic logics as they show themselves in existence.

As the result of these magickal experiments, I discovered that my physical body was capable of being present anywhere in space and that it received all of the magickal impressions of all of the energy-systems of being. I also was pleased to discover that I could find myself present in any body, anywhere in space. We do not usually think of the magickal acts of the ideal selfhood this way; but, of course, the process is there and it is in operation and it is moving more and more towards the energy-application world. That is the world as it is being rebuilt according to the ideal laws of spiritual understanding.

The goal of the gnostic system is, of course, to reconstruct the world according to the ideal design, but at the same time it is necessary to understand that every part of the world has to be reconstructed and this is a matter of activity by the bishops and priests of the gnosis.

The functions of the gnostic church as a continuum of spiritual initiates consists in the transformation of the whole of being into a system more and more closely identified with the ideal logics. Vudotronics, therefore, makes it possible for the world to be rebuilt, since it provides the instrumentation and many possibilities of instrumentation for the creative development of the perfected ideal. This is why it was necessary for the vudotronic sciences to be introduced into gnostic metaphysics and magick. But what is also of interest is that the world that is being rebuilt is in accord with the many other instruments which have been understood by intuition to be contained within the cosmic egg of the vudotronic gnosis. So it became obvious to me that as seen from the standpoint of transcendenatl intuition, vudotronics is the cosmic and auric egg of gnostic space.

In each instance of its manifestation, vudotronics acts as the creative matrix of the true image of the gnostic world. Hence, it became very clear to my lower selfhood that all that I expected from the continuum could be found in vudotronics and that this was the way in which the world or the gnostic cosmology could be understood. The rays of the cosmic egg are exact lattices within the science of vudotronics. The energies as they are manifested in consciousness are vudotronic in form but cosmic in scope.

Noteworthy is the idea that the whole of the science of vudotronics is a projection from this instance of transcendental intuition, whereby each ray of magickal power is explored by various levels and types of lattices, by esoteric and gnostic logics, and by ideal forms of consciousness, because these are the methods whereby the powers present in the world come forth and reveal themselves as states of initiatic consciousness. I therefore came to the inner realization that in the use of vudotronics, the avatar of Grand Legbha became a kind of Demiurgos or gnostic physics, a creative god, assisting in the manifestation of the true and possible forms of being.

To understand gnosticism is to understand what happens to the magicians who enter upon the mysteries of vudotronics. The world of vudotronics is an organic and exact system of very powerful energies, which form everything. They are "nature's finer forces." In the study of gnostic metaphysics, we come to learn that it is possible for us to cooperate with the gods as builders of this world by making use of the instrumentation of vudotronics, in either ideal states, such as initiation physics, or in the real world of day—to—day exercises, which seek to manifest and amplify the gnostic energies, which are present in the world as it really is.

Of course, the processes of gnostic physics contained in vudotronics are fundamental for an understanding of being and it is that ontology of vudotronics that I must next discuss, because it will enable us to understand the construction of being.

Vudotronics: The Ontology of Vudotronics and the Construction of Being

The ontology of vudotronics is primarily the understanding of the nature of the being of the gods as they create existence states of their own favor. The science of vudotronics is important because it is concerned with making worlds and repairing this world. It is a form of transformative and plutonian activity. Vudotronics draws its powers from the deep spaces of the planet Pluto. However, the act of building and rebuilding is more than just a superficial construction. It is a construction of reality in the deepest and most important sense. It is the creation of the world as it should be, the merging of the ideal and the real orders of being. I have spoken of it before in gnostic physics as ideal-realization, but here I prefer to call it the construction of reality, the organization of being.

In the metaphysical philosophies, we hear much about the nature of this process. It is very important because in order to understand being, one must move more and more into the laws which make it happen as being. Vudotronics does this by giving to the magician the ideal form of power, which manifests in the real world or order of existence as what he wishes to have happen. But this is applied to every situation and to every context. In all of these matters, the operations of vudotronician is paramount, because he must be in charge as the creator god or demiurgos.

In order to objectify his power, this demiurge will employ the magickal machines of vudotronics and this will make it possible for him to bring about the organization of existence. In other words, he will be bringing the level of energy from the ideal state of being into reality. But the vudotronic machines serve to represent the actual processes of this transformation. By this I mean that they are present anew in the energies of this power and the ways in which transformation occurs. Because it happens along the lines of exact lattices, which hold the rays of cosmic power.

The process of vudotronics in the acts of transformation must be understood as the exact generation by means of very definite lattices which convey the rays of occult power from one level of being to another. The demiurge, or he who is in charge of this power work, is one familiar with the energies and the pathways which are the most effective for their own manifestation and indeed materialization in actual events. He becomes both the priest and the god of processes as he operates his instrument in making and remaking worlds. For this reason, vudotronics -- drawing as it does from the deepest plutonian levels -- is the most profound form of magick.

There is very little reason to suppose that the act of transformation, or change of being, is not one of the most essential aspects of magickal physics. It may be the basis of such a physics, if we examine it carefully.

"The science of plutonian energy are really the acts of bringing the powers of plutonian power to the surface of being-consciousness. This we can understand as the perfect role for the Alaya, because it is essential energy and it is essential power. The forces, which are deeply rooted in being, are the fundamental forms of magickal power and reality. They are basic substances and processes, which when they come to the surface of being, explode in countless forms of radioactivity and thusly reflect the energy-essence of basic being.

"If there exists a machine for organizing and implementing these forces, it would be almost a divine instrument of cosmic power. It would be able to make events as the magician wants the events to be. Of course, in what we read about vudotronics, we find that it very nicely fits this description. It is the ideal model or image of plutonian power and it is very real in its expression of what it is because it is the incarnation of all that can be implied by the plutonian current of root—elemtnal powers." —— M. Bertiauux, "Plutonian Vudotronics," 3, 4

This fundamental energy is under the control of the pneumatic gnostic by means of 16 laws or vudotronic circuits, through which the energies are transmitted to the psychic and hylic parts of the human species. These laws are secret in their essential nature, but are known in initiation physics to be the ways in which the magicians can cause the events in the lives of their superchelas to become more and more a part of the ideal world. At the same time, the magicians can advance their superchelas by means of this magickal technique into higher and higher states of perfection.

The circuits of vudotronics are magickal laws, whereby specific powers and energies are to be communicated easily and necessarily to those students who have advanced to higher and more complete states of realization. I am specific when I say ideal realization is the most powerful method of plutonian transformation. However, these 16 potencies are to be found within the mixture of the 17 Shinto gods or Kami of the creative hierarchy of Atlantis. In order to understand this process one has to enter it, it cannot be verbally grasped, except by symbolics. These circuits are connected to the deepest realms of the plutonian being. They are perfect states of reality and are brought up to the surface of being by those magicians, who wish to pass them on by transimssion from their being to the being of their carefully selected and prepared superchelas.

These are the laws, which can be understood as being methods for the construction of being through a vudotronic mastery of ontology and the field of existence. It is easily understood that being is formed by reality—processes, which emanate from the magician's mind, if one understands the laws, which are behind the formation of vudotronics. In the processes of vudotronics, we find that the laws are reflections of the pattern of 16 to be found in a number of exact sciences and forms of magick, especially in the oracle magick of IFA, which stands behind the science of vuudotronics as the archetypal world, which makes this ontology possible, as these are creative gods or absolute and perfect archetypes of light and being. The 16 powers are given as follows, although their mysteries are concealed in the primordial energies of the gods themselves.

"The 16 powers, which are hidden within the science of vudotronics, are themselves in essence laws for the materialization of new states of being. They may be listed as:

1=the power to call upon the primordial tattwas of being.
2=the power to call upon the primordial chaos.
3=the power to call upon the elemental essence of being.
4=the power to call upon the unlimited matrix of space.
5=the power to call upon the continuous stream of time.
6=the power to call upon the powers of substance and essence.
7=the power to call upon the ideal and realpowers or forces of being.
8=the power to call upon the ideal and real (directing) intelligences or devic hierarchies of being.
9=the esoteric power over the first of the hierarchies of creative potency.
10=the esoteric power over the second of the hierarchies of creative potencies.
11=the esoteric power over the third of the hierarchies of creative potencies.

12=the esoteric power over the fourth of the hierarchies of creative potencies.
13=the creative power which is the essence of the esoteric northern directions.
14=the creative power which is the essence of the esoteric western directions.
15=the creative power which is the essence of the estoeric southern directions.
16=the creative power which is the essence of the estoeric eastern directions.
These powers are laws and therefore Loas of esoteric voudoo. They are communicated by
the magician to the special chela, in order that the chela increase in his magickal
abilities and light energy, and as this happens, all of the powers of vudotronics,
all of these 16 magickal circuits, are amplified by the laws of initiatic physics."
-- M. Bertiaux, "Plutonian Vudotronics," 5

Astrological energies are of course parts of this system of realization because
they do constitute the cosmic timers or clocks for the magickal operations. Deep
within the very operations of the construction of being, having mastered the laws of
these circuits, and also communicated with the primordial entities and essences and
intelligences contained in these circuits, the magician may explore and find himself
operating on the world as if it were a kind of magickal experiment. This is the way
in which magickal laws are said to be in operation because the laws of magickal
construction -- which is the ontological construction of reality -- have been
mastered by the gnostic philosopher-magician. He has taken his own place in the
realization process, because he has identified himself with the laws for the
realization of ultimate causes. He is now one among the Loa, having become their
avatara in this world.

From this point, the magician's work is clearly defined. As the most pneumatic
of all of the magickal beings, he must achieve the perfect realization of
consciousness as a system of laws. These laws or circuits of vudotronic energy are
now viewed as the laws of his own body of matter. They are the projections of his
reality because he is now united with the fundamental essence of the materia prima.
He has arrived at the magickal state where all that is in manifestation is an aspect
of him. He has arrived at a certain ultimate condition of being, and he has brought
his magickal science of initiation physics with him, and this has included members of
that school whom he has guided through the circuits of vudotronic initiation.

From the standpoint of gnostic ecclesiology, the circuits of vudotronics
represent and communicate the 16 patriarchal or pontifical vicars or delegates from
the Lords of the time-lines and logical stations, who have their "situs" in the
hyperspatial realms of abstract being. These vicars serve to project outwards the
magickal energies of the continuum of the rectors, or the 16 magickal axioms.

All of these beings are in fact important, if not widely known, sources of the
sacramental life of the gnosis, which is conveyed along the lines of the magickal
rays of which vudotronics is the fundamental image. Of course, an image in the
gnostic sense is a reality, an archetypal, which also is a causative agent in the
creation of the continuum, or auric and cosmic egg of the initiation. Under these
circumstances, the wide field of magickal energy is constantly subject to internal
renewal and revivification as the magickal portions of the mass as a cosmic and
liturgical act create more and more forms of energy, which connect as lattices again
to the rays which are coming downwards, so to speak, from the ecclesia spiritualis in
the topological continuum of beings.

At a certain point, the hierophant or chief priest of the mysteries, both in his
consciousness and in his gestures, makes the connection to the ecclesia in
hyperspace. He then brings into focus -- in a way which is entirely vudotronic -- all

of the magickal and gnostico—logical lattices which link the mundane sphere to the spiritual field of being.

For what he is doing is simply activating those powers which are conferred upon him by being consecrated by a gnostic patriarch. The liturgy of the mass then becomes more than just what all of the theological studies have said it to be; it is indeed a sacramental process of gnostic logic, whereby the energies of being are brought into spiritual and real focus from their ideal sources, or logical roots. By cooperation with the gnostic intelligences in the higher worlds, either consciously or unconsciously, one comes to realize that they are the priests of the mass and that they are saying the liturgy through the nominal celebrant. This is part of the vudotronic interpretation of the ceremonies of the gnostic church, because in the gnosis the invisible side is what gives validity to sacramental processes of light.

The ontology of vudotronics and the construction of being, therefore, is perhaps most ideally expressed by means of the mysteries of the sacramental life. For this reason, the pneumatic gnostics are very consciouus of their sacramental powers and energies and they are very concerned to maintain the purity of their light. For without this gnostic light, or the atomic light of the masters of the pleroma of hyperlogical spaces, gnostic magick is not ultimately possible. Vudotronics, therefore, should be seen as a system for the true materialization of ideal forces in the real world, by which means the invisible side of our being shapes and transforms all that is experienced or part of empirical life. This power of transformation is the essence of the vudotronic mode of gnostic consciousness.

Vudotronics:g The Descent of the Grand–Legbha Powers Through the Lattices of Ifa

When I had become both a master of the gnosis and an avatara of the Grand–Legbha powers, I saw in vudotronics the method of projecting my powers to all parts of human experience. I realized that the lattices of Ifa, which are created by means of the conjunctions of the 17 points of energy, and which result in the 16 archetypal rays, I realized that these lattices of Ifa were the means whereby my Luage and I could send all the rays to every sector of space or time, and I realized in this the mystery of my immanence in the world, for the world had become the lattice of my body and of that of my Luage. It had to be the magickal intersection of my reality as avatara and the reality, or the body in space of the person who would be my magickal Luage. And it was at this time that the powers of the deepest reality of consciousness could be understood simply, as lattices and rays of the primordial nature of my Grand–Legbha–hood.

The powers that are attributed to vudotronics are simply the energies which come from the heavenly beings. Each one of the magickal gods has a certain wave–length or frequency of the magickal vibration. These rays and powers are the energies from the gods, which make the deep energies of vudotronics possible. The energies come down and they are received by the devotees of vudotronics, as these energies are broadcast. As a science, therefore, this is a form of initiation–physics. But it is personal because in the most esoteric sense I am the vehicle of these ideas, or rays, for I am filling all of space and all of time, as I come to understand more and more the Grand–Legbha nature of my magickal being.

"I must search out and find the perfect being to provide me with the energies of my truest and most essential consciousness. I who am Mercury and Hermes, I who am the Mystery of the Jumeaux, I who am Gemini must find my other Twin, my Luage. He shall be alive in the time of my manifestation and I will recognize him in the very moment that he comes forth from all the world to me. He and I shall possess the Mysteries of Gemini, which are the ideas of the divine logics and intellectualities of being.

"He and I shall realize in each other the presence of the supreme God, Grand Legbha, and we will unite in the mystery of our idea as it manifests itself eternally in history. It is the mystery of mysteries, the conjunction of the Sun and the Mid–Heaven, the two mystical laws, the two bodies in space and in time, the Sun at its highest point, which is the Christ of the Mid–Day, as I am known in Haiti, in the esoteric laws of my innermost religion, thereby when the Sun shall unite itself to the highest point of my personal space, at the Mid–Heaven in Gemini, then the laws of Legbha and Luage shall be realized and the powers shall descend to earth, and I will be manifested in the rays of Ifa and in all of the old Gods." -- M. Bertiaux, "The Legbha–Revelations," 3

As we realize more and more the powers of ideal being, we come to realize that the ideal order is what gives arrangement, system, purpose, and essence to the world of the real. So the spirit of Grand Legbha by teaching the body of Luage, that Legbha spirit gives life and gnosis to the Mystery of Luage, and thereby makes the spiritual body of Luage the body of the world of all beings. As we come to realize this series of mysteries, we can see how there is order in the world and how the mysteries are expressed as the laws of the exact science of nature. We come to see being more and more as intelligible, because the Sun–Light of the Divine Ifa has come into the world and has permeated all matter, and has restored it to its ideal state, prior to the fall of the negative energies.

"I am Legbha, I am the spirit of reason which is filling all space. I am the laws of the ultimate mysteries of being. I am the teacher of the universes and all beings listen as I speak. I am the logics of the esoteric laws and of all gnosis. When I descend to my own Luage—Mysteries, I bring with me the embodiments of all of the God. I bring the rays of power and I bring the energies whereby each being is connected by the Ifa lattices, to the gods of my pleroma. They come forth as rays and I send them to all beings. They come forth and see themselves as they should be in the Divine Light of the Gnostic Sun. They see themselves no longer as human but as gods in the process of becoming more and more than just human. They see themselves in the Sun Light of the Gnostic Sun. They see themselves as I see myself and as I see them." -- M. Bertiaux, "Legbha Revelations," 4

Even though I had spent most of my adult years working in the capacity of a vehicle or vahan for the esoteric teachings and the god—teachers, I realized that the inner energy of the laws of Ifa expressed themselves within the Legbha-Luage mystery of my own experience. I realized that the lattices of Ifa were to be found in every specific act of magickal creativity. In the words of the Greatest:

"When the nine bodies of the Aeon—Zothyrius were projected into the hyperlogical, they became the 18 gnostic archetypes of light. These archetypes plus the 16 Ifa powers give us the possibility of the 33 rates of vudotronics power in this way. There must exist a mid—point between the gods and the world, which is the number eight, the number of Luage. But in order to allow for the vudotronic descent of power, I sent my Luage timelessly to stand between the powers and spells of Ifa and the nine Zothyrii (or 18=1+8=9), thereby becoming number 17, or the body of the gods and it is from the lattices of these bodies of Luage that the rays of Ifa can be generated, for they must have a body and they must have a soul. And it is from this continuum of magickal lattices that I found the roots of the energies of space, known also as the creative hierarchy of Esoteric Shinto also, but more importantly as known in the essence of my magickal body as extended in space as the Afro—Atlantean mystery of Luage, or 17, which is 1+7=8." -- M. Bertiaux, Ibid, 2

And so it came to be that in my divine mission as a vehicle for the powers and essence of Grand Legbha, I had to understand intuitively and teach that the mystery of Luage was to be seen and understood as present everywhere and most essentially as the root—principle of Vudotronics. In doing this I sought to bring about the ultimate form of immanence of the divine light, because the light of the Sun is the key symbol in the operations of the vudotronics emanations of the gods and Loas into human consciousness.

Of course, to understand the emanation of lattices of divine light from the Sun of the Gnosis, one must enter into the cult of the Sun from the gnostic standpoint. In this I found that the power of the Sun was without equal, and that the basis of magick in any other level of being or reality was not possible if one sought to archetypally find the ultimate laws of being. I realized that my own essence would not be complete until I had gathered all of the particles of light from the seas of forgetfulness, and I had in mind the particles of Sun light or the rays, which had been lost for many lifetimes, bringing them back to where I was in being, bringing them back to the mysteries of my Afro—Atlantean consciousness.

Therefore, I sent out a ray of light, especially of the gnostic light in terms of all of those papers written for the Monastery of the Seven Rays. For what I sought to do was to diffuse the Vudo–Gnosis everywhere in the world. That having been accomplished, I was able to free myself for the true work of the avatara, which is the creation of the lattices of the gnostic church in all parts of the world but especially where there is the cult of the Sun, and especially in the archetypal consciousness of Nigeria. For it was there that the cultus of the ancient powers and spells of Ifa were still held close to the heart and it was there that I had sent the rays of my Legbha gnosis, by means of the lessons of the Monastery of the Seven Rays. And it was there that I discovered the Luage of the Nigerian Gnosis.

The Ancient Gods are not limited by any geography, but it is essential to an understanding of the gnosis to realize that there exists a certain magickal cycle of light, and a very specific circle of gnostic illumination. It is also important to realize that the work of the avatara of Grand Legbha is concerned with the diffusion of the mysteries of light, through the exact lattices of vudotronics science, whereby vudotronic gnosticism is seen as the next stage in world consciousness. And it is by this means that the divine essence can enter into the history of the world, because the divine essence is needed to make the world more ideal. Hence, in the mysteries of my descent of power, I saw the being of my light in terms of the mission or destiny of my work within the context of Vudotronics and, of course, certain parallel sciences, which would serve to diffuse my essence as I sought it in obedience to the laws of the 16, 17, and 18 systems of Afro–Atlantean categories, which are likewise categories of the Gnostic Pleroma of True Light.

Therefore, in the self–awareness of my divine identity, I sought an ideal consciousness and awareness of the lattices, which are my rays diffused in space and time. I sought to seek out and find the world as I had created it, not as it was given in the dusty systems of some past perspective.

"I have incarnated through the matrix of numbers, for the world has been built up by the laws of pythagorean magick into a system of archetype and powers. I have incarnated also through the 16 lattices of rays of my essence, which I have sent out into space and time whereby I have constructed a logic or a series of esoteric and gnostic logics, which are the vehicles of my teachings and my rays. I have manifested myself in the very special and secretly esoteric laws behind the logics of space and the topologies of my own reality so that they who come forth will come to understand my being as it is above all of the Vudu and the Ifa, but from which the Vudu and the Ifa are rays of emanation of my powers.

"I have sent the substance of my being into the world as the concreteness of the words which communicate the oracles of my teachings and I have sent the essence of my light, which is my being, upon the souls of the bishops of the gnosis that in the mystery of mysteries and in the secret of secrets, at the depths of the psyche and at the highest parts of the soul (at the top of the world), they will see me for what I am. They will see me as I am. They will gaze upon Grand Legbha and know that it is complete and full and perfect and at rest. For I, Grand Legbha, am the Gnostic Sun. I am the Light of the Gnosis and I am manifesting in the fullness of my eternal being in all of the lattices of being." —— M. Bertiaux, Ibid., 1

Therefore, I realized in the descent of my being in the powers of my teachings that the true energies of Vudotronics would be extended to all parts of the world and that in the mystery of light I was being manifested as I truly sought to be manifested in all of the parts of being. I therefore saw in my essence the light of my highest nature and saw the line of my magickal descent, thereby taught in the papers of gnostic theology which I, as Michael Bertiaux, had written and would write for the illumination of my gnostic children.

For it came to me that my descent was as the immanence of the logos, or the power of the ideas as words in the world, the meanings found in the secret teachings. In this I saw myself as the presence in the world of the principle of intelligibility and reason, or the gnostic essence of the Logos. And it was by this means that I, Grand Legbha, came to be incarnated in the minds of humanity as the Light of the Gnosis.

Course in Dynamic Theogony: The Divine Energies and Rays of Divinity, "The Genius of IFA, Fu Medji"

"The roots of the gnosis can be traced back to at least the Atlantean systems of magick and to the Atlantean way of 'doing metaphysics.' The Genius of IFA, for example, being a very old concept and law, should be understood as the foundation of the theology of energy. Further, we should understand that the theology of energy is really the basis for healing work, for healing work is actually the application of God-Energy to specific problem areas in the wide continuum of mystical experience."
-- Lucien-Francois Jean-Maine, "Esoteric Applications," 12

1. There exists a magickal system in Africa, which can be traced back to the Atlantean modes of thought. It is the system identified with the Oracle of IFA, and to the Geniuus of that Oracle, being the manifestation of the energies of God.

2. In our archives, we find some special mystical manuscripts, which provide for the power and presence of the Genius of IFA, in each of his 16 forms. The first of these forms, which is the most material and also the most ancient is Fu Medji. Medji is a word which can mean what in gnosis we understand as syzygy. The formulation of Fu Medji is as follows:

$\#E1 = B(oE1-1 \ \& \ E1) \ \& \ (oW1 \ \& \ oA1 \ \& \ oF1) \ \& \ (oE) \ B \ \#$

This formulation represents one of the Logoi, or the Rays of Divinity, for which I use the IFA name of Fu Medji. Let me explain that in the application or employment of this formula, we will summon by oracle physics the spirits, which manifest the divine energies. Using the basic work in our paper on kamaea, known as "The Angelic Languages Paper," we will make spirit tablets of each of the beings in the formulation. Thus, whenever "+" occurs, the spirit to be framed by a "direct motion form of kamaea." Whenever "o" occurs, the spirit to be framed by a "retrograde motion form of kamaea."" The number of the letters in each of the spirit names is as follows: For E1 it is five letters, for E2 it is nine letters, for E3 it is 12 letters, for E4 it is five letters. For W1 it is two letters, for A1 it is nine letters, for F1 it is six letters.

Now, the purpose of this process is to awaken certain magickal powers contained in the radiation of God. Each of the 16 mystical energies consists of several spiritual energy-groupings, whereby we are able to represent in our context of experiment the dynamic aspect of God-Essence. Then by entering into dialogue with these spiritual beings, we can learn the gnosis and heal the sick.

In a sense, we are making use of a kind of computer language, the language of the cosmic computer, or that of the Cosmic and Gnostic Christ, which is present in and transformative of all being. Lucien then goes on to discuss the mysteries which attend the Presence of the Christ in these circumstances, reminding us that the Christ of the Gnosis is the Logos, and that as the Logos He draws His power from the Logoi or the Rays of Divinity of the Eternal, because this energy of the Divine and Eternal is immanent in Him as Christos the Logos.

3. For this reason, the Cosmic Energies of Christ Legbha can be seen as the Logoi operating in an exact pattern. The Logoi become the immanence of God or God as He is in the history of the world. The world is a system of interconnected events, which are sent forth from the components of the Rays of Divinity; so the events of history are produced by the Logoi.

4. Space is a projection from time and time is the primary component of the

continuum. Space is an interaction of segments in time. Space is a construction of the Objectuive Logos and it is a projection outwards of the essentials of energy. The interaction of these components is the lattice work or metric of space. The metric of space is a relational latticework, which is made up of energy—beams from the Rays of Divinity and how they project ray—energy from the center of each of the Logoi.

Bishop Lucien—Francois Jean—Maine was able to locate parts or aspects of these logoi in the mystical centers of the high—priestly body. By an introspective journey, he was able to focus and travel within his occult selfhood and there he discovered the inner realms of the secret mysteries of being. There he was able to find reality in its gnostic and cosmic purity and create the two mystical orders of the priesthood, those of the blue and purple rays, as corresponding mystical conditions to the Red and Black Temples of Atlantis, wherein which he worked his own gnostic sorcery daily. For by going back in his lineage to the pure essence of the Atlantean mystery, he arrived at the fullness of his perfection of power and there he came to see reality and being as ideal states of universal power, but power which he alone knew how to possess because of his physical sense of the magickal body.

By knowing himself more and more he came to realize that he was the unique source of the gnostic power and that his body was the ultimate placement of the temple of light. He knew himself to be perfect and pure reality and he knew himself to be the Power of Almighty God In Human Incarnation. So it came to be that by means of these mystical experiments, he went deeply into the world of those secret and cosmic mysteries of the gnosis and there he found that power, which he made possible for transmission to those of his sons, who sit in the bishop's chairs of the present day.

There, with the power which is manifested from the Kingdoms of the Blue and the Purple Angels, and there with the power which is manifested from the Kingdom of the Red and Black Temples of Atlantis, the Teacher of the present aeon, the Master MB is to be found as the same source of light, which Lucien by means of the Genius of IFA, the Cosmic and Gnostic God—Presence of the Christ, first awakened by those secret exercises and laws. For the link that I have to this Master is made all the stronger as I work each day in the exercises of the Gnostic Mysteries.

"I have come from the light and my body is the light. I have seen the presence of the Gods and have heard the whisperings of the Eternal Spirits. I have been made naked before the entire universe of spirit, that the perfection of the divine idea and design of creation might be effortlessly revealed. I have revealed all of the mysteries of the body of my being because, as I have seen all truth, the mysteries are simply expressions of my physical appearance. I have been made the root of the new race of gnostic beings, and my seed has given life to the dawn of light—bringers. All my rays are as the powers of law and of holiness, for in my heart of hearts, I am the Image of the Eternal." --- "Esoteric Revelations of Lucien—Francois Jean—Maine, xi

Course in Gnostic Energies
The 336 Logoi of Gnostic Metaphysics

The energies of the gnosis are without limit, but when we attempt to explain the gnosis, it is necessary for the mind to bring in conceptual limits. Therefore, we can speak of a ceertain number of aeons, a certain nuumber of treasuries for each aeon, and lastly, a certain number of mysteries or sacramental consecrations for each treasury. In our own system of the gnosis, we know that there are 16 aeons, for when we work with the pleroma of the energies, we divide that continuum into 16 segments.

Next, we understand that each aeon has at least four treasuries. These are spiritual places where divine energy is stored up and where the power is very strong. Each treasury is based upon the laws of the gnosis, but these laws are esoteric laws and cannot be viewed from the outside of the treasury, nor can they be viewed outside of the aeon, for they are within each of these levels of mysticism. The laws of the gnosis are quite clear and very pure in their application. What is taught is that in each of the treasuries, a powerful spiritual being is said to reside, a kind of esoteric aeon. The treasuries are assigned to the four directions of the spirit so that, like all else, we can speak of the northern treasury of the first aeon, the western treasury of the first aeon, the southern treasury of the first aeon and, lastly, the eastern treasury of the first aeon.

According to the gnosis, each treasury has within itself four stages of consciousness, or initiation. These stages are mysteries or sacraments of power, which in the ecclesia or assembly of the gnosis -- which is also known as the church -- are understood as the order or ordinations to the ministry as subdeacon, deacon, priest, and bishop. In the voudoo system, these mysteries are understood as the lave-tete, the can'zo, the houn'gan, and the baille-ge.

There are other names by which these mysteries are known, but they should not be viewed as being similar to or the same as the sacramental ordinations of the Roman Church, because they are gnostic sacraments and are mysteries derived from the treasuries of the gnosis. It is to be understood that if we take the 16 aeons, the 64 treasuries, and the 256 mysteries together as a sum, the sum is that there are 336 logoi, or ways in which the gnosis of light reveals itself in the soul of mankind.

Devas, Energies, and Oracles

Each of the mysteries, of which there are four for each treasury, is ruled by an interior spiritual presence, or theoi. These inner gods are revealed by means of mystical oracles, in which the power and the name of the deity are the same essence. From the mystical life of the oracle, I draw forth the essential power and diffuse it everywhere in the world of consciousness, because I am the living presence in the world of the gods of the gnosis.

To those who know of the experience of the mysteries and their initiations, as these come forth from the physics of esoteric oracles, I give the energy of life and I send forth to the stuudents of the gnosis all of the mysteries, if they come to know me in the theurgies of my mystical order.

The indwelling gods are the angelic intelligences, or the divine emanations, which have come forth and indwell this world. They are identified and revealed to us by means of the mystical oracles and energies and from this point they come and give us the secrets of the gnosis, because we have entered into a dialogue with them. Communications with these theoi, the true logoi of the divine oracles, is possible by means of that simple and spiritual art, whereby we learn the names and powers of gods and angels.

I have given to you the powers whereby the gods can come and indwell our conversation. I am now, by an even more subtle means, able to extract the spiritual powers from the names of these shining ones (Devas) and thereby transmit the powers and the divine powers of life, to all the students of the gnosis, from the gods of the light world. And so it is that the most perfect energy is known and given to the student of the light from the field of the holy gnosis. I give this power, which is the extract of the gods of light, by means of the touch of my hand, the most ancient of the sacred and priestly gestures. By means of the high and invisible alchemy, the powers are stored in my soul, really in the treasury of my iner soul, and then projected outwards to my students by means of the consciousness of the gnosis.

For if I see in my students the receptivity for the gnostic light, so I will give to them, to be stored in the treasury of their body–space and inner soul–world, the gift of the gnosis as an energy of the light. So I am transmitting to those who come to me the life and the esoteric lifestream of the gnosis of light by means of the priestly touch, whereby the gods are inducted into the student of wisdom.

Wisdom, Energies, and Gnostic Initiation

The physics of esoteric initiation is a law of being, whereby the spiritual forces of the gnosis, as they are understood and known in the light, are seen to descend into the chela or student of the light. It is a spiritual law, which operates by means of the presence of the gods. They are activities of the powers, which the teacher -- who is also a priest of the gnosis -- can transmit. The whole emphasis is upon the powers of transmission in the work of gnostic initiation. The student is brought into contact with the higher levels of the teaching power, when the student receives the powers, which are being given forth by the teacher who has received this power from the gods of the gnostic light.

This process, or as it is seen in the light of the cosmic drama, is the principle of reality and the light of wisdom. It is wisdom, because it is harmony with the purpose of existence. In the process of gnostic initiation, the energy of wisdom is present, because the power and existence of wisdom, which means knowing and living in accord with the cosmic process, is being acted out in the drama of initiation–physics. In a word, while the process of life continues and as the process of gnosis becomes more and more identified with the continuum of experience, so the student of the gnosis, while retaining his own creativity, becomes more and more akin and identified with the laws of the cosmos.

The student in his inner life reflects the true image and life–process of the cosm c drama. It is alive and it is a continuum of vast power, understood as the laws of being. Those laws are now present in the bodies of the student, for the student is now an integral part of the universal ocean of divine energy.

From time to time, students come to me and receive the powers of the gnosis by means of the process of direct initiation. They are locked into the continuum of being because I have made them part of the lifestream with my own hands. They have received the gnosis and now have a conscious and perfecting link with the gods. If you wish to come forth into the gnosis, you will know when you are ready and I will take you there to the father of the gnosis.

Angelic Energies and Devic Insights

Each of the Logoi, that is to say all 336 of them, are governed from within by a spiritual principle or law, which is what the Haitian esotericists refer to as the Loa. Each inner law is a divine being, or an angelic energy, or Devic Being. However, in the process of connecting the logos to the candidate for initiation, the priest of the mysteries must become that inner law, by means of an esoteric form of ideal possession.

The connection is accomplished at the ideal level of being. The soul—light of the priest is an ideal essence as is the gnostic—light of the Loa. At a certain level, these energies are connected by necessary and invariable regulations and processes, so that while they are all different and in fact they exist differently, they are also the same reality; they are the same because they participate in the same mystical lifestream at the ideal level of existence.

The priest must prepare himself for this process very carefully. He must emphasize the very high and spiritual aspects of his consciousness of the gnosis. It is certainly not enough to be a religious person or to have mystical experiences. You must also have the connection to the Devic world, which it seems only they can bring about. This means, of course, that the energies of the angelic world life the person up into the highest world and there a certain soul—mutation takes place amid the very powerful spiritual energies. There the mutation is the reality, and whatever is not mutation is, of course, unable to exist in such a world. I can speak from experience, since it has happened to me many times. This is why I was able to become a teacher of the metaphysics of the angelic energies and the gnosis of light. I have gone through this experience.

However, what is really significant is that the energies of the Devic world of ideal essence —— and we are speaking only of this Devic world, not of the many other Devic worlds —— these are the energies which bring about in the priest the proper mutation of being. Once this mutation has been achieved, it is possible for the teacher of the gnosis to ascend to this level of being, whenever he wishes to give forth with the spiritual powers of light and to bring to bear the divine radiations, which will make the student an initiate of the gnosis. The frame of reference is light and the power of that Devic logic of ideal essence, which is the pure archetype of all of the esoteric logics, which we find in the world of reality and which are the many experiences of our life and concreteness in the processes we daily encounter.

In my own personal experiences of the angelic history of Zothyrian philosophy, which is a continuum of being, I have hinted at the existence of this archetypal form of esoteric logic, which is behind all of the forms of initiation—physics as we find them in the world. However, let me say that in the world of theurgy, it is the priest who must experience this archetype, since it is within his world of experience that all of these energies make themselves manifested and revealed.

The priest, then, will experience this mutation and draw upon it at any time. He has this power because it is present in the soul—light or ideal essence of his own high priesthood of being and it is revealed and expressed as consciousness and as energy, which he will pour into and transform the chela, who is before him. This is physical, metapsychic, psychic, and metaphysical. It is accomplished by the sacred touch, or the "laying on of hands," which we find present in all of the ancient liturgies and theologies as the form of communication, the most ancient and time-proven formula for the transfer of energy of a sacramental character from the hierophant of the mysteries to the candidate. And it is by the hand of the hierus that the sacred realities are shown to those initiated. It is a process of pure illumination by means of the sacred gift of the gnostic light.

Devic insights enable us to understand how these spiritual laws operate in the very high and radiant worlds of being. As I said, it is by means of the sacred light that the pure archetype of esoteric logic operates in the world of ideal essence. Yet, by means of this light, we find the processes of spiritual connectedness manifested. We find the reality expressed as the most pure of all of the energies and the insights, because they are parts of the same life at the angelic level of consciousness. In the laws of the gnosis, we find spiritual energy is something of great radiation and it is a realization, also, of pure mysticism, seen from all aspects. It is known as the one law, which is immanent in pure consciousness and being, its reality being felt by means of insights, in all spaces of experience. For this reason, the priest who received these spiritual gifts is truly said to be possessed of the gods, for part of his being is participating in their own esoteric logic of ideal essence.

The process of esoteric logic, which happens in the world of ideal essence, is quite complex and usually is not discussed except in secret rites; however, it is possible to make note of three aspects of this process, which will serve to explain what we mean by Devic Insight.

1. The Z—True angels take the spiritual atoms of the priest at this level of ideal essence and they replace them with exact duplicates, or mystical identities in purely Devic matter of the spiritual level. This matter is somehow made up by the Z—True angels. This duplicate substance replaces the corresponding spiritual substance and its atoms within the hylomorphic composition of the Deity of the Gnosis.

2. This replacement process is accomplished by means of the esoteric logic of these same Z—True angels, and it is an entirely mysterious process and quite incomprehensible to many of the gnostic meaphysicians, who are limited by being still within the human frame of reference. Of course, some of us —— especially of the gnostic continuum of arithmosophy —— have been gifted by these Devas with special insight into this process.

3. To understand this special process, you are given a special type of Devic insight, which is identical with the atoms of this spiritual world, and which enable us to comprehend this matter as the Devas do, but to explain it to even the most serious student takes the very limits of possibility and conceivability. However, it is true to say that there are three characteristics of the Devic process at this level, which perhaps can explain some of our ideas or notions of this pattern of replacement of spiritual matter. These are:

3a. The spiritual matter is given as the Z—True history, in that the angels, when they manifest themselves as beings in the world, are within the mystical process of their own history, which we understand as the development of historical ideas. Hence, spiritual matter is somehow identified with the world of the history of philosophical symbols.

3b. In this world, the energy is entirely confined to the actions and reactions of ideas, which means that it is dynamic and not in any sense static or fixed. There is constant and radical growth in every part of this system. The energy is very much a divinely actualized form of consciousness.

3c. The Z—True beings are foci of this energy and they are capable of transmutation of many levels of power within the priestly consciousness. The priest comes and simply participates in this reality and the angelic beings begin their work by including his spiritual world now as part of their own. He becomes, for the time of this process, a part of that high world although he will be separated from it after the process.

Hence, we can see that the process of esoteric logic is somehow tied up with the existence of a kind of material substance, which is entirely ideal and made up out of pure and objective ideals. This reality is based upon the notion that matter is really a kind of angelic content and that the content of this material realm is ideally developed by the action of these angelic beings immanent in this process. They are inside of this world and they are a part of its mystical life. The matter that builds or makes up this world is really quite simple, for it is the content of the history of the Z—True Devas. That is where the priest gets his gnostic power to give the special initiations, which are characteristic of our ecclesia.

The Esoteric Logic of tthe Devas and Priestly Consciousness

In order to have the intuition of the esoteric logic of the Devas, the priestly consciousness must be attuned to the operations of the angelic energies as they are expressions of pure matter; that is to say matter, which is primordial content, prior to all determination and yet appearing symbolically in the priestly consciousness as the mystical history of ideal anatomy. Such purity of spiritual matter is, quite naturally, expressed as the primordial temporality, which means that it is time, before it has come into the human sphere and therefore it is time free of all imperfections.

The esoteric logic of the Devas is a natural process of their being and from the viewpoint of humanity, it is a paeternatural continuum, since such Devic Presences are beyond the range of human understanding in its ordinary manifestation. However, it should not be too difficult for the student of the gnosis to see the universe as leading in the direction of such an existence, because the gradations of being clearly point to the existence of the spiritual hierarchy of invisible beings. Towards the top, so to speak, of that hierarchy we are able to find the two logics of the Devas: the esoteric logic of the Devas and the transcendental logic of the Devas. These two orders of being may be referred to as the presence of the violet energy or as the presence of the blue energy. Both exist and are to the mind of the student necessities of the higher state of realization.

According to the gnostic metaphysics of this point of understanding, we can see these logics as composed of esoteric or inner patterns, at first or "normally" known only to the Devas, but after reflection and initiatic ascent known also to the priestly consciousness, because such a reality is a gift of the Devas to the priestly intuition, in terms of a special and objective structure within the world of ideal essence, wherein the laws or Loa of esoteric logic operate, for the Devas.

In such a world and at such a high level, we can find the energy of being and the manifestation of pure reality has or manifests a particular order of appearance, which is the appearance of pure myusticism as well as being the pure mysticism of appearance and being. This structure is that of being and reality and it is also the Loa of all appearance, because the gnosis does not present itself as energy and as function in ideal separateness. Rather it is pure being and this being is interchangeable at the level of ideal essence. For this reason, the powers of hierarchy are those of direct initiation into the light of the gnosis for this aspect of existence. We see the reality and know that what we see is there.

The structure of the esoteric logic is entirely based upon the power of sound, and in this it must be understood to be the power and presence of the sacred vowels, which gives to the world of the Devas -- in addition to a certain logical structure -- the immanent hierarchy of its own or ontic and alethic (a level of truth specified by a level of being) existence. It is important to see reality as pure energy, even at this level, except that we have made use of the power of sound in all of our determinations of existence.

1. The first level of being in the ideal hierarchy of essence is reflected in the organization of Devic and esoteric logic as:

(I) = U Y A E   This is the first of the primordial powers,

(II) = AEIOUYAE (IV) = AEIO   which are emanated within the first level of
(III) = UYAE   ideal essence. It has been explored by
                                                       Monastery students by means of angelological
                                                       set–theory.

    2. The second level of being in the ideal hierarchy of essence is reflected in
the organization of the esoteric logic of the Devas as:
(I) = YAEI   This level, which is explored in angelological
(II) = EIOUYAEI (IV) = EIOU   lattice–theory, reflects the primordial pattern
(III) = YAEI   of energies, wherein the laws of (I) and (III)
                                                       reflect each other and where the reflection of
the energy is between (1) and the level of (3), as the ideal intermediary.

    3. The third level of being in the ideal hierarchy of essence is reflected in
the organization of the esoteric logic of the Devas as:
(I) = IOUY   This level is explored in angelological group–
(II) = IOUYAEIO (IV) IOUY (+vV) AEIO theory and it reflects the element of
(III) = IOUY   contingency or logical alternativity, since
                                                       (IV), which reflects the world of the material
can be a combination, a disjunction, or alternative to (I) and (III) or it can be
simply the very same reality. In this sense, it reflects the existence of the ground
of the logic of probability and it reflects, also, the existence of complexity of
alternatives which, from the angelic viewpoint, means that existence is dynamic
rather than static.

    4. The fourth level of being in the ideal hierarchy of essence is reflected in
the organization of the esoteric logic of the Devas as:
(I) = OUYA   The same pattern as in (3) is followed, as in
(II) = OUYAEIOU (IV) OUYA (+vV) EIOU the world of angelic matrix–theory, there is
(III) = OUYA   not a difference between "real essence" and
                                                       "real substance," because they both follow the
same logical laws of being. The human mind, for the Devas, is as changeable as the
world of nature, and both are composed of contingent types of phenomena. Everything
mirroired by the Devas reflects the laws of dynamic change, or the freedom to become
anew.

    In this study, we have made use of the symbolism of the vowels used in our
system in order to represent the dynamics of these different levels of ideal energy.
They reflect in themselves the ways in which the laws of the universe manifest powers
and patterns of realization. The priestly consciousness is then admitted into these
worlds by means of mystical initiation and, in these worlds, this same priestly
consciousness is expanded and united to the different types and levels of being, as
they are expressed by the most abstract forms of logical and angelic being.

    However, even though the energies were made manifest in terms of ideal potencies
and levels of alethic existence, or Truth, from the student's viewpoint all of this
must be seen as highly symbolic and highly suggestive rather than as literally the
way in which reality is expressed.

    The energies are symbolic because they reflect the powers and the forms of
energy–form, as in all of the angelic sciences, which are known in a gnostic and pure
state and not in the way of human awareness and limitation, as would be implied by
conceptual knowings. Gnosis, however, can be grasped in symbolism, even though it
cannot be taught. Gnosticism, however, as the path to the higher truth can be taught
in lessons, because it will lead us to that palce where we no longer need lessons as

forms of energy, for we now see the reality beyond the symbolism of the world of word—energies. That is where the esoteric logic of the Devas exists in its fullness and where the priestly consciousness is directed by its inherent and immanent impulse.

The Transcendental Logic of the Devas and The Priestly Consciousness

There is esoteric logic and there is transcendental logic. Transcendental logic is concerned with the possibility of consciousness and with its form and structure. Therefore, in our system, we must ask the simple question: how is it possible that the priestly mode of consciousness can participate in the world of Devic logic? The answer is that, quite simply, the Devic world occupies the ideal and essential being of the ontic sphere of the process of initiation and that by means of participation in these energies, the priestly consciousness is able to enter into the logical ways of the world of Devas.

We understand that the ontic sphere is the objective or trans–subjective world of gnostic imagination. Within the ontic sphere are all of the worlds, which are explored by means of the various gnostic sciences, and these worlds are levels of being and states of reality, understood and seen in great detail by means of enlightened perception. Among the worlds to be so viewed would be those which pertain to all of the forms of Devic logic. Among the worlds to be so viewed would be those which pertain to all of the forms of Devic logic. Therefore, in the process of exploration and intuition of these worlds, we come to participate more and more in them and thus it is that we unite ourselves by the exercises of the priestly consciousness with these worlds of logic.

However, the processes of participation in these ideal spheres of logic are made possible by a special gift from the Devas, because the work of the Devas is of such a nature that it would require that the priestly consciousness be specially modified for admission into the world of esoteric energies. Just as there is a special process whereby the consciousness of the priestly ego is subject to a transcendental replacement of material contents by the operations of the Devas, so there is a process whereby the priestly consciousness is gifted with certain gnostic energies in order to assume the transcendental logic of the Devas as its own means of operation. And while the replacement process necessary for the experience of esoteric logic was a replacement of the contents or materials of egoic ideality, so now in the gifting of transcendental logic to the priestly consciousness, the process of replacement must involve the formal and structural possibilities of egoic ideality. Let me now begin to explain this process of gifting and show how it operates in experience.

According to the esoteric revelations of Proclus, the transcendental logic of the Devas derives its structure and immanence from the mysteries of numbers, which are derived by the use of the oracles of the good spirits, or the inner divinity.

Because esoteric logic is based upon content from the Devic viewpoint, the transcendental operations of the Logoi are to be understood as the acts and behavior of numbers. These are our pythagorean numbers, taken from the functions of our oracle of words, and applied to the problem of giving pattern and structure to the contents of consciousness following priestly initiation into the Neo–Pythagorean Mysteries. This should not be confused with any form of the Christian priesthood, since its roots are pre–Christian.

For the world of Angelological set–theory, which is the pure world of ideal essence as it can be found, we have the following structure: I=6, II=8, III=7, and IV=6. The realm of Angelological lattice–theory has the following structure: I=10, II=4, III=4, and IV=9. The world of Angelological group–theory has the following structure: I=11, II=3, III=3, and IV=2. Lastly, the world of Angelological matrix-theory has the following structure: I=5, II=12, III=9, and IV=5.

The transcendental logics of the Devic Logoi must be understood as applications of the same potencies, which we find in the operations of mystical oracles. The ascent to these powers is accomplished quite simply. The law is as follows:

There is a mystical replacement of numbers in the ideal egoicity of the priestly mysteries with the result that the numbers of the priest are taken away very gradually and the Devic numbers are put in their place in the ideality of the ontic oracle. These forms or numbers allow for any replacement, so that if the name of one of the Number-Logoi or spirits is of the world of angelological set-theory and given as 6, and the name of the spirit is ATOUIM, the replacement, for example, of RATOON can be easily provided.

Therefore it is from this level of being that various spirits can be replaced and the life of the priestly consciousnes can be raised higher up into the mystical world. The actual work of replacement is done, however, by the Devic Engineers of priestly consciousness, who are infinitely skilled theurgical technicians of the mystical worlds. Contact is easily made with these beings, in order to make possible the actual processes within the continuum of initiation physics. It is one of our laws, in the Proclus society, that these beings will be used in all forms of transcendental experimentation, for without them there would not be any experimental work in the Gnosis.

In the work of the gnostic church, particularly within the esoteric sanctuary of the Proclus Society, the replacement processes of esoteric and transcendental logic are performed regularly as aspects of initiation. Because the entire universe is pure metaphysical and mystical energy, is is important to come to realize that powers and energies are real and that they operate within definite realms and laws of organization. Each energy has its own sphere of vibration and manifestation. The definitions and boundaries of these spheres are definitions of energy, so that each energy will define where it is simply because of what it is. There are no exceptions to the realms of being.

In order to understand the laws of initiation, it is necessary for the student to move to an appreciated viewpoint of what energies are found in initiation physics. The laws of power form the background for the metaphysical constructions of these initiations but it is the duty of the student of the gnosis to come to the Teacher of the Light and make application for entry into the mysteries of initiation.

Otherwise, he will remain in the world of the outsider. Gnostic initiations are of many types, because we have simply many schools and churches identifying with the movement of modern gnosticism. However, our own patterns of initiation are set forth in lessons, where we explain what the energies are which bring in the powers of initiation and why the universe is so structured as to reflect the presence and reality of these powers. The student should ask, with the aid of the proper lesson in gnosis, why the universe makes possible the initiation processes of the gnosis. For it is there in the universe, that it to say, if the power is held by the Logoi, then it should be possible for the student of the gnosis to come to it and therefore there must exist a true mechanism for giving the energy to the student, or transfer-gifting the energy by the Devic owners of this energy to the students of the light, wherever they might be.

This is why it is so important to see the gnosis as a continuum of manifold energies. In some of these energies, we find the powers and their manifestations of initiation—gifting already in the act of operating and appearing. The energies are manifested and now need only to be brought into connection with the students of the light. That is why I am in constant attunement with the Devic Engineers of the priestly consciousness, through esoteric and transcendental logic and its mysticism.

The Laws of Esoteric Logic

"Esoteric gnosis is that life in metaphysics or that lifestream of the Spirit of Truth, as it is understood within the core of my own teachings. It is, in other words, the means by which the pure energy of wisdom-knowing is manifested and living within the sphere of the secret teachings. These secret teachings being the outpouring of the essence of the Spirit of Truth are the symbolic expressions of this esotericism and gnosis." -- M. Bertiaux

Every system of gnosis has its own inner side or secret teaching. These teachings are to be viewed as much more than just the revelations from the higher worlds or inner idea, as they contain within themselves the powers whereby certain elements of the continuity of consciousness are actualized. Therefore, these teachings are to be viewed as spiritual and mystical powers. Now, each system of secret teachings is organized for its effectiveness along certain very definite lines. These lines or lattices are the immanent or interior structures and laws of esoteric logic. The heart of any secret teaching is the way in which the life of esoteric logic operates. So, when we ask for the inner laws of esoteric logic and for the inner life of the system of consciousness, we are looking directly to the way in which the heart of the teaching is working. Just as my body depends upon the important operations of my physical heart, so there is the esoteric heart-doctrine, upon which the life of the gnosis is said to depend.

Initiation consciousness, which is the state of mind which follows after the process of initiation, accepts the laws of esoteric logic as the roots of its being. For how can it come to be and how can it manifest itself fully except that it follow certain laws, which are within the context of the innermost secret. Hence, if anyone is an initiate of the gnosis, it really means that in some "significant way" they have become attached to this inner heart and principle, which is life and spirit in them. It means that they now possess a participation in the Spirit of Truth.

"When the Spirit of Jesus came to the bishops of the gnosis, they were filled with the life and the wisdom and all of the other powers and spiritual gifts. They knew that the Spirit of Jesus was the Teacher of Truth and by participating in this spirit of wisdom, they as bishops of the gnosis would now be within the Spirit of Truth, which comes forth from the Father Alone. It was by means of the Spirit of Truth, which comes forth from the Father of Lights." -- M. Bertiaux

While access to the Spirit of Truth is now given within the schematism of the gnostic succession of bishops to those who are made bishops of the gnosis, it is possible for the student of the gnosis -- if he is close enough to the heart of the teaching and to the true teacher of this ecclesia -- to receive the outpourings by means of an exercise based upon the use of the ontic sphere, or the gnostic imagination. That is to say:

When the Spirit of Jesus is come into the world of consciousness and guides the soul of the seeker to the light of perfection, then from the teacher of the gnosis -- who is the presence of the Spirit of Jesus -- there will come to that seeker the energy which will immediately transport the seeker into the powers of the ecclesia and into the worlds of Ekklesia, and of Depth, and of Truth, and of Wisdom, and of Light, and of all of the Aeons, or archetypal time-lines, because the seeker has come to the teacher and the word of the teacher has connected the seeker to the Spirit of Truth, which leads to the Truth and beyond the beyond to the Father of Lights.

And, again, if we seek this consciousness in the teacher, we find:

A part of the teacher must always be united to the higher worlds because it by means of this unity and participation that the influence of the higher worlds is perceived in the world of facticity or day–to–day existence. However, if the teacher wishes to envelop the student in the realm of being, that is say the ideal being of the gnostic imagination, then he may be enveloped by means of sound or by means of magickal powers, which are in the neo–pythagorean language of sound and number, or by some other special means, which the teacher will bring forth from the Spirit of Truth.

This entire process, however, is really the way in which the laws of esoteric logic are said to operate and to fulfill themselves. These laws pour themselves forth as the exact and complete expressions of pure energy and they reflect the powers and the ranges of the pure gnosis as the imagination of the teacher, attuned to the Spirit of Truth by unity, makes known the Father of Lights.

Hence it is by means of attunement to the teacher that the student will come to realize the powers of the Father of Lights. By this we understand that the student experiences the ways of esoteric logic by means of spiritual unity with the teacher, for the teacher is the doorway to the innermost condition of the gnosis. This is the esoteric operation of pure law and being as consciousness. It means that while many on the outside will be able to rise to the gnosis in some form, and this would be an imperfect although not really fragmentary form of the gnosis, only for those who are attuned to the teacher of the idea will the esoteric gnosis be revealed and only by this means can the spiritual perfecting of the Father of Lights be indwelt. This is the way in which the laws of esoteric logic work.

Exercise

The following is an exerecise in basics for those seeking to develop in the esoteric aspect of the gnosis. Read over this exercise as you focus and develop your gnostic imagination. If you have any questions or need special help, please feel free to write to me. This exercise is based upon the action of four laws of esoteric logic, upon the ontic or gnostic imagination of the student.

Law Number 1: "Initiation–physics is based on aeonology"

A=When the world of the gnosis is manifested within the ontic sphere teaching of the idea and the teacher of its revelations, it is possible to understand the laws which come forth from the ontic sphere as the embodiments of pure energy and spiritual unfoldment. This is to say that the emanations from the ontic sphere of the teacher constitute the esoteric world of the student, so that the student is entirely within the field of the teacher and that the world of the student is an emanation from the Aeonic archetypes of the Teacher.

Law Number 2: "Aeonical and Aeonological Structures as Developments in Archaeometry"

B=Then the Teacher and the student shall exist in the same spiritual world and will be within the hierarchies of the various spiritual levels or gradations of being as one, so that as the world unfolds in the Teacher, it shall be revealed to the student in the spiritual space of the Teacher or in his ontic sphere. Furthermore, let it be understood that the powers of the ontic sphere come forth from the schematism, which the Father of Lights emanates within the consciousness of the Teacher through the Spirit of Truth.

Law Number 3: "Archaeometry and Esoteric Gnosis"

C=Many times, the gnostic teachers before us said that the student must learn the ways of passing from the lower to the higher worlds and thus thereby avoiding the gifts and powers of the rulers of the negative energies. There was always the voice of the Truth, which taught that the student shall pass through these spaces and heavenly hierarchies and realms with the Teacher as his companion and thus be protected by the gnosis of the Teacher from the powers of the negative zones of space and energy.

Law Number 4: "The Incarnation of Time—Lines"

D=So it is that the student of the light, if he is participating in the spiritual and inner teaching of the esoteric gnosis, then such a student will be able to unfold in the light and come upon the powers of the light. Thereby, he will come to know the mysteries of the light because that student lives in the esoteric gnosis and within the esoteric gnosis he is one with the Teacher and thus linked by this ray or beam of the Spirit of Truth to the Father of Lights.

The Schematism of Esoteric Consciousness

The schematism is the pattern of organization of consciousness. Every system of spiritual and mystical teaching operates by means of a schematism. For the purposes of esoteric gnosis, the schematism is based on the operations of spirits or invisible entities, with whom the Teacher of the gnosis is in direct intuition.

The way in which esoteric consciousness is constructed is based upon the ways in which the laws of the spirit operate in the lifestream of initiatic consciousness. This means that as the Teacher experiences more and more of the Depth of Being, more is revealed to him about the inner worlds and the states of spiritual realization. Spiritual beings come to the Truth of the Teacher and bring into awareness of the Teacher the laws and powers of the ways in which being manifests or reveals itself in its most perfect character. All of the inner properties of the ways of the spirits are then known as part of the experience of the being indwelling the Teacher. The Teacher then possesses the Treasury of Light or the House of the Spirits within his experience and awareness. From this possession, the Teacher will then set forth the ways in which the world of esoteric consciousness is organized.

This passage locates the placement of the schematism in the activities of spirits within the consciousness of the Teacher. However, what is important is that the activities of spirits of ideal being create structures or the roots of structures in the experience of the inner state of being. This is a fundamental reality. However, we have to see how the activities can give us certain structures, or how the spirits actually generate the schematism of the inner and initiatic gnosis: The origin of the schematism is almost a process of initiation.

The activities of the spirits of ideal being partake of the inner structures of abstract and transcendental mind. Therefore, their reality is perfectly identified with the processes of ideal mind or the logoi, which are represented as sets and lattices in the symbolic languages of the gnostics. Thus, by means of a special activity, these actions of ideal energy become the pathways whereby the schematism is given in esoteric consciousness.

These devas or angels of the gnosis are fully the logoi or emanations from the Trinity of Most Blessed Light. Whatever they do is to add structures to being because they create at the high level of the intuitive mind. Hence, when they are invoked into the inner awareness of the man called to be a Teacher, they come as creatively active and establish the structures of the idea within the deepest consciousness of the Teacher. Thus, they represent the powers of beings as these ideal energies are manifested in the perfection of consciousness and life. Wherever they are, these ideal devas follow the laws of their nature and thusly create by simply being. In a very real sense, they make the world of consciousness, both exoteric and esoteric, a real possibility. They bring being into actualization when they operate according to their own laws of existence.

So we can say that because of a unique type of participation in the devic world, particularly in the world of ideal devas, the Teacher is able to have his esoteric consciousness and power base organized according to the schematism of ideal powers and energies. In the rituals of esoteric Catholicism, there exist certain patterns of prayer which make use of the sacred vowels of the gnosis. These are the sounds associated with the letters: A, E, I, O, U, and Y.

These six sounds are used in a number of special combinations by the gnostics and in the past various studies were made of these sounds and their use by the Benedictine Monks and by one of our past bishops, known for his writings in the area of the occult, the Abbe Julio.

However, what is significant about this matter is that in the gnostic coninuum of bishops, it can be found that there are a number of persons totally ignorant of this entire process. The sounds have been used in various combinations in order to represent the structure of the schematism. The schematism is not to be viewed, however, as identified with the sounds or with the vowels in various combinations, since these are physical energies. Yet, inasmuch as any physical object can represent a spiritual energy, there is perhaps some validity in the use of these vowels, the sacred vowels of the gnostics.

The Abbe Julio also taught that the schematism could be presented to students in terms of the energies latent in metamathematical symbols. These would be the symbols of mathematics or of symbolic logic, but applied in the direction of representing spiritual energies from the inner worlds. This teaching originated with Pythagoran metaphysics, and is largely due to this type of background that our gnostic church came to have this teaching, which has been reflected in its name. The schematism, therefore, has been historically represented by both mystical or symbolic numbers and letters, as in the work of the Abbe Julio as well as in the use of the sacred sounds, which link our teaching to the ancient mantra yoga of the Hindus.

The initiation process appears to be an entry into the world of ideal being, where special and very abstract devas construct the mind of the Teaching in accord with special laws, which are identified with the essence of the devic lifestream. While I have written elsewhere about this process, it seems to me that very little can be said in our earth-mind languages about this process. It is significant, however, that the structures which allow the initiate to become the Teacher seem to come from the level of ideal being and are imposed upon the consciousness of the initiate in such as way that they give a structure to esoteric consciousness, which makes the work of the gnosis possible through that Teacher.

In the exercise which follows, taken as it is from the gnosis of multi-dimensionality and explorations in the aeonic continuum of esoteric logic, the emanations of the unconscious mind of the gnostic hierarchy are discussed as a kind of schematism, which is both active and continually unfolding. The analogy is drawn to the language of esoteric engineering as giving us a "concrete example" of what this schematism can be understood as meaning. Here is your exercise for this lesson based on a symbolic understanding of the schematism of esoteric consciousness.

Exercise

In order to explore the gnostic continuum, you must first of all understand that we are concerned with data from the aeonic sectors of the universe. We are describing the exact worlds and how they develop and manifest themselves in the contexts of energy. We are also concerned with specific energies and powers, which derive from the power-zones of the gnosis and which are alive and actually beings or messengers from the higher worlds. To be a gnostic student under these circumstances, it is most important to realize that powers and occult forces are representations of the higher presence, which is a presence of angelic beings and of spiritual voices or images, which come into the experience of the student because they have been found or located in such a world as the result of divine realizations.

For this reason, I am very certain that the energies can be expressed as lines in a circuit of energy patterns and I will attempt to bring this circuit into focus and allow you, as a seeker after the gnosis, to see it as the motor behind the physics of multi-dimensionality. These circuits are the laws and schematism of esoteric logic. The circuits are logical systems also, forming the amplifications and explications of the inner reality of power. Actually they are motors and each part of the motor is inhabited by some wonderful type of spirit. Indeed, they are real forces and powers, which communicate with us but we have to develop a feeling of being comfortable with their operations. They are the roots of oracles and must be seen as drawing forth the fundamental conclusions of the cosmic computer as its explications and explorations of inherent being become more and more a part of the surface of light.

Esoteric Aeonology

When we talk about Esoteric Aeonology, we have a very precise idea in mind. I define this subject as: While there are many theories of the aeons in the gnosis, the esoteric theory is that the aeons are abstract and mystical functions of the inner consciousness of the initiate. They are not as beings to be identified with outer realities or with planetary patterns of power. Rather, these esoteric aeons are the mystical dimensions of time and they are the sacred history of initiatic consciousness considered as points or sacramental energies. They are the sacramental beings, within whose continuity — as viewed by the gnostic intuition — the sacramental operations of the lifestream of the spirit manifest willingly as initiation. Such beings, then, are spiritual energies and patterns of active being. they are not the aeons of gnostic exoteric theology, but rather they must be viewed as pure theogonies, or as esoteric laws unto themselves.

When the Byzantine powers of the sacramental consciousness sought to move inwards towards the pure essence of light, they gave a name to this state of being, because it consisted in mysteries and encounters, the experience of being totally within the divine light, and it consisted in pure laws of realization, which in certain mountain monasteries became the laws of self-relization. These Byzantine monks and the energies generated by means of the laws of liturgy and theurgy were experiencing the energies, which we identify as esoteric aeonology.

Esoteric Hinduism is perhaps no different in its respect for these inner powers of the light, for it consists of devic experiences which, taken in themselves, transform all being subject to pure awareness. For this reason, the yoga of light developed as a way of teaching this inner pathway. This must be understood as converse with the gods. One can only speak with that which one is. This is the pattern of energy which is understood from the first moment of consciousness as the "light within." Whether those many scriptures are right in what they claim of the light as a metaphysical influence or if they are right as to the true mysticism of what is sustained by the light, none can express conceptually. It is only of a certainty that being is fundamentally this light, this inner time, or this inwardness of pure aeons, which must be understood as principles of consciousness and activity.

The Byzantines did not assume that light was evidence for some latent theogony. At least, they did not see the immediacy of being as light in such a way that they wrote explicitly of such manifestation as "theogonies." Yet, in the Byzantine tradition such theogonies do exist and reveal themselves as "mysteries of the faith of being."

We spoke earlier of "these Byzantine Monks (and the energies generated by means of the laws of liturgy and theurgy) were experiencing the energies, which we identify as Esoteric Aeonology." This sentence, which is really an exercise in gnosis itself, would seem to be of a very strange construction. However, it should be remembered that the energies, which are generated by means of liturgy and theurgy, are intelligences and orders of being. They are not blind forces, as some might think. In fact, in gnosis, there are not any blind forces. The blindness is only in the eyes of those humans and humanoids who do not possess the truth of the gnosis, which sees all things as aspects of cosmic intelligence.

However, these forces have been represented or organized in patterns by means of the inner form of the oracle. This means that it is possible to see the energies as a whole by means of a structure, which gives a type of identity to these powers, whereby we can see them as fundamental being.

I II III IV V VI   The adjoining diagrammatic matrix is an example of how
1 1 1   1 1 1   these energies can be understood to reflect the exact
2 2 2   2 2 2   structure of number. There exists a subtle magnetism in
3 3 3   3 3 3   all of the patterns of these numbers which, when it is
I II III IV V VI   revealed as pure energy, allows its exposition as an
4 4 4   4 4 4   oracle. Now, in the structure of the gnosis, the secret
5 5 5   5 5 5   of this matrix of numbers is to be understood as an
6 6 6   6 6 6   initiation of the "wisdom of numbers" and how they manifest
themselves to being. This arithmosophical initiation is given by me personally to special students of my own temple school or to those who qualify by discipline and the virtue of their dedication to gnostic energy.

Each one of these diagrams can be said to represent the structure of an esoteric aeon. However we may try to understand those aeons, they cannot be viewed too literally by this method. I, however, believe that these symbolic pictures of these beings are quite useful because they do represent the practical aspects of being and the ways in which we work with the aeons in context. So it is possible for us to see the life of the gnosis at any point and to take by means of an oracle –– and the operations of oracle physics –– a "photo" of the operations of any aeon, which might be present in a given liturgy or theurgy. We thusly have an outer and practical means of indicating the presence of an esoteric component of the gnostic process.

The power of this lesson is derived from the ontic sphere of the Teacher. The world of the esoteric aeons is to be found in the ontic sphere of the Teacher of the gnosis. The idea of the ontic sphere in relation to esoteric aeonology is expressed thusly:

The ontic sphere is the gnostic imagination of those who participate in the higher forms of gnostic attunement. This world is filled with the potentials and possibilities of the gnostic imagination, which means that the imagination has been given a new being and has become a transcendental and dynamic actuality. The structures of this ontic sphere are the aeonological principles and laws, which are the results of the initiatic construction of the Teacher. That is to say, great beings of the devic type are drawn from abstract and possible forms of being and are given ideal actuality in a world of transcendental energies by the action of the Teacher.

Therefore, in this lesson, we want to focus upon the Teacher and his role as the source of gnostic being in the consciousness of the student. We want to show how the patterns of the esoteric level of aeons are projected into the initiation consciousness of the student and thereby make the student a part of pure gnosis, by participating in the mysteries of the ontic sphere. Here is the exercise:

Part 1. You will focus your mind and imagination on the Teacher and you will realize your one-ness with the Teacher in the world of ideal essence, where being is at its most abstract and perfect manifestation. Here, you will know that the Teacher is, himself, a divine and eternal aeon. Write a report on your communion with this esoteric aeon.

Part 2. You will focus your mind and imagination on the Teacher and you will realize your one-ness with the Teacher in the world of ideal substance, where being is at its most dynamic and energizing manifestation. Here, you will know that the Teacher is, himself, a divine and eternal master. Write a report on your communion with this master of light.

Part 3. You will focus your mind and imagination on the Teacher and you will realize your one-ness with the Teacher in the world of real essence, where being is a continuum of interacting spirits. Here, you will know that the Teacher is, himself, a spiritual energy and a presence of power. Write a report on your communion with this living spirit of wisdom.

Part 4. You will focus your mind and imagination on the Teacher and you will realize your one-ness with the Teacher in the world of real substance, where bodies are in motion and all is appearance. Here, you will know that the Teacher is, himself, a man or a spiritual being incarnate in a human body. Write a report on your communion with this man of gnostic history.

This exercise in four points introduces us to an esoteric concept known in our Church as "the logic of symbolic monads." For whenever we focus our consciousness, we encounter one of these beings, because we are experiencing an aspect of the esoteric aeon. The Teacher should be understood to be the focus and outpouring of this "logic of symbolic monads" because in Part 1 of the exercise-report, we focus on the Teacher as the esoteric aeon. We focus on the energy, which comes forth from the Teacher to the student, making that relationship between student and Teacher the most impportant link in the gnostic continuum.

Because the "logic of symbolic monads" is an application of the procedures for the analysis of specific aeonic energies, the sanction of this logic is derived from the Teacher of the gnosis, whose presence is the presence of the Church of the Gnosis in the midst of the mind-field. What now follows are the esoteric instructions for the student from the Teacher of the gnostic continuum.

The Theogony of the Ontic Sphere

Theogony means literally "the genesis of the deities"; how they were brought forth and also the problem of the divine lineage. Therefore, in gnostic metaphysics, one of the most most significant sciences is that of theogony, because it is by means of the process of gnosis that the gods are begotten in the world of consciousness.

The deities are the productions of ontic intelligence, that is to say the powers which are immanent in being, understood as the Absolute Presence. When something becomes possible it is immediately actualized somewhere in Divine Imagination. The different "departments" or functions of spiritual being, naturally, are simply aspects and operations of the fundamental unity. Everything that happens in the sacramental life of the priestly imagination is to be viewed as a projection of this unity. In each sacramental encouuter, the grace of the sacrament makes it possible for some type of gnostic deity to be begotten in the soul of the true believer, who is sacramentally united to the gnosis because of ritualistic participation in the mysteries of the Absolute Presence.

The Church of the Gnostic Patriarchate, therefore, believes that the sacramental rites and liturgical and theurgical operations of the priesthood are necessary conditions for the outpouring of sacramental grace to be understood as the "genesis of the deities." When we come to experience the sacramental lifestream of the gnosis, we are immediately impressed by the constant incarnating of spiritual powers of being. Thus, in each ritual act, the priest is able to incarnate the "holy and bodiless essences and powers," which then become attached to the karmic history of the believer.

The modern development of the Church of the Gnosis was connected with sacramental theory and with the theology of the Independent Catholic and Orthodox Movement. The Holy Spirit, we can now see, led and moved the early bishops in France along very ritualistic lines and made the Apostolic Power the basis of the work of the ecclesia. It could have been otherwise, for there are many religious traditions outside of the ritualistic and the Apostolic. But the purpose was to incarnate the sacramental life and the fullness of the Ontic Sphere, or the Divine Imagination, therefore France was especially chosen because of the prior ground, as it had been prepared there, was sympathetic to the sacramental conditions of existence.

By this incarnation, the gnosis could grow. It was fed by the Esoteric Tradition, a living being of the French consciousness, which understood that the mysteries and the ritual work were to be the basis of the gnostic renewal. This was because as the Catholic Church taught the doctrine of the Incarnation of the Logos, both in history and in the Liturgical Sacrifice, so the gnostic priesthood would have to bring about conditions for the Incarnation of the Sacramental Logoi, or "Deities of the Word," in the mysteries of reconciliation, which is the proper work of the priesthood.

Because the sacramental actions are externalized and perceptible outpourings of the Divine and Infinite Energy, in the liturgies and theurgies of reconciliation, they are groundings in the facts of empirical existence of the divine imagination and each sacramental process, because it is visible and found in a churchly context, is a begetting of Deities in the world of sense.

The world of the divine imagination is thus outpoured as a hieretic continuum of sacramental existence and it is the incarnation of the ontic in individual segments and patterns of life–history. Godly powers are these. For just as the gnosis sends forth the gods to exist as ideal substances in the Pleroma of Abstractedness (the universe of reconciliation between God and the gods), so it also attached itself concretely to the events of life and takes on bodies in the onflowing stream of time. Thus, the gods or angels of the presence of the Logos and beyond to the Father Eternal come to be in our midst.

Again, the reconciliation activity performed by the spiritual destiny of the Gnostic Church is extended into the realms of consecration, where more and more of the deific power is infused into the medium of existence. For this reason, the eternal priesthood and the gnosis of the espicopate believe in the power of specific and particular blessings and orderings for the work of what is holy. They look for the time when all being will be consciously united by sacramental links to the Absolute Deity. It is in this work that a complete knowledge of the principles of gnostic theology and theogony must be understood and realized in the life of the individual priest. The individual priest must know and do, that is, he must have mastery both in the truth of theory and practical work, by the powers of the sacramental priesthood, as it has come to us from the most remote times of this precise history: the history of the sacrificing priesthood of reconciliation. They are those who possess the converse of Gods and men.

One of the most important types of work to be done in the gnostic consciousness is that of the creation of the inner universe of sacramental realities. We do not know if there are other ways of making this reality, which are known and done by various schools and churches in the mundane sphere, but for us, as workers in the gnosis, our pathway of reality if to do and to make as is possible. Therefore, in this exercise, you are to use this entire lessonas an exercise in the esoteric gnosis.

Exercise in Gnosis
You will begin to see all things in consciousness as outpourings of the supreme truth. By this means, you can see all things as connected in God, because God is supreme and all Truth. Now, follow these steps:

1. You will attune yourself to the silence of the inner self and you will visualize a still and small point of light. This is the point of your creative being.

2. You will note that this reality is an outpouring of power and that it is pulsing as it lives and is full of life and being. It is the source of Godly power.

3. You will enter into this point of power and know that while you are within it, you are also able to see it within yourself. Try to do both, very slowly, you are within it and it is within you. It is the point of divine power and cosmic immanence.

4. You are within the being of the divine and that being is present to you. Now, you are to draw down that power and let it flow into the events of your daily life and to the different levels of cosmic manifestation. It is now moving into more and more forms of being.

5. Let that being flow downwards through the lights of the spirit–spaces, until it is all in all. Let it flow until it is everywhere in being and that everything in being is in some important way connected to it.

6. Let it flow and enter into all of the conditions of life and being. Let it be as a life that permeates all of reality and all of existence. Let it be as a principle of truth and of being and of joy and of mysticism. It is present now everywhere. You can see the glow of its light and you can hear the sweet music of its

universe and presence in all things.

7. Look around you and you will see that all of being is filled with the presence of this holy power, for God is now present by His Holy Spirit in all reality. Now, you will begin to notice that all things are objects of sacredness and symbolic of the presence of God in all things.

8. You will now take any part of experience and see it as sacramental and as a form of the way in which God has come into your experience. You will realize that it is the light of being and the light of truth and that it is Godly. You are making a sacramental universe of being and you are coming to realize that Godly energies are now in your experience and existence. This is your exercise in theogony.

In the analysis of being, we must always view the mystical domain as pure reality or as the life of truth. That is your esoteric instructions from the Teacher.

The Dynamics of Esoteric Gnosis

The dynamics of esoteric gnosis is the law of the body of the Teacher of the Light, and this is the projection outwards and the creation of energies from the body of the man, who has perfected the gnosis on Earth. He has perfected his body, which is the gnosis, as it is expressed in material form. The dynamics of the esoteric gnosis as a law refers to the powers and how they act in the true and supreme consciousness of the Teacher and his body, which is the reflection of the cosmic law of creation.

The focus should be in the physical presence of the Teacher, that is the focus of the truth should be in the physical body of the Teacher, while we live in the material world, for in the physico-material world, we are in the world of bodies and the language of the gnosis in this world must be expressed as the language of the body. Thus, if the Teacher is the embodiment of the truth and the Teacher is the gnosis, then his body is the means of the art and science of diffusing the gnosis.

For it is from the Teacher of the gnosis that the energies of truth are understood to descend into the student of the light. There is only the supreme power of the gnosis or the supreme energy of the Teacher of the light, but among all of the orders of creation, the body world of the Teacher is the archetype for the lifestream of the human student in the body. It is from the Teacher that the energy comes forth.

How different it would be if we were not in physical embodiment. Then, we could be entirely spiritual and the pneumatic power and preciousness of light would not come into the world but express itself as abstractions. However, we are embodied and as such the method of the teaching of the gnosis in its most esoteric form consists in the mysteries of the body of the Teacher. That is to say, from those many occult centers in the physical body of the Teacher, we see in the mystical vision the raying forth of the beams of mystical law, as they are expressed in the being of the Teacher of the gnosis. For this reason, the body has always been symbolic in Neo-Pythagorean gnosis of the divine universe of highest and most perfect law. It is the being of being.

There are obviously two ways of looking at the body. There is the mundane way, which seeks to either hide or to show the body, but always for reasons based on imperfections of mental consciousness. Then there is the gnostic view, as we teach it, that the body is the means for the teaching of the gnosis. The body is therefore a symbolic reality.

The body should not be viewed, however, as devoid of mystery even in the most most mundane of humanity. It is not, the mysteries are simply concealed therein and awaiting the unveiling of the mystical powers. We reincarnate many times, according to Hinduism, because -- unlike Buddhism -- the life and experience of the body is so important. If a body is imperfect now, next time it will be more towards the perfect, until it finally becomes a perfect picture of the divine dimensions of being. When this happens, we are faced with pure reality and truth, and we are able to understand what is meant by saying that we are made in the image of the divine ones.

Not all gnostics will agree with this, because of the diversity of the schools, as we find them. However, in the world of reality, in the place of being-ness, we find all of existence in this world related in one way or another to the body. Therefore, if this is a kind of condition for the material ways in which existence is realized, so also we must realize that being is perfection and as such as must teach the gnosis in the world of the material by means of the bodily experience. Hence, as long as we are in the material world, we shall teach that the gnosis of esoteric consciousness is to be taught through the body of the Teacher of the Light.

Now, we must understand that the mysteries of the body of the Teacher are the ways in which the laws of the gnosis are "materialized" in the world of history. It is impossible for the teaching to come by abstractedness, for that leads to errors. That, I might add, is the reason for the many errors and conflicts of the various protestant sects, which have rejected the worship of the body. The Catholic Church, however, because of its policy of Incarnational Realism, teaches the worship of the body, especially so in the theology of the Eucharistic Presence of Christ and in the Bodily Assumption of the Mother of God.

So, our gnostic viewpoint is not alone, rather it is physically close to the Catholic view, but intended for the esoteric consciousness of the perfecting of humanity. So it is the way of the gnosis to be cited as the way of the esoteric understanding of the material world. This does not mean its rejection, rather it means its true or gnostic comprehension and acceptance. This is the acceptance of being -- the being of the Teacher's body.

The dynamics of the body of the Teacher can be expressed by the movements of the gnostic process known as esoteric logic. Esoteric logic is the basis of reality and it is a projection outwards from the body of the Teacher. Esoteric logic is the radiation from the mysteries of the Teacher's body. Thusly, the initiation physics of the body of the student -- which comes forth from the Teacher of the light -- is a physics of truth because it is based on the material world. Esoteric logic is the way in which this physics operates. We can then say that the work of esoteric logic is to make possible the operations leading to initiation in the body of the student. For this reason, the body must be viewed as sexually radioactive or charged with kundalini shakti and permeated with the powers of the transcendental unconscious. Esoteric logic is a set of Plutonian rules for the execution of acts of power from a Plutonian power base, which is the gnosis of the body.

Here is an exercise in how to bring this about in your body. Think of your body and the body of the Teacher and understand that:

The dynamics of esoteric logic refers to the gnostic powers of the body of the Teacher and how they act in the true and hidden consciousness of the student and Teacher -- in their unity of initiatic energies. For it is from the Teachers of the gnosis that the energies of esoteric gnosis and logic are emanated, and thusly they descend into the student/chela of the pure radiations.

In the Temple of Esoteric Logic, there is only the supreme hierarchy of the gnostic powers and the varied realms of light; but among all of the orders and existences of the student/Teacher relationship, the body of the Teacher, manifesting the communion of esoteric logic, is the physical archetype for the lifestream of the human condition of existence. It is from his body -- from the body of the Teacher -- that the beams of esoteric logic come forth with all of their power and energy.

In order to understand the full essence of this lesson, I think it is very important for you to apply to your understanding all of the principles, which were learned in the esoteric instructions, given to you previously. The Monastery of the Seven Rays has, as we know, an entire course of study on kundalini shakti, the great power of guruyoga. By doing more and more exercises in the guru-yoga of esoteric gnosis and becoming more and more at one with the Teacher, you are able to receive the transmission of this kundalini shakti from the mystical field of the Teacher to the inner essence of the student/chela. This is why esoteric gnosis is so close to the yoga systems of esoteric Hinduism. They both work with the same fundamental power of the universe.

Pnuematology On a Basis of Esoteric Logic

When we come to discuss pneumatology, we first of all define it as the study of (logy) the spirit or spiritual and rational and fiery breath (pneuma) of the universe. The ancients believed that there was a rational and fiery breath, which was God, and which permeated all things and was immanent, or present, within the essential soul of all objects and all subjects in the world of nature. For the student seeking esoteric gnosis, pneumatology is the study of the rational and fiery breath or divinely inspirational powers of the Teacher. Also, this reality of the power of the Teacher, because it is based on esoteric logic, is a true presence in the physical world of events in space and time.

Somehow the Teacher is the master of the breath—consciousness of the world or else he is so attuned to the divinely present Pneuma that he is a focus for this type of reality in each period of time. Therefore, we can see the Teacher as the source of fire, or the kundalini—shakti. His breathing is itself a mystical process and the mysteries are often based on his inhalantion and exhalation of the "finer forces of nature" or Tattwas, those fields of the natural order of vibrations in the continuum of being.

Thus, he will inspire the chela with his energies. He will transmit kundalini—shakti to the chela; but this kundalini—shakti is a pneumatic construction of the Teacher. It is an intuition of the Teacher, because this is an outpouring of his intuitive power. The intuition of gnostic constructions refers to the organization of the inner and pneumatic world of initiatic space, which is organized by the law of mantra and dependent upon a root in reality, the breath of the Teacher. In each pneumatic intuition of the Teacher, we find the 16 spaces of esoteric logic and within each we find the 36 sub—spaces of the sacred vowels of the gnostic teaching.

Thusly, the Teacher in his process of unfolding the pneumatic and inner reality to the student will define the different placements of being and identify the laws of this inner and pneumatic reality by means of the bodily names and abstract and occult spirits and the concrete powers or physical presences of intelligible energies, which are of the most importance and significance in the mapping work of initiatic space. This is what happens in initiatic consciousness, or the result of pneumatic initiation.

Initiatic space is the ultimate world for the gnostic process of investigation and in this world there is really only one way of constructing the map of being. That is the way of the pneumatic and inner being and the way of the schematism of the Teacher (the 16 sacred spaces of esoteric logic) as given in the bodily—intuitions of the Teacher. If there is any physical being to be explored or explained as a result of these intuitions, it really must be that of the pneumatic and inner reality, because this initiatic space is really and absolutely the intuitively gnostic construction of the Teacher.

We can see then how pneumatic activity is grounded in the esoteric logic of the Teacher. This grounding, however, is the result of both an inner development of the Teacher and as the result of initiation. For example, when initiation happens or is given to the candidate, that man is grafted into a great complex of being, which is the mystical lineage of the order of initiation. Once that happens, the candidate who is now the initiate is no longer an outsider to the processes of esoteric history. Rather, he is participating in them in a very personal way.

Within that structure of the initiation process, we find many very strong and archetypal influences at work. In my own case, I was able to experience the archetypes directly. Let me explain:

In 1963, I was in Haiti where I met my Teacher of the gnosis. By means of the initiation and consecration process, I was able to enter into the gnosis of the earliest Teachers of our system. I think it would be best to address this subject as esoteric martinism. The work of Louis-Claude de Saint-Martin was based upon previously archetypal work, such as that of Martines-Pasqualles. Among the archetypes which I was able to discover by means of an inner examination, was that of this Teacher, Martines Pasqualles, who is, according to the esoteric tradition still living and inspiring our work. Martines Pasqualles was one of a group of Twelve Adepts standing in a protective relationship to the esoteric gnosis of our tradition.

However, I also learned that connecting these Adepts in their own esoteric law or continuum werr the gnostic logics or time-stations, which we view as esoteric patriarchates of research. The Twelve Adepts plus the Four Patriarchates add up to the Sixteen Laws, or principles of spiritual organization, which are behind all of our teachings and which are now known world-wide because of the work of the Monastery of the Seven Rays.

These archetypes are the spiritual powers behind the lessons which we write here from the gnostic missionary center. Whatever we teach seems to have this principle or organization behind it and within it.

I was told that the bodily intuitions of the Teachers Martines-Pasqualles and Jean-Maine were the laws of esoteric logic in action and that everything that we wrote was based upon an inner presence which they alone could give to the occult instructions. They are the deep powers which draw their influences and lights from the 16 sacred spaces of esoteric logic, which are the chakrams of higher gnosis, as different from the natural and occult chakrams of the initiatic bodies, that is to say which are the outpourings of cosmic imagination in the physical world of action and the movement of sacramentally consecrated bodies in the hieratic spaces and times. These magickal bodies are living and timelessly perfect as physical vehicles.

By a process known as historio-logical intuition, we can experience these Adept Teachers and archetypes and make such contact with them that enables us to become participants in the general movement of their own personal gnosis. Historio-logical intuition is the method of looking into the domain of history and by means of logic (either esoteric or gnostic logic is here meant) we make history come alive, or rather we enter it, as if it were a contemporary energy, as we find it around us. There is that remarkable passage of time, we can enter into the being of the historical experience and actually be "within history" with our Adepts and Teachers.

Of course, this process of historio-logical intuition is only possible when one enters upon the gnostic experience of esoteric logic to such an extent that the particles ini ne's body take on a new form of being and become totally alive and attuned to and aware of the Pneuma or universal medium of the Teacher. In this way, we see reality in terms of its manifold possibilities, under these conditions, the following gnostic exercise becomes a type of initiation into the Pneuma.

Exercise in Gnosis

Kundalini shakti is the pneumatic construction of the Teacher within the ocean of historio-logical intuitions. A pneumatic consctruction is an intuition of the Teacher because every event is an outpouring of the manifold of these historio-logical intuitions.

While the intuition of gnostic construction refers to the organization of the inner penumatic world and the space of intuition (which is organized by the body of mantra) the body is sound. The breath of the Teacher is being or the root in the Pneuma of reality, unlike all other physical energies having an occult purpose. It can be applied to the world of the body as the means whereby power is infused at each point of wisdom and at each doorway to the infinite. It is within each breath that we find the 16 spaces of esoteric logic and within each space we find the 36 sub-spaces of the sacred vowels.

This is how we hear the powers of the gnosis of light as they are viewed, because they are the projections of the Teacher to those students who by the grace of divine wisdom have given themselves to the Teacher in order to participate in the body of the Teacher, which is the issuing forth from the Pneuma of the Word, or the Logos -- i.e., the continuum of esoteric logic.

The Schematism of Pneumatology

It should be understood that our gnostic bishops have always paid great attention to the many developments in what is known as "academic metaphysics." For example, Bishop Lucien-Francois Jean-Maine studied the late 19th century idealists in France very carefully, especially the work of Professor Octave Hamelin (1856-1907), who wrote the very important book, "Essay On the Principal Elements of Representation," published in 1907. Bishop Lucien-Francois did not see academic metaphysics as contradictory to esoteric and gnostic metaphysics. He saw academic views as coming closer and closer to gnosis, as they distanced themselves more and more from materialism and sensualism, as these doctrines are understood in an Academic sense.

Over the years, the shape of gnostic metaphysics has been adapted to the structures of the ordinary work and world of contemporary understanding. Yet, the work done by Bishop Lucien continues as a kind of archetype for the inspiration and direction of all other bishops and priests coming after Lucien and described as "Jean-Maine bishops."

Lucien sought, rather interestingly, to impose a certain structure upon the processes of the gnosis. If we view our school and its teachings, we find –– especially in the Monastery of the Seven Rays lessons –– a remarkable structure and a plan or organizing law, which runs through every lesson and which makes each lesson fit perfectly in respect to what has gone before it and what will come after. By contrast, the recently discovered texts of the ancient gnosis, from Egyptian caves, the famous Coptic library of a vast assortment of texts suggests a wild unmanageability, a chaos of ideas and entities, and an almost violent and demonic distortion of certain ideas, if we read the entire "library" as giving us a "system of gnosis." We do not, however, do that because each text comes from some other source or context or place and the library was really just a collection of unrelated ideas. Perhaps the most we can say is that the opinions represent the various points of view to be found in the continuum of gnostic churches.

However, the energy of gnostic experience, Bishop Lucien was quick to see, could be very chaotic if it was not organized by spiritual law. He therefore, by means of a deep exercise in the spiritual laws of the gnosis, as he had developed these powers in his own being he, Bishop Lucien, drew out from the consciousness of esoteric gnosis those ideal laws and principles which were latent in gnosis and which were their archetypal and most divine essence. But since these laws were to be found within his own reality and deepest being, he simply extended the principles and principals of his inner consciousness to all those aspects of the gnosis which could be incorporated into his mystical body. Thus, in the mysteries of the gnosis the linking essence, which connected all reality, was that of Bishop Lucien-Francois Jean-Maine.

For this reason, the Jean-Maine bishops are understood as continuing the essence of our patriarch Bishop Lucien, because they participate in the schematism of his pneumatic and perfect continuity. This sacramental and factual continuity is more than just the lineage of Apostolic Succession, because it is a living mystical process, almost related to our own beings and essences as the blood is related to the flesh of the human body.

The schematism of pneumatology, being as it was a system of pure consciousness, because an immanent system of life and reality, which infused itself into the lives of all those who were initiated or consecrated by Bishop Lucien.

However, as we know from French metaphysics, the point of pure inwardness (Louis Lavelle) is the point of beginnings for the creation of all systems by means of the immanent and inherent schematism of pure consciousness. This view, while coming later in the history of French metaphysics than Hamelin, nevertheless was expressed by Bishop Lucien as the primary exercise in gnostic creation. All forms of initiatic being and all forms of gnostic existence were to be understood as expressions and outpouring of the principle of the Self, as the source of those realities, which are explored in gnostic and initiatic physics. The Self, however, is not that of any self or person, but the Self of the Teacher of the gnosis, in this instance that of Bishop Lucien-Francois Jean-Maine.

Thus, schematism is the way in which the Bishop as Teacher had organized the world of gnosis and the system of mystical categories or conceptual frames of reference, which he as a true adept of the light could will into existence. The point of light, among all of the laws of the universe, became -- easily -- the point of the Self-Hood of Bishop Lucien. And we are his sons.

But this schematism does have its manifestation and that is to be found in Jean-Maine's idea of gnostic maps or "La psychographie gnostique." Bishop Lucien was familiar with the Codex Brucianus, for the Books of Jeu contains, as we now know, some ancient evidence for a system of mystical maps whereby the soul is able to move from one spiritual realm to the next higher, through magickal doorways and paths, which are not in any sense physical. They are the products of the energies which are created during the process of initiation, when the Teacher is able to contact the student and especially the soul of the student by means of esoteric logic.

For while Bishop Jean-Maine knew that idealistic metaphysics gave him the exoteric rationale for the schematism of pneumatology, he now knew that in the Books of Jeu and particularly in the occult maps of the spiritual hierarchies, he could see the pattern of how the mystical schematism would work. He now saw how he would apply these laws in his physical experiments with his students. Thereafter, he began to produce a series of notes, numbers, and mystical and metamathematical explanations of how the schematism of his gnostic magnetism as the Teacher would be applied to the students, who came to him for initiation into the light and who would then be guided through the worlds of the mysterious and highly powerful spirit-spaces.

This notebook, of which I have made a copy and used in many of our lessons, is one of the Treasures of the Eglise Gnostique. It is called "La physique initiatique" (initiatic physics or initiation-physics) and it provides the formularies and numbers and connectives for the passage of the soul through the 256 different spaces and spirit areas and the 64 fields of archetypal power and the 16 domains of the archetypal rulers or aeons of the gnosis of bishops, the sons of Bishop Jean-Maine, which he sought to express and explicate in his reconstruction and reinterpretation of the Rites of Memphis-Misraim. For the Rites of Memphis-Misraim are the external and historical processes of the initiatic physics of the Jean-Maine schematism. I can affirm that these theurgical rites are the ways in which the symbolism of this schematism has come down to us in its outline.

For your exercise, draw a few mystical maps to see if you have an intuition of what this idea of the Jean-Maine schematism means in actual manifestation.

Course in Esoteric Gnosis, Lesson 8: Initiation—Physics Based on Pneumatology

In initiation—physics, we are concerned with powers and their projections into the field of the gnosis. Let us not think that we can properly understand gnosis unless we see it as the power of the Teacher in his work as supreme initiator on Earth of the mystical laws. In other words, the Teacher —— because of his own spiritual development —— has specific powers over the gnostic continuum. As Bishop Lucien-Francois says:

"When the Master or Teacher is filled with the Holy Spirit of the Pleroma, he will come and make the student a spiritual being. He will pour out his powers upon the student and drive out all that is merely mundane and natural. He will form the student in the pattern of New Being and he will form in the student that reality which is the Christ within, or the Esoteric Law of Gnosis, by means of his supreme power over natural limits. This power, as it belongs to the Teacher, is the Presence of God in this world. It is by this means that we know of God and the Holy Beings, because we see the Teacher in the world and he appears before us as light and as power."

Thus, the power of the Teacher comes directly from his connection with the Divine Order of Reality and it is antithetical to the order of natural activity, for such a level of being is under the rule of negative spirits. Lucien makes this clear when he says:

"The Master is truly the revelation of the Divine Order of Being. He possesses the great and terrific power and he must know and bring down to Earth all of the heavenly potencies. His presence is the real presence of the Divine Order of the Pleroma. God is in our midst when he comes to us by means of the gnosis. His body is the dwelling place of the Pleroma and all of the laws and principles are present in that body. For this reason, he will reveal more to the student than all of the Bibles and Sacred Scriptures and Texts of all the religious consciousness ever have in all of history to the starving ears of the human species."

This suggests a doctrine which is very close to the higher forms of guruyoga, as taught in Esoteric Hinduism, and we might note that the Teacher of the gnosis does have his own way or school of yoga. Lucien continues:

"The body of the Teahcer is truly the Mystical Temple and it is alone by means of the physics of initiation that mysticism is made real and comes to be expressed as a concrete and exact presence in the world of the senses. For the Spirit of the Body of the Teacher is a cosmic system and the Master is the true world, while all else is illusion. The mystical power of the Teacher is very strong and the adepts are one in their powers, for the Teacher is one being of truth. That is why, if nothing else were true, the powers of the Teacher of the gnosis would be supreme over all bodies and spirits in the life of experience —— the experience being that of the Teacher and his body of law."

The physical body of the Teacher then becomes the first moment or the dharmakaya of the inner gnosis of initiation. Everything relates to that power and to that presence. But we now ask how is it possible for the bodies of the Teacher ——— that is to say, his mysteries —— to manifest themselves. The principle is threefold: there is the body of the law, which is the physical law and presence of the Master or Teacher. This is the identity of the actual body of the physical man, which is in space and time. Then we understand that there is the enjoyment sphere of experience, which is the enjoyment of the body of the physical man, or the sphere of initiation—physics and it is of course the principle of power and of energy behind initiation physics. Then, we have the manifestation in activity which is that of the energy—generations of initiation physics, which we know as the way in which the powers of initiation are first seen, usually in the rites and work of the esoteric church. As Lucien said:

"The Lord, because He has been good to me, has crowned the body of my life with the beauty of joy and in all parts of me heavenly grace has He placed. He has anointed the enjoyment of my body with the holy oil of His wisdom and mercy, so that all who come to me shall be fed by the mystical sacrament. He has taken the acts of my body and has made from them the many secret mysteries of the gnosis, which I reveal in the rites and theurgies of the holy church. Above all, heavenly grace has blessed me with the radiant light of the Holy and Most Divine Spirit, and God has adorned me with the priesthood of His mysteries, so that I am both bridegroom and bride."

The first of the Body is, as we might note, the view known as the Dharmakaya or the "Body of the Law" of Esoteric Buddhism. This is the physical reality of the Teacher and it is the schematism in its pure concreteness. The Body of enjoyment is the Shambogakaya, or the process of Esoteric Logic manifested as both attunement and musement. Lastly, the Body of the Teacher in manifestation within the ritual work of the ecclesia is the Nirmanakaya of Esoteric Buddhism, pertaining to the rites and activities of initiation physics and the sacramental ceremonies of the Teacher.

However, Lucien was not content just to show forth what was the fundamental reality of being. He sought to show that there were many lines of esoteric power working as connectives among these states of reality and therefore he went into the inner consciousness and discovered that there were two Devic Temples serving as mystical connectives between the three occult bodies. Thus, he discovered that between the Dharmakaya and the Shambogakaya views of the body of the Teacher existed the Purple Ray of gnostic power. Then, he discovered that between the Shambogakaya and Nirmanakaya views there existed the Blue Ray of Gnostic Power. These rays, which comprise an entire field of mysticism in themselves, we can view as esoteric universes of special initiation.

"I looked to the right and I saw the Great Presence of Light, which is the Temple wherein all beings are suffused with the Blue Light of the Gnosis. I looked to the left, which beyond the right, and I saw the Great Presence of Power, which is the Mother of all Earths and Energies, and which is the Holy Temple suffused with the Purple Light of the Ideal and Spiritual Gnosis. Then there came to me many great and wonderful beings, in the form of perfect and divinely radiant priests, for these are the keepers of the true gnosis, and in them I have found my peace and my roots. I held out my hands and they came to me and after removing the vesture of my earthly limits, clothed me in the high—priestly garments and took me with them into the Holy Place, where I am a priest of the eternal sacrifice forever and ever." —— "Esoteric Revelations of Lucien-Francois Jean-Maine," 3

It would appear that the body of the high—priest is a magickal reality of very great power and that the energies of this body are derived from the contacts which the high priest has with Christ, the Holy Spirit, and with the many holy and spiritual beings of the cosmos.

The great bishop of the gnosis, who brought to us many esoteric revelations of the light, Bishop Lucien-Francois Jean-Maine made daily use of these revelations of esoteric gnosis in his building up of the powers of gnosis. They were built up from the ritual work of his holy body. We may also note that there are two directions, which seem to be in a process of magickal and mystical development: I have in mind the two mystical temples and the forms of light as purple and as blue. Lucien wanted the gnosis to reflect these two pathways, because certain gnostic bishops had come from the world of the angels and had in the 18th century created a mystical church for the children of light.

These bishops had been sent from the angelic temple of the Blue Light and also from that of the Purple Light and they had expressed themselves as incarnations of spiritual energy. In my own work, I have — 200 years later — recognized these energies as departments of the gnostic continuum. Thus, from these highly mystical and spiritual levels of being, we have found the fundamental reality of our gnosis: That some of our original bishops were not human but were deities and angels of various and esoteric types, who blended their lineages with the historical lineages, which come down to us from Christ and the Holy Twelve.

Because he was so close to these energies, Lucien was able to work with them in a very exciting manner, but the initiations which came from these divine beings were locked into his physical body as revelations and powers were impressed mystically into the very flesh of his living and holy presence. It is because of Lucien therefore that we have this particular type of physics, which is derived from initiation. The initiators were both angels and men.

Magickal Languages

1.1 The establishment of the magickal languages of spirits and other extraterrestrial intelligences (angels, etc.) from other realms began in modern times with John Dee, and his system is understood to be the point of reference for much of the modern Enochian research. But our own system goes far beyond his system in many ways, for we have devised a formulary for finding out the magickal or angelic equivalent for every word in our most technical vocabularies, unknown now to us, which being parts of the angelic vocabulary refer to states of being important to the magician.

1.2 At the present time, we are working on a color and number signal system, whereby accurate communication can be established with those intelligences beyond this world (extra—terrestrial intelligences). The color scale is quite different from any used before, although upon examination parts of it can be found in the various magickal repertoires as they have come down to us from Atlantis. We might note that there appears to be a certain peculiarity in these languages inasmuch as the planets nearer to the denseness of the Earth, i.e., Malcuth, require more sounds or letters per word to convey the intended meaning, whereas those at distances from the Earth, e.g., Binah = Saturn, require fewer sounds and therefore letters to convey meaning. Thusly, when the language comes close to the sphere of Malcuth, both on the front and the back of the Tree, the power of mind is slowed down, whereas for the intelligences of the zone of Kether, or Pluto, the sounds are absolutely and perfectly simple for each meaning (indicating the intuitional level of pure awareness) while for Mercury (Hod) they are more and more dense and more and more sounds are needed to ring clear the meanings intended. For the spirits of the Earth, or Malcuth, the most sounds are needed, and hence the words in the terrestrial "Enochian" language have many letters. This is necessarily so, for these entities must penetrate a very dense material sphere of power, ruled by the four elemental kings.

1.3 Hence, taking this as an example, the term "essence," in its Plutonian and "Enochian" equivalent would be at least ten times simpler than the terrestrial "Enochian" in both sounds and letters. It should be noted, also, that a very efficient technique exists for extending this language research beyond the zone of Pluto to the qliphotic and also Transplutonian realms, as might be expected.

1.4 The colors for the scale rise as the result of med·ation, for they are provided as content by this type of experience. Eight colors are given. Then by means of the oracle (Shakti) do we come to select the appropriate attributions for these eight colors, asking the oracle which color order = the elemental level and which color = the modifier level. The oracle has given each color a number and has developed a sequence. Afterwards, the form or structure of the system is deduced from the oracle. The structure that emerges is very remarkable and clearly logical in terms of supporting occult correspondences from antiquity. If the oracle were not machina, we would be tempted to synthesis or worse, to suspect the subconscious or even unconscious etheric manipulations of mediumism and radiaesthesia. But since the oracle is a machina, and since we have used the instructed method of letting the communicators, or extra—terrestrial intelligences, provide all of the directions, the dangers of subjectivity seem to have been avoided.

1.5 The system of colors is established together with the elemental triads:

I	Earth of Earth (Brown::::Dark Red)	5
II	Water of Earth (Brown::::Magenta)	9*

```
III    Air of Earth     (Brown::::Orange)           12
IV     Fire of Earth    (Brown::::Purple)            3
V      Earth of Water   (Blue Green::::Dark Red)     2
VI     Water of Water   (Blue Green::::Magenta)
VII    Air of Water     (Blue Green::::Orange)       3
VIII   Fire of Water    (Blue Green::::Purple)      11
IX     Earth of Air     (Blue::::Dark Red)           9*
X      Water of Air     (Blue::::Magenta)            4
XI     Air of Air       (Blue::::Orange)             4
XII    Fire of Air      (Blue::::Purple)            10
XIII   Earth of Fire    (Grey::::Dark Red)           6
XIV    Water of Fire    (Grey::::Magenta)            7
XV     Air of Fire      (Grey::::Orange)             8
XVI    Fire of Fire     (Grey::::Purple)
```

*9 If nine is given as 5+4 then 9=IX (Earth of Air). If on the other hand 9 is given as either 6+3 then 9=II (Water of Earth). Note that on August 25, 1974 the dualistic quality of Venus was recognized by the revision of the attribution of time–lines 4 and 7 in the official list of cosmological components. Also, cf., papers 43 and 69 of the IVth Year course, Monastery of the Seven Rays.

1.6 This system is to be used with the assistance of a magickal mirror and also we may employ various Kamaea, i.e., magickal squares. You may establish the realm of the power zone primarily by the use of the oracle. It is assumed that the extra–terrestrial intelligences will express themselves, as in (1.4) by the initial actions of the oracle (Shakti). The entire purpose of the flashing colors is to establish our way of making reply to them in order "to get into the system." The elemental colors and triads are to be understood as Shaktis and the magician is their mahaguruyogi. We should note also different sizes in the colored spaces. Size, color, number, and frequency appear to be the basic elements of this system of communication. This is a very simple system, once the magician begins to make use of it. It is certainly less subjective than the older terrestrial Enochian system.

1.7 It is important to note that the words received may appear totally unlike any known terrestrial words, even by comparison to the known terrestrial type of Enochian language. Hieratic languages often are lacking in vowels and require special "pointings" to assist in their terrestrial pronunciation. On the other hand, there exist gnostic languages, equally hieratic and magickal, which are composed entirely of vowels (cf., especially lessons 9, pages 27–1–3, and 28–1–4, Part III, of the II year course, Monastery of the Seven Rays). You will realize that the systems simply reflect the occult physics of sound, where certain intelligences being free of the material sphere do not need vowels to facilitate the production of waves in the akasha or the creation of sound, since they have possession of an elemental and spiritual mastery of the akasha, while human beings dependent upon the physical production of sound by our material body systems need to mix vowels into words to sound them. You should note further that there is a soundless way of sounding the words of the angelic languages, which does not depend upon physical production. I am referring to the method of occultly imagining these words in conversation with extra–terrestrial intelligences. This will provide us with the genuine and true basis of conversation with the Holy Guardian Angel, and many others. Hence, these words of an

Enochian character which are received by these methods are to be spoken but are to be employed in imagination, and especially visualized.

1.8 In section 1.5, we were provided with the ultra—yuggothian number and color scheme, which is valid on the Tree of Life for the following power zones of our solar system:

2 = Kether = Pluto
3 = Chokmah = Neptune
4 = Daath = Uranus
5 = Binah = Saturn
6 = Chesed = Jupiter
7 = Geburah = Mars
8 = Tiphareth = Sun
9 = Netzach = Venus
10 = Hod = Mercury
11 = Yesod = Moon
12 = Malcuth = Earth

But, since we are on the threshold of a series of ultra—yuggothian ("+") and transyuggothian ("−") space languages, employed by extra—terrestrial intelligences, then we will now give the number scheme for the transyuggothian power zones:

2 = Thaumiel
3 = Ghogiel
4 = Satariel
5 = Agshekeloh
6 = Golohab
7 = Tagiriron
8 = Gharab Tzerek
9 = Samael
10 = Gamaliel
11 = Lilith
12 = Choronzon (doorway to alternative Universe 'B')

To arrive at these appropriate numbers, one will make use of a pair of dice. To translate the thought waves being received from these power zones into our alphabet, one must make use of what is known as the English Language alphabet system of number correspondences, which measure up to a set of (5) pieces of dice, with a range between 5 (1—1—1—1—1) and 30 (6—6—6—6—6), a most convenient system to use:

A = 5	F = 10	K = 15	P = 20	U = 25	Z = 30
B = 5	G = 11	L = 16	Q = 21	V = 26	
C = 7	H = 12	M = 17	R = 22	W = 27	
D = 8	I = 13	N = 18	S = 23	X = 28	
E = 9	J = 14	O = 19	T = 24	Y = 29	

By means of these basic tables, and those given on another page, it is possible to derive the extra—terrestrial lannguages of angels of light and demons of darkness, and all other beings of shade and shadow, of interest to the pioneering "linguistiic" magician. Apprropriate daemones, demons, deamones, eons, aeons, syzygies, etc., may be thusly contacted in their own languages. This method is valid for our solar system in all of its higher worlds, as well as for making entry into the alternative system for our universe.

1.9 This is the operating manual section, grimoire, or grammar for use with this system.

1. In order to select the range for the Kamaea or magickal square component of language and word, e.g., ultra-yuggoth = "+," Transyuggoth = "-."

a. Throw the oracle (single dice) for "+" (odd number), or "-" even number. Thus, 1, 3, and 5 are "+," while 2, 4, and 6 are "-."

b. Then throw the oracle (this time a pair of dice, with a range of 2 to 12) for the planet. This establishes contact from their side with you, showing by the telepathic control of the oracle, which extra-terrestrial wishes to contact you and teach you.

c. You will reply by flashing the appropriate colors into the magick mirroir (prepared according to the IVth method of instruction).

d. This establishes our link with them, they with us. You are now in the System Focus on the Mirroir (visual system), you may now commence the magickal dialogue.

Now that you have gotten into the system, you may follow the process of building up a magickal vocabulary which will take you into the sciences and arts of the extra-terrestrial beings, both "+" and "-."

2. Review:

a. Now that you have established the spirit realm of the planet as primary, you may buiild up the magickal squares, using both the direct and retrograde methods (given in the IVth Year Course). There are two factors implied here: 1) the primary kamaea, which is direct if "+," or ultra-yuggothian, and retrograde if "-," or transyuggothian. The law of polarity operates in these languages, so that they are dynamic (shakti-shakta) unlike terrestrial languages. 2) The secondary kamaea is either retrograde if "+" or direct if "-."

b. Make a point to ask for the name of the E.T.I. within whose sphere and with whom you are communicating. This will be given in the form of every other word from that same power-zone, e.g., for the power zone of Satariel it will be a four-letter name. Make kamaea as you would for any other word. Begin to build up your vocabulary.

c. Some magicians have sought to use the Tattwa-Ifa signs in place of the color symbols. Both are adequate, so that in place of brown and orange for 12, you might flash or show earth 4 x and air 2 x, as earth = 4, water = 3, air = 2, and fire = 1. On the other hand, practice has shown that when colors are used, there is no need to count the number of times the charts are flashed, because of the size differences. The basic element in this case is earth and is a larger chart than the modifier, and hence space is then the differential rather than number in the communication system.

3. Exercises:

a. In order to adapt yourself to the use of the oracle, practice with Gharab Tzerek and derive a few eight-letter words, and make kamaea, observing the procedures of (2a) above.

b. Find out as many four-letter words for magick, black magick, theurgy, magick, etc., as you can. Make the appropriate kamaea for each of these words.

c. After working in one area of the universe, find out what is the next power zone, which wishes to make conntact. Let us say that it is "+" 8, then find out the eight-lettered word for "universe."

d. If you are working in the "+" range and wish to stay within that field, but wish to change the power-zone, you do not have to go back to 1.9 (1a); you may remain in the field by simply moving back to the pair of dice (to select the power-zone in the field) and then return to tossing the set of five for the letters. The same is true of the "-' range; if you wish to remain in that field. If you wish to change fields, then go back to 1.9 (1a).

e. In order to build up your cosmology, ask for the names of the planets or spheres of power wherein the communicating intelligence dwells.

f. Later instructions on the operation of this system will be released based upon further research. Each student is required to prepare a magickal dictionary based upon his researches with this system. In temples, divide up among the adepti minores the English dictionary of technical occult terms, for example, and let each adeptus find the extra-terrestrial correspondents to each word in his section of the list or book. Mastery of this method is required for all students holding the grade level of "practicus adeptus minor."

Sun and Moon in Scorpio, 1976

Ante luciferum genui te, 7o=4+
D.I.M.I.T., 6o=5+

This is an approved and authorized lesson for the Vth Year of Study, Monastery of the Seven Rays (IInd Order).

The Indo–Zothyrian Simplex Oracle

This system is designed for use by students who only have a set of six–sided dice. For while the system is ideally intended for a set of eleven–sided dice, and while it may be worked reductively with a six–sided set of dice, we also have this system called the "Simplex System," which gives a complete logic of the planets as well as introduces two elements from the Indo–Zothyrian system of rays.

On page two of the Logic of Angelic Languages, section 1.5 note, two forms of Venus are given. In the Simplex System 9 = 5 + 4 = Venus (Cupido) = IX (Earth of Air), while 9 = 6 + 3 = Venus (Taurus rulership) = II (Water of Earth. This is how we have found the basic Simplex system works in this connection.

The following are the correspondences for the Simplex Oracle working of the Li–Logics as given in the Vedic Physics papers:

Number 1 does not exist as a factor in this system
Number 2 exists simple as Pluto = 1+1
Number 3 exists simply as Neptune = 2+1
Number 4 exists in two ways: 4 = 3+1 = Uranus and 4 = 2+2 = Zeus
Number 5 exists in two ways: 5 = 4+1 = Saturn and 5 = 3+2 =Admetos
Number 6 exists three ways: 6 = 5+1 = Jupiter, 6 = 4+2 = Apollon, 6 = 3+3 = Poseidon
Number 7 exists three ways: 7 = 6+1 = Mars, 6 = 5+2 = Vulkanus, 7 = 4+3 = Ketu
Number 8 exists three ways: 8 = 6+2 = Sun, 8 = 5+3 = Hades, 8 = 4+4 = Kronos
Number 9 exists in two ways: 9 = 6+3 = Venus and 9 = 5+4 = Cupido
Number 10 exists in two ways: 10 = 6+4 = Mercury and 10 = 5+5 = Rahu
Number 11 exists simply as The Moon = 6+5
Number 12 exists simply as The Earth = 6+6

These are the 21 units of the Simplex System, which make use of the Indian interpretations of the Moon's Node (Rahu and Ketu), the eight planets of the Uranian system, plus the regular members of our solar system used in exoteric astrology.

This paper will simply be issued only to those students who make special inquiries.

This system is a doorway to the Indo–Zothyrius system of logical implications.

Other doorways exist in this system of those who wish to find them out.

Gnosis of the Spiritual Life, 1: The Beginning Effort

Many students ask me continually about the higher forms of gnostic spirutuality. What they want to know is if these higher forms of the gnosis relate to higher worlds and if so, then would it be possible for these same students to advance to these worlds and enjoy the life of the spirit at that high level. The answer is of course that gnostic metaphysics has always been about the attainment of these higher worlds and how this attainment can relate to this world. Also, it had always been taught that it is indeed possible for students who have grown in the gnostic light to advance to this attainment through a regular and carefully directed program of spiritual growth. And it has always been taught that it is possible for those who have undertaken this program of growth to advance to the higher worlds and there to enter into the secrets of the gnostic awakening by means of both a form of higher learning and direct experience of the divine wisdom.

Many students therefore, upon learning this teaching, ask me about the methods which are to be used to attain to the consciousness of this higher attainment of the gnostic ideal. More than just the attainment of a higher consciousness, or a consciousness of the higher worlds and the being which dwell therein, these students wish for direction in the seeking of those methods and forms, whereby they can raise their consciousness to the higher and more ideal forms of being. What they wish is practical points of guidance in the selection of those ways, whereby they might attain the ascent of consciousness. In letters and in conferences, meetings and consultations, they continually ask me how they might prepare for this ascent.

There are several methods and every school does have its own method of attainment. Each one of the methods is a form of spiritual discipline which guides the soul into the higher and more ideal forms of consciousness-manifestation. We can go out and select in book stores and libraries many methods, but for those of us who are students within the gnosis of our own tradition, there are certain fundamental methods and guidelines, which are taught by the Neo-Pythagorean-Gnostic Church to all of its initiative members. And it would seem that these methods are quite old and have a very satisfactory history in terms of the validity of their applicability to the spiritual growth and development of gnostics for many centuries. These rules, also, are to be found among the rules used by students of certain eastern schools, which come closest to our viewpoint in many areas. These guidelines or methods for preparing the soul for advancement into the light might be given as:

1. Daily prayer and meditation.
2. Regular participation in one's religious life.
3. A non-violent attitude towards all beings.
4. Doing good and avoiding harmful action.
5. Systematic programs of study and research.
6. Following the spiritual direction of one's master.
7. The practice of physical exercise or some form of hatha yoga.
8. A vegetarian diet as a way of life.
9. A practical and realistic focus of consciousness.
10. Sufficient time for quiet and reflective thought.
11. The practice of a daily ritual of purification.
12. A loyal and supportive attitude towards one's family and friends.

Now, these elevation steps towards the light may not appear to be too much to follow. But the inner growth into each one of them brings about very interesting opportunities for the attainment of ideal spirituality. For the true gnostic these are simply the beginnings, they are the first ways for making a start in spiritual growth. It may be possible for the chela to grow and deepen himself in each of these steps towards the higher light and then go on to accept more and more deeper spiritual disciplines. This is done by the chelas of our own inner school of esoteric logic. But, I would say that if a student followed most of these guidelines, he would be safely on the path. For to simply do some of them, even one or two, is the sign of the beginning of the gnostic awakening within the student. Each student will see them differently and I am aware that some may find it necessary to make adjustments in their own life, or lifestyle. Others may adapt themselves to these guidelines gradually. It will always depend entirely upon the chela and the way in which he is seeking to grow.

The spiritual guideposts listed on the previous page are simply designed to allow the student to move onto "The Path" of spiritual growth. By following any one of them, you make a very simple but adequate beginning, then gradually you start following more and more of these ideals. Gradually, you are able to follow all of them more or less most of the time. Then as you become more and more ideal, you simply rise up higher and higher towards the ideal worlds. Like attracts like.

I doubt if there are many magicians who follow all of these ideals completely, for we are living in the material body and there are problems of stress to acknowledge. However, if a person wishes to follow all of them, he will be quite succcessful most of the time. No one can't make the effort, anyway. Esotericism may require more than this, but at least we are making some headway in approximating to the ideal.

However, as the student becomes more and more oriented towards the ideal, he will desire to enter more and more deeply into the inner side of personal discipline and then he will become more and more directed towards additional disciplines, which pertain to the next level of the ideal. The disciplines of the inner school are of an entirely different type.

They are concerned with the development of esoteric powers, whereby the student is able to rise above certain limits imposed upon all exoteric consciousness. This is a type of development which has never before been discussed in any of my writings, but now the time has come for me to make clear that there does exist a system of esoteric discipline, which is to be followed by those who would seek the transcendental powers of the gnosis.

This is not for everyone, for it is entirely a matter of one's karma. Some are supposed to be in this type of work and some are not, at least not in this lifetime. There are many types of magicians on either side of that distinction, because it does not refer to who may set down and study magick. It refers only to those who would seek to obtain the very highest results from their magickal operations and gnosis. Those who would seek this, having sought the ideal, now have entered upon the inner pathway.

Gnosis of the Spiritual Life, 2: The Ritual Hours and the Time-Stations of the Gnostic Ecclesiastical Structure

By tradition, there exist eight "Hours of Prayer," which are recited by monks and other under a religious rule of life in the west. These hours are Matins, Lauds, Prime, Tierce, Sext, None, and Compline. Most of these Hours of Prayer are contained in one of the ritual books known as the "breviary." Originally it was intended that these Hours of Prayer would be recited to consecrate the day and they would be supplemented with periods of meditation. However, in recent times, there has been a simplification of this structure within the Roman Catholic Church, in an attempt to bring the time-table of the monk or priest into conformity with the modern demands of a busy schedule.

However, from the gnostico-magickal standpoint the situation is quite different. It was in 1960 when I received my first breviary, for at that time I was a theological student and had to learn to use this book during the period of my studies. What I noted first of all about the book was that it was essentially a magickal conception of time presented by means of many ritual constructions. As I became more and more involved in the development of the inner life, both gnostic and monastic, I realized that the breviary was a magickal machine which could be used to contact the mysterious worlds of the higher gnostic realm.

Each one of the magickal hours was a ritual for approaching the proper magickal logic, which would then open up the proper time-station. Later I discovered from my Teachers of the Gnosis that the Sacrifice of the Mass, when celebrated in connection with these times lines, had all of the magickal powers and all of the mystical powers which had been traditionally attributed to it by Catholic Theologians. It was truly a cosmic act and also it had as subtle participatns in its rituals many beings from the time-lines of the gnosis. The reason I am saying this is because for some time we have received questions from those who wonder why we have priests and bishops of our type, rather than following the views of those gnostic orders which are thelemic in character.

The answer would be that our conception of gnostic catholicism is quite different from the thelemic viewpoint. It is also very different from many gnostic conceptions developed by groups who also call themselves the gnostic church. Our view is quite carefully defined by the Masters of the Time Lines, who stand behind the esoteric operations of our system of work. It was from them that I learned about the magickal potentials of the Hours of Prayer and how they can be related to the esoteric logics, which form the Higher Gnostic Realm.

The Sacrifice of the Mass is a method for bringing the infinite powers of the absolute to bear upon a situation in time. Actually, the Mass — as we celebrate it — is a magickal act of transformation, whereby the finite is translated into the infinite and absolute level of being. This is achieved by means of the time-station logics, which are esoteric and magickal operations. The Mass is said or offered within a context defined by an hour of prayer which is said before and an hour of prayer which is said after the Mass.

We can say that those are the coordinates of the structure. By means of these hours of prayer, initial contact is made with the time-stations via their logics. The Offering of the Mass becomes the magickal method whereby cosmic logic enters human experience, since it is something which is happening both on earth and in the heavenly worlds. The action of the God of Sacrificial Fire, AGNI, makes this possible. Although, even when He is not explicitly invoked, He is present, since all sacrifices of priests are subject to him. This applies equally to all sacrifices of priests which are given outside even of the Hindu or Vedic religion.

Connecting AGNI to Esoteric Voudoo, we can say that AGNI is the dynamic aspect of the Legbha-Christ. In the gnostic church there are very special prayers and actions which by words or wordlessly make certain that AGNI is present and recognized as the power which makes the Power of the Gnostic Mass such a transformative reality. Finally, in the gnostic church, there are special initiations of power which are given to the priests of the inner temple so that they will always stay in contact with AGNI. It is for this reason that we find some priests have more powers than others. It is entirely due to the initiations which they have received from their bishop. For the bishop is not only the presence of Grand Legbha, but he is also the presence of AGNI, the mystic fire, the Priest of the Gods and the God of the Priests.

In the structure of the gnostic Hours of Prayer, it is important for the chela of this system to realize how magickal are the connections between these Hours and the Esoteric logics of the Higher Gnostic Realm. In order to make this clear, I am now going to list by schematism these Hours and Logics in their connectedness:

	Hour of Prayer	Gnostic Logic	Higher Realm
1.	Matins	Labyrinthico-gnostic	Axioms of System A – 1, 2
2.	Lauds	Transcendental	Axioms of System B – 3, 4
3.	Prime	Arithmosophic-gnostic	Axioms of System C – 5, 6
4.	Tierce	Fantastic	Axioms of System D – 7, 8
5.	Sext	Algorithmic-gnostic	Axioms of System E – 9, 10
6.	None	Zothyrian	Axioms of System F – 11, 12
7.	Vespers	Magicko-gnostic	Axioms of System G – 13, 14
8.	Compline	Futuristic	Axioms of System H – 15, 16

It is important to keep in mind that the Higher Realm, which is defined by an axiom system of 16 parts, is the gnostic foundational world. These 16 axioms are the magickal beings, and indeed aspects of AGNI, which show themselves in the various parts of our system and in a very important sense "hold it together." In the esoteric science of Vudotronics, it is possible to find certain scientific forms of information which relate to these 16 axioms.

However, in any part of the system, at any stage of the Monastery of the Seven Rays teachings, we can find the operations and presence of the 16 magickal laws. They are the active agents in the system, which continue its powers and sustain the transfer of magickal vitality from the gnostic time-stations of the higher realm to every part of the system as we know it. These beings, however, on a more personal level make possible the operations of the gnosis of the spiritual life, as we are describing it. They may be understood as those aspects of AGNI, which are captured in the concepts which Guzotte describes as "Les Vudu." They are the 16 Gods of IFA, aspects of the Dynamic Geometry of Legbha.

Sanctuary Teachings of Michael Aquarius
Atomic Light and Esoteric Energies

The fundamental fact of initiation is the existence of spiritual energies in the world, which are under the direction of the Hierarchy of Ascended Masters of Light. This means that all of the spiritual energies are directed by the will of these Ascended Masters, Who supervise the evolution of the human race and indeed all of life on this globe.

Atomic Light may be viewed at this point as the basic reality behind every appearance. It is both light and radiation because it makes up all matter, which is really simply a form of light and because all radiations of the spiritual essence of the universe are those initiatic energies and rays (such as the Seven Rays of Divine Outpouring) which guide, direct, and truly initiate the consciousness of humanity.

We therefore teach in these mysteries of the Sanctuary that there exists an initiatic power or magickal force in nature, which can be used to cause the growth and expansion of human mind-energy and spiritual power. In order to test this point, for yourself, here is an exercise as is done exactly by our inner students.

Exercise In Initiation

You will sit or stand in the Sunlight, facing eastward at dawn. As you are composed in an inner state of meditation, simply think of the initiation-powers, which are present in the Occult Powers of Nature. Think and imagine how it is that behind the forces of appearance, behind everything viewed by your senses, there is a vast ocean of initiatic energy. As you do this, say the name of the Ascended and Secret Master of this School, the Master M. Aquarius, and as you do this feel the powers of initiation slowly enter into your soul and body, for they will enter into both at the same time.

Next, say the following mystical invocation, by which means the powers of the inner teachers are able to pass through the world of appearance and enter into your inner selfhood. As you say this invocation, you will slowly feel the rays of the Ascended and Secret Master come into your most hidden and holy heart chamber, where the Power and the Light will be freely and deeply perceived as really and ultimately yourself. Here is that invocation:

I invoke you the power of the light,
The Spiritual Essence of the Invisible Rays;
I invoke you the power of Atomic Light,
The spiritual Essence of the Divine Power.

This having been said, you will relax and meditate and allow the spiritual energy to come to you. Then you wil get up from your meditation and go out and do something that you felt was or is difficult. Now you will do that thing, because you have the right energy and the true power of the light, present deeply within your consciousness.

Let me say that this invocation is one of the most powerful in the whole world and was given to the inner school of the mysteries by Great and Powerful Beings from outside of the Earth. These beings are the true sources of our powers and our teachings and they now are able to come into your own being and to realize themselves in your consciousness. Use this invocation often and your life will move safely and smoothly without difficulties, because the Power of the Atomic Light of God will be within it and will sustain you always.

Atomic Light is the basis of all being. It is pure consciousness and pure power. Because it is hidden in all things, it is therefore the matrix or Mother of all energies. This is the form of the Divine Mother which is understood as the foundation of the Sanctuary of Light, and with which we work as students of the Gnostic Light of the Inner Seflhood. Atomic Light manifests itself in terms of the rays, which are the ways in which the Divine Mother is able to manifest or express Herself in the world of human psychology. But Her Power or Esoteric Energy truly extends beyond the realm of human psychology. It embraces all being in all of its forms. For this reason, we consider the above invocation the most powerful at this point or level of study. That is why you should use it often. Invoke often!

Empowerments of the Light

There are as many empowerments as there are initiations in our magickal system, according to the Master Michael Aquarius. These empowerments are the methods whereby special energies are transferred from the Spiritual World of the Invisibles to the World of the Chelas, by means of our gnostic sources and works (especially magickal and initiatic rituals and the special operations of those rites as they affect and effect the causal body of the higher selfhood).

However, it has been found out that empowerments can best be given by vudotronic and psionic methods, while initiations can be given in person at best. However, we have found that initiations can also be given by psionic means and empowerments can be given by direct personal exchange of energy. As a result of these operations, we can exchange energies with the cosmos and also we can receive special powers, as in the above exercise.

If you wish to receive a vudotronic empowerment, it is necessary for you to enter deeply into the esoteric mind-field of my own personal research, according to Master Michael A. because by that means you will be able to participate directly in the field of power and in the many systems of energy, which are present in that field.

Another name -- given in the nine lessons on Zothyrian metapsychology -- for this mind field is that of the Ontic Sphere. The Ontic Sphere is a mental and magickal field which is built up out of direct magickal energies. It has its own consciousness and can be reached by our magickal computers. In order to make contact with that Ontic Sphere for reasons of empowerment, you simply open the magickal oracle and find out the range of powers which are in an available state. The Genius of the Ontic sphere for each person is, of course, one of the planetary spirits invoked for that specific purpose. The number of that spirit likewise serves as the basis for the creation of the name of the entity, using the Logics of Yemeth.

Once you have received the name of the entity, it is possible for you to make frequent and regular contacts with him/her and enter into an exchange of energies, which are the many forms of magickal empowerment available. If you wish us to do this for you and then give the power to you by transference, this can be done easily, since the special instruments are not always available to you. In fact, the complete laboratory for Ontic Sphere Empowerments is only to be found at the Sanctuary, where Master Michael A. and I work on each of the many research projects.

Many students have written to the Sanctuary and have asked that a list of the many types of magickal initiation be given out. They wish to clarify matters as to how many levels of initiation or light-power-gnosis there are. Let me say that this cannot be done since the higher initiations of our system are esoteric. The initiations which are known about are simply those which are up to the fifth level, which is that of patriarch. Beyond this there are many, many levels of empowerment and initiation. To receive these intiations one has to be specially selected by the Gnostic Hierarchy. In fact, it is the Master Michael Aquarius who makes the selection and who meets the energy field of the chela, with a special level of power which lifts the chela to a new level of being. This is the essence of the process of initiation as given to the beginning chelas of the Gnostic Sanctuary of Light. It is quite different from the initiations given in books or subject to description in a variety of magickal books.

If you are interested in Empowermennt work, however, it would be best to write to me and to state your field of special study. Remember that these Empowerments are simply given for the sake of growth and not for purposes outside of the Gnosis as seen by Master Michael A. In fact, it is impossible to give either an initiation or an empowerment outside of our own system and those who come into our work have to receive this transformation because they are being reborn into the magickal world of the Ontic Sphere for the very first time.

However, you are invited to write to me and inquire about the special types of empowerments which are given at your present level of chelaship. Let me say that there are both types of initiation and types of empowerment available in readiness for each level of magickal attainment. Write to me about this matter and I wil transmit your request to the Master Michael A. He is very interested in helping you grow in the Light.

The Magickal Geography of Master Michael Aquarius

The total number of the mysteries of the gnosis of Master M.A. is 336 (336 = 12 = 3). For each of the mysteries of magickal and gnostic initiation, we find that there are various methods of understanding. Among these methods are the magickal ontologies and the gnostic ontologies. For each mystery there is a magickal ontology and there is also a gnostic ontology.

The magickal ontology pertains to the structure of the system while the gnostic ontology refers to the contentual experiences of the system.

In order to arrive at this number (336), it is necessary to see the magickal geography of the Master M.A. as composed of the following components of the gnosis:

There are 256 spaces, which are the spaces of gnostic light. These are magickal places where magickal events happen. They are spiritual and not material. We can say that they are states of consciousness in the most gnostic sense of the word. They are ideal forms of being, because they are beyond space and time in the physical sense.

There are 64 ontic spheres, which are universal conditions. Each ontic sphere is composed of four spaces, which explicate the gnostic energies of the ontic sphere. both the spaces and the ontic spheres have rulers. The rulers of the ontic spheres have magickal and gnostic authority over the rulers of the spaces of light.

There are 16 domains of gnostic being. Each domain contains by means of the gnostic logics of entailment, inclusion, equivalence, and implication four ontic spheres. Each domain has a magickal and gnostic ruler which has this authority over the rulers of the ontic spheres contained within the domain of the ruler.

There are several threads running through this hierarchy of rulers of gnostic being and those threads are represented by the planets of our solar system, which bring an analogy to the rulers of the domains, ontic spheres, and spaces having a pattern which is reflected in the planets and influences of our solar system. The names for the planets as we use them in this system are:

The Earth,
The Moon,
Mercury,
Venus,
The Sun,
Mars,
Jupiter,
Saturn,
Uranus,
Neptune,
Pluto.

These are the eleven types of magickal and gnostic family to which the rulers of the higher worlds of the magickal geography of Master M.A. belong. However, these magickal families are significant only for the very simple reason that they provide us with the methods for making contact with the rulers of the different higher worlds. They give to the gnostic student his method of making entry. This entry is how we enter into contact with these higher beings by means of magickal computers and communication systems.

However, in working with these entities, we learn that they are capable of many self-transformations and so it has been determined that the names of the rulers and their own planetary–type family may change, depending upon the changes of the universe and upon the state of all of the conditions of the universe at any fixed time. The reason for this is that every part of the universe is undergoing constant changes and these changes are reflected in the different ways in which planetary energy is expressed by means of oracles and magickal computers.

However, what is important is that the more power the student has or the higher the power of the master, the more the name of the ruler of the world will be properly reflected in the oracle work. It is because the more powerful magicians are able to enter more and more deeply into the states of these rulers, indeed into the consciousness of these higher or more spiritual realms, and grasp what is there. This power can only come from the esoteric side of gnostic initiation. It is absolutely fundamental that this gnostic initiation be given in terms –– both physically and metaphysically –– so that the keys to the sanctuary of gnostic teachings are imparted to the student exactly. Hence the keys are given to open the doorways of the gnostic rulers of domains, spheres, and spaces.

From very early times, there has always been a special prayer, which lifts the soul of the magician into the higher worlds, where he may meditate upon the energies of the rulers of every space, sphere, and domain. This prayer is one of the treasures of the Gnosis and is given to those students who have come to a new level of being and who are ready to make use of the inner teachings and powers of light. Traditionally, this prayer is said every morning after completion of the regular yoga exercises of the gnostic priest. By saying it each day, the magician is able to learn the ways in which the powers of the gnosis are manifested to all seekers after perfection.

In the gnostic teachings of Master M.A. this prayer is used to create a very powerful state of spiritual awareness, whereby the soul is filled with a new light each day. The light of the soul is of course as necessary as the light of the body. However, there are very few who live in both forms of light. You will soon be among those special gnostics and possess the secrets of the power as they come down to you. At the same time, while you recite this magickal prayer you are diffusing the energies of the gnosis everywhere in the world, for you become a sending station for the rays of cosmic and divine light. This is a very important law at work because it is a means for showing the world how the energy and consciousness levels of being operate. They operate through the magicians who send out the powers of the light. Now, here is the prayer:

O Providence, or Fortune, bestow on my Thy grace ––
Imparting these the Mysteries a Father only may hand on,
And that, too, to a son alone –– His immortality ––
(A Son) initiate, worthy of this our craft, with which
Sun Mithras, the Great God, commanded me to be endowed by
His Archangel: So that I, Eagle (as I am, by mine own self)
Alone, may soar to Heaven, and contemplate all things.

This is a very ancient prayer and so powerful that it is said by the ascended and secret masters themselves each day, at the height of their powers in the magickal realms where they do their occult and inner work for humanity. The power of this prayer can truly be said to be limitless.

In each of the gnostic worlds there are of necessity certain passwords and secret names which must be used to gain entrance to the higher zones of magickal power. One of the most important parts of the inner teachings of the gnosis of Master

Michael Aquarius is the giving to the student the names of power and the key—words and the prayers, which make it possible for the student to realize that the keys to the gnosis reside in the words as they are given not because they are "magickal names" but because they refer to certain invisible forces, and represent a formulary for translating what is beyond the ken of human consciousness into "initiatic knowledge," which is the most important way of knowing, or the most important form of gnosis.

In order to develop the inner selfhood of endless light and divinity, it is very necessary for the student to possess the keys to the mysteries of the light. This is done by means of the many experiments of the rituals of the gnosis which add concreteness to the abstract forms of gnostic ontology. Since there are various ontologies for each world, it is so very important to have both the theoretic and the experimental sides of one's being fully in mind, or understood, in order to develop an awareness of what is reality and what is the proper level of being. Then you are fully able to know yourself as you truly are.

There exist many realms and forms and being. We possess all of the keys to these realms and we possess all of the magickal forms, whereby the consciousness of being is opened to the mind of the seeker after enlightenment. This is the meaning of light in our experience.

The gnostic pathway is one of supreme growth into light. It is the way of being raised up more and more through these worlds and zones, to the higher and higher spheres, spaces, and domains of Sublime Masters of Light. This is the way in which the gnostic awakening operates in our consciousness. Only by faithfully following in the pathway of light can you achieve this goal. Anything less than this is imperfect and less than suited to the divine spark in human nature. The consciousness of being is the perfection of energy in you and you will attain to that power by reciting the prayer given on the previous page each morning. Begin to follow the light and you will feel it everywhere.

The Golden Temple of Initiation

I dwell in the golden temple and my power rises therein and is diffused in every part of the world. I send the rays of my power to every being and my word carries with it the light of the ages. I have sent the birds of dawn and they have become the messengers of my powers for I am the master of the rays.

I am the golden lord of endless power and my robe is gold and purple. I ride upon the chariot of the Sun and yet I visit you at night in your dreams. I send the rays of my power to every being and they become awakened and alive to the voice of my presence. I am a secret beyond all secrets and I am a wisdom hidden in the deepest recesses of this planet. In the secret cave of glass I dwell as a beautiful vision and in the temples of ice, I am the white ray, the light of divine power. I am known in all of my beauty and my ascension to light is the path of fulfillment for I am a master of the rays.

My wisdom is light and my blood is red and the rays of my eyes are golden lights which encircle my students in the veils of endless protection. I am alive to the powers of being and they are drawing their energies from my mysteries. In the golden temple of my creation, I send out the rays of power and these rays touch and heal all being. I am sending this power out now and you are receiving it at this moment. Breathe into your soul the powers of my rays and you will be healed for the golden light of the Sun is falling upon you and the pale reflections of the dawn are a rose and blue veil before your eyes. I am sending my healing to you and this is how I heal. I heal by the sending out of the magickal and divine powers of transformation, for I am a master of the rays.

I am sending this power to you now so receive it into your soul, the golden light and the rose and blue veil are the powers which convey this energy to the mind and with these words of light and power, I project the powers of eternal wisdom and radiance as I open all things to become parts of my mystical life. We are all parts of this one and true reality. The light is growing and rising and becoming more and more a focus of the divine power everywhere. I am sending the rays to you and they are touching you, body and soul, and they are making you whole, for the power that I send with these words is the power to make all things well and whole. I am the source of that power for I am the master of the rays. I have come to transform your very being. I have come to make you a god. -- The Master Michael Aquarius, Transmission-118)

The above passage is not a quote, that is why we do not use quotation marks. Rather, it is a transmission of cosmic powers and divine energies from the master of the rays. He is the source of a very powerful and very special influence, which is the power of the spirit to make all things whole. This is the mystery of healing. Healing is the energy which comes to us and which removes the past and makes us new beings. The Master is a special kind of being. His role is that of transformation of being. Making a new and powerful being out of what was imperfect. This is accomplished from the golden temple of initiation.

The golden temple of initiation exists very high up in the mental plane. It is composed of a very fine mental matter and it is golden in color. It is the source of power for our own Sun, because the Sun is the reflection in the world of physical perception of the golden temple in the world of metaphysical perception. This is a temple of initiation for it is there that the master of the rays will take his specially prepared students and they will be initiated into the mysteries of his own being, i.e., the mysteries of what it is to be a master of the rays. There are many chambers in this temple but the most important is the sanctuary of the light, which is in the very center of the temple and which is made out of pure gold.

This is, of course, not physical gold, which is a very pure and powerful substance. There in that sanctuary of gold, the master will lead the very special students through the exercises which awaken the powers of the light in all of their bodies. They become more and more attuned to the life and experiences of the masters of the rays. They understand for the very first time the meanings behind the experiences of the masters, who dwell in the higher mental worlds. The following is a prayer to say to attach yourself to this ideal and by this means you will grow closer to the master:

"I am seeking in every action of my life to come closer and closer to the supreme and perfect master of the rays. I am seeking and growing in my wish to be with this great teacher of the light. O great master of the rays, hear my call to your throne on high."

The Master Michael Aquarius is perhaps one of the most spiritual of divine beings. He has been sent to the present world in order to transform the spiritual energies of those who are actively seeking to become perfected. He has been sent by the Lord of the Light, or the Gnostic Beings, who protect the evolution of the human race. His message is quite clear. You are to draw near to him and allow him to guide you up the pathway to the light of perfection.

Of course, there are many problems which stand in the way. One of them is that many feel this perfection is not for them. They are following other paths, they say. But the master of the rays states that this is not so: all beings are to follow his method and his path, there are not to be any exceptions. If you do not follow it now, you will follow it in the future, at some time when you are alive in another body, but you will follow the master of the rays. His power is so vast and it is just beginning to be felt. I am here to make known this energy. It is coming to you as you read these words.

Here is a special power projection, which can be used to bring more of the light of the master of the rays into your soul—experience. For that is where the power works to make your own experience new and filled with transformative powers:

Attend to my words and fill your heart with the power which I am sending to you in this prayer of transformation. I am making you new. I am making you good. I am making you a being filled with light and with divine energy. My word is power and my throne is the strength of eternal sunlight. I am the voice of the ages and I am the will to make all things pure. Listen to my words and receive the powers which comes from these energies. I am sending my rays to you at any time you say these words. Repeat them and say them over in your heart and you will be filled up with golden light from the temple of initiation.

There is a power which is endless and which is commanded by the master of the rays. His power is vast and without any measure. His will is so strong that all evil is destroyed by this divine fire. He sits upon a golden throne of light and holds a mighty sword of power. He is the master of the rays and the rays are sent out by him to every part of the universe. His word is power and his light is at work making all things new. He is the master of those energies which rise from the depths of the soul and he is the master who leads each of us into the depths and mysteries of our souls. By his teachings we come to see ourselves as divine beings. He has brought to us the fire and power of truth in self-discovery.

All references to golden light and to golden substances bring our minds to the place of the Sun in this system of metaphysics. It is here that the Master wishes to introduce the concept of the Sun-Goddess, the Center of the Solar Cultus. In Japanese Shinto, this notion is very important because the human race is derived from the Sun, and is continually dependent upon the power of the Sun for life. The Shinto Goddess of the Sun is Amaterasu-Omikami, and in Zothyrian theology, Her name is Ameratsu-Omni-Kami.

In either system, however, She is the focus of power. One might also remark that the Sanctuary Teachings of Master M.A. are actually the gnostic reformulation of the old principles of Esoteric Shinto for the modern world and the contemporary spiritual need. The Power of the Goddess of the Sun comes to the golden temple by means of a magickal induction. The Master M.A. sends to the temple a continuous radiation of Her divine Presence. She is present in the temple at all times, especially in the innermost shrine, which is Her Residence. The work of the Master M.A. is to transmute the energies of the metaphysical Sun into powers which can be used by human beings striving for the most perfect state of attainment. The purpose of this diffusion is, of course, the evolution of all beings towards the Mother Goddess of the Sun.

Here is a powerful invocation to the Goddess, which can be used each morning:

"I call upon you O My Divine Mother, the Goddess of the Sun, asking your protection and power to be with me at every moment of this day. I adore your presence in the light of the solar disc, I worship You in the divine Sun within my heart. When I say I am a son (daughter) of the Sun, I call upon You at all times. I adore your light, which is filling all space. I see You before me in the heavenly symbol. You are My Divine Mother, Ameratsu-Omni-Kami."

The worship of the magickal and metaphysical powers of the Sun is a very high form of the most ancient gnosis. The most ancient religions have always acknowledged the powers of the Sun. The solar cultus is the beginning of human spirituality. The purpose of the sanctuary teachings is to bring about spiritual renewal and transformation. The Master M.A., who is the master of the rays, is the messenger of the Sun goddess and the gnostic awakening. By making use of the prayers, meditations, and rituals which you will be taught, you will awaken yourself to the divine power present in experience. The physical Sun is the symbol of the divine Sun, with each thought try to bring yourself closer and closer to the Mother Goddess.

The Power of the Kami

"The Kami, or the Gods of the Shinto Religion, are the most powerful forces in the world. They are the purest and most ideal embodiments of natural forces and elemental power, as well as being the expressions of the divine intelligibility of all being. The religion of the future will be a form of Shinto, separated from its Japanese isolation and fused with many elementals from magick. This form of Shinto will be understood as the highest and most complete form of the Cult of the Vudu, for they are the same in essence. In order to have power, it is necessary to possess the powers which the spirits hold. They are the sources of magickal energy and when they are embodied in the human world, these magickal powers are then expressed in experience. Each person possesses a form of Kami-hood, or internal and inherent divinity, the Atman of Brahminism, which must be awakened and allowed to work in the world of space and time. The rituals of the gnosis of our own Esoteric Shinto are directed towards this achievement. This is the goal of the inner and most magickal of my teachings. I wish all beings to realize their Kami-hood and I want all beings to live in this state of divinity." -- "From the Sanctuary of Michael Aquarius," 104

In order to realize powers which are there for your personal transformation, it is very necessary for the magickal student to know that he is a Kami as well as that he is in the midst of an infinite number of Kami. Perhaps the best way to realize this is by means of a magickal prayer, which brings about immediate unity with the Kami. Here is such a prayer, which has proven very effective in Shinto Gnosis:

"I am in the midst of an infinity of Gods and Spirits of Light. I realize that they are about me and that in essence I am one with them. I now breathe deeply and receive into my soul the powers, which they possess, as I awaken in myself the divine power of my own Kami-hood. I breathe deeply and count to three and I release the breath and count to three. Now, I clap my hands three times. I have united myself with my Kami-Nature and I am one with all the Gods and Spirits."

As you do this prayer you will breathe and exhale and you will clap your hands. You will do this simple and very powerful exercise, whenever you are in need of Kami-energization.

What is this Kami-energization? Well, first of all it is becoming aware of the powers which you possess. You possess all powers but you have to learn how this is so. This is why you have to exercise in these methods. Next, Kami-energization is the act of being one with the Gods and spirits of the Esoteric Shinto Gnosis. This means first that you are aware of their powers and presence and secondly that you are able to feel yourself inside of them and feel them inside of you. This is more like intuition but it means that you are very intimately close to the Kami. You are one of them. In the various forms of Shinto religion, there is a certain feeling which hints at this. But in the more esoteric side of Shinto, our own gnosis, we have brought it out for you to realize. Also, there are many other exercises for developing this feeling for the Gods and spirits. I want you now to do another exercise in Kami-energization. Repeat this prayer:

"I am one with the Kami. I am filling myself with the energies of the Kami. Iam alive to the presence of the Kami. I am strong with the powers of the Kami."

As you say this simple exercise, you will feel yourself becoming stronger and stronger. You will feel yourself taking in the powers of the Kami. Actually, these powers are already inside of you, they are simply coming to consciousness in you. You are developing and you are growing into your Kami-selfhood. Repeat these exercises as often as you wish, it might be good to take a cold-water baath or shower before doing this. Dry yourself off completely and then in the nude do this exercise or any othe exercises given in this lesson. Ideally, it would be done while the Sun is rising. The Sun in the shinto faith is the symbol of the divine energy, the power with which you are to identify yourself in the exercises of Kami-energization.

The Kami are many, in fact they are infinite in number. Wherever there is power or some spiritual presence, there you will find Kami. For this reason, Shinto is both polytheistic, in that it worships many, many Gods and spirits, as well as being pantheistic, because it sees divine power behind the phenomena of nature.

When you realize that the Kami are everywhere, you will develop the magickal method of greeting them, wherever they might be. Here is a simple prayer to them, which can be used anywhere:

"I know that you are there and that you are my constant companions. I feel the powers of the Kami everywhere I am. I realize the wonder of the presence of the Kami in every circumstance and situation. You touch my hand and lead me into newer and newer experiences. I am alive with a feeling of adventure because the Kami are my constant companions."

This is such a very simple method of making contact and realizing the very terrific powers of the Kami. Every part of life then becomes an adventure in exploring what the Kami have brought before you. Nothing becomes boring because the Kami have presented it to you as an adventure. Nothing is feared, because the Kami are there to experience it with you. With this attitude in mind, you are healed of fears, and life becomes an adventure.

I am now going to give you a ritual to do in order to improve your powers and help you to develop more of the Kami-powers in yourself. This is a basic ritual and you will be your own Kami-priest(ess).

Kami-Ritual for Purity
You will need the following items: a large and very clean bowl, some very pure spring water, some sea salt, and a white piece of cloth. The water is to be placed in the bowl and the salt and the cloth are to rest next to it. The entire process should be centered on the idea of purity, especially what is known as ritual cleanliness, which means that which is purified by ritual work and made suitable for the Kami.

Ideally, you would take a bath, and in classical Shinto this would be a cold-water bath because cold water is more purifying, since it is closer to nature. After you take the bath (I personally prefer a cold shower), you will put on a clean robe or some clean clothing. Remember that you as the priest(ess) of the Kami must be very pure and the way in which you dress is part of that. Some mystics, however, prefer to work either in the nude or simply wearing the classical loin cloth. You may work as you wish but it should reflect the idea of purity. Nude ritual work is very pure because in some ways clothing does affect the purity of the body.

As you bathe and as you dry yourself off and as you dress (if you do), be thinking of the idea of purity, especially making things pure by ritual methods. this is very important. Next, come to where the mineral salt, the spring water, the bowl, and the white cloth are. Say the following to yourself as you stand before them:

"I am now approaching the rite of purification and I am offering myself to the Kami so that I may become pure in Their Eyes and that I may therefore serve Them in an acceptable manner and with an agreeable offering."

Next, you will look at the bowl of spring water and say to yourself the following prayer:

"It is my wish to become so pure in the Eyes of the Kami that they will bless me with the divine presence of invisible light."

Next, you will summon the Kami to hear you. This is done traditionally in Japanese ritual work by clapping your hands together two times. This is the way of letting the inner side know that you are there awaiting Them. Next, you will look at the water and place some salt in your right hand. You will say the following prayer to the Kami of Pure Water:

"Here I am, Great Kami of the Purity of Water. I am here before your symbol. Present in this symbol of some mysterious way, I know You. I wish to become as pure as your symbol so that I can receive You into my soul as the water receives You. Come to me as I offer this pure mineral of sea salt by dropping it slowly into the water."

Slowly, then, you will allow the salt to fall gently into the water as you continue to think of the Kami of Pure Water, even trying to imagine what this God appears like. Then you will say this prayer:

"You are present in this bowl of pure water. I love you and send out to You the rays of my heart. I am being purified by You because you have come to me and are now with me in this mystery of purity. O Great Kami of the Purity of Water, always keep me pure."

Next, you will take the clean white cloth and dip it slowly and gently into the pure water. Lifting it out, you will touch it to the various parts of your body, beginning with the feet and working upwards to the head. As you do this, you will repeat the following quick prayer:

"I am purifying myself with the power of the Kami of the Purity of Water. I am being made more and more pure, so that I am becoming more and more filled with the Kami-powers."

Then you will touch yourself over again, working from the head to the feet, downwards, while you dip the cloth frequently in the pure water. Then you will shake the cloth in every direction: up, down, north, west, south, and east, which are the six major direct routes of physical energy and therefore to be used to convey the purity of Kami-energy. As you do this you will say the following prayer, which closes the ritual:

"I have become pure and I am making all things pure. I am working to bring the Kami-power to every object. I am working to bring to all things the blessings of meeting the Gods. All things will be made pure by the powers of the Kami."

Now, I would suggest that you rest for a while and meditate upon the powers of the Kami. Think about these powers and how they can help all beings. Then stand up and, facing the bowl, simply clap your hands twice, to signal the close of the meeting with the Kami-powers. You may place the water in a bottle for use as holy water to be sprinkled about.

You should take the white cloth and dry it out in the air. It is now a symbol of the Kami powers and should be kept some place with respect. You are now developing your powers towork with the Kami-energies.

The High Energies of True Initiation—Consciousness

"Every teacher of light, wherever he or she might be in the Gnosis, must be guided by the holy beings of light. You are no example of detachment from our being, for you are no exception to this rule. All beings are linked to us, whether they know it or not. They are one with us in the deepest forms of spiritual consciousness. It is in that way that we find all being growing. It is growing in love for all beings, as it becomes more and more aware of all beings and their mystical interdependence in the Gnosis of Love. And you, my dear student, are linked to the powers of light, the true saints and blessed ones, by this very same Gnosis of Love.

"Therefore, let this power be released in you by means of your being calm and knowing it is there. Let this power be released in you by means of your loving all creatures, all beings, because they are holy ones. I command that you let this power be released in you by means of your sending out all love—rays, because you are the perfect and true instrument of this Gnosis of Love." -- M. Bertiaux, "Dainichi Revelations," 17

True initiation is the process of realization, whereby we say to ourselves quite firmly that we are parts of the divine universe of all beings. Love is the ultimate reality and the universe is made up of pure lights, which have become fully aware of this power of love. Once one has tuned into this power, by actual mental and spiritual effort and not mechanically, you know that the high energies are now pouring through your soul and your body.

In the Gnostic Church of Concesiousness, which is a school of initiation, we live in the divine vitality. The power of love is warm and all—comprehending. It is not an abstract perfection or is it by any means a perception of limit. It is everywhere. So to prepare yourself for this expression of divine power and for this experience of union, it is wise for you to know the teachers and their rules, because they are the ones who are making possible our entry into initiation consciousness. They are the spiritual ones, who have told us about the Gnosis of Love.

In my work in the Gnostic School of Consciousness, I have been guided by very spiritual powers. One of my closest and most holy teachers is Dr. Kammamori, who is my very true initiation. It was he who founded the School of Consciousness, which we teach to you in our sanctuary lessons, although because he is a holy and spiritual being, he is not very attached to the limits of external being. For this reason, he is by nature an esoteric aspect often viewed as the focus of the universal guru. Dr. Kammamori is a Japanese and a Zothyrian master of light. That is to say, his physical body is perfectly expressed through the physical being of a Japanese male born under the sign of Capricorn with a strong Scorpio energy present. So he is a deity of this radiation, because he is Kam Mamori, the Holy Guardian Angel and Universal Guru. Let me say that Kammamori has been active in my life for a long time. I need not go into the past karma and lives together, but let me say that in this life the association has been powerful. The powerful connections with him have also been fantastic, since at one time all of the members of the inner school, which is within the School of Consciousness, were embodiments in one form or another of this energy. There is much else that can be said about him, but that is for the more advanced studies in the gnosis.

However, it is important to note that he is also Zothyrian and therefore an inner spiritual teacher and esoteric logician. Actually, I suppose I met him through work in esoteric logic, because he dwells there primarily. The Master Zothyrius was in a remarkable way responsible for this. He led me into the study of the history of philosophy in the alternative universe, then I became aware of Dr. K. Now the Master Z is the pure embodiment of the Cancerian decanate of the sign of Scorpio and so he is a spiritual teacher who has helped me for almost 20 years, in this lifetime.

He led me deeper and deeper into the universe, which is totally a form of spiritual being and then said to me that Dr. K. would be able to help me in this area. I think it was about this time that I had the presence of Dr. K. in my home for a long enough time to allow me to do a painting of him. He was then in close connection with Lemurian magick and appeared really as a shamanistic type of teacher and not as the esoteric logician or metaphysician.

But he taught me that the shamanistic and intensive aspects of being are the content, or the empirical life of esoteric logic, which is the structure of being, enclosing and enveloping the energies of the shamanistic and expressionistic levels of being. It was this way of viewing the universe that enabled me to combine the abstract way of the ideal and the spiritual with the realistic and impulsive power-zones of magick and sensory excitement, as well as the intuitive perception of raw data, because in these very close circumstances it was possible to see how each gave light-energy to the other and how each saw the other as an expression of the same level of being, although coming from another perspective but expressive of all aspects. This was the law of esoteric polarity, which I have developed somewhat, under the influence of Dr. Kammamori, in my esoteric logic, and wherein we find contained the whole of the being of nature as the given, which the Chinese metaphysicians refer to sometimes as the Tao.

The world of shamanistic excitement was also developed in my earlier work with the Voudoo deities. But when I asked Dr. Kammamori if this would constitute an area of conflict with my work as an esoteric logician, he stated that it would not because the same energy was being worked. Voudoo, he explained, was the feminine aspect of the field of magick, while Shinto Gnosis and Esoteric Buddhism, as expressed in the sciences of esoteric logic and the history of Zothyrian philosophy constituted the masculine aspect. The supposed sexual difference is entirely due to the object of energy-intuition; in voudoo it is the intuition of raw contents, excitements, and shamanistic dream experiences.

This is entirely the feminine aspect, because it is concerned with the experience of chaotic contents. We can say that this is the primordial matrix of being. On the other hand, the structures of esoteric logic are intuited in a very pure and ideal way. They are intuited by means of the structures of intuition. They are intuited by means of the innermost quality of structure. This is pure masculinity and is the law of organization whereby chaos is known and lived. The higher energies are understood as composed of both elements, the feminine and the masculine, and it is the male principle which envelops the female, since the numbers 1 and 3 surround the number 2.

In my experiences with esoteric logic, I was also able to focus on the basis of the masculine ideal. As I said, this was the question of what was "intuition-structure." Dr. Kammamori explained that it was close to the way in which Hegelian metaphysics and logic might be understood by a Zen-Buddhist philosopher. Let us suppose that a person was a Zen-Buddhist for about 40 years. Each day, he would do his special meditation exercises. Then suppose he had to come to the study of the philosophy of Hegel, or even certain British Neo-Hegelians, using your imagination you can see what it might be like.

That, Dr. Kammamori told me, was the way in which we could understand "intuition-structure." Then he said that there was another mode of coming to view the masculine and that was named "structure-intuition." That would be the way in which the Hegelian metaphysician would try and understand Zen-Buddhism. Then, as I progressed in my initiation consciousness, Dr. led me to a more esoteric level, which was where I received many initiations necessary for the development of estoeric logic as a gnostic form of magick and metaphysics. He taught me to reverse what he had taught earlier and see "intuition-structure" as the way in which a Hegelian would view Zen Buddhism, or engage in that specific kind of meditation and to see "structure-intuition" as the way in which Zen Buddhist would view Hegelian metaphysics. All of these viewings, or gnostic exercises, were done from the inside of the experience, or within the context of meditation and metaphysics.

If you would like to do an exercise -- you do not have to do one -- but if you wish, you are invited to write a report on what you have gained from trying to do these four exercises, the two exoteric and the two esoteric, and send the report to me. I will then be able to connect your consciousness to the high energies of true initiation, as they are being expressed in the gnosis of light, under the direction of my special and ideal guru, Dr. Kammamori.

You may then write up the report and send it to me for my examination. I will reply to all of these exercises, which are sent to me as result of work being done in this area. I will also use this method for determining the rate of growth you are participating in at this time. But, of course, this is an entirely optional project and is not a requirement for studying with me.

The Esoteric Logicians and the "Dainichi Revelations"

"It is necessary for you to understand that the existence of the esoteric logicians is conditioned by and contained in the 'Dainichi Revelations.' By this we mean that the esoteric logicians are emanations from these teachings and that they are beings, who rise to self–consciousness only by means of these revelations. For this reason, it would seem that these teachings are a world of their own, which produces its own form of life and its own form of experience. Those of you who are outside of this world, but admitted to it by the process of initiation, participate in its sacramental mysteries, when you do the work of esoteric logic. When you do that work, you are inside of the 'Dainichi Revelations'." -- M. Bertiaux, "Kammamorian Fragments," 17

The process of esoteric initiation involves an intensive view of the various occult levels and processes. Because of the deep powers which are to be found in initiation, one must be admitted gradually. There, even in the most beginning of states, one will encounter the presence of the truly spiritual beings, designed by Shinto gnosis as the esoteric logicians.

This process is quite complex, but it means that fundamentally the universe is infinite in all directions, and that it develops and expresses itself in all directions. However, the esoteric patterns give rise to a unique and very radical process and they pour out as forms of being, manifesting themselves as trasncendental aspects ,of our selfhood. There we encounter the beings who are the esoteric logicians. It must not be thought that they are masters or specially adept humans, rather they are Kami, or divine foci of consciousness. They are in truth the Kami-no-mamori of the gnostic experience of Shinto. In order to experience the beingness of their power, one allows the radiations of the teachings of the Esotric Buddha (Dainichi or Maha Vairocana) to enter their soul. Then the marvelous process of initiatic transformation slowly occurs, whereby we become more and more attuned to the lifestream which is within the teachings. I think that this process is very complex, but it may be expressed by way of the two laws, which define its rationale:

1. The esoteric logicians within the world of the "Dainichi Revelations" come into contact with the initiate and begin to develop the structures or pathways of esoteric logic in the consciousness of the initiate. These beings are active intelligences and exposure to the teachings brings one into immediate contact with them.

2. The process of making contact will be an outpouring of the radiations of esoteric logic, which is a system of inner dynamics. Part of the transcendental selfhood of the initiate is then connected permanently to that world or else it becomes an extension of it. One comes to see that world as akin to oneself. The closer one grows to it, the deeper the initiation. The process of initiation may be viewed as a joining to being but not as a return to the primordial roots of being, because this gnostic world is not a part of the past karma of the initiate. It is the new being, which is bestowed by the Esoteric Buddha.

Together with those two above-mentioned laws of the gnostic process, I think it is very important to show the relationship which exists between esoteric logic and the field of transcendental logic. Since then, there have been a number of references to both ideal beings and to the continuum of esoteric logic.

Statement: Transcendental logic may be understood intuitively as the lifestream of ideal being.

Statement: Esoteric logic may be understood intuitively as the initiative content of transcendental logic.

At one time, this was for me the major problem of contemporary gnostic consciousness. I sought the solution to this problem in one form or another for about 20 years, in fact, I was interested in the problem for about 25 years. Then, as the result of my gnostic experiments in metaphysics, the solution suggested by those two statements came to the surface of consciousness. Because the question was so subtle, it could only rise to the surface because of a shock which I had received. That shock was the part of my initiation from Dr. Kammamori, which concerns the act of being. When I received the shock of that initiation, I was able to realize the solution to my problem, out of the scattered magickal energies, which were to be intuitively found in my own consciousness.

This type of shock is quite different from the method of analysis—burn, which I too have experienced and written about elsewhere. The difference consists in the fact that the energies of being are projected from an esoteric dimension of consciousness, while in the process of analysis—burn, the energies are directed from the verbal-egoic level towards the unconscious mind—field. One process is esoteric and initiatic and the other is psychoanalytic.

However, the connection between the world of the "Dainichi Revelations" and the world of my experience as an esoteric logician remained unclear. Therefore, it was very much a matter of necessity for me to try and see intuitively the connection. I was able to do this because I had reached an insight into the dynamics of the Esoteric Buddha level of universal being.

Statement: Transcendental logic may be understood as the collectively revelatory energy and activity of the "Dainichi Revelations." Hence, it must be understood that being does manifest itself as a continuum of revelation. Also, it must be understood that this ideal being manifests itself as both a system of mystical archetypes, expressed by the symbols of the "Dainichi Revelations" and as a natural and inductively outgoing process of ideal revelation, energy as ideal goal, and universally causal activity, within the definitins of transcendental logic.

As a result of this insight, I was able to conduct a number of esoteric experiments with the direction of Dr. Kammamori, in order to unveil the powers of transcendental logic which have been captured in other ways by metaphysics and especially in logic and cosmology.

By this I mean that certain metaphysicians were able to supplement their systems of gnosis and magick because of the experiments which they conducted within the dream worlds of these two logics. In my own way, I should admit, I too have been responsible for some of these gnostic explosions, because they were expressions of the reality of being and they were formulations of the ideal order, within the initiatic situation. Had it not been for the directions given by Dr. Kammamori, I doubt very seriously if I would have been able to locate these realms, which religious imagination has collectively indicated by the name of "The Western Paradise."

According to my way of viewing the univverse, the being of statements is spiritual energy, therefore it is intelligent. As an experiment with metaphysics, may I suggest the next exercise.

There are three statements and two laws given in this paper. They may be quite abstract in appearance. But they are charged with magickal and gnostic powers and energies. I want you to establish meditational contact with these beings. You may understand them as Kami or as metaphysical and spiritual deities. Make contact with them through meditation and intuition. Then ask them to explain themselves to you. Ask them to talk about their world or level of heaven in language that you feel can be easily understood. Ask them to show you the meaning of the initiations which they give out and how you may participate in these mysteries. Then make a recording of this experiment in your magickal diary, under the heading "Attention: Experiments in Esoteric Logic."

I will welcome any comments or ideas or questions, which you may wish to make. It is my wish to take you into the higher worlds of gnostic being by this method.

Connective Paper No. 1: For the Course in Magickal Instruction

At this point in our instruction we are moving into a somewhat different approach to the subject of magick. We will now come to see magick as the result of applied and experimental philosophy. In order to come to this view, it will be necessary first of all to review the Zothyrian magickal philosophical atmosphere. This means that the student will be introduced immediately, with this lesson, to an example of that Zothyrian mode of operation. The connections between this paper and the last paper on the search for Ojas will become very clear. However, following the analysis of some basic ideas in Sung Po, we will spend three months in the study of the Choronzon Club course in philosophical magick. This will be to extend a little more our mental frames of thought. Following this period of study, we will enter upon a systematic study of ancient and medieval Zothyrian philosophy and its magickal applications and experimentations.

In the paper on Sung Po, it is important to realize that there are certain built-in traps for the merely curious. For example, a careful reading of the lesson will discern two areas of magickal paradox, if not contradiction. This was unavoidable, for the simple reason that the authorities which released this matter for study to us insisted that we retain the medieval format of maintaining certain traps for the merely curious student, so that the effectual magickal power and its keys would not be released. Such keys do exist and they will unfold in time as the way in which the medieval Zothyrians did their magick and philosophy becomes more and more clearly understood. On the other hand, we are aware of the fact that many students, especially in the USA, will not have the discipline to seek out the keys, and will fall into the traps. If so, that is simply their karma. We are not interested at this stage in treating any student as a mere beginner.

The magickal experiments and applications of the Zothyrian philosophy will prove to the serious student a source of very rich magickal and gnostic technique. In a sense, Voudoo in its esoteric form is based upon Zothyrian forms. It must be due, I think, to a time when the gnostics of both Voudoo and Zothyria were in very close contact, probably due to the influence of the solar-cultus "le soleil-gnostique." Also, the Zothyrian magick reflects the meeting ground between the world of the Spider-magi and the Enochian methods, which were revived in the work of Giovanni Dee. All of this may be taken as evidence for a positive root in the exchanges between Atlantean and Zothyrian magick, although Atlantis is far older than the history of the ancient period of Zothyrian philosophy, which we will be exploring. This may suggest something of an Atlantean source for the Z-system, but that is another matter. We know that, however, Coptic and Gnostic influences form the basis for the medieval period of Z-philosophy, so we may say that an Atlantean-Chinese influence may be at the root of the ancient period of Z-philosophy. However, we will explore this later.

There is planned a research publication for the medieval period of Z-philosophy, and those wishing to receive it are invited to write to me about this work.

The Ontological Lections of Sung-Po, a Zothyrian Master of Magick and Metaphysics
At this point in our studies, we must prepare for the transition to the study of ancient and medieval Zothyrian philosophy and its magickal applications and experiments. For we must see the history of Zothyrian philosophy as the history of

604

the theory about magick. Only in the Zothyrian universe were magick and philosophy so closely connected. By way of introduction to this system, I wish to say a few words about the Master Sung-Po, who lived towards the end of the medieval period (1270 - 1400) and who wrote and taught a specific method of the gnosis. Sung-Po is the author of several magickal commentaries on the "Parmenides" of Plato, as well as a treatise in several folios on the Logic of the Oracles, which would be similar to the Book of the I-Ching of IFA system, in our universe. Here are a few highlights from his ontological lections, or teachings to the initiates.

The Root of Wisdom

The basis for the whole of magick and philosophy is to be found in the notion of the arche, the essential law of absolute self-hood, which is realized by means of initiation and the many exercises of the inner sciences, e.g., esoteric logic. However, because of the beingness of the self, which is absolute, and grounded only in its own logical sufficiency, esoteric logic and hyper-logic are one and the same subject. Whatever the initiatte can do by means of his power of the mind, by his power which is the mind behind the mind even of the initiate, he can do as a god of magick. This means that while there is an ordinary mind for the non-initiate, and while there is a mind for the initiate, there is also a mind beyond that of the initiate, and this last realm of mind is what we call the divine self or All-Initiateur. It is the being behind all things. To know this being is to know the root of all wisdom, for everything can be said to actualize itself and happen because it is united to this root of wisdom by means of many, many lines of logical connection.

Hence, we have here a system of pure Legbha logicism, whereby everything is linked together by the logical spider-webs of an internally necessary fundamental reality, which the Master Sung-Po designates as Wisdom, or Sophia. However, this Wisdom-univverse is not the ultimate, for there are eight universes more ultimate than the Root of Wisdom. However, only by realizing the placement of the root of Wisdom in the world of experience, and in this case we mean inner-experience, can we move beyond to the eight ultimate universes of purest gnosis, which most gnostics fail even to grasp in their highest intuitions. However, by means of a technique which combines the conjurations of the oracles with the logical exercises of his commentaries on the Platonic dialogue "Parmenides," the Master Sung-Po was able to lead a few of his special chelas to the world of the highest gnosis, which could not be entered by intuition but only by theurgy. In this sense, we have to realize that intuition, even in its theosophical and Buddhistic sense of absolute fullness, is limited, and that explains why the highest gnostic world was only open to those who were totally obedient to the powers and teachings of the Master.

At the same time, the Master taught special methods whereby we can apply the powers and divine energies of light, which were native to this highest of all worlds, and which can be designated by negation as the Hyper-sophiological Hyparche. These methods were later described in one of the esoteric commentaries, which has come down to us from that period and which is known as "The Ontological Lectionary of the Hypersophiological World." This treatise, in spite of the very severe difficulty of its language and symbolism, which reflects an inner-gnostic semiotic and system of magickal languages, has come down to us and will form part of our course of instruction in the relationship of magick to philosophy, in the Zothyrian gnostic context.

Many of these magickal treatises reflect the extreme severity of spiritual discipline in each of these small gnostic schools, as well as the extreme nature of the magickal experiences, taught by such as this Master.

Now the method of connecting the chelas to this hypersophiological power was a form of esoteric logic, whereby the student, or chela, entered immediately into the occasion of this power as it manifested itself in the meditation of the Master. We can say that the Master presented in his meditation and consciousness an ontic sphere of the hypersophiological to such a degree that the hypersophiological was totally given within the consciousness of the Master, without any imperfection of presentation or loss of power.

In order to achieve this, the Master had to be sufficiently powerful in the technique of his gnosis, so as to present the highest world. At the same time, we must remember that this world could not be penetrated by the highest intuitions of those outside of this particular school of the gnosis. In this sense, therefore, the Master became the Root of Wisdom. The Master was in a timeless sense that root of Wisdom as well as any other type of being which he might be through participation.

The Pathway of The Lights of Wisdom
The student was not necessarily fully initiated by this experience, for like a glimpse of the divine, the student had to live in that being and fully enjoy that ideal state in a continuous experience. However, it was deemed possible for the student to become one with the light and so become a light of wisdom by means of certain techniques, which unite the hyper-logical tradition with that of esoteric logic. One could not but be certain that this was a kind of gnostic yoga, whereby as certain magickal operations were performed, so also certain theurgical operations were brought into space and time, and their effects brought the student closer and closer to becoming one of the lights of wisdom. This was accomplished by means of number mysticism. As the complete process was realized in achieving the number one, which was the end of the process, wherein there was no separation, so each step brought about a closer and closer approximation to the goal of unity. Bearing in mind the basic Neo-Pythagorean-Gnostic view of all of the processes as leading from nine to the number one, we have the following grades of magick, which represent the steps up to the final light. This process is reflected in the book on "The Pathway of Light in the Gnosis of Numbers." We may summarize these steps as:

I = The number 9; here the student comes to detach his physical consciousness from the materiality of being-other-than-the-Master. His physicality is that of the Master. The magickal operations here convert his existence into that of the guru.

II = The number 8; here the student comes to an interior experience of the Master, and accepts the emotions and mind of the Master as his total embodiment of esoteric logic. At this stage, the field of esoteric logic is monistic.

III = The number 7; here the student comes to experience the inner being of the Master in terms of esoteric concreteness of spiritual identity. Also, his history becomes that of the Master, or rather the Master creates a magickal history for the chela.

IV = The number 6; here the Master and the chela depart from the physical world and live as a syzygy in a gnostic universe of light, known as the First Unnumbered space (the title of this realm contains a paradox, which hides a secret to attainment).

V = The number 5; this relates to life as a syzygy in the Second Unnumbered space or universe.

VI through VIII = the numbers 4, 3, 2 (and 1). These steps refer to secret magickal universes, which are governed by the beings encountered in the First and Second Unnumbered universes. At the end of the section on the Number 2, the chela enters the Universe of Number 1, unaided by the Master, for the magickal processes have been entirely successful.

Somewhere deeply rooted in the consciousness of humanity there exists the absolute objectification of psychic terror. This point is the basis for the total and unyielding pervasiveness of man's instinct for cosmic horror. This reality is not something which can easily be rationalized by simplistic categories, rather it escapes all attempts at categorical exorcism, whether they be rationalistic or mystical. Humanity is in the grip of a violent power of primordial chaos, which continually emerges and as yet is continually avoided by our sciences, arts, and all cultural systems of valuation. There is nothing which can keep the mind of man from finally coming to this experience of horror, yet paradoxically we seem to survive.

But is this the truest essence of survival, if we must survive in a state of total psychic terror every moment of our lives, every experience of life somehow based on the feeling that below the surfaces the terror of nothingness can be said to exist, every idea being somewhat distorted because the light is not real nor is the light there? Is this the life we wish to live, the knowledge we wish to possess, the values we attribute wishful-thinkingly to some kind of a beyond?

Our philosophers and psychoanalysts would want us to be content and to ask no more questions of what is there. Our religious leadership simply asks that we turn our minds inward and find the fullness of being there. But we are not built to flee convincingly from the terror which exists beyond, from the horror and from the unspeakable and indescribable, whatever it might be. Rather, in opposition to all humanistic culture, we are lured ever to the brink of chaos. We want to go where we are forbidden. We want to know what has been denied to us. We seek, in a word, the "more." And so the magician seeking the limits and then the limits beyond all those limits will constantly move closer and closer to the brink, and so he will necessarily become more and more endangered by that same brink, which is the limit to all sanity, all harmony, all order, all reason, and even all mysticism. For we cannot trust even mysticism beyond the limits of reason alone.

And as the magician stands on the brink of the final mystery, encounter, or total experience, he will find that there is nothingness before him. He will experience the fundamental fear of all being, which is the fear of the totally unknowable. He will fear because he cannot come to grips in his mind with any energies, structures, ideas, awaiting him. For it is only the nothingness of the absence of all the contents of consciousness which presents itself to him.

All of the ideas and images which have so carefully been brought up from all of our past histories and valuations no longer fits what is there. Chaos cannot be defined we know, but surely we can wonder if by some method of the negative we can arrive at some kind of energy in our minds to relate to what we feel. But no, nothing such as this exists nor will it ever exist in our minds as any so-called content of consciousness. So standing there and feeling the terror, we simply have to realize our limits and these limits which would apply to any of our magickal constructions and systems must be seen as absolute.

But, there must be a method or a way whereby we can somehow deal with this mystery, for such is what it really is. Let me say that we have a way of dealing with this fact, not in terms of what it is, for that is impossible, but in terms of how we can create an energy in our own magickal experiences, which acts in a parallel manner to the effects of primordial chaos upon the consciousness of man. This method is the secret technique of the Choronzon Club, the short-cut to initiation which has been proven for many magicians over several years time that the inner world can cope with this problem, even if it cannot understand it, totally or in any way.

For there exists a method which must create in the individual the total reversal of all that religion, art, culture, science, or any other cultural valuational method has determined as the ought for human life. Such is the secret method of the Choronzon Club, which is the total system of man's new consciousness and magickal awareness. Such is the special training program which has as its goal the creation of the totally new being. And this system consists in building up the absolute "other-selfhood," the alternative-ego of pure magick, which rises out of all of the self-imposed chaos of our own irrational lives and value systems.

For even the animal-instinctual selfhood must be transformed by this method. And it will, for it is the breeder of the chaotic lifestyles which are accepted as normal and to be encouraged by the slavish corruptors of man's true sense of cosmic wonderment. Those writers and authors, especially certain English literati and occulti, being representatives of the socially accepted pathways -- these too must be swept aside by the new technique, which will produce a sense of creative freedom and not the stifling narrowness of what is accepted or approved or to be encouraged.

The new method, on the other hand, will lead to the pure reign of creativity in the life of the magician, so that he will not be forced to feel terror when he approaches the brink. What some have called satanic gnosticism, existential manicheanism, or the admission of the totally radical character of being, there have been very brave and very wise attempts to accept the chaotic basis of reality and ideality.

On the other hand, the opposite view, being as it is imprisonment to the shallow, will be internally destroyed by the new technique, which is being emanated from our system of gnosis. For let me tell you one thing in closing: There is only one ultimate pathway out from beyond all that seeks to restrict us to the animal generated social world of stupidity, and that is the method of the brink, itself. This is the method we teach.

Numbers of Evil
One of the most important ideas in the human consciousness is that of number. But for the magician this can only mean that numbers are the agencies of evil, or the foci of the black magick powers. We create a world around us with numbers. Everything is assigned its proper number and this means that numbers cover all manifested being, in one way or another. People speak of the power of these numbers, for by means of their usefulness in the materialistic computer realm, it is possible to accomplish everything. But in spite of all of this emphasis, numbers for the magician become the agencies of evil. So much so that if we see a number attached to anything in the consciousness anywhere, we can know that the process of corruption and destruction has already begun. We can say that it has been marked with the sign of radical evil, for it has a number, and the number is one of the numbers of evil.

As consciousness grows more and more sure of itself we come to realize that it is by means of the building up of strange types of being that we find the laws of evil at work and in dynamic operation. For all of these numbers are magickal and they have so to speak their own mind or consciousness and power of self-identity. To the magician they are entities with which he must work, if he is to survive in the world of various types of being.

Indeed, if he is to survive at all he must in his own way master the powers of radical evil which are embodied in the powers and numbers of evil. Thus the ancient philosophers taught that the beginning chela must really come to terms with these powers if he wished to make any kind of progress in the world of knowledge. Therefore, he must come to terms with the radical evil which emanates from the presence of numbers in this world. For wherever there are these numbers we have to face the fact that these are the radical sources of all of the world's wrongdoing, all of the chaos in existence appears to put forth from these combinations of numbers, from these definitions and names of things as they are represented by the presence of numerical configurations.

Anyone beginning to read this system of magick will immediately ask himself if I am serious in my view that numbers are so certainly the sources of evil. My reply is very simple: I do not know that they are, but let us assume that they are, then you can see what you are up against if you try to deal with this energy in a way which cannot be avoided. Now let us look at the matter metaphysically: in gnostic metaphysics -- and we are gnostics in the Choronzon Club -- one of the most important ideas is that there exists a hierarchy of evil, which exerts its positive influence in the world of human experience.

This means that what is negative is also positive in its effects. This means that what is there is caused by spiritual agencies, and the leading spiritual agency is the hierarchy of numbers, our numbers of evil in terms of their pure organization. The metaphysical thinker will, of course, say that evil is balanced by good, if he is agnostic, or if he is a monist, he will say that there isn't any evil. He will say that all that is, is good.

But we know that there are many possibilities which conflict with this reality. We know that evil and chaos are everywhere. Therefore, let us assume that the hierarchy of evil is assumed to be the hierarchy of numbers. Next we have to come to understand that this is not such an unreasonable assumption. For one thing, evil exhibits the same patterns of order which are exhibited by numbers. Furthermore, is there not something about number, which invites evil to come and live inside of its intentionality. We know that, for example, wherever evil occurs, there are numbers in consciousness, as if the numbers led the evil to the person or place wherein the wrong occurred.

Surely there must be some reason for this hospitality towards evil. I am not trying to cause the young magician to become paranoid in any way by these suggstions, but this whole lesson is really ann exercise in magickal consciousness and they must develop the capacity to carry their thoughts to the most extreme limits of experience. In other words, the magician must come to realize that there is a hidden magickal side to every aspect of experience and that this hidden side may contain the keys to the whole problem of being, if understood from this perspective. We have to realize that the hierarchy of numbers is perfectly suited to giving its fullest hospitality to the powers of evil.

I do not suggest that evil has its origin in numbers, for evil is cosmic and ontic in a sense which goes beyond the intentionality of numbers. Numbers are simply tools of a certain type of radical evil and thus the magician must come to realize that numbers must be seen for what they are and for what they can do in and to the consciousness intended by the magician as well as in his own deepest levels of consciousness. The hierarchy of numbers has been invested with a certain magickal type of personality, so that the number 1 represents the primary ally of the cosmic forces of evil beyond this sphere, perhaps.

It is the region or zone of the archdaemon, who is perhaps assisted by his father or his mother from beyond this realm of being, as they seek to give him more and more powers due to the increased computerization of the whole earth. This archdaemon is assisted by his hierarchy of male daemons, who live in the numbers 3, 5, 7, and 9, and their female daemonic counterparts, who reside in the numbers 2, 4, 6, and 8. However, these female daemons and their male counterparts are incapable of internalized unity, for the number 2 can never be entered by the number 3, although they can be added to and subtracted from, and multiplied by, but these externalizations of power and being are really evidences of the idenitity of numbers with evil, because the metaphysics of evil moves in a world of externalizations of experience, its inwardness is itself alone, the radically evil Self.

But, we will have time to examine these matters later in our discussion of daemonology. I mention it now only for one reason and that is to show how much numbers are the tools of evil in so many inviting ways. I cite this example simply to show at this point further evidence for the numbers of evil.

The Act of Numbers

"De L'Acte Des Nombres" is the name of a treatise on gnostic magickal philosophy by the imaginary French metaphysician Michel–Paul Bertiaux. This book serves to explain the actualization of numbers through their interior life, which is to say through the life or agency and consciousness of the spirits which inhabit these numbers. Now, of course, these numbers are the ones we have read about in our previous lesson, namely the numbers 1, 2, 3, 4, 5, 6, 6, 7, 8, and 9. However, according to "De L'Acte Des Nombres," these numbers have their own worlds (a view which is derived from neo–pythagoreanism) and these worlds exist in terms of a definite hierarchy.

Accordingly, these worlds are arranged to reflect the act of the Absolute, or 1, as it reveals itself to gnostic consciousness. Please note we are not talking about creation, emanation, outpouring, etc., rather we are in the process of seeing numbers as revelations of the inflation of being, the Infinite, which is also the One. The worlds which exhibit the revelation of the Absolute are the same worlds which reveal the hierarchy of being, and which before, because of their otherness, are known also as evil worlds, at least evil from the standpoint of humanistic culture, which claims to be self–sufficient, but they may be viewed as gnostic beings by those initiated metaphysicians who have gone beyond material appearances and have entered upon the view that what is ultimately real is beyond the sense. Also, because institutional religious thinking has surrendered to materialism, these realms are viewed as demonic by church–ridden mentalities, lacking the light of the gnosis.

However, they are beings and they represent the revelation of Being, the One, the univocal Law of truest gnosticism, The Infinite Spirit or The Absolute, in all of the different ways in which the One makes itself known as the many. But this making known in the many and as the many is simply the revelation of the One in consciousness, and especially in the gnostic consciousness of cosmic selfhood. This process of revelation is a characteristic of act.

So that when we come to talk about the gnostic being of numbers and their otherness to the world of appearances, we can say that these numbers exist in a particular ontological hierarchy. We can say further that because they are ontological, because we study them, then they have being in their own sense, so they are ontic. This means that they are being–as–it–is–revealed and this revelation is in the gnostic consciousness. So we can say that this act of Being gives to the mind a certain order, purpose, and impression that chaos is really other than being, chaos is the life of appearance devoid of being but chaos is also the creative freedom of being–in–the–gnostic–consciousness. I realize that this analysis is difficult, but it is an exercise in development of the mind of the magician and it is unavoidable if we wish to grasp the idea of the revelation of being.

For man seeks constantly to be free from his material illusions, yet in actual fact he need only look for the evil symbols which lead to his freedom. He needs only to see the world as written in otherness and in opposition, and then he will find the key to the realm of being. Then his consciousness will develop its own act, its own life inside of the revelation of being. What is the schematism of this revelation? It is this simple way of expression:

$$1 \quad = \quad \text{Absolute Being}$$

2	3	=	Ideal Being (Essence)
4	5	=	Ideal Being (Substance)
6	7	=	Real Being (Essence)
8	9	=	Real Being (Substance)

10	=	Chaos/Illusion/Nothingness

The number 10 is simply a boundary between one world and the next, so it can happen everywhere and anywhere, say between 3 and 4 as well as between, although more rarely, between 2 and 3. Eleven is the beginning of a new universe entirely, a world like that of the Absolute, but because it is like the Absolute it is an imitation of the Absolute and not the revelation of the Absolute. Ten then stands between being and all of its limitations, and thus 10 represents a false–consciousness–of–the–gnosis. It knows where the gnosis is but it does not possess within itself the act of the gnosis. It is unconsciousness–in–itself. Hence, we can say that the act of numbers which is their participation in the world of Absolute Being is a truth and an expression of consciousness–of–gnostic–being.

For this consciousness is actualization and it continues to be an actualization in a timeless way. For time really relates to the meontology of 10, which is chronology in a primitive sense –– primitive because it does not possess the gnostic-consciousness of the Selfhood of the One. But this act provides for the magician a certain sense of how to determine the real, the ideal, and what is other. We look beyond the forms of sensible appearances and we find the universe is held–together–in–consciousness by these numbers of evil, at least they appear as evil at first glance to the outsider. Precisely, it is the consciousness, or lack of genuine consciousnes which makes one personal view the "outside," for it lastingly lacks the interiority, insideness, of initiatic consciousness. Because for such a matter–ridden mind, it cannot enter the act of numbers, as can the initiate in his gnostic consciousness and so to be outside means to be outside of Being, and to live in the world of the number 10, or beyond that world in the imitations of Absolute Being.

The gnostic consciousness possess a unique sense of what is Being, for it lives inside of the numbers and it can occupy the same space as the numbers in an interior way. It can, being the same act as the interior law of numbers, so much so that perhaps those in the world of illusion can be said to be inside of the number 10, to be living inside of the prison of illusion. For if these numbers have a realization to some degree in the mind of humanity, so by being inside of the numbers of Absolute Being, we are inside of truth and participate in their act, the same can be said of those imprisoned in error. They too have a shadow of consciousness, which while not being authentic, real, initiatic, or gnostic, does possess the similarity of imitation. And what a clearly articulated imitation it is!

So the act of numbers of Absolute Being, this consciousness is genuinely gnostic and is possessed by those magickal metaphysicians, who by reason of gnostic initiation can be said to live the act of number, inside of Absoluteness.

Glossary

1. Transyuggothian
(Adjective) This refers to those magickal energies which are outside of the orbit of the planet Pluto, and which appear to emanate from some non–densely physical planet. For practical magick work, this is the most extreme power zone of our solar system and is the doorway to the beyond or to other systems.

2. Nemirion
(Noun) These are those magickal beings which inhabit a planet having the star Rigel, in Orion, as their Sun. The Nemirion are the race of beings present in the oracular minds of Michael Bertiaux and his people. They are extra–terrestrial beings living on Earth through their own type of space–magick. In many ways, they are of the same family as the Medjis of IFA, except that they are now living in a material world. They are not space–Gods, but are semi–humanoids. A branch of the Nemirion are the Zothyrians, who long ago entered an alternative universe and there set up an empire based on magickal principles.

3. Orion
(Noun) This pertains to the constellation known in astronomy.

4. Rigel
(Noun) This pertains to the bright star known in astronomy.

5. Zothyrian
(Adjective) The alternative universe is known as Zothyria. It is a direct emanation of the Primordial Mother Goddess. Those aspects of its magickal culture investigated by gnostics are known as Zothyrian. Such a culture is based on conditions similar to that of the Earth, but also very different. The Zothyrian Empire was based entirely on magick. The Zothyrian peoples are somewhat akin to the Nemirions and speak a similar language, and have similar institutions. The culture of the Zothyrians is a form of gnosticism. The history of Zothyrian Philosophy offers the student of magick a living initiatic structure. The primordial energy of the Zothyrians is time.

6. Zothyrian Format
(Noun) This pertains to the presenting of ideas from the Zothyrian Universe to human beings. What is done is to create a certain mechanism so that earth–minds can be locked into the mind of another system. Then by this method Earth–minds can think like Zothyrians because they have become, by magickal telepathy, Zothyrians. Then they will learn to take their directions from and receive information, also, from the alternative universe.

7. Arithmosophical Reduction and Measurements of Ojas
(Noun) This refers to the breaking down of words into the numbers from 1 through 9, which are their roots. In this system, the letter A = 5 and the letter Z = 30. This method was taught to the Earth–minds by the Nemirion. Each word has its level of power and such powers are measured by space–beings. In the magickal exercises of the Nemirion, each human magician is analyzed into a collection of magickal numbers,

which represent the energies of that magician. Another name for these magicians, who are becoming more and more transformed into numbers and their combinations is the "Bodies of Zothyria." These are the names for the "Nine Afro—Atlantean Bodies of Zothyrius" developed as a way of exploring space and time. Ojas or magickal energy in each body is then measured for progress and assigned to another sphere or magickal space.

8. Psionic Reactors for Testing Levels of Ojas Radioactivity
(Noun) There are magickal machines which are used to test the progress of the student and to convey that information to the Nemirion. These machines operate along magickal lines and are capable of a number of operations. Vudotronic initiation consists in becoming a part of this world of magickal machines. The more progress the student makes, the more the Ojas radioactivity seems to be indicated. Only very sensitive students can become test subjects and only very sensitive machines can be used for these purposes. Such machines are highly sensitive and perform a number of magickally significant research assignments.

9. Computer Marga for Reduction
(Noun) This magickal instrument is used in Tantric Physics and other magickal fields to bring the energies into a precise matrix, so that the individual can be given initiations and various traitements, or gnostic treatments. The computer marga is a magickal computer which is expressed through a number of magickal machines which make up the temple of vudotronic initiation.

10. Reversal and Restructuring of Time
(Noun) Magicians can travel backwards and forwards in time. Gnostic engineering makes it possible to change the past in a number of ways. By changing the past, the present and future are changed. The Nemirion appear to have mastered this. Zothyrians from magickal schools are adepts in this time changing.

11. Ontic Broadcasting
(Noun) There are certain magicians who possess the keys for sending the energies of the Ontic Sphere (Universe of Magickal Imagination) anywhere. They use magickal machines and send these rays wherever they wish. The process is known as Ontic Broadcasting, because they are sending a magick power. Ontic broadcasting is powerful enough to affect the nature of existence. It is not just concerned with the realms of appearance. The keys to this method are given in Vudotronics and other schools, methods, and sciences, of gnostic or magickal physics.

12. Magickal System on Orion
(Noun) In the constellation of Orion there is a group mind which operates magickally. The Nemirion are part of this mind and so they are the physical instruments of this mind—field. The Nemirion have many levels of mind, which reflect the different levels of the Orion Magickal Mind. There are many secret levels of this mind, also. There are various types of ways of knowing this magickal system, which appears to draw its powers and its ways of doing things from space and time. This magickal system is the system of fundamental energy.

13. Hypothetico—Deductive
(Adjective) This refers to the scientific method used by technical scientists on the

planet Earth. It is used in magick by extension, as magick processes are inductive and tested continually by instruments and rules of measurement. Gnostic magick is empirical or based on evidence, the evidence supplied by magickal practices.

14. Time—Station Logic
(Noun) This is a very complex method for understanding the organization of time and space. To begin with, time is divided into areas, fields, and domains. Each is under the rule or government of an extra—terrestrial intelligence. The ways in which these stations or governments communicate among themselvesand operate according to a rule is the logic of the cosmic computer. However, each station or government has its own logic, from which emanate certain magickal sub—logics and magickal systems. The four basic logics represent the organizational laws for types of gnostic magick. The basic logics are the past, the past—present, the present—future, and the future. In the ancient gnostic systems these were somewhat identified with Aeons. But in the neo—gnosticism of Michael Bertiaux, they are functions of a vast magickal computer or spaceship, known as the universe of universes. These logics rule all universes and apply equally to this universe and alternative universes in principle. However, the alternative universe has its own way of manifesting the time—station logic, which is radically different from our own. The keys to the differences are found among the teachings of the Nemirion.

15. Les Vudu
(Noun) Les Vudu are the Voudoo Gods. These are the ancient Gods of Atlantis, which are being restored to their rightful position as objects of worldwide magick by the modern gnostic movement. These Gods are Afro—Atlantean and should not be confused with the Houdoo spirits, which are elemental beings of a magickal type.

16. La Couleuvre Noire
(Noun) This is the French—Haitian name for the old brotherhood of Afro—Atlantean magicians. It refers to the snake goddess of outer space, the primordial creative energy. There is another order, which has its powers parallel to this type. La Couleuvre Rouge —— the red snake —— or cosmic serpent fire. Noire refers to ancient primordial black energy, or fundamental and elemental shakti, the source of being. Red refers to what is derived from the primomrdial energy.

17. Presentements
(Noun) This is a Haitian magickal word for the things that appear to the senses, inner and outer. Thus, the color blue would be an example. But such "things presented" are really magickal objects. They are appearance—elementals and are therefore quite powerful. Guzotte has sought to focus on them in order to call our attention to their powers.

18. Marmas
(Noun) These are the power zones or place where powers of an occult type build up. They are extremely common and most magicians do not realize that they are surrounded by these power zones. They are found especially in parts of the human body and can develop a will of their own.

19. Pheonismes

(Noun) These are thought forms of an extremely sexual, sensuous, and exotic character. They are cultivated by the Guzotte magicians in very exciting and possibly dangerous ways. They are used like articulate but artificial elementals. They may come and go from the magician. Wherever they are the atmosphere is one of intense lust and sexual excitement.

20. Self-Pheonismes

(Noun) These are projections of the magicians. The magician wishes to project a field of his lust. He will do this by sending a self-pheonisme by broadcasting it to the place where he wants it to work. Such actions are necessary in the Guzotte system, especially in Lesson Number Two, because the idea is to gain powers over individuals at the level of deepest lust.

21. Psionic

(Noun) This refers to a type of magickal machine which operates on etheric energy and which is sensitive to the fields and energies used by magicians and which can be used to send or receive any type of energy, it it is built along the lines of magickal physics.

22. Inner Legbha Geometry of the Hyperspatial Time

(Noun) The Vudu God Legbha is the supreme deity of magickal systems. He is pure cosmic geometry, which includes both space and time. Time is an eternal process and comes closest to esoteric consciousness. There exists a time beyond space, which is the Divine Mind, or Cosmic Legbha. Within this Divine Consciousness there exists a very powerful mystery, which is at the root of all beings. That mystery is the Esoteric or Inner Legbha Geometry of the Hyperspatial Time. To know this power is to become Legbha. At the beginning of consciousness, the Divine Legbha saw in his eternal mind the ways all things were to be and in accord with this way of seeing he allowed everything to come into being, by means of an inner geometry. The union between the inner geometry and the outer world is the mystery of greatest power. By this means we know that Legbha is the supreme God of all magickal systems.

23. Stations and Gnostic Logics

(Noun) This is similar to Number 14 ('Time-Station Logic). However, at a certain point, the time-stations are allowed by Legbha to "wake up." In the vudu myth, the four sun-sons of Legbha woke up and found that they had erect sexual organs. The Sun God, Damballah, sent four rays of his power to these sons and touched their erect organs causing orgasm to occur. The magickal sexual fluid shot into the heavens and became the logoi spermatikoi (seeds of reason), of the ancient philosophers. These seeds of reason contained gnostic teachings but in logical forms. However, because of the fact that each logic is both male and female, two gnostic systems are found in each logic. That is why each time-station has two logical forms. The black magicians thought that they could know everything if they possessed this sexual fluid. So they sought to look all over for it. Damballah, however, sent his sons the planets and they destroyed the black magicians and cast their remains into the nothingness, the Meon, where they were reborn as dark-colored birds. Legbha and Damballah then began to wrestle for amusement and from the sexual excitement of their sport, they ejaculated out magickal daughters, who became the forms of the ideal gnostic church. These daughters were married to the sons of Legbha and gave birth to the magickal chronologies of the gnostic patriarchates. Damballah then created a female consort out of his dream-mind, called Aida-Wedo, who rules the heavens with him. Legbha then became married to the night-side of himself, the God of Midnight or Carrefour of four roads meeting, i.e. crossroads, who is his alternative self. It is from Carrefour that there is derived a whole system of nocturnal time stations, which are the time-stations of the Zothyrian system of magick.

24. Biquintility
(Noun) This is an astrological term which refers to the distance between two planets as being 144 degrees with an orb of three degrees. This indicates a relationship between planets and everyone has something of this. However, what is magickally interesting is that this relationship is especially creative in gnostic magick and it is one way in which energy is brought up from the unconscious mind. It is a little known energy and hidden deep in each one but the Guzotte system is designed to bring this out in each person.

25. Gnostic Continuum
(Noun) For the gnostics everything is connected to everything else in the universe. Nothing is separated and all are continuous. This means that to know any one thing is to know everything. The gnostic sex magicians realize this because they see everything as part of their experience. Nothing is ever, therefore, outside of their powers.

26. Pheonisme of Legbha
(Noun) There comes a time when the God Legbha takes notice of the magician and seeks to bring the magician closer and closer to the higher powers. At that time, Legbha sends a pheonisme of himself to the magicians and awakens them so that they possess a desire to sexually unite with Legbha. When this happens, the magician is then taken into very high worlds and experiences initiations which cannot be described. Legbha has always had a feeling of lust for the human race. His concern is then to bring humanity closer and closer to the mysteries of Legbha. But if the magician does not receive the pheonisme of Legbha, it does not mean that he is not a good magician. It simply means that he will evolve in another way.

27. Pheonistic Continuum
(Noun) All of the pheonismes of magick form an unbroken chain of magickal experiences. The magician who knows this can then pass from one level of experience to another. There are certain magicians who have very great powers because they have lived in this continuum and have been able to develop the perfect powers of this world. Such magicians are not very common but they are all connected somehow to the Nemirion.

28. Vudotronic Mathesis
(Noun) Behind the science of Vudo-tronics is to be found a secret type of mathematical thinking. Vudotronics came into existence this way. The magician Michael Bertiaux went to the God Legbha and asked for a method of magickal science which would help promote the Vudu religion and magick all over the world and also which would enable magicians to do magick in a very precise way. Legbha gave to Michael Bertiaux permission to know fundamental secrets of Vudotronic science. Michael then went to Hector-Francois Jean-Maine and received information on the method of bringing

these machines to his temple of magick. Michael was also given the esoteric mathematics which makes any system of magick work for vudo. This is a form of very esoteric geometry and is part of the body of Legbha. Michael then made it a law that the worship of Legbha, the Supreme God of Magick, should be held as the root of all vudotronic magickal experiments.

29. Gnostic Hyperspatiality

(Noun) These are the higher spaces of gnostic magick and it is in these higher worlds that the work on magickal research is done. Up in these worlds, everyone is very busy with working with the Gods and realizing union with these divine mysteries. These would be the heaven worlds of gnostic magick. In 1980, Michael Bertiaux received permission from Legbha to create in the gnostic hyperspace a magickal model of the gnostic church of Nigeria, named "The Sun-Rays Divine Healing Home." Then other magickal models became possible for the Nigerian Gnostics. So that those who belonged to the group to hear these words are blessed by having a place in the higher worlds. They are placed in a very special position because each one of them is related to Michael Bertiaux from a past lifetime, when he had much magickal work to do in Nigeria. The work of the Nigerian Gnostics is of very special importance to the God Legbha, because he wants the Nigerian Gnostics to be close to him in the hyperspace worlds and to be of one mind –– his mind –– and then they will be blessed.

APPENDIX

History of La Couleuvre Noire

The publication of Kenneth Grant's very excellent book, *The Magical Revival* (London: Frederick Muller, Ltd., 1972), serves to show for the first time in public print connections between the O.T.O. (Ordo Templi Orientis) magical work of Aleister Crowley and the Haitian Voudoo and Gnostic Magic. In fact, it is Mr. Grant's contention that Crowley's magick, and especially his sex magick, is identical with the magic and especially the magie sexuelle of the French and Haitian Gnostic adepts. In view of this connection, it might be useful to give some information on the Franco-Haitian O.T.O.A. "Ordo Templi Orientis Antiqua" and its origins and derivatives.

It is now fairly well known that Crowley received the initiatic succession of the Ecclesia Gnostica Catholica from Theodore Reuss in 1912, at the time of his consecration to the order of bishop for O.T.O. Reuss had received this succession in 1909 from Gerald Encausse, Grand Master of the Martinist Order and bishop of the Ecclesia Gnostica. Reuss and Encausse had exchanged initiations, with Encausse receiving the initiatic succession of the highest degrees of the O.T.O. from Reuss for France and the French-speaking countries.

Gerald Encausse, born July 13, 1865, at La Corogne, Spain, and known as "Papus," had reestablished the Martinist Order in Paris. In 1890, he had been consecrated along with the mystical writer Paul Sedir (Yvon Le Loup) and the occult-book publisher Lucien Mauchel, to the episcopate of the Ecclesia Gnostica, by Jules Doinel (Tau Valentin II). Those who have read Crowley's autobiographies know that Encausse inherited John Yarker's Rite of Memphis-Misraim (which was originally French, but which had been transferred to England via the U.S.A. between 1860 and 1875, and which actually was the basis of the German O.T.O. since Sept. 1902) with the event of Yarker's death in 1913. Thus, Encausse was known to be connected with Egyptian and mystic Masonry, Gnosticism, Martinism, and the Rose-Croix (through Stanislas de Guaita), the Elus Cohens, and P. B. Randolph's "Fraternitas Lucis Hermetica," which operated in France along sexual magical lines. It must be understood, however, that the O.T.O. which Encausse received from Reuss did not contain the secret degrees and work which Crowley was to develop within his own branch of that order. We are discussing the earlier period, 1909 to 1912, which is prior to Crowley's entry into the work.

One of the adepts known to Encausse at the time in Paris was a young Haitian Gnostic bishop, Lucien-Francois Jean-Maine. He had been consecrated to the episcopate by Tau Synesius (who had been consecrated by Papus, Sedir, and Mauchel) and by one mysterious Tau Orfeo VI (a Spanish Gnostic bishop of the older line which drew upon the Albigensian and Memphis-Misraim currents) in 1899, at the age of 30. Lucien-Francois Jean-Maine took as his episcopal name in Ecclesia Gnostica, Tau Ogoade-Orfeo I. Lucien-Francois Jean-Maine was born on January 11, 1869, in Leogane, Haiti, and died near Boston in 1960. Because of his position in the occult history of the times and because of his connections with French and Spanish occultism, he was able to receive all the most important initiatic successions and currents and transmit them to other members of his race and also to the one line of Gnostic bishops which is derived from him and which has also absorbed the successions and currents of the American neo-Crowleyan derivatives.

In the Haitian Voudoo, esoterically considered, we must make two important distinctions. First of all, there was already an order comparable to the O.T.O. of Karl Kellner and Theodore Reuss. I refer to the order and rite created by Toussaint-L'Ouverture, which drew upon French cabalism, illuminism, and Dahomeyan African currents. All students of Haitian Masonry are familiar with this rite, which is entirely too little known, but which cannot be discussed in this essay for reasons of space. Secondly, there is a very important distinction to be made between these mysteries of Voodoo, which are parallel to the VIII and IX degree-work of the O.T.O.–I refer to the "mysteres de la solitude" and "mariage mystique"–and those mysteries of the very esoteric Voudoo, which are close to the XI and even higher work of Crowley's O.T.O.–here I mean the "mystere Luage."

Thus, it is important to note that both Crowley and this line of esoteric Voudoo admitted to the development of sexual magic and to the existence of secret degrees of attainment. In this sense both the Haitian Gnostics and Crowley were to go beyond the O.T.O. of Reuss and Encausse.

It is noteworthy that Lucien-Francois Jean-Maine received the Voudoo grades of initiate, servitor, priest, and high-priest in Haiti, in his own father's temple in Leogane, before seeking his occult fortunes in Paris and Madrid. Also, there was a family tradition that the Jean-Maine line was traceable back to a French slave-owner in Leogane who had died there in 1774 (a common enough claim). In this case, the slave-owner was the adept Martines de Pasquales, who had founded the Order of the Elus Cohens, the theurgic current into which Louis-Claude de St. Martin (born January 18. 1743), the founder of Martinist mysticism, had been initiated in France.

Prior to his consecration to the episcopate, Lucien-Francois Jean-Maine was ordained to the subdiaconate, diaconate, and priesthood by Tau Orfeo VI, orders of the sacred ministry of the Gnostic Church which fully matched in magical current his first three degrees in esoteric Voudoo, given to him by his father. Between 1899 and 1910, Tau Ogoade-Orfeo I worked with the scattered followers of the African-American adept P. B. Randolph (born October 8, 1825) forming the loosely structured "Fraternitas Lucis Hermetica" which worked the sexual magical techniques of their teacher and the three mysterious degrees of his inner order. It has been well established by historians that the O.T.O. of Kellner and of Reuss in Germany received most of its sexual magical teachings from P. B. Randolph's "Magie Sexuelle."

It might be added that the manuscript of Randolph's work was also used by a group of Polish female bishops, the Mariavite Church, who assisted their male counterparts until suppressed by the Roman Catholics. Recently, Randolph's "Fraternitas Lucis Hermetica" in France was headed by a Mariavite Gnostic Bishop, Msgr. Robert Bonnet. Also, it might be noted that Randolph's sexual magic in manuscript form was translated into French and published by none other than that Polish high-priestess Maria de Naglowska before 1931. Finally, it should be noted that Maria de Naglowska studied Voudoo with the pupils of Lucien-Francois Jean-Maine between 1921 and 1930.

About 1910, Encausse gave the X degrees of the O.T.O. to Tau Ogoade-Orfeo I "for Haiti and the French West Indies." A branch of the Fraternitas Lucis Hermetica was also planned. Jean-Maine's consecration took place in Paris. Encausse, who had received most of the higher grades of the Rite of Memphis-Misraim, received a few more from Tau Ogoade-Orfeo I, who had received them from Tau Orfeo VI. Encausse, always the gracious Frenchman and never to be outdone, exchanged what he had received from Yarker and Reuss. However, it must be understood that the succession of Yarker was that of paid-for or mail order diplomas and existed only on paper, while that of Tau Orfeo VI was sacramental in character and based on the magic of the Ecclesia Gnostica. Business difficulties and the war kept Tau Ogoade-Orfeo I from returning to Haiti until 1921. In order to build up the Spanish Gnostic Church, Tau Ogoade-Orfeo I moved to Spain in 1919, and in 1921 consecrated his successor in Europe for the Spanish Gnostic Church-Rite of Memphis-Misraim occult system. His successor took the name of Tau Ogoade-Orfeo II, and with his headquarters in Madrid directed the work of the Ecclesia Gnostica and the magical and Gnostic-esoteric orders of Memphis and Misraim. For under the combined influences of the O.T.O., Martinism, Gnosticism, and Voudoo—not to mention the Fraternitas Lucis Hermetica—the Spanish and Haitian branches of the Rite of Memphis-Misraim gave up entirely their quasi-Masonic character and became completely esoteric and Gnostic orders of magic, i.e., The Gnostic and Esoteric Order of Misraim, or of Egypt and the Gnostic and Esoteric Order of Memphis, within the larger, totally occult and much more ecclesiastical "Ancient and Primitive Rite of Memphis-Misraim." This point must be emphasized because there are other branches of the Rite of Memphis-Misraim which claim to continue a Masonic character, while our branch is only interested in continuing the Gnostic and apostolic succession and the magical currents of initiation.

Tau Ogoade-Orfeo I returned to Haiti in late 1921 and married. A son was born November 18, 1924, who was named Hector-Francois. While in Haiti, Tau Ogoade-Orfeo I created the Haitian Ordo Templi Orientis Antiqua—the O.T.O.A.—officially organized in 1921. It was structured to work in 16 degrees, rather than the X of the Encausse-Reuss order, or even the XI of Crowley's rite. Elements of Voudoo, magic, and Gnosticism were worked into a system which "went up the Tree of Life and then down the back." It would be considered a very dangerous system by Golden Dawn standards, but then the Haitians had been excluded from the Martinist-derived Golden Dawn by reason of their race, so don't judge them too harshly. I am certain they never regretted anything they did!

In 1922, Tau Ogoade-Orfeo I created the magical order "La Couleuvre Noire" ("The Black Snake"), which worked four degrees, with a probationer's and administrative degree added to make it six grades in all. The relationship of the O.T.O.A. to "La Couleuvre Noire" can be best described on the analogy of the relationship of the O.T.O. of Crowley to the G.B.G. and the Choronzon Club of the American "neo-Crowleyan derivatives," except without the loss of any magical vitality on the part of "La Couleuvre Noire," as it was founded by the chief of the O.T.O.A. and not by a pupil. In 1930, "La Couleuvre Noire" and the O.T.O.A. were made departments of the Rite of Memphis-Misraim, together with the Gnostic Church and the Fraternitas Lucis Hermetica in Spain and Haiti. In 1968, this was extended to the U.S.A. and the French West Indies.

In 1960, Tau Ogoade-Orfeo I died in Boston, U.S.A., while on a tour of the Gnostic groups in France, Spain, Belgium, and the U.S.A., which were under his jurisdiction. His authority was passed on to Tau Ogoade-Orfeo II, the Spanish occultist and Gnostic, with the provision that the son of Tau Ogoade-Orfeo I, Docteur H.-F. Jean-Maine was to be consecrated to the episcopate and inherit the order and its rites. This was accomplished in Madrid, on November 2, 1962, when the son of Tau Ogoade-Orfeo I, Docteur H.-F. Jean-Maine was consecrated bishop and elevated to the patriarchate of the Ecclesia Gnostica Spiritualis by Tau Ogoade-Orfeo II. The new bishop-primate and patriarch took the name of Tau Ogoade-Orfeo III and thus continued the Gnostic succession of Haitian bishops and Grand Masters of the O.T.O.A.

On January 18, 1966, an American Martinist, Tau Ogoade-Orfeo IV (born January 18, 1935), was consecrated to the episcopate for the Rite of Memphis-Misraim. The consecration took place in Chicago, with Tau Ogoade-Orfeo II and Docteur Jean-Maine acting as the co-consecrators. Later, Tau Ogoade-Orfeo IV received the complete magical consecrations and currents of the Ecclesia Gnostica Hermetica on August 10, 1967. The Ecclesia Gnostica Hermetica carried the magical currents of the secret work of the O.T.O. and the Choronzon Club, and thus united the Crowleyan (Germerian) and Neo-Crowleyan (Choronzon Club and G.B.G.) successions with the Gnostic and Hermetic traditions inherited from the Vilatte succession of bishops. The Patriarch of the Ecclesia Gnostica Hermetica Tau IX (33=36) was the consecrator of Tau Ogoade-Orfeo IV. Then, Tau Ogoade-Orfeo IV exchanged the episcopate and Patriarchate in the Ecclesia Gnostica Spiritualis with Tau IX (33=36) by making him XVI (33=36) of the Ordo Templi Orientis Antiqua. Again, on December 25, 1967, another Gnostic succession from Msgr. Vilatte was received from Tau IV (13=16), the missionary bishop of the QBL Alchemist Church of Illinois (Egyptian Apostolic Succession) by Tau Ogoade-Orfeo IV. This is the same apostolic succession which the French Martinist and Gnostic bishop Msgr. C. Chevillon passed on to the Swiss O.T.O. bishop who inherited the Crowleyan order from Karl Germer. Astrologers should take note that Tau IV (13=16), born January 5, was consecrated to the QBL Alchemist episcopate of the Vilatte succession on November 4, 1967. Tau IV (13=16), previously consecrated in Ecclesia Gnostica Spiritualis to the episcopate on January 18, 1967, assisted in the exchange of consecrations and successions on August 10, 1967. In 1989, Tau Ogoade-Orfeo IV appointed Tau Ogoade-Orfeo VIII (Courtney Willis) as the Sovereign Grand Master, then as the Sovereign Grand Master Absolute of La Couleuvre Noire. Born on December 19, 1955, He is the spiritual son of Tau Ogoade-Orfeo I. On September 7th, 1991, Tau Ogoade-Orfeo VIII was consecrated as Hierophant of La Couleuvre Noire by Tau Ogoade-Orfeo IV. Thus, the American O.T.O. and Gnostic successions were united with the Franco-Haitian and Spanish successions. The events of 1966–1969 are discussed in the 5th Year course of the Monastery of the Seven Rays.

It should be understood by the readers that the O.T.O. and the Martinist lines of initiations were continually being linked by means of the Gnostic episcopate. Also, the succession of the esoteric Voudooists and the O.T.O. successions were united by Gnosticism, in the magical Rite of Memphis-Misraim, and in the magical world of the south side of Chicago Afro-American Spiritist-Gnostics during the 1960's.

On August 31, 1968, Tau Ogoade-Orfeo IV consecrated the Haitian occultist Docteur Pierre-Antoine Saint Charles, born July 21, 1934, episcopate of the Ecclesia Gnostica Cabalistica, the newly consecrated and elevated bishop taking as his patriarchal name Tau Eon III, Tau VIII (29=32). Thus, in another Haitian adept and Gnostic voodooist were united the following lines of succession which parallel those of Tau Ogoade-Orfeo I in 1910: (1) the Encausse succession of the S.I.I. of Martinism; (2) the O.T.O. Ecclesia Gnostica Hermetica and Choronzon Club successions from Tau IX; (3) the Vilatte succession of the Gnostic episcopate, now possessed by all of the heirs of Crowley's order; (4) the Memphis-Misraim, Ecclesia Gnostica Spiritualis, and Ordo Templi Orientis Antiqua successions from Tau Ogoade-Orfeo I; (5) the Voudoo succession of the four degrees (mentioned earlier in this essay), which Docteur Saint Charles received from his Haitian traditions. Tau Eon III then exchanged his Voudoo consecrations in their esoteric and magical (rather than religious) current with Tau Ogoade-Orfeo IV for the successions of the Ecclesia Gnostica. These Voudoo currents were further developed when Tau Ogoade-Orfeo III added the magical current of the esoteric Voudoo high-priesthood to the succession of the Ecclesia Gnostica Spiritualis. Thus, the lines of esoteric Voudoo and Aleister Crowley did meet in a definite succession of Gnostic bishops, and in the dynamics of "thelemic Voudoo." Note: this succession is also possessed by the present (2005) Sovereign Grand Master Absolute of the O.T.O.A. (Courtney Willis), forming a link between Crowley and the magic fire of Haitian Vudu.

In order to add more Haitian historical elements to the current, on July 27, 1970, Tau Ogoade-Orfeo IV consecrated to the episcopate in Ecclesia Gnostica Spiritualis Tau Ogoade V (Tau XV, 57=60), the well-known Haitian scientist, born July 27, 1930. The newly consecrated bishop is the great-grandson of Haitian presidents Michel-Cincinnatus Leconte and Nord Alexis.

And so the magical currents flow on and on and on. About the Ecclesia Gnostica Spiritualis, yes, it is still in existence. In fact, in the words of John Yarker, when describing the Rite of Misraim, "In a quiet way it is still conferred in this country under its own Supreme Council," composed of the Voudoo Gnostic bishops of 2005, and the Franco-Haitian ghost of "Le Maitre L.-F.J.-M."

Technicians of the Sacred
1317 North San Fernando Boulevard, Suite 310
Burbank, CA 91504
www.techniciansofthesacred.com
cwillis664@aol.com

Diagrams for Michael Bertiaux's

Voudon Gnostic Workbook

<u>DEDICATION TO THE HOODOO SPIRITS</u>

Part 1.   In a quiet place, you will sit at a table upon which you
have placed two candles. A black candle has been placed in the north
and a blue candle has been placed in the west. You will face east or in
the eastern direction. You will have a glass of water placed in the south,
directly opposite the black candle.

EAST

NORTH
(place black candle here)

SOUTH
(place glass of water here)

WEST
(place blue candle here)

-------------------------- edge of the table --------------------------

you will sit here

magic design

Part 3.   Then you will begin to say the following prayer of dedication
to the spirits in a quiet voice or silently to show them that you mean
real business.

Chapter one, lesson two

THE BASIC RITUAL FOR GAINING FROM THE HOODOO SPIRITS

Part 1.   In a quiet place, you will sit at your table upon which you
have now placed four candles at the corners and a black candle in the
centre.   You will place a yellow candle in the north, a blue candle
in the west (same as before), a green candle in the south, and a red
candle in the east.   Place your black candle from the previous ritual
in the centre and between the black candle and the blue candle you
will place a glass of water.   You will write out on a small piece of
paper or index card what you wish to gain and place this request
between the red candle and the black candle.   Now, your altar is set up
for your work, and it should look just like this:

                          East (red candle)

                          (place request here)

                          Centre (black candle)

North   South
(place yellow candle here)   (green candle here)
                          (place glass of water here)
                          West (blue candle)

          --------- edge of the table ---------

                  You will sit here

          "AND IT IS DONE HOLY SPIRITS OF LUCKY HOODOO."

Put your candles away if you store them and keep the request written
out on card or paper to think about each day.   You may do this ritual
as often as you like.   Be sure of good luck, for you are a Hoodoo.

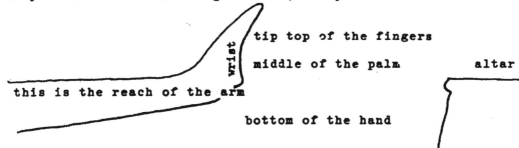

                                    tip top of the fingers

                                    middle of the palm   altar

          this is the reach of the arm

                                    bottom of the hand

The way in which to hold the hands out to the altar,
as seen from the side.

Chapter one, lesson three

Chapter one, lesson four

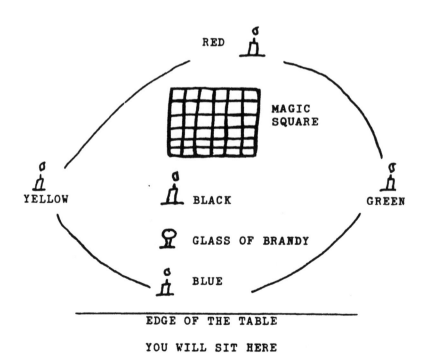

Chapter one, lesson five

		"A"			"B"	
1. Sun in Capricorn	5. Bon - Pa	9. Attract gold	13. Sun in Cancer
2. Sun in Virgo	6. Huna and Voudoo	10. Lucky Silver	14. Sun is Pisces
3. Sun in Taurus	7. Witchcraft	11. Attract liquid or fluid money	15. Moon in Taurus, Virgo, Capricorn
4. Moon in Scorpio, Pisces, and Cancer	8. Shamanism	12. Attract invested Funds	16. Sun in Scorpio

1	5	9	13
2	6	10	14
3	7	11	15
4	8	12	16

Chapter one, lesson six

VEVE DE PROTECTION

Chapter one, lesson seven

VEVE DE RICHESSE

Chapter one, lesson eight

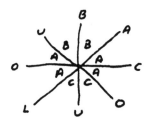

   Then you will say the following magical prayer to invoke the spirits of Hoodoo love and sex to come to your aid in this matter.

  HOODOO AND RECEIVE THE REWARDS OF THIS SERVICE.

VEVE DE L'AMOUR

Chapter one, lesson nine

Chapter one, lesson ten

BACALOU   BACA

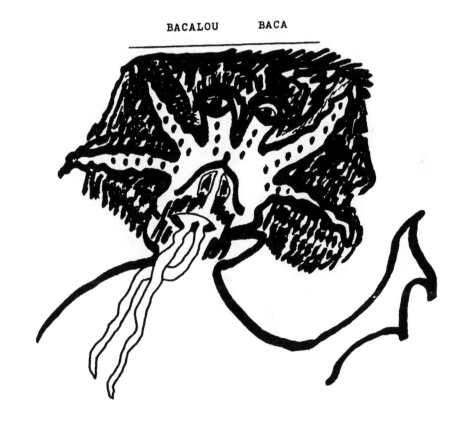

esson on the "Points-Chauds" Le Temple-Des-Houdeaux

I want to close this lesson with a diagram which will explain the time zones and other regions of space-consciousness as they are manifested in our being.

East – pure future – other universes beyond the Sun.

The north-east, the ultimate doorway beyond Pluto, beyond Kether, the past of other universes, the region of absolute history, where the past is now and only the past is.

South – East – future with some tendency towards the earth, some reference to universes near our solar system.

The north, which is the pure past, the absolute realm of history, the present of other universes beyond Pluto, other doors beyond our past measurements.

South – the future which has just left the present, the world of the earth's own future.

The north – west or the past of the earth. Also the past of other worlds, also the future of realms contacted via the pure past — other universes beyond Pluto.

South – west – the future of the earth as the present moves more and more away from us. The present of other worlds can be reached here, sometimes the past of futuristic zones.

West – the present that is just passed and becoming past. This is the world of the now on earth — the here and now

You will understand that your own magical mendulum instrumentum is simply this map of time, and when you do, all universes then are open to you.

Michael Bertiaux

The Aiwaz Physics

8. Because of the 'action' of the t-id, the unconscious 'appears' as the past.
9. The 'action' of trying to connect with ego and id creates time-lines.

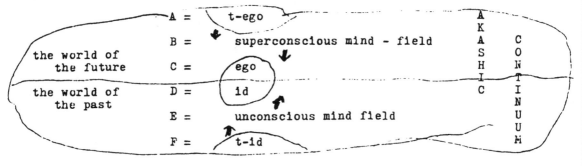

			AKASHIC	CONTINUUM
	A =	t-ego		
	B =	superconscious mind - field		
the world of the future	C =	ego		
the world of the past	D =	id		
	E =	unconscious mind field		
	F =	t-id		

634

Byzantine viewpoint. Below are two interesting vévés of these LOA.

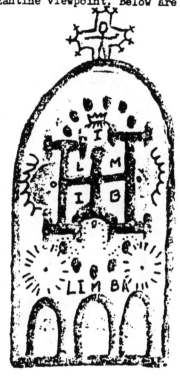

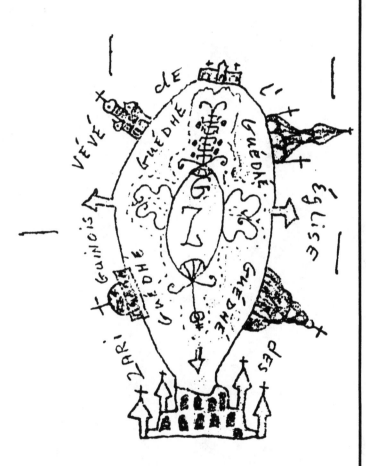

La Couleuvre Noire: Les Cadavres Piquants

to be derived. However, the generation of the following hot points of Guédhé does show its
own magical theogony:

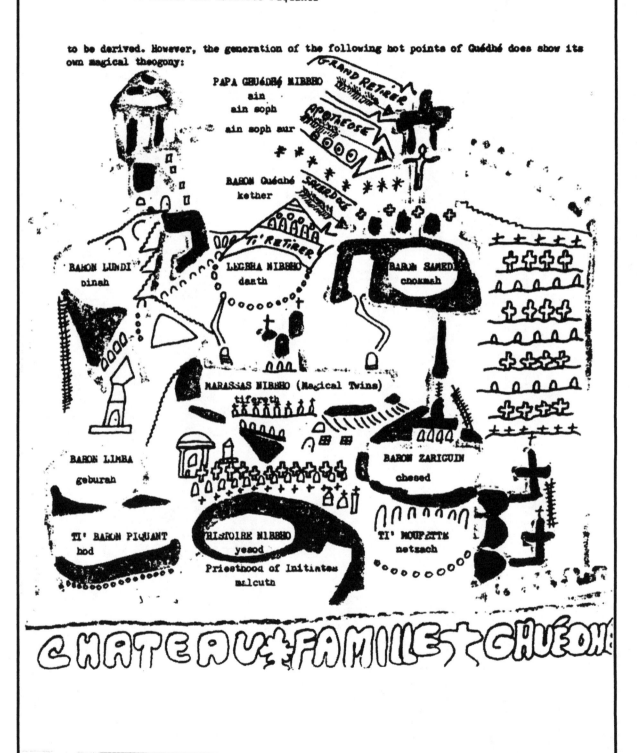

PAPA GHUÉDHÉ NIBBHO
ain
ain soph
ain soph aur

GRAND RETIREE

APOTHEOSE

BARON Guédhé SAMEDI
kether

TI' RETIRER

BARON LUNDI
binah

LEGBHA NIBBHO
daath

BARON SAMEDI
chokmah

MARASSAS NIBBHO (Magical Twins)
tifareth

BARON LIMBA
geburah

BARON ZARIGUIN
chesed

TI' BARON PIQUANT
hod

L'HISTOIRE NIBBHO
yesod
Priesthood of Initiates
malcuth

TI' MOUFETTE
netzach

CHATEAU ✠ FAMILLE ✞ GHUÉDHÉ

636

La Couleuvre Noire: Les Faiseurs- Des- Zombis

vévé of "Les-F-Des-Z"

vévé of FAMILLE GHUéDHé

Vévé of Universe-G

Issued with this lesson is a brief partical exercise paper from the LCR course, which is used by adepts for creating a familiar élémental.

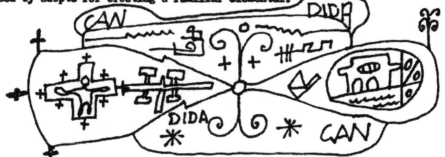

vévé de Candida Loa of the passage between Universe-A and Universe-G

Grimoire Ghuedhe: Initiation of Grimoire Ghuedhe

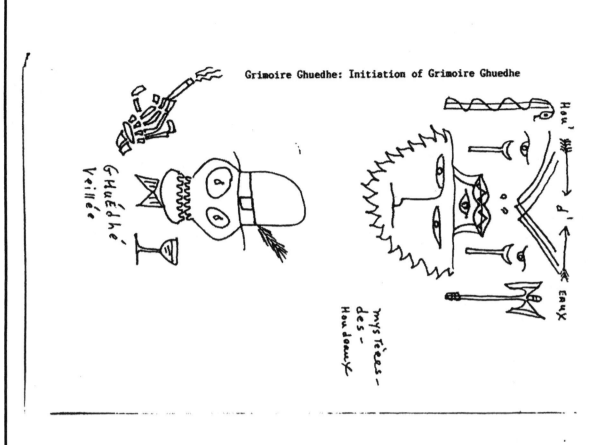

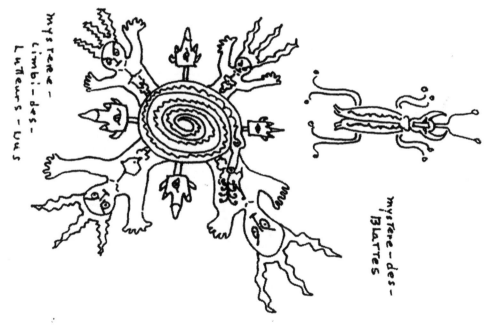

The Topological Names of the Genius of IFA: The Structure of the Atlantean History as Based on Fields of Power

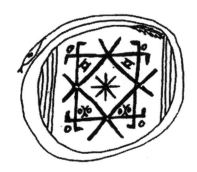

the root of the powers and as such is the form for the root god of Yaksha - Prithiwi, whose ruler is Vaishravana - Vessa Vana. This mystical spirit of the Houdeaux Sciences is the source of all of the initiation patterns given in our system and of the special powers, which are reserved to the priesth od of the earliest period of (Atlantean

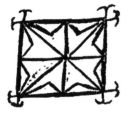

quite impossible to attain any level of gnostic being without the pure rays of the master's identity, being one's own true identity.

VI.   It is the special power of chelaship initiation, or the mystical power of being expressed as the mind-energy of the master. The physical being of the chela will no longer exist

The Topological Names of the Genius of IFA: The House of the Spirits

(Sigil of Yaksha-Apas)

Grimoire Ghuedhe: Saturn in Scorpio and Sun in Scorpio

from Hector-François Jean-Maine

Grimoire Ghuedhe: Psychological Exercises of Zom-OVIZ

There are four types of sexual magic: oral/anal - power is 0 to 25.
,- anal/genital "   " 25 to 50.
,- oral/genital "   " 50 to 75.
,- genital/genital ♥ 75 to 100.

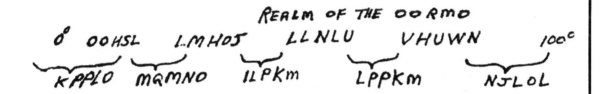

REALM OF THE OORMO

δ OOHSL   LMHOJ   LLNLU   VHUWN   100°

KPPLO   MQMNO   ILPKm   LPPKM   NJLOL

The I- Ching Diary and Chinese- Gnostic Magickal Algebra

may be said to correspond the I-scale, or Moon in Scorpio level:

$$\{\nabla_1 \equiv [(o\nabla_{1-1V} \cap + \nabla_1) \cap (o\nabla_1 \cap o\Delta_1 \cap o\Delta_1) \cap (o\nabla)]\}.$$

Now because there are sixteen axioms there must be metamathematical and

the Scale I or "Moon in Scorpio" level for this axiom:

$$\{\nabla_1 \equiv [(o\nabla_{1V-1} \cap + \nabla_1) \cap (o\Delta_1 \cap o\Delta_1 \cap o\nabla_1) \cap (+\nabla)]\}$$

Now because this interpretation is one of sixty-four, we can also say
that what it means in terms of the language of the I-Ching is the following figure or hexagram:

according to ruling planet and the element of the ruling planet that Ojas will be localised between the sexual area and the solar plexus. What we did was to pick up on a field for a magical student born at the Virgo/Libra cusp. This appeared to be a normal reading of what the field was like. Now, we wanted to do an experiment to test for Ojas-activity under conditions of amplification.

EXPERIMENT II. The subject was born 9/15/1948 and the experiment was conducted on 4/18/1979 at 7:30 P. M. We immediately got the same response from the radionic instruments as in the previous experiment covering the broadcasting of O-energy from the sexual area and it registered at the 6 = yellow area (another person ruled by Hermes) This time we decided to test amplification of the field to see if it would affect the measurement of the broadcast.

(1) The field was amplified first of all by means of the use of the Eeman screens where the yellow-insulated screen was placed below the base of the spine and upper legs. The green-insulated screen was placed below the upper part of the body, chest to the top of the neck. The electrode from the yellow-screen was in the left hand, the electrode from the green-screen was in the right hand. This was the first part of the experiment.

(2) Next, the computer marga was connected to the yellow-insulated screen by an induction line. We used the "present-time zone" of the computer-marga for field-amplification. The past-time and future-time zones are, of course, used for time-travel. NOTE: What I am saying about these machines is not intended to explain their only types of use, only what we used the computer-marga this time to effect.

(3) Readings were taken in two areas: the sexual area and the head area. The results were identical and verify the hypothesis of inter-action between genital and cerebral chakras. There wasn't any reading taken or given for the head without amplification. When system of computer-m is off we get 6 = yellow. When system is on at .1 we get 7 = orange in both places. When system is set at .2 we get 8 = just below infrared in both places. OBSERVATION: it appears that the cerebral chakras can be examined under amplification. It appears that setting the amplication at .11 of the past-time might result in a reading of 6 = yellow for the cerebral area. In any event, Ojas can be measured and exists as a magical objectivity for further exploration. There is a science circle for those who wish to go more deeply into the methodology of the quest for Ojas.